Exploring Japaneseness

Exploring Japaneseness
On Japanese Enactments of Culture and Consciousness

edited by

Ray T. Donahue

Civic Discourse for the Third Millennium
Michael H. Prosser, Series Editor

Ablex Publishing
Westport, Connecticut • London

Library of Congress Cataloging-in-Publication Data

Exploring Japaneseness : on Japanese enactments of culture and consciousness / edited by Ray T. Donahue.
    p. cm. — (Civic discourse for the third millennium)
    Includes bibliographical references and index.
    ISBN 1–56750–540–6 (alk. paper) — ISBN 1–56750–541–4 (pbk. : alk. paper)
      1. National characteristics, Japanese. 2. Japan—Civilization—1868– I. Donahue, Ray T.
II. Series.
DS830.E97 2002
952.03—dc21   2001045067

British Library Cataloguing in Publication Data is available.

Library of Congress Catalog Card Number: 2001045067
ISBN: 1–56750–540–6
ISBN: 1–56750–541–4 (pbk.)

First published in 2002

Ablex Publishing, 88 Post Road West, Westport, CT 06881
An imprint of Greenwood Publishing Group, Inc.
www.ablexbooks.com

Printed in the United States of America

The paper used in this book complies with the
Permanent Paper Standard issued by the National
Information Standards Organization (Z39.48–1984).

10 9 8 7 6 5 4 3 2 1

Contents

Introduction

Ray T. Donahue

At center stage in Japanese studies must be Japaneseness—what it means and how it is realized. These are important questions, not only for the Japanese themselves, but also for area-study specialists, including those in intercultural communication who seek greater understanding of the Japanese, their culture, and society. This present book, *Exploring Japaneseness,* part of the Ablex series, Civic Discourse for the Third Millennium, seeks to lay a foundation for inquiries into Japanese national and cultural identities by identifying aspects of Japaneseness as enacted through everyday discourse or communication.

MAIN TERMS

Discourse has attained such broad meaning in the social sciences that discourse and communication are now practically synonymous. Discourse has grown in scope to include both the verbal and the nonverbal, both speech and writing, as well as the "text" (Donahue & Prosser, 1997). Thus, discourse has gained much attention within the field of communication.

Civic is another term broadly defined. Contrary to its strong association with government, as in "civics," civic necessarily involves the community, the society, the public, as well as the relationship with the individual member or person. It broadly involves the interplay of public life and private life or, in a sense, culture and consciousness. Culture is meant here largely as "invisible" culture, thought patterns that are widely shared among a community of people, that are passed from one generation to the next, and that likely give rise to particular styles or means of communication (Prosser, 1978/1988). Consciousness refers to "the thoughts and feelings, collectively, of an individual or of an aggregate of people" (*Random House Webster's,* 1991). The interplay of culture and consciousness corresponds to Japaneseness. Work at the Japanese interpersonal level, then, necessarily entails the related social community, which in turn involves the greater society and culture. In keeping with this interplay of micro and macro levels (the interpersonal and sociocultural), as well as the broad conceptualizations of *civic* and *discourse*, this book covers a wide range of topics—from Japanese individual, personal, and national development to national ideology—as the context for cultural communication as manifested in phenomena traditionally studied in communication studies: language use, rhetoric, pragmatics, the mass media, and so on.

SCOPE OF TOPICS

Chapters in this book are written by authors from communication, linguistics, anthropology, psychology, and other fields, who attempt to document "Japanese enactments of culture and consciousness." They work at a descriptive level and use methods from their respective fields, such as participant observation, ethnography, content analysis, componential analysis, and various forms of discourse analysis (for a discussion of the latter, see Donahue & Prosser, 1997). The chapters are placed to form the following parts:

Japanese Core Cultural Concepts

Japanese Development: Person and Nation

Japanese Nation and State

Japanese Nationalism and Social Minority Relations

Japanese Language

Japanese Rhetoric

Japanese Pragmatics

Japanese Mass Media and Internet Communications

CONVENTIONS

Each chapter begins with an italicized section an an overview, similar to an abstract. Readers can choose whether to avail themselves of this aid or not. Romanization in the book generally follows Hepburn style, but not completely. Multiple styles are in use in Japan, but aesthetic and practical reasons may call for alternatives. For example, the original style used in source material, although non-Hepburn, might be advantageous to maintain for later retrieval purposes.

Macrons are used for vowel lengthening, but here again various conventions exist, which may make impractical uniform use across the many authors and fields included. Nevertheless, adjustments were made, but in the event of misses, we trust that the reader will ably bridge them. Lastly, because this book is focused on attributes of Japaneseness—national or cultural identity or character—an emphasis on cultural difference naturally results. With this background said, we now turn to a description of the chapters.

CHAPTER DESCRIPTIONS

Many chapters could apply to more than one part, and so organization followed the broad over the restricted in scope, macro over micro, historical over the contemporary, and so on. Other considerations also may have been applied to even out the parts or to balance the content.

Japanese Core Cultural Concepts

For a grasp of the state-of-the-nation conditions that gripped Japan at the start of the new century, Ray T. Donahue provides that in chapter 1. As a further aid to readers, he discusses essential principles and concepts deemed helpful for a serious study of Japan. Included are illustrative cases from the popular culture that reach to the core of Japanese culture and that present a challenge of cultural diversity to observers of culture.

Among all the Japanese cultural concepts, probably none have more utility than those of *soto* and *uchi* (outside and inside). Seiichi Makino shows why in chapter 2, in his compelling and comprehensive study of how these two concepts function throughout the fabric of Japanese society. Anyone familiar with the culture will surely recognize that Makino has his ear to the ground and his finger to the pulse of Japan. Because his work has such extensive connections to both micro and macro levels of Japanese discourse, one gets the feeling that one holds a veritable blueprint of the culture.

Japanese Development: Person and Nation

For a peek inside how Japanese schooling enculturates children to become "Japanese," see chapter 3. Tsutomu Yokota analyzes discourses of poetry across the elementary school years that inculcate important Japanese cultural values and ideals. His chapter is especially significant because his specimen texts are from a language arts class, which does not have a primary ideological goal as would civics; because his texts are approved by the Monbusho, the national department of education; and because they are taken from each of the grades second through sixth. His chapter is also methodical, in that he patiently lays a groundwork for the later "heavy duty" content of cultural values and ideals. This groundwork consists of discourse structure and process, areas that relate more to language than to moral development per se. But that is his intention, and Japanese cultural values become evident nevertheless. Overall, his is the rare work that so succinctly and so intimately deals with Japanese moral education.

The Japanese have an affinity for trains that becomes apparent to nearly anyone who lives among them. This special affinity likely led Sylvie Guichard-Anguis (chapter 4) to examine *kōtsū* (communications, transportation) and how hugely trains figure in early childhood literature, a subject found much less frequently in comparable literature in her native France, Japan's main competitor for high-speed train technology. From this basis of *kōtsū,* she traces its relation not only to Japanese everyday lives, but also to urbanization and city planning, areas in which Japan may make important contributions to postindustrial societies of the future.

Japanese Nation and State

A most fascinating sociolinguistic phenomenon is Japanese honorifics. Steeped in social hierarchy and rank, honorifics has no better starting place than at the very top—the emperor. Thus Noriko Sugimori and Masako Hamada (chapter 5) began their work to see what effect the institution of democracy has had on the use of imperial honorifics by the newspaper. In this way, one might be able to gauge, albeit indirectly, the growth of democracy in Japan. A remarkably novel idea, for this may be the first such study done. The authors chart out the changes in imperial honorifics that have taken effect and identify related patterns including those between the verbal and nonverbal elements of newspaper reportage. Also significant is that they come up with an important find—the Achilles' heel of the honorifics system.

Brian J. McVeigh in chapter 6 aptly calls *aisatsu* a social lubricant in his penetrating look at how Japanese politeness solidifies the nation and state of Japan. Sometimes the most obvious or most commonplace aspect of a society is the least understood. Japanese politeness might be one such example. Japanese politeness is so frequently observed that it might be considered by many as a given, and thus no longer noticeable. In this chapter, however, it is more than noticed. It is spotlighted, such that it can be seen permeating the populace interlinking person to nation to state.

Japanese authorities variously have come under fire because of their apparently poor crisis management in major emergencies, a topic of chapter 7. This inability, however, seems so uncharacteristic for a nation that has prided itself on the hard work ethic, social loyalty, and adherence to rules and planning. Surely of all people, wouldn't the Japanese be the most prepared for a major earthquake? But this was not to be for the great Hanshin earthquake of 1995, which put into relief how truly underprepared Japan was. Eamon McCafferty gives us a minute-by-minute account of the tragedy, laying bare the central government's inadequacy, while portraying sensitively how common people were able to cope.

Whenever translated texts differ considerably from their originals, they do so for a purpose. So reasoned Christopher Barnard (chapter 8) when he decided to compare how Japanese and American versions of *Newsweek* articles report news about Japan. Barnard found a peculiarity that occurred not infrequently: The Japanese version seemed to underreport negative information found in English about important Japanese officials or institutions. In other words, the Japanese version seemed to shield the most powerful in society from embarrassment. Could such cases merely be the correction of errors found in the original English reportage? If so, then the Japanese translations would be perfectly understandable. However, determining such error would be highly impractical because many news sources go unidentified and are therefore beyond the researcher's reach. Thus, Barnard came up with the next best thing: an intelligent selection of news events whose interrelatedness creates its own level of reliability. Although continued study is warranted, his findings are still provocative and may open new research avenues.

Japanese Nationalism and Social Minority Relations

In Japanese studies, a well-known Japanese discourse is *Nihonjinron*, both as an ideology and as an intellectual pursuit. This discourse, particularly the ideology, has gained notoriety for some of its extreme claims for Japanese cultural uniqueness. Among the scholars who have tracked this discourse is Rotem Kowner, who helps to turn a new page for the field in chapter 9. He turns attention onto the consumers of *Nihonjinron* and asks an important question: To what extent do consumers of *Nihonjinron* actually believe it? Based on survey research done in collaboration with others, most notably Harumi Befu, Kowner's chapter helps to clarify some of the finer points about Japanese nationalism and identity.

Soo-im Lee in chapter 10 interprets Japaneseness from her firsthand perspective as an ethnic Korean born and raised in Japan. Many people cannot understand why Koreans there would experience discrimination. She attributes at least part of this to Japanese insularity and to extreme views of *Nihonjinron*. She discusses the core issues while directed toward the question of Korean personal identity. Besides the importance for its own sake, the status of Koreans in Japan should lend insights to the question of Japaneseness in general.

Nikkei Brazilians also deserve attention because they constitute a relatively new social minority in Japan. But as Tomoko Sekiguchi shows (chapter 11), they also hold an inbetween status receiving preferential treatment based on their Japanese ethnicity. Yet they are more Brazilian—foreign—and therefore face discrimination. By no means are the Japanese special for engaging in discrimination of others. Discrimination is a universal problem. However, the case of *Nikkei* Brazilians helps to clarify the status of foreigner in Japan as well as what it means to be Japanese.

Japanese Language

The expression of emotions in a second language is acutely challenging, and Japanese is no exception. In particular, Japanese uses structural words to great effect as Senko K. Maynard shows (chapter 12). Doubtless the use of structural words in this way contributes to the Japanese reputation for being subtle. By also relating her chapter to the topic-comment grammatical frame, she helps to broaden the scope for this important schema in discourse relations. In a deeply thoughtful way, she illuminates Japanese aesthetics and poetics that naturally leads to her useful reflections on philosophical questions about language and thought.

How personal narratives are told in Japanese becomes Masahiko Minami's means for a psycholinguistic study of language (chapter 13). His study has special import for its focus on honorifics and sentence-final particles, two distinctive features of Japanese. Because his study involves mother–child interactions, one can see the budding of Japanese collectivism as reflected in elements that underlie the Japanese conversational trademark for high involvement and other-directedness. Such conversational elements help to form emotional or social bonds, in which linguistic structures play an important role, a point also made in the previous chapter.

Bates L. Hoffer (chapter 14) explains how the Japanese language has become inundated with foreign loanwords, even while the language is held as a pure symbol of Japaneseness. Perhaps it is to Japanese credit that they can accomplish these diametrically opposed ends of inclusiveness and exclusiveness about the native language. Hoffer shows how by the linguistic transformations performed on foreign loanwords. Sociocultural effects and issues of language policy are discussed as well.

Japanese Rhetoric

In chapter 15, Roichi Okabe takes an interesting journey into the history of Western rhetoric in Japan. This journey illuminates the dynamism of the Japanese even though they have yet to accept fully this Western import. After all, the West has had centuries to develop its rhetorical art and science. Unfazed, the Japanese intellectuals threw themselves into the enormous task of propagating such an alien system. Those individuals must have been lovers of ideas, a quality that transcends ages and cultures.

Competing views on rhetoric exist in Japan that lead to differing linguistic identities. Ryuko Kubota (chapter 16) discusses this matter in view of the major currents in thought in Japan today. She shows how views on rhetoric are deeply implicated with Japan's place in the world and how that place is perceived by the Japanese themselves. Thus, issues of identity are greatly involved and may greatly impact not just language policies and educational programs per se, but also the field of contrastive rhetoric. As Kubota suggests, these issues have yet to be fully recognized by researchers and practitioners in the field. She provides solid grounding for such contrastive studies.

The Sunday talk show of an informal political roundtable debate is found in both Japan and in the United States. The respective discourse, however, tends to differ in such aspects as conflict management and patterns of rhetoric or argument. Hiroko Furo (chapter 17) attributes such differences to culturally preferred schemas for political discourse in each country. At the very least, her study provides a window to some interesting (and sometimes comical) exchanges between the political figures in the respective countries. Her study also suggests how international flare-ups can sometimes have their cause in conflicting communication styles between the respective political leaders.

Japanese Pragmatics

Japanese have been variously described as indirect, especially with speech. Much less understood is how and when this indirectness takes place. Nagiko Iwata Lee (chapter 18) makes an advance forward by identifying the circumstances of Japanese indirectness in the context of social refusals. In order to do so, she combines a series of studies that have a triangulated effect in her comparison of data between Japan, Australia, and Canada.

Japanese are among the world's most polite people, if not *the* most polite. Understandably, therefore, there are intricate rules involved, and Naomi Sugimoto (chapter 19) provides a rare look at Japanese apology in teasing out some of the main distinctive features.

As important as politeness may be in Japanese society, Reiko Hayashi (chapter 20) reveals how the conventional use of vagueness as a politeness strategy can have negative effects and misunderstanding between Japanese themselves. Such effects are at least tied to the growing place of individuality in Japanese society.

Japanese Mass Media and Internet Communications

Every field or discipline needs its own self-criticism, and Brian Moeran, in chapter 21, helps in this regard by raising thoughtful questions about the popular impressions of Japanese advertising and, therefore, Japanese culture itself. He raises points that merit heed. Also, he opens the portholes to Japanese advertisers through his ethnography, made in whose offices he once worked. His attention to both cultural products and social processes is especially noteworthy in giving us a behind-the-scenes look at a Japanese advertising agency.

Foreign businesspeople going to Japan would be wise to consider chapter 22. Masayuki Nakanishi's kind of advice bears repeating because it all too often gets lost in the excitement of doing business abroad. For those in academic social science, his chapter is also applicable because theory is only as good as it can resonate in the real world. And Nakanishi illustrates aspects of Japaneseness through his study on TV commercials in Japan.

A sociocultural element integral to enculturation and socialization must be the self, which is the focus of chapter 23. Michael L. Maynard attempts to show how advertising constructs a self-image for the adolescent by a comparative study of advertisements in Japanese and American versions of the magazine *Seventeen*. By so doing, he illustrates how, respectively, collectivism and individualism can become primary ideals of the two societies.

What happens when Japanese carry on a newsgroup discussion on the Internet? Lots of interesting things, as Jane W. Yamazaki shows in chapter 24, for the form and content of communications are functions of the local and the global. That is, both particular (Japanese) and universal (the world) elements interact, expanding the Japanese repertoire of communicative strategies. In what direction does the Japanese choose, locally or globally? Even in the digital medium we can find that the sociocultural counts, and aspects of Japaneseness emerge.

These are the chapters included in this book. They do not provide the last word on Japaneseness, but rather form a basis for serious explorations of the subject. At the same time, it is hoped that readers will gain deeper appreciation of the culture and a sense of what it means to be Japanese.

ACKNOWLEDGMENTS

Thanks go to Peter Kracht, executive editor, Eric Levy, acquisitions editor, and Lindsay Claire, production supervisor, of Greenwood Publishing Group for their help in readying for production. Special thanks go to Meredith Phillips of Roundhouse Editorial Services, who expertly copyedited and typeset the manuscript, as well as to Ikumi Imani and Shigeki Suzuki for consultation on things Japanese.

REFERENCES

Donahue, R. T., & Prosser, M. H. (1997). *Diplomatic discourse: International conflict at the United Nations.* Greenwich, CT: Ablex.

Prosser, M. H. (1988). *The cultural dialogue: An introduction to intercultural communication.* Boston: Houghton Mifflin. (Original work published by SIETAR International, Washington, DC, 1978.)

Random House Webster's college dictionary. (1991). New York: Random House.

part I

Japanese Core Cultural Concepts

Chapter 1

Guideposts for Exploring Japaneseness[1]

Ray T. Donahue

In keeping with an interdisciplinary focus, this chapter acts as a primer for approaching Japanese studies. First, a background report about Japan on the threshold of the third millennium is provided, indicating a serious state of economic and financial crisis that impacted negatively on its institutions, as well as its people. The crisis was deep enough to raise questions among the Japanese about their national and cultural identities. Second, this state of affairs is explained with particular focus on the political leadership and shares some intriguing findings, as well as identifying why the study of culture looms so importantly even for topics economic or political in scope, topics sometimes considered beyond "cultural" interpretations. Third, basic principles for the observation and study of Japanese culture are discussed, including: (1) the linking of culture and behavior; (2) conceptualizing Japan as a hybrid culture; and (3) taking a cubist approach to Japanese studies. Illustrative examples are provided for analysis. These examples also provide the reader realistic stimuli for considering cultural diversity and issues of cultural relativism.

BACKGROUND TO THE STUDY OF JAPAN

State of Japan, 2000

Japan began the 21st century with record unemployment, bankruptcies, divorces, suicides, crime, and national debt, the amount of which was unseen in modern economic history ("Japan as No. 1," 2000)—an aggregated 130% of its GNP, doubled if local governments are included ("Japan's Debt," 2000). "To service the debt, Tokyo must devote an eye-popping 65% of central government revenue" (Zuckerman, 2000). What was supposed to be the start of a "Japanese century" of economic and technological preeminence came to a grinding halt during the "lost decade" of the 1990s. Japan had been considered nearly invincible, having resurrected itself from the ashes of war to become an economic superpower, as well as having been touted as number one from national health and education to longevity and lawfulness. These achievements underscored a United Nations study placing Japan first in the quality of life (Spencer, 1993). However, from burst of the economic bubble and protracted recession, Japan's fortunes reversed, befuddling its politicians and resulting in seven new prime ministers in just 8 years (1990–1998). The old formulas no longer seemed to work, and its political economy appeared unsuited—even dysfunctional—in the new era of globalization. Thus, a leading newspaper, the *Yomiuri Shimbun*, declared that Japan had a national identity crisis in that the Japanese had to ask themselves who they were and where they were headed ("Establish Common National Identity," 2000).

The 21st century is a turning point for Japan, its "third great opening" to the outside world (Masuzoe, 2000). The first opening was forced on them by the American Commodore Matthew Perry in 1853, a prelude to the Meiji period (1868–1912); the second opening, by the Occupation (1945–1952) by the Allied Powers; and the third, by "the wave of globalization" and pressure exerted by the United States (Masuzoe, 2000, p. 4). Each separated by about 50 years, these openings share a common theme: the challenge and crisis of international relations. Perry came with his famous "black ships" (steamers) to lull Japan out of its self-imposed centuries of isolation from the world. This xenophobia has been a backdrop to Japan's international and intercultural relations ever since. As a result, Prime Minister Nakasone in the 1980s promoted the idea of internationalization (*kokusaika*) for the nation to the extent that a national English teacher corps (Japan Exchange Teaching, or JET) was created to be staffed by hundreds of "imported" foreigners, who function not for their English teaching but more for their cultural diversity brought to Japanese junior and senior high schools, and whom the government hopes will return to their native lands as cultural ambassadors for Japan (Lai, 1999). Such purposes seem part and parcel of xenophobia, or as the Japanese sometimes refer to it, as a *gaijin konpurekksu* (complex about foreigners), particularly when cast alongside another highly homogeneous society, such as Hong Kong, whose Native-speaking English Teacher (NET) program uses foreign English teachers primarily for their English teaching, not as "cultural products" (Lai, 1999).

Another example of xenophobia is that up until recently a child of a Japanese mother married to a foreigner could not legally take the father's name. Even if the child, a Japanese citizen, went by the family name of, say, Smith from birth throughout his years of Japanese schooling, Smith was still not recognized by the Japanese government because it was a foreign name. Thus, when the child became 15 years old and needed his own Japanese passport, he needed proof of identification showing his *expected* use of his mother's Japanese name, an expectation not held for children whose fathers were Japanese. This occurred even if Smith had Japanese public school ID cards and bank passbooks showing his name was Smith (スミス), the only name he had ever gone by.

Another example: A child of mine, though part Japanese, looks decidedly Caucasian. When my wife, a Japanese, provided his photograph to obtain his Japanese passport, as a dual national, the government clerk vigorously tried to erase a "spot" he claimed to see on the child's photograph (of his face). My wife took offense, feeling that the clerk's claim and his exaggerated action were racist, for she did not see any such spot. (Needless to say, no "spot" actually appears on the child's face.) This is probably an isolated case, but Japanese women who out-marry become vulnerable because some Japanese may treat them as "traitors." This case also reminds me of the strong value of purity in Japan both concrete and symbolic. Ohnuki-Tierney (1984) observes that Japanese have a hypersensitivity about dirt and germs closely correlated with a spatial classification of in and out, which corresponds to a moral ethos that symbolically may cast outsiders as having "cultural germs." A case in point are the *burakumin* (a Japanese outcast group associated in the past with "unclean" occupations dealing with leather products and corpses). Historically, evil was believed to come from the outside (e.g., of a village), and strangers and foreigners were believed to be sources of disease and other misfortune (Ohnuki-Tierney, 1984).

Of course, that was then and Japan is a modern nation now. Japanese are well known for being hospitable to visitors, especially foreigners. But as has often been said, this openness toward foreigners is really only at "arm's length," so that foreigners cannot become integrated into Japanese society as they can in most Western societies. At the societal level, it is thought incongruous that a foreigner would settle in Japan. At the individual level, there are, of course, warm-hearted people who can accept foreigners of whatever national or ethnic origin. But once out of one's circle of Japanese intimates, foreigners, especially those without Asian features, are readily and continually marked as outsiders, such that they may be denied service in a restaurant or for rental of an apartment simply because of being a foreigner. An infamous case of Japanese discrimination occurred in New York City in 1992, where the Japanese restaurant, Tobata, repeatedly refused service to non-Japanese, which was filmed and documented by CNBC. For the foreigner in Japan, it is relatively rare but not inconceivable for such an event to occur at a restaurant. For access to bath houses and apartment rentals, the frequency of discrimination is much higher.

The third great opening of Japan involves the outside world because, as Masuzoe puts it,

[Japan's old way] of standardized education and mass production has reached a dead end. . . . New industries cannot be nurtured in the incubator of bureaucratic protection and guidance. . . . The keys to survival are deregulation, megacompetition, information disclosure, and freedom of choice. (2000, p. 3)

Masuzoe's "keys" imply a need for a loosening of the traditional social hierarchy and greater egalitarian relations. Such change essentially would involve greater openness to cultural diversity at school, at the market, and on the job. Japan's "group-think" mentality, borne from the people's high degree of homogeneity (see Donahue, 1998) and insularity, is antithetical to a democracy that offers equal protection of civil and human rights. Moreover, due to its rapidly graying population and low birth rate, Japan expects to require substantial numbers of foreign workers in the future. With increasing global competition, societies can no longer afford to bar many of its members from opportunity due to ethnic, racial, gender, or other social criteria. Because "the concept of human rights exists only vaguely in Japan" (Oshima, 1998, p. 202), the "third great opening" may become every bit as challenging as the other two.

Japan at 2000: Why and How

The Japanese economic miracle fizzled out by the 1990s. Famous for its export economy and "Japanese management style," which boasted the world's top efficiency rate in manufacturing (Katz, 1998), the domestic sector of the economy was nearly the opposite. Overall, the nation lagged behind most industrialized countries in productivity. Whereas the export segment of the economy operated on freely competitive principles, the domestic segment, from "smokestack" heavy industries to the services, were protected by practices known as convoy capitalism (Gyohten, 2000; Katz, 1998). Among the established players in the major domestic industries, no one enterprise could be left behind, necessitating that everyone keep the same pace within their industry, which included banks, the most central players of all.

A lack of oversight of banks (Japan's examiners numbered only a 10th of what the United States had) (Katz, 1998) and a public investment fervor led to hugely inflated valuations of real estate. Such overvalued assets underwrote more and more bad loans until eventually the house of cards had to fall. When it did, a major banking crisis ensued and equity values fell nationally as much as 70% or more. For many homeowners, it was a bitter outcome.

Convoy capitalism worsened the economic downturn because business executives are led to seek market share rather than company profit. They can do so because the interlocking relations between affiliated companies (*keiretsu*) enable them to divide business between themselves—without seeking independent bids—a collusion that may result in price fixing and cartels. Unchallenged by the weak Japanese FTC, the added costs of this "socialized market" get passed on to consumers. Such practices hardly enable the Japanese to compete in a globalized marketplace. This state of affairs partly, if not completely, explains why Japan, an electronics colossus, was ranked only 13th in access to the Internet in the year 2000, a ranking that actually may have been overestimated ("Japan Ranks 13th," 2000). An Internet expert estimated Japan then to be 5 years behind American

Internet technology (Kaneko, 2000), a huge gap in the digital age. Japan's relative slowness in embracing the Internet is attributable largely to high costs. Telecom charges for using the Internet in Japan were found to be nearly double to those in the United States ("Tokyo Internet," 2000). These high costs were set by Nippon Telephone and Telegraph (NTT), who owned the nation's network of telephone lines and whose majority stockholder was the state. NTT sought to recoup its investment costs, but critics argued that its fees were unreasonably high—the world's highest—and by deregulating, lower fees and higher revenues would be the result (Pawasarat, 2000). More telling of the issue was that Japanese hosts on the Internet were only 5% of the number of American hosts ("Japan Ranked 13th," 2000), undoubtedly due to the exorbitant costs of Internet start-ups in Japan. For example, a Japanese would-be entrepreneur had paid only $75 to register an Internet company in the United States, but found that in his own country the registry fee was over $6,000 ("Even the E-Rents," 2000).

Most countries would also compare unfavorably because the United States provides especially liberal conditions for entrepreneurship. However, among other industrialized nations, Japan still may be particularly unfavorable. Business start-ups in Japan, in general, not just for the Internet, produced proportionally less than half of the economic output that start-ups produced in France and in Germany due to government red tape that restricted the creation of new businesses (Wheatley, 2000). A Japanese advisory council, for example, led by the president of Sony, noted that for the Internet alone over 700 legal restrictions limited the growth of e-commerce (Sakurai, 2000). Such effects favor entrenched power, barring newcomers, Japanese and foreign alike. Japanese politicians knew this and have long called for reform. But change would be painful. The "old economy" represented traditional ways, and its restructuring could cost many workers their jobs.

The central government was ill-disposed to lead the restructuring. One and the same party—the Liberal Democratic Party (LDP)—held the leadership position for much of the postwar period. Only in later decades was it forced to form coalition governments, but it still clung to power nonetheless. A number of factors helped maintain the status quo in favor of the LDP. One factor that helped keep the LDP in power was the disproportionate power that rural/agricultural electorial blocs were allowed to have over urban voters, which long benefitted the LDP. Another factor was the power of political dynasties, by which political offices are practically inherited from one family member to another through the "well-oiled political machine." Many former prime ministers, largely LDP, advanced in this way. Indeed, one-third of the members of the Lower House, the most powerful of the two houses in the Diet, were family relatives of former politicians, whereas the comparable figure for other industrialized countries would be only 6 or 7% ("Novice Yuko Obuchi," 2000). Such political dynasties are said to be a throwback to prewar Japan when the then House of Peers consisted of appointed positions, most of which went to the inherited peerage (Yamaguchi, 2000).

A third factor that helped maintain the status quo was the huge disbursement of funds for public works, the amount of which exceeded "all other developed countries combined," leading Struck (2000) to call Japan the "pork barrel juggernaut." Japan has had large gaps in its infrastructure, and the government tried to spend the country out of its economic malaise, but the situation merited what one opposition leader aptly called a "hotbed of corruption" ("Novice Yuko Obuchi," 2000, p. 3). "With the possible exception of Italy, it can be said that money has corrupted democracy in Japan more than in any other major industrial nation" (Kerbo & McKinstry, 1995, p. 103). Curtis (1999) points out, though, that Japanese politics has less corruption than in the past and is working to reduce it. However, economic trade-offs made while attempting to jump-start the economy would likely lessen those attempts.

The fourth factor that helped the LDP stay in power had been the strong conservatism of the electorate. Despite the many stories of political corruption, Japanese voters had been reluctant to boot out the LDP completely because the party had overseen the growth of the Japanese economic miracle. This support for status quo, although gradually receding in recent years, makes me recall the nearly reverent feelings held for the state. After all, the state was a religion in recent history. A curious example of this reverence is how the city of Nagoya, the country's fourth largest, still identifies itself sometimes as Imperial No. 8 (八) for having been the site for the eighth imperial academy (*Dai-Hachi Kōtō Gakkō*) under the now-defunct prewar educational system. Thus, the city's subway system uses a stylized 八(8) as its mark of identity, as do certain highway signs for the city, and most recently, the city's soccer team in the nation's professional J League took the official name of Grampus Eight in partial reference to the city's old Imperial Academy No. 8 ("grampus" being an amalgam of meanings denoting "whale or dolphin" but also including school "campus" among others). A soccer team, of course, does not field 8 players but 11. My point is that Nagoya City, simply for having been part of the old imperial system, despite it having been only eighth, feels it to be honor enough to keep in warm memory (by at least the elders). To be sure, the imperial connection with 8 is not felt strongly among Nagoya residents today as it was decades ago. But it is the loyalty for the state in decades past that is most relevant here.[2]

Such loyalty seems akin to that which has sustained the popularity for the main political party, the LDP, even if corrupt, during its stewardship of the nation. Loyalty is strongly inbred among the Japanese as part of the social contract between *sempai* (senior) and *kōhai* (junior), the essential building block of Japanese society—the senior bestows paternalistic favors in exchange for the junior's unfaltering loyalty. This ethic underlies relations between siblings, between classmates, between coworkers, and even between organizations, such as companies. An essential aspect of the *sempai–kōhai* relationship is the paternalism that is usually involved. Thus, we can understand how convoy capitalism and political dynasties have become earmarks of Japan's political economy. Paternalism is exchanged for loyalty, a perfectly rational relation. The entrenched power that results makes effective political opposition that much harder. A shift in power still can happen as it did in 1993 when an opposition leader campaigning on a platform of reform won leadership of the coalition. His government, however, was short lived because, ironically, he was implicated in a corruption scandal himself and was forced to resign. The opposition gained the leadership only because of the succession of money scandals that were exposed involving LDP politicians and the economic bubble of the 1980s had burst miring Japan deep in crisis. However, in less than 3 years and two governments later, the LDP gained the prime ministership back, in 1996.

Japan's democracy, being still young, necessarily will have "growing pains," such as the weak enforcement of anti-monopoly or civil rights laws. Its democracy is much more a social democracy than a direct democracy, and so will inevitably differ from the type found in the United States. Operationally, the Japanese government is "the smallest among the industrialized democracies and thus [has] the fewest government officials relative to population size of an OECD country" (Curtis, 1999, p. 232). The Japanese government employs proportionally less than half the number as does the American government and a third less than what OECD (Organization for Economic Cooperation and Development) countries employ on average (Curtis, 1999). Understandably, therefore, Japanese politicians "lack sufficient staff to gather information and write legislation" (Kerbo & McKinstry, 1995, p. 104), which necessarily places extra reliance on the career bureaucrats to pick up the slack. And that they do: "Ministry officials issue ordinances that outnumber laws from the Diet by nine to one" (Kerbo & McKinstry, 1995, p. 104). Power therefore shifts toward these bureaucrats, and because they are known to have an "insular outlook" and "strong in-group identification" (Richardson, 1997, p. 245), each of the ministries becomes its own castle (see also "Government Aims to Pry Power," 2000). In effect, the Japanese prime ministership is probably the weakest among comparable positions in the Western industrialized world (Kerbo & McKinstry, 1995; Richardson, 1997).

It is little wonder then that the Japanese political leadership had trouble providing bold new steps during its economic and financial crisis at the turn of the new century. Nor did the electorate seem to mind—only "scant evidence" shows that the public wanted radical reform, which only encouraged indecisive government policy (Curtis, 1999, p. 39). And according to at least one economic theory (Ronald McKinnon's), Japanese leaders have had little choice anyway because external pressures for the Japanese yen to appreciate in the exchange rate as a trade imbalance corrective leads to a flight of Japanese capital to go abroad, reducing what is available for "pump priming" measures by the government ("Wading," 1999). Thus, a broader perspective is needed in viewing Japan. Explanations heavily based on a single factor, that of oppression (or corruption) by all-powerful social and political elites, which some Westerners seem eager to do, may be short-sighted.

A good example is how Western media covered the United States–Japan whaling dispute of 2000. The media typically gave the impression that Japan's scientific studies of whales were no more than ploys to put whale meat on the table in fashionable Tokyo restaurants (see Desai, 2000; McKillop, 2000). A journalist went as far as to call the Japanese government the "world's dumbest" for insisting on its right to hunt whales (McKillop, 2000). Yet, Japan not only had the right by dint of approval from the International Whaling Commission (IWC), but also was required by international law to produce whale byproducts—whale meat—so that the carcasses would not be completely wasted (Goodman, 2000). Moreover, the United States produced a similar quantity of whale byproducts as did Japan, which were also from an endangered species (Goodman, 2000). He also pointed out that Japan's harvest of whales would not adversely affect survival of the species and that Japan's scientific studies would contribute to the larger goal of effective management of the world's renewal resources (Goodman, 2000). If Goodman, a former Canadian representative to the IWC, is correct, then the Western media severely maligned Japan while helping to reproduce some of the worst stereotypes about the Japanese.[3]

In brief, a broad perspective is needed for viewing Japan by which the related context or situation is fully applied. "Corrupt political leadership," if that be the case, is probably just part of the equation in understanding Japan. Whatever ailed Japan at dawn of the new millennium had been begotten by the Japanese themselves—the whole society. Clearly "convoy capitalism," as practiced, seems a direct outgrowth of the well-known collectivism of the Japanese. So, too, does the central planning by the state, which produced the "world's most successful[ly] planned economy" (Cortazzi, 1998), as do other aspects of Japanese politics including the magnitude of public works, the electorial districting that favored ruralities, and perhaps the very weakness of the prime ministership. To this extent, the study of Japan's culture and national character merit all the more attention.

Linking Culture and Behavior

From whatever research or academic field we come, we are likely to share this task—the linking of culture and behavior. We would probably also agree that knowing how culture influences our behavior and that of others is essential for effective communication across cultures (see Brislin, 1993; Prosser, 1978/1988). Culture is meant here largely in the sense of "invisible" culture—thought patterns widely shared among a community of people that are passed from one generation to the next and that likely give rise to particular styles or means of communication (Prosser, 1978/1988). In this regard, however, culture is not held as *the* cause of behavior, but rather as a host of contributing and noncontributing factors (see Berry, Poortinga, Segall, & Dasen, 1992). From among such cultural components, the actual task becomes identifying specifically related factors, such as attitudes, socialization, and beliefs, that may impinge on a particular behavior or set of behaviors. Thus, when speaking of linking culture and behavior, I mean it in a shorthand way to represent the complex relations involved. It may prove helpful, therefore, given an interdisciplinary audience, to provide examples of how culture underpins Japanese behavior, as well as how culture may impact perception, especially that of the researcher. For the former, I share several cases, one immediately about the Japanese kimono culture, followed by cases from Japanese popular culture.

THE IMPACT OF CULTURE ON HUMAN BEHAVIOR

Japanese Walking Behavior

For ease of illustration, walking is chosen here because it is outwardly visible and both Japanese and North Americans have remarked that these peoples differ in how they walk. One such difference concerns the walk by Japanese females. Hinds and Iwasaki (1995) observed that Japanese females in Japan tend to walk pigeon-toed much more than Japanese American females in Hawaii or in California. Note that this observation does not apply to Japanese males, so presumably the intervening variable is not biological but cultural. The explanation is that the "kimono culture," being stronger in mainland Japan, can inculcate more effectively its female beauty ideal about walking. Although purely anecdotal, their observation has merit at least in regard, I believe, to this behavior 20 or 25 years ago, when this same behavior seemed rather apparent.

Even today, according to my international students in Japan, this behavior is especially apparent when Japanese females wear high heels. Wearing high heels, however, may require special practice and so should be discounted for present purposes. I have since informally surveyed Japanese college students of both genders on whether Japanese females walk this way while wearing modern attire. (I did not specify the shoe type.) More students disagreed than those who agreed about the prevalence of pigeon-toed females. This is not surprising because the recent generation of Japanese college students follow a behavioral code appreciably different than their parents. One example is that today it is no longer a taboo to blow one's nose in public, or at least in a classroom. Another example is walking down a street eating an ice cream. However, a finding that does give credence to Hinds and Iwasaki's observation is that some females, although only 1% of the females sampled, freely reported that their mothers specifically instructed them to walk pigeon-toed even when in modern attire (e.g., a dress or jeans). If this question had been directly asked to the respondents, it is likely that the 1% figure would have been higher.

Assuming that these self-reports were accurate, we do have tentative evidence for the behavior in question as having been learned (at least in some cases), which provides an apt case for the link between culture and behavior. Further validation is required, but if we remember the tentativeness of these claims, then we have a useful suggestion of how culture can impact human behavior. At the same time, we can see two grand conventions operating—modern and traditional. Both can be seen readily on the streets of Japan. More will be said on these different conventions in Japan, but first we consider the impact of culture on the perceptual behavior by researchers.

Effect of Cultural Bias on the Researcher

For the impact on the researcher by his or her own native culture, I have previously documented such cases for Japanese studies (e.g., Donahue, 1998), and so presently I go outside the immediate field for an illustrative case, such as one found in the book, *Reading National Geographic* (Lutz & Collins, 1993). Although the book documents culture's influence on behavior in the case of editorial decisions by *National Geographic*, I wish to focus more directly on how the two authors of the book, even while trying to be highly enlightened about such matters, succumb themselves to a blindness or ethnocentrism. And as I have shown, for example, with the case of North American TV broadcasters who behaved ethnocentrically with their Japanese counterparts (Donahue, 1998), such professional communicators and professional observers suggest that ethnocentrism can befall any of us. Our native culture becomes the sun for us in our perceptual universe. So central is our native culture to our perception that we probably cannot remove all the bonds of its mental programming. Perhaps the best we can do is continually remind ourselves of this influence. Through memorable examples, I hope to do the same, especially in the context of presenting bases for exploring Japaneseness.

Reading National Geographic is a laudable book that traces the impact of American cultural values on editorial decisions by the magazine. The authors also point out how the magazine appears to have helped its readers to enculturate a cultural ideal of female beauty through "the many ads [in the magazine] that use Pacific motifs" (Lutz & Collins, 1993, p. 152) to market products such as suntan oil in a sensual (or feminine) way. In ads such as the one for Hawaiian Tropic lotion included by the authors, a seemingly Hawaiian model is shown with long hair adorned with flowers, a feminine beauty ideal. They rightfully point out that such ads may encourage the formation of certain cultural beliefs. The point I wish to raise is how the authors themselves may have been unwittingly influenced in the same manner during their analysis. In fact, it seems as if one or both authors had an illusion about the contents of a photograph for study.

Such cases show both the powerful effect of culture on behavior, as well as the point it can happen to the best of us.

The photograph in question, originally from *National Geographic,* is of a Burmese woman working with plants in a field. Perhaps because of her floral patterned attire and the plants, the authors claim that the magazine portrayal "emphasize[s] her femininity *despite* her working" (p. 180, emphasis in original). They also say it could be because flowers are seen in the woman's hair (p. 180). The only problem is that no flowers can be seen in her hair, even in the original magazine issue. Nor did the original source, the magazine, make mention of any flowers. Rather, one or both of these two researchers may have imagined such presence in the photograph, either mentally transporting the flowers from the Asian woman's dress, from the image of the Hawaiian Tropic ad above, from the plants she worked with, or from all three sources. Regardless, the misattribution seems motivated by talk of "femininity" and an American (or Western) beauty ideal held for women, especially Asian. Here I would point out that "Asian" is a fluid sociocultural classification used by Westerners who may or may not correctly use it (Donahue, 1998). Thus, in Western culture, misclassification can occur between Asians and "associated" Polynesians.

To make clear, this error was not a mismatch of captions and photographs in their book. For two male authors, this error would seem almost inevitable, as remarked by one of a number of people with whom I discussed (and confirmed) the error about the photograph. But the two researchers happen to be women, showing how strong, indeed, cultural programming can be. Even when two conscientious and competent scholars tried hard to control their own biases and exercise critical analysis, their own native culture still stepped in the way, leading one or both authors to have an illusion. If such a possibility would seem too remote, I have only to remind readers of the classic findings by Gould (1981) of various research studies in the field of intelligence testing that had been nullified by unconscious biases of the measurers and researchers. Although Gould's study concerns errors of considerable degree, his cases do share one important commonality with the error raised about the photograph earlier: the impact of cultural bias on researcher behavior.[4]

Having shown how culture can affect behavior, I now offer two further essential principles useful in Japanese studies, while concurrently providing cases for application and analysis of Japaneseness. As pointed out previously, Japanese behavior is influenced by at least two major conventions—the traditional and the modern. These conventions, in turn, have been influenced by, respectively, Eastern- and Westernization, processes that Edwin O. Reischauer (1988) called bi-civilization. The bi-civilization of Japan lends itself to perceptual puzzles, contradictions, and paradoxes. It is also a way that the Japanese can integrate foreign cultural elements, a capacity long renowned and illustrated with a woodblock print from popular culture. In another illustration from popular culture, a storefront display based on a continuous Japanese custom of at least two millenniums provides further opportunity for readers to meet cultural diversity, as well as to identify aspects of Japaneseness.

FURTHER PRINCIPLES FOR THE STUDY OF JAPAN

Japan as a Hybrid Culture

Japan and the "West" differ in fundamental ways, largely because Japan has been "bi-civilized" between east and west like no other country, creating a "hybrid culture" (Yoshida, Tanaka, & Sesoko, 1984). Although Japan has shown an immense capacity to incorporate foreign elements, this incorporation often has had clear limits. Sharp distinctions are often made between Japanese and foreign things. Written Japanese, for example, uses separate written scripts for native Japanese and words of foreign origin. Thus, the difference is institutionalized, and the distinction is perpetuated. What probably made Japan's cultural hybridity distinctive is that its cultural borrowing could be made in "incubation," insulated from foreign invaders and therefore free to integrate culturally however it saw fit (Donahue, 1998). Except for sporadic periods of contact with China and Korea, and later the West, Japan was alone enough to adapt and integrate its cultural borrowing into a "set of characteristics more distinctive than almost any comparable unit of people in the world" (Reischauer, 1988, p. 32).

The Japanese genius for incorporation with limits has greatly advanced its culture. New technology and the associated language can be borrowed almost effortlessly because the foreign elements can be placed at a psychologically safe distance; native identity need not be threatened. For example, when some young Japanese come to the United States and see a McDonald's restaurant, they may say, "Americans have the same things as we do!" In Japanese, the name is written in *katakana,* script used for foreign words:

マクドナルド   (Makudonarudo).

Even though the original American name also appears in the Japanese locations, "McDonald's" is seen merely as a decoration, following the common use of English in Japanese commercial signs.

Blending Japanese traditional elements with the modern appears to be a useful strategy in commercial advertisements by Western companies, especially when securing a share of the market in Japan. To demonstrate this, but in the reverse case of a Japanese proprietor marketing Western products to Japanese consumers, I offer for analysis the case of a whimsical wall hanging in a Japanese multiplex movie house. By doing so, I also hope to show how seamless the traditional and the modern are interconnected in Japan. Furthermore, this case provides opportunity to consider various aspects of the culture.

A Wall Hanging at Vājin Shinemazu (Virgin Cinemas)

Right away, with the name Vājin (ヴァージン), we witness a change that has been happening recently in Japanese, if not a corruption of the language, by the entry of a previously missing sound /v/ and related orthographic symbol ヴァ. Most Japanese would still produce this with a /b/ sound unless they had had previous training in another language, notably English, from which the associated loanword comes. Indeed, "virgin," as in "Virgin Islands," is generally rendered as バージン (*bājin*). Linguistic loans tend to be lexical (vocabulary), so when new sounds or syntax are borrowed, it is rather remarkable. One example of new syntax borrowed from English is ザ (*za*) for "the," the definite article. Consider this use from an ad in an upscale department store: ザ三越バーゲンセール (*za Mitsukoshi bāgen sēru*/the Mitsukoshi bargain sale). Although such cases remain largely in commercial language, it reminds us of the well-known capacity of the Japanese to borrow from foreign cultures despite their having nearly an equally well-known xenophobia. It is this latter condition that I believe has relevance for the wall hanging in question.

The wall hanging is actually a modern woodblock print done in traditional or *ukiyoe* style, "a color print of everyday life in the Edo period" (*Kenkyusha's*, 1987). It hangs next to a concession in the lobby of the Vājin Shinemazu (Virgin Cinemas) in Nagoya City, a "megaplex" theater containing 10 or more screening areas for films. The very idea of this opulence seems Western, and indeed I was informed by an employee that this theater was bought as a franchise from a British developer, the same person who created the airline and record stores of the same name, Virgin. The interior design seems so Western that my children described it as Disneyesque: flashy ultramodern accents of chrome and bright colors that lead to an extra-long refreshments counter for popcorn and other Western snacks. But more pertinent was the souvenir shop, which sold various Hollywood paraphernalia. Indeed, the day of my visit, out of the 10 movies scheduled, only 1 was Japanese, 1 was French, and the rest were American.

On the opposite side of the lobby, and quite in juxtaposition, was a concession for *takoyaki* (fried octopus snacks). *Takoyaki* is a common traditional snack having a similar place in the culture as does the hot dog in American culture. Next to the concession hung a large woodblock print approximately 6 x 10 feet (see Figure 1-1) and is unrelated to any known Japanese story or film. A superhero samurai is depicted battling a giant red octopus that has in its clutches a Japanese female. The battle takes place on the surface of an inland sea framed by hilltops on either side. The only visible language is that of the name of the Japanese artist and presumably that of the movie theater: Vājin Takoyaki (Virgin fried octopus). This scene is identifiably Japanese because the faces of the characters are of such traditional appearance, and the samurai wears the traditional topknot and headdress associated with his social class. The sea setting is quite Japanese also, for Japan is an island country that makes great use of sea products, the octopus included.

Figure 1-1. Woodblock print displayed in the Vājin Shinemazu (Virgin Cinemas) in Nagoya City. Photo courtesy of Ray T. Donahue.

The whimsical arises with the notion that a red octopus, and therefore a cooked one, is giant enough to threaten people ashore. The further whimsy is that this scene is not historical but a present-day one: the samurai wears a watch and a scuba tank. Moreover, he sports a tattoo of the theater name, Virgin, written in English. Tattoos are taboo, associated with the underworld, but recently have gained popularity (at least the "wash-off" type) among young adults, who probably have been influenced by Western rock music stars who are known to wear them. Moreover, the female wears red hair, lipstick, and polished finger nails. So a traditional theme is made relevant to youth, who compose most of the movie-going audience.

Western influence is also found with the main theme: An action hero battles a monster to save a damsel in distress, a theme of romance and one relatively absent in Japanese fairy tales (Kawai, 1988). The basis for romance here resides partly in the hero's action and partly in the facial expression of this damsel. Plainly carefree, she seems to cast a flirtatious eye toward the hero. This theme is archetypical for the Western story and learned early in childhood. For sure,

Japanese have romantic stories, and *samurai* even come to the rescue of the help-less, including women. But the elements of the hero battling the monster and the flirtatious female, thereby suggesting a potential romantic pair, are overwhelm-ingly Western in comparison. Romantic love itself is a Western invention, at least in regard to marriage. While Westerners commonly marry for "love," the rest of the world marries through arranged marriages. The majority of Japanese did exactly the latter only until recently when the *renai* (love marriage) came into ascendancy. And just as the American Occupation allowed the Japanese to see the kiss on motion picture film for the very first time, so did it also help sow the seeds for growth of *ren'ai*, actually romantic liaisons in general.

Because of the romantic overtones of this octopus print, it would be useful to explore the implications that arise with this topic. First, romance itself suggests a *redii fāsuto wārudo* (ladies-first world), which could make some Japanese males uncomfortable because they are not socialized in that way. This term often was expressed jokingly to me by Japanese males in reference to how they perceived Western gender relations. Some of my female Japanese study-abroad students have returned impressed, telling me how American or other Western males fol-low common courtesies that women hardly ever received in Japan (which is probably due to shyness).

A second implication from the topic of romance is the kiss. The kiss is rather sensitive—nearly taboo—for depiction in visual media for general audiences. Generally, the kiss has been thought by the Japanese to be more properly per-formed in private, such as the bedroom. The kiss was banned from the cinema by Japanese authorities, and so Japanese audiences did not see their first filmed kiss until the American Occupation (Anderson & Richie, 1982). In Japanese films, it is not uncommon "for kisses to be faked, the act being taken from an angle where the spectator cannot tell that the principals are merely touching cheeks" (Anderson & Richie, 1982, p. 176). So even if kissing were shown, in whatever media, it may not always be completely convincing. A related case is that in the year 2000, the international studies office at a local Nagoya college received a complaint by two middle-aged male administrators that an American female stu-dent was seen in a prolonged kiss with a Japanese male in front of the library. An unfortunate development was that the "blame" was cast on the American; no action was taken toward the Japanese male student. She alone was summoned for advisement against such behavior. True, her foreignness made her easily identi-fiable, but she was never asked to help bring in the male for the same advisement. The implication therefore was that this behavior was "foreign" not Japanese. Note also that no official rule existed barring kissing. It simply is frowned on in public by the wider society, though it might occur on the most metropolitan cam-puses, those being in Tokyo.

Another relevant case is that of the long-lost fisherman at sea who did not kiss or embrace his wife at his return; rather he shook her hand (Donahue, 1998). A

Japanese woman observes what she sees is a lack of affectionate kissing even among family and her ambivalence about it: "American parents kiss their children . . . when they send them [off somewhere]. We Japanese cannot create the same kind of atmosphere, even in our own families. I envy American closeness with each other, but I also am embarrassed when I see Americans kissing each other" (Watanabe, 1994, p. 36). This Japanese view and related behavior is fine, of course. As we well know, it is relative. Relativism cannot hide the fact, though, that Japanese and Western cultures differ, sometimes widely, about gender, dating, marriage, and sexuality. These subjects are necessarily entailed in the octopus print because of the romantic hero motif, the "knight in shining armor."

Thus, this octopus print, though lowbrow, has implications that cut across the whole of Japanese culture. And casting this Japanese romantic hero in a traditional motif, as well as in humorous light, may function to neutralize anxiety from the romantic implications. I am generalizing here, for Japan also has its own share of romantics, but they may have different ways of expression. After all, romantic love is considered an important aspect of human growth in Western societies. Japanese society, however, simply does not regard it as developmentally important for young people as it is found in the West. Dating is fairly discouraged in Japan as a threat to school achievement and even to the social order. It is no coincidence, therefore, that sex education in Japanese schools did not gain attention by authorities until the 1970s, but still has yet to be fully implemented nationally (Nishijima, 2000). Despite these social restraints, however, a record one in three Japanese high school students reported having had performed coitus (Nishijima, 2000).

In sum, we have a Japanese art form executed by a Japanese for a Japanese audience utilizing traditional Japanese culture reconstructed to fit a modern Westernized situation—a multiplex movie house that predominantly shows Hollywood films, famous for adventure and hero worship wherein the male hero saves an attractive female. This woodblock print, a centerpiece in the movie house lobby, seems to act as a welcome mat for Japanese visitors, so they can feel at home in an otherwise alien atmosphere, if they happen to be so conservatively Japanese. For such people in particular, it seems to say: "We can function in a Western medium, but we may do so in our own way—the Japanese way. That may include eating Japanese traditional food, as well as having a superhero in modern times choose not a gun but a traditional weapon." The Japanese, incidentally, were the only major civilization in history to have truly given up guns in favor of the traditional sword (Perrin, 1988), occurring in the premodern era. Thus, a subtle message inheres that honors the traditional Japanese way, helping to avoid serious identity conflicts and paving the way for new experience. Such nearly seamless blends of traditional and Western or modern elements are found throughout Japan. It is remarkable how a people can be so harmoniously "bi-civilized." This aspect of Japaneseness may explain how the Japanese can so readily import foreign culture and transform it into their own.

The Cubist Approach

For the various points of view needed in understanding Japanese culture, Brian Moeran suggests taking what he calls a "cubist approach" (Moeran, 1990). Moeran points out that "any characterization of Japan will inevitably be partial" (p. 6). His statement is realistic given the complexity of Japan's bi-civilization. The cubist approach is particularly fitting for the ambiguity that must ensue in reaching only partial characterizations and for the idea that, at times, we may be dealing more with an "art" than a science, meaning that the subject may defy absolute certainties. For example, the concept of groupism is regularly misapplied by social scientists with the oft-cited personal opinion surveys that report that the Japanese overwhelmingly view themselves as being middle class. This abundant response by Japanese, however, is no different from how Americans and Europeans respond in similar surveys (see Donahue, 1998). In other words, Japanese cultural phenomena resist containment in a neatly wrapped package.

The Phallus

For application of our discussion thus far, consider Figure 1-2. This photograph is of a former establishment on Hirokojidori, a main thoroughfare in downtown Nagoya City. What do you make of this place where a large phallus stood at the entrance in broad daylight? In the immediate area are tall office buildings on the edge of a major shopping district. On the phallus is written the name, Irohanihoheto, as well as on the billboard above the entrance. Most people guess that this was at a museum, but in fact was at a restaurant. Given the location, most of the clientele were office workers from nearby companies. This was a typical *robatayaki*, a restaurant that specializes in grilled dishes along with other traditional foods, such as *sashimi* (raw fish), rice, and tofu. Additionally, they function as an ale house for groups of people to enjoy themselves. In a business district, these kinds of establishments help company employees enjoy their well-known custom of after-hours drinking together (*tsukiai*).

Apart from the phallus, it is rather curious that the name of this restaurant roughly would mean "Reciting our ABCs." *Iroha* is the traditional name for the Japanese syllabary, and *irohanihoheto*, I am told, was the first line of recitation of the syllabary in bygone days. Today, the first line(s) of recitation differs greatly—*aiueo – kakikukeko*—a much more systematic way. The name is also written in *hiragana*, the indigenous orthography and what children first learn to read and write. Thus, the name and the script lend a certain innocence to this setting, which, on the contrary, is far from erotic or raucous. Imagine, however, placing this same restaurant in a community in the United States, in China, or anywhere. In most places, I suppose, rather extreme reactions would arise. Yet Japanese react hardly at all; passersby and patrons alike seemed to ignore this phallic display. I had never seen passersby stop to inspect it, nor do I recall patrons around me having alluded much to it. Whereas the foreign reaction would be robust, the Japanese, rather calm. It is

Figure 1-2. A statue at an establishment in Nagoya City. Photo courtesy of Ray T. Donahue.

not that the Japanese are unfeeling. Rather, Japanese propriety applies especially when in eyesight of others. This case correlates with intriguing research (Ekman, 1972; Friesen, 1972, as cited by Matsumoto, 1996) that compared Japanese emotional reactions to an evocative film seen alone, seen with another American student, and seen with an American student and an "experimenter," an older male in a white lab coat (presumably an authority figure). Whereas the last condition all but blotted out most emotional displays by the Japanese in the former two conditions, the American reactions were essentially unchanged.

My point is that a similar restraint occurs in Japanese daily life when this "experimenter" is replaced by *seken*, the public world. *Seken* can induce fear in some individuals that they are being overly seen or watched by others, a fear akin to that of a shame culture as described by Benedict (1946) in her classic study. As I describe *seken* here, I don't mean that it causes Japanese to conceal their faces behind their coat collars when out in public. Rather, one makes an effort to be "clean-cut" looking, inconspicuous, and mindful of Japanese propriety. For urbanites (but not necessarily for ruralites), one wears fine clothes when out shopping or to the dentist. If not, what would people think? One does not cross the street when the light is red no matter how narrow the crossing nor how empty of cars it might be. One usually does not take notice of others, even if bodily contact is made—most people do not say *sumimasen* (excuse me) in a crowded area. One usually ignores people in difficulty—senior citizens, mothers with their babies. To do otherwise might attract too much attention or cause the other to incur an obligation. These statements are said in general; exceptions do occur. See chapter 2 for elaboration on *seken*.

How are these apparent conflicts explained concerning the name of the establishment, its storefront display, and the Japanese reaction? Furthermore, how does this display fit with the apparent squeamishness about the kiss, as noted previously, in terms of national character? Primarily, we need to engage a cubist approach by which we can accept the ambiguity from this "cognitive dissonance" to suspend judgment. And such suspension could be made indefinitely for certain phenomena, which so befits Moeran's metaphor. From this basis, one proceeds to collect information that may enlighten and help one gain deeper appreciation of the culture. At the same time, one needs to be cognizant of one's own native cultural influence on perception and reasoning that could be misleading. For this the various social sciences offer training, but many professionals realize that effective observations of culture require continued practice. No one is immune from ethnocentrism, as amply evidenced by even well-intended social scientists who unwittingly become entrapped by biases.

To return to the apparent cultural conflicts about the restaurant, first I note that its interior was designed not only in the typical rural motif, but it also included various antique agricultural implements throughout. The phallus on display was probably antique or at least a reproduction of such still found venerated today in a few Shinto shrines across the country, a practice that has continued for 2,000 years. Even without the huge phallus, Shinto, the indigenous religion, is replete with subtle symbols of phallicism (Nelson, 2000). This phallicism emanates not from a desire for male dominance but the worship of nature's generative power (Alles, 1988; Nelson, 2000). This worship is obviously connected with agricultural society and the desire for bountiful harvests. Such worship was made throughout the world in various guises through the ages. Examples are the ancient Celtic idols honoring gods of fertility, remnants found variously in Britain and Ireland (Cahill, 1995), not to mention similar artifacts found in India, parts of Africa, and elsewhere. It also should be pointed out that Shinto celebrates a "vulvism," a veneration of the vulva, outer female genitalia, which receives much less attention but is just as ancient, spiritual, and continuous in practice. What separates Japan from the other industrialized countries, which are largely Christian, is the continuity of these ancient fertility rites and practices of phallicism (and vulvism). A reason for this is a basic religious difference: "Concepts of 'sexual magic' are more harmonious with the polytheistic religions found among farming peoples than with . . . monotheistic ones" (Bolin, 1994, pp. 213–214). For those in the Christian world, especially Anglo, which has lost touch with its own similar ancient practices, it is hard to view the Shinto phallus (or vulva) worship as natural as do Japanese Shintoists. Some foreigners, including both Westerners and Asians, describe these practices as "bizarre," an understandable reaction given the cultural divide.

Another complication is that not all Japanese practice Shintoism, and even many of those who are Shinto may not have experienced actual rites and practices devoted to phallicism or vulvism. I have observed some Japanese go to a related shrine but stand outside while their partner made a momentary visit. They seemed to fidget as if concerned about who might see them. Japan has been influenced by Victorianism as has been the United States. For example, some Japanese women went about with breasts exposed and mothers openly breast-fed in public, practices that were discouraged with the influx of Christian missionaries a century ago. The state was concerned that Westerners see Japan as being "modern." Confucianism had similar effects on the relations between the sexes. Nevertheless, there is an undercurrent of naturalism about the exposed body. In some Japanese families today, girls continue to bathe at home with their father even through adolescence and beyond. This practice of mixed bathing, however, is not as prevalent in public baths as has been popularized in the Western media, at least not for young women. Here for the highly situationalized Japanese is the issue of *soto/uchi* (outside/inside), a subject taken up by Makino in chapter 2. So, for a number of reasons, Japanese could seem to ignore the phallus at Irohanihoheto, while its presence might confound the foreigner. Japaneseness is influenced by various traditions and "isms," such that applying the well-known archetypes about Japanese culture may be much more complex than generally thought.

CONCLUSION

Every culture is unique in its own way. Japan's uniqueness resides in its cultural hybridity, an integration of bi-civilizing influences from East and West. It was the first Asian nation to become a modern, industrialized power, greatly benefitting from Western science and technology. Yet Japan has done much to preserve its traditional ways and values. And at dawn of the new millennium, Japanese collectivism, as with the emphasis on senior–junior mutual obligations, was shown manifest in how the Japanese political economy operated, particularly with convoy capitalism. Parallel practices operated in national politics, whereby political dynasties, pork barrel politics, and an impaired prime ministership ruled the day. Because it also had an undersized government, Japan lacked proper oversight of its banking practices, which invited economic decline. Now pressured to function in a global marketplace, Japan faces its third great opening to the world by which it must rationalize its domestic economy and institute effective political reform. Such radical measures, however, were yet to be widely popular with the electorate. Thus, the state of Japan in 2000 represented for the Japanese a crisis in national and cultural identity, for they needed to redefine themselves in view of the new global realities.

Aspects of Japanese culture, such as the mutuality between seniors and juniors and the respective roles of the prime ministership and the electorate, tend to be lost on the outside observer. Instead, observers might fix on, say, the political corruption, while ignoring more relevant features, as seemed to be the case in Western media reports of the United States–Japan whaling dispute of 2000. Because journalists ignored vital elements of the dispute, they unjustifiably made Japan appear villainous, recreating negative images of the Japanese. Sensitive issues as these bring to the fore how easily one's own culture can color perception. Cultural bias, of course, is a universal problem and can arise even when least expected, as when two competent researchers had an illusion about the physical contents of a photograph of a foreign other. That case was used to show how strongly culture can impact perception. The relation between culture and behavior, of course, is of crucial concern in intercultural communication, for it governs, to a large extent, people's effectiveness across cultures.

Another key feature of Japan's cultural hybridity was illustrated by using cultural products found in Japanese popular culture. A modern *ukiyoe* print and a commercialized religious relic (a phallus) provided forays into Japan's nearly seamless bi-civilization of East and West and related discourses. These discourses reveal cultural conflicts, even if the bi-civilization appears so seamless. While the *ukiyoe* print served to bridge the cultural angst possibly felt by conservative Japanese in a heavily Americanized movie theater, the phallus seemed almost a lament over the loss of traditional culture by Japan's speedy industrialization and urbanization in recent history. The very use of this phallus and Japanese reactions to this use represent a particular worldview, one that may be beyond complete comprehension by non-Japanese (even if "intellectualized"). Here the cubic approach to Japanese culture is particularly useful, by which the foreign observer is helped to accept ambiguity—the ambiguity of the inexplicable. Another useful purpose served by both cases, but especially by the phallus, is the opportunity to apply cultural relativism. Can the related Japanese practice ultimately be accepted "as is" without being evaluated or judged? This acceptance does not necessarily mean approval. Rather, we treat the practice as meritorious for respect in its own right. One might personally disapprove of a cultural practice, but still grant others their right to it—at least to the extent that one tries to understand the basis for the practice in question.

Finally, one other point to remember about Japan: It is not a monolith. Considerable diversity exists among the population, even though many authors have been pointing out its high degree of homogeneity. Japanese have strong regional differences, such as that found between Tokyo and Osaka (Kanto and Kansai regions). Also, the very nature of being "bi-civilized" gives rise to dual, if not multiple, perspectives. One Japanese may do things in a "modern" or "Western" way while another is more traditional. Both are still Japanese, at least to a point. For many Japanese, it is not an either-or but a synthesis. Some Japanese, for example, practice both Buddhism and Christianity. Similar East–West combinations exist for medical services, schooling, marriage ceremonies, and so forth.With these various points made about Japan, it is hoped that the reader will be better equipped for further explorations in the chapters ahead.

NOTES

1. I wish to thank Chris Lewis, Bill Mansell, and Henry Reece for their comments about this chapter. Any error, of course, is entirely mine.

2. Although there are graduates of Imperial Academy No. 8 still living, in time this memory will fade if it has not already, for younger Nagoya people decipher Grampus Eight to mean "dolphin luck." Grampus in English generally denotes a large dolphin (*Random House Webster's*). For Nagoya, it refers to the golden dolphins perched on top of Nagoya Castle, which are known as *kin no shachi* (golden grampus or killer whale) (*Kenkyusha's*, 1987). I am unable to find any way that eight has a meaning of luck in Japanese. This association may derive from their misinterpretation of what the "eight ball" connotes in English.

3. Regardless of which side of the issue is correct, my point still stands. Western media generally were biased against Japan by ignoring such points raised by Goodman. Other arguments that Japan consumes an enormous amount of sea products or that the government and Green Peace have been in conflict are no excuses for the inadequacy found in Western media reports on the whaling issue. Where Japan may be faulted is its apparently weak public relations effort. As Michiko Wilson (personal communication) points out, the Japanese government did not publicize its view or argue its case by placing announcements in the Western media. This failure to do so seems to fit a Japanese value of conflict avoidance. Anecdotal evidence suggests that Japanese tend to withdraw from debating or arguing with someone even when correct. Exceptions do exist of course, but this characterization seems to fit based on my own observations and those of many others.

4. Gould's findings are termed "classic" here in the sense of being a textbook case of how research measurement can be adversely affected by the measurer's own bias. This matter concerns only that about the early methodology used for testing cranial capacity between social, ethnic, or racial groups, an aspect of his findings that has remained unchallenged. For other matters, I am not surprised that hereditarians, in particular, argue oppositely in the ongoing nature versus nurture debates. And while the hereditarians argue the finer points of Gould's statistical analysis or whether Cyril Burt, a father of British intelligence testing, deserves a new verdict after his debunking even by his ardent supporters many years ago, these are issues quite separate from the matter raised here. I wish to point out something that the hereditarians seem to ignore: How is it that it took someone outside the field of intelligence testing or psychology (Gould) to discover the gross biases of the cranial measurements concerned? Does this lapse on the part of psychology suggest an even greater problem than that assumed?

REFERENCES

Alles, G. D. (1988). Surface, space and intention: The Parthenon and the Kandāriya Mahadeva. *History of Religions, 27*(2), 1–36.

Anderson, J. L., & Richie, D. (1982). *The Japanese film: Art and industry (expanded edition).* Princeton: Princeton University Press.

Benedict, R. (1946). *The chrysanthemum and the sword.* Boston: Houghton Mifflin.

Berry, J. W., Poortinga, Y. H., Segall, M. H., & Dasen, P. R. (1992). *Cross-cultural psychology.* Cambridge: Cambridge University Press.

Bolin, A. (1994). Festivals and sex. In V. L. Bullough & B. Bullough (Eds.), *Human sexuality: An encyclopedia* (pp. 212–216). New York: Garland.

Brislin, R. (1993). *Understanding culture's influence on behavior.* Fort Worth, TX: Harcourt Brace College Publishers.

Cahill, T. (1995). *How the Irish saved civilization: The untold story of Ireland's heroic role from the fall of Rome to the rise of medieval Europe.* New York: Nan A. Talese.

Cortazzi, H. (1998, December 18). World's most successful planned economy. *Japan Times,* p. 20.

Curtis, G. L. (1999). *The logic of Japanese politics.* New York: Columbia University Press.

Desai, N. (2000, August 2). U.S. urges Japan to call off whale hunt. *Earth Times* [Online]. Available: http://www.earthtimes.org/aug/environmentusurgesjapanaug1_00.htm

Donahue, R. T. (1998). *Japanese culture and communication: Critical cultural analysis.* Lanham, MD: University Press of America.

Ekman, P. (1972). Universals and cultural differences in facial expressions of emotion. In J. K. Cole (Ed.), *Nebraska symposium on motivation, 1971* (Vol. 19, pp. 207–283). Lincoln: University of Nebraska Press.

Establish common national identity. (2000, August 13). *Yomiuri Shimbun* [Online]. Available: http://www.yomiuri.co.jp/newse/0813ed09.htm

Even the e-rents are outrageous in Tokyo. (2000, August 28). *Business Week* [Online]. Available: http://www.businessweek.com/2000/00_35/b3696206.htm

Friesen, W. V. (1972). *Cultural differences in facial expression in a social situation: An experimental test of the concept of display rules.* Unpublished doctoral dissertation, University of California, San Francisco.

Goodman, D. (2000, September 12). U.S. whaling sanctions smack of hypocrisy. *Japan Times,* p. 19.

Gould, S. J. (1981). *The mismeasure of man.* New York: W. W. Norton.

Government aims to pry power from bureaucrats. (2000, October 7). *Yomiuri Shimbun* [Online]. Available: http://www.yomiuri.co.jp/news/1007po17.htm

Gyohten, T. (2000). Japan's sheltered banks face the world. In Y. Masuzoe (Ed.), *Years of trial: Japan in the 1990s.* Tokyo: Japan Echo.

Hinds, J., & Iwasaki, S. (1995). *An introduction to intercultural communication.* Tokyo: Nan'undo.

Japan as no. 1 still rings true, but for different reasons. (2000, August 24). *Dow Jones* [Online]. Available: http://asia.biz.yahoo.com/news/asian_markets/article.html?s=asiafinance/news/000824/asian_markets/dowjones/Japan_As_No.1_Still_Rings_True_But_For_Different_Reasons.html

Japan ranks 13th in Net access rate. (2000, July 25). *Asahi Shimbun* [Online]. Available:

http://www.asahi.com/english/asahi/0725/asahi072511.html

Japan's debt tops 270% of GD. (2000, July 7). *The Business Times* [Online]. Available: http://business-times.asia1.com.sg/5/news/nwrld06.html

Kaneko, M. (2000, August 29). U.S. prodigy, 15, says Japan lags in IT. *Japan Times* [Online]. Available: http://www.japantimes.co.jp/cgibin/getarticle.pl5?nn20000829b1.htm

Katz, R. (1998). *Japan: The system that soured.* Armonk, NY: M.E. Sharpe.

Kawai, H. (1988). *The Japanese psyche: Major motifs in the fairy tales of Japan.* Dallas: Spring.

Kenkyusha's new collegiate dictionary. (1987). Tokyo: Kenkyusha.

Kerbo, H. R., & McKinstry, J. A. (1995). *Who rules Japan?* Westport, CT: Praeger.

Lai, M. (1999). JET and NET: A comparison of native-speaking English teachers schemes in Japan and Hong Kong. *Language, Culture and Curriculum, 12*, 215–228.

Lutz, C. A., & Collins, J. L. (1993). *Reading National Geographic.* Chicago: University of Chicago Press.

Masuzoe, Y. (2000). Introduction. In Y. Masuzoe (Ed.), *Years of trial: Japan in the 1990s.* Tokyo: Japan Echo.

Matsumoto, D. (1996). *Unmasking Japan.* Stanford, CA: Stanford University Press.

McKillop, P. (2000, September, 1). Letter from Japan: Whale of a problem. *Time* [Online]. Available: http://www.cnn.com/ ASIANOW/time/asiabuzz/2000/09/01/

Moeran, B. (1990). Introduction: Rapt discourses, anthropology, Japanism, and Japan. In E. Ben-Ari, B. Moeran, & J. Valentine (Eds.), *Unwrapping Japan* (pp. 1–17). Manchester, England: Manchester University Press.

Nelson, J. K. (2000). *Enduring identities: The guise of Shinto in contemporary Japan.* Honolulu: University of Hawai'i Press.

Nishijima, H. (2000, October 6). Lack of sex education leaves children in the dark. *Yomiuri Shimbun* [Online]. Available: http://www.yomiuri.co.jp/newse/ 1005so12.htm

Novice Yuko Obuchi is Gunma's heir apparent. (2000, June 21). *Japan Times,* p. 3.

Ohnuki-Tierney, E. (1984). *Illness and culture in contemporary Japan.* Cambridge: Cambridge University Press.

Oshima, H. (1998). Is Japan an egalitarian society? In J. Mak, S. Sunder, S. Abe, & K. Igawa (Eds.), *Japan—Why it works, why it doesn't: Economics in everyday life.* Honolulu: University of Hawai'i Press.

Pawasarat, C. (2000, October 10). NTT's lowered fees: The beginning of the beginning. *Japan Inc. Magazine* [Online]. Available: http://www.japaninc.net/mag/comp/ 2000/10/oct00_ntt.html

Perrin, N. (1988). *Giving up the gun.* Boston: David R. Godine.

Prosser, M. H. (1988). *The cultural dialogue: An introduction to intercultural communi-cation.* Washington, DC: SIETAR International. (Original work published Boston: Houghton Mifflin, 1978)

Random House Webster's college dictionary. (1991). New York: Random House.

Reischauer, E. O. (1988). *The Japanese today.* Cambridge, MA: Harvard University Press.

Richardson, B. (1997). *Japanese democracy.* New Haven, CT: Yale University Press.

Sakurai, J. (2000, September 1). Japan launches Internet strategy. Yahoo News: Associated Press [Online]. Available: http://dailynews.yahoo.com/h/ap/20000901/tc/japan_ Internet_1.html

Spencer, R. (1993, May 18). US ranks sixth in quality of life; Japan is first. *Washington Post*, p. A7.

Struck, D. (2000, September 10). Japan attempts to slow pork barrel juggernaut. *Washington Post* [Online]. Available: http://www.washingtonpost.com/wp-dyn/articles/A46255-2000Sep10html

Tokyo Internet costs almost double N.Y. charges. (2000, August 26). *Japan Times* [Online]. Available: http://www.japantimes.co.jp/cgibin/getarticle.pl5?nn20000826b3.htm

Wading in the yen trap. (1999, July 24). *The Economist* [Online]. Available: http://www2.gol.com/users/coynerhm/wading_in_the_yen_trap.htm

Watanabe, M. (1994). Enjoy your life in America. In K. Shirai, K. Komatsu, & K. M. Shimoda (Eds.), *To our friends and neighbors: Messages from Japanese women living in New York* (p. 36). Scarsdale, NY: Editors.

Wheatley, A. (2000, October 28). Analysis: Foreign pressure on Japan to reform won't go away. *Business Week* [Online]. Available: http://www.businessweek.com/reuters_stories/Asian2/10_28_2000.reuap-story-bceconomyjapanreforms.html

Yamaguchi, M. (2000, May 24). Dynasties vs. democracy in Japan. Associated Press [Online]. Available: http://sg.dailynews.yahoo.com/headlines/asia/aparticle.html?s=singapore/headlines/000524/asia/ap/Dynasties_Vs._Democracy_in_Japan.html

Yoshida, M., Tanaka, I., & Sesoko, T. (Eds.). (1984). *The hybrid culture.* Hiroshima: Mazda.

Zuckerman, M. B. (2000, September 11). The perfect storm. *U.S. News* [Online]. Available: http://www.usnews.com/usnews/issue/000911/11edit.htm

Chapter 2

Uchi and *Soto* as Cultural and Linguistic Metaphors

Seiichi Makino

Uchi *(inside) and* soto *(outside) have metaphorical extensions in Japanese like in no other major language. These metaphors have cultural, social, and cognitive implications and underlie key concepts of the culture. The fundamental semantic property of* uchi *is one of involvement. If* uchi *is so defined, it can provide a powerful tool for developing a unified explanation for both cultural and linguistic matters. Toward this end, this chapter identifies the metaphoric basis of* uchi *and* soto *for well-known cultural concepts of* amae, hon'ne, tatemae, giri, ninjō, miren, *among others, and for linguistic features, such as giving/receiving verbs, deixis, particles* wa/ga, *honorific usage, tense switching, and nominalizers. Additionally, application extends to temporality and other patterns of discourse in Japanese. To interrelate such diverse cultural and linguistic phenomena shows the vital importance of the* uchi *and* soto *concepts, while enhancing our analytical tools in Japanese studies and contributing as well to the study of metaphor at large.*

Concepts especially intrinsic to Japaneseness are *uchi* (inside) and *soto* (outside). Although universally found across cultures, these concepts are variously interpreted. Some people would say that *uchi* (inside) space is up to one's skin, and beyond lies the vast space of *soto* (outside). Others might argue in a Cartesian way that one's brain is what *uchi* is all about. For the average Japanese, *uchi* is far more. It is space for interacting freely with others in an informal, friendly, or intimate relationship. *Uchi* is taken to such heart by Japanese that it can even mean one's house or home, the only culture I know that does this. This custom is certainly not found in Korean, perhaps the most closely affiliated language. It is worth noting also that the people of Osaka, in western Japan, have taken this *uchi*-"centricism" a step further. In the Osaka and neighboring dialects, *uchi* can also mean one's self—"I"—in addition to the *uchi* = "one's house/home" equation (not to mention "inside," of course). Again, this custom appears to be found only in Japanese culture.

If the *uchi* = "one's house/home" equation appears nowhere else, and spatial metaphors are so basic to human thought, then the *uchi–soto* concepts must be particularly distinctive of the Japanese language and culture. In making the case that *uchi–soto* is particularly distinctive of Japanese, and thereby identifying an important aspect of Japaneseness, this chapter proceeds as follows. First, the traditional Japanese house is briefly considered to identify certain spatially related Japanese customs or rituals, related, of course, to inside and outside concepts. Second, this conceptualization of *uchi–soto* is clarified by comparison with other research and expanded by application to other key concepts of Japanese culture, such as *hon'ne, tatemae,* and *amae.* If there can be any single or combined concept most integral to Japanese culture, *uchi–soto* seems to be it. Third, a comprehensive survey is made of the language to show various linguistic facts related to *uchi–soto* spatiality. Lastly, a rather significant finding is shared related to temporality as based on *uchi–soto* thinking

UCHI AND *SOTO* AS CULTURAL METAPHORS

As has been said, *uchi*, "inside," also means "house" or "home." This metaphor thus has various sociocultural, as well as linguistic, implications. Let us now take a brief look at the prototypical Japanese house. Regardless of size, a Japanese house is surrounded by either brick walls or, more traditionally, hedges, both five to nine feet tall. There is always a gate (*mon*) through which you reach space just in front of the house. When you go through the gate, you feel the first sense of *uchi*-ness from being enclosed by the walls. This space is still ambivalent, however, because it is still between the *soto* and the *uchi* of spatiality. This ambivalence still continues after entering the *genkan*, the entrance of the house.

In the *genkan*, it might seem like the inside because it is under the roof. But you are not quite "inside" because you have yet to take off your shoes, which may not necessarily be your option. The *genkan* is somewhat of a "holding station," a transitional point before gaining the inner entrance to the house. This holding station is also literally lower in height than the inner entrance, which is a step higher. You as a visitor can only proceed further by being invited. Once you are invited, and have removed your shoes, you can step upward into the house. You might then feel strongly that you are in *uchi*. But not really. On a first visit, you typically would not be invited into the innermost areas. It takes time before you are allowed to enter the space of the family room.

Three levels of height are discernable: ground level at the gate, the level of the *genkan*, which is 2–3 inches higher, and the level of the inside living area, higher than the *genkan* by 2–10 inches. An intriguing new development in the past decade or so is that the difference in height between the *genkan* and living area has become smaller and smaller. In the event that the level of *genkan* and that of the living quarters become equal in the latter half of 21st century (if my prediction is right), then the *genkan* might lose its purpose for the removal of shoes. The custom could disappear except for when entering rooms of *tatami* (straw mat) flooring.

Uchi space is not just physical but also social—the space for close, intimate relations, often with those of blood relations. This space is, in a word, one of involvement. There a person primarily tends to be defined as a member of the house or collective before being defined as an individual person. As with collectives, he or she relies on expanded rather than on individualized ego. Although singles living alone (*tandoku kazoku,* "single families," i.e., unmarried people aged between 25 and 40 years or elderly widows), which account for 20% of the nation's households, may have reduced social contact, *uchi* space still remains for most Japanese as a space of involvement.

Clarification of Terms

Before venturing further, it is necessary to emphasize a point I made about *uchi*, in view of Quinn (1994). Based on his extensive analysis of Japanese compounds and phrases that involve *uchi* and *soto*, Quinn has defined *uchi* and *soto* as follows:

Judging from the concepts *uchi* participates in expressing, this word has been associated with notions such as fully bounded; indoors, nearby, enclosed, concave, dark; domestic, family, intralineal, "us"; casual, comfortable, informal, familiar, private, indulgent, free; concealed, secret, privileged, detached, known, shared, mutual, benefit; local, limited, controlled, specifiable, enumerable, part of larger whole, sacred, special, and primary. A summary review of *soto* finds it used in the company of such concepts as outside an enclosure, outdoors, open, protruding, convex; extralineal, nondomestic, "them," secular, profane, removed, exposed, visible; customers, well-behaved, restrained, maintaining appearances; "on the town"; peripheral, foreign; less known, less detailed, undifferentiated; uncontrolled, and secondary. (pp. 63–64)

As can be seen, the concepts of *uchi* and *soto* have very broad meanings indeed.

Although Quinn usefully charted many of the semantic features involved, his analysis, however, contains an oversight that bears directly on my present work and requires clarification. Among all the features for *uchi* listed by Quinn above, "detached" seems crucially wrong for two reasons. First, the space of *uchi*, as I have explained above, entails involvement as a central feature. If "detached" were one of the *uchi* features, then its opposite, "involvement," must necessarily be entailed by *soto*, but it is not listed as such by Quinn. Second, while he captures an essential element of "us versus them" in distinguishing *uchi* and *soto*, his analysis seems contradictory for including both "us" and "detached" for *uchi*. He places "detached" in association with "known," "shared," and "mutual," suggesting that this "detached" corresponds to relations with one's significant others. If so, that could not be any farther from the truth. Thus, it was incumbent on me to emphasize the utility of my analysis and the distinctive feature drawn about *uchi* and *soto*.

In passing, an important caveat is warranted whenever it concerns language. We must recognize that a gap may necessarily inhere between reality and its description. As society changes, so does language. Certain linguistic analyses may turn out to describe language more conservatively than what is actually the case. With this in mind, I hope to ensure, as best as I am able, that my analysis accords with contemporaneous changes in Japanese language and society.

Uchi and *Soto*: Bases for Key Cultural Concepts

Well known to many in the field of Japanese studies are certain concepts presented as keys for understanding the culture and its people. Actually, many of these concepts manifest themselves either in the spheres of *uchi* or *soto*. Here we consider seven of these concepts, some of which come in paired relations:

1. *hon'ne* (real wishes) versus *tatemae* (stated reason)
2. *ninjō* (humane feeling) versus *giri* (social obligation)
3. *amae* (physico-psychological dependence)
4. *haji* (sense of shame)
5. *miren* (lingering attachment to a thing of the near past)

Hon'ne and *tatemae* have clear parallels to *uchi* and *soto*. One's true wishes (*hon'ne*) hardly can be expressed in *soto*, especially in a formal situation talking with one's superior. In *soto*, a Japanese tends to put on a public persona and to suppress his or her true feeling. In other words, self-assertion has been strongly discouraged in *soto*. So a typical Japanese obeys a social norm for a given social situation and gives vent to his or her true feeling when he or she comes home (i.e., *uchi*). Societal views, however, appear to be changing by a weakening of *tatemae* and a strengthening of *hon'ne*, especially among young Japanese people. Shintaro Ishihara, a then-future Governor of Tokyo, and Akio Morita, cofounder of Sony Corporation, wrote the best-selling book, *No to ieru Nihon* [*The Japan That Can Say No*] (Ishihara & Morita, 1989), which was intended to encourage Japanese politicians and diplomats to express their *hon'ne* to American counterparts on the international front. This book has been harshly criticized as being too nationalistic, but I believe that this book has created a feeling that it is politically correct to stick to one's *hon'ne* even in international contexts (with one's allies). That is, the imperative to be diplomatic need not completely rule out telling another how things really are. Japanese culture is changing toward placing more emphasis on *hon'ne*, but the distinction between the two concepts still remains potent in the Japanese mentality.

Ninjō, in (2) previously, is akin to *hon'ne* in that both of them refer to one's true feelings. But *ninjō* is contrasted not with *tatemae* but with *giri*, social obligation. *Ninjō* is basically *uchi*-oriented, but *giri* is definitely *soto*-oriented. *Giri* specifies an array of behaviors that one should observe to maintain good relations with *soto* people. *Ninjō* and *giri*, however, are not always mutually exclusive. When you really feel thankful toward your boss (a manifestation of *ninjō*) you give a gift during the socially instituted gift-giving seasons (i.e., midyear and end of the year), satisfying your true feeling. *Giri*, though, entails such a strong canon that one must honor it even when not accompanied by *ninjō* feeling. Thus, all sorts of conflicts may emerge between *ninjō* and *giri*, and heightened by the related *uchi–soto* relations. On the other hand, within *uchi* itself, especially with the immediate family, a host of unwritten obligations prevail, but these are not considered an aspect of *giri*. Rather, Confucianism provides the applicable code, such as with *oya-kōkō*, filial piety, and spells out how children should return love (called *on*) to one's parents. Japanese youths tend to go by *ninjō* alone, but as they become adults, they learn how to conform to *giri*, a mark of the fully socialized Japanese.

Amae, the third concept, has become a key cultural principle for explaining Japanese behavior since the work of Doi (1971). He defined it as: "to depend and presume upon another's benevolence" (p. 78). There are three significant facts about *amae*. First, *amae* shares its stem with *ama-i*, meaning "sweet." In other words, the Japanese psychology of dependency is fundamentally sense-based. The derived verb *ama-eru* means to depend on one's superior, who ideally is as sweet as candy. An equally important fact about *amae* is that it is psychological dependency not on a *soto*-person, but on an *uchi*-person older than oneself. Its prototypical sense is that of an infant feeling cozy in its mother's arms. Thus, Doi's definition of *amae* ought to be amended to become: "to depend and presume upon an *uchi*-person older than oneself." Third, a point neglected or downplayed by scholars is that the basis of *amae* is not exclusive to Japanese culture. *Amae* phenomena are clearly observable even in nonhuman, animate beings (especially mammals). *Amae* is largely a matter of nature. Then, if so, what would be the part that nurture has which relates to cultural difference?

Regarding the nurture of *amae*, we need to consider the earliest days when an infant begins to acquire cultural codes. Two related studies, now rather old but still relevant, were published in the latter half of the 1960s, an era marked by Japan's successful hosting of the Olympic games and its emergence as an economic giant. Neither of these two studies addressed *amae* specifically, but they nonetheless provide evidence for its genesis.

One of the studies is Caudill and Weinstein (1969/1986), which examined how infant care by a mother differs between Japan and the United States. The two anthropologists recorded the relationship between the infant and the mother in great detail using a time sampling procedure by which observations were made at regular intervals during a day. The participants included 30 middle-class mothers and their infants from each country, totaling 60 pairs. Some of the most revealing findings include the following:

• Japanese mothers tend to lull their infants to sleep rather than talking with them.

• Japanese mothers are with their infants as often as three times more than American mothers with theirs. Japanese mothers take care of a sleeping infant almost five times as often as do American mothers. Aside from regular care-taking, Japanese mothers are still with their awake infants twice as often as that for American mothers.

• American mothers give their infants half-solid food at 1 month of age, whereas Japanese mothers wait until their infants become 4 months old.

• Sixty percent of the Japanese mothers were found to breast-feed, whereas only 16% of the American mothers did so.

What can the findings tell us about *amae*? Japanese mothers tend to keep close physical proximity to their infants, as long as they can, and as the result of this, Japanese infants likely develop a stronger psycho-physical dependency on their mother, who is always available to them. Close physical proximity, which fosters development of Japanese *amae*, is essentially nonverbal. You can surely *ama-eru* using language, but action speaks louder than words. And, of course, infants have yet to acquire a language anyway.

The other study of note is Caudill and Plath (1966/1986), which made the following observations based on the co-sleeping patterns within 323 Japanese households in cities of Tokyo, Kyoto, and Matsumoto:

• In a household of young couples with an infant 3 to 4 months old, 86% will cosleep with each other regardless of the number of rooms for sleeping.

• Even when a child is 13 years old and the husband and the wife are 45 and 40, respectively, the rate of cosleeping is 62%.

• The rate of cosleeping is lowest (20%) when the child is between 16 and 26, a period during which the suicide rate happens to be the highest.

In a nutshell, Japanese tend to sleep in a group. Here again, physical proximity during the sleeping hours (which is one-third of one's life time) reinforces the psychology of *amae*. I do not know any specific research on co-bathing in Japan and the United States, but my impression is that co-bathing between parent and child in Japan extends much longer in the child's age than that practiced in the United States. It is not accidental that Japanese coined the word, *sukinshippu* ("skinship"), meaning physical contact with the skin of another as an important means of communication.

Why do Japanese *uchi*-persons love physical proximity? I simply don't know. It is almost like asking why certain cats (e.g., Siamese cats) are more aloof than others. Japanese culture has been undergoing restructuring since the 1960s in the direction of American culture of "anti-*amae*" (or culture of independence), but my observations seem to confirm that Japanese mothers still intently take care of their infants even at sleep, and Japanese still love co-sleeping and co-bathing, albeit less frequently than before.

Amae still appears to be a driving force in the culture. Japanese people tend to dislike the idea of leaving *uchi* and becoming independent. Perhaps economic factors enter, but Japanese college students don't leave home unless they really have to do so. They feel much less an imperative than American students to live on their own. For the American, becoming independent from the parent is well sought after, as is well known. On the contrary, for the Japanese, dependency is more positively valued.

Now we move to the next concept for consideration, *haji,* or shame. It was Ruth Benedict (1948) who stated that Japanese culture is not a culture of guilt but one of shame. According to Benedict, such a culture operates on standards of morality that are not absolute but relative to a given situation. One can criticize Benedict's dichotomous classification of shame versus guilt as being too simplistic, but she zeroed in on one of the most important features of Japanese ethics, for their situational (or spatial) quality. In other words, *haji* arises when one violates a community's ethical rules and gets caught in the act by *seken* (the public, society), which then leaves the person caught in the middle between *uchi* and *soto*. If one is free from the eyes of *seken*, then he or she may feel free to violate societal rules and be much less scrupulous than when he or she is in his or her own community, as epitomized by the proverb, "*Tabi no haji wa kaki-sute*" ("When one is on a trip one can throw away *haji*"). A sense of *haji* is caused by one's shameful exposure of himself or herself to the eyes of *seken*, and *seken* (often called *seken-sama*) is positioned nearly like God but not omnipresent as in the Judeo-Christian tradition. Rather, *seken-sama* is immobile and located somewhere between *uchi* and real *soto*.

Finally, number (5), *miren*: The word came from Chinese, but the original meaning of "not well trained" is far from its current meaning in Japanese. Today, it means "lingering attachment to someone/something of the (near) past." A typical *miren* behavior manifests itself universally in a situation where young lovers have to split but feel unable to. In our spatial terms of *uchi* and *soto*, *miren* is a centripetal psychology, which entrusts that the person will return to *uchi* again—someone who is about to go to *soto*. You are thus better able to let him or her go. In general, however, social departures seem to take longer for Japanese to complete, especially the ritual of seeing off a guest from one's home. Suppose you were the visitor. Just as there are at least three stages of entering *uchi* as a guest, so there are several stages when leaving. At each stage, there are various thank-yous and good-byes said; at the first stage, initially in the room where the social-izing took place; the second stage, at least, at the *genkan* to put on your footwear; and the third stage, but not necessarily the last one, as you go through the outer gate and, perhaps also, from your car, or at the nearest train station or a bus stop as well. What makes this "stage-like" is that the host almost mandatorily must see the guest completely from the house through the garden and out onto the street, even waiting until the guest drives off. Americans usually limit their thank-yous, because to do so repetitiously might suggest to them a wish for more favors of the same sort.

Miren as a psychological vector is not limited to parting situations. The Japanese guest thanks the host or benefactor again after the event, their next time meeting each other. By doing so, he or she will bring back a thing of *soto* (i.e., the past) to *uchi* (i.e., the present).

Instead of looking forward, Japanese like to look back. In the Judeo-Christian tradition, *miren* would carry a negative implication. In fact, in Genesis (19:15–29), Lot's wife was turned into a pillar of salt when she looked back at the towns of Sodom and Gomorrah. And the successful moon landing by American astronauts in 1969 (Apollo 7) was an embodiment of American fron-tier spirit or spirit of looking forward into the future. In contrast, psychology of *miren* usually makes Japanese very hesitant about becoming a pioneer into *terra incognita,* a total *soto* space. They would rather stay in *terra cognita,* a familiar space of *uchi* where they can make creative stylization based on something already existent in Japan or imported into Japan.

Miren actualizes itself in all sorts of ways. Nobody has statistics on this, but Japan probably has a higher per capita amount of people who keep personal diaries than elsewhere. Japanese schoolchildren are required to keep a diary (*nikki*) during their summer holidays. Indeed, the origin of Japanese modern nov-els can be traced back to the first major diary literature by Kino Tsurayuki (ca. 872–945) called *Tosa Nikki* (*Tosa Diary*) (Porter, 1976) written around 935. Subsequently, a major literature of diaries, *nikki bungaku* (diary literature), appeared. Some of the representative works include Fujiwara no Michitsuna's *Kagerō Nikki* (974), Izumi Shikibu's *Izumi Shikibu Nikki* (ca. 1010), Murasaki Shikibu's *Murasaki Shikibu Nikki* (ca. 1010), and *Sarashina Nikki* by Sugawara no Takasue no Musume (ca. 1060). The diary, according to some literary schol-ars, gave birth to a further important literary development in Japan, the I-novel. The question then becomes, why do Japanese love to keep a diary?

One of the nonliterary reasons, I would argue, is that a diary allows easy remembrance of the past and so satisfies the psychology of *miren*. For that mat-ter, the short poetry of *haiku* (5-7-5 syllables) and that of the more traditional *tanka* (5-7-5-7-7 syllables) provide similar satisfaction of *miren* by being useful records of a poet's momentary psychological experience, enabling him or her to recall such past sentiments through, perhaps, the shortest of artistic expression. *Nikki, haiku,* and *tanka* are all literary forms that express a writer's inner feelings, or psychology of authentically felt *uchi.*

Another example is the curious role of cameras in the everyday lives of Japanese. Japan produced its first box camera for nonprofessionals in 1903 using imported lenses and shutter mechanisms. Since then, Japanese have become infatuated with cameras and now produce and export various high-quality camera equipment. Cameras can capture some of life's most meaningful moments, and thus become important media for *miren.* The significance here is the degree to which Japanese use cameras in their everyday lives. It is an intensity of use that I simply have not observed in the United States or elsewhere. Photographing is, in my judgment, so culturally motivated that it is now a Japanese icon.

THREE PIVOTAL FACTORS

At this juncture of my presentation between cultural metaphors and linguistic metaphors, I present three factors that help to bridge the sections, as well as to summarize some of the previous key concepts. These three pivotal factors are social sensitivity, linguistic empathy-focus, and *seken.*

Social Sensitivity

Japanese culture often has been said to be a *sasshi no bunka* (a guessing culture) (see, for example, Wilson, 1998), meaning that a Japanese must either anticipate or conjure the intentions of another because social indirectness is an ideal for interpersonal relations. I would argue that underlying this *sasshi*-culture are *uchi–soto* relations unique to Japanese culture. Even within that most basic of *uchi* spaces, the family, various *uchi–soto* relations operate, simply because the Japanese family historically has been strongly hierarchical in structure. For example, one does not refer to one's siblings as brother or sister but as older/younger brother or older/younger sister. This sibling order is a microcosm of the age-based hierarchy of Japanese society that one continually experiences in Japanese daily life. Other aspects of this hierarchical language are explored later in this chapter. One becomes aware that, in general, one cannot completely share the same social space with another, even one's siblings. One thus holds a distinct social role—*uchi* space—within the family that is apart from the social roles of other family members—*soto* space. In the larger society, such hierarchical relations "resist clear, verbal communication" (Wilson, 1998, p. 216). So, one can understand why "guessing" about the intentions of others requires needed social sensitivity at one time or other in Japanese society.

It is this sensitivity that underlies *amae,* best typified between the child and mother. *Ninjō* also requires this sensitivity, as does *hon'ne. Miren* can be redefined as "sensitively engaged with someone or something that belongs to the (near) past." Whether this social sensitivity is called "empathy," "sympathy," or whatever, it is fundamentally of universal nature. However, some conceptual difficulties surround the application of the term empathy (Donahue, 1998). Nevertheless, a component probably shared by empathy, sympathy, and other pro-social capacities is involved here; namely, the perspective taking by one person of another. On a linguistic level, such perspective taking is referred to as empathy-focus.

Linguistic Empathy-Focus

Kuno (1987) proposed empathy-focus to refer to perspective taking as reflected in certain linguistic structures. Kuno compared this "linguistic empathy" to be like a camera angle. I adduce a few of his examples below. Suppose that a man named John hit his brother Bill:

(a) Then John hit Bill.
(b) Then John hit his brother.
(c) Then Bill's brother hit him.
(d) Then Bill was hit by John.

In (a), the camera angle is equidistant from both John and Bill. This is more or less an objective description. Sentences (b) through (d), however, are rather subjective, because the speaker as a "cameraman" seems much closer to John than Bill in (b) and the reverse in (c) and (d). It is this kind of empathy-focus, at least linguistically, that speakers of Japanese are often called on to operate according to *uchi–soto* relations in a particular social situation.

Seken

Related to the hyper-social sensitivity of many Japanese is the important concept of *seken*, mentioned briefly in discussion previously. *Seken* is situated between *uchi* and *soto,* according to the social psychologist Inoue (1977). *Seken* consists of people who are watching you. They are people living in the same town as you. You don't know them, but you are conscious that they are there. Japanese reinforce the centrality of *seken* by adherence to *seken-tei,* the keeping-up of appearances. So as long as one stays within the reach of *seken,* one cannot commit evil deeds, but once outside *seken,* one may want to do evil things. This feeling of *seken* may at least partly account for the relatively low crime rate in Japan. The combination of social sensitivity at an affective level and empathy-focus at a linguistic or cognitive level, which in turn are heightened by *seken* within the *sasshi-bunka* (guessing culture), provides us with the pivot that interlocks the cultural and linguistic phenomena of *uchi* and *soto* that this chapter attempts to chart out.

UCHI AND SOTO AS LINGUISTIC METAPHORS

Having discussed some of the major indexical meanings of *uchi* and *soto* within culture per se, I move now to some of the basic Japanese grammars that interface with culture based on *uchi* and *soto*.

A. Giving Verbs

Just as Japanese gift exchange has its behavioral complexity of rules, so does the associated language. The language of giving and receiving is relatively more complex in Japanese than in other major languages. The key to its complexity is the perspective taking assumed by the participants and is rooted in frameworks of *uchi* and *soto*. For the language of giving, Japanese uses, to simplify, two basic verbs: *ageru* and *kureru*. Both mean "to give." A choice is made between these verbs depending on whose perspective is taken—the giver's, the receiver's, or that of other principals involved. In A-1, both verbs are translated identically in English.

A-1 (a) *Hanako wa Tarō ni chokorēto o **ageta**.*

　　　　Hanako - to Tarō - chocolate - gave

　　　　(Hanako gave Tarō a chocolate.)

(b) *Hanako wa Tarō ni chokorēto o **kureta**.*

　　　　Hanako - to Tarō - chocolate - gave

　　　　(Hanako gave Tarō a chocolate.)

Absent from these English "equivalents" are the nuanced social relations conveyed in Japanese by the perspectives respectively taken between Hanako or Taro. To help see this, consider A-2, which demonstrates it using the respective cases of the recipient being either a stranger (a) or a sibling (b).

A-2 (a) *Hanako wa shiranai hito ni chokorēto o **ageta**/*****kureta**.*

　　　　Hanako - to a stranger - chocolate - gave

　　　　(Hanako gave a chocolate to a stranger.)

(b) *Hanako wa otōto ni chokorēto o **kureta**/*****ageta**.*

　　　　Hanako - to [my] little brother - chocolate - gave

　　　　(Hanako gave a chocolate to my little brother.)

In A-2a, the receiver of the chocolate, a stranger, is by definition a *soto*-person, and in A-2b, the receiver is an *uchi*-person. As indicated by an asterisk, the verbs *kureta* in A-2a and *ageta* in A-2b are not acceptable in the respective sentences. In other words, *kureru* and *ageru* require an *uchi*-person and a *soto*-person, respectively, as the receiver of a gift. Kuno and Kaburaki (1977) argued that a sentence like A-2a is uttered from the viewpoint of the subject/giver (i.e., Hanako) and A-2b from the viewpoint of the indirect object/receiver (i.e., little brother). Because such perspective taking is akin to the vicarious assumption of roles such as in empathizing with someone, Kuno talks about the speaker's "empathy focus." In A-1a and A-1b, the empathy focus is on Hanako and Taro, respectively. What I am proposing here is nearly the same as Kuno and Kaburaki's generalization, because *uchi*-person is with whom the speaker "empathizes," and *soto*-person, with whom the speaker does not. My proposal, however, is much wider in scope than Kuno and Kaburaki's account as is soon evident.

The notion of person as a grammatical concept in Indo-European languages is anything but fluid. The first person (the speaker) is always the first person, and the second person (the listener) is always the second person, and the third person (neither the speaker nor the listener) is always the third person, regardless of linguistic or social contexts in which they are used. And the elaborate agreement rules are very sensitive to the person. This is not the case in Japanese, however. *Uchi*-person and *soto*-person are highly fluid. About the only static or nonfluid aspect involved is that the *uchi*-person always has the self at its core.

To exemplify the relativity of personhood in Japanese, linguistically speaking, consider the case of A-3, which compares reference to one's wife and that for one's ex-wife.

A-3 (a)   *Rhōshin wa tsuma ni nekkuresu o **kureta**/***ageta**.*

My parents - to my wife - necklace - gave

(My parents gave my wife a necklace.)

(b)   *Ano otoko wa wakareta tsuma ni kane o tanmari to **yatta**/***kureta** rashii.*

The guy - to my ex-wife - money - a lot - gave

(It appears that the guy gave a large sum of money to my divorced wife.)

In A-3a, *tsuma* (my wife) is the speaker's *uchi*-person, so the verb *kureru* naturally agrees in use. But once the same speaker is divorced from his wife, she is no longer his *uchi*-person, so *kureru* would not be acceptable in use. Instead, *ageru* (or its equivalent) is the appropriate choice. Note that in both A-3a and A-3b, the third person—my wife—in the Indo-European language maintains its "personhood" linguistically in relation to the speaker. In Japanese, however, this third person requires different linguistic measures according to the changed social relations between the speaker and his wife. In other words, a shift must be observed between *uchi*-person and *soto*-person in agreement with the related social context.

Thus, for example, if the receiver is a total *soto*-person, then it is rather impossible for the speaker to use *kureru* as found in A-4.

A-4 *Mika wa tsūkōnin ni bara no hana o **ageta**/***kureta**.*

Mika - to a passerby - a rose - gave

(Mika gave a rose to a passerby.)

Here the relation of stranger as presented would raise no eyebrows. However, consider the next case, A-5. Both sentences are correct, but how would you explain them?

A-5 (a) *Chichi wa haha ni nekkuresu o **ageta**.*

my father - to my mother - necklace - gave

(My father gave my mother a necklace.)

(b) *Chichi wa haha ni nekkuresu o **kureta**.*

my father - to my mother - necklace - gave

(My father gave my mother a necklace.)

Normally, *kureru* would be the appropriate choice of verb when speaking about one's mother. Thus, A-5a raises surprise. It is acceptable because it depends on a speaker's psychology at the time of utterance. If she sides with her father, she will utter a sentence like A-5a, but if with her mother, A-5b. If the daughter, however, feels closer to her father than to her mother, then she cannot utter A-5b. Or for that matter, if she happens to be closer to her mother, then she can really utter only A-5b. In short, the acceptability of A-5a and A-5b depends on the speaker's psychological distance to the giver and to the receiver, at the time of utterance.

Equally curious is the case of A-6, which turns on the difference between quoted speech and its opposite. Here the same speaker reports about Kenta, who gave an item to the speaker's brother. In A-6a the speaker directly quotes Kenta as doing so. In A-6b the speaker does the same but by indirect speech (unquoted). Note that "your brother" in (a) must change to "my brother" as a result of the speaker changing from a direct quote to indirect speech.

A-6 (a) *Kenta wa "Kimi no otōto ni kamera o **agetta**/***kureta** yo" to itta.*

Kenta - "to your little brother - camera - gave" said

(Kenta said "I gave a camera to your little brother.")

(b) *Kenta wa [boku no] otōto ni kamera o **agetta**/**kureta** to itta.*

Kenta - to (my) little brother - a camera - gave - that - said

(Kenta said that he gave my little brother a camera.)

In A-6a, the giving verb has to be *ageru* because the entire sentence is uttered from Kenta's viewpoint. But in the indirect quote version, the giving verb can be either *ageru* or *kureru*. Why? My explanation for this intriguing phenomenon is this: If the speaker (not the utterer of the original quote) thinks that he or she is reporting from his or her viewpoint, then he or she naturally regards his or her own brother as an *uchi*-person, and chooses *kureta*. Because indirect quoting has a function of rephrasing the direct quote from the viewpoint of the speaker's viewpoint, the choice of *kureta* should be an automatic choice. But the curious fact is that the giving verb can be *yatta*, too. It sounds as if the original *yatta* in the direct quote version of A-6a is carried over in the indirect version. This observation seems to support an interesting argument that there is a third version for a quote, that is, a quote caught in the middle between direct and indirect quotes.

I have shown that the third person can be either an *uchi*-person or a *soto*-person. And it has been assumed all along that under normal circumstances, the first person is constantly *uchi*-person, unless the self is schizophrenically divided into ego and alter ego as illustrated by the following example.

A-7 *Ore wa jibun ni motto jiyūna jikan o **yara**nakarereba naranai na.*

    I - to myself - freer time - give - have to

    (I believe I have to give myself freer time.)

This sentence is most likely a monologue in which the speaker is talking with his alter ego. What can we say about the second person? The second person can be theoretically either *uchi*-person or *soto*-person, but the tendency is that in Japan when two people are conversing, the listener is the *uchi*-person.

A-8 (a) *Dare ga hon o kashite **kuremashita**/***agemashita** ka.*

        Who - book - loaning - gave?

        (Who loaned you the book? [lit. Who gave you a favor of loaning the book?])

    (b) *Otōsan wa kuruma o tsukawasete **kuremashita**/***agemashita** ka.*

        Your father - his car - using - gave

        (Did your father allow you to use his car? [lit. Did your father give you a favor of using his car?])

In the above sentences, the verb of giving, *kureru,* is not used as a real verb but as an auxiliary verb, and the entire structure means that someone gives some action as a favor to someone. The receiver of a favor is the second person in both A-8a and A-8b and the speaker utters these sentences from the receiver's viewpoint, resulting in the exclusive use of *kureru*.

B. Receiving Verb

Analysis of the receiving verb yields interesting facts regarding *uchi*-person and *soto*-person. The focus is on the choice of the particles *ni* and *kara* affixed to the giver. Before I discuss *ni* and *kara* as the particle that indicates the giver, let me discuss semantics of each particle. *Ni* is a highly polysemous particle, so all sorts of seemingly unrelated basic senses are given in a dictionary, as shown in B-1. These functions of *ni* include those usually translated as "on," "in," "to," "from," "by," and "at."

B-1 (a) Direct contact (on)

      *Yōshi **ni** namae o kaita.*

      on form - name - wrote

      (I wrote my name on the form.)

   (b) Locational existence (in)

      *Princeton Daigaku wa Princeton **ni** aru.*

      Princeton University - in Princeton - exist

      (Princeton University is in Princeton.)

   (c) Direction (to)

      *Boku wa New York **ni** itta.*

      I - to New York - went

      (I went to New York City.)

   (d) Purpose (to)

      *Watashi wa oyogi **ni** itta.*

      I - to swim - went

      (I went there to swim.)

   (e) Indirect object (to)

      *Mika wa kanojo **ni** hon o kashita.*

      Mika - to her - book - loaned

      (Mika loaned a book to her.)

   (f) Source (from)

      *John wa o-kane o Mary **ni** moratta.*

      John - money - from Mary - received

      (John received money from Mary.)

   (g) Agent (by)

      *Boku wa sensei **ni** homerareta.*

      I - by teacher - be praised

      (I was praised by my teacher.)

(h)   Point of time (at)

*Ashita gozen 9-ji **ni** kite kudasai.*

tomorrow - a.m. - at 9 o'clock - come please

(Please come at 9:00 a.m. tomorrow.)

Makino and Tsutsui (1986, p. 303) have identified the most basic meaning of *ni* as "contact" from which the rest of the meanings derive. Notice that B-1a through B-1c are all spatial and the rest can be assumed to be metaphorical extensions from the spatial notions of contact. Time expressions such as B-1h are universally derived from spatial expressions. If we substitute "contact" for another expression that is relevant to our discussion of *uchi* and *soto*, it would be "involvement," which, as you recall, characterizes the space of *uchi*. In a nutshell, the particle *ni* is essentially an *uchi*-oriented particle.

In contrast to *ni*, the paired particle *kara* is almost as polysemous.

B-2 (a)   Point of departure (from)

*Taitei 6-ji goro ni kaisha **kara** kaeru.*

usually - at 6 o'clock - company - from - go home

(I usually go home at about 6 o'clock from my company.)

(b)   A person as source (from)

*Sono hon wa Yamada **kara** moratta.*

that book - from Yamada - received

(I received the book from Yamada.)

(c)   A thing as source (from)

*Sake wa kome **kara** tsukuru.*

sake - from rice - make

(Sake is made from rice.)

(d)   After a point in time (from)

*Kaigi wa gozen 9-ji **kara** da.*

meeting - from a.m. - 9 o'clock - is

(The meeting is from 9:00 a.m.)

After a point in time (after)

*Gohan o tabete **kara** terebi o mita.*

meal - eating - after - TV - watched

(I watched TV after eating the meal.)

(e)   Reason/cause (over)

*Tsumaranai koto **kara** kenka ni natta.*

trifle matter - from quarrel - began

(We started to quarrel over a trifle. [lit. It became a quarrel from a trifle.])

Reason/cause (to)

*Nihon e iku **kara** Nihongo o benkyō shite iru.*

to Japan - go - so - Japanese - study

(I'm studying Japanese because I'm going to Japan.)

(f) Agent (by)

*Boku wa sensei **kara** chūisareta.*

I - by teacher - was warned

(I was warned by my teacher.)

B-2a is the only use with spatial meaning and the rest are again metaphorical extensions. The basic meaning is opposite to *ni*. It indicates space out of which someone or something comes out. The something or someone thus loses contact with the space. The space is metaphorically perceived as a source of various kinds. My conclusion about the semantic nature of *ni* and *kara* is that the former is "+ involvement" and the latter is "– involvement." Now with this in mind, let us look at the case of the receiving verb.

B-3 (a) *Atashi ne, ano hito **ni/kara** daiya no necklace o moratta no.*

I - from - that person - a diamond necklace - received

(I got a diamond necklace from him.)

(b) *Watashi wa Princeton Daigaku **kara**/****ni** shōgakkin o moratta.*

I - from Princeton University - scholarship money - received

(I received scholarship money from Princeton University.)

When the source is not an individual as in B-3b with whom one can hardly empathize, then *ni*, which is "+ involvement," is not acceptable. Rather, *kara*, a particle of "– involvement," has to be used. Extrapolating on this distinction, the choice of particles in B-3a cannot be arbitrary. If the speaker feels very close to the giver, then he will use *ni* to mark the giver, but if he feels distant from the giver, he will use *kara*. In fact, if *ano hito* is replaced by "fiancé," the speaker would choose *ni* over *kara*, unless some problem lies between the speaker and her fiancée. We can say that *ni* and *kara* mark the giver as *uchi*-person and *soto*-person, respectively.

When the receiving verb is used as an auxiliary verb, meaning that someone receives some action as a favor from somebody, the receiver is marked only by *ni* for unknown reasons.

B-4 *Boku wa tomodachi **ni**/***kara** ongakkai no kippu o katte moratta.*

I - friend - from - concert ticket - buying - received

(I had my friend buy a concert ticket. [lit. I received from my friend a favor of buying a concert ticket.])

In some restricted passive sentences, however, a choice or near-choice develops between *ni* or *kara* as I discussed in Makino (1999). Consider B-5.

B-5 (a) *Boku wa shōgakkō no dōkyūsei **ni**/***kara** yoku ijimerareta.*

I - by elementary school classmates - often - was bullied

(I was often bullied by my elementary school classmates.)

(b) *Watashi wa kinō tomodachi **ni?**/**kara** eiga ni sasowareta.*

I - yesterday - by friend - to movie - invited

(Yesterday, I was invited to a movie by my friend.)

(c) *Watashi wa kōkō shika dete inai noni, Tōdai de no josei to kekkon shita node, ryōshin **ni***/**kara** iroiro iwaremashita.*

I - high school - only - finished - but - Tōdai [University of Tokyo] graduate - woman - married - so - by parents - many things - were said

(I have finished only high school, but I have married a University of Tokyo graduate woman, so I have been criticized in all sorts of ways by my parents.)

(d) *Watashi wa kōkō shika dete inai noni, Tōdai de no josei to kekkon shita node, seken **kara**/***ni** iroiro iwaremashita.*

(I have finished only high school, but I have married a University of Tokyo graduate woman, so I have been criticized in all sorts of ways by people.)

Normally, the agent of a passive sentence is marked not by *kara* but by *ni,* as shown in B-5a. But when the final passivized verb expresses something related to verbal communication, both *ni* and *kara* are acceptable. I don't know the exact reason why the verbal communication creates a favorable context in which one can use *kara,* but my educated guess is that verbal communication is important human interaction of different degrees of closeness. The close interaction is marked by *ni,* and distant one by *kara.*

Be that as it may, what is interesting is the fact that here again the speaker's psychological distance to the person marked by the particle is at issue. If the speaker feels close to the person, then *ni* is chosen over *kara* and vice versa. Even one's father, a typical *uchi*-person, as an agent may take *kara,* depending on the context. In the following example, the speaker Takahashi didn't like his father, who didn't allow him to become a film actor. So *oyaji* (my dad) takes not *ni* but *kara.*

B-6 *Kazoku-kaigi de, oyaji **kara** wa "Haiyū nante erabu michi de wa nai" to tsuyoku hantaisaremashita.*

at family meeting - by father - actor - choose - path isn't - strongly - was opposed

(At a family meeting, I was strongly opposed by my father who said that I shouldn't choose a path to be an actor.) *Asahi Shimbun* (1997, May 15)

If Takahashi chose *ni* over *kara*, it would have been an inadequate choice of the particle. The subtle relationship between young man and woman is subtly expressed in the following *waka* poem by Machi Tawara.

B-7 *Anata **kara** "Aitsu omae no nan na no" to kikarete ki ni narihajimeru aitsu.* (Tawara, 1987)

By you - guy - your - what is he - was asked - started to think - guy

(When I was asked by you on my relationship with the guy I started to think about the guy.)

Even though *waka* is a short poem, the reader can comprehend the subtle relationship between Tawara, "you," and "the guy." At the point when she made this poem, her mind is already fleeing from "you," whom she addressed. The status of "you" was switching from *uchi*-person to *soto*-person for Tawara. It is amazing that the almost subconscious choice of such a tiny particle can index human psychology.

C. Polite Expressions

Japanese is a language highly sensitive to speech levels. Speakers of Japanese must give accord in their speech to relative differences in social position or rank between themselves and others. As with various spheres of the culture, this situationality is found par excellence with politeness. Because politeness essentially accentuates the psychological distance between interlocutors, this "space" has strong divisions in terms of *uchi* and *soto*. To illustrate, two areas of politeness are briefly sketched here: terms of kinship and honorifics.

Terms of Kinship

Two separate sets of kinship terms exist in Japanese, depending on to whom and about whom one speaks. To simplify, one can view these sets roughly related to family and nonfamily, respectively: family being *uchi*, and nonfamily being *soto*. In reference to one's father, separate terms for "father" are generally differentiated: *otōsan* when among family; *chichi* when among nonfamily. Note that this difference is not a matter of familiarity (e.g., dad versus father), for familiar forms exist for *otōsan* while *chichi* is not one of them. Rather, *chichi* and other terms of the *soto*-set honor the addressee by humble reference to one's own family (*uchi*). Such semantic sets (see C-1) help inculcate continual concern for the proper regard of other (*soto*) while keeping fast the sense of *uchi*.

Yet, as has been noted, *uchi*-person remains fluid, such that role-perspectives can be assumed by which one identifies with that of the other effecting an enlargement of *uchi* space. Thus, the *uchi* set generally is used also when referring to the other's (*soto*) family members: *otōsan* can refer to one's own father, as well as to the father of someone else. In fact, these same *uchi* kinship terms can be used to address complete strangers in a fictive way: *otōsan* or *okāsan* in address of a man or woman in the presence of their children, an obvious sign. This fluidity explains my use of terms *uchi*-oriented and *soto*-oriented in the chart in C-1. Although Japanese are called on to maintain an *uchi–soto* focus to social interactions, these terms vary in conception across situations.

C-1	*Uchi*-Oriented	*Soto*-Oriented
Father	*o-tōsan*	*chichi*
Mother	*o-kāsan*	*haha*
Grandfather	*o-jīsan*	*sofu*
Grandmother	*o-bāsan*	*sobo*
Older brother	*o-nīsan*	*ani*
Older sister	*o-nēsan*	*ane*

Honorifics

Honorifics in Japanese are richly varied. Some of this was seen in how one must refer to the members of one's own family in humble terms. More extensively, honorifics are found with the verb. Verbs are inflected according to the honorific gradations associated with social differences. In an honorific polite expression, that is, an expression that is intended to be polite to one's superior, the verb is marked by polite markers typically as in C-2.

C-2 *Tanaka-sensei wa computer o **o-kai-ni-narimashita**.*

   Professor Tanaka - computer - bought

   (Professor Tanaka bought a computer.)

The verb phrase *o-kai-ni-narimashita* is the honorific "exalted" polite form that relates to the subject of the sentence, Tanaka. If the predicate is stripped of the honorific *o-*[Vstem]-*ni-narimashita*, then it becomes just *katta,* the past (plain) form of "buy." What is interesting about *o-*[Vstem]-*ni-narimashita* is that the underlining verb *naru* (to become) expresses an autogenic change (i.e., someone or something changes to someone else or something else spontaneously). This change is a matter of course, one that corresponds with the generative power of nature. This power is inexplicable, and so nature forms an ultimate force in the Japanese worldview. That is one way to explain why a verb of "autogenesis" is used as the polite exalted marker. When reference, however, is to an *uchi*-person as the subject, the honorific becomes a humble polite expression. As with *uchi* kinship terms, the humble variant bestows honor on the addressee.

C-3 *Sensei, sono o-nimotsu, watashi ga **o-mochi-shimashō**.*

   Professor - that luggage - I - will carry

   (Professor, I will carry your luggage for you.)

The humbleness is expressed by *o*-[Vstem]-*shimasu*, which is the maximally unnatural, agentive verb "do." It is maximally unnatural because "do" represents activity not produced by nature but by humans.

   When a *soto*-person calls a senior member of a company, the receptionist shifts her ordinary face-to-face speech level of exalted politeness for her superior within *uchi* to humble politeness when speaking about the same superior as in C-4.

C-4 *Yamada de gozaimasu ka, mōshiwake gozaimasen ga, tadaima kaigichū de gozaimasu ga. . . .*

   Yamada - is? sorry - but - right now - conference - in - is - but

   (I am sorry, but Yamada is in a conference right now, but. . . .)

Again, this humble expressiveness conveys honor to the *soto*-person. But if she speaks directly to her superior, she uses exalted expressions.

D. Demonstrative Pronouns

   In Japanese, there are demonstrative pronouns that index a space where a given animate or inanimate object exists. *Ko-, so-,* and *a-* index an object in the speaker's territory, an object in the listener's territory, and an object in neither the speaker's nor the listener's vicinity, respectively. *Ko-* definitely does so for an object in *uchi* space. *So-* indexes *soto* space closer to *uchi* space, while *a-* does so for space further away. *Ko-, so-,* and *a-* indicate the gradation of *soto*-ness very neatly. A possibly related semantic domain is the *do-* series of question words, but this is outside my present discussion.

   The use of *ko-* reveals that *uchi* space is not physically but psychologically determinable as shown by the following range of examples in D-1.

D-1 (a) *Koko de matte imasu.*

      Here - be waiting

      (I will be waiting here.)

   (b) *Kono apāto wa kinō-teki ni dekite imasu ne.*

      This apartment - functionally - is built - isn't it?

      (This apartment is functionally built, isn't it?)

(c) **Koko no sushi wa oishii desu ne.**
here - of - sushi - delicious - isn't it?
(The sushi is good here, isn't it?)

(d) **Kono machi wa totemo sumiyasui.**
this - town - very - easy to live
(This town is very easy to live in.)

(e) **Kono chikyū no jūmin to shite chikyū o daiji ni shinakereba naranai.**
this Earth - of - as inhabitant - earth - take good care of - have to
(As an inhabitant of this Earth, I have to be kind to the earth.)

Ko- space can be as small as the space currently occupied by the speaker as in D-1a or as large as the planet he or she lives on. For an environmentalist, the Earth is an empathy-focus, which can become his or her territory. On the other hand, there are cases where *ko-* cannot be used even when one refers to something very close to him, as demonstrated by D-2. Let's suppose that this is a dialog between a doctor and her patient.

D-2 Doctor: *Senaka ga itaitte, dono hen ga itai n desu ka.*
*Chotto akaku natte iru keredo, **ko**ko desu ka?*
back - painful - you say - about where - painful - a bit reddish - is - but - here - is it?
(You say your back is painful; about where is it? I can see a reddish spot here, but is this the spot?)

Patient: *Hai, [**so**ko-/***ko**ko/***a**soko] desu.*
Yes, there/here/over there is
(Yes, that's it.)

Although one's back is clearly in a person's physical proximity and therefore seems fit for *ko-*, the case of A-2 requires the use of *so-*. *So-* is required here because the spot is out of easy reach by the patient and falls within the proximity of the doctor even though their respective spaces overlap.

In other situations, the choice may be more ambivalent, making *ko-* and *so-* equally acceptable, as D-3 demonstrates.

D-3 (a) *Boku wa ima dōkyūsei no onna no ko to tsukiatte iru n da.* [**Ko**-/**So**-/***A**]no
onna no ko wa ima made tsukiatta dono onna no ko yori hanashite ite
tanoshii n da.

I - now - classmate - girl - become friends with. [This/That/*That over there] - girl - up until now - became friends - any girl - more - talking - enjoyable - is

(I have become friends with a girl in my class. This/The girl is more enjoyable to talk with than any girl I have become friends with before.)

(b) *Sono kaisha ni wa zettai ni hito ni aisatsu shinai otoko ga ita.* [***Ko/So/*A***]*no otoko wa itsu mo shita o muite aruite ita.*

that company - at - never - people - greet - not - guy - was. That guy - always - looking down - was walking

(There was a guy at that company who never greeted people. This/The guy was always walking with downcast eyes.)

This is a question of how to anaphorically refer to someone or something that has already appeared in the preceding sentence. In both D-3a and D-3b both *ko-* and *so-* are acceptable. To understand why, we need to first consider the unacceptability of *a-*. We naturally would think that *a-* would function here because the referents—the girl in D-3a and the guy in D-3b—are physically out of view. It is also the case that the referents are retrievable to be "at hand," even if only in a psychological sense. So because such anaphoric referents can be mentally brought to the fore, if not already, *a-* does not apply. A more important question is why both *ko-* and *so-* are equally acceptable. *Ko-* is a natural choice because the referents are originally part of the speaker/writer's territory. The plausible reason for the correctness of *so-* is that the speaker/writer assumes that referents have moved into the territory of the listener/reader. The choice of *ko-* yields a subjective impression, whereas *so-* yields an objective one. Or, in other words, *ko-* and *so-* indicate *uchi-* and *soto-*orientations, respectively.

Taboo Words and Other Unmentionables

Every culture has its share of taboos and unmentionables. Such inauspicious matters are typically related to birth, sex, menstruation, and death. They definitely belong to *soto*. Their avoidance includes at least several strategies. The first strategy for avoidance is simply to leave them unmentioned, as with *shi* (death) or *chi* (blood). The second strategy is to make use of nicknames, as, among many examples, do fishermen in calling their hateful *hebi* (snake) by *nagaimono* (long object), or as do hunters in calling their equally hateful *kuma* (bear) by *yama-oyaji* (the old man of the mountains). A third strategy, which concerns us most, is to make such reference by the demonstrative pronoun *a-*, which is, after all, supremely *soto*-oriented as shown as follows. This *soto*-ness is especially apparent when the reference is made to bodily functions or one's private parts.

D-4 (a) *Kyō atashi **are** na no.*

Today - I - that [thing]

(I have my period now. [lit. Today I got it.])

(b) *Are ga shitai.*

that - want to do

(I want to make love. [lit. I want to do it.])

(c) *Asoko ga kayui.*

over there - itchy

(That "private" area is itchy.)

Memory Lapses

For something forgotten, the *a-* demonstrative applies because it is considered a matter out of one's memory.

D-5 (a) *Are nan dakke, kinō tabeta mono?*

What - was it - yesterday - ate thing

(What was it? You know, the stuff we ate yesterday.)

(b) *Ano hito dare dakke, kinō atta hito?*

person - who - was - it yesterday met person

(Who was that person I met yesterday?)

Interjections

Ko-, so-, and *a-* are often used as an interjection. *Ko-* indicates an exclamation about something that has happened in the speaker's territory, as in D-6.

D-6 (a) *[Ko/*So/*A]-ra, dare da!*

Hey - who is it

(Hey, who is it?)

(b) *[Ko/?So/A]-nō, saikin, karada no chōshi ga warukute ne.*

Ah - recently body's - condition - bad

(Ah, I haven't been feeling well these days, you know.)

(c) *[Ko/*Sore/*A]-re wa, konna tokoro de o-ai suru nante, odorokimashita na.*

Oh! - at such a place - meet - was surprised

(Oh, I didn't expect to see you here!)

So- as an interjection is listener-oriented. The use of *sonō* in D-6b is marginal, because the bodily condition has nothing to do with the listener. Examples of *so-* as interjections follow.

D-7 (a) **[*Ko/So/*A]**-re, iku zo!

      go

      (Here we go!)

  (b) **[*Ko/So/*A]**-ra yappari dame darō?

      See - as expected - no good - right?

      (See, I told you so! [lit. See, you failed just as I had said.])

  (c) **[*Ko/So/*A]**-nō nante itta kke, kimi no musume-san no namae?

      Ah - what call - your daughter's - name

      (Ah, what was your daughter's name?)

  (d) **[*Ko/So/*A]**-re wa **[*Ko/So/*A]**-re wa, o-medetō gozaimasu.

      (Oh! Congratulations!)

In these cases, so- indicates something that relates to the listener, so they are out of bounds for ko- or a-.

If ko- and so- relate to the speaker and the listener, what does a- relate to? It has the function of relating to both the speaker and the listener. In other words, it has a function of drawing the listener's attention to something and creating a shared experience. This is, actually, a metaphorical extension of the regular demonstrative use of a-, that is, reference to something both the speaker and the listener can see. Examples follow.

D-8 (a) **[*Ko/*So/A]**-tto ikenai!

      (Oh, no!)

  (b) **[*Ko/*So/A]**-re! Tasukete!

      (Ah! Help!)

  (c) **[*Ko/*So/A]**-nō, Makino to mōshimasu ga.

      (Ah, my name is Makino.)

  (d) **[*Ko/*So/A]**-ra mā, o-hisashiburi!

      (Oh, we haven't met for a long time!)

E. Informality versus Formality: *Uchi* Forms versus *Soto* Forms

It is well known that when in *uchi* space with *uchi*-persons, Japanese use the so-called informal forms, but in *soto* space, they use the formal/polite forms (or *desu/masu* forms). As argued in Makino (1983), the informal forms are used when the utterance is speaker-oriented, by which one's true feeling is expressed without much attention paid to the listener(s), whereas the formal/polite forms are listener-oriented. Clear-cut evidence for this argument is that Japanese never speak using formal/polite forms in a monologue. They are speaking to themselves truthfully, as in E-1 where I am assuming that the utterance takes place in front of a *soto*-person.

E-1 (a)   [A bee stings the speaker while he is giving a formal lecture]

        Ā! Itai/[Itai desu]!*

        Painful

        (Ouch!!)

   (b)   *Ā, samui/*[samui desu]!*

        is cold

        (Oh, it's cold!)

   (c)   *Ā shimatta/*[shimaimashita]! Kasa o motte kuru no o wasureta.*

        gosh - umbrella - bring - forgot

        (Oh, gosh! I forgot to bring an umbrella with me.)

   (d)   *Ā, kore wa oishii/*[oishii] desu!*

        Wow - this - is delicious

        (Wow, this is good!)

Japanese children acquire formal forms only when they start to speak to *soto*-persons, especially their teachers in elementary schools. Henceforth, I call the informal form, *uchi*-form, and the formal form, *soto*-form.

Now, how would you explain the Japanese use of *uchi*-forms in what Lebra (1976, chapter 7) called an anomic situation, one in which *soto* and *ura* (the rear; underside) are combined? The contradictory combination of *uchi*-forms in *soto/ura*, I believe, is only superficial. For an anomic situation, Lebra thinks of one in which a person behaves "anomically" in a public place. The most appropriate expression for it is *bōjaku bujin ni furumau* (lit. to behave outrageously as if there were no *soto*-persons around). I would argue that this is a case when a public *soto* space just mentally turns to a private *uchi* space.

And while on the subject of switching of forms, an intriguing case concerns that from *soto*-forms to *uchi*-forms, as some switching can be found in most formal dialogs. In a formal dialog, the participants use *soto*-forms 99% of the time. However, there are times when they switch from *soto*-forms to *uchi*-forms. I wrote about this phenomenon in Makino (1983), a long time ago, but revisit it here. In my examples below, the italics represent the switch to *uchi*-forms. The examples are taken from a magazine's roundtable discussion on cooking.

E-2 (a) In my house, my mother made cakes and things. The villagers made bean paste and soy sauce together, you know. When we had company, *my father would make noodles, and on such a day a chicken would be missing (from its pen)*. That was actually my father's feast for us.

(b) What I still remember is that usually my grandmother cooked, but before the end of the year, my great grandmother was in charge. *A pot of beans was cooking all day long, and its sweet smell was floating softly in our rooms.*

(c) When I wondered which plate I should choose to place a cake on for our guest, I made a small plate on which I painted my angelic youngest daughter. *When we ate, we looked at the plate and we felt cheerful and happy. We could enjoy our food better because we could eat in a dimension different from our daily life.* I actually make utensils [his profession] with this enjoyment in mind.

(d) *Nowadays [people] often talk about human bonds (*kizuna*), but they cannot talk about a means of living (*yosuga*). The latter we create using our hands and feet, and we need a lot of effort, I think. Currently, women rather than men are quick to say "it is cumbersome to do something, so let's simplify it" and the mass media is agreeing with them.* Anyway, I feel that no matter how much one attempts to simplify the human bonds and means of living, it all boils down to human efforts.

In E-2a, E-2b, and E-2c, *uchi*-forms are used to describe some frozen images in the minds of the speakers. Such images are supposed to be inaccessible to a *soto*-person. They are inner images that have been cherished for an extended period of time. In E-2d, however, *uchi*-forms are used to describe the speaker's long cherished conviction. But what is common to all the italicized parts is that they are directly related to the real *uchi*, that is to say, the self or internal consciousness of the speaker. Japanese self seldom manifests its individualistic side, but does come through in the way *uchi*-forms are used.

Take another case in which an *uchi*-form is chosen over a *soto*-form, as in E-3. The verbs in *uchi*-form in the examples are placed in all capitals. The verbs in *soto*-form are all unacceptable.

E-3 (a) *Ashita wa [HARERU/*haremasu] **deshō**.*
Tomorrow - clear up - probably
(It will probably clear up tomorrow.)

(b) *Mō [KAERU/*kaerimasu] **n desu** ka.*
Already - go home
(Are you going home already?)

(c) *Mō Tokyo ni [TSUITE IRU/*tsuite imasu] hazu da.*
     By this time - to Tokyo - has arrived - is expected
     (It is expected that he has arrived in Tokyo by this time.)

(d) *Eiko-san wa kenchikuka ni [NARU/*narimasu] yō da.*
     Eiko - architect - become - appear
     (It appears that Eiko will become an architect.)

(e) *Rainen wa Oxford daigaku ni [IKU/*ikimasu] tsumori da.*
     Next year - to Oxford University - to go - intend
     (Next year, I intend to go to Oxford University.)

So far, no adequate explanation has been given to the reason why only *uchi*-form is permissible in sentences such as those given in E-3. But extrapolating on our analysis of E-2, the choice of *uchi*-form can be explained plausibly by the assumption that due to the boldfaced sentence-final modality predicate (i.e., guessing [*deshō* in E-3a and *yō da* in E-3d], involvement [*n desu* in E-3b], expectation [*hazu da* in E-3c], and intention [*tsumori da* in E-3e]), the use of *uchi*-forms is mandatory.

F. *Wa* and *Ga*

Every language has markers that distinguish important, new information from relatively unimportant, old information. In English, the indefinite article "a(n)" and the definite article "the," among other markers, are used to indicate important, new information and unimportant, old information, respectively. Japanese *ga* and *wa* are something like English "a(n)" and "the." *Ga* is used to mark important information as the subject of the sentence, and *wa* to mark relatively unimportant information as the topic of the sentence. Originally, such distinction between *ga* and *wa* was made by Masaharu Kasuga (1919/1978), but more recently by Kuroda (1964/1978). Kuroda put the issue in much more universal perspective. Kuno (1973) has also dealt with the two particles in a detailed and systematic way.

Information carried by a noun marked by *wa* is either situationally or contextually shared by both the speaker and the listener. Consider the following examples.

F-1 (a) *Watashi [wa/*ga] Makino desu. Dōzo yoroshiku.*
          I - Makino - am. Nice to meet you
          (I'm Makino. Pleased to meet you.)

     (b) *Dono hito [ga/*wa] Makino-san desu ka?*
          Which - person - Makino - is
          (Which person is Mr. Makino?)

(c) *Watashi [ga/*wa] Makino desu.*

    I - Makino - am

    (I am Makino.)

In a typical self-introduction, as in F-1a, the speaker himself is in front of the listener, so he is marked by *wa*. In F-1b, however, in which the speaker is asking a question not knowing which person is Makino, the question word "which," the subject of sentence, has to take *ga*. If F-1c is the answer to the question in F-1b, then the subject can take *ga*, because it is brand new information to the questioner.

Consequently, I can generalize that *wa* indexes a temporary or permanent interiorization (i.e., stored in the brain, the ultimate *uchi*) of some information shared by both speaker and listener. More examples follow.

F-2 (a) *Tanaka-san no kuruma **wa** dore desu ka.*

    Tanaka's - car - which one - is

    (Which one is Mr. Tanaka's car? [lit. Speaking of Tanaka's car, which one is it?])

(b) *Dore **ga** Tanaka-san no kuruma desu ka.*

    Which one - Tanaka's - car - is

    (Which one is Mr. Tanaka's car?)

F-2a presupposes, for example, a situation in which the interlocutors are looking for Tanaka's car in the parking lot. They are sharing the same, interiorized information. What is not known to the questioner is which car is Tanaka's. So the subject/topic is marked by *wa*. Actually, if the interlocutors know very well that they are looking for Tanaka's car, then the entire *wa*-marked phrase can be omitted. If F-2a is inverted by fronting the question word *dore* (which one), then we derive F-2b. This inverted version sounds very abrupt in comparison. It also takes *ga* because the fronted question requests new information. Such inversion is not always acceptable, as found with those that involve a demonstrative pronoun.

F-3 (a) *Kore **wa** dare no hon desu ka.*

    this - whose - book - is

    (Whose book is this? [lit. Speaking of this, whose book is it?])

(b) **Dare no hon **ga** kore desu ka.*

    Whose - book - this - is

    (Whose book is this?)

F-4 (a) *Sore **wa** nan desu ka.*

    it - what - is

    (What is it?)

(b) *Nani **ga** sore desu ka.
     What - it - is
     (What is it?)

The reason why F-3b and F-4b are unacceptable apparently is due to the use of a demonstrative pronoun. But why can't we use *ko-so-a* here? My explanation is that *ko-so-a* have such a high degree of topicality that they cannot be placed at a nontopical position of sentence.

Narrative discourse commonly is begun with a *ga*-marked noun phrase that later switches to use of the *wa* marker with the noun phrase as in F-5 below. To simplify, I constructed the example using English and inserted *ga* and *wa* where appropriate.

F-5 There was my classmate-**ga** who was awfully good at math. The classmate-**wa** was apparently more advanced in math than his teacher. But one day, my friend-**ga** got a zero on an exam. He simply didn't solve the problems because they were such stupid ones.

At first mention of the writer's friend (i.e., the subject in Japanese), *ga* enters because this friend, the classmate, is new information. On next mention, this same person takes *wa* because the reader can be assumed to have already stored the classmate into at least temporary memory. From the reader's viewpoint, a natural flow exists from *soto*-information (marked by *ga*) to *uchi*-information (marked by *wa*). An interesting thing happens, however, with the third sentence: Despite the presumed storage into the reader's memory, the protagonist of the story takes not *wa* but *ga*. Why is that? The reason is that the unexpected happened when the classmate got a zero on the math exam. In general, if discontinuity occurs between the preceding and subsequent parts of the story, then the *wa*-marked subject noun phrase can switch to use of *ga*. The discontinuity is signaled by the disjunctive "but"-conjunctions, such as *shikashi, demo, tokoroga,* among others.

In contrast to F-5, in which the protagonist is introduced with help of *ga*, he or she can be introduced as a *wa*-marked noun as in F-6.

F-6 My classmate-**wa** was awfully good at math. The classmate-**wa** was apparently more advanced in math than his teacher. But one day, my friend-**ga** got a zero on an exam. He simply didn't solve the problems because they were such stupid ones.

Such abruptness in introducing the protagonist is more commonly employed by modern novelists. What is implied is that the reader should have known him or her. The writer adopts this strategy to get the reader involved in the story from the very beginning. Metaphorically speaking, the reader feels as if he or she got into a house without going through the gates and the *genkan*.

Another important matter regarding *ga* and *wa* is that *wa* can be omitted in discourse, because *wa* marks relatively unimportant information recoverable from context. Therefore, F-5 can take the form of F-7. Note that ( ) indicates deletion of *wa*.

F-7 There was my classmate-*ga* who was awfully good at math. ( ) was apparently more advanced in math than his teacher. But one day, my friend-*ga* got a zero on an exam. He simply didn't solve the problems because they were such stupid ones.

Notice, however, that the *ga*-marked noun in the third sentence cannot be omitted, because it indicates very important information. Universally speaking, linguistic deletion occurs where the information carried by the omitted noun phrase (or whatever elements) has been interiorized.

Getting back again to syntax, I would like to draw the reader's attention to a well-known syntactic phenomenon that occurs within a subordinate clause. Consider the following sets of examples, which, taken together, demonstrate the role of syntactic placement in the choice between *wa* or *ga*.

F-8 (a) *M-sensei [ga/*wa] kaita hon wa taihen fuhyō deshita.*

 Professor M - wrote - book - very - unpopular - was

 (The book that Professor M wrote was very unpopular.)

   (b) *Chosha [ga/*wa] Princeton daigaku no kyōju da to wa shirimasen deshita.*

 author - professor of Princeton University - the fact - didn't know

 (I didn't know that the author was a professor of Princeton University.)

Consider what happens when the sentence subordination in F-8 is removed:

F-9 (a) *M-sensei wa hon o kakimashita. Sono hon wa taihen fuhyō deshita.*

 Professor M - book - wrote. The book - very - unpopular - was

 (Professor M wrote a book. The book was very unpopular.)

   (b) *Chosha wa Princeton daigaku no kyōju desu. Sono koto o shirimasen deshita.*

 Author - professor of Princeton University - professor - is. The fact - I didn't know

 (The author is a professor of Princeton University. I didn't know that.)

The *wa*-marked noun phrases in F-9 are marked by *ga* in the subordinate clauses of F-8. Why is this? The reason seems simply spatial. The topic marker *wa* shouldn't be hidden in an inner syntactic space such as the relative clause of F-8a or an appositive clause in F-8b. The topic marker *wa* should be brought to the initial position of a main clause, a syntactic space that is most transparent to the listener/reader.

G. Temporality: *Uchi*-Time versus *Soto*-Time

Despite views to the contrary (e.g., Sadanobu, 1999), we have assumed that spatiality is a more basic concept than is temporality. I do so because there are numerous examples by which spatial words are used to convey temporal meanings but not the reverse. In Japanese as well as in English, locational postpositions or prepositions, such as *ni* (at/in), *kara* (from), *de* (at/in), and *made* (no English counterpart) can be used as temporal postpositions or prepositions. It is well known that in Japanese, a locational noun *tokoro* (place) is frequently used as a temporal noun. This area needs closer examination that only a separate paper could do justice. So suffice it to say here that there is some evidence showing the precedence of space over time.

Given this apparent precedence for spatiality, the next logical step seems that of *uchi*-time and *soto*-time. This distinction is what I have been building toward all along. *Uchi*-time is when one is currently involved in something, whereas *soto*-time refers to either past time or future time. *Soto*-time (past) is closer to *uchi*-time because it entails real events (usually) when the speaker/writer was previously involved with something. It is harder for the future to match the intensity of actual involvement, so the future seems farther away from *uchi*-time than does the past. This psychological difference between these zones underlies an interesting cultural difference to be shown between Japanese and English. But first, let us consider grammatical tense in the two languages.

Japanese has just two tenses—the past and the non-past—which, believe it or not, is the same for English—technically speaking. Both languages use grammatical aspect (e.g., progressive aspect, "I am going") and other features, such as adverbs, to convey various temporal meanings. In the sentence "I go tomorrow," the non-past tense (the present) is used with an adverb to convey future time. It is this variable use of a present-tense form that necessitates using the term non-past. On this point, the two languages are similar, but they soon depart as you further investigate their verb-aspect systems. Japanese, for example, has fewer specific forms of perfective aspect to use as in English (e.g., past perfect: "I have gone"), and so uses other word forms to convey a similar meaning.

Another way the two languages differ is the relative use of the non-past in narrative discourse. Japanese appear to use the non-past (the present) relatively more than do English speakers. Of course, Japanese appreciate a past event as the past, just as any other people. English speakers are not entirely immune to this impulse either. The historical present is commonly found in spoken narratives in English (e.g., "He gets in his car and takes off") for past events. English is also known to use the "backgrounding present," whereby a speaker orients his or her listener to the story being told. What I am saying, however, is that this tendency is much greater in Japanese than in English, and particularly in the function of the backgrounding present. In trying to explain this difference, I find that what best accounts for it is what I call *uchi*-time. Before further explanation, let us consider an intriguing example found in a novel by Kawabata and its English version in translation.

The following is a passage from Yasunari Kawabata's novel called *The Sound of the Mountain* (1952) translated by Seidensticker (1970). Curiously, Kawabata used the non-past (the present) in certain places, but Seidensticker chose to render them all in the past tense. Such places are marked in italics.

Though August *had only begun*, autumn insects *were already singing*. He *thought* he *could detect* a dripping of dew from leaf to leaf. Then he heard the sound of the mountain. It *was* a windless night. The moon *was* near full, but in the moist, sultry air the fringe of trees that outlined the mountain *was blurred*. They *were* motionless, however. Not a leaf on the fern by the veranda *was stirring*. In these mountain recesses of Kamakura the sea *could* sometimes be heard at night. Shingo wondered if he might have heard the sound of the sea. But no—it was the mountain. It *was* like wind, far away, but with a depth like a rumbling of the earth. Thinking that it might be in himself, a ringing in his ears, Shingo shook his head. The sound stopped, and he was suddenly afraid. A chill passed over him, as if he had been notified that death was approaching. He wanted to question himself, calmly and deliberately, to ask whether it had been the sound of the wind, the sound of the sea, or a sound in his ears. But he had heard no such sound, he was sure. He had heard the mountain. (Seidensticker, 1970, pp. 7–8)

Kawabata used non-past tense in a special way where Seidensticker chose to render it all into past tense. Most instances of the non-past were not for actions by the protagonist but for elements of the setting or atmosphere. Here the present (or non-past) tense functions as what might be called the *backgrounding present* as opposed to the *historical present* (see, for example, Celce-Murcia & Larsen-Freeman, 1999). Whereas the historical present might be availed to by novelists in English, it is the backgrounding present that would seem most peculiar, as demonstrated above by Seidensticker's avoidance of it. In Japanese novels, however, this device is frequently found. Its function in the Japanese novel is one of orientation in support of the main thread of the story.

Hopper's (1979) conception of foregrounding information and backgrounding information provides an explanation. Compare use of the non-past with that of the past tense by Kawabata. The key sentence in the passage, which happens to be in the past tense, is the third one: "Then he heard the sound of the mountain." This is a crucial event for the protagonist Shingo, which caused him to think about death. This instance of past tense, which occurred between instances of the non-past (present), provides foregrounding information. The non-past (or present) signals the backgrounding information in support of the foregrounding, the latter of which is indispensable for tracking the major event line of the protagonist's psychological experience. The backgrounding helps give the reader a physical setting by which a psychological event—the sound of a mountain—took place. In my terms, the reader enters into involvement with the story or character(s) by use of *uchi*-time—the present tense. *Uchi*-time helps produce an illusion as if the narrative events happen in real time, similar to the effect of watching a stage play.

This phenomenon of *uchi*-time, or non-past backgrounding, appears to be a cultural inclination by the Japanese as compared to Americans, especially in literary novels. Seidensticker's choosing to avoid the device is quite telling in this regard. If it appears in English novels, it is likely for a special creative intent, whereas in Japanese, it is more common, perhaps part of everyday thinking. This appears so from an experiment (Makino, 1978) I conducted between 20 Japanese college students and 20 American students, in which they wrote the same narrative (Cinderella). Whereas all the Japanese used the non-past for certain instances, not one American did so. Because backgrounding and foregrounding are not binary but continuous in concept, a clear distinction is not always possible. Nevertheless, my preliminary analysis of the Japanese student narratives shows that the backgrounding non-past was much in evidence. Thus, strong grounds appear to exist for proposing that this phenomenon is an inclination in Japanese culture as compared to American English overall. And this inclination may very well be given impetus by the temporality of *uchi*-time.

CONCLUSION

This chapter shows highly distinctive aspects of Japanese language and culture—spatial metaphors related to *uchi* and *soto*. We found how the Japanese make inside–outside concepts supremely social by the extension of *uchi* to mean house or home. With strong correspondences between space and social relations found practiced at the Japanese house, we also found that *uchi–soto* metaphors underlie many key cultural concepts in Japan. Further inquiry found that these metaphors also help to explain various linguistic phenomena, as well as a fascinating difference about Japanese temporality. Thus, we found strong grounds for considering *uchi* and *soto* as core concepts of Japanese culture.

This chapter contributes in another way. Metaphor, based on analogical cognition, has been marginalized in linguistics ever since the birth of modern linguistics with Saussure's theory of language. His linguistic theory was essentially inherited by Cartesian linguist Noam Chomsky, who has marginalized the analogical faculty of the human mind by promoting a rather digitalized view of human language. Exactly in sync with postmodernistic deconstruction of various "centricisms," Lakoff and Johnson (1980) took a really fresh look at the hitherto marginalized field of metaphors. My attempt to explain Japanese culture and language as metaphor of *uchi* and *soto* is intended to be a part of this new wave of metaphorical reinterpretation of human and nonhuman matters.

In the abstract, we don't know yet to what extent spatial concepts are basic to human cognitive processes, but the fact that my attempt has been fairly successful in presenting an interesting alternative to explain piecemeal phenomena in a unified way attests to basic correctness of my metaphorical application of the spatial concepts of *uchi* and *soto* to nonspatial matters. There are many other areas that were left untouched due to the limit on the space, I mean, literal space on which I can write. Some of them are, for example, animism as a human endeavor to expand *uchi* into nonhuman entities and to interact closely with them. Or some of them are *soto-ka* (exteriorization) of Japanese language, which in my view is still kept in *uchi*. Japanese is seldom used as a common language for communication between two or more nonnative speakers. After living in the

United States for more than half of my life, I feel as if I were caught between *uchi* and *soto*, but I realize that I am now in a position to think hard about *uchi*, my native culture, and *soto*, my adopted American culture, with a reasonable amount of objectivity.

REFERENCES

Benedict, R. F. (1948). *The chrysanthemum and the sword: Patterns of Japanese culture*. Boston: Houghton Mifflin.

Caudill, W., & Plath, D. (1986). Who sleeps by whom? Parent-child involvement in urban Japanese families. In T. S. Lebra & W. P. Lebra (Eds.), *Japanese culture and behavior: Selected readings* (pp. 247–279). Honolulu: University of Hawai'i Press. (Reprinted from *Psychiatry 29* (1966), 344–366)

Caudill, W., & Weinstein, H. (1986). "Maternal Care and Infant Behavior in Japan and America." In T. S. Lebra & W. P. Lebra (Eds.), *Japanese culture and behavior: Selected readings* (pp. 201–246). Honolulu: University of Hawai'i Press. (Reprinted from *Psychiatry 32* (1969), 12–43)

Celce-Murcia, M., & Larsen-Freeman, D. (with Williams, H.). (1999). *The grammar book*. Boston: Heinle & Heinle.

Doi, T. (1971). *Amae no kōzō* [Anatomy of dependence]. Tokyo: Kōbundō. Also available as *Anatomy of dependence* (J. Bester, Trans.). (1973). Tokyo: Kodansha International.

Donahue, R. T. (1998). *Japanese culture and communication: Critical cultural analysis*. Lanham, MD: University Press of America.

Hopper, P. J. (1979). Aspects and foregrounding in discourse. In T. Givón (Ed.), *Syntax and semantics: Vol.12. Discourse and syntax* (pp. 213–259). New York: Academic Press.

Inoue, C. (1977). *Sekentei no kōzō* [Structure of *sekentei*]. Tokyo: Nihon Hōsō Shuppan Kyōkai (NHK Books).

Ishihara, S., & Morita, A. (1989). *No to ieru Nihon* [The Japan that can say no]. Tokyo: Kobunsha.

Kasuga, M. (1978). Shukaku ni tsuku *ga* to *wa* (*ga* and *wa* attached to the subject). In S. Hattori, S. Ono, A. Sakakura, & A. Matsumura (Eds.), *Nihon no gengogaku* [Linguistics in Japan] (pp. 563–568). Tokyo: Taishukan. (Original work published 1919)

Kawabata, Y. (1952). *Yama no oto* [The sound of the mountain]. Tokyo: Chikuma Shobō.

Kuno, S. (1973). *The structure of the Japanese language*. Cambridge, MA: MIT Press.

Kuno, S. (1987). *Functional syntax*. Chicago: University of Chicago Press.

Kuno, S., & Kaburaki, E. (1977). Empathy and syntax. *Linguistic Inquiry 8*(4), 627–672.

Kuroda, S. (1978). *Generative grammatical studies in the Japanese language*. New York: Garland Press.

Lakoff, G., & Johnson, M. (1980). *Metaphors we live by*. Chicago: University of Chicago Press.

Lebra, T. S. (1976). *Japanese patterns of behavior*. Honolulu: University of Hawai'i Press.

Makino, S. (1978). *Kotoba to kūkan* [Language and space]. Tokyo: Tokai University Press.

Makino, S. (1983). "Speaker/listener-orientation and formality marking in Japanese. *Gengo Kenkyū* [Journal of the Linguistics Society of Japan] 84, 126–145.

Makino, S. (1999) Oto to imi no kankei wa yuuen ka? [Is there necessary relationship between sound and meaning?]. In Y. S. Alam (Ed.), *Gengogaku to Nihongo kyōiku* [Linguistics and language pedagogy] (pp. 1–32). Tokyo: Kurosio Shuppan.

Makino, S., & Tsutsui, M. (1986). *A dictionary of basic Japanese grammar*. Tokyo: The Japan Times.

Porter, W. N. (Trans.). (1976). *The Tosa Diary*. New York: AMS Press.

Quinn, C., Jr. (1994). The terms *uchi* and *soto* as windows on a world. In C. Quinn, Jr., & M. J. Bachnik, *Situated meaning—Inside and outside in Japanese self, society, and language*. Princeton: Princeton University Press.

Sadanobu, T. (1999). Kuukan to jikan no kankei—"kuukanteki bunpu o arawasu jikan-goi" o megutte [Relationship between space and time: On time vocabulary that expresses spatial distribution]. *Nihongogaku, 18*, 24–34.

Seidensticker, E. M. (Trans.). (1970). *The sound of the mountain.* New York: Alfred A. Knopf.

Tawara, M. (1987). *Toretate no tanka desu.* Tokyo: Kadokawa Shoten.

Wilson, M. N. (1998). The guessing culture of Japan: Gain or Pain? In R. T. Donahue, *Japanese culture and communication: Critical cultural analysis* (pp. 215-218). Lanham, MD: University Press of America.

part II

Japanese Development:
Person and Nation

Chapter 3

The Sociocultural Discourse of Poetry: Japanese Moral and Personal Development as Reflected in Elementary School Textbooks

Tsutomu Yokota

This chapter provides an inside glimpse of Japanese elementary school education and the enactments of Japaneseness through the teaching and learning of poetry as part of language and culture education. Poetry, in particular, has a facilitative role in the development of personal identity, as well as guiding children's perceptions of nature, life, and the society around them. The present chapter reveals how poetry helps cultivate Japanese values and beliefs integral to a Japanese cultural worldview. To do so, representative poetry from across the grades are sampled and analyzed.

This chapter has two main purposes: (1) to provide insight to Japanese early education, and (2) to show how Japaneseness becomes enacted through the teaching and learning of poetry. Poetry is well suited for developing a cultural worldview in the minds of the young because its lyrical and semantic properties can make vivid and memorable complex rhetorical messages. Rhythm, rhyme, and metaphor are just several of such properties that help make the rhetoric of morality and character building both interesting and comprehensible to the young Japanese mind. To demonstrate, samples of poetry from grades 2 to 6 were selected from Japanese elementary school textbooks currently used nationwide, textbooks all compiled and approved by Monbusho (the Japanese Ministry of Education). The present rationale is that children's awareness of national culture, as well as their view of the world, is strongly influenced by their school education in which school textbooks play a major role.

The poetry selected consists of both fixed form and free verse and are analyzed in view of structure, process, and content. Structure corresponds to the styles or forms of poetry, namely fixed form or free verse, as well as related mode and genre including monolog, dialog, narrative, and expository types. Process involves the specific linguistic strategies to present the theme of the poetic text, while content is concerned principally with values and norms expressed through language. These components of poetry are integrated in order to generate socio-cultural discourses through which the Japanese moral code and philosophy for well-being are taught to Japanese school children.

This chapter first considers the aims of both Japanese elementary education and of the teaching of poetry. Therefore, texts from various poems are excerpted for present review and analysis for locating aspects of Japaneseness. Excerpted texts are necessary because they are practically the most efficient means for providing a cross-section of Japanese schooling within the narrow confines of this one chapter. I freely excise this poetry with this sole intention and am confident the reader will be the wiser.

POETRY IN EDUCATION

The Aims of Elementary School Education

The pedagogic aims of elementary schools in Japan include those to help children acquire essential knowledge and skills and to develop attitudes toward healthy social life as an individual as well as a member of society. Children are encouraged to develop a deeper humanity, recognize their own strong points and individuality through interactions with others, foster self-reliance, and deepen their understanding of national, as well as local, history, culture, and tradition. They are also encouraged to appreciate different cultures and to cultivate the spirit of cooperation in the international community (Monbusho, 1998a, pp. 4–7).

In response to these pedagogic aims, Japanese language teaching at elementary schools places great emphasis on students' having their own ideas and on the development of their ability to reason, express themselves appropriately depending on the purpose and the situation, develop communicative competence, and comprehend the content of reading accurately. In this way, students can deepen their interest in language, develop thinking skills, generate imagination, and foster an attitude of respect for the Japanese language (Monbusho, 1998c, pp. 6–14). These pedagogic aims are meant to develop children into good citizens having Japanese cultural and moral orientations.

Teaching Poetry

Poetry can help carry out these educational aims by encouraging children to see their everyday experiences from different angles, turn their own knowledge into a rich personal encounter, and find pleasure in expressing their own ideas, emotions, and feelings. In such ways, children may develop a fresh outlook on the ordinary things that surround them, helping to foster personal individuality, a goal of the Japanese educational system today. Based on these pedagogic themes, teaching poetry is recommended as one of the most important strategies that develop children's attitudes in understanding their everyday lives, appreciating Japanese culture, and expressing themselves in their own way.

Japanese children are encouraged to perceive the sounds and meaning messages of poetry through their five senses and express them in their own way for effective communication. Their rich perception of sound becomes the basis for creating their own poetry. In learning poetry, listening to the sounds in everyday situations, expressing them through their own perceptions, and having versatile sound experiences are what constitute main tasks for the children. The various aural experiences of poetry encourage children toward enhancing their language sensitivity and cultural perceptions, major instructional goals in early education.

STRUCTURE OF POETRY IN TEXTBOOKS

The arrangement of poetry helps to impart meaning. Specimen texts in this section show the use of indentation, repetition, and sequencing as strategies of arrangement. The significance of arrangement is that it demonstrates rather clearly the rhetorical function—the attempt by the authors to affect the readers in some way. Even if this way is merely to help make information comprehensible, it helps to show motivated choices by the authors. Once establishing this function, we then have grounds for considering how rhetoric functions for larger purposes, such as moral development or theenculturation of the young. Please note that throughout, the punctuation of poetry may differ widely between English an Japanese.

Indentation for Style

Text 1 (Tsurumi, 1996) demonstrates how indentation is used to highlight the major theme by partitioning it from the supportive details.

Text 1 (Grade 2)
Ame no uta   *A Song of Rain*

Ame wa hitori ja utaenai,   The rain can't sing alone,
kitto dareka to isshoda yo.   (it) always sings with someone else.
   Yane to isshoni yane no uta   (It sings) a song of the roof with it.
   tsuchi to isshoni tsuchi no uta   (It sings) a song of the earth with it.
   kawa to isshoni kawa no uta   (it sings) a song of the river with it.
   hana to isshoni hana no uta.   (it sings) a song of flowers with them.

The first two lines, which describe the theme of the poem, start from the margin, while the lines thereafter are indented. The indented lines provide details in support of the theme, namely how the rain needs others to sing with. This strategy of indentation indicates the qualitative difference between the introductory or thematic part of the text, a text that also serves to inculcate Japanese values of collectivism and love of nature.

In Text 2 (Sakata, 1993), the setting sun urges children to go back home, because the time is late. In this text, a narrative explanation of the situation precedes the lines directly connected to its theme. Here, indentation is employed to distinguish the narrative from its dialog.

Text 2 (Grade 3)
Yūhi ga senaka o oshite kuru   *The Setting Sun Pushes Us*

Yūhi ga senaka o oshite kuru	The setting sun pushes us
makka na ude de oshite kuru	with (his) red hands
aruku bokura no ushiro kara	from behind
dekkai koe de yobikakeru	(he) calls out to us loudly
sayonara sayonara	Good-bye, boys, good-bye
ban-gohan ga matteru zo	(your) dinner is ready (for you)!
ashita no asa nesugosu na	Don't oversleep tomorrow morning!

In Text 3 (Shimada, 1996), indentation is used to emphasize the theme of the text, in which a specific meaning and the emotions of young girls carrying a portable shrine are embedded in both structure and rhythm of the basic five-five syllables.

Text 3 (Grade 5)
Doitenka   *Make Way, Please*

Doitenka	Make way, please!
doitenka	Make way, please!
onna no mikoshi ya	A girls' portable shrine!
doitenka	Make way, please!
minna de hayase ba	If celebrated by all
tsuyuzora hareru	even a rainy sky will clear up
wasshoi wasshoi	Heave-ho, heave-ho!
doitenka	Make way, please!

In this text, the last line, "*doitenka,*" is indented by about 1 inch from the margin. The indentation reinforces the theme of the text, in which a group of young girls' reserved but confident expression of identity is outspoken in the last phrase, "*doitenka.*" The indentation distinguishes the festive mood (the outside world) from the girls' intention to express their own identity (the inside world). The structure functions to convey their positive attitudes for their own self-assertion by young girls carrying a portable shrine. We can see that indentation is one of the effective strategies that indicate qualitative differences in both style and meaning of texts, which for poetry may be uniquely Japanese, at least compared to English.

The rhetorical function of this indentation conflicts with exaggerated views of Japanese communication as being wholly convoluted, mysterious, or opaque.

Repetition for Emphasis

Repetition is employed to emphasize the psychological and internal state of the protagonist, the theme of which figures in the next poem (Text 4, from Bundo, 1996). The great disappointment of the protagonist is emphasized by the repetition of the phrase, "*Nihai mo shita*" (I even lost twice in this battle).

Text 4 (Grade 5)
Kibasen   *A Mock Cavalry Battle*

Boku wa maketa!   I lost!
nihai mo shita.   (I even lost) twice.
Nanbyakunin mono mae de   In front of hundreds of people
nihai mo shita.   (I lost) twice.
Torakku no mannaka de   Right in the middle of the track
akagumi no yowai taishō ga   a lost leader of the red team
dekai karada o chiisaku shite   with his fine-built body shrinking
hazukashi sō ni   bashfully
tatte ita.   (he was) standing alone.

When repetition is combined with rhythm as in Text 3 and Text 4, the combination creates a special meaning. In Text 4, the special meaning is the extra anguish of failing in front of others, heightened because it occurred in front of hundreds. In a collectivist culture such as Japan's, this is one of the worst fears. "*Maketa*" (to have lost at) even goes unspoken in the last lines though it is understood as such: The unspeakable happened twice. By these few lines, we can sense a connection to the famed Japanese work ethic and their widely acclaimed achievement motivation.

Instead of repeating a whole phrase or sound as in previous texts, the same word "*hatahata*" (sandfish) is repeated six times in Text 5 (Murou, 1996). In this poem, the poet describes the color of the fish, the weather when fishing, and the cooking when done best, all said in which the name of the fish is repeated.

Text 5 (Grade 5)
Hatahata no uta   *The Song of Sandfish*

Hatahata to ifu(u) sakana,   A fish called *hatahata* (sandfish),
usubeni iro no hatahata,   a slightly rouged sandfish,
hatahata ga toreru hi wa   the day (we) have a catch
hatahatagumo to ifu (u) kumo
 ga araha(wa) reru.   sandfish-clouds appear.
hatahata yaite taberu no wa   Grilled sandfish are

kitaguni no kodomo no gochisō nari.	delicious food for children in the north.
Hatahata o mireba	Whenever (I) see sandfish
haha o omofu(u) mo	(I) think of (my) mother
fuyu no narahi nari.	as is usual in winter.

This repetition of the name of the fish (*hatahata*) throughout the poem conveys the fisherman's deep feeling toward the fish. This feeling can be understood in the sense of an adversarial respect but more importantly the gratitude that the fisherman feels to fish at large in providing him a livelihood. This sentiment explains why special shrines are made in Japan to recognize the contributions by living creatures to the benefit of humankind. Thus it would not be unusual if, in this particular fisherman's village, a religious shrine had been made to recognize the gifts received from the sea. In this respect, one can grasp how the Japanese traditional worldview conceives humankind as a part of nature, in contrast to the Western view of the separation, or the opposition, between the two entities.

In addition, and perhaps more significantly, the fisherman in the poem invokes the memory of his mother in association with the fish in a cherished way, not once but on a regular basis ("as is usual in winter," probably the season for this particular fish). Just as the fisherman recognizes the sacrifices made by the fish on his behalf, so he recognizes the same done for him by his mother.

Repeating the same phrase or sentence helps give readers a clear visual image of content. In Text 6 (Yamamura, 1996), for example, the phrase "*Ichimen no nano hana*" (Outstretched rape (mustard) blossoms), which is repeated seven times in each of the three stanzas, is used in describing beautiful rape blossoms spread out like a yellow mosaic carpet in a field.

Text 6 (Grade 6)
Hūkei—Jungin mozaiku   *Scenery—Pure Gold mosaic*

Ichimen no nano hana	Outstretched rape blossoms
Ichimen no nano hana	Outstretched rape blossoms
Ichimen no nano hana	Outstretched rape blossoms
Ichimen no nano hana	Outstretched rape blossoms
Ichimen no nano hana	Outstretched rape blossoms
Ichimen no nano hana	Outstretched rape blossoms
Ichimen no nano hana	Outstretched rape blossoms
Kasuka naru mugibue	Faint sounds of an oaten pipe

While the multiple repetitions about the rape (mustard) blossoms convey their abundance, the single mention of faint sounds of an oaten pipe (a reed used as a flute) in the eighth line conveys the solitude, the silence, a Japanese aesthetic, as well as a moral and spiritual value. In contrast to the sometimes overbearing social group relations, as with extreme cases of fixations on one's mother, Japanese religiosity, especially Buddhism, seems founded on solitary excursions, either outwardly on a mountain retreat or inwardly in meditation, as ways for spiritual cleansing. Moreover, this state of solitude can bring present-centered-ness as a way to fully appreciate nature, a spiritual as well as aesthetic value deriving, perhaps, from the indigenous religion, Shinto.

The same poem continues the subject of nature in its later stanzas by which the chirping of skylarks, "*Hibari no oshaberi,*" and "*Yameru wa hiruno tsuki*" (Only the midday moon shining dimly) occupy the eighth line of the later stanzas, respectively. This three-stanza poem follows a consistent pattern in repeating the same key phrase of "*Ichimen no nanohana,*" which incorporates three lines describing the atmosphere of the fields, each of which is placed at the eighth line of each stanza. Each line is composed of a five-four syllable pattern that creates the same rhythm throughout the poem.

The children's sense of beauty is stimulated simultaneously through their own minds' eye and through their sense of rhythm in appreciating a peaceful and beautiful scene of nature. At the same time, a consciousness develops for impor-tant Japanese cultural values. Patterns of poetry provide a memorable means for this acculturation through the combination of indentation, repetition, and rhythm.

Perceiving the Orderly Sequence of Communication

Observing an orderly sequence of our actions related to social events and sit-uations is an early task for children in the language arts. Children in early ele-mentary school are encouraged to read by paying attention to the order or sequence of events described in texts (Monbusho, 1998c, p. 7). Although this is a basic task for young children developing skills in communication, some poems also encourage moral or civic education. In Text 7, "*Aki no kamakiri*" (A Mantis in Autumn) (Sakamoto, 1996), the protagonist's behavior is described clearly in sequence. Related instructional aims for cognitive/psycholinguistic and moral development are schematically displayed in Table 3-1.

Text 7 (Grade 2)
Aki no kamakiri   *A Mantis in Autumn*

Kōen ni ittara,   I went to the park, and
susuki no nemoto ni,   at the roots of Japanese pampas grass,
kamakiri ga ita.   (I) found a mantis.
Kaze ga fuku tabi ni,   At every autumnal breeze,
te to ashi ga furuete ita trembling were his tactile organs and his legs.
Nemutte iru noka na   (Is he) asleep, (I wonder)?
boku datte   even I myself
janpā o kite iru noni,   wear a jacket
kamakiri wa   it
hadaka da.   has nothing on.
ohisama ga ataru yōni,   so that the sun may shine on (the mantis),
happa no ue ni   on the surface of a leaf
sotto oite yatta.   (I) softly place (him).

Table 3-1
SPRE and Cognitive Mapping of the Poem, *Aki no Kamakiri*

Structure (Discourse)	Text	Process (Cognition)
Situation	1 *Kōen ni ittara*	
	I went to the park	Initial behavior
	2 *susuki no nemoto ni*	
	at the roots of Japanese pampas grass	Discovery
	3 *kamakiri ga ita*	
	I found a mantis	Object
	4 *Kaze ga fuku tabi ni*	
	At every autumn breeze	
Problem	5 *te to ashi ga furuete ita.*	
	[he was] trembling.	Observation
	6 *Nemutte iru noka na*	
	Is he asleep, I wonder?	Inference
	7 *boku datte*	
	even I myself	Comparison
	8 *jampā o kite iru noni,*	
	wear a jacket,	
	9 *kamakiri wa*	
	it	Observation
	10 *hadaka da.*	
	has nothing on.	Description
Response	11 *ohisama ga ataru yōni*	
	so that the sun may shine on it	Assessment
	12 *happa no ue ni*	
	on the surface of a leaf	Interpretation
	13 *sotto oite yatta.*	
	I softly place him.	Willful action

In this poem, a boy visits a park, which is his initial behavior (1). There, the child finds a mantis—the object (3)—which he closely watches. He learns that the insect is motionless in an autumnal breeze, demonstrating his observation (5). Based on this observation, the child comes to decide that the insect must be cold—assessment (11). This assessment results in a behavior—a plan of action (13). The poem gives an orderly sequence of the boy's behavior. He perceives that the mantis might be cold in the cool autumnal breeze—an inference (6)—because he deduces an internal state of another on the basis of observed external events. Although verbal communication was absent between the boy and the insect, he presumably perceived correctly the state of the insect (line 11). Thus, the poem contributes to a child's cognitive or psycholinguistic development, however small that contribution may be.

In addition to these cognitive or psycholinguistic elements, the poem is arranged in a common pattern of cultural discourse—*ki-shō-ten-ketsu*—or perhaps even a universal one, known as SPRE (see, for example, Donahue, 1998), by which a text is arranged in segments corresponding to situation, problem, response, and evaluation, or in variations thereof. *Ki-shō-ten-ketsu,* which had been borrowed from China centuries ago, has since developed as a similar, general, all-purpose discourse pattern. The poem presently under study could be analyzed by either format, SPRE or *ki-shō-ten-ketsu,* because it happens to fall in between as a variant. I have chosen to use the SPRE pattern, partly because it is probably more familiar to readers.

Briefly, the events of this poem are arranged in the order of situation-problem-response. The individual in the poem is placed in a situation, namely finding a mantis at a park. He perceives a problem involving the mantis and makes a response in reaction. Evaluation of the response is absent probably because the poet felt no need for it. Or one could argue that evaluation is understood here as having been successful. At the same time, moral development comes into play in this poem whereby children's pro-social behavior is fostered by stimulating within them a sympathetic response or fellow feelings for others in need, even though in this case it is an insect. Although Japanese education is not unique for such moral development, it still prides itself for attention to this area. One aspect that could be particularly Japanese is to do so through poetry, though not limited to this alone, which exemplifies, perhaps, the keen sense for aesthetics that the Japanese have. This poem is typical of the poetry used in school textbooks in Japan, exemplifying here common aims for psycholinguistic, discursive, and moral development.

PROCESS OF POETRY IN TEXTBOOKS

Sounds for Meaning

The rhythm created by the manipulation of different sounds offers children a good opportunity to learn poetry. The rhythm of words intuitively attracts a child's attention toward "word wonderments" (Denman, 1988, p. 113). Of particular note here about Japanese is the special place in the language held by onomatopoetic words. Onomatopoeia in Japanese "play a much more important role than do corresponding words in English" (Itō & Mester, 1999, p. 63). Onomatopoeia give an affective quality to Japanese that otherwise might be assumed absent due to the relatively greater restraint that Japanese people exercise in public than do their Western counterparts. Text 8 (Yamada, 1996), the first of several related examples here, describes people trying to live undaunted by a heavy rain.

Text 8 (Grade 5)

Ame	*Rain*
Ame ame ame ame	Rain rain rain rain
ame ame ame ame	rain rain rain rain
ame wa bokura o zan zaka tataku	The rain hits us heavily,
zan zaka zan zaka	(onomatopoeia)
zan zan zaka zaka	(onomatopoeia)
ame wa zan zan zaka zaka zaka zaka	(it) falls heavily, (onomatopoeia)
hottategoya o neratte tataku	(it) hits (our) shanties directly and mercilessly
bokura no kurashi o bishi bishi tataku	and (our) life without mercy.
sabi ga zarizari hageteru yane o	(It) hits (our) roof with its paint peeled off
yasumu koto naku shikiri ni tataku	without stopping.

This first stanza describes how the merciless rain hits the people's humble house, while the seventh and eighth lines of the second stanza describe how the rain beats upon them:

mimi nimo mune nimo shimikomu hodoni	as if (it) penetrates into (our) ears and heart
bokura no kurashi o kakonde tataku	surrounding our whole life

"*Zan*" expresses the quantity of the rain falling in the real world, hitting poor people and their shanties without mercy. It describes the objective sound of rain. "*Zaka*," on the other hand, conveys the quality of rain falling on the poet's heart, or his "inside" world. The distinction between the actual rain falling outside and the imaginary rain falling inside is simultaneously expressed through the contrast between "*zan*" and "*zaka*." The two different meanings of the sounds repeated five times each, embedded in rhythmical seven-seven and eight-seven syllables, respectively, emphasize the text's theme. The personified rain presents readers with a concrete image of the rain hitting people heavily. Through oral reading, children begin to notice the rhythm and alliteration in "*zan zan*" and "*zaka zaka*." The sounds and rhythm of this poem, coupled with its fixed form verse style, lead to its meaning and theme.

Besides the onomatopoeia, another item for notice is the rural or agricultural setting: Shanties here are reminiscent of a rural past, one that historically is more recent for Japanese than it is for Westerners, despite that proportionally more Japanese live today in urban areas than do Americans (Donahue, 1998). Although social hierarchy is honored relatively more strongly in Japan than in the West, rural life is greatly celebrated in the literature for Japanese children, as is also that of everyday service and manual occupations. Such positive regard might surprise Westerners, given the strength of social hierarchy in Japan, so let Text 8 be one such example.

Text 1, already mentioned, is also an example of the celebration of nature through rain and may remind Japanese readers of associated onomatopoetic sounds. Text 9 (Kudo, 1996a) does so through the wonderment of fast moving "*medaka*" (small fry fish) in water.

Text 9 (Grade 4)
Ogawa no māchi   *The March of a Brook*

Tsun tata tsun ta   (onomatopoeia)
migi muite pin   turn to the right, *pin*
tsun tata tsun ta   (onomatopoeia)
hidari muite pin   turn to the left, *pin*
bokura ogawa no tankentai   we are an expeditionary party of the brook
sebire soroe te tsun tatta   neatly dressed, *tsun tatta* (onomatopoeia)

In the second stanza, the group of fish swiftly pass a frog: "*kaeru yokome ni tsun tatata*" (with a sidelong glance at a frog, *tsun tatata* [onomatopoeia]). In the third stanza, they make their way through water grass: "*mizukusa chon*" (making our way through water grass, *chon* [onomatopoeia]).

Here "*medaka*" (small fry fish) have just started to explore a brook. "*Pin*" describes the fish turning to the right; "*tsun tatta*," marching through the water; "*chon*," passing swiftly through water grass. "*Tsun tatata*" also describes them quickly glancing at a frog. All these sounds describe each different motion of the fish. Like the fish in this poem, children are expected to start exploring a brook and understanding the outside world through various sound experiences.

Even ants communicate with children through onomatopoetic sound. In Text 10 (Kudo, 1996b), ants move their tactile organs and legs to convey their feelings and emotions.

Text 10 (Grade 4)
Sanpo   *A walk*

Tōku made aruita   (I) walked far
amai aji sagashite   looking for sweet taste.
boku no hige puru puru   My whiskers go *puru puru* (onomatopoeia)
boku no ashi shaka shaka   my legs go *shaka shaka* (onomatopoeia)
asoko nimo koko nimo   here and there
amai aji iroiro   various sweet tastes
bokuno hige iso iso   my whiskers go *iso iso* (onomatopoeia)
boku no ashi achikochi   I walk here and there
ouchimade kaerō   (I) must go home
amai aji tappuri   (I am) full of the sweet taste
boku no hige pin pin   my whiskers go *pin pin* (onomatopoeia)
boku no ashi don don   I walk briskly back home.

"*Puru puru*" describes ants busily moving their tactile organs in search of sweets; "*shaka shaka,*" the ants walk busily in search of sweets. These lively images are of ants that have just started their search. The first two lines of Text 10 describe the ants' initial action, while the remaining lines describe their different motions. "*Pin pin*" describes their antennas as cocked and motionless, while "*don don*" describes ants walking briskly back home, vigorous and satisfied with their bellies full.

These various onomatopoeia convey both the motion and emotions of insects. The five-four syllable meter employed throughout creates rhythm, which contributes to the wonderment of nature. We can see how sound structure functions to help readers generate lively images of ants, as well as helping to understand how the so-called Japanese love of nature can be actualized and extended even to the "lowly" world of insects.

Text 11 (Tanigawa, 1996) similarly employs onomatopoeia to describe the successive leaps by a young frog from its home and then eventually outward into the mechanized world of cars and trains, and even beyond that, though only the first stanza is presented here.

Text 11 (Grade 2)
Kaeru no Pyon   *A Frog Pyon*

Kaeru no Pyon   Frog *Pyon*
tobu no ga daisuki   (he) likes jumping very much
hajime ni kāsan tobikoe te first (he) jumps over (his) mother
sorekara tōsan tobikoe ru   then (he) flies over (his) father
pyon   (onomatopoeia)

"*Pyon,*" the onomatopoetic sense for a frog's leap, increases in frequency with each subsequent stanza, showing that the frog hops from the nearest to the farthest objects away, from its home to the outside world until it flies into the future. In the second stanza, the frog jumps over cars and the *Shinkansen* (the "bullet" train); in the third stanza, airplanes and the sun; in the fourth stanza, today and into tomorrow. Instead of a detailed explanation, "*pyon*" helps children imagine such concrete objects and the natural progression involved over space and time. This use of sound encourages children to find pleasure in reading poetry orally. Oral reading of poetry in Japan, either individually or in groups, has become widely recognized as an integral part of language learning. It allows children to develop both reading and communication skills in an effective manner. Through practicing oral reading, children are exposed to Japanese rhyme and rhythm, as well as correct pronunciation. The pedagogic functions of oral reading enable children to acquire selective reading skills, rhythm and styles of the language, and production skills, all of which directly connect sound to meaning and language awareness.

Personification for Interaction

Personification can affect children in meaningful ways, especially when placed in dialog as with Text 12 (Kawai, 1996).

Text 12 (Grade 6)
Yuzuriha   *Leaves of* Yuzuriha *Tree*

Kodomotachi yo,   Hello, my dear children,
kore wa yuzuriha no ki desu.   this is the leaf of a *Yuzuriha* tree (speaking).
Kono yuzuriha wa   This leaf of the *Yuzuriha* tree,
atarashii ha ga dekiru to   when a new leaf comes out,
irekawatte furui wa ga ochite
    shimau no desu.   will give place to the new one.
Konnani atsui wa   Even thick
konnani ookii wa demo   and big like this, though
atarashii wa ga dekiru to muzōsa
    ni ochiru   (I) easily fall when a new leaf sprouts, (and)
atarashii wa ni inochi o yuzutte   (I) hand over my position in favor of my junior.

The leaf of this tree addresses children as if already on intimate terms. This direct address arrests attention. The implicit message for the children is that someday they will inherit all that their parents have accumulated, including the natural environment. Underlying the theme of the poem is consciousness for the child–parent relationship, which is rooted in Confucian thought.

Other examples of the personification of nature for instructional purposes follow. The setting sun, for example, can be personified in order to urge children to return straight home, as we have discussed for Text 2. This text also employs dialog for extra effect: The moral instruction is clear here, as well as the potential to put personification in like service as with Text 13 next.

Text 13 (Kawasaki, 1996) shows the use of personification to present an adult philosophical viewpoint about life but also social relationships, including respect for elders and community as conveyed through the imagery of ancient cedar trees.

Text 13 (Grade 6)
Yakushima no sugi no ki   *Cedar Trees on Yaku Island*

Kimi wa ikutsu?   How old are you?
Kimi no tōsan wa ikutsu?   How old is your father?
Kimi no obāsan wa ikutsu?   How old is your grandmother?
Oretachi Yakushima no suginoki wa   We the cedars on Yaku island
sensai de yatto ichininmae   become adults at the age of 1,000 years.
7,200 sai datte iruzo   Some of us are as old as 7,200 years old.
kaminari ni utarete   Hit by a stroke of lightning

bokiri to orete taorete mo	even if stricken down
ki ni abura ga	(we have) resin
gicchiri to tsumatte iru kara	packed to the full
kusara nai	and (it) prevents us from decaying.
oreta tokoro ni	At the broken scar
sugi no tane ga ochite me ga dete	cedar seeds fall and sprout
mata	once again (and)
nanzen nen mo ikiru no da	(they) live for thousands of years.

The trees remark how they have endured hardships for thousands of years while implying a long nurturance or growth period. Being like the good cedar trees, we are sure to take heed from our elders—our parents and teachers especially—and endure life's struggles.

In Text 14 (Takami, 1993), even the grass tells children how to lead positive lives.

Text 14 (Grade 5)
Ware wa kusa nari   *I Am the Grass*

Ware wa kusa nari	I am the grass.
nobinto su	(I am) making efforts to grow by myself.
nobiraretu toki	When (I) can grow,
nobinto su	(I) make an effort to grow.
nobirarenu hi wa	On the day (I) can't (grow),
nobinu nari	(I) won't.
nobirareru hi wa nobiru nari	On the day (I) can, (I) grow.

In these poems, elements of nature assume the roles of elders in teaching children a moral code as well as a life philosophy. Use of dialog permits, though vicariously done, "direct" communication with nature. In this way, an individual may conceive of humankind as being in harmony with nature as much as it may be opposed. The issue of how much this sentiment is actually practiced is not of concern here. I merely wish to point out the Japanese cultural values that inhere, some of which that pertain to the prizing of nature. This reverence represents an ideal and, like with all cultures, may or may not be fully realized. Nevertheless, cultural ideals provide important insights for understanding a culture.

Metaphor for Imagination

Poetry can create powerful images in only a few words, and once metaphors have been incorporated into them, they allow readers to generate strong imagery of its content. In Text 15 (Shouda, 1993), the author, perhaps as a boy, describes his impression when parents visited his class.

Text 15 (Grade 6)
Kenkyū jugyō   *Class Open to Parents*

Kinō,   Yesterday,
kenkyū jugyō ga atta.   (parents visited) our class at work.
Minna ishi ni natta.   Everyone turned into stone.

The children's tense psychological condition is clearly described by three simple sentences. The "*ishī*" (stone) conveys a tense atmosphere prevailing in the classroom. Parental observation of class is regarded as an important educational strategy to promote school education. The recommendation submitted to the Ministry of Education by the Curriculum Council in 1998 proposes that schools, parents, and local communities need to incorporate each other in order to promote Japanese education for the 21st century (Monbusho, 1996, pp. 61–65). Children are expected, however, to perform before their parents: They are not supposed to make mistakes nor behave rudely in class. If a child makes a mistake in his or her performance, he or she is likely to feel guilt as we have seen in Text 4. The sense of guilt lies heavily on both the child and the parent. Therefore, children become nervous and passive, and tend to remain silent, which is referred to as "*ishī*" (stone) in the text. The fact that both teachers and parents expect too much of their children helps create this unwelcome situation. This is one aspect of Japanese culture found in the Japanese school system. The poem is very short, but the third line tells much about Japanese education today. Here we see a close relationship between metaphor (process) and theme (content), which describes school culture.

Metaphor can help expand our consciousness. In Text 16 (Sugano, 1993), the sequence of actions looking through a magnifying glass reveals a surprisingly different outlook on our everyday world. The poet's discovery impresses her so much that she feels as if she were in a different world. Her surprise is described in metaphorical expressions (as broadly defined).

Text 16 (Grade 3)
Mushimegane   *A Magnifying Glass*

Mushimegane de soto o mita.   (I) saw through a magnifying glass.
Me kara don don hanashite iku to,   When (I) kept the magnifying glass apart
                                             from my eyes,

patto kyūni masshiro ni natte,   a flood of white light came (into my eyes),
yuki no sekai ni haitta yōda.   and (I) felt as if (I) got into a world of
                                             snow.

Tsuzukete hanashite iku to,   When (I) kept the glass further away,
kurutto keshiki ga sakasama ni natta.   the scenery turned round to upside down.
Marude, chikyū ga,   As if, the earth
sakadachi shita mitai da.   stood on its head.
Ie ga kumo ni kuttsuita.   And the house reached the clouds.

The text presents the world as seen from different angles and reveals quite a different world to the child through the power of metaphor. We can see how our common action or behavior becomes a new experience and gives us a fresh look at our world.

CONTENT OF POETRY IN TEXTBOOKS

Poetry is a treasure trove of Japanese cultural values, as has been indicated already. This section pursues the subject more directly with four major values: interdependence, self-sustenance, cosmic unity, and maternal love. Other values, of course, can be found, but these four values correspond to the basic principles of moral education (Monbusho, 1998c, pp. 90–94) and hold a central position in early moral development of the child as reflected in the poetry of Japanese elementary school textbooks.

Interdependence (*Kyōsei*)

In Text 7, the boy in the poem says to himself, "*bokudatte*" (even I myself), showing how he equates himself with the insect in the chilly autumnal wind. He is not conscious of the biological differences between the insect and himself. His perception has something in common with the view held by the Tendai Buddhism sect in the 8th century, that all life, including human life, is basically of the same value in this world. In the Japanese educational environment, the view has been applied to create a value of "interdependence," a value with both a sympathetic response to others and cooperative attitude integrated on an equal footing with other person(s), thing(s), or object(s) (Monbusho, 1998b, pp. 22–24).

Children are encouraged to respond to animals and plants, and any other objects, in much the same manner as they do to their peers and familiar others in their everyday lives. The sun (Text 2), a mantis (Text 7), fish (Text 9), an ant (Text 10), a frog (Text 11), a leaf (Text 12), a tree (Text 13), grass (Texts 14 and 17), cranes (Text 18), and a locust (Text 19) are viewed as children's close friends or familiar others. In school discourse, this interdependence is so embedded in the curriculum that it enhances children to nurture a rich humanity through cultivating a healthy mind to respect others, to appreciate beauty, and to protect the environment and the like (Monbusho, 1998b, pp. 54, 70).

Self-Sustenance (*Ikiru Chikara*)

Highly valued in Japanese education today are self-esteem and self-sustenance. A mere observation of grass growing may make children aware of the meaning of life or life through self-sustenance. Text 17 (Nakamoto, 1993), written in a free verse style, describes how the poet, perhaps as a child, marvels at the grass growing by itself.

Text 17 (Grade 2)
Kusa   *Grass*

Kusatte tsuyoi na.   How strong is the wild grass!
Datte, nanimo shinai demo,   Because without any help, though,
sukusuku sodatte iru.   (it) grows everyday.
Kusa wa,   It
jibunde jibun o sodatete iru.   rears itself.

The theme of the poem, self-sustenance, corresponds to one of the pedagogic aims in Japanese education today: to help children cultivate mental independence (Monbusho, 1997, p. 15). The poem expresses for the child the importance of self-sustenance through the example of grass. It presents a little child's view of life, while Text 14 presents an adult's view. Both texts are representative of a pedagogic theme to teach children how to face their own life. The poet, perhaps as a child, inquires into the reasons for the rigorous, superb power of grass growing by itself and becomes aware of the importance of self-sustenance, the theme of the text. What is expected from children in the poetry class is their own awareness of the wonder of life, their own view of the world, and their own interpretation of the tasks, for example, reading or writing poetry. The task directly leads to the pedagogic theme of motivating children to learn by themselves and helping them develop abilities to learn, reason, judge, and express themselves accurately (Monbusho, 1996, pp. 31–33).

Cosmic Unity (*Shizen Tono Ittaikan*)

Nature in poetry is beautiful and quiet with life in it. In Text 18 (Shintani, 1996), life with nature is described as follows:

Text 18 (Grade 5)
Tsuru ga wataru   *Cranes Migrate*

Tsuru ga wataru   (A flock of) cranes are migrating,
wataru   migrating,
shitsugen no sora o nakinagara
   wataru   crying high over the moor.
kō kō to wataru   Migrating, whooping *kou kou.*

In the first stanza, cranes and the moor are mentioned, and in the first and the second lines of the second stanza, the sky, the sun, and the mountains are also.

Yūhi ga moeru   (The skies) are aglow with the setting sun
yamanami ga moeru   and tinged are the peaks of the mountains, too.

In the third stanza, a man (the poet) sets his heart on the cranes:

shitugen niha mō sugu kibishii
fuyu ga kuru   A severe winter will soon come to the moor
itetsuku yuki mo kuru darō   and freezing snow, too.

In the fourth and fifth lines of the fourth stanza, the poet describes the whooping of the cranes as follows:

nakikawashi nagara wataru   with calling to each other.
tsuru ga wataru   Cranes are migrating
kō kō to wataru   migrating, whooping

In this text, a flock of cranes migrating over the moor are described along with the sunset and mountain peaks tinged with a rosy flash by the setting sun. Flying high, like white flowers, the cranes and the rosy mountains are beautiful to look at, but approaching winter suggests that the beautiful cranes face life in a severe environment. Also, the calling out by the cranes to each other en route to their destination indicates mutual help and regard. Elements from across the spectrum of nature—cranes, the setting sun, the peaks of the mountains, the moor, and man himself, the poet, through his thoughts of the cranes—are integrated to create a landscape within an "all-in-one scene." This all-in-one scene represents cosmic unity, a particular aspect of the Japanese poetic spirit. This perception of cosmic unity is also found in Text 6, where rape blossoms, the moon, the sound of an oaten pipe, skylarks, and the poet in the field create an all-in-one scene like a beautiful landscape picture. These poems describe a peaceful life embraced by nature, while Text 19 (Mado, 1996) also concerns cosmic unity but is suggestive of how nature follows the dictum of "the survival of the fittest."

Text 19 (Grade 6)
Inago   *A Locust*

Happa ni tomatta   On a leaf
inago no me ni   in the eyes of a locust
itten   just a single point
moete iru yūyake   glowing is the setting sun.

demo inago wa   But the locust
boku shika mite inai noda   watches only me,
enjin o kaketa mama   with (his) engine going,
itsudemo nigerareru shisei de   and preparing to fly away at any moment.

ā, tsuyoi ikimono to   Oh, between a stronger life
yowai ikimono no aida o   and a weaker life
kawa no yōni nagareru   flows like a river
ine no nioi   the fragrance of the ears of rice.

In this text, the poet looks at a locust in the setting sun, with a faint scent of rice plants in the air, and he becomes aware of the relationship between the locust and himself. In the eyes of a locust, staring at the poet, are reflected the blazing red sun and rosy skies. The description suggests a quiet and colorful world in which the strong (the poet, humanity) and the weak (the locust) face each other in a state of tension, even as we seek a harmonious, interdependent world. This tense atmosphere coupled with the fragrant rice engulfing the entire scene creates the poetic spirit.

Children are advised to describe animals, plants, or human beings with reference to nature in their own poetry (Monbusho, 1999, pp. 37–38). Even the humble, rural life can become a noble topic for poetry as we have seen in Text 8. It is one aspect of the Japanese mentality. The poetic spirit, well embedded in poetry, is linked to such Japanese pedagogic themes as fostering children to seek harmonious living with others, to appreciate beauty, and to sympathize with other living things (Monbusho, 1998c, pp. 90–94).

Maternal Love (*Hahagokoro*)

Japanese mythology teaches that Japan was created by the sun goddess *Amaterasu*. History teaches that Japan had a matrilineal society in ancient times. The mother figure has loomed large in Japanese consciousness, at least symbolically, for a long time. Today, a mother's love for her children is one of the most familiar themes found in the poetry in school textbooks. We saw this already in Text 5 with the fisherman's remembrance of his mother. This value is more fully considered by Text 20 (Yagi, 1992), in which a daughter notes what her mother says to each family member as they start their day.

Text 20 (Grade 3)
Okāchan no kotoba   *My Mother's Words*

Kotobatte, takusan aru.   Words are so versatile.
uchi no okāchan ha,   My mother (says),
asa, minna ga dekakeru toki,   when everyone leaves for school or for work,
otōchan niha   To my father,
"Gokurousan, ohayō okaeri yasu"   "Have a nice day, and come back early."
onēchan niha,   To my sister
"Kisha ya densha
    ni kiotsukeru none. "   "Be careful about trains and streetcars."
onīchan niha,   To my brother,
"Shikkari benkyō shite kunno yo."   "Study hard, you see."
watashi niha,   To me,
"Jidōsha ni kiotsukerunon yo."   "Be careful about traffic."
soshite, chiisana koe de,   And in a low voice,
"Shikkari sensei no ohanashi   "Listen to your teacher attentively,
    o kiitena akane."   you know."
to, kimatta youni iwaharu.   Always (she) says to me.
obāchan ni dake,   Only to my grandmother,
"Goyukkuri."   "Please relax."

to,	like this,
yasashii koe de iwaharu.	(she) says gently in a soft voice.
okāchan mo, taiteiya nai.	Indeed she is always full of family cares.

When the mother in the poem says a few words to each member of her family, she tries to encourage and motivate them in the hope that they can start their day with a sense of security and in a relaxed mood. This sympathetic concern by Japanese mothers helps maintain their family unity through the close attention to the personal needs of others (Monbusho, 1998b, pp. 28–35).

The image of one's mother in poetry is a typical manifestation of mother-centered consciousness in the Japanese community, although this text shows us a child getting to be independent of his or her mother. In the poetry class, for example, children are encouraged to collect as many words as possible uttered by their mother, and to think about and discuss their mother's roles in the family or activities in the community.

In Japanese traditional thought, the mother–child relationship is central to the family, more important than that between the two parents. In actuality, the mother–child relationship in Japan may become quite intense by Western standards, even verging on the abnormal in some extreme cases by which a child remains overly fixated on the mother or her image well into adulthood (e.g., Text 5). In most cases, however, the child develops the independence to leave home to start a family but still remembers the parents in order to take care of them in their old age, a scenario happening less and less over recent decades. Similarly, the centrality of the mother–child relationship in the family may be changing in the future, as daycare centers and women careerists become more prevalent in the years ahead.

CONCLUSION

The poetry in textbooks was presented to show the relationship between structure, process, and content in relation to pedagogical themes in Japanese education. Poetry presents Japanese cultural values expressed in simple but refined Japanese. Learning poetry in the language class is greatly encouraged to help children internalize the values embedded in poetry because they need to enact them in their daily lives and develop them through their own initiatives in the future. The pedagogic themes of poetry in textbooks facilitate children to construct their own personality and national/cultural identity in their early years. The unique links between poetry and Japaneseness can be seen as the building blocks for Japanese civic discourse and the budding of a Japanese social being.

REFERENCES

Bundo, A. (1996). Kibasen [A mock cavalry battle]. In J. Kinoshita et al. (Eds.), *Kokugo 5* (pp. 92–93). Tokyo: Kyoiku Shuppan.

Denman, G. A. (1988). *When you've made it your own . . . :Teaching poetry to young people*. Portsmouth, NH: Heinemann.

Donahue, R. T. (1998). *Japanese culture and communication: Critical cultural analysis*. Lanham, MD: University Press of America.

Itō, J., & Mester, A. (1999). The phonological lexicon. In N. Tsukjimura (Ed.), *The handbook of Japanese linguistics* (pp. 62–100). Malden, MA: Blackwell.

Kawai, S. (1996). Yuzuriha [The leaves of Yuzuriha]. In K. Kurihara et al. (Eds.), *Kokugo 6* (pp. 98–101). Tokyo: Mitsumura Tosho.

Kawasaki, H. (1996). Yakushima no sugi no ki [Japanese cedar on Yaku Island]. In K. Kurihara et al. (Eds.), *Kokugo 6* (pp. 26–27). Tokyo: Mitsumura Tosho.

Kudo, N. (1996a). Ogawa no māchi [A march in the brook]. In J. Kinoshita et al. (Eds.), *Kokugo 4* (pp. 31–32). Tokyo: Kyoiku Shuppan.

Kudo, N. (1996b). Sanpo [A walk]. In J. Kinoshita et al. (Eds.), *Kokugo 4* (pp. 30–31).Tokyo: Kyoiku Shuppan.

Mado, M. (1996). Inago [A locust]. In J. Kinoshita et al. (Eds.), *Kokugo 6* (pp. 4–5). Tokyo: Kyoiku Shuppan.

Monbusho (Ed.). (1996, August 20). 21seiki o tenbōshita wagakuni no kyōiku no arikata ni tsuite [Education for the 21st century]. *The Monthly Journal of the Monbusho, 1437*, 61–65.

Monbusho (Ed.). (1997, July 25). 21seiki o tenbōshita wagakuni no kyōiku no arikata ni tsuite [Education for the 21st century]. *The Monthly Journal of the Monbusho, 1449*, 15.

Monbusho (Ed.). (1998a, October 30). *Chuōkyōiku shingikai tōshin* [The central education council's recommendation]. *The Monthly Journal of the Monbusho, 1466*, 111–113

Monbusho (Ed.). (1998b, October 30). Chuōkyōiku shingikai tōshin [The central education council's recommendation]. *The Monthly Journal of the Monbusho, 1466*, 28–35.

Monbusho (Ed.). (1998c). *Shōgakkō gakushō shidō yōryō* [The course of study for elementary school]. Tokyo: Okurashō Insatsukyoku.

Monbusho (Ed.). (1999). *Shōgakkō gakushū shidō yōryō kaisetsu* [Commentary on the course of study for elementary school]. Tokyo: Tōyōkan Shuppansha.

Murou, S. (1996). Hatahata [Sandfish]. In J. Kinoshita et al. (Eds.), *Kokugo 5* (pp. 6–7). Tokyo: Kyoiku Shuppan.

Nakamoto, K. (1993). Kusa [The grass]. In J. Kinoshita et al. (Eds.), *Kokugo 2* (pp. 20–21). Tokyo: Kyoiku Shuppan.

Sakamoto, K. (1996). Aki no kamakiri [A mantis in autumn]. In J. Kinoshita et al. (Eds.), *Kokugo 2* (pp. 22–23). Tokyo: Kyoiku Shuppan.

Sakata, H. (1993). Yūhi ga senaka o oshite kuru [The setting sun is pushing us from behind]. In J. Kinoshita et al. (Eds.), *Kokugo 3* (pp. 4–5). Tokyo: Kyoiku Shuppan.

Shimada, Y. (1996). Doitenka [Make way, please!]. In J. Kinoshita et al. (Eds.), *Kokugo 5* (pp. 32–33). Tokyo: Kyoiku Shuppan.

Shintani, A. (1996). Tsuru ga wataru [The cranes migrate]. In J. Kinoshita et al. (Eds.), *Kokugo 5* (pp. 4–6). Tokyo: Kyoiku Shuppan.

Shouda, K. (1993). Kenkyū jyugyō [Parents' visit to class]. In K. Kurihara et al. (Eds.), *Kokugo 5* (p. 75). Tokyo: Mitsumura Tosho.

Sugano, Y. (1993). Mushimegane [A magnifying glass]. In J. Kinoshita et al. (Eds.), *Kokugo 3* (pp. 14–15). Tokyo: Kyoiku Shuppan.

Takami, J. (1993). Ware wa kusa nari [I am the grass]. In K. Kurihara et al. (Eds.), *Kokugo 5* (pp. 22–24). Tokyo: Mitsumura Tosho.

Tanigawa, S. (1996). Kaeru no Pyon [A frog Pyon]. In J. Kinoshita et al. (Eds.), *Kokugo 2* (pp. 26–27). Tokyo: Kyoiku Shuppan.

Tsurumi, M. (1996). Ame no uta [The song of rains]. In J. Kinoshita et al. (Eds.), *Kokugo 2* (pp. 4–5). Tokyo: Kyoiku Shuppan.

Yagi, J. (1992). Okāchan no kotoba [My mother's words]. In H. Inoue et al. (Eds.), *Atarashii kokugo 3* (pp. 58–59). Tokyo: Tokyo Shoseki.

Yamada, I. (1996). Ame [The rain]. In J. Kinoshita et al. (Eds.), *Kokugo 5* (pp. 30–31). Tokyo: Kyoiku Shuppan.

Yamamura, B. (1996). Fūkei—Junkin mozaiku [Scenery—Pure gold mosaic]. In J. Kinoshita et al. (Eds.), *Kokugo 6* (pp. 6–8). Tokyo: Kyoiku Shuppan.

Chapter 4

Communications as Connections Between Different Japanese Realms: *Kōtsū* and the Case of Children's Illustrated Books

Sylvie Guichard-Anguis

Kōtsū, in a general sense for communications, has special meaning for Japan. Historically, travel within the archipelago was, and is still, far from easy due to the mountainous terrain and, of course, its island makeup. The special place of communications for the Japanese can be gleaned from an examination of their illustrated books for children. Leaving one's own locale to get to another is to go through the experience of finding something different, encountering the other, and creating unity through this process. The scale of those differences has changed through the centuries, but whether it be the pilgrimages to famous places in days gone by or as part of present-day "Discover Japan" travel packages, Japanese are reminded of the natural barriers created by their mountainous land and the unity achieved through kōtsū. Bridging these barriers may lend itself all the more to fantasy, and the special sentiment felt by Japanese for kōtsū. Further enhancement of its symbolic value has come about from the part played by kōtsū in recent Japanese movements to preserve national cultural heritage, as well as its part played in introducing innovation and internationalization.

The Japanese word *kōtsū* has several meanings, such as traffic, communication, transport, and navigation (Nelson, 1987), which have special relevance for Japanese culture as shown here. The two *kanji* (written characters) for this word each have their own broad range of meaning:

kō	*tsū*
coming and going	to pass
to associate with	to be understood
to mingle with	

So the association of these two characters includes the ideas of moving and mingled with, as well as the one of becoming familiar with. In this chapter, I refer mainly to *kōtsū* as ways that create connections between different worlds, different spheres of activities, and realms of reality and fancy. No clear equivalent word exists in English, so for convenience's sake, *communications* is sometimes used in translation and to refer broadly to the wide range of phenomena involved.

My hypothesis starts from the abundance of literature on *kōtsū* for very young children in Japan, a variety of which that cannot be found in Europe. Analysis of such books[1] can provide clues as to how communications are perceived in Japan nowadays. From a child's very young age, the vital importance of transport and communications is stressed in an archipelago whose development has long been hindered by its geomorphology. This trend goes back at least to the Edo period (1603–1868) and has led to the preservation movement that intends to protect remnants of *kōtsū* from a bygone age. The *kōtsū* of today, however, involve networks outside the boundaries of the archipelago and play a key role in the innovation and internationalization of Japan.

COMMUNICATIONS BETWEEN REALITY AND FANTASY

Child: Mother, where does the blue train come from?

Mother: From the country of the very, very long night, where everybody's sleep is transported. (my translation)

These few words that begin the children's book *Goodnight Blue Train*[2] (my translation) by Mutsumi Matsuzawa and Sadao Kimura (1981) introduce us to a part of children's literature that seems rather important in Japan, but the likes of which is not encountered in Europe (or perhaps North America as well). The importance of this theme reveals a conscious or unconscious need to familiarize children with communications in the Japanese archipelago. This need of the Japanese would be seen as fundamental by those in the fields of geography or environmental studies, for the need implies educating very young children in regard to the perception of physical space. In comparison to French children's literature, as far as realistic characteristics of the country are concerned, some of it is dedicated to famous historical landmarks, places, or other important features of culture, but relatively little about French trains, even France's most remarkable transport achievement—the French version of the bullet train called TGV (*Train à Grande Vitesse*), the long-time rival of the Japanese *Shinkansen*. There seems to be no need to familiarize French children with the communications in their country. In Japan, on the other hand, illustrated books on famous temples, shrines and castles, and even historical landscapes or places (*meisho*), barely exist.

In other words, if the theme of gothic cathedrals has to be addressed for young French children, the theme in Japan must be the railway station and associated trains. Japanese illustrated books (*e'hon*) focus on practical everyday life through the different kinds of connections between places, rather than on historical events and strict cultural identity. Cities in Japanese children's books, generally speaking, are introduced as homogeneous environments devoid of any aesthetic dimension and are dedicated to the activities of men (Guichard-Anguis, 1993). Functions of the city play the main part in the description of those urban spaces, while little interest is given to their visual quality. Most descriptions of the urban environment are realistically detailed with little need to be filled in by the reader. The contemporary city is stressed through drawings of landscapes that serve as Polaroids of reality. Such renditions could play the part of ethnographic or sociologic documents by their precision. As dynamism through transport is enhanced in these evocations, the railway station seems to be the core of the urban spaces presented (Guichard-Anguis, 1997).

Eight illustrated books for young Japanese children became the subject of this chapter and were published between 1980 and 1990. Seven are devoted to train transport, the other to airplane. These books came into my possession as the result of having children in kindergarten in Japan, where for a small fee a new book was delivered to the schoolchildren every month. Although the theme of train transport was not the topic for most books available, I was still struck with the multiple of titles on the topic. That probably had influenced the choices I had made for the purchases. Regardless, I believe it is safe to say that trains hold a special place in young children's literature in Japan, probably even more so than that found in other industrialized societies. The exception in my collection is the book *Fly to the Sky, Little Plane* (Kokaze & Yamamoto, 1989), which follows a topic atypical for children's literature: going abroad. This book shows illustrations of a little plane leaving Japan and going to a different land. The last image shows the little plane flying into the blue sky over the ocean, leaving behind the seashore, which is supposed to be that of the Japanese archipelago. Curiously, this book is still set entirely in Japan although this plane is overseas bound. What does take up a foreign location in my collection is a train book—*My First Trip by Train,* the location being India (Noma & Ishiodori, 1989). The appeal to the Japanese reader of this book is that the story is told in a culturally Japanese way, very similar to the other books set in Japan. The need to stress a Japanese view of communications through a foreign setting exemplifies its importance. It is also obvious that the choice of India, famous worldwide for the use of trains, was made for good reason considering that communications has its own unique situation there as it does in Japan. Compared to the many books available about trains, those centrally devoted to airplanes are much fewer. The same can be said for the attention paid to the automobile for its role in everyday life. These facts reflect the conception and the history of Japanese networks of communications. Young Japanese children still have comparatively very few opportunities to take planes and, for that matter, cars also, because congested highways and related costs encourage many Japanese to choose trains rather than cars for their travel needs.

The train books in this study give complementary views of the part that trains play in the living environment. Historically, the first actual railway line in Japan started between Tokyo and Yokohama in 1872 and ran 28 kilometers. Two years later, the Kansai area (Kyoto, Osaka, and Kobe) had its own line from Osaka to Kobe. At the turn of the 20th century, in spite of the privatization that took place in 1987, railway networks played a key role in the country's planning. The networks of the JR (Japanese Railways) lines, of the private local lines, and of the subways account for a huge operation totaling 26,895 kilometers of track as of 1990. City development in Japan cannot be understood without this transport system in mind. Although the number of registered motor vehicles is growing steadily, railway lines connecting railway stations in the heart of the cities benefit from the daily urban traffic congestion (Unyushō, 1993). The service industries (hotels, department stores, cultural or leisure amenities, etc.), in which railway companies, especially private ones, are actively involved, add to the impact of this system of transport on the nation's activities. In the Kansai area, private lines such as Hankyū, Hanshin, or Kintetsu became synonymous for a kind of living environment specific to this part of the country, for there railway companies are not just for train service but for major hotels, department stores, housing developments, even professional baseball teams. So the names Hankyū, Hanshin, or Kintetsu play an enormous role in the lives of many people.

From this background sketch, let us proceed to a discussion of the storybooks in question as related to communications between the real and the unreal. To begin, we return to the story of the blue train, a dialog from which we saw previously. Blue train, the familiar name for the sleeping car train, all but vanished from the railway network in December 1994 when the timetable was modified, and those trains were reduced from service. Except for rush holiday periods, sleeping car trains were eliminated due to the extension of the bullet train *shinkansen* network. The peak popularity for the blue trains, the so-called "running hotel," was between the mid-1960s and mid-1970s, beginning with the introduction in 1958 of the train called "Morning Wind" (*Asakaze*). The storybook about the blue train unfolds with the conversation of a child and his mother. Following their words, the illustrations show the sleeping cars running from the land of sleep and of dreams to the world of fantasy. Evoking the world of fantasy through everyday settings has appeal for Japanese readers and is a characteristic means for this type of story in Japanese children's literature.[3] Answering the child's questions about the places where the blue train goes leads the mother to the world of imagination. But the last question of the child in the story is a realistic one:

Child: When will father be back?

Mother: He will be back tomorrow at daybreak, from a faraway city, riding the blue train and carrying a lot of presents. (Matsukawa, 1992; my translation)

In a few phrases, the real utility of the blue train is explained to the child. It connects faraway cities to the place where one lives and is a means of travelling for the men—fathers—who take part in the active world. Trains sustain their livelihood.

This connection between the world of reality and the one of fantasy is also emphasized in the book *Kyubē* [*The Steaming Locomotive*] (my translation). According to its author, Hiroyuki Takahashi (1984), the steam locomotive No. 9 displayed in a recreation of a Meiji-era village, Meiji Mura, in Inuyama[4] was the starting point of this story. (Meiji Mura, which actually exists, is an outdoor museum recreating the atmosphere of Western industrialized Japan in the 19th century and is full of Westernized buildings and other artifacts.) Instead of coal, bags of dreams are fed to the engine, which begins to move the coaches again, but this time up into the sky to a leisure land on a planet. Magic is the dominant impression of the world opened to the children's eyes by the steam locomotive train. It is a little reminiscent of the famous work by Kenji Miyazawa (1896–1933), *Night Train to the Stars* (1927), which, in turn, gave inspiration to a very popular animation in the 1980s. Riding trains provides opportunities to meet the unknown, to visit places for fun and leisure, and to inspire dreams in the minds of Japanese, young and old alike.

Two other books that present the commonplace theme of riding trains are *I Took the Train* (Nishimura, 1984) and *Our First Train Trip with Father's Wheelchair* (Shiraishi, Imaki, & Nishimura, 1989) (my translations). Illustrations in the former give the most realistic approach. The story goes with the help of only a few sentences through familiar images of a train boarded by a mother and her two children. The train is shown running through landscapes unembellished. The charm of this book lies in the accurate details given in the illustrations, which a young child can recognize. The second of the two books tells the story of a father in a wheelchair accompanied by his young son. They ride a train in order to see the boy's grandmother in the countryside. The whole trip, from leaving the house to riding a bus, getting to the train station, boarding the train, spending time inside the train, and so on, is depicted with much accuracy in a succession of mini-adventures. The same type of story is told in *My First Trip by Train* (Noma & Ishiodori, 1989), mentioned previously as being set in India, in which a young boy goes to Calcutta with his father and mother. Indian trains are depicted in a realistic manner as well.

Another feature of note about these train books is the direction of the travel: It is always from a big city to the countryside. In *Our First Train Trip with Father's Wheelchair* (Shiraishi, Imaki, & Nishimura, 1989), the grandmother is supposed to be living in the "countryside," but in fact lives in the city of Kōriyama (pop. 310,000). What explains this attitude is that Kōriyama is in Tōhoku, a region in northeastern Japan having a strong rural image. As far as my research is concerned, I did not find any contemporaneous illustrated books telling the story of a young Japanese child coming from the countryside and discovering the world of the big city. So this literature stresses that most young people live in big cities and that the elderly are to be found in the cities in the countryside. In fact, those descriptions correspond largely to the population demographics according to the census. This storyline is underscored also by the absence of criticism of the part played by transport in the urban environment. Generally speaking, transport is always introduced in a positive way to the young child.

An unusual feature, at least to French readers, is that a Japanese story might even be about an entire day spent in a train station. *A Snowy Day* (Sasaki, 1980) shows a whole day from sunup to sundown in a tiny train station somewhere in the countryside, in the most poetic and dramatic way, without a single word. As the title says, snow is falling all along the pages of this book. The loneliness of this train station without any significant activity (only two trains stop, one for passengers and one for freight) contrasts with the lively character given by the book *A Busy Platform* (Akiyama, 1990). Nevertheless, the lonely setting in *A Snowy Day* is the type of scene cherished by the Japanese and finds its way in various works of literature, including screenplays for stage and TV.

A Snowy Day and *A Busy Platform* are notable also because they represent the two opposite roles played by trains in the Japanese archipelago, between the underpopulated areas, *kaso,* and the overpopulated, *kamitsu.* The latter book obviously depicts Tokyo, as its foreword indicates that its chosen subject was Shinjuku Station, the namesake for a well-known section of the city. The book starts with the delivery of the morning newspaper and the description of the train tracks at 6 a.m. The book ends with the closing of the gate at half-past one in the morning. Based on the author's direct observation, the book stresses daily life in metropolitan areas with accuracy. It introduces young children to a world that will be soon theirs, as many Japanese children depend on transport in their daily commutes to school, whether that be kindergarten or university.

Familiarized with urban life from a very young age, the growing child is acculturated in certain ways. Aspects of Japanese city life are justified to the young child, whose opinion is at least partly formed through these books. As young French children are initiated by their books to the importance of the quality of physical space and to the existence of a cultural heritage linked to the past, Japanese young ones are made aware of the vital character of transport within and between cities. The plain, ordinary views of Japanese life add charm to this theme. The flowing activity of city life is emphasized rather than the motionless structure of physical space. The physical surroundings are secondary to what happens there. By this approach, the cultural conception of a city is created for the present, devoid of a past memory. This reflects the situation of most of the large Japanese cities and the cultural attitude of their bureaucratic leaders. In the present state of affairs, one of the main consequences is the unavoidable destruction of urban land-scapes for the sake of communications. Historic or natural environments may be sacrificed in the name of transport. In this perspective, all the big operations of urban development (*saikaihatsu*) around the railway station, conceived as the main gate to the city, are justified. To name a few cases, Kanazawa (pop. 427,000), in spite of the opposition from citizen movements, lost one of its oldest parts in this reshaping of its so-called entrance to its center. In Matsue (pop. 140,100) and in Matsumoto (pop. 196,300), places proud of being ancient castle-towns (*jōka-machi*), the ward around their railway stations got new urban landscapes, similar to the ones of large cities. During the 1970s and the 1980s, the fierce competition for attracting new businesses and commerce produced a phenomenon of homog-enization of urban landscapes in the core of many cities.

KŌTSŪ AS NOSTALGIA AND INNOVATION

The tendency to show communications as connections between different worlds, mainly represented nowadays by trains in young children's literature, goes back at least to the Edo period (1603–1868). In this perspective, communi-cations connect worlds set on opposite sides, the one of everyday reality and the other of leisure, dream, and fantasy; in other words, cities and countryside, the latter generally represented as the realm of nature and of nostalgia for the past that vanished from the large cities. This leads us to examine *kōtsū* in a wider per-spective through history. It is obvious that the geological relief of Japan has given a tremendous importance to communications, compared to other countries, for leaving one valley or island to get to another is still far from easy. The complex-ity and the breaking up of the relief has led to the development of different regional entities that tend to resist unity, a major trend in Japanese history. Leaving one's own place to get to another is to go through the experience of find-ing something different, of encountering the other. In this process seems to lie the origin in meaning for the two characters of *kōtsū*.

The scale of those regional differences has changed through the centuries. Different networks appeared on the archipelago, stretched from the different cap-itals following one after the other. During the Edo period, pilgrimages, travels to famous places (*meisho*) or hotsprings (*onsen*), may be referred to as one of those experiences suggested by the meaning of *kōtsū*. The numerous works of Andō Hiroshige (1760–1849), which include *Fifty-Three Stations of the Tōkaidō Road, Eight Views of Omi,* a set of famous places in Kyōto and Osaka or of the Nakasendō or Kiso Kaidō Road, *One Hundred Views of Edo,* and *Thirty-Six Views of Mt. Fuji,* are linked with the idea of connections. The themes of those works may be divided into two: the descriptions of two of the most famous roads belonging to the network of Gokaidō ("five roads"), which extended its branches from Edo (now Tokyo) and the famous places (*meisho*). During the Edo period, since walking was the usual means of transportation, those woodblock prints illustrate an idea rather similar to the children's books of today: They suggest that going along those major roads may mean leaving big cities and everyday life for the purpose of encountering a world of dreams and imagination (through, for example, the legend of a given place). The illustrated guide books (*meisho zue*) published during the same period give numerously detailed information from history to famous products (*meibutsu*) of a given place.

The post-station towns (*shukuba machi*) that lined up along those roads lost their main function with the construction of new networks of roads and railway lines at the end of the 19th century (Miyazawa, 1987). For over 100 years, they suffered economically from their isolation away from the new networks of transit, or, in the worst cases, simply fell into decay, surrounded by a rather harsh environment. At the end of the 20th century, they were given a new part to play in the history of transport as assets of cultural heritage linked with *kōtsū*. It is rather interesting to note that in Japan, the local movements to protect sites of cultural heritage started with those towns. Such movements led to the protection of historical urban landscapes and became models for preservation of small cities in Japan (Sorifu, 1994). This preservation movement presents a challenge to bureaucratic policies centered around the idea of development (*kaihatsu*) through continued redevelopment of towns into modernized landscapes.

To name a few of the local movements of historical preservation, Narai, Tsumago, Magome, and Seki are towns that retain historical landscapes, characterized by a consistency of traditional architecture difficult to find even in such famous tourist places as the old capital of Kyoto. Located far from the industrialized regions or the mid-sized cities, their remoteness made possible the permanence of those traditional forms. This situation became a great opportunity for a new form of development based on their identity. Since the end of the 1960s, this new form of development has made them enter slowly into networks of small cities to be visited for their quaint atmosphere of the past. These post-station towns are enlarging by mergers with other towns or villages into bigger administrative units as a means of economic viability. The post-station town of Seki (pop. 7,300) in Mie prefecture benefitted from the crossroad between the Tōkaidō and the Isekaidō (Torizawa, 1991). Designated as an Important Preservation District for Groups of Traditional Buildings according to the law of 1975, it may be one of the first places where awareness of the value of old urban landscapes took place. The station prospered also as the temple-town of the Jizōin. The authentic character of the restoration is not even troubled by the new post office built in 1984, because it was built using materials similar to those available during the Edo period. As in every town of this category, a few shops retain traditional craft activities: a confectionery, the making of wooden buckets, and a blacksmith.

The village of Narakawa (pop. 4,200) is composed of several clusters among which the post-station town of Narai is set along the Kisoji, a section of the

Nakasendo line. This small village, remotely located, became so famous after being designated that it became a leader of a Japanese delegation of like communities to France to attend the French–Japanese Symposium on Urban Amenities in 1990. The cultural impact of Narakawa in the making of cities (*machi zukuri*) in Japan is by far much bigger than its size would normally allow.

Tsumago, located in the town of Nagiso (pop. 6,100), south of Narai, belongs also to the underpopulated *kaso* regions of Japan, with 94% of its area occupied by mountainous forests (74% in Narakawa). Tsumago was one of the leaders in the awareness of the preservation of historical landscapes issuing a charter on the protection of the post-station town in 1971. In the village of Yamaguchi (pop. 2,100), the town of Magome is one of the 11 Kiso post-station towns along the Nakasendo. Built along a steep mountain road, the little town is covered by snow several months a year, which did not prevent it from being one of the post-station towns favored by tourists. Those collective approaches and sense of responsibility give way to numerous initiatives all over Japan.

As was noted, various buildings associated with the ancient transit highways entered as the first of the *kōtsū* memorials into Japanese cultural heritage. They were followed rather recently by the trains, vehicles that are considered by themselves as mobile cultural assets, while a new category of cultural assets makes its way through protection: industrial heritage. In Meiji Mura, opened in 1965, a steam locomotive was later added in 1974 and began to run along 744 meters between recreations of Tokyo Station and Nagoya Station. This steam engine was originally imported from England in 1874 and was the first one to operate within the archipelago, running between Shimbashi and Yokohama (Matsukawa, 1992). A second steam locomotive at Meiji Mura, used as an alternative engine, is the famous No. 9, which also happened to be the inspiration for the story in *Kyubē (The Steaming Locomotive)*. Engine No. 9 was imported from the United States in 1913. About the recreated stations there, the one called Tokyo Station was originally built during the Taishō period (1912–1925) for service on the Meitetsu line, a private railway local to Nagoya. The rails used in the Meiji Mura recreation are Russian and were used in Noto, a peninsula on the north-central coast. As a result, this exhibit at Meiji Mura consists of materials coming from several parts of the country as well as from abroad and from different time periods. This feature adds a touch of exoticism and nostalgia to this main tourist attraction, but is in fact a recreation. The ticket to the attraction is a reproduction of a train ticket of the Meiji period and gives the visitor access to travel through the past. This railway line was recreated in the same spirit as that which originally constructed the buildings around it. Scattered among the rural slopes that surround Meiji Mura, this recreation is devoid of a true urban identity. The original buildings, having become useless in Japanese cities and having been a hindrance according to the Japanese bureaucratic model of development, were reunited in this natural environment, as in a kind of reserve for historical buildings. The same phenomenon happened to the old transport.

In recent years, the attitude for the protection of *kōtsū* shows signs of evolution. The Japan National Trust for Cultural and Natural Heritage conservation, created in 1968, modeled after the British one, took as a motto: "Protection of Nature and Culture by Everybody." Granted tax exemption in 1986, its activities center on protection, research, and communications. The JNT works in collaboration with the Agency of Culture and the Minister of Transport. It has to be differentiated from the Association of National Trusts of Japan, created in 1992 by authorization of the Agency of Environment. Pursuing the aims of the Nationaru Torasuto o Susumeru Zenkoku no Kai created in 1983, it embodies most of the local movements of citizens to protect the natural environment.

A component of the JNT, the Railway Preservation Society in Japan (Torasuto Torein), works for protecting obsolete trains by keeping them operational. Maintained by volunteers, a C12 steam locomotive and three passenger carriages bought by the trust have run since 1987 once a month from April to November in Shizuoka prefecture along the Ohigawa railway. Those 40 kilometers of local lines give opportunities to enjoy the countryside, landscapes that do not belong to the everyday life environment of most of the tourists or enthusiasts who ride this train. Nostalgia comes not only from the train itself, but from a way of life that is vanishing from the archipelago and may be seen from the windows of the carriages. The activities of JNT also concern constructions linked with transport. The Odaira staging post in Nagano prefecture is being restored progressively.[5] As the only stage post along the Odaira road, which connected Tsumago to Iida in Nagano prefecture, it fell victim to the depletion of the local population by migration to the cities, and was nearly turned into a ghost town.

KŌTSŪ AS INNOVATION AND INTERNATIONALIZATION

Nowadays, *kōtsū* still offers the opportunity to "discover Japan" as the Japan National Railways publicity campaign stressed in the 1980s, through the country's most nostalgic aspects. But modern transport offers ways to leave the archipelago and travel to foreign countries. The little train in children's books that leads to a world of fantasy became a plane in the world of adults that allows one to hop to Singapore, Hawaii, or Guam, as well as to stream Japanese people into the world community.

Publications by transportation companies offer insight into the role given to transport by Japan's international strategies of development. In 1990, the transportation sector garnered the highest number (19%) of Official Development Assistance (ODA) commitments. The urban transport infrastructure of numerous countries in Asia rely greatly on Japanese financial assistance. Those projects supported by Japan in the recipient countries are distributed among roads (38%), railroads (29%), seaports (21%), and airports (5%) (Evans, 1993). Among them, southeast Asian countries rank first, with Indonesia receiving 47% of the total, Thailand 21%, and the Philippines 14% (Iwata & Kidokoro, 1993). Those three countries absorb over 80% of the ODA aid in the transport sector. Japan's experience in the transport field particularly benefits countries that have severe problems of urban traffic congestion similar to the ones in the Japanese archipelago.

The solutions provided through master plan studies for urban development tend to promote the Japanese transport infrastructure as a model. This Japanese globalization carries the Japanese perception of physical space in the field of transport. The hierarchy of railways applied in Japan, which includes medium distance JR lines, private railways that manage local lines and intracity subways, allows the population that live in some of the world's biggest metropolitan areas to commute rather conveniently (Morichi & Kubota, 1994). The division of train transport services into super-express, express, and semi-express is another original feature of the Japanese railway network. In that perception of Japanese urban space, the railway station becomes the core of an urban center. The concept of the urban railway station plaza, applied in most medium-sized or large cities today, owes its existence to the conception of a railway station being linked with commercial activities in Japan.

The construction of the Kansai international airport built on the sea continued in this vein of Japanese innovation of transport. Another recent example is Osaka prefecture's building the suspension bridge of Akashi, the longest in the world with its 3,910 meters. Both the airport and the bridge are spectacular ways for the Osaka region to promote its attractiveness through economic competitiveness and increased internationalization. There lies a historical trend in a country compelled to develop an archipelago composed of nearly 4,000 islands, which also happen to be largely mountainous, that to overcome the associated problems of disconnectedness, it has had to conceive daring projects. Today, those daring projects in turn become showcases for Japanese technology and the way Japanese planning is undertaken. These projects pave the way for Japan's internationalization.

CONCLUSION

Trains play such an important part in Japanese society that the need to get young children familiarized with them and their different aspects lead to abundant literature patterned in one way. Those books of illustrations model a specific perception of physical space, governed by the supremacy of train transport in the urban and nonurban environment. According to this perception, the railway station, with its plaza and its commercial facilities, becomes the core and the main gate of the cities, where people work and live.

Tourism is the new function fixed to the obsolete constructions linked with transport and to the old trains. Once devoid of any practical value, they are reunited in a kind of reservation for the past of the cities and of the country, set aside from the everyday environment. The voyage through those places is not only a trip through bygone periods, but also a trip inside parts of the country where old ways of living can still be discovered. Nostalgia that is enhanced through this schema cannot find room in the cities themselves because of Japan's modern urbanization.

Japan's vision of *kōtsū* and urban space has begun to be applied globally through foreign aid and associated programs for city and regional planning in southeast Asia and elsewhere. The positive aspect of this implementation cannot be denied, but the conception of urban development that is at work in Japan can endanger existing cultural assets linked to the past. Preservation movements have risen as a result, but the issue about the price of urban growth will be perennially felt. How Japan deals with this issue in the 21st century is sure to impact the world and could well provide lessons for civic culture on an international scale.

NOTES

1. These books are Akiyama, 1990; Kokaze and Yamamoto, 1989; Matsuzawa and Kimura, 1981; Nishimura, 1984; Noma and Ishiodori, 1989; Sasaki, 1980; Shiraishi, Imaki, and Nishimura, 1989; and Takahashi, 1984.

2. The original English titles of the children's books are given in the text; otherwise, they are indicated as my translation.

3. The close relation of trains with the world of fantasy is further developed in Guichard-Anguis (2002).

4. The village of the Meiji period (1868–1912), Meiji Mura, was opened in 1965 about 20 kilometers from Nagoya to the northeast. It includes buildings selected from all around the archipelago, scattered among green hills, and some transport like the old tram of Kyoto. Those physical elements help evoke nostalgia for a bygone period.

5. The Masuya house was restored in 1983 and the Kamiya house in 1985, beginning the restoration of the whole village and its opening to the public.

REFERENCES

Akiyama, T. (1990). *Densha ga mairimasu* [A busy platform]. Tokyo: Fukuikan-Shoten.

Evans, P. C. (1993). New directions in Japan's international economic cooperation. *The Wheel Extended, 86,* 3–9.

Guichard-Anguis, S. (1993). Sensibilisation à l'aménagement de l'espace urbain chez les enfants au Japon [Awareness to urban planning among Japanese children]. In F. Blanchon (Ed.), *Aménager l'espace* [Land development] (pp. 89–101). Paris: Presses de l'Université de Paris-Sorbonne.

Guichard-Anguis, S. (1997). Enfance et villes japonaises [Childhood and Japanese cities]. In F. Blanchon (Ed.), *Enfances* [Childhood] (pp. 361–376). Paris: Presses de l'Université de Paris-Sorbonne.

Guichard-Anguis, S. (2002). Trains et perception de l'espace dans la littérature enfantine japonaise [Trains and perception of space in Japanese children's literature]. In F. Blanchon (Ed.), *Aller et venir: Faits et perspectives* [To come and go: Facts and perspectives]. Paris: Presses de l'Université de Paris-Sorbonne.

Iwata, S., & Kidokoro, T. (1993). Foreign aid and urban transports in Asia. *The Wheel Extended, 84,* 11–15.

Kokaze, S., & Yamamoto, T. (1989). *Tobe! Chisai puroperaki* [Fly to the sky, little plane]. Tokyo: Fukuikan-Shoten.

Matsukawa, K. (1992). Meiji Mura tetsudō bunkazai ni tsuite [About the cultural assets of the railway line in the Meiji Village]. *Nihon Nationaru Torasuto, 282,* 5–7.

Matsuzawa, M., & Kimura, S. (1981). *Oyasumi burūtorein* [Goodnight blue train]. Tokyo: Froebel Kan.

Miyazawa, H. (1987). *Machinami hozon no netto wāku* [Network of protection of urban landscapes]. Tokyo: Daiichihōki.

Morichi, S., & Kubota, H. (1994). Improving railway networks and interconnecting transport modes. *The Wheel Extended, 88,* 3–11.

Nelson, A. N. (1987). *The modern reader's Japanese-English character dictionary.* Tokyo: Tuttle.

Nishimura, K. (1984). *Densha ni notta* [I took the train]. Tokyo: Fukuikan-Shoten.

Noma, A., & Ishiodori, K. (1989). *Kisha ni notta Bini* [My first trip by train]. Tokyo: Fukuikan-Shoten.

Sasaki, H. (1980). *Yuki no hi* [A snowy day]. Tokyo: Kodansha.

Shiraishi, K., Imaki, M., & Nishimura, S. (1989). *Otōsan to isshōni obāsan no uchi he* [Our first train trip with father's wheelchair]. Tokyo: Fukuikan-Shoten.

Sorifu. (1994). *Kankō hakusho* [White book on tourism]. Tokyo: Okurashō.

Takahashi, H. (1984). *Kikansha kyubē* [The steaming locomotive]. Tokyo: Popurasha.

Torizawa, M. (1991). *Machinami saiken* [Close inspection of urban landscapes]. Tokyo: Nihon Kōtsū Kōsha.

Unyushō. (1993). *Unyushō hakusho* [White book on transport]. Tokyo: Okurashō.

part III

Japanese Nation and State

Chapter 5

Discourse and Cultural Attitudes: Japanese Imperial Honorifics and the Open Society[1]

Noriko Akimoto Sugimori
Masako Hamada

Honorifics, distinctive of Japanese, function to distinguish between people of higher and lower social status. Because Japan has preserved its emperor system for more than the past millennium, Japanese values—aspects of Japaneseness— should be reflective of the attitude held toward the emperor as found in the associated imperial honorifics. Moreover, Japanese society has immensely changed since the pre–World War II days, affecting the emperor's status. Being reduced from a god status to that of a mortal must have profoundly affected Japanese civic discourse as well as the related language honorifics. It would be instructive, therefore, to document these epic changes as a way to gauge the growth of democracy in Japan. The authors do so by analysis of a long tradition of Japanese newspapers: the celebration of the emperor's birthday. Published texts and pictures about the emperor on this annual event provide a systematic method of comparison and reveal remarkable changes, both verbal and nonverbal. Besides identifying these changes, the authors also present an actual case revealing the "Achilles heel" for Japanese honorifics and the open society: how imperial honorifics can shield an imperial person from personal responsibility.

The complex system of honorifics (grammatical encodings of the social status of a person) (Brown & Levinson, 1978) is a major characteristic of the Japanese language (Kindaichi, 1990; Reischauer & Jansen, 1995), and the use of honorifics has risen and fallen over time, reflecting changes in Japanese society in general. This system includes, for example, different levels of speech in terms of politeness, formality, and deference among which the speaker must choose according to the social situation; the relative social levels of the speaker, addressee, and audience; and the attitude of the speaker toward the addressee and audience.

When we try to understand honorifics over time, we are led to their origin and their use toward gods and the emperor. Throughout history, the emperor has been a recipient of the highest form of honorifics. Given that Japan has preserved the emperor system for more than 1,300 years, Japanese values should be reflected in the attitude of the Japanese people toward the emperor, as shown by the honorifics they use to refer to him. Thus, an examination of newspaper use of honorifics for the emperor is a kind of microcultural analysis that can help us explain and understand Japanese society as a whole.

Toward this aim, this chapter examines changes in articles in a major newspaper, the *Asahi Shimbun*,[2] about two Japanese emperors from 1942 to 1999. These two emperors are Emperor Hirohito, who reigned from 1926 to 1989, and his direct successor, Emperor Akihito.[3]

Although Japanese newspapers generally do not use honorifics in news reports, one exception had been when referring to the emperor (Donahue, 1990). Ever since the start of the postwar era, Japanese newspapers gradually have modified their use of honorifics for the emperor until 1993 when honorifics for him were all but eliminated. This chapter charts this evolutionary change in use over the last half of the 20th century by analysis of an annual event in Japan—the press coverage of the emperor's birthday, typically by a photograph and accompanying texts. Linguistic and especially paralinguistic aspects of this coverage are quite revealing of a patterned decline of honorifics for the emperor. Before proceeding, a background sketch about the Japanese language, society, and the emperor's birthday would be helpful.

HISTORICAL BACKGROUND OF JAPANESE LANGUAGE AND SOCIETY

Japanese, like other languages, developed within a particular social and cultural system (Loveday, 1986). Japanese society is hierarchical (Nakane, 1973). The remnants of feudal times, from the 12th to the 19th centuries, can still be seen in strong values concerning hereditary authority, duty, and loyalty among the contemporary Japanese (Reischauer & Jansen, 1995). The Japanese language has rigid rules of usage that depend on the social position of those speaking and those addressed (Kindaichi, 1990), and its development was influenced by the long history of hereditary power and aristocratic rule in Japan. One's status relative to other people was very important, and this was reflected in the Japanese language.[4]

Japanese society, however, has greatly changed since the 1940s. Democracy came more widely to Japan than ever before, and brought with it new pressures on society in general. One result of democratization was a trend toward simplifying the language (or, a "rudeness of expression" as some have said) (Haga, 1990), which tended to work against the use of honorifics in the language. According to Tsukishima (1990), one result of these changes is that expressions that highlight one's social class status are used less frequently now than before the war. However, polite forms (and especially ultrapolite forms) are still used because Japanese people still tend to see others as being either superior or inferior to themselves in a hierarchical social framework.

PRESS REPORTS ON THE EMPEROR'S BIRTHDAY

In 1889, the Meiji Constitution institutionalized the emperor's absolute and sacred status, and the government emphasized the role of the emperor as the head of the Japanese state and the father of all Japanese people. After Japan's defeat in WWII, the postwar constitution of 1947 defined the emperor as "the symbol of the State and of the unity of the people with whom resides sovereign power" (Reischauer & Jansen, 1995, p. 242), depriving him of the political power and sacred status he had had in prewar Japan.

Reflecting the changes in the emperor's status, newspaper reports on the emperor's annual birthday have also changed. Until 1946, the emperor's birthday was called *tenchōsetsu*, a special imperial word that literally means "heaven long celebration." It was in 1873 that this national holiday was created by the Meiji government. Each year the *tenchōsetsu* marked the continuation of the emperor system, which supposedly reflected the nation's uniqueness and superiority. After WWII, however, the Occupation authorities ordered that the term *tenchōsetsu* be changed to *tennō tanjōbi* (the emperor's birthday). In regard to newspapers, they were censored by the government before and throughout the war, and by the Occupation authorities thereafter, in the latter case because the Occupation authorities feared a resurgence of Japanese ultranationalism (Eto, 1982).

As previously mentioned, the *Asahi Shimbun* typically published a photo and accompanying article each year at the time of the emperor's birthday. A special mystique had surrounded the emperor's portrait especially in the prewar period and during the war. The emperor's picture, together with the empress's, was treated as sacred until the war's end and received special care in schools by school principals throughout Japan. Usually, the pictures were covered, and they were shown only on special occasions. The imperial honorific word *goshin'ei* (lifelike picture) was used specifically to address the pictures of the emperor and empress.

Given this history, newspaper treatment of the emperor's photo is likely to mirror the generally held attitude toward him.[5] Paralinguistic aspects, such as the size of the photo or of the related text, may be so reflective because they can serve as persuasive devices (Gruber, 1997). Other important paralinguistic or nonverbal clues may be found in how the photos were composed, including the bodily appearance of the imperial person, and in how press conferences were conducted with the emperor, the rules of the meeting with him, and the permissible range of topics or content. These paralinguistic clues, as well as the linguistic, are scrutinized in turn starting with the size of the newspaper text and photo.

To anchor our analysis, we used newspaper coverage from the period of World War II because the strongest homage toward the emperor likely would have been then. For the postwar period, we divided it into two, corresponding to the respective reigning years of Hirohito and Akihito. Thus, we discuss the newspaper coverage according to these three time periods.

Paralinguistic Aspects

Paralinguistic aspects here are treated as the nonverbal presentation including length of the printed text, the size of the photo, and other related characteristics. To measure length or size, we used the Japanese orthographic character as a convenient unit of measurement by counting how many written characters were used in the texts, and for photos, how many written characters could reasonably fill the physical space taken by the photos, ascertained by counting the characters in the nearby edge of print and then calculating the spatial area of the photo. As can be seen in Table 5-1, the length and size of the texts and pictures (or photos) steadily declined from the wartime to the most recent period. This decline was especially dramatic for the photos in the recent period by its twelvefold decrease in mean size from that of the war years and by its nearly twofold decrease from the intermediate period. Although the emperor's birthdays were typically marked by a news article including both a photo and text, there are some exceptions. In some years, either one or both were absent in the newspaper. For example, the tradition of birthday coverage was altogether not followed in 1947.

In Table 5-1, the years correspond to the appearance of the emperor's birthday articles, not actual period distinctions. For example, WWII ended in August 1945. Therefore, the wartime period continued until this date, and the period after belonged to Hirohito Later Years. In January 1989, Emperor Hirohito died, and the Akihito Early Years soon began. Therefore, the data in 1989 comes from the article about Emperor Akihito's birthday, which appeared in December 1989.

The treatment of the emperor's photos during the Occupation, in particular until 1950, was distinct from that of the rest of the postwar period. In these five years, the emperor was shown as an unrecognizable figure at the palace or not at all. Since at least 1948, the imperial palace has been open to the public on the emperor's birthday. The emperor has greeted the well-wishers on that day ever since. Pictures of this event in the newspaper have differed in what became the main focus. From 1948 to 1950, the main focus was the crowd, but afterward it became the emperor's private moments, such as his walk in the garden or his pursuit of a hobby.

Location of the picture in the newspaper underwent change also. During the war, the picture always appeared above the fold, for the government ordered the

Table 5-1
Spatial Measurement of the Emperor's Birthday Article (by Orthographic Spaces)

	War in Pacific 1942–1945	Hirohito Later Years 1946–1988	Akihito Early Years 1989–1999
Mean text size	1814.8	676.2	562.2
No. of texts	4	42[a]	11
Mean picture size	3521	582.2	273.2
No. of pictures	3[b]	41[c]	11

Notes: [a] In 1947, no emperor's birthday article appeared.
[b] In 1943, the text appeared, but no picture accompanied it.
[c] In 1946 and 1947, no pictures appeared.

newspaper to use this eye-catching location. The location of course was on the first page. During the postwar period, however, the picture has appeared largely inside the newspaper and has appeared on the front page only 9% of the time.

Another noticeable aspect about the emperor's pictures was the etiquette followed about what was allowable for photographic images. Generally, wartime photos emphasized the gap between the emperor and the commoner, whereas recent ones emphasize the opposite. This difference arose from the status of the emperor projected, his relationship to the empress, their facial and bodily expressions, and costume. As would be expected, during the war, the emperor was always shown in military uniform, in full body length. Only the emperor could have a full body pose; commoners would be photographed only in part. Another peculiarity practiced, even to recent time, is that if an emperor were shown walking, the photograph had to show both feet on the ground (Kumakura, 1988). In wartime, the emperor's facial expression was mainly serious, though some pictures in the postwar period showed him smiling. Still, his mouth was always shown closed. In contrast, Emperor Akihito has had a smile with his teeth showing in 9 out of 11 pictures. It is worth noting that this emperor is unusual for another reason: He is the first emperor to have married outside the imperial blood lines, though the empress did come from an elite background.

How the empress has been photographed has differed as well. She never appeared with the emperor in the war period because only the emperor's public, official life was shown. Thereafter, however, if the emperor were shown with another person, it was usually the empress. The etiquette for photographic images of her and other females of the imperial family has eased somewhat, such that in recent times the coat of the empress was shown blown in the wind revealing her skirt; or more recently, the empress, while seated, was shown with her knees exposed. This ease of imperial etiquette about photographic images is now in line with that applied to other elite, nonimperial figures in society.

THE WAR IN THE PACIFIC (1942–1945)

For a taste of a wartime article on the emperor's birthday, an excerpt from one in 1942 follows. Excessive honorifics have been cut in our translation to ease the presentation while focusing on the main content:

His Majesty the Emperor, today the twenty-ninth, celebrated his forty-first birthday happily. . . . Nothing is comparable to the deepest excitement we, one hundred million of the emperor's children, feel when we hear that the emperor is in the best health and in the highest spirits. . . . Responsibilities of an emperor in politics and the military encompass various fields. . . . We wish the prosperity and the long life of the emperor. . . . Hearing that the emperor is paying attention to us day and night, the only thing that we, the entire nation, can do is to be moved to tears to find the depth of [the emperor's] kindness. . . . We promise [you] to make further efforts to complete this sacred war, thus making [you] feel relieved. ("Daitōa," 1942, p. 1)

The emperor was the only person who received such congratulatory remarks about his health and birthday in newspapers. Such remarks for the emperor often appeared throughout the war period. We can see from this text that the Japanese people were expected to be tearful in joy by the thought of being in the heart and mind of the emperor. WWII was being fought by the people to please the emperor. The emperor was portrayed as being always busy with politics and the military.

As shown above, appositive constructions involving the plural first pronoun "we" (as in "we, one hundred million of the emperor's children") functioned to suggest that the readers and the newspaper all stood on the same ground: That is, the "we" (the Japanese people) promised to complete the war for the emperor. By doing so, the newspaper invited the readers to pay homage toward the emperor. These statements also told readers how good Japanese citizens were supposed to act in this national crisis.

Other characteristics of the emperor's birthday articles in the Pacific War period were the use of positive adjectives to refer to the emperor. Examples include *yūakunaru* (benevolent), *omedetai* (auspicious), and *ogosokani* (solemnly). These terms were usually accompanied by intensifiers such as *iyoiyo* (more and more) and *hitoshio* (especially) to emphasize their positive meanings.

After Japan's defeat in WWII, however, the Occupation authorities tried to end this homage. This homage was such that until the end of the war, the Japanese media had never thought of interviewing the emperor and so were astonished to hear that American and British press agents made such requests of the emperor on the same day that Douglas MacArthur arrived in Japan in 1945 (Takahashi, 1988). Inspired by their Western counterparts, the Japanese media soon followed suit. Until they did, the Japanese media had to rely on indirect sources about the emperor. Since this change in the process of information gathering had a significant impact on the subsequent emperor's birthday articles, the next section discusses in detail the emperor's press conference with the Japanese media.

FORMAT OF THE EMPEROR'S PRESS CONFERENCE

The emperor's first press conference with Japanese newspaper reporters occurred on May 1, 1947, two days before the new constitution came into effect.[6] The Imperial Household Agency's (IHA's) policy was to keep exposure of the emperor to the media at a minimum. The IHA ordered reporters not to ask any questions regarding politics, the military, or other public matters. Fearful the press conferences would become regular events, the IHA required the Japanese newspapers to say that the event happened "by chance." This explanation, however, meant that the meeting had to have happened outside the palace, so the palace garden was chosen as the place plausible for a press conference. Picture taking, note taking, and tape recording the event were all prohibited.[7] Nevertheless, this "press conference" became a precedent, and related restrictions continued to be enforced until 1975 when taboo questions about such topics as the emperor's war responsibility, the atomic bombs, and his plan to visit Okinawa were asked at last. However, such questions tended to be asked more directly by foreign reporters (Takahashi, 1988).

The IHA screened all questions before the conference, deciding what questions could or could not be asked (Takahashi, 1988). The IHA sometimes even closed a conference early if it found something inappropriate in a reporter's follow-up question to the emperor. In a 1977 conference, the emperor spoke an inappropriate word, and the IHA ordered the newspapers to change the word. Although all newspapers followed the order, the September 9, 1977, issue of *Shūkan Asahi*, a popular weekly magazine, disclosed the IHA's intervention in the media. This angered the IHA, and it cancelled the emperor's regular press conferences for more than a year (Ichikawa, 1993). This tense relationship between the IHA and the press led the media to impose greater self-censorship.

Gradually, press conferences with the emperor resumed and led to two new developments: (1) starting in 1985, the emperor regularly held a press conference right before his birthday so that newspapers could publish the article on the morning of this special day (Takahashi, 1988); (2) birthday articles in the 1990s have been based on information gained from the press conference without having to go through the emperor's chamberlain.[8]

HIROHITO LATER YEARS (1945–1989)

The defeat in WWII brought about a drastic decrease in the use of honorifics and words of glorification. However, honorifics still continued to be used at a stable low rate in the newspapers (Sugimori, 1999). Until the late 1970s, when press conferences for the emperor's birthday were irregularly held, the emperor's birthday articles were written based on the information from the emperor's chamberlains. Ever since the first press conference, the press had been obliged to limit their topics to noncontroversial, trite, and uncritical matters such as the emperor's health, hobbies, and daily life. Because of the nature of these topics, the contents of their articles were repetitious, inviting the dissatisfaction of some readers.

In the 1977 article, the newspaper quoted the emperor's words, which were spoken, reportedly, through the chamberlain:

Some people say that [my thoughts] are the same every year, but nothing special happened and [my basic feeling does not change, so] I have nothing to add. ("Tennō," 1977, April 29, p. 22)

The first part of this statement shows that the emperor may have been aware that some readers were not satisfied with past articles because he repeated the same answers every year. The last part of the statement functioned as the emperor's rationalization. The emperor stressed the interviewee's points of view, that is, that it was natural to stick to the same answers to the questions because his feeling remained the same. By saying so, the emperor implied that it was the media, which continued to ask similar questions year after year, that was to blame for the dissatisfaction of some readers. Was the emperor's rationalization valid? Was he ready to answer any question about whatever the readers really wanted to know? Could it be that he didn't know that the IHA imposed restrictions on the media's choice of topics and their questions? To all these larger questions, the answers could be both yes and no.[9]

First of all, we are not sure whether the emperor's words were accurately reported because they were conveyed through his chamberlain. Any quotation is a creation of the person who quotes it (Tannen, 1989). It is also possible that the emperor was not informed of the IHA restrictions on the media, and what he said may have reflected his genuine feelings. In some cases, the emperor declined comment, but in some others, the IHA interrupted the emperor's answer, possibly against his will. Thus, because the relationship between the IHA and the emperor appears murky, uncertainty has always surrounded reports about the emperor. This uncertainty is found at many levels, including the issue of Emperor Hirohito's war responsibility.[10]

AKIHITO EARLY YEARS (1989–   )

The early years of Emperor Akihito brought about further democratization in many aspects of the emperor's birthday reports. The most significant change started in 1993 with the discontinuation of honorifics except for address terms such as "His Majesty." Before discussing the impact of this loss of honorifics, we consider this loss in terms of its linguistic features such as verbals, adjectives, and topical content.

Verbals

According to the IHA, *kaiken* (meet) should be used only when someone of equal status meets the emperor, such as the head of a nation, not reporters in a press conference (Takahashi, 1988). In the report about Emperor Hirohito's last press conference, however, *kaiken*[11] appeared ("Okoe," 1988, p. 31). This word was placed in parentheses, showing *Asahi Shimbun*'s reservation about using this word in conjunction with press reporters. In Emperor Akihito's first press conference for his birthday in 1990, *kisha kaiken* (meeting the press) was treated as part of a verb phrase with honorifics ("Tennō," 1990, December 23, p. 22). Two years later, *kisha kaiken* was used as a sentence-final noun phrase ("Tennō," 1992, December 23, p. 26). By using this noun-phrase ending, the use of honorifics was avoided. From 1993 to the present, plain verbs without honorifics have been used. The use of plain verbs has not been limited to these press conferences, however. Honorifics (except for address terms) have been nonexistent in virtually all verbs and nouns since 1993.

Adjectives

As shown earlier, adjectives with positive connotations were used when referring to the emperor. After the war, the variety and the frequency of these adjectives decreased drastically. In Emperor Akihito's years, the only adjective that appeared consistently in the first four years of birthday reports was *tabōna* (busy), in reference to the emperor at work. This evaluative term, however, has since disappeared in the *Asahi Shimbun* birthday reports. Let us compare this use of *busy* with its disappearance in the following excerpts.

It is said that [the emperor] could hardly enjoy his fish research, which was his specialization, because he was too busy. ("Tennō," 1989, December 23, p. 30)

It was a busy year [for the emperor] because he was the first emperor to visit three countries in Southeast Asia [and because of other activities]. ("Tennō," 1991, December 23, p. 26)

It was a busy year with many domestic "business trips." ("Tennō," 1992, December 23, p. 26)

[The emperor] said [that] time for his fish research and tennis had decreased. . . . According to the Imperial Household Agency, the emperor invited the Mayor of Hyogo Prefecture and other officials to the palace a total of twenty-three times, and he listened to their reports. His visits to country areas, including a visit to see the victims of an earthquake, . . . extended to as many as ten prefectures. ("Kokoro," 1995, December 23, p. 26)

The 1995 excerpt could imply that the reason the emperor had spent less time on his hobbies was that he was too busy with his work. This reason, however, was much less explicit as it was in the 1989 excerpt. Thus, a growth of objective reporting by the newspaper is evidenced by how readers were left to evaluate the content of the articles for themselves. If some readers of the 1995 article wished to conclude that the emperor was busy with his work, then that was their own prerogative. The main point here is that the newspaper did not impose its evaluation on its readers.

Topics

Health has not been a topic reported in the articles during the present Emperor Akihito's years. This contrasts with those in Emperor Hirohito's years, both before and after WWII, in which the emperor's birthday articles always mentioned his good health. Apparently, at that time, the emperor just being in good health was considered newsworthy. Some may argue that the good health of Emperor Hirohito had news value because he was the longest reigning emperor, but his good health was reported even when he was young. In contrast, the good health of commoners is hardly reported, except for very old people and athletes. The absence of any mention about Emperor Akihito's health may indicate that the newspaper intends to treat the emperor nearly like any other citizen.

THE LOSS OF HONORIFICS AND ITS IMPACT

Influenced by a ban on emperor deification by the Occupation forces, the National Language Council stated in 1952 that honorifics in general should reflect everybody's basic human rights and mutual respect. This new policy, however, did not make an exception for imperial honorifics. Thus, a limited number of imperial honorifics are still in general use today. For the media, the IHA and the Japanese media reached a new agreement on the use of imperial honorifics. They agreed to discontinue imperial honorifics in favor of the highest form of honorifics in general use. Although a step downward, the emperor was still being accorded the highest form of honorifics at any given time. This use of honorifics in the mass media continued but invited criticism from the foreign press as being a form of self-censorship that hindered free speech in postwar Japan (Hara, 1994). The time came for the press to dispense with honorifics toward the imperial family after the death of Emperor Hirohito in 1989. So, in 1993, when Crown Prince Naruhito married Masako Owada, related news reports were devoid of most honorifics (Sugimori, 1999). Owada was the third commoner who married a major member of the imperial family since Michiko married Emperor Akihito in 1959.

A question thus arises as to how newspaper readers are impacted by the use of honorifics toward the imperial family. For this we turn to a veteran of the Japanese press corps quite familiar with the issue. Ishii (1993), who handled briefings from the IHA for the *Asahi Shimbun*, pointed out the essential problems. The use of honorifics may prevent objective reporting because users of honorifics may develop special feelings for the imperial family that could lessen the necessary distance between reporters and their object for reporting. Furthermore, objective reporting is needed if readers are to make reasoned decisions in the whole debate about the emperor system.

Are honorifics really obstacles to objective reporting, as Ishii claims? The following incident gives us insight into the relationship between the use of honorifics and its possible hindrance to objective reporting: On October 11, 1965,
Emperor Hirohito's brother, Mikasanomiya, caused a traffic accident
("Mikasanomiya," 1965). His car hit a taxi and triggered a multiple-car collision.
The media must have been perplexed as to how to report this accident, because
the sentence, "Mikasanomiya-sama hit a taxi," becomes ambiguous if involving
an imperial person. The corresponding sentence in Japanese,

Mikasanomiya-sama wa taxi ni tsuitotsu sareta
Mikasanomiya-(honorific title)-topic taxi-on/by hit-honorific/passive-past

has two contrary but possible readings:

Reading 1: Mikasanomiya hit a taxi.
Reading 2: Mikasanomiya was hit by a taxi.

The different readings depend on the verbal, a derivative of *(ra)reru*, and whether
or not Mikasanomiya is viewed as imperial. For imperial persons, the verbal
(ra)reru becomes active; for commoners, passive.

Reading 2 is, by far, more familiar for commoners because that is what is said
for themselves and nearly all others. Moreover, the honorific title *-sama* is not
exclusively used for imperial persons. Thus, imperial culpability can blur, if not
outright vanish.

Considering the built-in ambiguity, the *Asahi Shimbun* did a reasonably good
job of reporting, especially if solely judging the headline. The headline was
absent of any honorifics, and Mikasanomiya was treated as the cause of the accident. Potential conflict arose, however, in the text of the article because some
honorifics for him were used. The very idea of addressing Mikasanomiya with
-sama, an honorific title, presupposes a state of honor and, therefore, might preclude a negative interpretation. Thus, honorific discourse could help shield such
an imperial person from culpability even if not intended.

This rare incident makes us realize the relationship between the use of honorifics toward the imperial family and the related discourse. It demonstrates that
sentences with honorifics pragmatically can inhibit the use of verbs with negative meanings such as "hit," making one interpret such sentences in the passive
(not active) voice. Why is this so? Grammatically speaking, there should be an
equal possibility for each reading. However, we find that the nature of verbs in
the Japanese language with negative meanings is not compatible with honorifics.
This instance illustrates that honorifics can hinder negative reports on the imperial family, thus being obstacles to objective reporting. We can assume, therefore,
that readers repeatedly exposed to a positive slant on the imperial family experi-

ence the honorific feelings toward imperial actions vicariously, thus making it difficult to judge the reports objectively.

PRESS CONFERENCE ON THE WEB

Beginning with the 1998 birthday press conferences, the *Asahi Shimbun* began to publish on the World Wide Web the entire transcripts of press conferences held with several major members of the imperial family, prior to the day of the observance. The following is an English translation of an excerpt from the transcript of the 1998 emperor's birthday press conference that was published on the Web. This excerpt literally shows the direct interactions between the emperor, press, and the IHA official(s):

Reporters: One more question.

IHA official: You may have a question, but the time has run out, so no more for today.

Emperor: Well, if you have a question, why don't you ask it? ("Tennō," 1998, online)

The extra space created by the Web enabled the newspaper to include the entire transcript, thereby showing what happened in the conference in detail, word for word. Note also that the inclusion of the entire transcript does not automatically suggest its criticism of the IHA. Rather, judgment of the transcript is left for its readers.

CONCLUSION

Newspapers are mirrors of society. This chapter has taken one aspect of Japanese culture, the use of honorifics in newspaper articles referring to the emperor, as illustrating associated changes in the social structure, values, and norms of Japanese society in general. As the civic discourse about the emperor has changed, so has society's attitude toward the imperial institution. In so doing, the Japanese have redefined the status of the emperor, shifting power to themselves. If Japan is to have a truly democratic society, it must free itself further from the mystique of the emperor system and its strictures on a free press. For this reason, the decline in the use of honorifics in referring to the emperor has helped the Japanese demystify the emperor system and explore the meaning of objective reporting in the civic society.

ACKNOWLEDGMENTS

We are especially grateful to Mary Catherine O'Connor and Merry White for their insightful advice during the writing of this chapter. We also thank Michiko

Aoki, Gregory Guelcher, Ken'ichi Nagura, Scott North, Richard Showstack, Pam Siska, and Sumiyuki Yukawa for their helpful comments.

NOTES

1. The introductory paragraph was written jointly. The section on historical background was written by Hamada. Sugimori is solely responsible for all other parts of the chapter.

2. *Asahi Shimbun* is one of Japan's leading newspapers with a circulation of 8.5 million. The political slant of this paper is considered to be liberal.

3. Although the correct practice is to refer to the emperor by the name of his reign (such as "Emperor Showa" for Emperor Hirohito) after his death (Aoki, 1991), for convenience's sake, we refer to Emperor Showa as Emperor Hirohito and the current emperor as Emperor Akihito in this chapter. Their reigning periods are also named using their first names.

4. The social structure is reflected in the flowery language used, as well as in complex methods of address and ritualistic manners (Gudykunst & Nishida, 1994), the related social status (including one's age and gender), and the level of formality that is appropriate for a situation. These features are all influenced by the cultural values of the society (Condon & Yousef, 1975).

5. Japanese handle expressions of respect and humility not only through spoken language, but also through body language (Williams, 1998). Bowing is one of the key social behaviors that reinforce the vertical hierarchical structure of Japanese society. According to DeMente (1993), bowing is a significant part of the physical and psychological cultural conditioning of the Japanese people, and, like their spoken language, their body language also shows different degrees of respect depending on to whom they speak or greet. Bowing, for example, depends on relative social position: People bowing to the emperor do so at a 90 degree angle while the emperor acknowledges them by merely nodding slightly.

6. The emperor talked to 2 of 17 Japanese reporters very briefly in December 1945 (Takahashi, 1988). However, in this case, reporters did not ask the emperor any questions, so we did not consider it the first press conference.

7. The IHA balked at note taking in the 1970s, but it became allowed in Akihito's period. Picture taking and audio- and videotape recording were allowed in 1975 (Ichikawa, 1993).

8. One exception was in 1999 when the emperor did not hold a press conference and he responded to the reporters' questions in writing.

9. Our personal communication with *Kyodo News* staff reporter Ken'ichi Nagura indicates that it is possible that the emperor did not know the IHA restrictions on the media.

10. According to Reischauer and Jansen (1995), the basic ambiguity of the Meiji Constitution on the role of the emperor left it uncertain as to his power and responsibility. According to the constitution, all power stems from the emperor but his power is not de facto.

11. *Kaiken* appeared in the headline of the report on the emperor's first press conference ("Tennō Heika," 1947) for the first time. This practice, however, did not continue after the end of the Occupation.

REFERENCES

Aoki, M. (1991). Women *tennō* of Japan. In C. I. Mulhern (Ed.), *Heroic with grace* (pp. 60–76). Armonk, NY: M.E. Sharpe.

Brown, P., & Levinson, S. (1978). *Politeness: Some universals in language use.* New York: Cambridge University Press.

Condon, J. C., & Yousef, F. S. (1975). *An introduction to intercultural communication.* Indianapolis, IN: Bobbs-Merrill.

Daitōa senka hatsu no tenchōsetsu [The first emperor's birthday during the War in the Pacific]. (1942, April 29). *Asahi Shimbun,* p. 1.

DeMente, B. (1993). *Behind the Japanese bow.* Lincolnwood, IL: Passport Books.

Donahue, R. T. (1990). *Japanese non-linear discourse style.* New York: Applied Linguistics Research.

Eto, J. (1982). The censorship operation in occupied Japan. In J. L. Curry & J. R. Dassin (Eds.), *Press control around the world* (pp. 235–253). New York: Praeger.

Gruber, H. (1997). The rhetoric of trivialization: The coverage of right-wing extremism and Neonazism in Austria's most read tabloid. In J. Blommaert & C. Bulcaen (Eds.), *Political linguistics* (pp. 139–156). Amsterdam: John Benjamins.

Gudykunst, W. B., & Nishida, T. (1994). *Bridging Japanese/North American differences.* Thousand Oaks, CA: Sage.

Haga, Y. (1990). *Shakai no naka no Nihongo* [Japanese language in society]. Tokyo: Taishukan.

Hara, T. (1994). *Journalism wa kawaru* [Journalism changes]. Tokyo: Banseisha.

Ichikawa, H. (1993). *Kōshitsu hōdō* [Reporting on the imperial family]. Tokyo: Asahi Shimbun.

Ishii, T. (1993). Kōshitsu keigo o kangaeru [Thinking about imperial honorifics]. *Shimbun Kenkyu, 505,* 74–77.

Kindaichi, H. (1990). *Nihongo* [The Japanese language] (U. Hirano, Trans.). Tokyo: Charles E. Tuttle. (Original work published 1957)

Kokoro no omoi toshi deshita [My heart was heavy this year]. (1995, December 23). *Asahi Shimbun,* p. 26.

Kumakura, M. (1988). *Genron tōseika no kisha* [Reporters under control from the freedom of speech]. Tokyo: Asahi Shimbun.

Loveday, L. (1986). *Explorations in Japanese sociolinguistics.* Amsterdam: John Benjamins.

Mikasanomiya tsuitotsu shite kega [Mikasanomiya slams (car) and is injured]. (1965, October 12). *Asahi Shimbun,* p. 15.

Nakane, C. (1973). *Japanese society.* Berkeley: University of California Press. (Original work published 1967)

Okoe ni hari yodominaku [Sonorous voice]. (1988, April 29). *Asahi Shimbun,* p. 31.

Reischauer, E. O., & Jansen, M. B. (1995). *The Japanese today: Change and continuity.* Cambridge, MA: Belknap Press of Harvard University Press.

Sugimori, N. A. (1999, June). *Newspaper honorifics.* Paper presented at the annual meeting of the New England Association of Teachers of Japanese, New London, CT.

Takahashi, H. (1988). *Heika, otazune mōshiagemasu* [Your Majesty, I would like to ask some questions]. Tokyo: Bungeishunju.

Tannen, D. (1989). *Talking voices: Repetition, dialogue, and imagery in conversational discourse.* Cambridge: Cambridge University Press.

Tennō . . . tanjōbi [Emperor's . . . birthday]. (1942–1999). *Asahi Shimbun,* (April 29, 1942–1946 and 1952–1988; April 30, 1948–1951; December 23, 1989–1999). [Ellipses in the title represent variable information that pertains to his particular age. Page number and date for an article specifically cited are found in the chapter with the citation.]

Tennō heika kisha to hatsu no kaiken [His majesty the Emperor's first meeting with reporters]. (1947, May 3). *Âsahi Shimbun,* p. 1.

Tsukishima, K. (1990). *Bunka no kōzō to kotoba* [Structure of culture and language]. Tokyo: Taishukan.

Williams, S. N. (1998). *The illustrated handbook of American and Japanese gestures.* Tokyo: Kodansha International.

Chapter 6

Aisatsu: Ritualized Politeness as Sociopolitical and Economic Management in Japan

Brian J. McVeigh

The chapter focuses on why civility acts as a "social lubricant" for helping run the machinery of capitalism, nationalism, and statism in modern Japan. To what degree civility actually increases the production of capitalism, national identity, and statist projects in Japan is debatable, but one fact is certain: Civility is heavily promoted within diverse social arenas and this advocacy is in no small measure generated by economic nation-statist forces. In order to illustrate how politeness acts as the "lubricating oil" for Japan's grand projects of modernity, the author introduces the nexus of business, bureaucracy, and national identity, which are all conveniently summed up in the term "economic nation-statism." Next, in order to focus on the role of the state in advocating etiquette, he examines how manners are taught in school. Then, he examines the paradoxical nature of civility in Japan as it relates to "civil society" and "publicness" and contends that aisatsu (sociolinguistic practices) takes the place of an impartial public arena. Finally, he concludes by arguing that aisatsu should be regarded as a key institution in Japan that promotes sociopolitical management and control. An "invisible institution," civility links together ethics, education, and etiquette, vertically arranging "cells" that share a nationalist ideology and are primed for politico-economic reproduction.

Question: In Japan, what do moral education, secretarial training, a "new religion," and etiquette guidebooks have in common? Answer: A mandate for Japanese civility. This civility, as mandated in several sociocultural domains, is explored in McVeigh (1997, 1998a, n.d.) and is revisited in this chapter by a focus on the etiquette training in Japanese schools. The common ideological source found for the prescriptions on civility or politeness is an array of statist and capitalist forces. Regardless how diverse the group goals, social settings, values, and other variables, various spheres of Japanese society share an ethnomorality about civility that is contoured by state projects and corporatist concerns. This ethnomorality is most visible in *aisatsu,* which covers an entire range of sociolinguistic practices, from perfunctory greetings to complex ceremonials.

In this chapter, I focus on why civility acts as a "social lubricant" for helping run the machinery of capitalism, nationalism, and statism in modern Japan. *To what degree* civility actually increases the production of capitalism, national identity, and statist projects in Japan is debatable, but one fact is certain: Civility is heavily promoted within diverse social arenas, and this advocacy is in no small measure generated by economic nation-statist forces. Codes of politeness, of course, are found elsewhere, but what may separate them are the politico-economic motivations that drive them.

In order to illustrate how civility acts as the "lubricant" for Japan's grand projects of modernity, I introduce the nexus of business, bureaucracy, and national identity, which are all conveniently summed up in the term "economic nation-statism." Next, in order to focus on the role of the state in advocating etiquette, I examine how manners are taught in school. Then, I examine the paradoxical nature of civility in Japan as it relates to "civil society" and "publicness" and contend that *aisatsu* takes the place of an impartial public arena. Finally, I conclude by arguing that *aisatsu* should be regarded as a key "institution," among others, in Japan's political economy.

LINGUISTICALLY LINKING CAPITAL, ETHNOS, AND STATE

The major projects of the state and the corporate world generate minor projects visible on a more local, immediate, and personal level, so that the daily practices of *aisatsu* affirm, support, and reproduce (though often implicitly and unawares) massive political economic arrangements through numerous institutional linkages. In this section, I note these arrangements.

By "political" (in the title), I specifically mean state attempts to instill statist notions of modernity within individuals. The state organ most obviously committed to this endeavor is the Ministry of Education. Subsumed under the political is also national identity and ethnocultural sentiments[1] ("Japaneseness"), which the state is committed to protecting and propagating and whose linkages to manners are discussed. By "economics" (in the title), I specifically mean capitalism and the large corporations that run the offices, factory floors, and numerous branches and outlets employing individual workers who must deal with the public on a daily basis. In addition to the highly capitalized corporations, there are smaller companies and shops that must ensure their employees are treating client patrons in the appropriately polite manner.

Viewed together, Japan's "politics" and "economics" form a powerful deployment of ideo-institutions whose grand project may be termed economic nation-statism. One should not exaggerate the interconnections between state and business (i.e., the "Japan, Inc." image). However, regardless of the friction caused by occasional divergences, statist and capitalist concerns do share key projects (e.g., accumulation of capital, aggrandizement of nation-statist power, belief in general social progressivism, "Japaneseness") and are clearly interlinked. These linkages have been described in various ways; for example, "capitalist developmental state" (Johnson, 1993), "state-assisted capitalism" (Bello, 1996), "strategic economy" (Huber, 1994), and "strong capitalist state" (Dower, 1990, p. 66). Institutionally, the most important organization that bridges the *zaikai* ("financial world" or "capitalist circles") and the state is the Federation of Economic Organizations. Other important organizations are the Japanese Federation of Employers' Associations, the Japanese Committee for Economic Development, and the Japan Chamber of Commerce and Industry. It should be noted that members of these prestigious organizations sit on state advisory councils (and more specifically for my purposes, Ministry of Education advisory councils), as do other individuals from various sectors of the *zaikai*. In addition to the well-known top organizations, there are about 3,000 local business associations that advocate capitalist values.

Civilizing Capital: Economics and Language

Sociolinguistic practices such as *keigo* (honorific language) are prescribed, deployed, and employed to assist economic production and rationalization. Specifically, exalting (*sonkeigo*) and humbling languages (*kenjōgo*) construct hierarchical lines of authority while polite language (*teineigo*) maintains clear in-group/inclusionary and out-group/exclusionary categories. Schooling experiences prime individuals to be ideologically receptive to the rationalizing demands of labor. For instance, group-dividing linguistic practices reflect the rationalization of breaking workers down into atomized "small" or "self-management" groups and "quality control circles."

Not surprisingly, in banks, institutions most associated with capital, very polite language is used in interactions between clerks and customers, "while clerks at post offices often use the plain form" (Mizutani & Mizutani, 1987, p. 7). Thus, the more capital involved in a transaction, the higher the level of civility that is expected. "Generally speaking, those who sell costly merchandise talk more politely than those who sell inexpensive articles. Salesman [people] who deal with merchandise such as jewels, cars, and expensive clothes talk very politely." The same salesperson "can change language depending on the price of the merchandise" (though all customers receive at least a minimal level of respect). Fish and vegetable sellers "use a rather rough language." Taxi drivers, it might be pointed out, ordinarily use plain language (Mizutani & Mizutani, 1987, pp. 6–7).[2]

Emitting Japaneseness: The Nation and Language

The Japanese language is frequently regarded as the essential element in making the Japanese "Japanese." The use of *aisatsu* and *keigo* are frequently used as national and/or racial identity markers. Some note with pride how difficult it is to use polite Japanese correctly and how "unique" Japanese is. For example, Kitagawa points out that there are twelve ways to say "good-bye" in Japanese (1985, p. 35). In a section of *How to Write Letters* called "Japanese and a Sense for the Seasons," nature (Japan as place) and norms (Japanese values) are linked. In the same book, aesthetics and ethics are connected through a discourse about Japanese and a *bi-ishiki* (consciousness of beauty), *iki* (stylish, chic), and *kejime* (discernment, i.e., of social relations and affairs) (Yasuda, 1978). *Aisatsu, keigo,* and terms of respect "are associated with the original Japanese language, and are a unique and important part of this culture. There are a lot of special words for expressing respect, and I think their sounds are soft and really beautiful" ("Respecting Terms of Respect," 1997, p. 6).

Some express the fear that *aisatsu*, as an essential aspect of Japaneseness, is on the decline (see, for example, Kitō, 1995, pp. 38–71) and that measures should be taken to preserve it: "It is very important that we protect our culture so that we can pass it on to future generations." After all, losing an institution such as *aisatsu* will tear at the fabric of society: "We have to work hard to communicate with others, and using polite language can only serve to make all parties feel more comfortable." As for those who use inappropriate language forms: "I am sometimes a little surprised or upset, and feel pity for those who have made mistakes and caused others discomfort" ("Respecting Terms of Respect," 1997, p. 6).

Japanese are somehow essentially and morally linked to the Japanese language (unlike *gaikokujin* or "foreigners"); that is, Japanese *should* speak Japanese because they are born Japanese. For many, those who are not racially Japanese but speak Japanese are remarkably out of place (see Miller, 1982). Because being Japanese is so tightly tied to national and racial identities, non-Japanese who emit signs of Japaneseness (i.e., use the Japanese language) are calling into question linguistic boundaries; they are challenging what are often regarded as immutable and essentialist identities.

If speaking Japanese signals one's Japaneseness, speaking *keigo* and properly using *aisatsu* loudly announces one's Japaneseness. However, it must be stressed that though the average Japanese is familiar with the basics of honorific language, we cannot assume that all Japanese have mastered it. There are, after all, strong ideological reasons, motivated by an ideology of "cultural homogeneity," behind the notion that "all Japanese" use *keigo* (Miller, 1989). *Keigo* "is a formally learned, specialized code not available to all members of Japanese society. And, even among those expected to be proficient in it (white-collar workers) the use of *keigo* is somewhat restricted" (Miller, 1989, p. 41). This "is indicated by the fact that much of it is learned as an adult. The pages of daily newspapers are full of advertisements for specialized schools that offer language training." After all, "if all Japanese had the same competence in this code, there would not be a market for special language training and for 'how to' books" (Miller, 1989, p. 40).

LEARNING OFFICIAL JAPANESENESS: THE STATE, SCHOOLING, AND LANGUAGE

In today's world, "the assumption that different languages 'naturally' exist illustrates just how deeply nationalist [and statist] conceptions have seeped into contemporary common sense" (Billig, 1995, p. 10). The *Wagakuni no Bunka to Bunka Gyōsei* (*Our Country's Culture and Culture Administration*) devotes one chapter to the Japanese language (1988, pp. 175–206). The history of language reform is outlined and the conclusions of the various councils that have met to deal with the Japanese language are explained. Also, problem areas such as language "corruption" (*midare*), changes in verbal conjugations, honorific expressions, and how information technology affects language are identified.

The reform and rationalization of the Japanese language has also been thought of as a necessary tool in building an economically powerful nation-state (Gottlieb, 1996; Twine, 1991; Unger, 1996). Schools, the educatio-socializing arm of the state, have as one of their primary missions the teaching of Japanese. *Kokugo* (Japanese language, literally, "national language") is one of the core subjects of the Ministry of Education–ordained curriculum that students must master for examinations. Number 4 of Article 17 of Chapter II of the School Education Law states that one of the purposes of primary schools is: "To cultivate ability to understand and use correctly words and expressions of the Japanese language needed in everyday life" (*Fundamental Law of Education,* 1977). Other state-authorized sites concerned with the "official" language include the National Language Research Institute, which is attached to the Agency for Cultural Affairs (under the Ministry of Education) and publishes a wide range of books about the Japanese language, and the National Institute of Japanese Literature, which is attached to the Ministry of Education. This institute publishes the annual *Language Series* (*Kotoba Shirīzu*). These books are distributed by the state to schools, libraries, and citizens' halls and sold at bookstores. The Agency for Cultural Affairs has also produced videos and every year publishes *Collection of Questions and Answers about Language* (*Kotoba ni kansuru mondōshū*).

MORALS AND MANNERS IN SCHOOLS

Though there is regional and urban/rural variation, in general schools are a key site in which individuals are socialized to use proper language. Such language use is stressed by the Ministry of Education which, through the Agency for Cultural Affairs, publishes and distributes guides on how to teach Japanese, or *kokugo*, and works on *aisatsu* and *keigo*.

The teaching of Japanese language and its sociolinguistic use must be understood within the context of "moral education" and the values it advocates. I have examined moral education and its linkages to the state elsewhere (McVeigh, 1998b, 1998c), but here it suffices to point out two values embedded in the discourse of moral education as they relate to manners: thoughtfulness (*omoiyari*, sometimes glossed as consideration or empathy) and belongingness.

Many have commented on the role of thoughtfulness in Japanese society (see, for example, Donahue, 1998; Gerbert, 1993; Lebra, 1976; Lewis, 1995). *Omoiyari* is called the "foundation of morality" and is tied to love of family, friends, patriotism, and respect for law. The importance of *omoiyari*, which literally means "giving thought" (to others), is seen in the Ministry of Education's recommendation of books such as *Guidance for Cultivating a Heart of Thoughtfulness in Primary School* and *Guidance for Cultivating a Heart of Thoughtfulness in Middle School* (Ministry of Education, 1986a, 1986b) and the great frequency with which this term is employed in other materials. Clancy notes that "empathy and conformity may be seen as two sides of the same coin" (1986, p. 235). By "telling their children what other people were thinking and feeling, the mothers encouraged their children to empathize with others; by warning them that certain behaviors were strange, frightening, or shameful in the eyes of others, they indicated the importance of conformity" (p. 245).

Kitagawa explains that *aisatsu* contains the feeling that "perhaps, because I am a person who is not perfect, I unintentionally did something that was rude. Or perhaps I said something in such a way that I hurt your feelings. If I did do such a thing, I am sincerely sorry" (1985, p. 43). Moreover, as I have argued elsewhere in more detail, because everyone is so busy performing social roles enacted through etiquette practices, it is often difficult to discern what another is really thinking, feeling, or experiencing (McVeigh, 1997, pp. 45–46); that is, politeness erects walls between individuals, and social interaction becomes a guessing game. Kitagawa writes that the trick of *aisatsu* is to "put yourself in the place of the other" (1985, p. 23). Because thoughts are often not expressed directly—veiled behind appearances and masks of self-effacing courtesy—social meanings and subtle messages must be deciphered. Therefore, successfully decoding the costuming and posturing on the social stage strongly encourages individuals to be thoughtful. Consequently, empathy and etiquette reinforce each other, and how one looks is essential for social order, because by observing a person's appearance, others are able to calibrate their treatment of that person. Such calibrations are taken quite seriously. For instance, an incident in which a woman who was shot with a crossbow set off a debate about whether the media should have referred to her as *kaishain* (company employee) or *shufu* (housewife) (she was in fact a working housewife). According to the author, Nozomu Hayashi,

the Japanese trait of asking one's title or age arises from the fact that we have to use a language which requires the use of many different levels of politeness according to the relative positions of the speaker and the other party. There may be some who advocate the banishing of this intricate and irksome habit in favor of a flat, uniform politeness set somewhere in the middle of the present complex strata. But we must remember culture does not grow out of something flat. Born in the Japanese culture, we work every day to avoid sounding either insolent or stand-offish. We must watch whether the other party is satisfied with the level of politeness expressed. We have to judge and interpret on our own the delicate nuances conveyed via newspaper and TV news. To tell the truth, I have come to enjoy this tough task. (1993, p. 15)

How does belongingness relate to sociolinguistic practices? Guide books on morality advise that students learn "feelings of solidarity," "feelings of belonging," "feelings of unity," "respect [for] the rules of the group," "awareness as a member of a group," "mutual understanding," and "cooperation" so as to instill belongingness and groupism (McVeigh, 1998b, 1998c). Such sentiments are indispensable for eventual laboring as members of work groups and loyal company workers who should have "whole-hearted devotion" (*seishin sei-i*). Maintaining clear group boundaries and smoothly exiting/entering groups—joining corporations, being assigned to departments and work details, being rotated, visiting other offices and companies, retiring—are accomplished through *aisatsu*. Just as in the case of thoughtfulness, the more emphasis that is placed on belongingness, the more central etiquette becomes in social interaction, and vice versa. *Aisatsu*, it needs to be pointed out, performs a paradoxical role: Though it brings individuals together, it also separates, fragments, even atomizes society (McVeigh, n. d.).

The Morality of Manners

An example of the importance schools assign civility is evident in an internal document compiled for teachers by a middle school called *Manners for Young People* (*Wakai hitotachi no manā*). In this document, we learn that *aisatsu* is a lubricant for "deepening human relations" and that there are basically two types of situations in which it is used: *nichijō* (everyday) and *tokubetsu na baai* (special situations). Properly executed *aisatsu,* which should be an embodiment of "sincerity" (*sei-i*), has three components:

1. posture and attitude (*shisei* and *taido*),
2. speed of speaking and use of pauses, and
3. facial expressions and where one looks.

Aisatsu should manifest "rationality, aesthetics, and efficiency": "Correct posture could be called posture that is rational (*gōriteki*), beautiful (*utsukushī*), and is not wasteful," and walking, if done well, should be "beautiful." Students are taught how to execute the three types of bows depending on the occasion and to whom:

1. *shinrei,* a deep bow that is the most respectful,
2. *gyōrei,* an ordinary bow, and
3. *sōrei,* a bow in which the angle is not so steep.

These three bows also each have their respective sitting versions. As for sitting on one's heels (*seiza,* a respectful way to sit that can be rather painful for the unpracticed), students are told what to do if their feet fall asleep and how to stand up from the *seiza* position. Instructions are gendered; individuals should move their bodies in certain ways depending on whether they are male or female, with special attention given to women in order to be "feminine." *Aisatsu* also embodies national distinctions; Japaneseness is embedded in discussions of how to act, depending on whether they are in *yōshitsu* (Western-style) or *washitsu* (Japanese-style) rooms.

Manners for Young People is divided into two parts. The first is "Basic Manners," which includes sections on "Posture and How to Walk," "How to Sit," "How to Stand," "How to Bow," "How to *Aisatsu*," "How to Carry and Present Things," and "How to Speak." Under the latter section (which is accompanied by diagrams), students are advised against making "big gestures" when speaking, to "speak with your chest out," to talk confidently with a smile, and not to look down. One piece of advice, illustrated by a diagram with a dotted-line square superimposed over a young woman's face, explains that one should speak while focusing one's gaze within the dotted lines (i.e., look at the other person's eyes and face). Other points for speaking: Organize your thoughts before speaking; use pauses and intonation correctly; and use many types of facial expressions. Under "How to Introduce Oneself," students are told to avoid speaking in a low voice, the tendency to look downward, and moving one's eyes too much, since such people are thought of as "crooked" and "gloomy." Under "How to Use Honorific Language," students are warned "not to mix up" exalting language (*sonkeigo*) with humble language (*kenjōgo*). Under "Manners at School," students are reminded that "When you wear your clothes neatly, you feel steady and give a good feeling to those you meet" and that good manners give "a delightful feeling to those around one." They are also told to carry their book bags in their left hand and umbrella in the right (which should not be "pointed at people").

The second part of *Manners for Young People,* called "Manners for Visiting and Receiving Others," is divided into sections called: "Dos and Don'ts for Visiting," "Manners for the Entrance (*genkansaki*)," "Manners for When Admitted into a Room," "How to Open and Close a Paper Sliding Door (*fusuma*)," "Manners Concerning Cushions (*zabuton*)," "Dos and Don'ts for

Receiving Others," "How to See Off a Guest," "Dos and Don'ts for Returning Home," and "How to Telephone Someone." Under the latter section, students are told to "make a memo of what you will say before calling, confirm with the listener what you have said, and don't stay on the phone too long." They are also told what to do if they receive a wrong number: "don't cover the receiver with your hand," "don't cover the mouthpiece," "keep the TV turned down low," "don't eat while speaking," "don't call too late or too early, and avoid calling during meal time." Under "How to Receive a Telephone Call," they are advised that "after hearing it ring, catch your breath and calm down before picking up the phone," and "don't forget the caller's name." Rules about using public phones are also explained.

A memo passed around among middle school teachers called "On Entering and Exiting the Faculty Room" offers another example of how schools view the significance of civility:

I. Have a Proper Attitude

(1) Say "excuse me" and "I'm leaving now" clearly

(2) Pay attention to proper speech

(3) Don't speak in a loud voice (this also applies when meeting guests and speaking on the phone)

II. For People Who Have Business

(1) Don't have others accompany you (it is important for those in charge of lessons to properly fulfill their roles)

(2) When many individuals want to speak with the same teacher at the same time, consider using another place (the faculty room is not a happy, noisy home)

III. Maintain Etiquette

(1) When entering the room, what should you do with your cap, gloves, coat, and book bag? [place in appropriate place]

(2) How should you speak toward your superiors? [politely]

Another document, sent to various schools in the Gero area, reported the results of a six-day "*aisatsu* contest" (*aisatsu no torikumi*) among a number of schools. The same language employed for students was used for those schools that did not fare too well: They were asked to *hansei* or "reflect" (i.e., on their weak points) and *gambaru* ("continue to try hard") the next time.

The themes of primary and secondary schooling discussed previously continue through to the university level. Elsewhere I have explored the teaching of *aisatsu* at a women's junior college (McVeigh, 1997), but here it is worth mentioning how manners are not only an issue of concern at some junior colleges, but are also given attention at some four-year co-ed universities. On a form for instructors on how to interview university applicants, faculty are told to check for "points of positiveness" (*sekkyokusei*) and to ask applicants to *jiko*-PR ("self-

PR") within 1 minute. Under the item of "attitude" (*taido*), faculty are told to check for: (1) "The *aisatsu* of entering and exiting the room," (2) "Speech" ("can the student use exalting, humble, and polite language?"), and (3) "Does the student's personal appearance have a sense of cleanliness (*seiketsukan*)?"

DISCUSSION: THE PARADOX OF JAPANESE CIVILITY[3]

Does Japan have a "civil society"? This is a complex and contentious issue, and elsewhere I have explored the meaning of Japan's "civil society" and "publicness" in a more detailed and nuanced manner (McVeigh, 1998a), but here I focus on the paradoxical nature of civility in Japan.

All the attributes usually associated with civil society are evident in modern Japan. Democratic institutions, a media with a large readership, a relatively open market of ideas, residents' movements (*jūmin undō*), and citizens' movements (*shimin undō*) certainly indicate some type of "publicness" or "civil society." However, my contention is that in spite of any similarities, public and civil society possess various configurations in different places. "Public" and "civil society" are concepts so basic and interwoven into the Anglo-American political experience that they are often taken for granted.[4] They are, in fact, a type of "common sense." But such concepts are anything but commonsensical, and they are, in fact, quite historically specific. For instance, Williams notes that "Whatever hopeful resonance the word 'public' may evoke in the English ear, it must be stressed that 'government of the people, by the people, and for the people' is not a Japanese administrative tradition. At best, the Confucian bureaucratic tradition is about paternalistic benevolence, not power-sharing with the masses" (Williams, 1994, p. 111). Moreover, Williams notes that "civil society" (*shimin shakai*) "translates only poorly into the Japanese language" (p. 165). Stated simply, my contention is that in the case of Japan, rituality and staged formalities take the place of a neutral public space. The lack of a clearly defined public space encourages a social theatrics of formalized etiquette (*aisatsu*), which mediates personal encounters. Indeed, I contend that the lack of a strong civil society, which buffers the private sphere from state action (as in Anglo-American societies), enhances the power of Japan's bureaucrats, who, in the words of Isomura and Kuronuma, administer "for the sake of the citizenry," but not necessarily with the "participation of the citizenry" (1974, p. 11).

A WALL OF DENSE RITUAL AND SOCIOPOLITICAL CELLS

I contend that in place of a well-conceptualized civil society as conventionally understood in Anglo-American societies, Japan has the institution of *aisatsu*. Practices associated with this sociolinguistic behavior, driven by sociopolitical and economic rationalization and bureaucratization, are seen in staged formalities which erect thick walls of rituality. According to Obana and Tomoda, "politeness in English language is often associated with barrier-breaking features whereas in Japanese language, politeness initially sets up a social barrier" (1994, p. 46). Terms such as *uchi/soto* (inner/outer) and *ura/omote* (inside/exposed) form a discourse that comment on this ritualization. This discourse is driven and shaped by modernity; it is not an ahistorical "tradition," but shaped by very present practices, and is not comprised of depoliticized "customs," but politicized socioeconomic relations and structures.

If the individual feels pulled between an array of groups—some demanding formalized performances, others requiring more personal expressions—then society is perceived as an aggregate of well-sealed boxes. Leaving one box and entering another requires care, since the space between them is perceived as asocial and anomic and is not an area in which one would usually want to become stranded. Consequently, particular groups with specific interests are privileged over an all-encompassing collectivity composed of individuals with common interests ("public" in the Anglo-American sense). Anomic spaces are where unknowns and strangers (*tanin,* literally, "other people") dwell who are not necessarily deserving of attention or help. This characterization should not be exaggerated, but there is a sentiment (to what degree it exists is impossible to gauge) that one should not aid strangers because then they would "feel indebted" (see Kiritani, 1997). Neither should one move out of the way unless specifically told to do so (see, for example, the case of crowded trains in "Teaching Train Etiquette," 1996).

Lacking a culturally sanctioned sphere where an individual's opinions, interests, or self may be expressed readily before a collectivity that safeguards such expressions, Japanese society requires certain social practices to facilitate exchanges. In Japan, *tatemae,* meaning stated policy or the rules or conventions that have been established and agreed on within a group and often refers to attempts to create an atmosphere of amiable consensus, is employed to construct a type of publicness and thereby serves a similar function as "public" does in Western societies. *Tatemae* serves as a collectively agreed-on neutral or buffer area where the individual is, in at least a certain sense, protected from others.

If, for many Japanese, intimate situations involve "insiders" and ritual situations involve "outsiders" but require *tatemae* practices and face-maintaining maneuvers, there are situations that cannot be defined clearly as inside or outside. These are ambiguous social spaces, betwixt and between family and nonkin group-regulated settings. It is in these areas, described as anomic by Lebra (1976, p. 112), that an individual regards someone as an "outsider" but feels no need to maintain face, since there is no hierarchy-observing behavior and thus no rules to uphold. It may be argued that, ideally at least (and I emphasize "ideally"), there should be no anomic areas in Anglo-American conceptions of the social landscape. Rather, as the basic unit of society, the individual is expected to move between different settings. All space between intimate or nonintimate situations is recognized as an arena regulated by agreed-on codes of conduct. In Japan, however, it is the group setting (whether intimate or ritualized) that establishes the rules. Any space between these groups is incidental to the groups themselves, a sort of marginal area unregulated by significant social concerns.

If we speak in the most general terms, "society," in Anglo-American conceptions, is conceived as an all-encompassing community composed of individuals who move about in a buffer or "social public" area (distinguished from "official public") that fills the gaps between islands of private domain. This public space nurtures a civil society, or publicness, that is distinct from the state. If ideally (again, I emphasize "ideally") the public in Anglo-American societies are spaces in which grids demarcate agreed-on routes traveled by individuals who temporarily leave their privacy behind, in Japan, the public is a somewhat more disordered place where atomized individuals take their privacy with them and try their hardest to coolly disregard others. The implications are political: See Abe, Shindō, and Kawato (1994), who note that "'Freedom,' in contemporary Japan, is less a value to be realized through the unremitting efforts of human beings than it is simply a condition in which people are living tranquilly by coincidence" (p. 210). Japanese society may be conceived as being composed of numerous small cells or "mini-societies," each with its own subculture and particular rules.

It sometimes seems as if the bureaucracies encourage pockets (*uchi*) of privacy because it is suspicious of collectivities coalescing that might come between the state and the individual citizen, a sort of "divide and rule" strategy. Though interest groups exist in Japan in great numbers, "there is no theory of pluralism that legitimates their political activities" (Johnson, 1982, p. 49). Consequently, "civility"—rather than being codes that maintain personal inviolability while not in the private domain—is primarily a matter of managing the movement between these many societies. The focus is on maintaining clear boundaries between in-groups (*uchi*) and out-groups (*soto*) and fostering impressions and practices (*tatemae*) that expedite intergroup traffic. Areas betwixt and between groups are anomic and ambiguous. Because the area between groups is socially ambiguous, groups must clearly carve out and continually reinforce their perimeters in order to define (or as the case may be, defend) themselves. This is why passing between groups demands entrance and exit rituals symbolized by elaborate sociolinguistic codes. Thus, rather than complex codes of behavior designed for a neutral, mediating space, navigating the Japanese social world emphasizes boundary-clarifying practices.

CONCLUSION: CIVILITY AS INTERSTITIAL "SOCIAL STUFF" AND "COMMON SENSE"

I conclude with three points. The first point concerns why so much attention is paid by Japanese to manners: What drives and motivates the practices of *aisatsu*? I have already linked *aisatsu* to larger projects in the introduction, but it is worth reiterating that sociolinguistic practices in Japan are driven in no small measure by politico-economic rationalization—not by timeless "tradition"—and should be regarded as generated by Japan's brisk march into modernization. *Aisatsu*, then, is part and parcel of bureaucratization (statism), rationalization (economic endeavors), and ritualization (daily manners). Though such processes are by no means limited to Japan, they are certainly salient in the Japanese sociopolity, and hierarchization, categorization, and standardization are better described as constituting a very modern "bureaucratic ethos" implicated in nation-state construction rather than premodern, feudalistic "traditional values." The patina of "tradition" provides current forms of civility with legitimacy, and sociolinguistic practices are an "aestheticization" of the state/capital nexus. *Aisatsu* is a grand project because it lubricates modern Japan's economic machinery, ensures statist control, and affirms Japanese ethnocultural heritage.

A second point concerns the close association between *aisatsu* and "common sense"; to violate civility indicates a lack of "common sense," or what is natural, normal, and socially expected. This "common sense of society" (*seken no jōshiki*) (Kitagawa, 1985, p. 38) is something that everyone should know, a theme reflected in etiquette guides such as *To Be a Member of Society with Common Sense: Encyclopedia of Etiquette* (Tanabe, 1989). Moreover, its practices are so ubiquitous and it is so embedded in the realm of taken-for-grantedness that it is pushed to the background of daily life, far from critical analysis. Civility is a hegemonic institution par excellence in the sense that it is best characterized as "natural": Very few Japanese would argue that less of it is needed, though not surprisingly many complain that there is not enough of it. It is also hegemonic in the sense that it is so deeply implicated in the grand projects of modernity; the flow of capital, rationalized social interaction, statist visions of order, ethnocultural "tradition," and national identity all converge in and are reproduced by civility.

The final point concerns the key role *aisatsu* has performed in building modern Japan. Gao writes that "the Japanese state has been able to achieve its policy objectives through nonstate institutions" and that "the development of many economic institutions that are usually labeled as private has in fact been driven by the industrial policy of the Japanese state" (1997, p. 295). I propose that *aisatsu* qualifies as an institution that in no small way assists the state/capital nexus in its policy objectives. Unlike other institutions as conventionally understood, *aisatsu* is admittedly very diffused and it is not always easy to discern the linkages between sociolinguistic practices and the sociopolity (though as state-sanctioned and -monitored sites, schools certainly qualify as official *aisatsu*-teaching organizations). As a practice that is ubiquitous and practiced by everyone and yet highly patterned and structured in its reproduction, acts of civility and *aisatsu* can be described as "interstitial institutions," the "social stuff" or "filler" that interlinks the array of institutions that form Japan's politico-economic system. *Aisatsu*, as a mundane practice, is an invisible institution tied to Japaneseness that provides a sense of "we-ness" and interlinks national identity with capitalism and statism.

NOTES

1. "Ethnocultural" refers herein to knowledge about a group of people, especially as it relates to the group's identity.

2. However, Tsuda reports that Japanese salespeople, with very few exceptions, treat customers with extreme courtesy (1984).

3. A more comprehensive treatment of the issues explored in this section can be found in McVeigh (1998b).

4. For my present purposes, it suffices to state that "public" has three meanings: (1) anything related to or for the collective interest and open to communal use; (2) institutions associated with state authority or officialdom; and (3) a socially recognized and organized forum in which an individual's opinions, interests, or self may be readily and freely expressed in front of a collectivity that safeguards such expressions. Civil society "can be applied to all those social relationships which involve the voluntary association and participation of individuals acting in their private capacities," and it is "a coming together of private individuals, an edifice of those who are otherwise strange to one another." Significantly, civil society is "clearly distinct from the state. It involves all those relationships which go beyond the purely familial and yet are not of the state" (Tester, 1992, p. 8).

REFERENCES

Abe, H., Shindō, M., & Kawato, S. (1994). *The government and politics of Japan.* Tokyo: University of Tokyo Press.

Bello, W. (1996). Neither market nor state: The development debate in south-east Asia. *The Ecologist, 26*(4), 167–175.

Billig, M. (1995). *Banal nationalism.* London: Sage.

Clancy, P. M. (1986). The acquisition of communicative style in Japanese. In B. Schieffelin & B. Ochs (Eds.), *Language socialization across cultures* (pp. 213–250). Cambridge: Cambridge University Press.

Donahue, R. T. (1998). *Japanese culture and communication: Critical cultural analysis.* Lanham, MD: University Press of America.

Dower, J. (1990). The useful war. *Daedalus, 119*(3), 49–70.

Fundamental law of education and school education law (F. Nakane, Trans.). (1977). EHS Law Bulletin Series. Tokyo: Eibun-Horeisha.

Gao, B. (1997). *Economic ideology and Japanese industrial policy: Developmentalism from 1931 to 1965.* Cambridge: Cambridge University Press.

Gerbert, E. (1993). Lessons from the *kokugo* (national language) readers. *Comparative Education Review, 37*(2), 152–180.

Gottlieb, N. (1996). *Kanji politics: Language policy and Japanese script.* London: Kegan Paul.

Hayashi, N. (1993, November 28). Naming and the power of suggestion. *Japan Times,* p. 15.

Huber, T. M. (1994). *Strategic economy in Japan.* Boulder, CO: Westview Press.

Isomura, E., & Kuronuma, M. (1974). *Gendai nihon no gyōsei* [Contemporary Japanese administration]. Tokyo: Teikokou Chihō Gyōsei Gakkai.

Johnson, C. (1982) *MITI and the Japanese miracle.* Stanford, CA: Stanford University Press.

Johnson, C. (1993). Comparative capitalism: The Japanese difference. *California Management Review, 35*(4), 51–67.

Kiritani, E. (1997, September 13). Some cultural peculiarities of politeness. *Daily Yomiuri*, p. 8.

Kitagawa, K. (1985). *Aisatsu no kotoba: kore dake shitte ireba jūbun* [Words of greeting: If you know just this it's enough]. Tokyo: Escargot Books.

Kitō, N. (1995). *Kokoro ni nokoru aisatsu—Words that remain in my heart.* Tokyo: The Japan Times.

Lebra, T. S. (1976). *Japanese patterns of behavior.* Honolulu: University of Hawaii Press.

Lewis, C. C. (1995). *Educating hearts and minds.* Cambridge: Cambridge University Press.

McVeigh, B. (1997). *Life in a Japanese women's college: Learning to be ladylike.* London: Routledge.

McVeigh, B. (1998a, December 5). *Manners, morals, and modernity: The political economics of Japanese politeness.* Paper presented at the conference of American Anthropological Association Meeting, Philadelphia, Pennsylvania.

McVeigh, B. (1998b). *The nature of the Japanese state: Rationality and rituality.* London: Routledge.

McVeigh, B. (1998c). Linking state and self: How the Japanese state bureaucratizes subjectivity through "moral education." *Anthropological Quarterly, 71*(3), 125–137.

McVeigh, B. (n. d.). "Lubricating" modernity: How political economy drives Japanese politeness (unpublished manuscript).

Miller, L. (1989). The Japanese language and honorific speech: Is there a *nihongo* without *keigo? Penn Linguistics Review, 13,* 38–46.

Miller, R. A. (1982). *Japan's modern myth: The language and beyond.* New York: Weatherhill.

Ministry of Education (1986a). *Shōgakkō: Omoiyari no kokoro o sodateru shidō* [Guidance for cultivating a heart of thoughtfulness in primary school]. Tokyo: Ministry of Finance.

Ministry of Education (1986b). *Chū gakkō: Omoiyari no kokoro o sodateru shidō* [Guidance for cultivating a heart of thoughtfulness in middle school]. Tokyo: Ministry of Finance.

Mizutani, O., & Mizutani, N. (1987). *How to be polite in Japanese.* Tokyo: The Japan Times.

Obana, Y., & Tomoda, T. (1994). The sociological significance of "politeness" in English and Japanese languages—Report from a pilot study. *Japanese Studies Bulletin, 14*(2), 37–49.

Respecting terms of respect. (1997, October 4). *Daily Yomiuri*, p. 6.

Tanabe H. (1989). *Jōshiki aru shakaijin de aru tame ni wa: Echiketto hyakka* [To be a member of society with common sense: Encyclopedia of etiquette]. Tokyo: Tsuchiya Shoten.

Teaching train etiquette. (1996, November 20). *Japan Times*, p. 20.

Tester, K. (1992). *Civil society.* London: Routledge.

Tsuda, A. (1984). *Sales talk in Japan and the United States.* Washington, DC: Georgetown University Press.

Twine, N. (1991). *Language and the modern state: The reform of written Japanese.* London: Routledge.

Unger, J. M. (1996). *Literacy and script reform in occupation Japan: Reading between the lines.* New York: Oxford University Press.

Wagakuni no bunka to bunka gyōsei [Our country's culture and culture administration]. (1988). Tokyo: Agency for Cultural Affairs.

Williams, D. (1994). *Japan: Beyond the end of history*. London: Routledge.

Yasuda T. (1978). *Tegami no kakikata* [How to write letters]. Tokyo: Kōdan-sha.

Chapter 7

The Great Hanshin Earthquake: The Japanese Response

Eamon McCafferty

The Japanese authorities were criticized at home and abroad for being unable to provide a timely and effective response to the Great Hanshin Earthquake of January 1995. Various institutional, legal, and political factors were identified as the primary causes, including contention surrounding Article 9 of the constitution, a wide diffusion of power, a weak prime minister, bureaucratic sectionalism, and a decision-making system characterized by consensus. By examining reactions during this crisis, as well as drawing parallels to previous and subsequent crises, salient aspects of what might be termed "Japaneseness" are highlighted: groupism; the hierarchical structuring diffused throughout society; and conflict (often resulting from the previous two) that is routinely checked by the high value placed on consensus and harmony. An examination of the debate in Japan in the immediate aftermath of the disaster unveils certain examples of this carefully restrained conflict, as well as types of discourse commonly used to reinforce what it means to be a good member of Japanese society.

At 5:46 a.m. on Tuesday, January 17, 1995, an earthquake measuring 7.2 on the Richter scale struck the city of Kobe and the surrounding Kansai area. The quake caused widespread devastation and a final death toll of more than 5,400 people, with more than 27,000 injured, approximately 300,000 made temporarily homeless, and over 100,000 buildings either destroyed or damaged (Sassa, 1995). For a country living under the constant threat of such types of natural disasters, both local and central authorities demonstrated a remarkable failure to respond effectively.

In this examination of the Japanese response to the earthquake, some distinctive features of "Japaneseness" are discussed. These cultural ideals are maintained by their enactment in daily life, as shown in both the government's lack of effective response to the devastating earthquake and in the ensuing debate that emerged. Also, an acknowledgment of the institutional, legal, and political factors that contributed to this situation can provide a rational approach to the study of Japaneseness. In so doing, I hope to avoid the kind of mystification of cultural differences prevalent in many studies of Japan (Ben-Ami, 1997).

JAPANESENESS

Often discussed in the literature on Japan are the attempts to explain Japanese "difference" by its "uniqueness." In fact, such is the quantity of debate on this topic that the notion of Japanese uniqueness has acquired its own label— *Nihonjinron*. Revell (1997, p. 53) defines *Nihonjinron* as "a body of literature, emanating from within Japan, that describes the character of the Japanese people and explains why they are different from other people or unique." Although Japanese culture is no more or less unique than any other, there are certain modes of behavior that are highly valued within it and, as such, are reinforced through discourse in everyday life. These ideals—what Befu (1980) calls "behavioral ideology"—are representations of Japaneseness in the same way certain reinforced values represent any culture. They qualify what it is to be a good member of society by following "the subtle codes, cues, and expectations set out in daily life to guide us to virtuous and acceptable human behavior" (Pharr, 1990, p. 21).

An examination of the manner in which both the Japanese government and the victims of the Great Hanshin (or Kobe) Earthquake responded to the disaster reveals a number of such "codes, cues, and expectations." These enactments of Japaneseness tended to fit the group model of Japanese society. Although this model recently has been criticized for failing to account for behavior not falling under its rubric, many of its main tenets form the idealized behavior within society. The model sees Japanese people acting within the framework of a hierarchically organized group that fosters interdependence among its members.

A key feature of the group model of Japanese society is that members are expected to conform to the norms of their group and preserve harmony within it by avoiding conflict. One way that this is achieved is by following formal and ritualized behavior, often with the purpose of reaching consensus before embarking on a given course of action. Implicit in these ideals is a concern for others before oneself. Emphasis is placed on cooperation rather than conflict and open competition (Befu, 1980, cited in Moeran, 1986).

THE AUTHORITIES RESPOND

The Prime Minister's Official Residence did not receive formal news of the quake until approximately 7:30 a.m., nearly two hours after the trembler struck. To put this in perspective, it was reported that Isao Nakauchi, chairman of the Kobe-based Daiei, Inc., supermarket chain, was already giving orders to his staff a full 30 minutes before this time ("Tokyo Response Shackled," 1995).

When the Japanese authorities did react, attention often focused on the process rather than the product. On January 19, more than 48 hours after the quake, Prime Minister Murayama decided to shift authority for the relief efforts from the National Land Agency (NLA) to a new Emergency Countermeasures Headquarters. This was set up the following day. Essentially, this was a liaison committee to coordinate relief efforts by government agencies overseeing economic affairs. This was changed from an Emergency Disaster Countermeasures Headquarters that the prime minister had claimed would be established the day before. The difference was that the latter would have given the prime minister much wider powers, such as being able to impose price controls and consolidate command over the separate relief activities of the Fire Defense Agency; Ground, Air, and Maritime Self Defense Forces; and police riot squads (Sassa, 1995). This unwillingness to concentrate power was shown by a cabinet minister's response to criticism over the inability to set up such a special task force with discretionary authority. Chief Cabinet Secretary Kozo Igarashi stated that under the "current situation" such a task force would give the prime minister too much power, which might lead to a restriction of the people's rights (Ueda, 1995). In an even more illuminating instance, when Kazutoshi Ito (director of the NLA's Disaster Prevention Coordination Division) was questioned at a news conference as to whether Japan should change its system, he angrily responded:

In an emergency like this one, if you are referring to the central government having the power to suppress and suffocate the will on the part of the local municipalities, it reminds me of the rebirth of Japanese militarism. In the name of the state of emergency, our country restricted the rights of the people and even trampled on the rights of the people. . . . I am firmly resolved we shall never, ever return back to the state of affairs that we were in fifty years ago. (T. Watanabe, 1995a, p. 2)

Several organizations in the strongest positions to help survivors of the earthquake, such as the Self Defense Forces (SDF) and the ministries, seemed to concentrate more on getting approval for their actions than on responding promptly to victims' needs. For example, the SDF, the only real nationwide organization trained and equipped to deal with disasters, did not begin organized mobilization until 4 hours after the quake struck (Yoshida, 1995). This was in spite of the fact that there was an SDF base within the immediate area that had already sent out helicopters to survey the scene. Although this survey team reported to their headquarters that the area had sustained considerable damage, no one there reported these findings to higher authorities. The prime minister was not informed. Neither was the Defense Agency chief, nor the National Disaster Prevention Bureau of the NLA, the organization assigned with supervision and coordination of government rescue operations in natural disasters. The reason for the 4-hour delay was that the SDF, acting under the SDF law, decided that it had to wait for a direct call for assistance from the prefecture of Hyogo. But as Atsushi Shimokobe, former vice minister of the NLA stated, "It must have been almost impossible for the Hyogo Governor, especially just after the quake, to draw up the necessary paperwork to ask for assistance from the Self Defense Forces" ("Response: Crisis Management," 1995, p. 19).

Many examples of bureaucratic delay, especially in connection with foreign offers of help, hampered rescue efforts. The central government received many international offers of emergency relief aid immediately after the quake, many of which were repeated after receiving no response. As of January 25, of the 52 countries, as well as the United Nations (UN), the World Health Organization (WHO), and the European Union (EU), that had offered help, 14 had been accepted ("Tokyo's Response to Offers," 1995). For example, the Health and Welfare Ministry substantially delayed an offer from Switzerland to send a res- cue team equipped with specially trained tracker dogs. It was reported that this was due to the ministry insisting on the usual requirement of temporary quaran- tine (Ueda, 1995). The Hyogo Prefecture government reportedly declined offers of help from several other Japanese prefectures, saying that they were not pre- pared to accept medical teams. Similarly, a French medical team was informed that they would not be allowed to help survivors because their doctors were not licensed under Japanese law. This was later overturned when the Health and Welfare Ministry announced that the Japanese laws concerned were not applica- ble in emergencies ("Lives or Laws," 1995). The England-based International Rescue Corps (IRC) were unable to receive prompt permission to enter Japan, despite their initial request being made at 6:16 a.m. (Japan time), only 30 min- utes after the quake. Despite trying all conceivable methods open to them, the IRC were unable to break through heavy bureaucratic resistance until they finally were requested by the Japanese government to attend relief duties on the morn- ing of Saturday, January 21. This was only after a direct appeal from the cousin of Sir Winston Churchill, a close friend of Japan's deputy planning minister (Holland, 1995). Naval vessels carrying food and other relief equipment were prevented from docking at Kobe port for several hours, because workers at the dock had not received any official orders to receive them ("Faith," 1995). A Japanese doctor, trained in disaster relief, told how he was unable to get SDF hel- icopters to ferry critically injured victims to hospitals in Osaka. The SDF office insisted that he follow normal bureaucratic procedures involving a five-step process involving several organizations. The doctor claimed to have lost 10 hours trying to unravel red tape (T. Watanabe, 1995a).

These examples are better understood with an examination of relevant aspects of the Japanese political system. Since the executive, the bureaucracy, and the SDF drew most criticism, they are examined further. Distribution of power, the decision-making process, and constitutional limitations all contributed to their responses.

The Japanese Political System

Power and Decision Making Within the Executive

Power is widely diffused among political actors in Japan. Indeed, Karel van Wolferen (1989) contends that power is, and has been for centuries, something that has been shared among various semiautonomous groups. There is, he claims, "a hierarchy, or, rather, a complex of overlapping hierarchies. But it has no peak; it is a truncated pyramid. There is no supreme institution with ultimate policy-making jurisdiction. Hence there is no place where, as Harry Truman would have said, the buck stops. In Japan the buck keeps circulating" (p. 7). Certainly, in the case of the earthquake, there was little evidence of anyone, including the prime minister, taking control of the situation quickly.

Within political parties, power is widely diffused among hierarchically organized factions. In his study of Japanese political parties, Kitaoka (1993, p. 35) calls this system, "a prescription for followership, not leadership." An emphasis on consensual decision making has also tended to produce leaders who are reactive rather than strong and assertive. The selection of leaders tends to place emphasis on long-serving politicians (nearly always faction leaders) who have worked within the system, establishing good relations with other faction leaders. This process tends to produce leaders who are hard-working and have a relatively low public profile (Hayao, 1993).

Central to decision making is the concept of *nemawashi*. Literally translating as "cutting around the roots of a plant before it is transplanted," it refers to the practice of careful consultation that takes place when a decision is needed, so that a consensus can be reached. It can be argued that *nemawashi*, by its very definition, stifles initiative in a crisis situation where timely responses are crucial.

The Bureaucracy

In a similar vein to the factionalization of political parties, prompt responses from ministries are hindered by deep sectionalism. In an elitist and exclusive system, bureaucrats have a strong sense of solidarity toward their individual ministries. In terms of responding to a crisis, this can lead to obvious pitfalls. As Kitaoka (1993, p. 39) states, "This sectoral approach works well when one policy or another needs minor adjustments, but it comes up short when problems with a broad scope must be resolved." This was the case in the aftermath of the earthquake. What was highlighted was the lack of any clear command structure to deal with the emergency. An editorial criticizing the response explained it in this way: "We hear too many complaints that for several days after the quake, officials at both high and low levels failed to comply with inquiries or requests from citizens because they had received no 'instructions from above.' This Japanese mind-set inherent in the vertically divided bureaucracy has been hampering the progress of relief efforts as badly as the politicians' insensitivity" ("Crisis Calls," 1995).

The Pacifist Constitution and Article 9

The Japanese Constitution is one of the most vital components in the make-up of postwar Japanese politics. The debate surrounding Japan's pacifist constitution has been central to the platforms of the major political parties and, in turn, to the direction taken on many major foreign policy issues. Article 9 is the most contentious. Its first paragraph states that the Japanese "forever renounce war," with paragraph 2 stating that "land, sea, or air forces, as well as other war potential will never be maintained." The rather ambiguous role of the SDF, therefore, has long been a hotly debated issue among the political parties and among the general public. In light of this, the SDF's initial timid response to the earthquake becomes more understandable.

THE PEOPLE RESPOND

As already noted, the media response to the government's crisis management was harsh, with many commentators pointing to the peculiarities of a political system that hampered speedy, coordinated relief efforts. Many of these comments were directed at aspects of Japaneseness that manifest themselves in organizational settings.

The behavior of the victims also received noteworthy remarks. Not only were they praised for their "characteristically Japanese" conduct, but they also were criticized when it was seen to be lacking. When interviewed, the words used by the victims themselves also highlighted what they saw to be proper behavior. In this way, a large part of the discourse concentrated on the aspects of Japaneseness that were seen to contribute positively or negatively to the overall handling of the disaster. This can be seen in the following examples, as reported in the national press.

Survivors of the quake often emphasized the importance of group or community spirit in overcoming their hardships. One resident of a temporary housing area that had formed its own "town council" commented: "Our council holds *karaoke* contests and events to promote communication among residents here. I think it is essential to form good relationships in a new place. This experience will help us build a new community after moving into permanent houses" (Nakamura, 1996, p. 3).

The importance of one's contribution to, and benefit from, the community was a strong theme. An elementary school headmaster said of his students: "Through the quake, they must have learned through experience how to deal with everyday life earnestly and pay due consideration towards others" ("Survivors Look Back," 1996, p. 2). A reverend at a memorial service said: "Some people have lost everything, but here in the ruins things are born anew, and we learn that even with nothing we can live if there is someone beside us" (Nakamura & Hay, 1996, p. 2). A year after the earthquake, one victim appealed for continued support in this way: "I think people outside quake-hit areas are losing interest in us. The national and local governments are also getting cool, and that's tough for us. We hope many people will look on us with warm hearts from now on" (Nakamura & Hay, 1996, p. 1).

In all of the above comments, the importance of the dependence on others is emphasized as an essential part of Japaneseness. This dependence is an essential part of belonging to a group, whose boundaries can change depending on the circumstances. For example, the last comment was an appeal to the Japanese as a people with a common national identity, for he expected widespread help.

The earthquake also highlighted the ordered way in which people conduct themselves, even under the worst of circumstances. A South Korean reporter noted that there were not any reports of looting or robbery of the kind seen in other countries. In commenting that a similar disaster would create chaos in his own country, he wrote: "I could not help admiring their spirit of perseverance, solidarity, civility, and, above all, voluntary observation of their civic duty and law and order" (Cho, 1995, p. 19). The need for order was even used as an excuse for slow responses to foreign offers of assistance by a foreign ministry official, who said: "Some people may say that the government should have invited the rescue teams in anyway. But it is important to first identify how and where foreign rescue teams can operate in detail, otherwise more confusion would arise after their arrival" ("Tokyo's Response to Offers," 1995, p. 4).

Highlighting the importance of order in establishing harmony, a politics professor wrote of "confused and restless conditions" when he bemoaned the lack of smooth administration by the coalition government headed by Murayama: "Specifically, the quake touched off 'disorder' throughout Japan's politics, economy, and society. In other words, there are some signs that the interlocking political, economic, and social network is beginning to loosen . . . underlying all of this is a spiritless atmosphere prevailing in the political world and a lack of leadership on the part of individual politicians in high places" (Uchida, 1995, p.18). Showing little regard for the victims of the disaster, one reader suggests rather strongly that their behavior was inappropriate. He accused them of "cowering in the emergency shelters, whining about how hungry and cold they were, without lifting a finger to join in helping the emergency rescue operations" (Iwamoto, 1995, p. 18).

Much discourse centered on the nature of Japaneseness itself. This may not be considered particularly surprising given that, "the Japanese manifest consuming interest in the question of who they are in a cultural sense, so much so that the discourse on Japanese identity may even be called a minor national pastime"

(Befu, 1993, p. 107). One reporter wrote, "The response of its officials and workers, victims and volunteers, mirrors the strengths and weaknesses of Japanese society itself. The disaster has illuminated the national psyche—a complex emotional tapestry of shame and pride, of dependence and fatalism, of the celebrated ability to "endure the unendurable" as the Emperor Showa urged his nation defeated by war" (T. Watanabe, 1995b, p. 19). In the same report, a doctor quoted a Japanese proverb to explain the shame in showing weakness: "Even samurai who don't eat hold a toothpick in their mouths." One young lady who considered canceling her overseas trip was hailed as having "exemplified the Japanese custom of cancelling trips, parties or sports events after a calamity. The practice is known as *jishuku* or self-restraint. . . . Mitsuru Inuta, professor of social psychology at Tokai University near Tokyo, said Japanese tend to feel guilty about conspicuous consumption, and self-restraint comes readily at times of national crisis" (C. Watanabe, 1995, p. 3).

Highlighting the custom of reaching agreement without resort to legal measures, one journalist reported on the slow speed with which some areas were being rebuilt: "Some people whose homes collapsed are finding it difficult to reach a consensus on the best way to rebuild, and the cost they are prepared to pay" (Nakamura, 1996, p. 3). In an offer to preserve harmony in possible disputes, "the local government is recommending that householders who need to repair a roof first check the cost carefully and consult with city officials. . . . [They] will mediate between consumers and companies over unfair pricing" ("City Warns," 1995, p. 2).

A final aspect of Japaneseness that media coverage illuminated was hierarchy, or rank consciousness. This area has been touched on already in the discussion of the authorities' response, but this rank consciousness was also shown to extend to the outside world. That is, the Japanese showed great concern for their place in the international community. Many reports referred to how things were done in other countries and showed an interest in what foreign observers thought of the Japanese response. Unfortunately, foreigners were often labeled as one large, indistinguishable group, reinforcing the idea of "us" and "the rest of them," an attitude that bolsters the myth of Japanese uniqueness (see Editorial Sampler, 1995, in *The Japan Times* for such examples from Japanese mass media).

CONCLUSION

In discussing the question of Japaneseness, one must be careful not to stereotype cultural ideals or values. Indeed, there is no doubt that examples could be given to contradict the relative importance of the aspects of Japaneseness I have highlighted. However, the point is that they are ideals—examples held up as proper ways to behave. Schwartz (1998, p. 18) puts it this way: "Values are neither heritable nor immutable. They are maintained and transmitted, and their reproduction allows for their recreation by power holders." I have shown the reproduction of ideals to some extent with the examples used here. How they might be manipulated by those involved in that process is a separate question, not within the scope of this chapter.

In the examples that have been presented, we have seen how particular qualities, lauded as appropriate ways to conduct oneself, do not always help in crisis situations requiring prompt decision making. Indeed, many lives were probably lost in the immediate aftermath of the Great Hanshin Earthquake due to delays caused by heavily bureaucratized responses, in part influenced by notions of "acting correctly." It can be assumed that when cultural ideals (having the wider purpose of keeping order within a given society) are seen to be ineffective in particular situations, it will be difficult to institute the kind of changes needed to allow more appropriate responses in the future. Such changes might be deemed common sense to those who have assimilated different values in another culture. However, common sense is culture specific. In a recent article that marked 4½ years passing since the earthquake's terrible destruction, the focus was on the repeatedly delayed construction of a large, five-story police box equipped with disaster-prevention equipment. With the half-completed project due to be tendered out for the fourth time, Tsunekawa (1999, p. 7) concluded: "Thus, preparations for dealing with disasters continue, and I hope that the police box project will eventually go smoothly." I would argue that the writer's measured response is, in itself, indicative of Japaneseness. The features of Japaneseness highlighted in this chapter, primarily the desire for harmony and consensus, and the results that this has on the way institutions organize and make decisions prevented a more efficient response to the devastating earthquake of 1995. Paradoxically, these same features also helped contribute to the dignified and ordered response of its victims.

REFERENCES

Befu, H. (1980). The group model of Japanese society and an alternative. *Rice University Studies, 66,* 169–187.

Befu, H. (1993). Nationalism and Nihonjinron. In H. Befu (Ed.), *Cultural nationalism in East Asia* (pp. 107–135). Berkeley: Institute of East Asian Studies, University of California.

Ben-Ami, D. (1997). Is Japan different? In P. Hammond (Ed.), *Cultural difference, media memories: Anglo-American images of Japan* (pp. 5–24). London: Cassell.

Cho, S. H. (1995, January 28). Lessons in disaster decorum for Korea. *The Japan Times,* p. 19.

City warns against inflated repair charges. (1995, January 29). *The Japan Times,* p. 2.

Crisis calls for a drastic change. (1995, January 26). *The Japan Times,* p. 20.

Editorial sampler. (1995, January 22). *The Japan Times,* p. 18.

Faith in the authorities fades. (1995, January 21–22). *Financial Times* (Asian edition), p. 9.

Hayao, K. (1993). *The Japanese prime minister and public policy.* Pittsburgh: University of Pittsburgh Press.

Holland, J. (1995). *International rescue corps: Team leader's report—Japan earthquake January 1995.* London: International Rescue Corps.

Iwamoto, S. (1995, January 22). Quake has exposed deeper problems. *The Japan Times,* p. 18.

Kitaoka, S. (1993). The bureaucratization of Japanese politics. *Japan Echo, 20*(2), 33–39.

Lives or laws. (1995, January 27). From the vernacular press [column]. *The Japan Times*, p. 18.

Moeran, B. (1986). Individual, group, and seishin: Japan's internal cultural debate. In T. S. Lebra & P. L. Lebra (Eds.), *Japanese culture and behavior: Selected readings* (Rev. ed., pp. 62–79). Honolulu: University of Hawai'i Press.

Nakamura, A. (1996, January 17). Kobe still struggling a year after the quake. *The Japan Times*, p. 3.

Nakamura, A., & Hay, C. (1996, January 18). Hanshin area remembers the quake. *The Japan Times*, pp. 1–2.

Pharr, S. J. (1990). *Losing face: Status politics in Japan.* Berkeley: University of California Press.

Response: Crisis management system questioned. (1995, January 23). *Nikkei Weekly*, p. 19.

Sassa, A. (1995). Fault lines in our emergency management system. *Japan Echo, 22*(2), 20–27.

Schwartz, F. J. (1998). *Advice and consent: The politics of consultation in Japan.* Cambridge: Cambridge University Press.

Survivors look back on lessons learned. (1996, January 17). *The Japan Times*, p. 2.

Tokyo response shackled by bureaucratic roadblocks. (1995, February 6). *Nikkei Weekly*, p. 1.

Tokyo's response to offers of help draws fire. (1995, January 27). *The Japan Times*, p. 4.

Tsunekawa, T. (1999, June 23). Lessons from killer quake. *The Daily Yomiuri*, p. 7.

Uchida, K. (1995, March 24). Spiritless politics prevail. *The Japan Times*, p. 18.

Ueda, T. (1995, February 3). Central authority lacking—scorn heaped on government response to quake. *The Japan Times*, p. 3.

van Wolferen, K. (1989). *The enigma of Japanese power.* London: Macmillan.

Watanabe, C. (1995, April 11). Self-restraint emerges in aftermath of quake. *The Japan Times*, p. 3.

Watanabe, T. (1995a, January 28). Official lashes out over quake criticism. *The Japan Times*, p. 2.

Watanabe, T. (1995b, January 28). Kobe's citizens forced to endure the unendurable, again. *The Japan Times*, p. 19.

Yoshida, R. (1995, January 22). SDF's role in rescue queried. *The Japan Times*, p. 4.

Chapter 8

Through the Ideological Filter: Japanese Translations of a Western News Source

Christopher Barnard

A critical linguistics approach is taken in this chapter to compare the language of the English-language Newsweek *magazine, and the Japanese-language version of the same. The author shows that there are considerable differences in the meanings created by the language of these two magazines that cannot be explained in terms of production constraints. It is argued that in the process of translation from English to Japanese, there are forms of ideological adjustment that take place in the dimension of power and in the dimension of information. Regarding the former, it is shown, for example, how Japanese* Newsweek *minimizes structural corruption in Japan. Regarding the latter, it is shown, for example, how voices of protest that are present in English* Newsweek *are silenced or muted in Japanese* Newsweek. *The research reported here seeks to answer questions regarding the media's role in the formation of public opinion in modern Japan, as well as its connections to governmental, bureaucratic, and business interests, and at the same time considers the potential ideological uses of translation.*

In recent years, there have been several well-known cases of the Japanese public learning about news related to Japan only after such news had been taken up by the foreign press. Examples of this are the revelations concerning the irregular financial affairs of former prime minister Kakuei Tanaka (Farley, 1996, pp. 146–148; Sherman, 1990, p. 38), the revelations concerning former prime minister Sōsuke Uno's liaison with a *geisha* (Farley, p. 142; Sherman, p. 38), and the news regarding the decision of crown prince Naruhito and Masako Owada to get married (Cooper-Chen, 1997, pp. 39–41; Farley, p. 138). Prior to the international reporting of these stories, the mainstream Japanese media knew about them but chose to maintain silence (Cooper-Chen, pp. 39–41; Farley, pp. 138–140; Sherman, p. 38). It thus seems likely that the news media in Japan practice a form of self-censorship that supports the power elite.

Although the full extent of this self-censorship is unknown, Japanese broadcast and print media are believed to be integrated with the power centers of Japanese society, including the bureaucracy and big business (Akhavan-Majid, 1990, p. 1006). Cooper-Chen (1997, p. 23) suggests that the journalists from mainstream media companies tend not to adopt a confrontational attitude to politicians or bureaucrats whom these journalists are covering and that the press traditionally has been allied with the government, rather than with the public (p. 26).

Revisionist writers (for a discussion, see Krauss, 1996, pp. 243–273), such as van Wolferen (1989), argue that the media in modern Japan practice a system of self-censorship that often actively serves the state and its governmental and administrative organs, as well as business interests. Yasunori Okadome, a non-mainstream Japanese magazine owner and editor, makes a similar point in a *Newsweek* interview ("Digging up Dirt," 1999):

I wanted to challenge the kind of issues that Japan's mass media consider taboo, such as the imperial family, powerful ministries, advertising giants and some religious organizations. I wanted to print the kind of articles that reporters in the field were dying to write but knew would be killed by their own editors.

In this same interview, Okadome says that the front pages of major Japanese dailies are almost identical since these dailies just print what they are given by politicians and bureaucrats.

To give a specific example of one of the taboos mentioned by Okadome ("Digging up Dirt," 1999), namely that concerning the imperial family, Irokawa (1995, p. 115), a Japanese historian, discusses how the Japanese press censored themselves with respect to the way they dealt with the illness and death of Emperor Hirohito in 1988 and 1989, and, furthermore, were uncritical when writing about the emperor's role in the war. Irokawa claims to see similarities with the behavior of the press at this time and its behavior during the wartime period. Pharr (1996), adopting a more balanced position, sees the Japanese media acting in a dualistic fashion—sometimes as an establishment mouthpiece, while at other times challenging and attacking the establishment.

A consideration of this range of positions sketched out above suggests that a data-based study is likely to throw light on the role of the media in Japan. For example, if indeed there is self-censorship, to what facts, opinions, and views does this self-censorship extend? Can an elucidation of the nature of putative news management give us a hint as to the issues or values that are at stake within Japanese society?

Outside Japan, a number of writers have looked at the nature of news reporting and media language from sociologically or politically oriented perspectives (e.g., Gitlin, 1980; Hallin, 1986; Herman & Chomsky, 1988), and have shown that the media certainly do not report events in an objective fashion. Linguistically grounded analyses of the media, particularly in the Australian, British, and continental traditions of critical discourse analysis and critical linguistics (e.g., Bell & Garrett, 1998; Blommaert & Verschueren, 1998; Fairclough, 1995; Fowler, 1991; Hodge & Kress, 1993), support the view that the media do not report the news exactly, "just as it is." My work, as reported in this chapter, is an example of the latter approach—an example of a linguistically grounded analysis.

Kress (1989, p. 7) suggests that we can ask the following three questions of any text: Why is this topic being written about? How is this topic being written? What other ways of writing about this topic are there? The first of these questions deals with the motivation for writing about the topic, the second with the slant or emphasis put on the way the topic is written, and the third question, by highlighting the multiplicity of ways of writing about the topic, reminds us that any text can be challenged by readers; its selection, presentation, and interpretation of information, as well as the taken-for-granted assumptions of the writer, can be held up to examination, and readers themselves are free to strive toward their own interpretations by, for example, reading between or behind the lines.

AN IDEOLOGICAL FILTER

Thompson writes (1990, p. 7) that ideology is *"meaning in the service of power"* (emphasis in original). He develops this as follows:

The analysis of ideology . . . is concerned with the ways in which meaning is mobilized in the social world and serves thereby to bolster up individuals and groups who occupy positions of power. Let me define this focus more sharply: *to study ideology is to study the ways in which meaning serves to establish and sustain relations of domination.* (p. 56; emphasis in original)

In this chapter, it is argued that in the translating of news from English *Newsweek* to Japanese *Newsweek* there are consistent adjustments of the message such that the translation produces meanings that bolster up individuals and groups who occupy positions of power in Japan. The metaphor I use for this is translation as an ideological filter.

I will say that an ideological filter is in operation if I can (a) identify consistent differences, both in content and grammar, between English *Newsweek* and

Japanese *Newsweek*, and (b) show that these differences potentially serve the interests of particular sections of society and, as a corollary, are likely to work against the interests of other sections of society.

TRANSLATION STUDIES

The "cultural turn" in translation studies (Bassnett, 1998; Lefevere & Bassnett, 1995) addresses such questions as (a) how knowledge is produced in one culture and then transmitted, relocated, and reinterpreted in another culture; (b) how translation affects both the originating and, more importantly, the receiving culture; and (c) how a culture translates material that in its original form is perhaps uncomfortable, or contrary to, well-established beliefs that exist within that culture.

The translator, the mediator between two languages, makes choices regarding what to transfer to readers in the receiving culture. These choices, as Álvarez and Vidal (1996, p. 5) write, are meaningful, culturally significant, and culturally determined:

It is essential to know what the translator has added, what he has left out, the words he has chosen, and how he has placed them. Because behind every one of his selections there is a voluntary act that reveals his history and the social-political milieu that surrounds him; in other words his own culture.

This is, as it were, the "translation version" of Kress's third question: What other ways of translating this are there? And, as a corollary: What other meanings would have been created by other choices that the translator could have made?

Bassnett (1998, p. 136) highlights the potential political uses of translation, while at the same time reminding us that translations can dissemble:

Translation, of course, is a primary method of imposing meaning while concealing the power relations that lie behind the production of that meaning. If we take censorship as an example, then it is easy to see how translation can impose censorship while simultaneously purporting to be a free and open rendering of the source text.

Both Álvarez and Vidal's (1996) position, as well as that of Bassnett (1998), would suggest that a comparison of original news articles with their translated versions might tell us much about societies; their social values, political values, and sensitive or taboo subjects; the differing limits of reasonable or possible debate within the different societies; and so on.

DESIGN OF THE STUDY[1]

In this chapter, I compare original news articles and their translations and attempt to ascertain what this tells us about the role of the media in present-day Japan. In order to do this, I examine the difference between the original English

Newsweek and the translated Japanese *Newsweek*[2] and seek to establish the nature and significance of this difference.

It is important to stress that this chapter is not an investigation into whether English *Newsweek* or Japanese *Newsweek* is more truthful, nor is English *Newsweek* being set up as a benchmark of truth, against which Japanese *Newsweek* is judged. What I wish to do is to identify patterns of difference between English *Newsweek* and Japanese *Newsweek*, argue that these patterns of difference produce meaning differences, and suggest that what we see is an example of an ideological filter in operation. Thus, such meaning differences, rather than involving questions of right and wrong, or truth and falsity, involve omission of material, completeness or incompleteness of information, frankness of the message, emphasizing or deemphasizing certain points, and so on. It must also be mentioned that TBS-Britannica, the publisher of Japanese *Newsweek*, is a Japanese company (*TBS-Britannica,* 1999), whose ties to Newsweek Incorporated, the American company, are of a contractual and commercial nature.

This chapter is based on my research into all articles dealing with Japan and Japanese-related matters that appear in both the English version of the American weekly magazine *Newsweek* (the Asian edition available in Japan) and the Japanese version of this magazine, within the period 1/1/99 to 8/31/99. This comprises a total of 15 articles, accounting for a total of approximately 30 pages (including photographs, graphs, illustrations, etc.) in English *Newsweek*.

My analysis takes two mutually reinforcing approaches. First, I examine content, looking particularly for omissions or abridgements of English *Newsweek* material in Japanese *Newsweek*. Second, I examine vocabulary and grammar and show that the differences in the meanings created by the language of English and Japanese *Newsweek* support the content analysis and cannot simply be explained away in terms of differences between the English and Japanese languages.

The word "translation" as used in this chapter includes translation proper, as well as such processes as selection, rewriting, and editing. Thus, it covers all the processes that change English *Newsweek* into Japanese *Newsweek*. My assumption is that the process of translation is from English to Japanese. This is obviously a simplification and, in some cases, must be incorrect—especially with reference to articles about Japan, where, say, a Japanese informant was perhaps interviewed by a Japanese journalist and then the interview translated into English; in such cases, Japanese would be the original language and English the target language. In fact, there are several permutations of interviewing, interpreting, and translation, concerning which I cannot know the details.

In a study such as this, there are two problems that have nothing more than unsatisfactory solutions. First, there is the question of what data to choose to analyze and discuss. Selecting widely from among the 15 different articles in order to illustrate particular points is likely to confuse readers. What I have done is to arrive at general conclusions based on an examination of all the articles, and then illustrated these general conclusions using a small number of articles. The second problem concerns how to present the data. The solution I have used is to present extracts from English *Newsweek*, but with the parts that do not exist in the Japanese translation printed in bold. Thus, it is possible to get an accurate idea of the information contained in Japanese *Newsweek* by reading the English, skipping over the parts that are in bold. Sometimes the nature of the English and Japanese texts makes this rather difficult to do and confusing. In such cases, instead of using bold, I have made literal translations from Japanese into English.[3] The appendix contains the romanized version of this Japanese material.

All quotations are referenced by page, with the page reference to Japanese *Newsweek* given even when only the English article is quoted. When material does not exist in the Japanese version, I have referenced where it would probably be, if it were there. References are enclosed in parentheses, with "EN" standing for English *Newsweek*, and "JN" standing for Japanese *Newsweek*. The articles I discuss are:

1. *FSA* (Financial Supervisory Agency): An article on the recently established government agency charged with sorting out Japan's banking and financial problems (Kattoulas, 1999;[4] "Ginkō Kirisute," 1999).

2. *Konishiki*: An article on the American sumo wrestler (Kattoulas & Wehrfritz, 1999;[5] "Sumō ni Miru," 1999).

3. *Viagra*: An article comparing the ease with which Viagra won approval with the fact that the Pill has not yet been approved (Itoi, 1999a,[6] 1999b).

ANALYSIS OF THE DATA

In looking at these three articles, I show that there are consistent ideological adjustments related to the *dimension of power* and the *dimension of information*.

The Dimension of Power

The dimension of power deals with the structure of power within Japanese society and considers such questions as where power is located, who the power holders are, how their power is structured and shared, and how it is used. This dimension is divided into *insider networks* and *uses of power*.

Insider Networks

This refers to the existence of networks of insiders who have access to power, authority, prestige, money, and so on—perhaps in some morally questionable or favored way, and especially in a way that is the result of existing structures within Japanese society. The existence, membership, or workings of such insider networks may not be known to ordinary Japanese people. First, let us consider an example from the FSA article:

1. In November, the FSA forcibly nationalized Nippon Credit Bank—**reputedly a major underwriter of Finance Minister Kiichi Miyazawa's political faction**—for failing to put its balance sheet in order. (EN, p. 18C; JN, p. 20)

Reference to the possible existence of a collusive financial–political complex within Japan has been omitted from the Japanese version, as well as an important politician's name. It could be argued that this is a parenthetical, and unsupported, aside by the writer, and to cast doubts on the integrity of the Japanese finance minister in a Japanese-language magazine published in Japan is a very different matter from doing the same thing in an international English-language magazine. Therefore it is quite natural that this aside is omitted from Japanese *Newsweek*.

But the point is that the above omission is part of a pattern of omission; in Japanese *Newsweek,* there are *consistent* omissions with respect to insider networks, as in 2 and 3 below. Number 2 refers to an insider network within the world of sumo itself; 3 refers to the general existence of insider networks (i.e., "cronyism") within Japan and suggests that these networks extend their influence to the world of sumo (and thus, much of what goes on in the stadium lacks "transparency"):

2. Watching over sumo's rituals with a protective eye is the ultraorthodox Sumo Association, **made up of leading members of Japan's business, cultural and political elite**. (EN, p. 51; JN, p. 53)

3. **As Japan comes under pressure to abandon the cronyism of the past and embrace globalization, fans are clamoring for more transparency in the stadium, too.** (EN, p. 53; JN, p. 53)

In 4, the power and influence of the Sumo Association are frankly stated in English *Newsweek*, but, with the absence of an equivalent to "stranglehold" in the Japanese, minimized in Japanese *Newsweek*:

4. Some fans would like to break the association's stranglehold over the sport, which seems frozen in ancient times. (EN, p. 52)

Translation: From among fans, a voice has started to come forth that the Sumo Association should change its outmoded ways. (JN, p. 53)

Putting 2, 3, and 4 together, we can see that readers of Japanese *Newsweek* are not told, as readers of English *Newsweek* are, that an "elite" has a "stranglehold" over sumo such that much of what goes on in the stadium lacks "transparency." Instead, readers of Japanese *Newsweek* are told that the Sumo Association is "protective" of sumo and some fans want it to change its "outmoded ways." Surely these are very different stories.

Money, or more precisely structurally organized flows of money, is something that Japanese *Newsweek* consistently shies away from mentioning, as in 1 earlier.

But in fact, according to English *Newsweek*, it exists in the sumo world, as well as in the political world:

5. Sumo's **old guard** resisted Konishiki to the finish. When he decided to retire in 1997, they tried to take his fighting name, claiming it wasn't his to use. **The dispute was about money. The association, which once banned wrestlers from doing sideline promotional work, lifted the restriction in 1995 but demanded a huge cut of any deal. In response, Konishiki resigned from the association. After a fight,** the association allowed Konishiki to use his ring name, but only in English. **In the symbolism-drenched world of sumo, it was the ultimate denial of his legitimacy as a wrestler.** (EN, p. 54; JN, p. 54)

The English story and the Japanese story are very different. The Japanese version has minimized the insider element (omission of "old guard"), removed the money element (and by so doing clouded the whole matter of why the parties behaved as they did), minimized the acrimony of the dispute (omission of "After a fight") as well as the relegating of Konishiki to the role of an outsider to the world of sumo ("denial of his legitimacy as a wrestler"). Note also how the English writer's disapproving attitude conveyed in, for example, "demanded a huge cut of any deal," which suggests an unfair practice, is not present in the Japanese version.

Together with the minimizing of structurally organized flows of money, Japanese *Newsweek* is also very careful about the way it handles structural corruption, by which I mean corruption that is built into the system. Individual cases of corruption can be freely reported, systemic corruption is another matter altogether. I interpret 6 to mean that stable masters fix fights in sumo, at least occasionally:

6. **To stalwarts, his [Konishiki's] ascent violated sumo's rigid ranking system, a hierarchy that requires young warriors to pay heavy dues and wait their turn, even when that means heeding a stable master's order to throw a bout.** (EN, p. 53; JN, p. 54)

The whole idea of low-interest financing to certain sections of the economy (another example of structurally organized flows of money) is carefully dealt with, as we see in the FSA article:

7. Japan's banks never really outgrew their postwar assignment, which was essentially to dole out policy loans. Under the so-called "convoy" system, they channeled funds to strategic industries while the Finance Ministry shielded them from outside competition and guaranteed every bank in the convoy a profit. (EN, p. 18C)

Translation: Japanese banks, which after the Second World War, under the so-called "convoy system" played the role of supplier of financing to key industries, did not grow beyond such an existence. The Ministry of Finance excluded competition from outside and guaranteed every bank a profit. (JN, p. 20)

"Playing the role of a supplier of financing" is certainly not the same thing as "doling out policy loans." The writer's disapproving attitude toward this system is hinted at in English *Newsweek* by the use of "essentially" (i.e., "this is pretty much all they had to do"), but absent from Japanese *Newsweek*. We see an omitting of the same idea of structurally organized flows of money in 8 below:

8. The Long Term Credit Bank's **spectacular** collapse last October sank the convoy system forever. **Established after the war to write cheap loans for heavy industry, it branched into real estate, and during the go-go 1980s bankrolled everything from Australian vacation resorts to French Impressionist masterpieces.** (EN, p. 18C; JN, p. 20)

The pattern shown in the two preceding extracts from the same article, of either downplaying cheap loans (as in 7) or of omitting reference to them (as in 8), suggests a consciously motivated choice.

Uses of Power

This refers to the fact that, with the concentration of power in the hands of the government, the bureaucracy, economic interest groups, and individual companies, there is the possibility that such organizations do not use this power wisely and may abuse it by committing irresponsible, immoral, or criminal acts.

In 9, a striking difference appears between English *Newsweek* and Japanese *Newsweek*. As in 8, the Japanese version minimizes abuse of power and authority and the irresponsibility that contributed to Japan's banking crisis:

9. It wasn't a merry Christmas for Japan's troubled bankers. On Dec. 25, the new Financial Supervisory Agency issued a scathing report on the scale of Japan's bad-debt crisis. It criticized the country's 17 largest banks for underreporting—even hiding—nonperforming loans valued at $600 billion. (EN, p. 18B)

Translation: It was not at all a merry Christmas for Japanese bankers. Last year on Dec. 25, the Financial Supervisory Agency announced the results of its intensive investigation into Japanese banks. According to this, 19 [sic] leading banks together underreported nonperforming loans of 7.3 trillion yen. (JN, p. 19)

In the Japanese version, there is almost no criticism directed at the banks from the FSA; there are no equivalents of "scathing" and "criticized." Also, the obfuscation and possible illegal behavior of the banks are not present in the Japanese version (omission of "even hiding"). English *Newsweek*, furthermore, suggests some calamity in the banking industry by referring to bankers as "troubled." So, between the two, the English article suggests the greater possibility for criticism of bankers than does the Japanese article. This is important, since these are the first sentences of the respective articles and, thus, set the tone for these articles.

In 9, the banks are absolved of responsibility by Japanese *Newsweek*. In the following extract, the Ministry of Finance is likewise absolved of responsibility:

10. The FSA, established last July **to relieve the policy-oriented Finance Ministry of its sweeping supervisory powers,** has moved quickly to facilitate—and even demand—reform. It's led by Masaharu Hino, former senior prosecutor at the Justice Ministry, **who won the post because the Finance Ministry and Bank of Japan are so tarnished by scandal. Hino has attacked the job with a lawman's zeal.** (EN, p. 18C; JN, p. 20)

Not only is the implication that the Finance Ministry had too much power and did not use it wisely omitted from the Japanese version, but the thrust of the whole paragraph disappears: namely that the ministry was so tarnished by scandal that a "lawman" was needed. I think we all know how serious the situation has become when a "lawman" is needed to sort things out.

The Japanese version gives no explanation of *why* a prosecutor was needed for what would seem to be normally an economist's job. Omissions have thus left readers of Japanese *Newsweek* less informed than readers of English *Newsweek*, perhaps even confused.

The minimizing of references to irresponsibility and possible abuse of power in Japanese *Newsweek* are common, and it is easy to find examples:

11. In the 1980s, when some of their traditional clients started needing them less, the bankers began funneling vast fortunes into speculative real-estate schemes. They skipped the credit analysis and simply accepted the overvalued properties as collateral. When Japan's asset bubble burst in 1992, hundreds of billions of dollars' worth of debt turned bad. (EN, p.18C)

Translation: In the 1980s, when some of their traditional clients started needing them not as much as previously, the banks provided financing with overvalued real estate as collateral, and this turned to non-performing loans with the bursting of the bubble at the beginning of the 1990s. (JN, p. 20)

There is a difference between the English and Japanese not only in information given (e.g., the fact that the Japanese banks skipped the credit analysis), but also the tone of the first sentence of the English version, which conveys the disapproving attitude of the writer of the English version, with its image of money sloshing around in a rather irresponsible manner, is absent from the Japanese version.

Note that the omission concerning the skipping of credit analysis results not only in loss of information, but avoids suggesting untoward action on the part of the banks by omitting "skipped" and "simply." These two words in English *Newsweek* give the impression that the banks' actions were purposeful, rather than just unavoidable error.

In the English version, responsibility is placed on the banks, who are portrayed as not only "speculating," but actually speculating in "schemes." In Japanese *Newsweek*, the use of the word "overvalued" (without mentioning who was responsible for this overvaluing) does not necessarily place responsibility on the banks.

In short, the English version portrays bad banking practice and irresponsibility; the Japanese version is a story of reasonable banking practice and bad luck. I provide another example but reserve comment on it until later:

12. Management consultant **and best-selling author** Kenichi Ohmae warns that Japan's banks remain so intertwined that one major collapse could bring them all down. **"There's no such thing as good banks and bad banks," he says, "only bad practice." And, at least until recently, those bad practices have been nearly universal.** (EN, p. 18C; JN, p. 20)

These examples illustrate the consistent way Japanese *Newsweek* minimizes irresponsibility, bad banking and supervisory practice, and abuse of power within the financial world. These examples, considered together with 13 below, strongly suggest conscious motivation on the part of Japanese *Newsweek*:

13. Another sign of a changing climate: Japanese officials are finally acknowledging both the depth of their nation's banking crisis and the Finance Ministry's complicity in creating it. (EN, p. 18C)

Translation: Japanese officials have finally come to acknowledge the depth of the financial crisis and the Finance Ministry's responsibility. (JN, p. 20)

In 13, the Finance Ministry has been absolved of responsibility by Japanese *Newsweek*, this time by a subtle shading of the translation. The Japanese language is capable of differentiating between "complicity" and "responsibility," if not by rather direct translation, at least by some sort of explanatory circumlocution.

The Dimension of Information

The dimension of information deals with the dissemination of information within Japanese society and considers such questions as who has access to information, what kinds of information are widely broadcast or not widely broadcast, how information is adapted or altered, why this occurs, and how people, groups, or organizations who wish to present information to the general public are muted or silenced. This dimension is divided into "information control" and "silencing others."

Information Control

This refers to the existence of a form of information control that includes not making known to the general public information that they may reasonably believe to be in their interest to know. The information that information itself is being controlled also falls under this heading, as shown by this example:

14. **Anti-Pill propaganda has been so effective that only 7 percent of Japanese women say they even want oral contraceptives.** (EN, p. 17; JN, p. 27)

Also, the fact that information, whose dissemination is probably in the public interest, is not disseminated is mentioned in English *Newsweek*, but not Japanese *Newsweek*:

15. More than 70 percent of women polled cited fear of side effects as the reason they wouldn't use the Pill. Horiguchi [a gynecologist] blames such attitudes on a lack of public information. "Most women don't know what the effects are, or what improvements have been made over the years," she says. (EN, p. 17; JN, p. 27)

Thus, putting 14 and 15 together, we have a picture of the Japanese people being actively propagandized, as well as not being given information that any responsible person might think it is his or her right to have. This latter point we see again in the following example:

16. If the [women's-rights] activists didn't help, perhaps international pressure will. **Hope springs eternal**: there are rumors that the ban will be lifted later this year. **Neither the Health Ministry nor pharmaceutical firms will comment.** (EN, p. 17; JN, p. 27)

Certainly, there might well be a good reason for the disinclination of the Health Ministry and pharmaceutical firms to comment. But the point is that while readers of English *Newsweek* can question this reason, readers of Japanese *Newsweek* cannot, since they are not told about this disinclination in the first place.

The possibly arrogant and unsympathetic position of the ministry and the pharmaceutical firms toward the Japanese people is not conveyed by Japanese *Newsweek*. Also, the linking of the Health Ministry and the pharmaceutical firms may raise questions in the minds of readers of English *Newsweek*: Do these two parties themselves constitute an insider network that regards the general public as the outsider? Why is there this positioning of the Ministry of Health and pharmaceutical firms on one side of the fence and, by implication, the general public on the other side of the fence ("will not comment to the general public")? Surely the Ministry of Health should represent the interests of the general public more than the interests of pharmaceutical firms. English *Newsweek* allows readers to question all this. Such lines of questioning are completely shut off to Japanese readers.

Silencing Others

This refers to the silencing or partial silencing of the voices of people who demand certain rights, assurances, or protection, or who question, object, or protest. This is done by omitting them, their objections, the strength of their feelings, the capacity or role in which they are acting, or the qualifications and expertise they may possess. This includes cases in which the voice of the writer of the article in English *Newsweek* is silenced (or partially silenced) in the Japanese translation—simply by omission or, more subtly, by a process of muting or toning down. Numbers 5, 10, and 14 contain examples of this.

In Japanese *Newsweek*, advocacy is very often minimized. There is an example in 15, in which Horiguchi's voice, when she is assigning blame, is not present in the Japanese version. In the following example, the advocacy role of Kitamura is present in English *Newsweek*, but not in Japanese *Newsweek*:

17. According to Kunio Kitamura, a gynecologist and family planning advocate, 40 percent of women who have abortions end up having another—and another. (EN, p. 17)

Translation: According to Kunio Kitamura, Head of the Japan Family Planning Association Clinic, 40 percent of women who have an abortion receive another abortion operation. (JN, p. 27)

In the same Viagra article, Japanese *Newsweek* omits the fact that a pro-Pill activist is a pharmacist (and therefore presumably capable of making judgments based on training and expertise). In other words, voices are not allowed to be too loud or too insistent, and ordinary people are not allowed to be too expert. An example of this exists in number 12. Kenji Ohmae's status ("best-selling author") is omitted and his voice is muted. His words in reported speech that describe the current situation are given in the Japanese version, but his actual words given in quotation marks, which describe the reasons for the situation, are omitted from the Japanese version. This is followed by the silencing of the comment by the writer of the English article: "And at least until recently, those bad practices have been nearly universal."

This silencing of the voice of English *Newsweek* writers by the translators of Japanese *Newsweek* is one of the most interesting types of silencing that occurs in Japanese *Newsweek*. One would expect the opinions of the writers of English *Newsweek*, and the fruits of their journalistic expertise, to be heavily relied on by Japanese *Newsweek*. But such is clearly not the case when these writers step over the line by speaking too frankly or saying too much about insider groups, money flows, abuse of power, and information control in Japanese society.

In the Viagra article, the first example of this is in the headline, "The Great Viagra Emergency." For me at least, this is related to expressions of the type that are used in a joking, tongue-in-cheek way to suggest that there is no emergency at all. The translation of the Japanese headline is "Contradictions That Viagra Exposed" ("*Baiagura ga abaku mujun*").

This same attitude on the writer's part is suppressed in 18 below, where the writer is suggesting reasons why Viagra was approved so quickly:

18. Others speculate that the aim is to help boost Japan's birthrate **(currently only 1.39 children per woman) and avoid a population crash. The government has its own explanations. Lots of them.** The Ministry of Health and Welfare says it's trying to shorten the review process for all drugs, **not just Viagra.** And impotence is a medical problem, meaning official action on Viagra is a matter of public urgency. **Without cracking a smile,** the bureaucrats say the Pill can wait because it's for *healthy* women. (EN, p. 17; JN, p. 27)

This paragraph criticizes the government and bureaucracy in the same tongue-in-cheek way, and at the same time suggests that they are arrogant and less than honest and forthright when giving information. "Lots of them" suggests that the government can make up any kind of explanation it wishes, whenever it wishes;

"Without cracking a smile" suggests that the bureaucrats are laughing up their sleeves, while holding the public in low regard.

In 19, the cynicism expressed in "Hope springs eternal," suggesting that nothing will ever change, is absent from the Japanese.

19. If the activists didn't help, perhaps international pressure will. **Hope springs eternal:** (EN, p. 17; JN, p. 27)

It is certainly possible to argue that this kind of cynical, tongue-in-cheek humor cannot be translated easily into Japanese, or even if it could be, it would be inappropriate in a magazine like Japanese *Newsweek*—irrespective of whether it is appropriate or not in English *Newsweek*. However, this does not alter the fact that the English article by means of its cynicism criticizes the Japanese establishment and holds its actions up to questioning and examination. The Japanese article does nothing like this; it makes no attempt to pierce the facade of the establishment.

Even if there are reasons for not translating the cynical humor of the English text, surely the writer's loud cry of anger and indignation, in the last sentence, could be conveyed in the Japanese version of the following—but is not.

20. Reviewing a new drug for sale in Japan usually requires a minimum of two years. The manufacturers of Viagra won approval in an unprecedented six months. Meanwhile, despite decades of clinical research, Japan remains the only member of the United Nations where the Pill is banned. **The blatancy of the legal double standard is not only frustrating—it's infuriating.** (EN, p. 17; JN, p. 27)

The frustration of the writer is also present in the following extract, although not so loudly.

21. Japan's health minister opined in 1992 that the Pill might increase risk of AIDS infection because people would stop using condoms. **Last year the Health Ministry announced yet another concern: the risk of environmental pollution by chemical hormones that are flushed out of Pill takers into waste water.** "I don't know how many times we heard it was getting close," recalls Horiguchi, "but they always come up with some excuse." (EN, p. 17; JN, p. 27)

The writer's cynical view that "the government can always think up something or the other" is most strongly signaled by "announced yet another concern." The signaling of this attitude, followed by the other concern (namely hormones in waste water), suggests that this other concern is not a real one, but has been thought up just to block the introduction of the Pill. The comment by Horiguchi must be seen in this light: She is frustrated because she knows that the government can always block arguments for introducing the Pill by thinking up one more excuse. Thus, Horiguchi's frustration is more vividly portrayed in English

Newsweek than in Japanese *Newsweek*. In this one paragraph, the translation conveys neither the cynical attitude of the writer nor the full frustration of the gynecologist. Their voices have been silenced or muted.

CONCLUSION

The "translation version" of Kress's (1989, p. 7) third question is: What other ways of translating this are there? The design of this study allows us to answer this question with respect to the Japanese *Newsweek* articles, by referring to the corresponding English *Newsweek* articles. When we find that there is a conspicuous difference between the English article and the corresponding Japanese article, we must ask: If there were not this difference, what would the Japanese article look like, and what meanings would it convey to readers? Both the differences between English *Newsweek* and Japanese *Newsweek*, and the realization that Japanese *Newsweek* could have been written in other ways, allow us to strongly question, to challenge, the position of Japanese *Newsweek*.

Since these differences constitute a *pattern*, it is not tenable to say they are mainly due to differences between the English and Japanese languages, time constraints in translation, space constraints in Japanese *Newsweek*, design and layout decisions, other matters related to the production process of Japanese *Newsweek*, and differences regarding background knowledge or interests of Japanese readers as opposed to English readers, and so on.

To argue that an ideological filter is in operation, I have said that it is necessary to (a) identify consistent differences, both in content and grammar, between English *Newsweek* and Japanese *Newsweek*, and (b) show that these differences potentially serve the interests of particular sections of society and, as a corollary, are likely to work against the interests of other sections of society.

In a linguistically grounded discussion such as this, it is easier to satisfy (a), which I believe I have done. However, given the nature of the phenomena that have to be investigated, to satisfy (b) is a harder task. Nevertheless, my claim is that the analysis presented here does very strongly suggest that what we see in the Japanese *Newsweek* data presented in this chapter is the conscious manipulation of language for political purposes, by which I mean a manipulation of facts, opinions, meanings, and nuances that serves the interests of certain sections of Japanese society and probably works against the interests of others.

A simple thought experiment will go a long way toward satisfying (b) above. Readers can go back and look at the data presented here, comparing the English versions and the Japanese versions, and ask themselves the following kind of question: Would Mr. Miyazawa, the Ministry of Finance, Japanese bankers, the Sumo Association, sumo stable masters, and the Ministry of Health prefer the stories as they are written in English *Newsweek* or in Japanese *Newsweek*? In almost all cases, the answer is "Japanese *Newsweek*."

Readers can then ask themselves these kinds of questions: Would Japanese tax-payers who are bailing out the banks, people who are angry with the Ministry of Finance, ordinary sumo fans, and people who want women to have access to the Pill find the stories as written in English *Newsweek* or Japanese *Newsweek* more interesting? Which stories would make such people angry or indignant—the stories in English *Newsweek* or the ones in Japanese *Newsweek*? In almost all cases, the answer is "English *Newsweek*."

Thus, when we answer these questions, it is clear that Japanese *Newsweek* is, at least as far as the three articles considered in this chapter are concerned, consistently representing certain interests within Japan. The fact that a preliminary study based on all 15 articles informed the present study of just three articles suggests that the conclusions drawn from these three articles are typical and representative of Japan-related articles in Japanese *Newsweek*. Of course, to what extent the findings of this study are generalizable to Japanese mainstream media as a whole is a subject that requires further research.

APPENDIX: ROMANIZED VERSION OF THE JAPANESE EXAMPLES

The numbers in parentheses refer to the numbering of the examples in the body of the chapter.

(4) Fan no aida de wa, Sumō Kyōkai wa furukusai yarikata o kaeru-beki da to iu koe mo dehajimete iru.

(7) Dainiji-taisen go, iwayuru "gosōsendan-hōshiki" no shita de jūyō-sangyō no shikin chōtatsu-yaku o tsutometa Nihon no ginkō wa, sore ijō no sonzai ni wa seichō-shi-nakatta. Ōkurashō wa gaibu to no kyōsō o shadan-shi, subete no ginkō ni rieki o hoshō-shite kita.

(9) Nihon no bankā-tachi ni totte wa, chittomo "merī-kurisumasu" de wa nakatta. Sakunen 12-gatsu 25-nichi, Kinyūkantoku-chō wa ginkō ni taisuru shūchū-kensa no kekka o happyō. Sore ni yoru to, ōte 19-kō wa awasete 7-chō 3000-oku en mo no furyō-saiken o kashō ni jikosatei-shite ita.

(11) 1980-nendai ni natte jūrai no kokyaku no ichibu ga izen hodo ginkō o hitsuyō to shi-naku naru to, ginkō wa kadaihyōka-sareta fudōsan o tanpo ni yūshi o okonai, sore ga 90-nendai hajime no baburu-hōkai ni yotte furyō-saiken to ka-shita.

(13) Kinyū-kiki no shinkokusa to Ōkurashō no sekinin o, Nihon no kanryō mo tsui ni mi-tomeru yō ni natta no da.

(17) Nihon Kazoku Keikaku Kyōkai Kurinikku no Kitamura Kunio shochō ni yoru to, chūzetsu-shita josei no 40% wa futatabi chūzetsu-shujutsu o ukeru to iu.

NOTES

1. I wish to express my sincere thanks to my friend Stephen Church, who with his knowledge of the health-care industry and his detailed readings and interpretations of *Newsweek* articles ("E. Coli Alert," English *Newsweek*, pp. 36–41, Sept. 1, 1997, and the

equivalent article in Japanese *Newsweek*, "Hanbāgā ga kieta," pp. 28–31, Sept. 3, 1997) dealing with an E. coli O157 contamination (food poisoning) incident in the United States, demonstrated to me that there were substantial differences between these two articles and that there were grounds for believing that these differences reflected a system of self-censorship in Japanese *Newsweek*, in this case related to the Japanese Ministry of Health and Welfare's concern with slaughterhouse regulation.

2. I use the term Japanese *Newsweek* for ease of citation. This magazine is actually *Nyūzuwīku Nihonban (Newsweek Japan-Edition)*.

3. My wife, Masako Barnard, a native Japanese speaker and technical translator of German and English, has been through these data with me many times, untiringly answered my questions, listened to my interpretations, and corrected me when I have gone off the rails. Tsutomu Katsumi, a former high school English teacher, and presently a freelance textbook writer and translator, has also been through earlier drafts of this chapter with me—suggesting, amending, correcting, changing. He has also checked all my uses of bold lettering and my literal translations from Japanese to English. I have discussed with him in detail the attitudinal differences between English *Newsweek* and Japanese *Newsweek*, and any of my interpretations that he was not in agreement with do not remain in this chapter. Ikuo Koyama, associate professor of English language and literature in the Department of Anglo-American Language and Culture at Teikyo University, Tokyo, has read the relevant English *Newsweek* and Japanese *Newsweek* articles and answered an 18-item questionnaire focusing on the attitudinal differences between English *Newsweek* and Japanese *Newsweek*. In all cases, his responses were in agreement with those of the two previously named informants. Thus, in terms of interpretations of the language at the level of both informational differences and attitudinal differences, there is a high level of what may be termed consensual validity. I wish to express my thanks and gratitude to these three people, without whom this chapter could not have been written. Of course, all argumentation that moves out from the language itself to the wider society and culture is mine alone.

4. From *Newsweek*, February 8 © 1999 Newsweek, Inc. All rights reserved. Reprinted by permission.

5. From *Newsweek*, June 21 © 1999 Newsweek, Inc. All rights reserved. Reprinted by permission.

6. From *Newsweek*, February 1 © 1999 Newsweek, Inc. All rights reserved. Reprinted by permission.

REFERENCES

Akhavan-Majid, R. (1990). The press as an elite power group in Japan. *Journalism Quarterly, 67*(4), 1006–1114.

Álvarez, R., & Vidal, M. C.-Á. (1996). Translating: A political act. In R. Álvarez & M. C.-Á. Vidal (Eds.), *Translation, power, subversion* (pp. 1–9). Clevedon, U.K.: Multilingual Matters.

Bassnett, S. (1998). The translation turn in cultural studies. In S. Bassnett & A. Lefevere (Eds.), *Constructing cultures: Essays on literary translation* (pp. 123–140). Clevedon, U.K.: Multilingual Matters.

Bell, A., & Garrett, P. (Eds.) (1998). *Approaches to media discourse*. Oxford: Blackwell.

Blommaert, J., & Verschueren, J. (1998). *Debating diversity: Analyzing the discourse of tolerance*. London: Routledge.

Cooper-Chen, A. (with Kodama, M.) (1997). *Mass communication in Japan*. Ames, IA: Iowa State University Press.

Digging up dirt in high places. (1999, August 23). *Newsweek*, p. 54.

E. coli alert. (1997, September 1). *Newsweek*, pp. 36–41.

Fairclough, N. (1995). *Media discourse*. London: Arnold.

Farley, M. (1996). Japan's press and the politics of scandal. In S. J. Pharr & E. S. Krauss (Eds.), *Media and politics in Japan* (pp. 133–163). Honolulu: University of Hawai'i Press.

Fowler, R. (1991). *Language in the news: Discourse and ideology in the press*. London: Routledge.

Ginkō kirisute de shin no kaikaku ga hajimaru [By sacrificing the banks a real reform starts]. (1999, February 3). *Nyūzuwīku Nihonban*, pp. 19–20.

Gitlin, T. (1980). *The whole world is watching: Mass media in the making and unmaking of the new left*. Berkeley: University of California Press.

Hallin, D. C. (1986). *The "uncensored war": The media and Vietnam*. Berkeley: University of California Press.

Hanbāgā ga kieta [Hamburgers have disappeared]. (1997, September 3). *Nyūzuwīku Nihonban*, pp. 28–31.

Herman, E. S., & Chomsky, N. (1988). *Manufacturing consent: The political economy of the mass media*. New York: Pantheon.

Hodge, R., & Kress, G. (1993). *Language as ideology* (2nd ed.). London: Routledge.

Irokawa, D. (1995). *The age of Hirohito: In search of modern Japan* (M. Hane & J. K. Urda, Trans.). New York: The Free Press.

Itoi, K. (1999a, February 8). The great Viagra emergency. *Newsweek*, p. 17.

Itoi, K. (1999b, February 10). Baiagura ga abaku mujun [The contradictions which Viagra exposed]. *Nyūzuwīku Nihonban*, p. 27.

Kattoulas, V. (1999, February 1). Squeeze them 'til it hurts. *Newsweek*, pp. 18B, 18C.

Kattoulas, V., & Wehrfritz, G. (1999, June 21). Selling sumo. *Newsweek*. pp. 50–55.

Krauss, E. S. (1996). Media coverage of U.S.–Japanese relations. In S. J. Pharr & E. S. Krauss (Eds.), *Media and politics in Japan* (pp. 243–273). Honolulu: University of Hawai'i Press.

Kress, G. (1989). *Linguistic processes in sociocultural practice* (2nd ed.). Oxford: Oxford University Press.

Lefevere, A., & Bassnett, S. (1995). Introduction: Proust's grandmother and the thousand and one nights. The "cultural turn" in translation studies. In S. Bassnett & A. Lefevere (Eds.), *Translation, history and culture* (pp. 1–13). London: Cassell.

Pharr, S. J. (1996). Media as trickster in Japan: A comparative perspective. In S. J. Pharr & E. S. Krauss (Eds.), *Media and politics in Japan* (pp. 19–43). Honolulu: University of Hawai'i Press.

Sherman, S. (1990). Pack journalism, Japanese style. *Columbia Journalism Review* (September/October), pp. 37–40.

Sumō ni miru Nippon [Looking at Japan through sumo]. (1999, June 23). *Nyūzuwīku Nihonban*, pp. 50–55.

TBS-Britannica corporate profile 1998/1999. (1999). Tokyo: TBS-Britannica.

Thompson, J. B. (1990). *Ideology and modern culture: Critical social theory in the era of mass communication.* Stanford, CA: Stanford University Press.

van Wolferen, K. (1989). *The enigma of Japanese power: People and politics in a state-less nation.* London: Macmillan.

part IV

Japanese Nationalism and Social Minority Relations

Chapter 9

Deconstructing the Japanese National Discourse: Laymen's Beliefs and Ideology

Rotem Kowner

Nihonjinron *is a currently vast discourse that takes place within the Japanese society and seeks to account for the particular characteristics of its culture, behavior, and national character.* Nihonjinron *also serves as a broadly based ideological support for Japan's nationalism through its ethnocentric emphasis on the nation as the preeminent collective identity of the people. In recent decades, many studies have critically examined the world of* Nihonjinron *and its producers. This chapter, by contrast, reviews the rather neglected realm of* Nihonjinron *"consumers," namely, the people who adhere to* Nihonjinron *as a national ideology and believe in its tenets. Based on the results of several surveys, the chapter examines the contemporary functions of* Nihonjinron *and speculates about its future trends.*

The Japanese have a consuming interest in their national and cultural identity, almost unique in its magnitude. The current vast discourse that seeks to account for the particular characteristics of Japanese society, culture, and national character is called *Nihonjinron* (but sometimes also referred to as *Nihonron, Nihon Bunkaron,* or *Nihon Shakairon),* which means literally "theories of the Japanese (people)." *Nihonjinron* also serves as a broadly based ideological support for Japan's nationalism through its ethnocentric emphasis on the nation as the preeminent collective identity of the people. Overall, it has become a societal force shaping the way Japanese regard themselves. As a reflection of the concern for Japan's cultural and ethnic identity, contemporary *Nihonjinron* discourse can be tracked back to prewar writings, the late Meiji era quest for identity, and even earlier texts (for review, see Minami, 1976, 1980, 1994). Nevertheless, only in the last three decades has *Nihonjinron* emerged as hegemonic ideology, an "industry" whose main producers are intellectuals and whose consumers are the masses.

A dated compilation of monographs in this genre published between 1945 and 1978 contains 698 titles, of which 25% were published in the three years that preceded the compilation (Nomura Sōgō Kenkyūjo, 1978). Although in recent years *Nihonjinron* literature may have leveled off a bit, it still seems to be extremely popular. Numerous studies have explored the content of these writings critically, scrutinizing the motives and background for their "production." In this chapter, however, I review a rather neglected aspect of *Nihonjinron*: its "consumers," Japan's mainstream population. My focus is to identify the adherents of *Nihonjinron* and to examine the extent to which their profiles match the functions *Nihonjinron* is supposed to serve. In order to deal with these issues, I initially review the content of *Nihonjinron* and its role as national ideology.

PREMISES OF *NIHONJINRON*

Nihonjinron deals with a wide range of social phenomena (from "race," social structure, and language, to ecology, economy, psychology, and even international relations) under a common denominator. This varied and complex discourse treats Japanese culture as a unique and unparalleled product of racial, historical, and climatic elements that underlies the essence of current social phenomena. This fundamental approach is followed by several premises about the nature of Japanese society (for extensive inquiry of *Nihonjinron* tenets, see Befu, 1987; Dale, 1986; Miller, 1982; Mouer & Sugimoto, 1986).

The first premise is that the Japanese are homogeneous people (*tanitsu minzoku*) and that Japan as a nation is culturally homogeneous (*tōshitsu*, or *dōshitsu*). This notion implies that the Japanese invariably share a single language, religion, and lifestyle, and belong to a single race. Although this assumption is based, at least culturally, on certain aspects of reality, *Nihonjinron* writers tend to overlook class, gender, regional, and other variations, to mention only a few, as well as to ignore the existence of underprivileged minorities within Japanese society.

The second premise asserts a strong nexus between the land of Japan, the people, and their culture. *Nihonjinron* writers maintain that Japanese culture, as manifested by language and social customs, can be carried only by Japanese who are the result of the specific amalgam of the Japanese archipelago. These people share the same genetic pool ("blood"), the assumption goes, and only they can master the language and all the nuances of the culture. As such, the second premise equates land, people, and culture in such a way that people defined as non-Japanese ("foreigners") not only can never master Japanese culture and language, but due to their "foreignness" can never become "real" Japanese (Befu, 1993).

The third premise treats the Japanese society as a vertically constructed group and regards the Japanese as group-oriented. It states that the Japanese prefer to act within the framework of a hierarchically organized group in which relations are based on warm dependency and trust. The hierarchical structure of the Japanese society is often perceived as the basis of social order as well as the mold of behavior and personality (see the writings of Ben Dasan, 1970; Doi, 1971; Nakane, 1967; Yoneyama, 1976).

Given these premises, *Nihonjinron* is profoundly ethnocentric. Although physical anthropology does not recognize a "Japanese race," *Nihonjinron* thinkers have long tended to perceive the Japanese as a distinct group in racial terms and to elaborate on the special relations between race and culture in Japan (Oblas, 1995). There are some unpleasant similarities between this approach and earlier ideology. During the ultranationalistic period that ended with Japan's surrender in 1945, racial homogeneity was associated with the ideology of "family-nation," according to which all Japanese were related by "blood." Japan's "racial vigor," it was then maintained, was the predominant factor in Japan's attainment of a distinguished position among nations (Dower, 1986; Hayashida, 1976).

The current ethnocentric character of *Nihonjinron* is amplified by its reliance on comparisons between Japanese culture and other referent cultures, predominantly Western ones. These comparisons with other cultures lead to a fourth premise focusing on uniqueness. Japan and consequently the Japanese people are perceived as "unique," a notion that principally, but until recently not explicitly, has implied superiority over other cultures. At the same time, due to their emphasis on "we" (in-group) versus "them" (out-group), *Nihonjinron* has a special place for foreigners. They, and especially Westerners, are used as an antithetical representation of the essence of Japaneseness, and only through comparison with them, through the construction of their (foreign) image, Japanese identity can be defined and affirmed.

NIHONJINRON AS MANIFESTATION OF JAPANESE NATIONALISM

The short review of the scope of *Nihonjinron* should be sufficient to suggest that it represents the very ideology of contemporary Japanese nationalism. It offers a comprehensive worldview that deals with and accounts for all that nationalism is about: tradition, culture, nation, and stance vis-à-vis the outside world. By continuously confounding race, ethnicity, and nation, *Nihonjinron* creates a strong source of nationalism uniting society, culture, and "blood."

There is wide agreement among various critics of *Nihonjinron* on the inseparability of *Nihonjinron* from Japanese nationalism. They may differ on the degree to which it reflects nationalism, partly because no one has defined or thoroughly examined contemporary Japanese "nationalism." In his controversial critique of *Nihonjinron* promulgators, Peter Dale contends that *Nihonjinron* constitutes "the commercialized expression" of modern Japanese nationalism (Dale, 1986, p. 14). In contrast, Kosaku Yoshino (1992) refers to *Nihonjinron* as cultural nationalism and distinguishes between this form of nationalism (which he also refers to as "secondary nationalism") and original nationalism ("primary nationalism"). Befu (1987, 1993) argues that *Nihonjinron* is the core ideology of Japanese national-ism, but like most discursive nationalism or nationalistic ideologies, it represents passive nationalism, in a sense that they lack an intense emotional element. *Nihonjinron* evokes only a modicum of emotive content, and yet may be an indis-pensable precursor to a full-fledged, emotion-laden nationalism. It is almost inevitable that its emphasis on cultural uniqueness and racial distinctiveness, especially when used to account for Japan's indisputable achievements in recent decades, is destined to enhance nationalist sentiments.

To stress further the role of *Nihonjinron* in Japanese nationalism, I argue that it is, in fact, the hegemonic ideology in contemporary Japan. Not only are its tenets endorsed by the political establishment and the economical elite, as Yoshino claims, but also there is virtually no other ideology that competes with *Nihonjinron* (Befu, 1993). For this reason, *Nihonjinron* thinker, Yamamoto Shichihei (Ben Dasan, 1970) went as far as to call it "Japanese religion" (*Nihon-kyō*). Regardless of their religious affiliation, he argued, all Japanese subscribe to the cultural theology of Japan because they invariably accept the basic tenets of Japanese culture.

The Worldview of *Nihonjinron* Consumers

While some *Nihonjinron* is serious academic discourse, a great bulk of it is produced by academics, journalists, critics, businessmen, and politicians for pop-ular consumption. Since the early 1980s, there have been an increasing number of studies that critically examined the world of *Nihonjinron* and its producers, their historical and ideological milieu, and the methodology and social function of their writings (e.g., Befu, 1987; Dale, 1986; Kawamura, 1982; Miller, 1982; Mouer & Sugimoto, 1986; Sugimoto & Mouer, 1982; Yoshino, 1992).

In contrast, only a few studies have examined the characteristics of *Nihonjinron* "consumers," that is, the people who adhere to *Nihonjinron* as a national ideology and believe in its tenets. The most extensive and well-known research endeavor in this category is the massive nine national surveys conducted every 5 years since 1953 by the governmental Research Committee for the Study of the Japanese National Character (Tōkei Sūri Kenkyūjo Kokuminsei Chōsa Iinkai, 1961, 1970, 1975, 1982, 1992, 1994). The "National Character" surveys are an especially invaluable source of information because they have sampled the whole adult pop-ulation of Japan, have been conducted every 5 years over a period of four decades, and have supplied a breakdown of each response according to gender, age, educa-tion, region, city size, and even (occasionally) cohort comparison (e.g., Tōkei Sūri Kenkyūjo Kokuminsei Chōsa Iinkai, 1985).

Nevertheless, because these surveys have dedicated only a few questions to attitudes toward the nation and race, they offer limited insight to the character and reception of the central tenets of *Nihonjinron* among the Japanese population. Pertaining to *Nihonjinron*, the National Character surveys examined self-images, national status vis-à-vis the West, and evaluation of Japan's economic achievement, standard of living, and emotional life. Reflecting the new trends toward internationalization in Japan, two recent surveys conducted in 1988 and 1993 for the first time incorporated questions on attitudes toward marriage with a foreigner and whether the respondents had been abroad.

Also, the Japan Broadcasting Corporation (NHK) conducted two national surveys regarding the "consciousness of the Japanese people," which incorporated a few nationalism-related items (NHK Sōgō Hōsō Yoron Chōsajo, 1975, 1980). The NHK surveys found high correlation between positive attitude toward the emperor, attachment to Japan, and feeling of national superiority. More important to our case, they provided a breakdown of the responses according to several variables. Age and, to a lesser extent, gender, education, profession, and political affiliation were the most important factors in determining attitude toward the emperor, and feelings of national superiority, yet were barely significant in regard to attachment to Japan (because the response was very high across all respondents). Although only seven questions were used and responses were somewhat contradictory, the NHK surveys indicated that younger, more educated respondents, members of left-wing parties, and women had weaker nationalistic attitude. They also revealed a slight increase in nationalistic attitudes (but a decrease in respect for the emperor) within the 5-year period from the first survey in 1975.

Using data from seven National Character surveys conducted between 1953 and 1983, as well as the two "consciousness of the Japanese people" NHK surveys, John Gano (1987) examined in his doctoral thesis the effect of generational change, maturation, and period (change with the lapse of time) on Japanese postwar nationalistic attitudes. Gano found age (labeled as "experiential effect") to be the crucial factor in determining nationalistic attitudes. In 10 out of 16 questions Gano examined, he found that the oldest generation, those who experienced the war as adults, expressed stronger nationalistic attitudes than the younger generations, whereas in two questions, the younger generation's tendency to converge with the attitudes of the old ("maturation effect") was the main factor determining attitudinal change. In addition, in nine questions he found attitude change in all groups with the lapse of time ("period effect"). Overall, Gano concluded that postwar Japanese public opinion "shows strongly declining support for every element relating to the 'layer' of the modernizing ideology, both by period and by experiential effects" (Gano, 1987, p. 439) and, at the same time, maintains or increases its level of support for "the elements of the 'core' social system underlying traditional Japanese nationalism" (p. 442).

Yoshino (1992), in his important book *Cultural Nationalism in Contemporary Japan,* approached *Nihonjinron* as a discourse of "thinking elites" who mobilize the ordinary sections of the population by transmitting to them their ideas of national identity. To illustrate his thesis, Yoshino examined responses to ideas of national distinctiveness among a sample of 71 educators (mainly high school headmasters) and businesspeople, the majority of whom were males and of middle age or above. Based on interviews and a few quantitative questions, Yoshino found various differences between the businesspeople and educators in the way they were exposed to and reacted to *Nihonjinron* tenets. Compared with the educators, the businesspeople indicated much more "active interest" in *Nihonjinron* literature (75% vs. 29%), whereas relatively more educators indicated "no interest at all" (17% vs. 3%). Moreover, the businesspeople tended to express their ideas regarding Japanese uniqueness in abstract and holistic terms, whereas the educators did so also in terms of arts and everyday customs. Yoshino also observed that younger educators were more informed on *Nihonjinron* than older educators, and that younger respondents, in general, were more indifferent toward the subject of nationalism and "old" nationalism in particular.

Yoshino concluded that *Nihonjinron* stimulated, if not created, the active consciousness of Japanese identity of some of the respondents as well as their perceptions and expressions of it. As for the differences found between the two groups, he suggested that the fact that businesspeople showed greater interest in *Nihonjinron* was because they deal with organizational and crosscultural issues. As for individual differences, Yoshino argued that a person's inclination to become a social bearer of cultural nationalism depends on the presence of conscious critical attitudes toward ideas of Japanese uniqueness. Despite the pioneering character of this study, its results are suggestive at best. This is largely because of its empirical shortcomings, such as the absence of comparative raw data and statistical analysis, the small and nonrandom sample, as well as the limited range of respondents, which preclude further comparisons.

Another contribution to the study of *Nihonjinron* consumers is Leo Loveday's (1990, 1997) research on Japanese attitudes toward contacts with foreign language and their relation to cultural ethnocentrism. Loveday identified, among other things, the social features (age, educational level, gender, and occupation) of 461 adult respondents who disclosed their attitudes toward contact with foreign culture and language. He found that respondents with higher educational background and higher occupations, and those aged 18–29, were somewhat more tolerant to foreign culture and language contact with English, although attitudinal disparity did not feature prominently in his study.

The Nishinomiya Survey

The most prominent endeavor hitherto to explore the Weltanschauung of *Nihonjinron* consumers was set forth at the end of the 1980s by a team led by American anthropologist Harumi Befu and Japanese sociologist Kazufumi Manabe. These researchers composed a questionnaire comprised of more than 200 items regarding familiarity with *Nihonjinron* ideas, adoption of its general attitudes, and belief in its tenets. The questionnaires were then distributed to a random sample of 2,400 adults in Nishinomiya, a city with a population of nearly a half million, serving as a "bedroom community" being midway between Osaka and Kobe. Nearly 1,000 adults from a wide range of age, occupation, education, and level of standard of living responded to the questionnaire and their answers were analyzed. The huge amount of raw data accumulated in this survey has yet to be fully exhausted as to its yield or relevant studies. For further details on the method, demographic structure of the sample, and descriptive results, see Manabe and Befu (1992); for statistical analysis, see Kowner, Befu, & Manabe (1999); McConnell, Kweon, Befu, and Manabe (1988); and Manabe, Befu, and McConnell (1989).

The findings of the Nishinomiya survey are highly important since it has been the only research to examine thoroughly the permeation and acceptance of *Nihonjinron* tenets into the mainstream Japanese population. The Nishinomiya survey revealed high familiarity of the respondents with *Nihonjinron* literature, promulgators, and ideas. Many of the respondents were familiar with *Nihonjinron* writers such as Kindaiichi Haruhiko (70%), Aida Yuji (50%), and Doi Takeo (20%), and a surprising number of them read *Nihonjinron* material such as *The Japanese and the Jews* (Ben Dasan, 1970) (30%) and *The Structure of Amae* (Doi, 1971) (20%). They were also familiar with *Nihonjinron* tenets such as homogeneity of the people (72%) and uniqueness of the culture (57%).

At the same time, this survey also indicated that not all Japanese, as often has been claimed by *Nihonjinron* critics, think and behave in the way *Nihonjinron* authors write about Japan. When asked, for example, whether they espoused the proposition of homogeneity of the Japanese, only 38% of the respondents said "yes." Thus, although much has been made of the homogeneity notion in *Nihonjinron*, it seems to only apply to a third of the population, while most other people either know about it but do not believe in it, or do not even know about it.

The Nishinomiya study identified two distinct features of Japanese public attitudes toward *Nihonjinron*: interest and belief. Naturally, interest in *Nihonjinron* surpasses belief: While 82% of the sample expressed interest in *Nihonjinron*, only about half of the sample expressed belief in its tenets. Thus, a clear message is that interest in *Nihonjinron*, such as that reflected by the sale of *Nihonjinron* books, does not mean that all who read about it necessarily agree with it. In contrast, perhaps to what one may expect from nationalistic attitudes, interest and belief seem to be correlated negatively. In other words, those who show high interest in *Nihonjinron* tenets do not believe in its tenets as much as those with lesser interest, and vice versa. This distinction is of great importance because interest in *Nihonjinron*, especially the widespread availability of books on this topic, has been often taken as an indicator of the strength of Japanese nationalism in general and ultranationalism in particular (Kowner, Befu, & Manabe, 1999).

The Nishinomiya survey also examined the idea of a "true Japanese," namely, what are the requisites for being Japanese and how strict are they? A few studies have sought to identify the requirements for being Japanese. In a survey conducted in 1973, Cullen Tadao Hayashida asked a sample of 313 adults, mainly from

Tokyo and its vicinity, to indicate the most important conditions for being considered a Japanese. Of the six conditions specified, respondents rated national character as the most important, blood relations with other Japanese second, and then particular physical characteristics, Japanese citizenship, and birth in Japan, with language fluency being the least important condition (Hayashida, 1976).

Louise Kidder (1992) sought to identify those subtle criteria by interviewing youth who, after a long stay abroad, found they were no longer considered "real Japanese" and felt marked as marginal. Their experiences of being discriminated as different stemmed from their insufficient adherence to certain social norms. First, they were somewhat physically marked, often by a different hairstyle or even color and by a different code of dress. Similarly, they behaved differently, acting more confident and expressive, while becoming more direct and less polite.

The Nishinomiya survey asked its respondents to rate their personal ("self-norm") and public ("societal") view regarding the relevance of 10 criteria to one's Japaneseness. The most relevant ("absolutely necessary") criteria were: Japanese citizenship, Japanese language competency, Japanese name, having both parents Japanese, having a Japanese father, having a Japanese mother, living in Japan for some duration, and Japanese physical appearance. The least relevant criterion was to be born in Japan, and yet, none received 100% endorsement. In fact, many of the criteria, especially when rated as a public view, received less than 25% endorsement, a finding that underscores the point made earlier that *Nihonjinron* tenets are not uniformly supported by the majority of the Japanese population. Interestingly, although the ranking order of the criteria in the personal and public view was virtually identical, respondents believed that the public view is more conservative than their own personal opinions (Manabe, Befu, & McConnell, 1989).

Finally, it is interesting to illustrate the profile of the people who are interested in *Nihonjinron* ideology and believe in it. The typical person found to be highly exposed to *Nihonjinron* tenets and to manifest a greater interest in this topic tend to be an older and more educated male, who has been abroad, and has foreign acquaintances. By contrast, the person found to believe in *Nihonjinron* tenets and support them tends to be an older and less educated person, who has not been abroad, and does not have foreign acquaintances. The survey did not find appreciable sex differences, and the few statistically significant differences found were small.

FUNCTIONS OF *NIHONJINRON* AS REFLECTED BY ITS CONSUMERS

The resurgence of the *Nihonjinron* discourse in recent decades is an outcome of its ability to fulfill much of the needs of both its producers and consumers. Further, the tremendous popularity of *Nihonjinron* at present suggests that there has been a continuous process of mutual feedback between these two parties, a process that inevitably culminates into a multifunctional discourse.

Certain *Nihonjinron* writings are evidently the outcome of an identity quest. Befu (1995) places the current *Nihonjinron* in historical perspective, in which the present is only one phase in the long swing that has characterized the Japanese identity. The relative strength of Japan vis-à-vis a referent civilization, China in the past and the West since the Meiji Restoration, has been instrumental in defining Japan in a positive or negative light. Since the 1970s, Japan's economical "miracle" and social stability prompted the decline of postwar negative introspection and the reemergence of national self-confidence. It is in this milieu, Befu asserts, that *Nihonjinron* has attempted to challenge perceived Western dominance by demonstrating the singular character of Japanese culture and social institutions (1984).

Despite its strong emphasis on national supremacy, *Nihonjinron* betrays some doubts as well. Yoshino (1992) argues that the main purpose of *Nihonjinron*, as cultural nationalism, is to regenerate the national community, by strengthening and even recreating the Japanese cultural identity in an era when it is felt to be lacking or threatened. Although this contention seems at first to be at odds with the economic success and international prominence Japan has gained recently, it is hard to miss the identity crisis Japanese society has experienced in the same period. Among the manifold reasons for the urgent quest for identity one may point out rapid urbanization; loss of traditional values and instead a full-fledged acceptance of values and behavior of a postindustrial, postmodern (but not necessarily "Western") society; and growing regional and global responsibility despite the existence of ambiguous attitudes toward foreign contacts (Befu, 1984; Oe, 1989; Stronach, 1995).

Japanese tradition plays an important role in *Nihonjinron*'s account for current characteristics of Japanese society. It often presents an idealized picture of the old family system, communal life, and the past in general, stressing their unbroken ties with present institutions (Crawcour, 1980). This attempt to reconstruct the past and to link it with present circumstances is not particular to Japan. Hobsbawm (1983) went as far as to note that "the national phenomenon cannot be adequately investigated without careful attention to the 'invention of tradition'" (p. 14; cited by Yoshino, 1992). As a discourse that weaves old and newly invented tradition into current national identity, *Nihonjinron* fills an acutely felt vacuum, partly due to the absence of clearly defined and accepted major national symbols in contemporary Japan, such as the flag, the national anthem, and even the imperial institution (Befu, 1992). For this function, *Nihonjinron* attracts particularly the old generation, which seems to be more at loss at times of rapid transition. Moreover, members of "the war generation" group formed their national identity during a period of ultranational consciousness and seem to keep a positive disposition toward symbols and practices associated with "old nationalism." Thus, it is no wonder that in a period characterized by constant transitions, urban alienation, and destruction of the old family structure, members of the old generation show the greatest need for traditional values and firm national identity.

Wide agreement exists among *Nihonjinron* critics regarding its ideological role, even though they may differ on the question as to which segments of society benefit from its promulgation (Befu, 1987; Mouer & Sugimoto, 1986). There is no doubt that the establishment and big corporations (and, one may argue, the society as a whole) do benefit from the masses' belief in a hegemonic ideology, such as *Nihonjinron*, that advocates social harmony and homogeneity and consequently reduces conflict and threat to the status quo (Halliday, 1975; Kawamura, 1982). Indeed, the government and large firms in Japan have offered active support to various institutions that promote *Nihonjinron* tenets (Mouer & Sugimoto, 1995). The findings of a gap between consumers with high interest and consumers with strong belief in *Nihonjinron* tenets indicate that *Nihonjinron* is perceived by a wide range of the elite and adjacent classes as an agent of social control. Promulgated by a large number of educated middle-class Japanese, *Nihonjinron* reinforces the norms of the society. Notwithstanding its descriptive stance, the normative overtones of *Nihonjinron* writings are rather explicit and tell the Japanese, in John Davis's words, "who they *ought* to be and how they *ought* to behave" (1983, p. 216).

The people the Nishinomiya survey identified as showing greater interest and exposure to *Nihonjinron* largely belong to the Japanese "intelligentsia" (which may correspond to Yoshino's category of "thinking elites"). These people, similar to members of any intelligentsia, "possess some form of further or higher education and use their educational diplomas to gain a livelihood through vocational activity, thereby disseminating and applying the ideas and paradigms created by intellectuals" (Smith, 1981, p. 108). Thus, through their knowledge of *Nihonjinron* tenets, but not necessarily because of their belief in them, they fulfill their role as members of a specific social strata, lower in hierarchy than the thin layer of genuine progenitors of ideas, but much above the gullible masses who are more prone to accept *Nihonjinron* tenets.

Finally, the fact that much of the *Nihonjinron* writings have been generated out of the authors' own experiences in foreign countries or their encounters with foreigners in Japan prompted Davis (1983) to suggest that *Nihonjinron* is aimed primarily at a reading public with some international experience. This may be an overstatement, yet indeed over the last few decades, *Nihonjinron* has increasingly dealt with the domain of international relations and Japan's "internationalization," chiefly because of Japan's ever-growing involvement in the international arena (Befu, 1983; Mouer & Sugimoto, 1983). *Nihonjinron* writings furnish Japanese who live overseas or merely maintain foreign contacts, and to a lesser extent also foreigners who deal with Japan, with cultural explanations regarding their difficulties in intercultural communication with each other, as well as justification for Japanese "national" behavior (Inamura, 1980; Ishihara & Morita, 1989).

Here, too, the establishment has assumed a substantial role in promoting *Nihonjinron* concepts overseas in various ways, such as funding translation of *Nihonjinron* publications, supporting foreign and local scholars who conduct research on issues within the umbrella of *Nihonjinron*, and sponsoring performances of "unique" Japanese art forms around the world (Sugimoto & Mouer, 1989). This function may account for the greater interest in *Nihonjinron* found among those who represent Japan vis-à-vis the world: members of the intelligentsia and, in our case, those who have been abroad and have foreign contact. Having knowledge of *Nihonjinron* tenets not only provides them with instant solutions to questions and even threats from foreigners, but also supplies them with simplified answers to doubts they may have regarding their own identity.

CONTEMPORARY ATTITUDES AND FUTURE TRENDS

In view of the multiple role the *Nihonjinron* discourse plays for either the establishment or individual consumers, its tremendous prevalence and acceptance in contemporary Japanese society should not be a surprise. What is the course of *Nihonjinron* in the near future?

The Nishinomiya study provided a few clues regarding certain trends among *Nihonjinron* consumers. The fact that both exposure and interest to *Nihonjinron* are greater among older people suggests perhaps that adherence to *Nihonjinron* may decline in the future. This is not as simple as it appears to be; first, because age is only one out of many determinants of adherence, and second because adherence may change with time. Gano (1987) demonstrated that there is a slight tendency for generations to converge with the attitudes of the old ("maturation effect") and, more importantly, an attitude change in all age groups with the lapse of time ("period effect"). For this effect, Gano concluded that "the 'core' values of traditional Japanese nationalism are alive and strong and growing stronger among all generations of postwar Japanese." (1987, p. 443).

There are other indications for probable weakening of *Nihonjinron* beliefs in the future. Since the Nishinomiya survey was conducted, a large number of Japanese traveled abroad (38% of the respondents in the National Character Survey of 1993 traveled abroad vs. 28% in the survey of 1988, and in 1995 alone, about 16 million Japanese went abroad), a phenomenon that suggests a slight reduction of the belief, but not necessarily interest, in the tenets of *Nihonjinron*. Likewise, the widespread educational attainment in contemporary Japan may decrease the acceptance level of *Nihonjinron* tenets among the emerging young generation.

These trends notwithstanding, the future of *Nihonjinron* inevitably will be affected predominantly by the domestic and international situation of Japan. Continuous affluence, stability, and successful involvement of Japan in global affairs may decrease consumers' need for *Nihonjinron*. In contrast, increasing international competition or economic depression, among other things, may intensify adherence to its tenets. A case in point may be the recent economic stagnation in Japan since the mid-1990s. My thesis suggests that such a situation should intensify, at least slightly, nationalistic attitudes as reflected in an increase in *Nihonjinron* tenets. While continued research into current *Nihonjinron* beliefs is encouraged, there are recently some indirect indicators to support this contention, such as the growing acceptance of the Kimigayo national anthem and use of the Hinomaru (the rising sun) flag in schools, wartime symbols once disapproved by many Japanese.

REFERENCES

Befu, H. (1983). Internationalization of Japan and *Nihon bunkaron*. In H. Mannari & H. Befu (Eds.), *The challenge of Japan's internationalization: Organization and culture* (pp. 232–266). Nishinomiya: Kwansei Gakuin University.

Befu, H. (1984). Civilization and culture: Japan in search of identity. In T. Umesao, H. Befu, & J. Kreiner (Eds.), *Japanese civilization in the modern world* (*Senri Ethnological Studies*, No. 16). Osaka: National Museum of Ethnology.

Befu, H. (1987). *Ideorogī to shite Nihon bunkaron* [The theory of Japanese culture as an ideology]. Tokyo: Shiso no Kagakusha.

Befu, H. (1992). Symbols of nationalism and *Nihonjinron*. In R. Goodman & K. Refsing (Eds.), *Ideology and practice in modern Japan* (pp. 26–46). London: Routledge.

Befu, H. (1993). Nationalism and *Nihonjinron*. In H. Befu (Ed.), *Cultural nationalism in east Asia: Representation and identity* (pp. 107–135). Berkeley, CA: Institute of East Asian Studies.

Befu, H. (1995). Swings of Japan's identity. In S. Clausen, R. Starrs, & A. Wedell-Wedellsborg (Eds.), *Cultural encounters: China, Japan, and the West* (pp. 241–265). Aarhus, Denmark: Aarhus University Press.

Ben Dasan, I. (1970). *Nihonjin to Yudayajin* [The Japanese and the Jews]. Tokyo: Yamamoto Shoten.

Crawcour, S. (1980). Alternative models of Japanese society: An overview. In R. Mouer & Y. Sugimoto (Eds.), *Japanese society: Reappraisals and new directions* [Special Issue]. *Social Analysis, 5*(6), 184–187.

Dale, P. N. (1986). *The myth of Japanese uniqueness*. London: Croom Helm.

Davis, W. (1983). The hollow onion: The secularization of Japanese civil religion. In H. Mannari & H. Befu (Eds.), *The challenge of Japan's internationalization: Organization and culture* (pp. 212–231). Nishinomiya: Kwansei Gakuin University.

Doi, T. (1971). *Amae no kōzō* [The anatomy of dependence]. Tokyo: Kobundo.

Dower, J. (1986). *War without mercy: Race and power in the Pàcific war*. New York: Pantheon.

Gano, J. V. (1987). *Generational change in Japanese nationalism* (Vols. 1–2). Unpublished doctoral dissertation, Massachusetts Institute of Technology.

Halliday, J. (1975). *A political history of Japanese capitalism*. New York: Pantheon.

Hayashida, C. T. (1976). *Identity, race, and the blood ideology of Japan*. Unpublished doctoral dissertation, University of Washington.

Hobsbawm, E. J. (1983). Introduction: Inventing traditions. In E. J. Hobsbawm & T. Ranger (Eds.), *The invention of tradition*. Cambridge: Cambridge University Press.

Inamura, H. (1980). *Nihonjin no kaigai futekiō* [The Japanese inability to adjust to life overseas]. Tokyo: Nihon Hoso Shuppan Kyokai.

Ishihara, S., & Morita, A. (1989). *No to ieru Nihon* [Japan that can say no]. Tokyo: Kōbunsha.

Kawamura, N. (1982). *Nihon bunkaron no shūhen* [The environs of theories of Japanese culture]. Tokyo: Ningen no Kagakusha.

Kidder, L. H. (1992). Requirements for being "Japanese." *International Journal of Intercultural Relations, 16,* 383–393.

Kowner, R., Befu, H., & Manabe, K. (1999). The human profile of Japanese nationalism: A study of *Nihonjinron* followers. *Journal Komunikashi, 15,* 73–95.

Loveday, L. J. (1990). *The sociolinguistic evolution and synchronic dynamics of language contact in Japan.* Unpublished doctoral dissertation, Essex University, England.

Loveday, L. J. (1997). *Language contact in Japan: A sociolinguistic history.* Oxford: Clarendon Press.

Manabe, K., & Befu, H. (1992). Japanese cultural identity: An empirical investigation of *Nihonjinron.* In *Japanstudien: Jahrbuch des Deutschen Instituts für Japanstudien der Philipp-Franz-von-Siebold-Stiftung* (Vol. 4, pp. 89–102). München: Iudicium Verlag.

Manabe, K., Befu, H., & McConnell, D. (1989). An empirical investigation on *Nihonjinron*: The degree of exposure of Japanese *Nihonjinron* propositions and the functions these propositions serve. *Kwansei Gakuin University Annual Studies, 38,* 35–62.

McConnell, D., Kweon, S.-I., Befu, H., & Manabe, K. (1988). *Nihonjinron*—Whose cup of tea? *Kwansei Gakuin University Annual Studies, 37,* 129–133.

Miller, R. A. (1982). *Japan's modern myth: Language and beyond.* New York: Weatherhill.

Minami, H. (1976). The introspection boom: Whither the national character. *Japan Interpreter, 8,* 159–184.

Minami, H. (1980). *Nihonjinron no keifu* [The development of *Nihonjinron*]. Tokyo: Kodansha.

Minami, H. (1994). *Nihonjinron.* Tokyo: Iwanami Shoten.

Mouer, R. E., & Sugimoto, Y. (1983). Internationalization as an ideology in Japanese society. In H. Mannari & H. Befu (Eds.), *The challenge of Japan's internationalization: Organization and culture* (pp. 267–297). Nishinomiya: Kwansei Gakuin University.

Mouer, R., & Sugimoto, Y. (1986). *Images of Japanese society.* London: Routledge & Kegan Paul.

Mouer, R., & Sugimoto, Y. (1995). *Nihonjinron at the end of the twentieth century: A multicultural perspective* (*La Trobe Asian Studies,* 4th ed.). Bundoora, Victoria, Australia: School of Asian Studies.

Nakane, C. (1967). *Tate shakai no ningen kankei* [The human relations in hierarchical society]. Tokyo: Kodansha.

NHK Sōgō Hōsō Yoron Chōsajo (Ed.). (1975). *Nihonjin no ishiki-NHK yoron chōsa* [The NHK survey of the consciousness of Japanese people]. Tokyo: Shiseido.

NHK Sōgō Hōsō Yoron Chōsajo (Ed.). (1980). *Daini Nihonjin no ishiki-NHK yoron chōsa* [The second NHK survey of the consciousness of Japanese people]. Tokyo: Shiseido.

Nomura Sōgō Kenkyūjo [Nomura Research Institute] (1978). *Nihonjinron: Kokusai kyōchō jidai ni sonaete* [Theories of the Japanese: The groundwork for an era of international cooperation]. Kamakura: NRI Reference (No. 2).

Oblas, P. B. (1995). *Perspectives on race and culture in Japanese society: The mass media and ethnicity.* New York: Edwin Mellen Press.

Oe, K. (1989). Japan's dual identity: A writer's dilemma. In M. Miyoshi & H. D. Hartoonian (Eds.), *Postmodernism in Japan* (pp. 189–213). Durham, NC: Duke University Press.

Smith, A. D. (1981). *The ethnic revival.* Cambridge: Cambridge University Press.

Stronach, B. (1995). *Beyond the rising sun: Nationalism in contemporary Japan.* Westport, CT: Praeger.

Sugimoto, Y., & Mouer, R. E. (1982). *Nihonjin wa "Nihonteki" ka* [Are the Japanese "very Japanese"?]. Tokyo: Tōyō Keizai Shinpōsha.

Sugimoto, Y., & Mouer, R. E. (1989). Cross-currents in the study of the Japanese society. In Y. Sugimoto & R. E. Mouer (Eds.), *Constructs for understanding Japan* (pp. 1–35). London: Kegan Paul International.

Tōkei Sūri Kenkyūjo Kokuminsei Chōsa Iinkai. (1961). *Nihonjin kokuminsei* [The Japanese national character]. Tokyo: Shiseido.

Tōkei Sūri Kenkyūjo Kokuminsei Chōsa Iinkai. (1970). *Daini Nihonjin kokuminsei* [The second study of the Japanese national character]. Tokyo: Shiseido.

Tōkei Sūri Kenkyūjo Kokuminsei Chōsa Iinkai. (1975). *Daisan Nihonjin kokuminsei* [The third study of the Japanese national character]. Tokyo: Shiseido.

Tōkei Sūri Kenkyūjo Kokuminsei Chōsa Iinkai. (1982). *Daiyon Nihonjin kokuminsei* [The fourth study of the Japanese national character]. Tokyo: Idemitsu Shoten.

Tōkei Sūri Kenkyūjo Kokuminsei Chōsa Iinkai. (1985). *Kokuminsei chōsa no kohoto bun-seki-daisanban* [Application of Beyesian cohort model to the Japanese national character study data, 3rd ed.]. (Research report No. 62.) Tokyo: Tōkei Sūri Kenkyūjo.

Tōkei Sūri Kenkyūjo Kokuminsei Chōsa Iinkai. (1992). *Daigo Nihonjin kokuminsei* [The fifth study of the Japanese national character]. Tokyo: Idemitsu Shoten.

Tōkei Sūri Kenkyūjo Kokuminsei Chōsa Iinkai. (1994). *Kokuminsei no kenkyū dai kyukai zenkoku chōsa* [The ninth national survey of study of the Japanese national character]. (Research report No. 75.) Tokyo: Tōkei Sūri Kenkyūjo.

Yoneyama, T. (1976). *Nihonjin no nakama ishiki* [Group consciousness of the Japanese]. Tokyo: Kodansha Gendai Shinsho.

Yoshino, K. (1992). *Cultural nationalism in contemporary Japan.* London: Routledge.

Chapter 10

Koreans—A Mistreated Minority in Japan: Hopes and Challenges for Japan's True Internationalization

Soo-im Lee

As the new millennium dawns, Jōhō (information) is the latest buzzword in Japan, succeeding the catchy kokusaika *(internationalization). Collapse of the Japanese economy in the 1990s forced the Japanese to seek greater accountability and information disclosure in business and in other spheres of society. One area, however, has remained only dimly, if at all, lit in Japanese consciousness: the status and plight of the Korean minority in Japan. Few Japanese know about the Koreans' historical background and the cause of their presence in Japanese society. Because Koreans are physically indistinguishable from Japanese and many use Japanese assumed names to avoid likely discrimination, their existence has become practically invisible in Japanese society. Japanese lack awareness of minority problems in their own country, influenced by myths of cultural homogeneity and racial purity, which are still firmly believed by many Japanese. This chapter focuses on two related topics: (1) the superiority and inferiority relationship between Japanese and Koreans from historical perspectives, and (2) the changing consciousness of national identity held by young Japanese and Koreans. Young Japanese have fewer negative feelings toward Koreans than do older people, while young Koreans experience an identity crisis as they try to work out an ethnic identity. Also discussed is government policy concerning foreign residents in light of naturalization procedures, that is still obscured from public view.*

Koreans form the largest foreign minority group in Japan, accounting for 42% of foreign residents, as well as being a well-known target group for Japanese prejudice and discrimination. This large Korean presence goes back to the turn of the 20th century when the colonial takeover of Korea by Japan induced many Koreans to seek work in Japan out of economic necessity, if not as captured laborers, as was the case before and during the Second World War. As it was also Japanese policy, individuals from colonized areas could obtain a kind of limited Japanese citizenship that also carried voting rights.

Koreans in Japan, however, were stripped of their citizenship in 1952 when the San Francisco peace accords were signed between Japan and principally the United States. Because Japanese citizenship is based on lineage, it matters little that many Koreans have known no other country but Japan, having been born and bred there. Despite the fact that many Koreans live their lives as Japanese—speaking the language and following the same customs—their legal status is limited and they are still considered foreigners.

The Japanese word *gaijin* often refers to foreigners and has a negative nuance of an exclusion of foreign elements. Under the Japanese nationality law based on lineage, Koreans must remain *gaijin* no matter how many generations of them have lived in Japan. Leaving Japan is impractical for most Koreans because they only know one home—Japan—and their ancestral home has long been in divided chaos as a result of the former Japanese colonialization and the subsequent division between the Cold War powers. Among Japan's 1.5 million foreign residents,[1] the elderly Korean minority in particular are the victims of Japan's adherence to ideas of racial and cultural homogeneity and deserve to have their case heard. Through such cases of the Koreans, we can gain insight into Japaneseness that we might not otherwise.

As an ethnic Korean myself, born and raised in Japan and currently on the faculty of a Japanese college, I believe I have a unique perspective to share on this topic. I was raised as if I were Japanese, but my Korean ethnicity was such that the "as if" quality could never be permanently removed, often putting me in intercultural situations at a moment's notice. Continually having to function between intra- and intercultural communication with the Japanese gives Koreans much insight into Japanese character from both "insider" and "outsider" perspectives. Koreans gain the "insider perspective" because many of them are physically indistinguishable from Japanese and, if native born to Japan, can pass themselves off as being truly "Japanese."

Average Japanese citizens are naïve about the Korean issue, about their plight and that of other ethnic or social minorities. Consciousness raising is long overdue in Japan, and if the nation is ever to internationalize, it must face these matters. It so happens that with the dawn of the new millennium, a new openness appears to be developing in Japan. *Kokusaika* (internationalization) has been joined by *Jōhō* (information), the newest buzzword, as national goals. With the collapse of the Japanese economy in the 1990s, Japanese institutions have been pressed to accept higher accountability and disclosure. In a more open society, ordinary Japanese may finally come to grips with the increasing ethnic and racial diversity in Japan and seek common ground with their foreign brethren.

This chapter looks at the extent to which Japan has actualized its goal for internationalization, while illuminating Japanese values and beliefs in relation to the Korean minority group. The foci of my analysis include the power relation between the two groups and the Korean identity formation process. My method is through personal introspection and a qualitative account of culture-specific discourse. I am a second-generation Korean in Japan and hid my own roots until 18 years of age by using an assumed name of Japanese origin. Such a personal account may be the most direct and revealing way to examine identity issues for social minorities in Japan.

HISTORICAL OVERVIEW

This overview is a bit unusual because I present my own personal history and that of my family. This way may be more meaningful for the reader, for I have directly lived the story. To begin, as a second-generation Korean born and bred in Japan, I went to Japanese schools from the elementary to the university level, so that my environment was quite different from that of Koreans who were formally educated in the *Chongryun* (General Federation of Korean Residents in Japan). Because *Chongryun* is viewed by Japanese as a "formidable Phongyang lobby in Japan" or a "highly disciplined Korean Communist organization in Japan" (Ryang, 1997, p. 11), *Chongryun* Koreans are isolated from mainstream Japanese society and have created their own ethnic culture. I, however, was brought up in an assimilated environment. I speak no Korean and believed that I was the same as any other Japanese until I began to experience discrimination and prejudice later in my childhood. Being discriminated against caused me to question my own identity, leading me, and others like me, to develop an in between consciousness—one neither "Japanese" nor "Korean." Korean youths typically develop their consciousness of being non-Japanese and non-Korean under a fully assimilated system in their first phase of identity formation. The experience of discrimination awakens them and forces them to face the social reality and associated problems.

Compared to the first-generation Koreans who had strong ties to their own country, the second-generation Koreans who were raised in a Japanese environment, like me, have been culturally and socially assimilated into the dominant society. However, most of them have had traumatizing experiences of direct or indirect discriminatory treatment and prejudice in Japanese society, even though the degree of discrimination and prejudice differs depending on their situation. I was born in 1953 as the oldest daughter in my family. Because the Alien Registration Law was implemented in 1952, I was born as a Korean despite the fact that my father had Japanese citizenship up to that point. My father's family background depicts a typical case of the plight of the Korean migrants during the period of colonial rule from 1910 to 1945. There was a large influx of Koreans into Japan in search of jobs as a direct result of land confiscation managed by imperial Japan from 1910 to 1918 (Fukuoka, 1996; Kan & Kim, 1994; Lee & De Vos, 1981). Many married men left their families behind in Korea and migrated to Japan alone. My grandfather was one of these men.

After my grandfather left for Japan, my grandmother soon followed him without his knowledge. She took along with her my father, then only 4 years of age. Hers was a brave act because Korean women were not easily permitted to migrate to Japan. My grandmother hid herself and my father in the bottom of a fishing boat for the whole trip. Somehow they caught up with my grandfather and began to live in a small village in Wakayama, south of Osaka, Japan. My father tells us that the most difficult time for them was when no one in the village wanted to rent a house to this newly arrived Korean family. They still managed, and in time, my father learned the language and literacy, becoming a guide for his parents in this foreign land. My father calls Wakayama his hometown despite the hard life that they had.

My maternal grandfather also migrated to Japan under similar circumstances. He, however, was to lose his life during the hysteria in Tokyo during the Great Kanto Earthquake in 1923. He was victimized as one of the 6,000 Koreans massacred by Japanese rioters who believed an ill rumor that Koreans would rise up to take over Tokyo. Japanese vigilantes forced Koreans to speak certain sounds[2] (Kuboi, 1996) to detect and, on this basis, kill those who were believed to be Korean. This case is a tragic reminder of how language can become a powerful weapon by which the mainstream or majority exercises control over a minority. Those with speech impediments and also those with different Japanese regional accents, even if Japanese, were victimized during the 6-day massacre.

Politically and Socially Deprived Status Given to Koreans

After Japan's defeat in World War II, about 2 million Koreans were given the choice of either going back to Korea or remaining as secondary citizens in Japan. Relatives on both sides of my family wanted to return to Korea, but my mother's parents, who were financially stable, decided to remain in Japan. My father's parents went back to Tegu, their Korean hometown, with their seven children. My father, 21 years old at the time, could not adjust himself to the unfamiliar culture and language. In Korea, people mocked his accented Korean and bullied him because of his Japanized behavior. The Korean hostility was understandable, but it still forced my father to return to Japan by himself, leaving his family and siblings behind. Soon after, in 1950, the Korean War broke out, which meant that he and his family did not see each other for 15 years, until Japan normalized diplomatic relations with South Korea in 1965. One of his younger brothers was drafted into the South Korean army, became a prisoner of war, and was taken as a captive to North Korea. On reflection, my father cynically laughs that his Japanese identity saved him from becoming a casualty of war.

Yun (1992) points out that the native Korean identity for first-generation Koreans served as a bulwark against the social injustices received. For the sake of their children, they struggled within the gap between assimilation and separation and survived despite being outside the mainstream. They knew that they could never return to their home country and would likely lose some of their own Korean culture and identity.

Few Japanese know that Koreans held limited Japanese citizenship until 1952. Even though they were considered Japanese nationals, colonial subjects were not to be accorded the same respected status as Japanese citizens. The *koseki* system (family registry), as applied to Koreans, meant that their family registry (*chōsen koseki,* Korean family registry) was clearly distinguished from the Japanese koseki (*naichi koseki*) (Tanaka, 1990). Lee and De Vos criticize the discriminatory treatment against Koreans using the different *koseki* under the assimilation policy for colonial subjects. However, as imperial subjects, 38,912 Korean men were eligible to vote in the election of September 1931,[3] and a few Koreans were elected to the Japanese Diet (Lee & De Vos, 1981, pp. 136–137). Understandably, these Korean politicians were loyal to the imperial Japanese government and supported the government's policy on Koreans.

As mentioned before, Japanese citizenship was stripped away without giving Koreans the choice, in contrast to Germany's humane treatment of citizens from countries it had colonized during World War II. Such people in Germany were offered citizenship, and many took it. In Japan, the Alien Registration Law restricted the lives of Koreans, and they have been treated as foreigners ever since. As foreigners, they were subjected to being fingerprinted periodically, having to be in possession of an alien identity card at all times, and having to apply for a reentry permit anytime they went abroad for a visit. Violation of any of these provisions could mean severe legal punishments, including compulsory expulsion.

THE NATIONAL IDENTITY CREATED
FOR POLITICAL PURPOSES

In spite of Japan's obsession with internationalization over the past two decades, the Japanese still implicitly consent to the inferior status accorded Koreans in Japan. Historically, Japanese believed that they were biologically superior to Koreans (Lee & De Vos, 1981). Given that Japanese and Koreans are of the same "race," how did the racism against Koreans develop?

The Japanese national identity has been politically and economically created for the swift promotion of industrialization and militarization ever since Japan's postrestoration Meiji era (Kan & Kim, 1994; Suh, 1987; Yoshioka, 1995; Yoshioka, Inui, Kawase, & Yamamoto, 1984). The Japanese national identity consists of a complexity of feelings of superiority toward the East and inferiority toward the West as a direct result of its historical drive to surpass Western civilization. It makes sense that if Japanese felt inferior to Westerners, then they might seek a compensatory way to shore up their pride through other Asian countries. Korea, being Japan's closest neighbor and economically behind Japan, became a convenient target for ego gratification while reinforcing Japanese ethnocentrism before and during World War II. This ethnocentric outlook formed a basis for Japanese national identity to be politically harnessed for the swift advancement of the nation.

Concomitant with the nation's militaristic periods in the 1930s and 1940s, an ethnocentric fever swept Japan producing a mass literature that celebrated Japanese racial purity. For example, "the putative relationship between blood and culture was made more explicit in Tetsuji Kada's *Jinshu Minzoku Senso* (Race, Ethnicity, and War), published in 1938" (Weiner, 1997, p. 2). Kada consistently affirmed the biological basis of *minzoku* (ethnicity) by distinguishing it from *jinshu* (race) and supported belief in the purity of Japanese blood. Purity of blood, as expressed in "racial" homogeneity, reinforced Japanese collectivity, and it was politically used to change the family-state into a militarized nation.

This racialized ideology explains the mistreatment of minorities, even of their own people—the *burakumin*, formerly outcasted Japanese. It was a common belief early this century that "*burakumin* were racially distinct from mainstream Japanese; that they were the descendants of slaves from the ancient period, descendants of Koreans, or even descendants of the lost tribes of Israel that somehow ended up in Japan" (Neary, 1997, p. 53). Others were categorized on the basis of their non-Japanese blood, regardless of quantity. For example, even if Ainu (an indigenous people) were able to conceal their ancestry, they might still be marked by physical appearance. Even if they succeeded in passing as Japanese, they often must live in fear of discovery (Siddle, 1997). This is a similar pattern to that of the naturalized Koreans who hide their ethnic origins by erasing the evidence from their newly formed family registry (Kim, 1990). The popular literature on *Nihonjinron* ("discussions of the Japanese" or "theories of Japaneseness," which appeared in the late 1960s and 1970s) was a reflection of a revitalized cultural nationalism (Yoshino, 1992) and indicated Japan's struggle for power as the society became increasingly Westernized (Befu, 1987). This literature emphasized not only Japanese uniqueness, but also the superiority of Japanese culture over other cultures (Weiner, 1997).

Whether or not Japanese cultural nationalism is racially based, the Japanese still maintain today a superiority complex, even if in a new form. Hicks (1998) observes that

even though the Japanese are proud of their own uniqueness they do not necessarily look down on others as inherently inferior, but rather judge them in terms of "perceived achievement." Successful Western countries are looked up to, but Asian societies seen as less successful than Japan are looked down upon. Korea is ranked rather low, because of its former status as a Japanese colony. (p. 5)

Ryang (1997) also questions why and under what circumstances "certain foreigners are politely treated and others are bluntly insulted, exploited, and looked down upon" (p. 9). Japanese swiftly changed their perceptions toward Americans from devils to the most admired group in the postwar period, as the most popular foreign culture for Japanese is American (Hagiwara, 1998). Many Caucasians confess that they are treated politely by Japanese, and one American woman even described her own experience in Japan as being treated as if she were a queen. Of course much depends on people's situations and their expectations. Still, within Japan's hierarchy of social minority groups, Caucasians as a group receive more respect than do other non-Japanese groups.

The Lack of Intercultural Understanding

The first-generation Koreans brought their own culture and lifestyles into the Japanese communities and "Japanese could not comprehend that the observable behavioral differences of the first-generation Koreans were because of differences in cultural heritage" (Sato, 1991, p. 21). Hoffman (1992) points out the difference in communication style between the two groups. The Korean direct and straightforward style causes Japanese to perceive them as being aggressive or rude. Conversely, Japanese are famous for their high-context communication style (Hirai, 1994; Samovar & Porter, 1991), and "the two attitudes of *hon'ne* (true feelings) and *tatemae* (face value) cause Koreans to distrust Japanese because they appear two-faced to Koreans" (Hoffman, 1992, p. 483). Most of the first-generation Koreans who migrated to Japan were uneducated and illiterate in both languages. On top of the extreme poverty in their lives, their attitudinal and behavioral patterns looked aggressive to many Japanese. Japanese parents told their children to stay away from the Korean communities, which implicitly instilled fear in their young minds.

The Development of a Korean Inferiority Complex

The second-generation Koreans who were educated and assimilated into Japanese society became ashamed of their own roots after realizing who they really were. When out with my Japanese friends, I often ignored my grandparents, if they came into eyesight, and hoped that they would not notice or talk to me in front of my friends. Many second-generation Koreans share similar memories, which indicates the social stigma they must face. The power relationship between Japanese and Koreans turns on this social stigma and is fueled by Japanese belief of their homogeneity and exclusionary attitudes toward foreigners. For Japan-born Koreans, the likely result is alienation from their own Korean ethnicity and an insecure identity. This is the price that must be paid for assimilation into Japanese society, for Hoffman (1992) can attest that Korean newcomers to Japan (and thus not yet assimilated) have strongly intact Korean identities.

THE DEVELOPMENT OF KOREAN PERSONAL IDENTITY

Personal identity is based on various elements, such as gender, race, religion, ethnicity, nationality, and sexual orientation (Tajfel, 1981, 1982). Martin and Nakayama (1997) distinguish ethnic identity from national identity. They note that even though the ethnic roots of the minority groups in the United States are diversified, their nationality is American. The majority of second- and third-generation Koreans do not share much cultural and social identity with Korean nationals, but rather with Japanese (Fukuoka, 1996; Fukuoka & Tsujiyama, 1991). The primary difference between Japan-born Koreans and Japanese is the deprived legal status of Koreans.

Martin and Nakayama (1997) state that identity consciousness of the minority groups develops earlier than that of the majority group (pp. 76–77). If this view also applies to Japan-born Korean youth, then their ethnicity will likely become a sensitive issue, one not shared by Japanese youth. They will realize that they are discriminated against in many aspects of their lives and may feel alienated in Japanese society. The identity held by assimilated Koreans, however, is an ethnic one because they have embraced few Korean cultural values or beliefs. Kim (1999) is one of the few sociopolitical researchers who has conducted a statistical analysis on the formation of ethnicity in Korean youth in Japan, and his findings indicate that family, Korean community, language use, and education have significant causal relationships with ethnicity formation. He also found that the experiences of suffering discrimination and prejudice had an indirect influence on their development, causing deprived and negative feelings.

Different Acculturation Patterns

A large number of case studies were conducted based on interview data gathered from over 150 Korean youth by Fukuoka and Tsujiyama (1991) and Fukuoka (1996). The Korean youth in the study were categorized under four different patterns of acculturation according to family beliefs and environment. Fukuoka's purpose was to investigate the changing awareness or consciousness of the new Korean generation including the diversified values and beliefs of the Korean minority, which cannot be generalized into one pattern.

The first type, called the Nationalists, are those who want to maintain their status as resident foreign nationals and are not interested in being assimilated into Japanese society. Many of those who were educated in the *Chongryun* environment fit into this group. The second type, the Pluralists, are those who aim to solve the problem of social discrimination through social and political activities initiated in their own communities. The third type, the Individualists, are represented by those who believe that financial success in society is achieved by using one's ability, and that their chosen values and beliefs are to fight back against social discrimination by liberating themselves. They are not particularly concerned with ethnic Korean history or their roots; nor do they feel an attachment to either Japan or Korea in their relationship as individuals to the state. The last type is the Naturalization Oriented Individuals, and their main concern is to become Japanese. They believe that by assimilating they can live without experiencing ethnic discrimination. Japan-born Koreans chose an acculturation pattern in order to survive in their exploited lives, and some of them are satisfied with attaining a materialistically comfortable lifestyle.

In my case, I declared myself a Korean (*honmyō sengen*) at my high school graduation ceremony. My high school teacher gave me a choice of whether I would be called by my Japanese or Korean name. It was a difficult choice for me because I thought I might lose my friends if they found out my ethnic roots. If I recalled my own experience, the inferiority complex was deeply rooted in my mind and the best way to protect myself was to pretend to be Japanese using my Japanese assumed names.

However, my coming out experience in using my own Korean name was the second phase of my identity formation. My internal struggle forced me to be sensitively aware of my own personal identity and my Japanese friends' supportive attitude was the main factor that strengthened my confidence and self-determination.

OVERCOMING THE WE–THEY RELATIONSHIPS

Now more than 50 years have passed since the end of World War II, and with increased internationalization and globalization within Japan, a shift in power relations with minorities has occurred. Until recently, naturalized Koreans were required to take Japanese names in compliance with the government assimilation policy (Kim, 1990). These Korean Japanese became an invisible social minority while the myth of complete homogeneity was maintained under this policy. However, the victories of naturalized aliens who sued to keep their ethnic names have resulted in gradual changes in government policy.

Recently, Koreans have become eligible to apply for the national pension, government housing loans, and child allowances, when the Japanese government modified its domestic laws to accommodate Vietnamese refugees in the early 1980s. The human rights movement has also led to one Korean's refusal to be fingerprinted, becoming a mass movement of 10,000 Koreans. The fingerprinting requirement was eventually scrapped for foreign residents, who mostly consist of Koreans, and the government scheduled its complete abolishment in the year 2000 (Nihon Keizai Shinbun, 1999, Aug. 15). Recently, I often have been invited by Japanese junior and senior high schools to give a workshop for their students regarding the situation of Koreans in Japan. I have come to realize that many of the teachers do not know how to deal with the situation, but they still feel obligated to help Korean students, who generally hide their ethnic roots by using Japanese names. Although I found a few who use their Korean names—and courageously so—most still use Japanese names and pretend to be Japanese.

Japanese consciousness toward Koreans is gradually changing, and intellectuals, scholars, and educators are particularly concerned with this long-lasting social stigma in Japan. Many Japanese youth do not necessarily have negative ideas about Koreans, even though they may be unaware of the historical facts (Hicks, 1998; Tanaka, 1995; Uchiyama, 1982). Along with this softening of attitudes in youths, the increase in intermarriages between Japanese and Koreans (Sakanaka, 1999) indicates that belief in the purity of blood is not as strong as before. Another factor is the reassessment by Japanese of traditional management practices in business, due to the stagnant economy of the 1990s. Japan's first modern experience with sustained slow growth affected Japanese values and beliefs. The Japanese public has demanded accountability and information disclosure from official authorities. Such trends have influenced practices in the schools as well. Individuality, originality, creativity, critical thinking, and self-expression are values or goals gaining attention, which could eventually diminish certain traditional practices, practices that ultimately encourage belief in Japanese complete homogeneity, such as emphases on cooperative attitude, harmonious relationships, and group-oriented thinking.

In English education in Japan, for example, the importance of cultural understanding is included in educational guidelines set forth by the Ministry of Education for the junior and the senior high school levels (Hatori, 1996). Cultural understanding and intercultural communication are now considered two of the most important research and pedagogical interests in ESL. The purpose of learning English is seen more and more as communicating with the outside world in the global network. The Internet, of course, has had a great impact in this regard, especially by making global communications available for all. This development will remove English ability from the sole province of social elites (Sugiura, 1999). The potential equalizing effects in Japanese society appear bright. Japan may have an unprecedented opportunity to overcome the we–they relationships with others within Japanese society and in the world at large.

Technological innovation, especially the Internet, helps Japanese and Koreans to communicate on an individual level (Tsuji, 1999). Exchange programs through e-mail are increasing between Japanese schools and Korean schools. It is apparent that today is the most promising time to deepen cultural understanding between the two countries. Because Koreans know what happened to them during Japan's colonial period, they have tended to get too emotional about Japan. Nevertheless, when it comes to business and economics, Koreans readily can view Japan as a model. In this regard, a book written by a Japanese businessman, Momose (1998), titled *Kankoku ga shindemo Nihonjin ni oitsukenai 18 no riryū* (Eighteen Facts Why

Korea Would Never Catch Up with Japan in Business), became a best-selling book in Korea. Although this may drive some nationalistic sentiment, more importantly the interest shows a willingness to view Japan more realistically. Economic emulation could lead to more positive feelings for the nation.

HOPES AND CHALLENGES FOR TRUE INTERNATIONALIZATION

Korean scholars Kan and Kim (1994) suggest the continued social stigma of Koreans would be alleviated by the automatic granting of citizenship to them. Some optimism has emerged in a published book by a Japanese immigration official, Sakanaka (1999), who encourages the betterment of relations between Japanese and Koreans and predicts that the Korean disadvantages would eventually disappear if Koreans were afforded more moderate legal treatment, such as simplified procedures for naturalization. De Vos and Wetherall (1983) suggest that one effective, but revolutionary, solution would be to adopt an *ius soli* basis for awarding citizenship to all those born in Japan and, thus, grant most Koreans automatic citizenship (p. 11). Sakanaka warned that the forced assimilation policy would not help solve minority problems, and he implied that the more moderate immigration laws are implemented toward the Koreans, the faster their genuine assimilation into society would be. This would also lead to an accelerated acceptance of the new identity by Korean residents. He even added that ethnic cultural preservation would be possible if naturalized Koreans start using their ethnic names after being naturalized.

Koreans, however, are often surprised and discouraged to learn about the Japanese ignorance of historical facts. It is apparent that the Japanese way of teaching the historical facts is different from the Korean way. The Korean high school students who were interviewed on a Japanese TV program said that "Japan's sincere attitude would be assessed from now on because our friendship has just started and we are obliged to develop it further" (Nippon Hōsō Kyōkai, 1999, Aug. 15). The bilateral relationship between Japan and Korea significantly affects the status of Korean residents in Japan and Japan's policy will be evaluated in many aspects, not only by Korea, but also by the international community. The treatment given to Koreans is one of the most crucial tests of Japan's efforts to demonstrate its true internationalization.

NOTES

1. The largest group, Koreans (South Koreans and North Koreans, including newcomer Koreans), accounts for 42.2%; the second largest, Chinese (including Taiwanese), accounts for 18%; and the third largest group, Brazilians (which is drastically increasing), accounts for 14.7% of the total number of foreign residents in Japan (Hōmushō, 2001).

2. Koreans could not pronounce particular voiced sounds, so that they were forced to pronounce "*Jyugo en Jyugo sen*" (Fifteen yen and fifteen sen) or "ga gi gu ge go" sounds.

3. Korean voting rights were taken away right after the war ended in 1945.

REFERENCES

Befu, H. (1987). *Ideorogī to shite no Nihon bunkaron* [The theory of Japanese culture as an ideology]. Tokyo: Shiso no kagaku-sha.

De Vos, G., & Wetherall, W. (1983). *Japan's minorities: Burakumin, Koreans, Ainu, Okinawans* (Report No. 3). London: The Minority Rights Group Ltd.

Fukuoka, Y. (1996). Beyond assimilation and dissimilation: Diverse resolutions to identify crises among younger generation Koreans in Japan. *Saitama University Review, 31*(2), 1–30.

Fukuoka, Y., & Tsujiyama, Y. (1991). *Dōka to ika no hazamade: Zainichi wakamono sedai no identity no katto* [Assimilation and dissimilation: Korean youth's identity crisis]. Tokyo: Sofukan.

Hagiwara, S. (1998). Japanese television as a window on other cultures. *Japanese Psychological Research, 40*, 221–223.

Hatori, H. (1996). *Kokusai kano nakano Eigo kyouiku* [Japan's internationalization and English education]. Tokyo: Sanseido.

Hicks, G. (1998). *Japan's hidden apartheid: The Korean minority and the Japanese.* Burlington, VT: Ashgate Publishing.

Hirai, K. (1994). Kotoba to bunka. In N. Honna, B. Hoffer, K. Akiyama, & Y. Takeshita (Eds.), *Ibunka rikai to communication* [Cross cultural communication]. Tokyo: Sanshusha.

Hōmushō. (2001). *Zairyugaikokujin tokei, Heisei 12nen* [The year 2000 statistics in immigration]. Japanese Ministry of Justice.

Hoffman, D. (1992). Changing faces, changing places: The new Koreans in Japan. *Japan Quarterly,* (October–December), 479–489.

Kada, T. (1938). *Jinshu minzoku sensō* [Race, ethnicity, and war]. Tokyo: Keio Shobo.

Kan, J., & Kim, D. (1994). *Zainichi Kankoku, Chōsenjin rekishi to tenbō* [The history of Koreans in Japan and their future perspectives]. Tokyo: Rodo Keizaisha.

Kim, M. (1999). *Minzokuteki kyushinryoku no keiseiron LISREL o mochiita ingakankei-bunseki* [Ethnicity formation in the analysis of structural equation modeling using LISREL]. Available online: http:www.han.org/a/vita.html

Kim, Y. (1990). *Zainichi Chōsenjin no kika* [Naturalization of Koreans in Japan]. Tokyo: Akashi shoten.

Kuboi, N. (1996). *Chōsen to Nihon no rekishi* [The history of Korea and Japan]. Tokyo: Akashi shoten.

Lee, C., & De Vos, G. (1981). *Koreans in Japan: Ethnic conflict and accommodation.* Berkeley: University of California Press.

Martin, J., & Nakayama, T. (1997). *Intercultural communication in contexts.* Mountainview, CA: Mayfield Publishing.

Momose, T. (1998). *Kankoku ga shindemo Nihon ni oitsukenai 18 no riryū* [Eighteen facts why Korea would never catch up with Japan in business]. Tokyo: Bungei Shunshu.

Neary, I. (1997). Burakumin in contemporary Japan. In M. Weiner (Ed.), *Japan's minorities: The illusion of homogeneity.* New York: Routledge.

Nippon Hoso Kyokai. (1999, Aug. 15). *NHK special: Tonari no kuni wa partner, kako o norikoe kyusekkin* [Neighboring country, Korea: Overcoming the past] (TV program).

Ryang, S. (1997). *North Koreans in Japan: Language, ideology, and identity.* Boulder, CO: Westview Press.

Sakanaka, E. (1999). *Zainichi Kankoku Chosenjin seisakuron no tenkai* [Japan's policy regarding Korean minority]. Tokyo: Nippon Kajo Shuppan.

Samovar, L., & Porter, R. (1991). *Intercultural communication.* Belmont, CA: Wadsworth Publishing.

Sato, K. (1991). *Zainichi Kankoku Chosenjin ni tou* [Questions to Koreans in Japan]. Tokyo: Akishobo.

Siddle, R. (1997). Ainu: Japan's indigenous people. In M. Weiner (Ed.), *Japan's minorities: The illusion of homogeneity.* New York: Routledge.

Sugiura, M. (1999). *Internet to gaikokugo no jyugyou* [The Internet and its effect on the English education in Japan]. Available online: http://lang. nagoya u.ac.jp/~ sugiura/ed1997-06-30 gengobunkadayori.html

Suh, Y. (1987). *Kankoku Chōsenjin no genjyo to shōrai* [The present and future of Koreans in Japan]. Tokyo. Shakai Horon-sha.

Tajfel, H. (1981). *Human categories and social groups.* Cambridge: Cambridge University Press.

Tajfel, H. (1982). *Social identity and intergroup relations.* Cambridge University Press.

Tanaka, H. (1990). *Kyomo no kokusai kokka Nippon: Asia no shiten kara* [Illusionary internationalization in Japan: From Asian perspectives]. Tokyo: Rodo Keizaisha.

Tanaka, H. (1995). *Zainichi gaikokujin* [Foreign residents in Japan]. Tokyo: Iwanami Shoten.

Tsuji, Y. (1999). Internet o tsukatta Kankoku to no kokusai kyoryu [Intercultural communication with Korean students via the Internet]. *Education and Information, No. 490* (January), 8–11.

Uchiyama, K. (1982). *Zainichi Chōsenjin to kyōiku: Chosen o shiru kyōzai to jissen* [Education regarding the Korean minority: Related materials and pedagogical practices]. Tokyo: Sanichi Shobo.

Weiner, M. (1997). The invention of identity: "Self" and "other" in pre-war Japan. In M. Weiner (Ed.), *Japan's minorities: The illusion of homogeneity.* New York: Routledge.

Yoshino, K. (1992). *Cultural nationalism in contemporary Japan.* London: Routledge.

Yoshioka, M. (1995). *Zainichi gaikokujin to shakai hoshō* [Foreign residents in Japan and their social welfare]. Tokyo: Taihei Insatsu-sha.

Yoshioka, M., Inui, S., Kawase, S., & Yamamoto, H. (1984). *Zainichi Chōsenjin to shakai-hoshō* [Koreans in Japan and their social welfare]. Tokyo: Shakai Horon-sha.

Yun, K. (1992). *Zainichi o ikiruto wa.* [Living as a Korean in Japanese society]. Tokyo: Iwanami Shinsho.

Chapter 11

Nikkei Brazilians in Japan: The Ideology and Symbolic Context Faced by Children of This New Ethnic Minority

Tomoko Sekiguchi

This chapter examines the symbolic status of the children of Nikkei *Brazilian migrants to Japan. Analysis of their social position and the stereotypes about them in relation to Japanese attitudes toward foreigners indicates that, although ethnically favored,* Nikkei *Brazilians are socioculturally stigmatized and experience both ethnic inclusion and exclusion under the Japanese multifaceted stratification system. By focusing on the social categories reflected in the Japanese ethos, the way in which* Nikkei *Brazilian children are recognized and labeled, and by examining their ambiguous "in between" status as an ethnic Japanese anomaly, a deviation from "normal Japanese" but "not completely foreign," the author explores the vexing issues of who is Japanese and what constitutes one. It also reveals the blurred borderline between "Japaneseness" and "foreignness," the marginality into which the children of* Nikkei *Brazilians are placed, and from where they struggle to find out what and who they are.*

This chapter examines the symbolic context of *Nikkei-Burajirujin* (Japanese Brazilian)[1] children as members of a conspicuous, new ethnic minority in Japan, having grown in number to nearly a quarter of a million residents, largely over the last several decades. Although sharing in an ethnicity with Japanese nationals and receiving preferential treatment for entry into the country, *Nikkei* Brazilians still suffer the handicap of being a social minority in Japan. By examining their ambiguous status of *Nikkei* Brazilians as an "ethnic Japanese anomaly," a deviation from "normal Japanese" but "not completely foreign," the author intends to explore the vexing issues of who is Japanese and what it means to be Japanese. It also serves to reveal the blurred borderline between "Japaneseness" and "foreignness," the marginality into which the children of *Nikkei* Brazilians are placed, and from where they struggle to find out what and who they are.

Nikkei Brazilian children have become salient as *gaikokujinshijo* (foreign children)[2] in Japanese public schools, as the result of the influx of *dekasegi* (seasonal migrant) *Nikkei* migrants after the 1990 revision of the Immigration Control Law and Refugee Recognition Law, which made *Nikkeijin* (foreign nationals of Japanese ancestry) and their spouses eligible for long-term residence and employment in unskilled labor. In the Japanese public education system, however, these children are classified as quasi-*kikokushijo* (Japanese returnees who have been long abroad because of their parents' business) (Monbushō Kyouiku joseikyoku Kaigaishijokyouikuka, 1991, p. 59), and under the same remedial education program for *kikokushijo*, Japanese language education and guidance for adapting to the Japanese school are given in principle to these "ex-Japanese."

The current number of *Nikkei* Brazilian children in Japan is said to be about 50,000 ("Imakoso towareru Nihon," 1999), and because of their demographic upsurge, the system for receiving these Brazilian students has been gradually improved during the last decade, with such additional features as hiring part-time bilingual teachers and setting up a separate class named *kokusai kyoushitsu* (international classroom) for the students of limited Japanese proficiency and special sessions for *kokusai rikai kyouiku* (education for international understanding) to show and share particular Brazilian culture such as folk plays, songs, dances, and ethnic foods. However, as they proceed into junior high school, when schooling takes on rigid rules for conduct and academic performance and heavy demands for Japanese literacy, *Nikkei* Brazilian students generally come to lose interest in school and begin to cluster with fellow Brazilians, while becoming susceptible to socially deviant behaviors. Reported cases of school absences, school withdrawals, and juvenile delinquency have increased among *Nikkei* Brazilian teenagers, becoming one of the most prevalent concerns in the present-day *Nikkei* Brazilian community.

Such school problems have been attributed by educators to several causes.

1. the "transmigrant"[3] status of the parents by which they seem to live in limbo about their future plans for themselves and for their children's education;

2. intercultural differences between Japanese nationals and *Nikkei* Brazilians; and

3. the general antipathy for diversity that still exists in Japanese schools today.

In related discussions, however, the social significance of being *Nikkei* Brazilian in Japanese society and discursive labels that come attached receive little notice, warranting our present look. Thus, this chapter focuses on the role of social categories reflected in the Japanese ethos, the way in which *Nikkei* Brazilian children are recognized and labeled, and argues that the identity conflict and social problems now faced by the older children of *Nikkei* Brazilians result in part from the symbolic status accorded them in the Japanese belief system. This status indirectly, but fundamentally, defines the socio/psychological discourse of the environment in which these children are placed and structures the way they adapt to the host society.

JAPANESE STEREOTYPES OF *GAIKOKUJIN*: IMAGE AND IDEOLOGY

The Relative Status of *Nikkei* Brazilians: In Between the Admired and the Despised

When I speak to clerks in Portuguese at the Japanese department store, they just ignore me. But, when an American speaks to them in English, they will attend to him very quickly. The Japanese hate, avoid, and discriminate against the Brazilians. The only people the Japanese like and respect are the Americans.[4]

So says a Brazilian student attending public junior high school in a highly concentrated area of *Nikkei* Brazilians, where they comprise 30% of the total residents. Indeed, one *Nikkei* American resident of the area, who speaks limited Japanese but looks Japanese, claims being poorly served several times because he was mistaken as a *Nikkei* Brazilian. His claims gain credence because he once revealed that he was an American and a store clerk apologized saying, "I am sorry, I thought you were a Brazilian. . . ."[5] A question arises: Is being Brazilian perceived as negative in Japan?

The purpose of this section is to explore the relative position of the *Nikkei* Brazilian among other "foreigners" in Japanese perception today (Table 11A-1, in the Appendix) and to examine the general image of each "foreign" group held by the Japanese (Tables 11A-2, 11A-3, and 11A-4, in the Appendix), leading to a discussion about the psychological, social, and political effects of such images on the acculturation process of *Nikkei* Brazilian children. The intent here is only exploratory, for most of the data presented relied on nonrandomized sampling of attitudes through questionnaire or interview assessments. Still, certain patterns emerge consistent with generally accepted views of Japanese. Moreover, my own survey (Sekiguchi, 1999), if anything, is a conservative estimate of Japanese attitudes toward "foreigners" because my sample was taken from *kikokushijo* at a private sectarian school in the Nagoya metropolitan area, given the assumed name herein of *Kita Kokusai Gakuen* (Kita International Junior High/High School), whose enrollment is largely *kikokushijo* (90%) and the rest, foreign students (10%), including a few *Nikkei* Brazilians. The school's international basis is derived from the fact that it caters to children who have had experience living abroad or have international heritage and do not fit easily into the Japanese school system. Given its openness to diversity and its students' own crosscultural experiences,[6] and the fact that it is near a community of *Nikkei* Brazilians, this school was considered ideal to tap relevant attitudes among its students. Although *kikokushijo* are probably more positive in attitude toward "foreignness" and therefore less representative of Japanese attitudes in general, we can expect them to have more realistic views and to be more capable of distinguishing various cultures and nations of the world, including *Nikkei* Brazilians, from their inside/outside perspectives.

Also, in this study, the term "stereotype" is defined as "an exaggerated image (mental, verbal, or visual) of the characteristics of a target group, which is motivated by intergroup tension or conflict" (Donahue, 1998, p. 90), and the term "foreigner" is deliberately used for the vague concept of so-called "*gaijin*" or "*gaikokujin*" in Japanese ideology: a miscellaneous image of "others" signified as "foreign" or "non-Japanese," mixed with feelings toward "*gaikoku*" (foreign countries). Although I am well aware of the flaw in the "foreign" group categorization on the tables, for the sake of comparison and in order to tap "stereotypical" images, I decided to use the same categories as had been used in the previous studies. Therefore, the "foreigner" label on the tables represents an inaccurate but typical labeling of "*gaijin/gaikokujin*" in the minds of Japanese, which does not solely involve nationality, but also "race," ethnic origin, or any group status marked as "outsider" in Japanese society.

The preference for and the traits perceived in each group are oversimplified or overgeneralized, revealing aspects of the Japanese ideology concerning "foreigners." Analysis of each group is interesting in its own right, but the discussion here is focused on the *Nikkei* Brazilians and their major reference groups. Table 11A-1 confirms the well-known Japanese preference for Westerners, especially for British and Americans.[7] Also notable in Table 11A-1 is the improvement of blacks in rank over time, in contrast to the stable positioning of the best-liked and the least-liked groups. Even though the changing climate cannot be generalized across generations,[8] "black"-styled popular culture is becoming "hip" among young Japanese, such as *ganguro* (an abbreviation of "*gangan kuroi*" or "super black"), a style marked by faces tanned golden brown and hair styles imitative of "afro" fashion.

The principal source of information for the "black-is-cool" image is from the highly sensationalized visual images of black (mostly African American) pop musicians, basketball stars, world-class athletes, models, and movie stars in the mass media that appeal to young Japanese. The effect of these visual images presented in television and movies is important. For, if the media deals primarily in sensationalized images, whether positive or negative, and the viewer has little opportunity for personal contact with the related ethnic or racial group, the probability of the stereotype becoming the reality to the viewer becomes likely. The improved image of blacks seems still to be distorted by their being cast as the "super athletes and/or entertainers" and underrepresented for "intellectual pursuits." While certain traits such as having "quick reflexes" and being "cheerful" remain undeniably associated with blacks across time as shown in Table 11A-2, the "clever/bright" attribute is completely absent for black people.[9]

Indeed, Tables 11A-2 and 11A-3 reveal how we tend to perceive each foreign group with certain traits, how the visual image of *kawaii/kakkoii* (cute/cool) is becoming a key attribute of person perception among young Japanese,[10] and how negative attributes are fixed on particular groups over the years. The tables reflect *honne* (private inner feeling), making explicit the stratified ethnic/racial/national valuations hidden in the Japanese mind, which usually underlie *tatemae* (public behavior, socially desirable attitude). The important point here is that these stereotypes are more or less based on ignorance or misrepresentation, but easily become the reality of intergroup relations if reinforced and maintained by media images or by hearsay knowledge. Without critical consciousness, Japanese may interpret a person's behavior and speech based on ethnicity, "race," and/or national origins, as viewed through the lens of stereotyped images grown, developed, and absorbed uncritically within a Japanese social milieu. (Such practice, of course, can be seen anywhere. As Maeyama [1996] points out, if individual [A] had a fight with individual [B] in Brazil, it would be described as "*japonés*" [Japanese] had a fight with "*italiano*" [Italian].) With these various points in mind, we now consider the *Nikkei* Brazilians with reference to other "foreigners."

Table 11A-1 shows the seemingly good position of Brazilians in 1999, as compared with other major nationalities in Japan, such as Koreans, Chinese, and Filipinos.[11] Iranians, with the least favorability, became visible as foreign workers in Japan from the late 1980s to the early 1990s, like *Nikkei* Brazilians. Comparing the images of Iranians in Table 11A-2 with the ones of *Nikkei* Brazilians in Table 11A-3, however, it is clear that Iranians have a negative image. The difference in favorability might result from the media's "priming effects"[12] (Zebrowitz, 1990) by their sympathetic tone toward *Nikkei* Brazilians, who are portrayed as "legal" workers, who have ties with Japanese heritage, and who are working hard despite their difficulties. In contrast, an unfavorable tone exists toward Iranians, who are depicted as "illegal" workers and who commit crimes ranging from the selling of tampered telephone cards to that of illicit drugs.[13]

This ethnically privileged position of the *Nikkei* Brazilians in the Japanese psyche is exhibited, to begin with, in the enactment of an open immigration policy toward "ethnic Japanese." (Note, however, that this policy applies only up to the third generation of ethnic Japanese, unlike Germany's almost unlimited admission of ethnic Germans [Kajita, 1999].) The *Nikkei* Brazilian privileged status is based on a vague Japanese premise that *Nikkeijin* of Japanese blood lineage are assumed to be "culturally" as well as "physically" related to Japanese nationals, as expressed by this Japanese factory worker:

Discrimination and disparagement is less toward the Brazilian *Nikkeijin* because they have a Japanese face. . . . Since we see them as people who were originally Japanese, we are more sympathetic. There is much more discrimination toward the *zainichi Kankokujin* [Korean Japanese]. (Tsuda, 1998, pp. 322–323)

And speaking of Korean Japanese, although Tsuda translated *zainichi Kankokujin* into "Korean Japanese," there is no vocabulary in Japanese to refer to such a person of multicultural heritage, and thus, the conception of Korean Japanese has not yet been generally established. Koreans born and raised in Japan are both culturally and phenotypically indistinguishable from Japanese, but because of their Korean lineage, they continue to be regarded as "foreign" residents and not accepted as Japanese (Fukuoka, 1993). See chapter 10 for a first-hand report on this issue.

The Mixed Status of *Nikkei* Brazilians: *Kikokushijo* from the Third World and *Hāfu*

Actually, the image of *Nikkei* Brazilians is nearly as good as that for *kikokushijo* (see Table 11A-3). The lower frequency for each attribute in my survey, as compared to Takao's, may suggest a decline in the positive image for *Nikkei* Brazilians over the last decade, or the general lower frequency for the "typical" image could suggest more realistic views by my respondents. Although the relatively good attributes such as being "active, amiable, cheerful, and cute/cool" are common to both groups, the attributes of clever/bright, individualistic, and progressive appear reserved for *kikokushijo* in comparison to *Nikkei* Brazilians. Here, Brazilian nationality and socioeconomic factors outweigh whatever positive pull their Japanese ethnicity may have for these *Nikkei*.

The image of the *kikokushijo* is almost identical to that of Americans in both Takao's and my results, but not because they have all returned from the United States. Rather, it is because the United States is the typical ideological model of *gaikoku* (foreign country) in the mind of Japanese youths today. This is concretely shown in the conventional discourse in our casual conversation of "*gaikoku, tatoeba Amerika*" (foreign countries, for example, the United States) (Lummis, 1997). The distorted formula in Japanese perception of *gaikoku* = *Amerika* = *eigo* (English) = *hakujin* (whites) = *shinpoteki* (progressive) is also confirmed by the remarks of Japanese returnees, such as: "Whenever Japanese meet a foreigner, they think he or she is American, even if British, French, or any other nationality"; "When Japanese friends find I am from Belgium, they say '*Eigo pera-pera de ii ne*'" (You are lucky to be able to speak English fluently).[14] Naturally, the image of the *kikokushijo* is predominantly represented by children returned from the United States. This has functioned to develop the special "brand image" of *kikokushijo*, as the Japanese who can speak "cool" English, an image pervasive in Japan (*Kaigaishijo Kyouiku Shinkou Zaidan*, 1998), and who have positive characteristics analogous to those perceived for Americans, and who have the "privileged class image of an international elite."[15]

Brazil, in contrast, has historically and psychologically held little attention for Japanese (Maeyama, 1997).[16] The lack of interest in Brazil among the Japanese becomes evident in the fact that in the longitudinal study of national preference among university students (Nishikawa, 1992),[17] Brazil has never been among the top 15 countries either in the list of favored countries or of those disliked. Also, in the previous studies on Japanese national/racial distance (Wagatsuma & Yoneyama, 1967; Izumi, 1953), Brazilians never have been included in the list of nationalities to be chosen. Even with the increased mania over the J League soccer teams and the many human interest stories in the media about *Nikkei* Brazilians, little has changed in the Japanese perception of Brazil as being the "Third World country with the Amazon, the Samba Carnival, great soccer players, and coffee." The majority of Japanese continue to be indifferent to Brazil and see the *Nikkei* Brazilians as "peculiar" Japanese returnees, who speak a "strange" language,[18] have a "jovial Latino character," and are "unfortunate" *dekasegi* people from a culturally, socially, and economically underdeveloped nation.[19]

What then is the image of the Japanese held by people outside Japan? Be it *kikokushijo*, *Nikkei* Americans, or *Nikkei* Brazilians, they are all seen as representative Japanese within their respective locales. A sizable literature on *kikokushijo* and overseas *Nikkei* tells us that no matter where they grow up in an environment detached from Japanese society, local people's perception of them is strongly interrelated with the image of Japan/Japanese and its international status and power. Thus, stereotypes of the Japanese must have some impact on the self-perception of those ethnic Japanese living overseas either temporarily or as a result of long-term immigration. In Table 11A-3, the typical traits for the Japanese include "mass psychological, polite, clever, methodical, and quiet." These traits are rather congruent with the stereotype of *Nikkei* American students in the United States as being "quiet, conforming, hardworking, and highly motivated" (Kitano, 1997, p. 113), and of *Nikkei* Brazilians in Brazil as being "ugly, but intelligent and hard working" (Maeyama, 1996, p. 494). The *Nikkei* stereotype seems to be consistent, but at the same time, we should keep in mind the fickle nature of stereotypes when combined with changes in a social context. In the history of *Nikkei* Americans in the United States, under the influence of wartime hysteria, the stereotype of "sly, sneaky, tricky Jap" shaped the cry "Japs Must Go." In March 1942, because they were considered to be of an "evil race," persons of Japanese ancestry, defined as anyone with as little as one eighth Japanese blood, were made to evacuate to relocation camps (Kitano, 1997). After WWII, coupled with Japan's rising international status as an economic power, both *Nikkei* Americans and *Nikkei* Brazilians have established an image of a successful "model minority" by their educational and occupational achievement. However, we should be mindful that these so-called "model" minorities are rarely found among the top elites in each country, for they are positioned in the second tier of the social stratification system as "middleman," due to their racial/ethnic origin.

Ironically, when they return to Japan, both *kikokushijo* and *Nikkeijin*, who were formerly seen as representative Japanese, are contrarily seen as "strange Japanese" who had lost their Japanese culture in favor of alien behavioral patterns and languages. The crucial point here, however, is that these "Japanese anomalies" are not treated equally. In the mind of the majority Japanese, they are ranked along national, social, and cultural characteristics. *Kikokushijo* are positively valued as potential elites; *Nikkei* Americans, backed by the American image, as relatively positive but less fashionable *Nikkeijin*;[20] and *Nikkei* Brazilians, as negative *Nikkeijin* with unprogressive undertones associated with the Brazilian image and the low socioeconomic status of *dekasegi* in Japan. Table 11A-3 does not reveal this distinction, probably because the young Japanese in my survey were not familiar enough with Japanese emigration history to develop negative perceptions of *Nikkeijin*.[21] The table does show, however, how national image casts a shadow on the social perception of the *Nikkei* Brazilian. Among those of ethnic Japanese origin, only the *Nikkei* Brazilians are not seen as being "smart-Japanese," which is ironic because the very image of being "smart" is firmly attached to *Nikkeijin* in Brazil, at least until recently.[22]

People of mixed parentage are also an important reference group, because "mixed blood *Nikkei*" now describes the majority of *Nikkei* Brazilian teens. "Marrying out of the ethnic group" is the most visible change in today's *Nikkei* Brazilian society, and the out-marriage rate has been increasing generation by generation: among *Nisei* (the second generation), 6.03%; *Sansei* (the third generation), 42.00%; and *Yonsei* (the fourth generation), 61.62% (Oyama, 1995a).

Although out-marriage historically was disapproved of in Japan, statistics show a fivefold increase in intermarriages over the last 30 years, going from just 5,546 (0.5% of all marriages) in 1970 to 29,636 (3.8% of all marriages) in 1998 (Kouseishou, 2000), indicative of changing social conditions, though still slow. One particular pattern of intermarriages to note is that of arranged marriages through introduction agencies that match Japanese men and Asian women (largely from the Philippines, China, and Thailand). These women generally are viewed as "foreign brides" or "brides from Asia," and their offspring receive a peripheral status in Japan, for which Tsutusmi (1997) applies the term of "marginal child."

At least among young Japanese, more receptive attitudes toward people of mixed heritage seem apparent. Such people, as shown in Table 11A-4, are not cast in a negative light by at least the young Japanese in 1999, showing improvement in the image of "mixed black" as compared to that in Wagatsuma and Yoneyama's study in 1967. The history of labels attached to them also tells us of the change in the image and social connotation of being mixed (see Table 11A-5),[23] from *ainoko* (half-breed: derogatory), *konketsu-ji* (mixed blood[24] child: derogatory, but becoming more a neutral term as a technical description), *hāfu* (the Japanese pronunciation of the word "half": the most popular term), to that of *kokusai-ji* (international child: the term to celebrate an international heritage) and *daburu* (the Japanese pronunciation of the word "double": the term to stress the positive aspects of a bicultural heritage).

Indeed, being *hāfu* in today's Japan is not so stigmatic as it used to be;[25] rather, it has become almost fashionable, in that the viewing public is now exposed to numerous good-looking *hāfu* entertainers and models in the mass media. Murphy-Shigematsu (1996) also points out the idealized image of *hāfu* perceived by young Japanese as having the ideal physical attributes plus being bilingual, bicultural, and intelligent, associated with bilingual English instructors, TV announcers, and radio disc jockeys. For another example: "I am a 'half.' While in Japan, I want to be looked at as a non-Japanese, because everybody regards a half positively here," as viewed by a high school girl of an Italian father and a Japanese mother, enrolled in an international school in Japan (Minoura, 1995, p. 199). This is all well and good, but we ought to be mindful also that there are important class and racial distinctions among the *hāfu* images and that *hāfu* still remains a marked status in Japanese society. A social hierarchy among mixed-race people exits in Japan, in which Japanese Caucasian individuals are given much greater status than individuals of other mixed racial backgrounds (Hall, 1996). In Table 11A-4, too, there is a subtle difference in nuance attached to the different racial categories. The typical cute/cool image accorded to "mixed white" is absent in "mixed Asian," where the traits usually attached to Asians seem to predominate, while in "mixed black," the black's athletic and emotional image explicitly shown in Table 11A-2 still seems to remain. The power of the stereotypes ought not to be underestimated, for its influence on person perception, even if not permanent, fights to persist. Whether these epithets are phrased positively or not, as long as people are uncritical of their irrational nature, such stereotypes can encourage social avoidance and discrimination when motivated by intergroup tension.

COMPLEXITY OF ETHNICITY AND IDENTITY

Within-Culture Diversity: From Fully Foreign to Fully Japanized

Table 11A-6 shows the multifaceted reality of ethnic *Nikkei* Brazilian society in Japan. Generally speaking, for the *Nikkei* Brazilian teens, *Issei* are their grand-parents, *Nisei* and non-*Nikkei* Brazilians are their parents, and *Sansei/Yonsei* (mainly *hāfu*) are themselves. We should note the multiple appearances (fully Japanese, partly foreign, or fully foreign) and the within-culture diversity well represented by the presence of "full-foreign" Brazilians. Also, the growth in the number of *Sansei/Yonsei* born and raised in Japan adds further intergenerational, intercultural gaps. Their identities, molded from the start in contemporary Japan, must be far different from their own grandparents, parents, and older siblings. Nevertheless, that is the reality the *Nikkei* Brazilian community now faces, which elucidates the current cultural transition of Japanese society from the mythical "stability, homogeneity, and purity" toward the reality of "fluidity, multiplicity, and hybridity."

AMBIVALENT ETHNICITY: IN BETWEEN THE POSITIVE AND THE NEGATIVE

Nikkei Brazilian teens, especially those who look Japanese in appearance, experience ambiguous social categorization in their everyday lives. Having been called *japonés* (Japanese) or *chinés* (Chinese) in Brazil, and called *Burajirujin* or *gaijin* (foreigner) in Japan, their ethnic identity reflects ambivalence, inner conflict, and situational dissonance, which is exemplified in typical statements such as "In Japan I am Brazilian, but in Brazil, I am *Nikkeijin* or *Nihonjin* (Japanese)" (Sekiguchi, 1999, p. 172). They are made conscious of being ethnically different and marginal in both countries.

In Brazil, "*Nikkei*ness," however, is a racial categorization that entails the status of a "positive minority," while in Japan, it is an out-group distinction placing them in the status of "weak negative minority,"[26] ethnically privileged but socio-culturally denigrated. This subtle minority status is well reflected in the consciousness of *Nikkei* students, as shown in the following student voice by a "full" *Nikkei* junior high school girl, who came to Japan at the age of 6 and is now perceived by her teachers and parents as "totally Japanized":

I feel a bit ashamed of being *Nikkei* Brazilian. . . . Having a Brazilian background is perceived as slightly negative, at least here in Japan. I wish I could become a Japanese. Or, I wish I could have stayed in Brazil in the first place, so I wouldn't have to feel this way.[27]

Usually, the negativity of being *Nikkei* Brazilians is not activated in public, as long as they stay "invisible" by conforming to Japanese behavioral patterns. However, once they become "visible" as a "non-Japanese" critical mass, it may lead Japanese nationals, who had since been tolerant or indifferent, to feel anxiety, fear, and hostility. Confronted with conspicuous "Brazilianness," Japanese nationals erect mental barriers between "us" and "them." Brazilian language, communication style, and ways of behavior are depreciated within Japanese society. Their freer interpersonal expressions and less restrained behavior are frowned on. Moreover, when certain Brazilians engage in undesirable conduct such as "partying" until midnight on weekends, throwing garbage out recklessly, and clustering in groups in the streets or around a corner, those behaviors are prone to be over-generalized[28] as "Brazilian cultural characteristics," which leads to more negative stereotypes such as the traits "ill-mannered, wild, and horrible."[29] Gradually, the image of "noisy Brazilians indifferent to the rules of the Japanese society" becomes the standard perception, and by then, the whole group of *Nikkei* Brazilians are likely viewed as "that bunch," a collective disturbance in the neighborhood.

During this process, combined with the reinforcing effect of rumor and media coverage of a recent increase of juvenile delinquency and crimes among *Nikkei* Brazilians, mere symbolic prejudice based on latent stereotypes of Brazilian culture and language has been amplified to actual discriminatory acts of social avoidance or residential segregation. The general neglect by the municipal government and the housing corporation of the "*Nikkei* Brazilian problem," the *Nikkei* Brazilians' lack of commitment to the local community by being "transmigrants," and the exodus of Japanese residents from the fieldwork area all worsened the situation, in addition to the multiplying mechanism of prejudice when it reaches a critical mass among in-group members in view of outsiders. Under this condition, Brazilian youth find themselves unwanted and socially unaccepted. The bottom line for Japanese society is that "Brazilianness" must yield in favor of "Japaneseness"—the "proper" Japanese way—if these *Nikkei* wish to live in Japan. However, in the process of conforming to the Japanese way, two separate courses are laid before *Nikkei* Brazilian children.

Japanese Face and *Gaijin* Face: Two Disparate Discourses of Inclusion and Exclusion

Among the multiple "faces" of *Nikkei* Brazilians in Japan, which type can be accepted as "Japanese" in Japan? The answer is only those who are fully ethnic Japanese, having a "Japanese face," a "Japanese blood line," and a "Japanese name." Neither a non-*Nikkei* Brazilian who decides to get Japanese citizenship to settle in Japan and changes his or her own name to a Japanese one nor a mixed-*Yonsei* born and raised in Japan and culturally indistinguishable from other Japanese nationals can ever be considered as being "full-fledged Japanese," because of their non-Japanese phenotype and blood lineage. The latter is approximated as such by virtue of the *koseki* family registry, a municipally held record of one's genealogy.

Social expectation, social acceptance, and social treatment toward *Nikkei* Brazilian children are structured according to this principle. The "full" *Nikkei* (in contrast to "mixed" *Nikkei*) who have a "Japanese face" but are culturally foreign are viewed as "incomplete Japanese" in the eyes of Japanese nationals, just as *kikokushijo* used to be. The internal/external psychological pressure on the fully ethnic Japanese to assimilate into becoming "normal Japanese" is strong, especially within the culturally intolerant public school system. Therefore, as "full" *Nikkei* students adapt to the school culture, they soon choose to become "invisible" by using a Japanese full name so that they will not stand out as "I-am-from-Brazil." This symbolic choice of using a full Japanese name is a political strategy of a mono-ethnic *Nikkei* family to expand their life opportunities in Japan.[30] It is also tacitly understood by Japanese teachers that a "full" *Nikkei* student will not use a Portuguese name, so as not to be differentiated from the "normal Japanese." The ultimate choice for a mono-ethnic *Nikkei* family is to become "authentic Japanese" through naturalization, by which they will complete the process of normalization and obtain a "ticket" to join the majority group in Japanese society.

In contrast, the "mixed" *Nikkei* students use a mixed name with a Japanese family name and a Portuguese first name and continue to be treated as *gaijin*, even if they are acculturated enough to have forgotten Portuguese and feel more socially comfortable with Japanese. They are not expected to act like Japanese as the "full" *Nikkei* are. Their *gaijin* looks function as an internal/external brake on the process of their further assimilation. Their physical face, however, can also function as a cultural asset in today's Japan, as we have seen earlier. A *hāfu* face, not too exotic but cute enough with some Japanese features, is now in high demand by the Japanese advertising industry and entertainment media (Oyama, 1995b). Mixed *Nikkei* Brazilians, therefore, tend to dream of becoming a model or a celebrity, knowing full well that by being good-looking they might gain a "ticket" for success in Japan. Nonetheless, being sociopsychologically excluded from the track of becoming Japanese, mixed *Nikkei* who cannot "pass" into the mainstream find life easier by adopting a separate identity, just as they are, one oriented toward being bicultural or transcultural (Sekiguchi, 1997). However, except for the fortunate ones with competence and high motivation plus the dedicated support from parents, teachers, and peers, most average students, placed in powerless and frustrated settings as being "unsure when to return to Brazil, where to fit in, and what goals to set," tend to adopt an "oppositional identity" (Davidson, 1996; Ogubu & Simons, 1998) that resists Japanese schooling and leads to delinquent behavior.

CONCLUSION

Multiculturalism, a view of national/social integration, presumes an appreciation of diverse cultures. Such a view has been disseminated in Japan since the 1980s as a "liberal/cultural pluralist approach" (Gordon, 1981; Sekine, 1994), which at least tries to guarantee "equality of opportunity" and allows cultural diversity within private spheres (Sekine, 1994). This view, along with the notion of *uchinaru kokusaika* (internal internationalization), has been circulated as a politically correct slogan and has come to acknowledge the long-neglected ethnic cultures within Japanese society. However, if my findings are valid, then Japan still has a long way to go before multiculturalism makes any headway on the islands. The consistent pattern of negative or positive stereotypes of certain "foreign" groups over three decades, as we have seen, suggests that those categorical valuations or biases are more or less shared and accepted as a social norm in Japan. As Wagatsuma and Yoneyama (1967) observes, prejudice and discrimination are social norms and aspects of culture that lead its members, overtly or covertly, to so treat a target group. In fact, the pattern of stereotypes identified is even supported, though also revealing of a new upward trend for the black image, by a supposedly "progressively minded" group of Japanese that is *kikokushijo* who view "Japaneseness" with critical eyes.

The concept of "Japaneseness" is itself an exclusionary ideology deeply linked with "blood" or racialized beliefs, which is employed by the mainstream majority Japanese to identify themselves when contrasted with "foreignness." The imagined symbol of "Japanese blood," signified as the boundary marker for the "Japanese identity," is associated with an exclusive entitlement to "Japanese language and cultural competence" (Yoshino, 1997), which makes social assimilation by foreigners, even those having partial Japanese ethnicity, more difficult and denies them full participation in Japanese society. Most Japanese, who live in a monocultural setting in everyday life, seem uninterested in questioning the social practices that manifest this ideology. However, facing the social reality of increasing numbers of foreign residents from diverse cultural origins and "mixed" children in the cultural margins, the conventional view of "Japaneseness" is ripe for serious challenge. A case in point is the *Nikkei* Brazilians who embody its boundary dissonance and categorical dilemmas themselves. Perhaps because of their preferential treatment as "Japanese," yet who still receive foreign, marked status, they may help to pinpoint the real issue involved.

Japanese school programs for Brazilian folk dance or samba festival under the name of *kokusai rikai kyouiku* (education for international understanding), no matter how well intentioned, could end up simply reinforcing cultural stereotypes rather than fostering a sense of multiculturalism, if they take place in the unquestioned supremacy of mainstream Japanese discourse. The identity and social problems faced by *Nikkei* Brazilian teens are a collective problem common to all culturally stigmatized ethnic minority youths in Japan, such as the Koreans, the Chinese,[31] the *burakumin* (a historical outcast group of Japanese), the *Ainu* (an indigenous people), and the *Okinawans* (another indigenous people).[32] The fundamental issue is not differences in language and culture per se, but the symbolic status conferred on the minority by mainstream Japanese, a matter embedded in the history and the structure of Japanese society.

Appendix Tables 11A-1 through 11A-6 follow.

Table 11A-1
Ranking of *Gaikokujin* by Young Japanese[33]

Rank	Wagatsuma & Yoneyama (1967) (univ. students) $n = 80$	Takao (1992) (young people: age 18–29) $n = 55$	Sekiguchi (1999) (*kikokushijo:* age 15–18) $N = 50$	Average rank*
1	British	American/British	American	2.44
2	German	—	British	4.32
3	French	Italian	Italian	4.94
4	American	German	French	5.52
5	Italian	French	Black	5.68
6	Asian Indian	Chinese	Swiss	5.88
7	Russian	Indonesian	German	6.20
8	Chinese	Thai	New Zealand	6.24
9	Thai	Black	Australian	6.28
10	Indonesian	Asian Indian/Russian	Brazilian	6.80
11	Filipino	—	Filipino	8.52
12	Black	Korean	Chinese	8.68
13	Korean	Filipino	Asian Indian	8.76
14	—	Iranian	Indonesian	8.96
15	—	—	Russian	9.70
16	—	—	Thai	9.80
17	—	—	Korean	10.74
18	—	—	Iranian	11.26

*Average rank: total of ranking/50, e.g., for American, total ranking number 122 was divided by 50, rendering 2.44.

Table 11A-2
Japanese Images of *Gaikokujin*[34]

	Wagatsuma & Yoneyama (1967) (10s–60s: mainly 20s–40s) $N = 270$			Takao (1992) (10s–70s: mainly 20s–30s) $N = 94$			Sekiguchi (1999) (*kikokushijo*: age 15–18) $N = 50$		
	Adjective	N	%	Adjective	N	%	Adjective	N	%
British	Polite	197	73.0	Polite	62	65.6	Polite	17	34.0
	Conservative	163	60.4	Conservative	39	41.5	Calm	13	26.0
	Calm	94	34.8	Rational	33	35.1	Cute, cool	12	22.0
	Rational	94	34.8	Calm	22	23.4	Clean	9	18.0
	Moral	67	24.8	Intelligent	22	23.4	Intelligent	9	18.0
American	Cheerful	147	54.4	Cheerful	52	55.3	Amiable	16	32.0
	Amiable	99	36.7	Active	34	36.2	Friendly	15	30.0
	Active	86	31.9	Amiable	33	35.1	Cute, cool	15	30.0
	Progressive	85	31.5	Progressive	28	29.8	Progressive	14	28.0
	Individualistic	77	28.5	Friendly	23	24.5	Cheerful	12	24.0
							Active	12	24.0

(continued)

Table 11A-2 *(continued)*

	Wagatsuma & Yoneyama (1967)			Takao (1992)			Sekiguchi (1999)		
	Adjective	N	%	Adjective	N	%	Adjective	N	%
French	Artistic	164	60.7	Artistic	52	55.3	Artistic	15	30.0
	Cheerful	107	39.6	Individualistic	26	27.7	Cute, cool	11	22.0
	Individualistic	78	28.9	Talkative	20	21.3	Lovely	10	20.0
	Amiable	73	27.0	Argumentative	15	16.0	Amiable	8	16.0
	Emotional	62	23.0	Rational	15	16.0	Clean	7	14.0
							Individualistic	7	14.0
Black	Quick reflexes	86	31.9	Quick reflexes	49	52.1	Quick reflexes	22	44.0
	Cheerful	68	25.9	Cheerful	34	36.2	Cheerful	14	28.0
	Superstitious	65	24.1	Active	19	20.2	Healthy	11	22.0
	Impulsive	51	18.9	Emotional	16	17.0	Good natured	9	18.0
	Unsophisticated	50	18.5	Frightening	16	17.0	Talkative	9	18.0
							Gentle	9	18.0
							Cute, cool	8	16.0
							Emotional	8	16.0
Filipino	Cheerful	69	25.6	Mass psych.	21	22.3	Gentle	7	14.0
	Emotional	48	17.8	Slovenly	20	21.3	Talkative	6	12.0
	Unsophisticated	47	17.4	Unsophisticated	17	18.1	Active	6	12.0
	Conservative	40	14.8	Filthy	17	18.1	Lovely	6	12.0
	Lazy	40	14.8	Amiable	16	17.0	Good natured	5	10.0
	Unattractive	40	14.8				Amiable	5	10.0
Chinese	Patient	59	21.9	Polite	20	21.3	Short tempered	10	20.0
	Shrewd	57	21.1	Conservative	20	21.3	Clever	10	20.0
	Superstitious	57	21.1	Shrewd	19	20.2	Emotional	8	16.0
	Sly	49	18.1	Mass psych.	18	19.4	Active	7	14.0
	Conservative	49	18.1	Unsophisticated	16	17.0	Stingy	6	12.0
							Talkative	6	12.0
Korean	Filthy	87	32.2	Emotional	25	26.6	Short tempered	13	26.6
	Sly	79	29.3	Conservative	23	24.5	Calm	7	14.0
	Subservient	77	28.5	Shrewd	20	21.3	Clever	7	14.0
	Bad mannered	66	24.4	Sly	19	20.2	Talkative	6	12.0
	Mass psych.	64	23.7	Mass psych.	19	20.2	Mass psych.	6	12.0
				Polite	19	20.2	Emotional	6	12.0
Russian	Evil minded	47	17.4	Sly	26	27.7	Frightening	8	16.0
	Shrewd	47	17.4	Evil minded	20	21.3	Sly	7	14.0
	Artistic	46	17.0	Gloomy	17	18.1	Evil minded	7	14.0
	Scientific	44	16.3	Conservative	17	18.1	Active	7	14.0
	Sly	42	15.6	Reticent	15	16.0	Conservative	6	12.0
							Scientific	6	12.0
Iranian				Frightening	28	29.8	Short tempered	9	18.0
				Superstitious	26	27.7	Frightening	9	18.0
				Mass psych.	22	23.4	Law breaking	7	14.0
				Sly	18	19.1	Active	7	14.0
				Weird	15	16.0	Impulsive	6	12.0
							Violent	5	10.0
							Talkative	5	10.0

Table 11A-3
Japanese Images of *Nikkei* Brazilians and Other Reference Groups

Group	Takao (1992) (10s–70s: mainly 20s–30s) N = 94			Sekiguchi (1999) (*kikokushijo*: age 15–18) N = 50					
	Adjective	N	%	Adjective	N	%	Adjective	N	%
Nikkei Brazilian	Cheerful	42	44.7	Good natured	9	18.0	Cheerful	15	30.0
	Amiable	34	36.2	Active	9	18.0	Emotional	11	22.0
	Active	24	25.5	Amiable	9	18.0	Active	11	22.0
	Good natured	23	24.5	Cheerful	8	16.0	Amiable	10	20.0
	Friendly	23	24.5	Cute, cool	8	16.0	Quick reflexes	9	18.0
kikokushijo	Active	46	48.9	Clever	19	38.0	Mass psych.	21	42.0
	Individualistic	43	45.7	Amiable	16	32.0	Polite	17	34.0
	Progressive	40	42.6	Cheerful	15	30.0	Clever	16	32.0
	Cheerful	39	41.5	Progressive	15	30.0	Methodical	15	30.0
	Amiable	28	29.8	Cute, cool	15	30.0	Quiet	10	20.0
				Active	13	26.0	Reticent	9	18.0
American	Cheerful	52	55.3	Amiable	16	32.0	Cheerful	10	20.0
	Active	34	36.2	Friendly	15	30.0	Active	10	20.0
	Amiable	33	35.1	Cute, cool	15	30.0	Amiable	10	20.0
	Progressive	28	29.8	Progressive	14	28.0	Kind	9	18.0
	Friendly	23	24.5	Cheerful	12	24.0	Talkative	8	16.0
				Active	12	24.0	Clever	8	16.0

(For Sekiguchi 1999: first adjective set = *Nikkei* Brazilian / *kikokushijo** / American; second adjective set = Brazilian / Japanese** / *Nikkei* American)

* Because the participants in the Sekiguchi sample were *kikokushijo*, the question became "What image do you think the Japanese around you have of the *kikokushijo*? It does not have to be relevant to your own perception."

** The question asked was "What image do you think foreign people have for the general Japanese?"

212

Table 11A-4
Japanese Images of People of Mixed Parentage

	Wagatsuma & Yoneyama (1967) (10s–60s: mainly 20s–40s) N = 270			Sekiguchi (1999) (*kikokushijo*: age 15–18) N = 50		
	Adjective	N	%	Adjective	N	%
Mixed Black	Subservient	72	26.7	Gentle	12	24.0
	Healthy	55	20.4	Cute, cool	9	18.0
	Quick reflexes	53	19.6	Good natured	8	16.0
	Emotional	42	15.6	Healthy	8	16.0
	Reticent	41	15.2	Cheerful	7	14.0
				Amiable	7	14.0
				Short tempered	7	14.0
Mixed White	Cheerful	80	29.6	Cute, cool	15	30.0
	Emotional	51	18.9	Gentle	11	22.0
	Active	49	18.1	Cheerful	10	20.0
	Friendly	40	14.8	Kind	9	18.0
	Amiable	39	14.4	Amiable	8	16.0
	Individualistic	39	14.4	Polite	7	14.0
Mixed Asian				Gentle	9	18.0
				Clever	7	14.0
				Methodical	7	14.0
				Polite	6	12.0
				Good natured	6	12.0
				Healthy	6	12.0

Table 11A-5
Japanese Labels for People of Mixed Parentage

Japanese Label	English Translation	Image	Implication
Ainoko	Half-breed, Cross	Negative	Pejorative label toward the offspring of U.S. servicemen and Japanese women after WWII, associated with images of poverty, illegitimacy, and impurity; now obsolete and politically incorrect in public usage. *Ainoko* indicates "a child of unlike things put together" in the way used for hybrid plants/animals. Since "*ai*" meaning "love" is a homonym, the term was sometimes wittily mistranslated as "Love Child" to transform its negative connotation in this period when they were discriminated against socially as well as legally.

(continued)

213

Table 11A-5 *(continued)*

Japanese Label	English Translation	Image	Implication
Konketsu-ji	Mixed-blood child	Negative, neutral	Once considered derogatory under the ideology of pure bloodline; becoming a more neutral term as literal description in current usage. But, as the historical residue of social problems caused by the U.S. military and of overrepresented image in single-mother families and school dropouts, the negative nuance still lingers, especially when referring to the "Amerasian" fathered by U.S. servicemen in Okinawa, where 75% of the U.S. military installations in Japan are concentrated, and also to the offspring of "brides from Asia," which have been increasing recently.
Hāfu	Half	Negative, neutral, positive	Currently the most accepted term to describe persons of mixed heritage. The term *hāfu*, a borrowed word from English meaning "half foreigner and half Japanese," was created to avoid emotionally laden Japanese terms with history of negative associations and to signify a brighter image. Though the denigrating implication of "half-breed Japanese" still has not evaporated, the stylish image of being "cute/cool" and "bilingual" has become the popular stereotype of *hāfu* and for now used most often as a trendy label without a sense of its original English meaning.
Kokusai-ji	International child	Positive	Advanced in 1979, the International Year of the Child, as an alternative label for children of mixed ancestry to emphasize their positive aspect with the international quality of their parentage and their cultural background. This term is preferred by some awakened parents and journalists but never has been widely used and acknowledged.
Daburu also	Double	Positive	Another borrowed word from English to imply the positive aspects of double heritage. Considered as politically correct and as a term of empowerment, *daburu* is preferred by progressive people to the term *hāfu* because of the latter's less-than-whole connotation. This term is not yet established as general Japanese usage.

Table 11A-6
Multiple Faces of *Nikkei* Brazilians in Japan

	Japanese Nationality	"Pure" Japanese Bloodline	Japanese Face	Japanese Name	Japanese Language Competence	Japanese Cultural Competence	Birth in Japan	Current Residence in Japan
Issei	+/–	+	+	+	+	+/–	+	+
Nisei Full *Nikkei*	–/+	+	+	+/–	–/+	–/+	–	+
Sansei Full *Nikkei*	–/+	+	+	+/–	–/+	–/+	–/+	+
Yonsei Full *Nikkei*	–/+	+	+	+/–	–/+	–/+	–/+	+
Sansei Mixed	–/+	–	–	–/+	–/+	–/+	–/+	+
Yonsei Mixed	–/+	–	–	–/+	–/+	–/+	–/+	+
Non-*Nikkei* Brazilian	–/+	–	–	–	–/+	–/+	–	+

Note: + indicates having the attribute, and – indicates absence of the attribute. *Issei:* first generation (Japanese emigrant to Brazil); *Nisei:* second generation; *Sansei:* third generation; *Yonsei:* fourth generation. Full *Nikkei:* of "full" ethnic Japanese descendant; Mixed: of "mixed ethnic heritage" between *Nikkei* and non-*Nikkei*; Non-*Nikkei:* nonethnic Japanese heritage, who came to Japan as a "spouse of *Nikkeijin.*"

Notes and References follow.

NOTES

1. *Nikkei-Burajirujin* refers to Japanese emigrants to Brazil and their descendants. The term *"Nikkei"* here is defined as persons of Japanese descent and their descendants, who have returned to Japan where they constitute separate identities from the majority Japanese. The data in this chapter are based on the author's fieldwork in the most concentrated area of *Nikkei* Brazilians in the suburbs of Nagoya, Aichi prefecture (approximately 3,100 Brazilians out of 11,000 total residents as of December 31, 1998), from May 1994 to October 1995 and the follow-up from September 1998 to October 1999.

2. The word *shijo*, a classic administrative term meaning children, has been controversial, due to its nonneutral implication (*shi* for children and *jo* for women, literally translated). Thus, the term *gaikokujin-jidouseito* (foreign student) has replaced the term *gaikokujin-shijo* more recently in the literature.

3. A "transmigrant" pattern is emerging among *dekasegi Nikkei* Brazilians as their prolonged status of being "in between temporary and permanent," which is accompanied by the ambiguous stance of "one day, I'll go back to Brazil, but I don't know when," an ambiguity reinforced by the harder social/economic conditions in Brazil. For more details, see Mori (1999).

4. From a personal journal (n. d., approximately 1998) of a *Nikkei* Brazilian junior high school student writing about life in Japan and provided through the courtesy of Kimiko Nii. Originally written in Portuguese and translated by the author.

5. From an interview on June 25, 1999, with a Japanese American resident in the suburb of Nagoya.

6. I should add that quite a few students in my sample had declined taking this questionnaire because they thought such surveys induced prejudice, feeling that they could not comment on any group of "foreigners" without knowing individuals from each group. These students show at least a budding of their own critical consciousness.

7. A recent Yomiuri/Gallup poll done in Japan in 1999 (a stratified random sample of nearly 2,000) also reveals the Japanese favorable feeling toward Western countries, particularly the United States and England. The result in answer to the question "Among the following 25 countries, choose 5 countries you think most trustworthy" shows that the top 3 countries are the United States (43.9%), England (35.3%), and France (25.0%) (*Yomiuri Shimbun*, 1999, December 19, p. 13). The 1997 results to the same question of Yomiuri poll were the United States (40.6%), England (26.2%), and Switzerland/Australia (19.4%) (*Naikakusoridaijin Kanbo Kohoshitsu*, 1998, p. 534).

8. In Takao's data (1992, p. 33) for the cohorts in their 30s–40s and 50s–70s, no significant change was found: "black" was ranked by both cohort groups at 12, just ahead of Russian and Iranian.

9. In my data, nobody chose the clever/bright attribute for blacks. The distorted stereotypes of blacks in Japanese mass media are well analyzed by Russell (1991).

10. McVeigh (1999) indicates how *kawaisa* (cuteness) is a potent theme in Japan, permeating numerous spheres of Japanese daily life.

11. As of December 31, 1998, Koreans totaled 638,828; Chinese, 272,230; Brazilians, 222,217; and Filipinos, 105,308; and these groups constitute 81.9% of all foreign-registered residents in Japan (*Houmushou Nyūkokukanrikyoku*, 1999). Most Koreans are permanent residents, and those born and raised in Japan are called "old-comers"; those who

came to Japan as foreign workers after the 1970s are called "newcomers."

12. Priming effects are cognitive phenomena whereby perceivers' impressions of a person reflect those descriptive terms that are most accessible because they have been frequently activated.

13. Because the word *fuhou* (illegal) itself has a strong priming effect for inducing an impression of "bad guy" in the perceiver, alternative terms such as *hiseiki* (unofficial) and *shikakugai* (uncertified) recently have been suggested. Consider how the general image of *Nikkei* Brazilians is becoming negative because of the increased coverage of juvenile delinquency and crimes, such as car robbery and stealing among Brazilians in Japan. See the National Police Agency report, *Keisatsuchou Rainichi-gaikokujin Hanzainado Taisakushitsu* (1999).

14. From an interview with junior high school students in the Nagoya metropolitan area, on July 26, 1999.

15. See Goodman (1990) for a study of *kikokushijo* from a class perspective. The reality is that there is more diversity of family backgrounds than that put forward in Goodman's view, but the image of international elite for *kikokushijo* is still dominant among the general Japanese.

16. The public opinion poll by *Jijitsūshinsha* (a stratified random sample of 1,398; January, 1998) confirms the general lack of interest toward Latin America including Brazil. To the question of "Which country or area will become most significant to Japan about 5 years from now?" only 2.1% chose Latin America, in contrast to 64.5% for the United States, 57.9% for the People's Republic of China, 28.0% for Southeast Asian countries (*Naikakusoridaijin Kanbo Kohoshitsu*, 1998, p. 576).

17. For instance, among 641 respondents in a 1990 questionnaire (Nishikawa, 1992, p. 34), only 3 students chose Brazil as their favorite country.

18. Most Japanese don't know what language the *Nikkei* Brazilians speak. Compared to the attention and status given to English in Japan, Portuguese is ranked low, as one of the anonymous languages hardly familiar to the general public (see for example, *Naikakusoridaijin Kanbo Kohoshitsu*, 2000, p. 480). Portuguese media in Japan, however, has grown to meet the demand within the ethnic *Nikkei* Brazilian network. For the striking development of Portuguese media in Japan, see Ishi (1996).

19. The public opinion survey by *Naikakusoridaijin Kanbo Kohoshitsu* (1998) (a stratified random sample of nearly 2,100) also confirms these images. To the question of "What images do you have for Latin American countries?" 45.4% chose "countries suffering from socioeconomic difficulties such as inflation and terrorism"; 31.7% for "countries that are geographically distant and have not had close ties with Japan, except the emigration legacy"; and 27.9% for "countries that have jovial national character represented by the rhythm of Samba and Soccer" (*Naikakusoridaijin Kanbo Kohoshitsu*, 1998, p. 92).

20. *Nikkei* American informants reveal how hard it is for Japanese nationals in Japan to see *Nikkei* Americans as full-fledged Americans because of their facial appearance, and how they tend to value white Americans as the model representative for Americans, when, for example, hiring an English teacher or accepting the home-stay of a foreign student. A similar prejudice is held by mainstream Americans in the United States, when they see *Nikkei* Americans or phenotypically visible ethnic minorities as a whole.

21. Some of the student informants did not even know the term *Nikkeijin*. But older informants seem to have a certain image of *Nikkeijin*, based on the stigmatized emigration

legacy, as poor, unfortunate, and pitiful. For the complexity of ethnic prejudices on *Nikkei* Brazilians, see Tsuda (1998).

22. The academically top image of *Nikkeijin* in Brazil is well documented in previous literature, but the image also seems to be fading somewhat because many young Brazilians have dropped out of high school or college and come to Japan as *dekasegi*, and many school-age children have been in Japan in their formative years and find it hard to be reintegrated into the Brazilian educational system.

23. For additional background, see Murphy-Shigematsu (1996) and Kich, King, Shinagawa, and Shizue (1998).

24. Here it is interesting to note comparatively that in the United States, offspring of intermarriage couples are usually described as being of a "mixed race," whereas "mixed blood" is used in Japan, suggesting what matters in each country.

25. For the stigmatized image by racial/class prejudice until around the 1970s, see Wagatsuma (1976).

26. For details, see Tsuda (1998, p. 321). In Japan the image of the term "minority" never includes Americans, if a positive minority is defined as Tsuda did: As numerically smaller, not a dominant power holder in society but enjoying a relatively higher socioeconomic status, and respected for their distinctive cultural qualities and social position, the first candidate for such a positive minority in Japan would be the English-speaking American.

27. From an interview in Japanese on October 16, 1999, and interpreted by the author. The child's 13-year-old brother also answered the same way, perceiving Brazilianness as slightly negative with the wish to become a Japanese and to marry one.

28. These problems have always been included in the discourse of the "*Nikkei* Brazilian problem" but partly may be due to "illusory correlation effects" (Zebrowitz, 1990, p. 68), a tendency by which evaluations of physically salient persons become polarized in the direction of the most salient behaviors.

29. From interviews with Japanese residents in the fieldwork area where the proportion of Brazilian residents is perceived as overwhelming. In fact, one symbolic incident to indicate rising hostility in this area occurred when young Japanese right-wingers were clamoring "Brazilian Go Home" to a group of young Brazilians ("*Gaikokujin to Uyokura*," 1999, June 8, p. 27).

30. The present discussion describes the dominant patterns seen among "full" *Nikkei* families. Some "full" *Nikkei* individuals choose to use their Portuguese first name out of conscious Brazilian pride.

31. This category also includes those who are technically "ethnic Japanese" but "culturally Chinese," that is, *Chūgoku kikokusha* or *Chūgoku zanryūkoji* (Japanese children who were left behind in China during the chaos of the WWII evacuation and who had grown up in China but have returned to Japan as adults) and their descendants. The offspring are usually of mixed blood having Japanese and Chinese parents.

32. For the studies concerning the related issues of these minority children in Japan, see De Vos and Wagatsuma (1996); Nakajima (1998); and Nakagawa (1998). For cross-national parallels, see, for example, Cummins (1986); Davidson (1996); and Matute-Bianchi (1986).

33. In the Wagatsuma and Yoneyama study (1967, p. 119) ($N = 270$: mainly 20s–40s middle class with relatively higher academic background and 30 farmers in Tokyo and Kansai area), British, Asian Indian, Korean, Indonesian, French, Chinese, Filipino, American, black, Italian, Thai, Russian, and German were presented as the list of "for-

eigners" to be ranked in order of liking from 1 to 13. In Takao's study (1992, p. 33) ($N =$ 94: mainly 20s–30s middle class with relatively higher academic background in Tokyo area), Iranian was added to the list. In my study, Iranian, Brazilian, Swiss, Australian, and New Zealand were added to the list, considering the recent expansion of the Japanese psychological world map. While in previous studies participants were Japanese across generations (the results of university students shown here in Wagatsuma and Yoneyama's study are basically the same as that of the total samples; the data in Takao's also show a similar pattern as that of the total samples, except for the better rank of blacks in 10s–20s cohort), all the participants in my data are *kikokushijo.*

"Koreans," stated in Japanese as *Kankoku Chōsenjin,* is a vague ethnic term without distinguishing between South Koreans, North Koreans, and Koreans living permanently in Japan; "blacks," stated in Japanese as *kokujin,* is a vague "racial" term with no distinction of nationality; "Asian Indians" is used here for the people of India, to distinguish them from Native Americans.

34. Wagatsuma and Yoneyama and Takao asked respondents to choose from a list of 64 and 50 adjectives, respectively, the top five descriptors for each "foreign" group. In my study, the following 61 adjectives (the less chosen adjectives in previous studies are omitted and "cute/cool," one of the most-often used words among young Japanese is added) are presented with the question "What image do you have for the following people generally? Choose 5 adjectives, which are closest to your image": honest, sly, kind, unkind, polite, bad mannered, amiable, unsociable, evil minded, good natured, generous, stingy, argumentative, cheerful, subservient, progressive, unsophisticated, prompt, lazy, emotional, dull, calm, impulsive, rational, artistic, materialistic, short tempered, patient, gloomy, talkative, law breaking, active, conservative, scientific, superstitious, cruel, gentle, lovely, clean, filthy, clever, reticent, moral, stoic, friendly, weird, frightening, imprudent, prudent, violent, quiet, quick reflexes, intelligent, methodical, slovenly, healthy, arrogant, shrewd, individualistic, mass psychological (i.e., being highly cliquish), and cute/cool. The order of adjectives presented in my study basically followed the one of Wagatsuma and Yoneyama.

REFERENCES

Cummins, J. (1986). Empowering minority students: A framework for intervention. *Harvard Educational Review 56*(1), 19–22.

Davidson, A. N. (1996). *Making and molding identity in schools: Student narratives on race, gender, and academic engagement.* Albany: State University of New York Press.

De Vos, G. A., & Wagatsuma, H. (1996). Cultural identity and minority status in Japan. In L. Romanucci-Ross & G. A. De Vos (Eds.), *Ethnic identity: Creation, conflict and accommodation.* London: Altamira Press.

Donahue, R. T. (1998). *Japanese culture and communication: Critical cultural analysis.* Lanham, MD: University Press of America.

Fukuoka, Y. (1993). *Zainichi Kankoku Chōsenjin: Wakaisedai no aidentiti* [Koreans in Japan: The identity of young generations]. Tokyo: Chūokōronsha.

Gaikokujin to uyokura tairitsu [Conflict between foreigners and right-wingers]. (1999, June 8). *Chunichi Shimbun,* p. 27.

Goodman, R. (1990). *Japan's "international youth": The emergence of a new class of school children.* London: Oxford University Press.

Gordon, M. M. (1981). Models of pluralism: The new American dilemma. *Annals of the American Academy of Political and Social Science, 454,* 178–188.

Hall, C. C. I. (1996). 2001: A race odyssey. In M. P. P. Root (Ed.), *The multiracial experience: Racial borders as the new frontier* (pp. 395–410). Thousand Oaks, CA: Sage.

Houmushou Nyūkokukanrikyoku. (1999). *Zairyūgaikokujin toukei* [Foreign residents statistics]. Tokyo: Houmusho Nyūkokukanrikyoku.

Imakoso towareru Nihon no ukeiretaisaku—*Nikkei* fusyūgakujidouseito no gekizou ni dou taisho surunoka [Japan's measures to accept foreign students; now critically questioned—How to cope with the upsurge of *Nikkei* non-attending students]. (1999, April). *Frontier,* p. 1 (Newsletter produced by Frontier Toyohashi, an NPO for multicultural/multilingual matters, in Aichi prefecture, Japan).

Ishi, A. A. (1996). Dekasegi keikensha no manga kara Hanshin-Daishinsai houdou made: Porutogarugo media no kaishingeki [From the *manga* of a *dekasegi*-experiencer to the reports on the Great Hanshin Earthquake: Striking advancement of Portuguese media]. In S. Shiramizu (Ed.), *Esunikku media: Tabunka shakai Nihon wo mezashite* [Ethnic media: Toward multicultural society Japan] (pp. 95–145). Tokyo: Akashi Shoten.

Izumi, S. (1953). Tokyo shoushimin no iminzoku ni taisuru taido [The attitude of Tokyo residents toward different ethnics]. In Nihon Jinbun Kagakukai (Eds.), *Shakaiteki kinchou no kenkyū* [Studies on social strain] (p. 430-1). Tokyo: Yūhikaku.

Kaigaishijo Kyouiku Shinkou Zaidan. (1998, April). Eigo wo oshieru: Gogaku-kyoushi to natta kikokushijo tachi [Teaching English: Kikokushijo who became language teachers]. *Kaigaishijo Kyouiku, 302,* 33.

Kajita, T. (1999). Kairi suru nashonarizumu to esunishiti: "Nikkeijin" niokeru houtekishikaku to shakaigakuteki genjitsu tono aida [Estrangement between nationalism and ethnicity: Between legal status and sociological reality of "Nikkeijin"]. In K. Aoi, T. Takahashi, & K. Shouji (Eds.), *Shiminsei no henyou to chiiki/shakai mondai—21 seiki no shiminshakai to kyoudousei: Kokusaika to naimenka*—[Civic change and community/social problems—Civic society and cooperation for the 21 century: Internationalization and internalization] (pp. 139–165). Tokyo: Azusa Shuppansha.

Keisatsuchou Rainichi-gaikokujin Hanzainado Taisakushitsu (1999, September). *Rainichi gaikokujin mondai no genjou to taisaku: Heisei 11nen kamihanki* [Situations and measures of the foreigners problem in Japan: The first half of 1999], pp. 11–13, 29–30.

Kich, G. K., King, R. C., Shinagawa, L. H., & Shizue, S. (1998). Intermarriage and *hapas*: An overview. *Nikkei Heritage, X.4,* 4–7, 16–17.

Kitano, H. H. L. (1997). *Race relations* (5th ed.). New Jersey: Prentice Hall.

Kouseishou. (2000). *Jinkou doutai toukei* [Vital statistics]. Tokyo: Kosei Tokei Kyokai.

Lummis, C. D. (1997). *Uchinaru gaikoku: "Kiku to katana" saikou* [Internal foreign country: Rethinking of "The chrysanthemum and the sword"] (E. Kaji, Trans.). Tokyo: Chikuma Gakugeibunko.

Maeyama, T. (1996). *Esunishiti to burajiru Nikkeijin: Bunka jinruigaku teki kenkyū* [Ethnicity and Japanese Brazilians: Cultural anthropological research]. Tokyo: Ochanomizu Shobou.

Maeyama, T. (1997). *Ihou ni "Nihon" wo matsuru* [Worshiping "Japan" in a foreign country]. Tokyo: Ochanomizu Shobou.

Matute-Bianchi, M. E. (1986). Ethnic identities and patterns of school success and failure among Mexican-descent and Japanese-American students in a California high school: An ethnographic analysis. *American Journal of Education, 95*(1), 233–255.

McVeigh, B. J. (1999, May). *What cuteness, cleanliness and consumerism say about the "Group Model" in Japan.* Paper presented at the meeting of Anthropology of Japan in Japan, Sophia University, Tokyo.

Minoura, Y. (1995). Culture and self-concept among adolescents with bicultural parentage: A social constructionist approach. In J. Valsiner (Ed.), *Child development within culturally structured environments. Vol. 3: Comparative-cultural perspectives* (pp. 191–209). Norwood, NJ: Ablex.

Monbushō Kyouikujoseikyoku Kaigaishijokyouikuka. (1991, January). *Kaigaishijo kyouiku no genjou* [The current situation of education for overseas Japanese students]. Tokyo: Monbushō, p. 59.

Mori, K. (1999, November 20). *Transmigrant patterns of migrant labor: 15 years of Nikkei Brazilian "Dekasegi."* Paper presented at the international symposium, Globalization of Labor Mobility and Settlement Patterns of Migrants: Network Formation and Policy Issues, Institute of Comparative Economic Studies, Hosei University, Tokyo.

Murphy-Shigematsu, S. (1996). Representations of Amerasians in Japan. *Japanese Society, 1,* 61–76.

Naikakusoridaijin Kanbo Kohoshitsu. (1998). *Seron chousa nenkan* [Annual public opinion survey]. Tokyo: Ōkurasho Insatsukyoku.

Naikakusoridaijin Kanbo Kohoshitsu. (2000). *Seron chousa nenkan* [Annual public opinion survey]. Tokyo: Ōkurasho Insatsukyoku.

Nakagawa, A. (Ed.). (1998). *Mainoriti no kodomotachi* [Minority children]. Tokyo: Akashi Shoten.

Nakajima, T. (Ed.). (1998). *Tabunka kyouiku: Tayousei no tameno kyouikugaku* [Multicultural education: Pedagogy for diversity]. Tokyo: Akashi Shoten.

Nichibei kyoudou seron chousa [Japan–US joint public opinion poll]. (1999, December 19). *Yomiuri Shimbun,* p. 13.

Nishikawa, N. (1992). *Kokkyou no koekata: Hikakubunkaron josetsu* [A way to transcend national borders: An introduction to comparative culture theory]. Tokyo: Chikuma Shobou.

Ogubu, J. U., & Simons, H. D. (1998). A cultural-ecological theory of school performance with some implications for education. *Anthropology and Education Quarterly, 29,* 155–188.

Oyama, T. (1995a, April 29). Japonēs puro é raridade na 4ª geração de descendentes [Pure Japanese are rare among the 4th generation of descendants]. *Folha de S. Paulo,* sect. 3, p. 4.

Oyama, T. (1995b, April 29). Mestiças são favoritas dos fotógrafos [Mixed are favorites of photographers]. *Folha de S. Paulo,* sect. 3, p. 4.

Russell, J. G. (1991). *Nihonjin no kokujinkan* [Japanese ideology of blacks]. Tokyo: Shinhyouron.

Sekiguchi, T. (1997). Zainichi *Nikkei* burajirujin-shijo no esunikku aidentiti: Ibunkakan kyouiku no shiten kara [The ethnic identity of Japanese-Brazilian children in Japan: Anthropological/sociopsychological perspective on intercultural education]. *Imin kenkyū nenpou, 3,* 61–85.

Sekiguchi, T. (1999). Baikaruchuraru chirudoren no aidentiti keisei: Nigenteki bunkaka no shiten kara [The identity formation of bicultural children through a dual enculturation process]. *Kokusai Kaihatsu Kenkyū Fōramu, 13,* 159–178.

Sekine, M. (1994). *Esunishiti no shakaiseiji-gaku* [Political sociology of ethnicity]. Nagoya: Nagoya Daigaku Shuppankai.

Takao, M. (1992). *Nihonjin no ijinkan* [Japanese ideology of foreigner]. Unpublished manuscript, Housou Daigaku, Japan.

Tsuda, T. (1998). The stigma of ethnic difference: The structure of prejudice and "discrimination" toward Japan's new immigrant minority. *Journal of Japanese Studies, 24,* 317–359.

Tsutusmi, K. (1997). Esunishiti, Jendā, shakaikaisou: Sanhensū no kanren no kaimei nimukete [Ethnicity, gender, and social class: To uncover the interrelationship of three variables]. In M. Okuda (Ed.), *Toshi esunishiti no shakaigaku: Minzoku/bunka/kyousei no imi wo tou* [Sociology of urban ethnicity: Questioning the meaning of ethnicity/culture/coexistence] (pp. 243–273). Tokyo: Mineruba-Shobou.

Wagatsuma, H. (1976). Mixed-blood children in Japan: An exploratory study. *Journal of Asian Affairs 2,* 9–16.

Wagatsuma, H., & Yoneyama, T. (1967). *Henken no kouzou: Nihonjin no jinshukan* [Structure of prejudice: Japanese ideology of race]. Tokyo: NHK Books.

Yoshino, K. (1997). *Bunka nashonarizum no shakaigaku: Gendai Nihon no aidentiti no yukue* [Sociology of cultural nationalism: The future of identity of contemporary Japan]. Nagoya: Nagoya Daigaku Shuppankai.

Zebrowitz, L. A. (1990). *Social perception.* Buckingham: Open University Press.

part V

Japanese Language

Chapter 12

Sources of Emotion in Japanese Comics: *Da, Nan(i),* and the Rhetoric of *Futaku*

Senko K. Maynard

This chapter addresses how feelings and emotional attitudes are expressed in contemporary Japanese popular culture, specifically comics. Instead of overtly expressing their feelings by emotive words, Japanese often employ grammatical strategies for emotional expressivity. The author analyzes two such strategies— certain uses of the so-called copulative verb da *(and* ja-nai*) and the* wh-*question word* nan(i). *It is argued that* da *functions not only as a copulative predicate, but also, and more relevant to the present investigation, as a strategy signaling the speaker's conclusive and assertive attitude toward his or her verbal performance.* Da *brings to speech the effect of emphasis and desire for control. It is also argued that the non-interrogative* nan(i) *signals unspeakable moments in communication, while at the same time it signals significant expressive functions. These functions include marking attitudes of anticipation, surprise, exclamation, confrontation, and so on. The meanings of* da *and* nan(i) *are indexically and interactionally motivated as well as contextually and negotiatively interpreted, and both offer a means for emotional expressivity. They also contribute to the realization of the Japanese preference toward the topic–comment relationship. The author emphasizes the inherent importance of emotive meanings in language and foreground the rhetorical figure of* futaku *as a key for sharing the sources of feelings expressed without emotion words in Japanese.*

How is emotion expressed in Japanese popular culture? Is the way of expressing emotion explainable in terms of the sociocultural and rhetorical preferences in Japan? I explore these themes by examining two linguistic strategies used in

Japanese comics. Themes of language and emotion have been explored under the heading of the expressive function of language. Yet, as pointed out in a number of studies (e.g., Caffi & Janney, 1994; Foolen, 1997; Günthner, 1997; Maynard, 1993a, 1995; Ochs & Schieffelin, 1989), the expressive function of language has occupied a marginal position in dominant theories of modern linguistics. Only in recent years have studies on expressivity (especially emotive and attitudinal meanings) become readily available under headings such as *affect* (Ochs & Schieffelin, 1989) and *involvement* (Tannen, 1982).

Studies touching on emotion and the Japanese language have tended to center around emotion words, often in association with metaphor (see Kövecses, 1995; McVeigh, 1996; Wierzbicka, 1991, 1997), and emotive interjections (see Ishigami, 1981; Moriyama, 1996). In the course of this chapter I argue that seemingly emotionless linguistic devices express significant feelings and emotional attitudes of the speaking subject.

The discussion is based on the observation made on expressions of emotion appearing in Japanese comics. Comics are expected to contain interactions in which emotional stakes are high. They provide not only verbal expressions, but also graphic and visual cues useful for interpretation. Unlike naturally occurring speech, comics foreground contextual features particularly relevant to the action. Although artificial, these features often offer cues for understanding otherwise hidden internal emotions. Facial expressions and a variety of icons (e.g., a puff of air, dark shadows, wavy background, sharp multiple lines) are useful for interpreting emotive expressions.

Among the comics chosen are a science fiction comic *Kōkaku Kidōtai* (Shirow, 1991) and its English translation *Ghost in the Shell* (Shirow, 1995), as well as two volumes of *Chibi Maruko-chan* (The Little Girl Maruko) (Sakura, 1995, 1996), about a character who provides a wistful, sometimes humorous take on family life from the perspective of a third-grader. Obviously, the data chosen for this study are limited, and, therefore, it should be kept in mind that the result reported herein must ultimately be tested against data collected from other genres and vehicles of contemporary Japanese popular culture.

This study focuses on two linguistic strategies usually dissociated from expressivity—the so-called copulative verb *da* (and *ja-nai*), and the *wh*-question word *nan(i)* (what). These two strategies are chosen because their emotive use is prominently observed in comics and they co-occur creating the kind of emotive discourse that has not received much attention in the past. Take, for example, the utterance *Nani zureta koto yatte n da yo* (Shirow, 1991, p. 138), translated as "What the hell do you think you're doing, Togusa!" (Shirow, 1995, p. 140). The use of *nani* and *da* both contribute to the emotive reading. In addition, as I discuss later, this utterance exemplifies the nominalization-plus-commentary structure critical to the kind of Japanese expressivity explored in this chapter.

The study's methodological framework primarily follows conversation analysis, but with the implicit conceptualization of interactional context as situated in discourse analysis, pragmatics, and rhetoric. The analysis uses concepts of turn-taking context, sequencing of moves, adjacency pair, the speaker's utterance design, as well as discourse- and pragmatics-based principles. The organizational principle of topic–comment especially offers a framework for understanding the sources of emotion in Japanese discourse. I take the figure of *futaku* from traditional Japanese rhetoric as a means for interpreting the nominalization-plus-commentary structure. I also explore the Japanese sociocultural context as a possible key for understanding the observed expressive preference. Last, I reflect on the issue of linguistic ideology as I assess the content of this chapter in light of the relativism/universalism of knowledge and understanding.

EMOTIVE *DA* AND *JA-NAI*

The Japanese predicate *da* often has been considered the counterpart of the English verb "to be," functioning primarily as a copulative predicate within the proposition. For example, consider a sentence *Asoko ni iru hito ga sensei da* (there-is-person-*ga* (subject marker)-teacher-*da*; or, The person over there is the teacher), where *da* functions as a copulative predicate. Although scholars often have identified *da* as being unrelated to emotive expressivity, certain uses of the Japanese predicate *da*, that is, "emotive *da*," offer a strategy for expressing the speaker's conclusive assertive attitude, indicating varied kinds and shades of emotion.

More specifically, I take the position that *da* is indexical and offers a means to signal the inherent stativity and situationality relevant to the speech occasion.[1] *Da* indexes the speaker's assertive commitment to the speech act with regard to content as well as performance. In addition, while *da* indexes an assertive posture in favorable situations, in certain cases of its negative counterpart, *ja-nai*, that is, "emotive *ja-nai*," indexes an assertive posture in unfavorable situations. Because of this expressive function, certain uses of *da* and *ja-nai* make prominent the speaker's participation in the speech event, often involving emphatic intent and a strong desire for controlling the situation under discussion. In what follows, I discuss emotive *da* used for emphatic purposes in relation to the speaker's utterance itself as well as in quotation responding to the partner's utterance. I also examine *da* and *ja-nai* used for expressing the speaker's strong wish to control the situation.

Unlike copulative *da*, emotive *da* often appears outside a propositional structure, frequently in a nominal predicate form as in *Omae mo ippen sonna me ni attemiro tte n da* (Shirow, 1991, p. 74). This utterance appears as a part of a speaking turn in English, "How'd you feel if yer [sic] wife sprung a divorce notice on you? Probably do the same thing as me, hey?" (Shirow, 1995, p. 76). *Sonna me ni attemiro* (lit. "Go through such an experience") ends with a verb imperative form and can appear without *tte n da*. However, when *da* is added (either as a part of *tte n da*, or singularly), the utterance takes on the emphatic effect. This interpretation is supported by the speaker's defiant facial expression as well as the exchange of moves in progress.

Significant to this utterance (as well as to the utterance *Nani zureta koto yatte n da yo* mentioned at the outset of this chapter) is the use of the nominalizer *n(o)*. The nominalized portion presents information as a concept, now encapsulated in the form of a noun. The emotive *da* following it expresses the speaker's commentary toward that nominalized concept in an assertive manner, indexing the speech act itself. The nominal predicate structure represents a topic–comment structure in a broad sense in that it presents a topic in discourse, and the speaker's performatory comment about that topic follows.

The emotive *da* may accompany a nonsentence as well. For example, in "Humph, Mom, you understand, don't you? The smell of *natto*" (Sakura, 1996, p. 22), Maruko utters *Fun da-tt. Fun* (humph) is an interjection and *da* immediately follows it. *Da* expresses Maruko's desire to emphasize her feelings, by punctuating her annoyance and resentment. Note that it is difficult, in fact impossible, to interpret this *da* as a copulative predicate since *Fun da-tt* lacks the subject corresponding to *da*. Here *fun* is presented as if it is a noun, followed by *da*, indexing the speaker's comment of strong assertion. In the original, *da* is followed by a small orthographic *tsu* (transliterated above as *tt*), which represents a glottal stop, signaling the phonology-based emphatic effect. This *tsu* indicates the strong and forceful enunciation of the syllable *da*, exhibiting a case in which multiple levels of linguistic strategies achieve a concerted emotive and attitudinal effect. In addition, the emotive interpretation of *da* is supported by contextual information as well. Because she is upset since her father teased her dislike of *natto*, a pungent soybean food, Maruko shows defiance and immediately solicits approval and support from her mother. One side of Maruko's face is shadowed, a classic cartoon cue indicating that Maruko is in emotional jeopardy.

The echo question, when the speaker responds to the partner by quoting the partner's speech, is another assertive attitude the emotive *da* brings to discourse. For example, a speaker has difficulty believing what the ghost said in the prior turn and responds with *Seimeitai da to!?* (Shirow, 1991, p. 246). This response from Aramaki (the boss of Major Kusanagi, the heroine of *Kōkaku Kidōtai*) occurs in the following conversation. (The angle brackets < > mark a speech balloon, and a slash / is inserted at line changes.)

(1.1) Ghost: <. . . What you / witness **here** / is my will.>

<As a self-aware / life-form . . . / a ghost . . . I / formally / request / political / asylum.>

(1.2) Aramaki:<What?! / A / **ghost**?!> (Shirow, 1995, p. 248)

Aramaki repeats the phrase *seimeitai* (ghost) followed by *da* and the quotative *to*, creating an echo question. *Da* is not a copulative predicate of *seimeitai*;

it indexes the ghost's verbal performance. When the echo question appears with *da* as in Aramaki's speech, it conveys acceptance of the ghost's statement as conclusive, and the certainty of that acceptance is communicated through Aramaki's own assertive attitude. *Seimeitai*? ("Ghost?") is possible, but this utterance fails to express the strong conclusive tone associated with the ghost as well as with Aramaki.

Here is a case in which assertiveness is dialogically and negotiatively realized. *Da*'s indexicality makes two different speech situations come alive, so to speak, first when the ghost speaks, and then when Aramaki quotes the ghost's speech. In both instances, the assertiveness is reinforcingly expressed as a result of a dialogic interaction between both parties in two different situations. Two separate voices are represented here—that of "You're telling me?!" and that of "I'm telling you!" from two intersubjective perspectives. In the English translation, the emotive expressivity is indicated by interjections and bold letters, although no bold letters appear in the Japanese original. The emotivity expressed through different strategies in English translation provides indirect evidence in support of the emotive reading of *da*.

A similar example is observed in Sakura (1996) as in *Kusō-tt, tabako ga neagarisuru da tō* (lit. "Shit, the price of cigarettes going up?!") (p. 106). In this situation, Maruko's father, annoyed by the antismoking atmosphere, rails against the price increase. This utterance starts with a cursing word *kusō* ("shit") followed by the glottal stop. Visually, a puff of air comes out of the father's head, an icon of anger. Additionally, in the next turn, the father says *Atama ni kuru nā* (lit. "I'm totally upset/mad, almost blowing my top"), an emotion metaphor that captures his emotional state. The combination of this contextual information supports the emotive reading of *da*.

Another emotive effect associated with both *da* and *ja-nai* is the desire for control. First, consider *da* in *Sā shigotobeya e iku n da!!* (Shirow, 1991, p. 19) translated as "Now move it! To your work stations!" (Shirow, 1995, p. 23), with "To your work stations" in large bold letters. *Da* in this command does not function as a copulative predicate, but rather, indexes the speech act as an imperative. However, instead of using a direct imperative such as *Sā zen'in shigotobeya e ike!* (lit. "Now you all, go to your work stations!") intended to the addressees, the statement with *da* expresses the speaker's posture toward the situation, that is, his desire to control the situation such that everyone goes back to the work station.

This desirative *da* also takes the negative form, *ja-nai*. For example, in the following speaking turn, the speaker orders his subordinate by saying *Kora soko! Shateki tesuto ja-nē n da. Ningen mitaina dekē hyōteki ni kakkotsukete nerai sadamete n ja-nē-tt. Ute ute* (Shirow, 1991, p. 155). As seen in the English translation, "Jesus, you useless pukes! This ain't the stinking Olympics! With big targets like humans, don't worry so much about putting five in the same hole—Just blast away at the center of mass!" (Shirow, 1995, p. 157), *ja-nai* appearing in *sadamete n ja-nē-tt* expresses the speaker's wish that the situation were otherwise. *Ja-nai* expresses the speaker's denial of what is occurring or, more accurately, the speaker's desire that the situation were opposite of the current status.[2]

The use of emotive *da* (and emotive *ja-nai*) reinforces the "here-ness" of the interaction among speech participants. Emotive *da*'s meaning is associated with *da*'s indexicality to the performance—emphasis, assertion, and desire for control. And because of this indexicality, *da* reminds the reader that there is a speaker lurking behind the utterance, assessing and conveying how his or her verbal performance is expressed. The speaker's voice, intricately connected with the situation at hand, strongly reverberates, giving personal authenticity to the words. In the process, the speaker's emotivity is foregrounded.

Given the account of *da* presented herein, an overreaching implication comes to mind regarding the entire picture of the Japanese language. In my earlier studies (Maynard, 1992, 1993b, 1997a, 1997b), I reported that Japanese discourse is rife with nominal predicate accompanied by nominalized clause.[3] As I argued in Maynard (1997b), the use of the emotive *da* in the *n(o) da* expression reinforces the topic–comment structure in the Japanese language. In topic–comment structure, the perspective the speaker takes toward what is being expressed takes precedence over the grammatical subject. The use of the emotive *da* in Japanese discourse is likely to be associated with the preference toward linguistically identifying topic as a target of emotional commentary, leaving the grammatical subject only as secondary. I return to this issue later.

EMOTIVE *NAN(I)*

The expressive function of the *wh*-question word *nani* (what) and its colloquial version *nan* in Japanese has attracted little attention from linguists. A casual perusal of the data, however, reveals that *nan(i)* appears not only in the context of interrogatives, but also, and more significant to this study, in noninterrogative emotive contexts of expletives and exclamatives.[4]

As a sample discourse segment, observe the following utterance that one of Major Kusanagi's subordinates makes.

(2.1)   <Hey! / Isn't that / Ishikawa's / Fuchikoma?>
(2.2)   <What / the / hell's / going on?>
(2.3)   <Now **that's** / one shitty / Goddamn / sighting / mecha- / nism.>
(2.4)   <Ishikawa! / **Ishi/kawa!**>
(2.5)   <What / the hell / are you / doing?!> (Shirow, 1995, pp. 40–41)

For (2.3), *Nante aimaina shōjunsōchi o tsukatte-yaga n da* appears, and for (2.5), *Nani nebokete yagaru!!?* (Shirow, 1991, pp. 36–37) occurs. The line (2.3) is a representative case of expletive use of *nan(i)*, and (2.5), exclamatory use, as reflected in the English translation. *Nante* is a combination of *nan* and the quo-tative marker *to/te*. In the comic, both (2.3) and (2.5) appear with visual signs that support such emotionally charged interpretation.

I should point out that in (2), an answer to (2.5) is notably absent. In fact, an answer is not expected, and this turn-taking interaction fails to meet the expecta-tion of the question–answer adjacency-pair recognized in conversation analysis (Schegloff, 1968). Thus, *nani* in (2.5) is noninterrogative. Note also the use of the verbal suffix *-yagaru* appearing in (2.3) and (2.5), which expresses an attitude of mockery, hatred, and perhaps even disdain. The use of *nante* and *nani*—not fol-lowed by relevant answers and co-occurring with this attitudinal suffix—sug-gests that these phrases are associated less with information and more with emo-tional attitude. It is true that the emotion-involving interpretation of *nan(i)* is sup-ported by various linguistic and pragmatic factors, and, therefore, *nan(i)* by itself does not guarantee the expletive and exclamatory reading. It is also true, howev-er, that noninterrogative *nan(i)* plays a major role in bringing about the said effects.

Nan(i), as observed in (2.5), functions as an "anti-sign." In the classical Saussurean understanding of sign, the sign's internal structure is dyadically char-acterized, through a signifier and a signified (Saussure, 1966). In this under-standing, analogous with the relationship between two sides of a coin, a sign is a sign because it is mutually supported by a signifier and a signified. Interestingly, in the case of emotive *nan(i)*, the signified is definable only by its absence. *Nan(i)* has no supporting concrete concept (e.g., the concept of a tree corresponding to the signifier *tree*). This, of course, does not mean that *nan(i)* is an empty sign sig-nifying nothing. On the contrary, *nan(i)* signifies the situation in which one can-not or does not find an appropriate signifier. One may characterize such *nan(i)* as being in an oppositional relationship with the entire network of signs. *Nan(i)*, failing to function as a sign in the Saussurean sense, speaks for the unspeakable in the language, functioning as anti-sign.

Thus, *nan(i)* indexes unspeakable moments of language, and yet, or because of this characteristic, it affords a significant expressive function. More specifi-cally, I find nine expressive functions of noninterrogative *nan(i)* associated with three different levels of communication, that is, cognition, emotion, and inter-action. *Nan(i)* functions to mark one's attitudes of anticipation and recognition on the cognitive level—surprise, criticism, exclamation, as well as confrontation on the level of emotion. It also functions, on the interactional level, as a device for replacing speech, marking negative response, and signaling vocative expres-sion. The source of *nan(i)*'s expressive functions is traced to the peremptory nature of some of *nan(i)* interrogatives, to not expecting the other's response, specifically.

Let me focus on those cases where *nan(i)* most clearly indexes emotivity, including surprise, criticism, exclamation, and confrontation. In addition, I briefly discuss *nan(i)* used for participatory design. The surprise *nan(i)* indexes the speaker's surprise when faced with unexpected and/or extraordinary facts, while the criticism *nan(i)* conveys the speaker's critical and/or accusatory attitude giving an impression that the utterance is made as a complaint. As for the exclamatory effect, the use of *nan(i)* expresses the speaker's amazement toward unusual, unexpected, and extraordinary situations, and finally as expression of confrontation, *nan(i)* is used to challenge the partner's action and speech in conflict situations. On the interactional level, *nan(i)* helps realize participatory design when used to avoid specification and, instead, to fill space, often functioning as a conversation filler.

The surprise *nan(i)* is used in "What?!! Even though I'm not going through a dedicated deck, I'm being visually transformed" (Shirow, 1995, p. 276), with the original Japanese *Nani!!?* (Shirow, 1991, p. 274) for "What?!!" When addressed with this kind of utterance, it is impossible to provide information, although *nan(i)* is a *wh*-question phrase. And, in fact, in the comic, *Nani!!?* remains unanswered. Its use here indexes the emotional response of being unable to accept immediately the relevant information. *Nani* fills in when one cannot find specific words, that is, when experiencing surprise and bewilderment. The surprise *nan(i)* in comics is often accompanied by typical graphic and visual icons (e.g., large vacuous eyes, lines of rays radiating from face), further supporting this interpretation.

The criticism *nan(i)* occurs in an utterance "What the hell are you doing?!" (Shirow, 1995, p. 41), the original for which is *Nani nebokete yagaru-tt* (Shirow, 1991, p. 37). Similar examples are "Boss! Why're you slowing down?" (Shirow, 1991, p. 140), for which *nani* is inserted in Japanese: *Shachō! Nani yukkuri hashitteru n desu?!* (Shirow, 1991, p. 140). The exclamatory *nan(i)* appears in an utterance *Maruko yo . . . chotto minai aidani . . . iya chigatta, mainichi miteru noni nante rippani natta n ja* (lit. "Oh dear Maruko, while I haven't seen you, no, while I've been seeing you, how mature has she become!") (Sakura, 1995, p. 76).

As for *nan(i)* indexing confrontational attitude, observe the following segment that occurs in the context of an emotionally charged conflict/argument.

(3.1) Sister: *Nani, ima no uta . . . Dassā . . .*

                   what-now-of-song corny

(3.2) Maruko: *Nani-tt monku aru-tt*

                   what-complaint-you have

(3.3) Grandfather: Kora kora. (Sakura, 1996, p. 11)

                   hey-hey

Maruko was happily singing a song, to which her sister confronts her by saying *Nani, ima no uta . . . Dassā . . .* (lit. "What the heck is this song [you were singing]? How corny!"). Maruko, defiant of her sister's unkind remark, confronts the sister by using *nani* in *Nani-tt monku aru-tt* ("What, you got a problem with that?"). Here both interactants choose *nani*, although *nani*, in propositional terms, refers to nothing. It is clear, however, that *nani* brings to the fore the emotive meaning in this interaction.[5] The confrontational reading is supported by visual signs as well. The sister's embarrassment over Maruko's helplessly silly song is signaled by a drop of sweat falling down her cheek. Maruko's confrontational attitude is signaled by two lines placed next to her face indicating a challenging head movement. And the dark background of the cartoon frame implies that something ominous is happening. The sibling confrontation is also evidenced when, in (3.3), the grandfather, also with a drop of sweat dribbling down his forehead, utters *Kora kora* (lit. "Hey, hey") attempting to calm down the girls.

Nan(i) functions as an anti-sign most clearly in the case in which it is used as a conversational move. In an utterance "Now, about this issue you raised" (Shirow, 1995, p. 46), the Japanese expression uses *nan* as in *Kimi no itteta nan datta ka na, sono nan da* (Shirow, 1991, p. 42). *Sono nan da* (lit. "Uh, that, what, uh") functions as a filler, filling in the pause, while communicating nothing informationally. Inserting verbalization without a specific reference creates an interpersonal space, rendering the conversation less abrasive. *Nan(i)* functions as a kind of delay device often placed as a preface to the dispreferred seconds within the preference organization (Levinson, 1983; Pomerantz, 1984).[6]

I should add in passing that anticipatory *nan(i)* on the level of cognition also utilizes the nonspecificity facilitated by *nan(i)*. The anticipation *nan(i)* marks the speaker's cognitive attitude of eager curiousness and anticipation of an imminent occurrence of the event. The speaker is about to learn something, one such example being *Nani nani . . . hajimemashite* (Sakura, 1996, p. 5). Here Maruko is holding a letter addressed to her and is about to read it. Maruko signals her readiness to face something new by uttering *Nani nani* (lit. "What what"), the duplication of *nani*. *Hajimemashite* (lit. "How do you do?") is the first sentence appearing in the letter. By adding *nan(i)*, the speaker points to other unspecified possibilities. Just as *nan(i)* is used for conversation fillers, *nan(i)* in the duplication context not only fills in the discursive space, but also functions to avoid unnecessary specificity and yet still manages to say something.

As discussed previously, noninterrogative *nan(i)* indexes the speaker's emotional attitudes—surprise, criticism, exclamation, confrontation, and anticipation. Despite, or because of, the fact that *nan(i)* functions as anti-sign, it foregrounds emotive and psychological aspects of communication. Emotive *nan(i)* is a device dedicated to expressivity, and it brings to Japanese comics significant emotive effects.

TOPIC–COMMENT AND THE RHETORIC OF *FUTAKU*

So far, I have discussed Japanese emotivity expressed by seemingly emotionless strategies. Naturally, it is possible in Japanese to express one's emotion directly. But evidently another mechanism is at work when expressing emotion in Japanese discourse. Consider that *da* and *nan(i),* along with the nominal predicate structure, realize a fundamental discourse principle recognized in the

Japanese language, that is, topic–comment. In addition to the subject–predicate relation, Japanese is known to follow the topic–comment principle (Li & Thompson, 1976; Maynard, 1980, 1994; Mikami, 1960). How is this principle related to the interpretation of emotion?

One way of understanding how emotive meanings are realized in Japanese discourse is to tap into the traditional Japanese rhetorical figure of *futaku*. According to Amagasaki (1988), *futaku* (lit. committing, referring) is a method for expressing one's feelings by borrowing something else. In the art of Japanese *waka*, one avoids using overtly emotive words that state too clearly what one is feeling (e.g., "I am sad" is too overt); rather, the technique encourages an indirect route, by which, through the "borrowing" of another element and then ascribing to it an emotional feeling, one communicates to others one's own emotion.

Through reference to nature, for example, one is able to express emotion indirectly and thus more movingly. If a person is sad, the moon is seen as being sad. By presenting a sad moon, one intends that the reader will see the moon from the same emotional perspective. Amagasaki (1988, p. 120) suggests that if presented through the person's direct expression of emotion, interpersonal empathy becomes problematic, but if presented through an object or image that reflects the same emotion, the partner will see the object with the same eye (*onaji me de miru*). The feeling projected on a third object offers a way of revealing one's own emotion since the reflected emotion is shared by the partner.

The third object, the target of *futaku* is realized through the nominalized concept in the nominal predicate, and through the topic–comment relation. The concept is first broached in discourse as the target of emotion and is followed by the commentary *da*. In this manner, the topic–comment symbiosis offers an ideal means for expressing emotion indirectly. Recall that emotive *da* functions not as a copulative predicate but as an index of the speaker's speech acts. The shift of focus compelled by the emotive meaning realized by *da* and *nan(i)*, among others—from propositional to commentary aspects of communication—requires contextual information for interpretation. And such communication inevitably involves emotion, more prominently than in communication where the propositional information is in primary focus.

The case of *nan(i)*, of course, presents a peculiar situation. *Nan(i)* itself does not provide a concrete object to serve as the target of *futaku*. However, because *nan(i)*'s indexicality intrudes emphatically into discourse, it encourages, at minimum, the participants to point their views in the same direction. By speaking for the unspeakable, *nan(i)* supplies an undefinable yet identifiable object/source of emotional experience. The speaker and partner, by experiencing shared perspectives, find themselves in a common place. In this process, feelings associated with *nan(i)* become foregrounded, ironically because the target of *futaku* remains unspecified, rendering the communication less information-centered.

Still, one may ask: How exactly does one interpret emotion through *futaku*? To answer this question, I should refer to the concept of shared perspectives.

Discussing, from cognitive psychology, how perspectives function in human perception and understanding, Miyazaki and Ueno (1985) introduce two types of perspectives, namely, the perspectives of "seeing" and of "becoming." In their view, for understanding one's partner in communication, first one needs to "see" (recognize) an approximate appearance of the world as viewed from the partner. Second, one recreates the world seen by the partner by "becoming" (i.e., taking the identical perspective of) the partner. Ultimately, understanding requires one to "become" like the partner, by "seeing" (vicariously) the world as if seen by the partner. Miyazaki and Ueno (1985, p. 144) call this process of understanding *mie senkō hōryaku* (optical-world-first strategy).

Following the idea that shared-perspective–based experience leads to interactional and negotiative interpretation of meaning, I take the position that *da* and *nan(i)* facilitate just such experience. These strategies offer a means for aligning perspectives. They help the partner share the speaker's world, which, in turn, encourages the partner to gain empathetic understanding of the speaker's cognitive and emotional attitudes. Both the rhetoric of *futaku* and the theory of shared perspectives emphasize the importance of coexperience, and one strategy facilitating this is the emotive expression without using overtly emotive words. Rather than describing one's emotion in emotion words, the speaker expresses emotion in a roundabout, yet effectively moving, manner.

REFLECTIONS: EMOTION, CULTURE, AND LINGUISTIC IDEOLOGY

Given that expressivity is realized in Japanese in seemingly emotionless words, and this preference is necessitated by the rhetoric of *futaku*, one must bring up the issue of relativism/universalism regarding language and emotion. Is Japanese expressivity particular to itself? Is it explainable in terms of Japanese sociocultural tendencies?

Toward the end of the Edo period, Mitsue Fujitani, a Japanese language scholar, offered significant insight into the poetics of Japanese *waka*. In his essay (Fujitani 1817/1986), Fujitani introduced the concept of "reversed words" (*tōgo*) and explained it as the following. The art of reversed words refers to saying "not going" when one means "going" and saying "not seeing" to mean "seeing." But the art of reversed words involves more than words referring to actions such as going and seeing. It applies to human emotions as well. In order to appeal to the partner emotionally, one must learn the logic of ancient *waka* poetics. In fact, in *waka*, avoiding direct expression of emotion, one expresses emotion by referring to nature (*ka-chō-fū-getsu*, lit. flower-bird-wind-moon). Fujitani (1917/1986) emphasized the importance of learning this art of indirect emotion-rich expression. As in the rhetorical figure of *futaku*, in the art of reversed words, the emotive meaning ricochets back and forth between participants through the target of emotion.

Although the art of reversed words is discussed in relation to the creation and interpretation of *waka*, the Japanese cultural desire for not addressing one's emotions through emotion words is often observed in contemporary popular culture as well. In fact, as discussed in this chapter, this aesthetic preference remains to be coded in contemporary Japanese language, of which the nominalization, *da*, and *nan(i)* are only a part. In this sense, the way the Japanese express emotion through seemingly emotionless words is explainable in terms of the Japanese cultural preference.

However, one must not be satisfied with discovering Japanese particularities alone. A question remains: What is the significance of making a claim that Japanese emotivity is often expressed by words seemingly unrelated to emotion, and that this preference is in agreement with traditional Japanese poetics?

Let us take a moment to reflect on the relationship among language, culture, and the knowledge/understanding of them. Such reflection applies to this chapter as well. The theme associated with the relationship between language and theory has been discussed under the heading of linguistic ideology as reviewed by Woolard (1992). According to Silverstein, "ideologies about language, or linguistic ideologies, are any sets of beliefs about language articulated by the users as a rationalization or justification of perceived language structure and use" (1979, p. 193). To appreciate how linguistic ideologies are likely to influence our own understanding of and theorizing about language, let me cite Rumsey's (1990) work.

Rumsey (1990) argues that seemingly important areas of English language structure (the grammar of reported speech and of textual cohesion) are related to the Western ideology of clearly distinguishing language from reality, particularly talk from action. Rumsey's study on Ngarinyin, an aboriginal language spoken in northwestern Australia, reveals that such ideology is notably absent. The idea that there are formal distinctions between direct and indirect discourse (on which the grammar of reported speech is based) is likely to develop along with linguistic ideologies that convincingly distinguish speech from action, words from things.[7] In short, the language one theorizes in, that is, the meta-language, influences the theoretical and methodological position one takes.

Given the concept of linguistic ideology, it seems important also to reflect on the content of this chapter. I analyzed two strategies in Japanese comics based on methodological frameworks developed for English by English-speaking scholars, while incorporating interpretive principles of *futaku* and reversed words grown out of traditional Japanese rhetoric. At the same time, analysis and interpretation advanced in this chapter are made possible, in part, by examining Japanese data, which enabled such an undertaking in the first place.

It is not the case that all theories are consistently in agreement with the linguistic ideology recognized for a specific language (this is abundantly evidenced by conflicting views on language based on identical language and meta-language). Linguistic ideologies are, after all, more complex. It is true, however, that theories of language tend to correspond to its language and meta-language. It becomes critically important, therefore, that studies on Japanese language and culture are reflexively examined in the context of Japanese language ideologies that are both enabling and restricting. Ironically, because of their ideological restrictions, studies focusing on particular language and culture (e.g., Japanese) potentially become increasingly more meaningful. After all, insight into language obtained by examining Japanese can challenge available theories and views toward other languages (and vice versa, as well). Consider that the emotive *da* is prominently coded in Japanese and is repeatedly observed. Recall that the Japanese *wh*-question word *nan(i)* helps realize expressivity in varied ways. And consider the forces surrounding topic–comment and nominalization-followed-by-commentary structures. Functions associated with these features are prominently coded in the Japanese language but may not be in other languages. The mode of expressivity generated through nominalization, *da*, and *nan(i)* may occupy a less significant place in other languages and, therefore, may not receive sufficient analytical attention.

Since any theory of language must be grounded in a specific language, when speaking of how language is theorized in different cultures, it is impossible to avoid relativism. On the other hand, the forced universalism of certain available theories (both Western and non-Western) must also be avoided. Somewhere at a point between this relativism and universalism I hope to locate the ideological boundedness and possibilities inherent in this study. And my discussion on the sources of emotion in Japanese comics is hoped to add, in some ways, to the understanding of emotivity in Japan—and beyond.

NOTES

1. See Maynard (1999) for a detailed account on stativity and situationality associated with *da*.

2. Note that *ja-nē* appearing in *Shateki tesuto ja-nē n da* is a copulative predicate, and not an emotive *ja-nai*. The utterance final *da* is an emotive *da*, indexing strong assertion.

3. For example, the frequency of the *n(o) da* predicate in 10 published *taidan* (dialog) conversations was 25.82% of all sentence-final forms—520 out of 2,014 sentences—(Maynard, 1992). Likewise, the frequency of *n(o) da* in 3-minute segments of 20 casual conversations resulted in 25.48% of all sentence-final forms—317 out of 1,244 utter-ances—(Maynard, 1993b). I also examined Commentary Questions (interrogative sentences based on the [nominalizer + *da*] structure) in Maynard (1995) and reported their relatively high frequency (more than 30% in comics and fiction).

4. Curiously, the use of *nan(i)* in information-seeking interrogative sentences is rather limited in *Kōkaku Kidōtai*. Instead, cases of *nan(i)* occurring in expletive and exclamatory expressions abound. *Nan(i)* (including cases of *nani*, *nan*, *nanto* and *nante*) occurred a total of 76 times. *Nan(i)* appeared in the information-seeking interrogative 29 times (38.16%), while the remaining 47 cases (61.84%) occurred in expletive, exclamative, and

otherwise emotive context. In addition, there were 30 cases of *nani ka* (something) and *nani mo* ([not] anything) in noninterrogative sentences.

5. The use of *nan(i)* occasionally illustrates elaborate interaction where referentially meaningless but emotionally rich discourse is at work. For example, in a television drama, *Ōoka Echizen, Adauchi Yūreikago* (TBS Television, 1992), the following interaction takes place. Okatsu answers the investigator who suspects that her husband, Kumakichi, and the business partner are involved in a homicide.

Okatsu: Sir, my husband and Hachi don't have the talent to commit such a complicated crime. If they did, we won't be engaging in this line of business.

Kumaichi: Hey, what do you mean (*nan dē*) by this line of business?

Okatsu: What do you mean by what is this? (*Nan da to wa nan dai*)

Kumaichi: What do you mean by what do you mean by what is this? *(Nan da to wa nan da to wa nan dē)*

Okatsu: What are you talking about? (*Nani itte n da yo, Omaesan*)

As the expression *Nan da to wa nan da to wa nan dē* epitomizes, the repeated use of *nan* (and *da*) makes possible the emotive interaction, while conveying little information. Here, saying something, or anything, is important, and what is being said remains secondary.

6. I should note here that *nan* in *nan datta ka na* is an interrogative *nan(i)*, functioning as a part of the interrogative utterance.

7. Curiously, investigation of the Japanese quotation has revealed that the distinction between direct and indirect discourse is blurred (this point summarized in Maynard [1997b]). Even more interestingly, Tannen (1989), by using the concept of constructed dialog, argues that English quotation does not support a strict direct/indirect paradigm either. Linguistic ideologies do not totally explain the relationship between the meta-language and theory.

REFERENCES

Amagasaki, A. (1988). *Nihon no retorikku* [Rhetoric of Japan]. Tokyo: Chikuma Shobō.

Caffi, C., & Janney, R. W. (1994). Towards a pragmatics of emotive communication. *Journal of Pragmatics, 22,* 325–373.

Foolen, A. (1997). The expressive function of language: Towards a cognitive semantic approach. In S. Niemeier & R. Dirven (Eds.), *The language of emotions* (pp. 15–31). Amsterdam: John Benjamins.

Fujitani, M. (1986). Kadō kyoyō. In K. Miyake (Ed.), *Fujitani Mitsue zenshū* [Collected works of Mitsue Fujitani] (Vol. 4, pp. 765–777). Tokyo: Shibunkaku. (Original work published 1817)

Günthner, S. (1997). The contextualization of affect in reported dialogues. In S. Niemeier & R. Dirven (Eds.), *The language of emotions* (pp. 247–275). Amsterdam: John Benjamins.

Ishigami, T. (1981). Kandōshi ni tsuite [On exclamative interjections]. *Shinshū Daigaku Kyōyōbu Kiyō, 15,* 1–11.

Kövecses, Z. (1995). The "container" metaphor of anger in English, Chinese, Japanese and Hungarian. In Z. Radman (Ed.), *From a metaphorical point of view: A multi-disciplinary approach to the cognitive content of metaphor* (pp. 117–145). Berlin: Walter de Gruyter.

Levinson, S. (1983). *Pragmatics.* Cambridge: Cambridge University Press.

Li, C. N., & Thompson, S. A. (1976). Subject and topic: A new typology of language. In C. N. Li (Ed.), *Subject and topic* (pp. 450–490). New York: Academic Press.

Maynard, S. K. (1980). Discourse functions of the Japanese theme marker *wa*. Unpublished doctoral dissertation, Northwestern University, Evanston, IL.

Maynard, S. K. (1992). Cognitive and pragmatic messages of a syntactic choice: A case of the Japanese commentary predicate *n(o) da. TEXT: An Interdisciplinary Journal for the Study of Discourse, 12,* 563–613.

Maynard, S. K. (1993a). *Discourse modality: Subjectivity, emotion and voice in the Japanese language.* Amsterdam: John Benjamins.

Maynard, S. K. (1993b). Interactional functions of formulaicity: A case of utterance-final forms in Japanese. *Proceedings of the 15th International Congress of Linguists* (Vol. 3, pp. 225–228). Quebec City: Laval University Press.

Maynard, S. K. (1994). The centrality of thematic relations in Japanese text. *Functions of Language, 1,* 229–260.

Maynard, S. K. (1995). Commentary questions in Japanese: Cognitive sources and pragmatic resources. *Studies in Language, 19,* 447–487.

Maynard, S. K. (1997a). Synergistic structures in grammar: A case of nominalization and commentary predicate in Japanese. *Word: Journal of the International Linguistic Association, 48,* 15–40.

Maynard, S. K. (1997b). *Danwa bunseki no kanōsei: Riron, hōhō, Nihongo no hyōgensei* [Possibilities of discourse analysis: Theory, method, and Japanese expressivity]. Tokyo: Kuroshio.

Maynard, S. K. (1999). Grammar, with attitude: On the expressivity of certain *da* sentences in Japanese. *Linguistics, 37,* 214–250.

McVeigh, B. (1996). Standing stomachs, clamoring chests and cooling livers: Metaphors in the psychological lexicon of Japanese. *Journal of Pragmatics, 26,* 25–50.

Mikami, A. (1960). *Zō wa hana ga nagai* [As for elephants, their trunks are long]. Tokyo: Kuroshio.

Miyazaki, K., & Ueno, N. (1985). *Shiten* [Point of view]. Tokyo: University of Tokyo Press.

Moriyama, T. (1996). *Jōdōteki kandōshi kō* [Thoughts on emotional exclamative interjections]. *Gobun, 65,* 51–62.

Ochs, E., & Schieffelin, B. (1989). Language has a heart. *TEXT: An Interdisciplinary Journal for the Study of Discourse, 9,* 7–25.

Pomerantz, A. (1984). Agreeing and disagreeing with assessments: Some features of preferred/dispreferred turn shapes. In J. M. Atkinson & J. Heritage (Eds.), *Structures of social action* (pp. 57–101). Cambridge: Cambridge University Press.

Rumsey, A. (1990). Wording, meaning, and linguistic ideology. *American Anthropologist, 92,* 346–361.

Sakura, M. (1995). *Chibi Maruko-chan* [The little girl Maruko] (Vol. 13). Tokyo: Shūeisha.

Sakura, M. (1996). *Chibi Maruko-chan* [The little girl Maruko] (Vol. 14). Tokyo: Shūeisha.

Saussure, F., de. (1966). *Course in general linguistics* (C. Bally & A. Sechehaye, Eds.; W. Basken, Trans.). New York: McGraw-Hill.

Schegloff, E. (1968). Sequencing in conversational openings. *American Anthropologist, 70,* 1075–1095.

Shirow, M. (1991). *Kōkaku kidōtai* [Ghost in the shell]. Tokyo: Kōdansha.

Shirow, M. (1995) *Ghost in the shell* (F. Schoot & T. Smith, Trans.). Milwaukie, OR: Dark Horse Comics. (Original work published 1991)

Silverstein, M. (1979). Language structure and linguistic ideology. In P. R. Clyne, W. F. Hanks, & C. L. Hofbauer (Eds.), *The elements: A parasession on linguistic units and levels* (pp. 193–247). Chicago: Chicago Linguistic Society.

Tannen, D. (1982). The oral/literate continuum in discourse. In D. Tannen (Ed.), *Spoken and written language* (pp. 1–16). Norwood, NJ: Ablex.

Tannen, D. (1989). *Talking voices. Repetition, dialogue, and imagery in conversational discourse.* Cambridge: Cambridge University Press.

TBS Television. (1992, October 5). *Ōoka Echizen, Adauchi yūreikago* [Ōoka Echizen, Revenge of the ghost paranquin, television drama]. Tokyo, Japan.

Wierzbicka, A. (1991). Japanese key words and core cultural values. *Language in Society, 20,* 333–385.

Wierzbicka, A. (1997). *Understanding cultures through their key words.* Oxford: Oxford University Press.

Woolard, K. A. (1992). Language ideology: Issues and approaches. *Pragmatics, 2,* 235–249.

Chapter 13

Narrative as a Reflection of Culture and Consciousness: Developmental Aspects

Masahiko Minami

Personal narratives not only involve a description of a past experience as an ubiquitous aspect of human behavior, but they simultaneously embody culturally specific modes of telling a story or recollection. This chapter examines the means by which Japanese—both children and adults—encode their own perspectives and emotions. The chapter specifically explores Japanese children's and their mothers' oral personal narratives, in order to analyze what kinds of linguistic means and rhetorical devices they deploy in narrative. The findings of this study suggest that: (1) early mother–child conversational interactions are important contributors to children's acquisition of how to express their emotions in socioculturally appropriate ways; and (2) telling a narrative on their own as a socioculturally situated activity does not seem to be an easy task for young children. Overall, this chapter focuses on how the sense of being Japanese gradually comes to emerge, becomes manifest, and is effectively delivered in narrative discourse.

People from virtually all cultures tell stories because narrative functions not only informationally, but also socially as a self-presentation. Personal narratives help describe our past events or experiences while embodying specific sociocultural modes for doing so. This chapter examines how Japanese do so—both children and adults—in expressing their own perspectives and emotions. Although Japanese spoken communication is generally said to be subtle or vague, personal voice is a prominent feature of the language (Maynard, 1993). While research on Japanese conversation mounts, little work has been done on how Japanese acquire their culture-specific consciousness (i.e., Japaneseness) in verbal communication.

Studies on child language acquisition suggest that, like children elsewhere, Japanese children acquire their language very early (Clancy, 1985). In terms of pragmatics, however, children must go through further developmental stages, sometimes through to adulthood, before being able to tell a well-formed story or becoming a full-fledged social being. For the Japanese, two sociolinguistic devices of the language necessary to become such a social being, but relatively absent in many other languages, are its honorifics (largely verb endings) and sentence-final particles (remotely similar to tag questions in English). These two devices appear crucial for telling a story competently, for they enable one to participate in the famed Japanese "group-oriented society," as well as making self-presentations. Charting just when such devices are acquired by the Japanese would provide a foray into acquisition of Japaneseness itself. Completely doing so, of course, is well beyond the scope of one chapter, even several. For present purposes, I provide a snapshot in the development of this Japaneseness by comparing the storytelling between very young children and adult Japanese in view of honorifics and sentence-final particles. Such a snapshot shows how Japanese storytellers encode their own perspectives and emotions at the very crux of culture and consciousness. Before doing so, I present the generally understood view of narrative structure followed by a look at the sociocultural factors related to the Japanese narrative.

Among the authors whose work particularly inspired me to write this chapter are sociolinguist William Labov (1972) and Japanese linguist Senko Maynard (1993). While differing in focus, these two scholars share an important aspect; both took a sociocultural approach to the study of verbal behavior. In particular, they both interpreted narrative as a socioculturally situated activity. Much of our knowledge about narrative comes from the work of Labov and his associates. Besides identifying a model of the "naturally occurring narrative," its parts and how they work, Labov gives insight into the evaluative function of narrative. The evaluative function tells us about the narrator's attitude toward the events of the story or the significance they may have. This matter of evaluation is what I equate herein with emotion or emotional expression, which may vary in explicitness or implicitness for a story. The importance is that without evaluation, thereby emotional expression, many of our stories would have but an empty feel.

Bruner's (1986) view of narrative structure as analogous to landscape painting consists of two major landscapes: the landscape of action and the landscape of consciousness. The latter the narrator "paints" to show "how the world is perceived or felt by various members of the cast of characters, each from their own perspective" (Feldman, Bruner, Renderer, & Spitzer, 1990, p. 2). Developmentally, the child's acquisition of these two vehicles for thought and language production—the landscape of consciousness in particular—is crucial to understanding his or her progress in narrative production, because, according to Bruner (1986), it tells the listener about "what those involved in the action know, think, or feel, or do not know, think, or feel" (p. 14). Developing clear landscapes is not easy and involves knowing how to properly foreground and background information.[1] Previous research (Berman & Slobin, 1994; Minami, 1996; Reilly, 1992) has revealed developmental changes in children's ability to foreground information (i.e., restricted narrative clauses) and to background information (i.e., free narrative clauses) as a function of increasing age. Developmentally, therefore, there has been an interest in the relationship between the older an individual becomes and the more nonsequential informa- tion—because evaluation in particular is closely connected to emotion—he or she adds to the narrative, in order to emphasize why he or she wants to tell the narrative. Hence the added impetus for me to study and compare both young children and adults.

NARRATIVE AS SOCIOCULTURALLY SITUATED: THE CASE IN JAPAN

When turning our attention to sociocultural factors, which are also considered important contributors to differences in linguistic style, it is critical to examine how the meaning-creation and self-presentation process, which is conducted by an individual who lives in a specific culture, reflects socioculturally accepted norms. Psychological studies have recently focused on the process by which peo- ple construct the meaning of the world and of their own experience (e.g., Mandell & McCabe, 1997). Some of these studies particularly investigated how these processes emerge from the interplay of mind and culture (e.g., Minami, 1997). In this regard, Bruner (1990) advocated that psychology "must be organized around those meaning-making and meaning-using processes that connect man to cul- ture" (p. 12). Conversely, it is also crucial to explore how the social norms shape an individual's meaning-making and self-presentation. For example, speech acts and politeness not only share some universal features (Brown & Levinson, 1987), but they simultaneously vary crossculturally as well as crosslinguistically (Matsumoto, 1993). These referential choices and issues of politeness are con- sidered important because they are closely related to issues of subtlety and vagueness not only in the Japanese language, but also in Japanese society at large. That is, the Japanese language, which is often affected by a culturally meaningful context, is a highly contextualized language; the speaker must be fully aware of (1) whether the relationship with the listener is intimate, or (2) whether the communication is impersonal. In this respect, Hall (1989) writes:

In sharp contrast, high context peoples like the Pueblo, many of Africa's indigenous cul- tures, the Japanese, and apparently the Russians . . . inhabit a "sea of information" that is widely shared. . . . The "sea of information" group lives in a unified, very high context world in which all or most of the parts interrelate. (p. 39)

In a relatively homogeneous society like Japan, even if what the speaker talks about or the meaning and self-presentation the speaker wants to convey is not explicit but vague, it is often said that the similarity of background allows (or at least Japanese people believe it allows) for more accurate inferences on the part of the listener. Similarly, Azuma (1986) states: "In contrast to the West, where it is the sender's responsibility to produce a coherent, clear, and intelligible message, in Japan, it is the receiver's responsibility to make sense out of the message" (p. 9). Even vague utterances may thus result in successful communication in Japan because interlocutors believe that they have the shared experience necessary to make sense out of the vague uses of the language (Donahue, 1998).

In many other areas, the Japanese also show behavioral patterns that differ greatly from those identified in Western cultures. For instance, the guiding principle of the Japanese can be characterized as social relativism, within which the individual is defined by the reference groups to which he or she belongs (Holloway & Minami, 1996; Lebra, 1976; Maynard, 1993). Social relativism, however, does not necessarily imply that the Japanese do not possess the notion of independence or individualism. Rather, traditionally they have defined each individual, and his or her function, on the basis of the human relationships within the society of which he or she is a part; each individual is thus allowed to enjoy individualism and independence within a certain framework of group. In this way, in contrast to American culture, which is characterized by the guiding principle dominated by the pursuit of individual autonomy and self-interest (Lebra, 1976), it is somewhat difficult for an individual to nourish a Western sense of individuality on Japanese soil.

As a reflection of such sociocultural uniqueness, those who have conducted research on Japanese conversational discourse (e.g., LoCastro, 1987; Maynard, 1989, 1993; White, 1989; Yamada, 1992) have described a variety of its characteristic features. Among them, Maynard's (1993) study is particularly relevant to the current topic. Advocating that personal voice is prominent in Japanese, she identified certain Japanese linguistic devices and manipulative strategies that essentially convey a subjective emotion as well as an individual's shared feelings with others. Contrary to Westerners' stereotyped misconception of Japanese individuals as quiet, showing little emotion, Maynard emphasized that a variety of emotive signs—for example, interactional particles, discourse connectives, modal adverbs, and verb forms—are deployed in the Japanese language so that an individual can convey his or her emotion effectively to the listener.

As seen in the studies conducted by Maynard (1993) and others described above, although research focusing on Japanese conversation already exists, little work has been conducted on how speakers of Japanese acquire such culture-specific consciousness (i.e., Japaneseness in this case) in verbal communication.

Studies on child language acquisition, for example, suggest that Japanese children begin to use a variety of linguistic signs very early, such as "formal" *des(u)/mas(u)* verb-ending forms (i.e., suffixes) at about 2 years of age (e.g., Clancy, 1985). Yet, even if young children have learned the social pragmatic functions or interactional dimensions of such linguistic means and communicative devices, they might not have acquired the subtleties of those devices expected in telling oral personal narratives, such as the effective use of proper verb-ending forms to encode the narrator's perspective (Minami, 1998). Designed to address a gap that currently exists in this body of research, therefore, the present study assumes that early mother–child interactions set the pattern for subsequent emotional manifestations relating to the possible roots of Japaneseness. This assumption is based on Vygotsky's (1978) social interaction approach, which states that humans are fundamentally social and cultural beings and that, therefore, any cognitive skills have a social interactive origin. Accordingly, to examine the emergence of Japanese consciousness, this study examines young Japanese children's personal narratives in two different contexts, monologic (i.e., telling a narrative alone) and dialogic (i.e., coconstructing a narrative with someone else). With a focus on linguistic devices and strategies in Japanese narratives, the overall goal of the study is to explore how the sense of being Japanese (i.e., Japaneseness) gradually comes to emerge, becomes manifest, and is effectively delivered in narrative discourse.

METHOD

Subjects

A total of 20 middle-class Japanese preschool children participated in this study, along with their mothers. Of these children, 10 were in 5-year-old children's classrooms in preschool at the time of data collection, whereas the other 10 were in 4-year-old children's classrooms; in each of the subgroups, half of the children were males, half females, so that any relationship between gender of the child and lexical development could be examined.[2] These children's oral personal narratives—both monologic (a child alone) and dialogic (a mother–child pair)—were studied in order to analyze what kinds of linguistic means and rhetorical devices they deploy in narrative discourse. The reason that this study focused on preschoolers is due to age constraints that emerge from analysis of the development of children's narratives. Children begin telling personal narratives from the age of 2 (Sachs, 1979), but in any culture, these early productions are quite short through the age of 3½ years (McCabe & Peterson, 1991). By about age 4, however, children become able to produce fairly complex narratives (McCabe & Peterson, 1991; Ninio & Snow, 1996; Peterson & McCabe, 1983). Preschool years thus represent the period of extremely rapid development in the child's acquisition of narrative discourse capacity.

Data Collection and Procedures

Monologic Narrative Production

Monologic narrative activity is based on Labov's (1972) methodology for elic-iting personal narratives, specifically, danger-of-death or scary-event narratives, a child version of which was later developed by Peterson and McCabe (1983) for analyzing children's developing narrative skill. Before eliciting narratives, rap-port was established by an adult Japanese interviewer with the child, through activities such as drawing pictures. When children were judged to be comfortable initiating conversation with the interviewer, they were asked in their native lan-guage, Japanese, prompting questions related to injuries, in the manner devel-oped by Peterson and McCabe (1983). This elicitation technique had previously proved to be effective with Japanese children (Minami, 1990; Minami & McCabe, 1991, 1996). Questions about personally experienced events were asked, such as "Have you ever gotten hurt?" in children's native language, Japanese. However, no specific questions were asked; only nonspecific social support, such as "Uh huh," "Tell me more," "Then what happened?" was offered. The narratives elicited from the children were thus *without scaffolding*[3] and rel-atively *monologic* in nature.

To understand language-specific styles of narrative discourse, we need to con-sider how differently young children and more mature speakers of the same lan-guage deploy their language. To examine the relative narrative competence of young children, therefore, narratives were also elicited from adults, the children's mothers in this study. Adult narratives are expected to provide the culturally appropriate, full-fledged, rhetorically well-formed narrative with fully developed Japanese-specific consciousness that children eventually will accomplish in telling personal narratives.

Dialogic Narrative Production

Mothers who participated in this project were supplied with tape recorders and blank cassette tapes. They were asked to elicit interesting past events or experi-ences from their children in a relaxed and informal situation. In this way, moth-ers and their children were audiotape-recorded in their homes. Recall in the inter-viewer's narrative elicitation described above, nondirective general cues were given and thus narratives were elicited from the children without providing any scaffolding. In this mother–child conversational activity, on the other hand, mothers were expected to scaffold the narratives of their young children. In this project, therefore, following the methods McCabe and Peterson (1991) used in their studies, mothers are expected to ask their children to relate stories about per-sonal experiences, about real events that have happened in the past. However, mothers were also instructed to do this narrative elicitation in as natural a way as possible, like they ordinarily behave when they ask their children to talk about past events. In contrast to the adult interviewer's monologic narrative elicitation, therefore, this task is dialogic (or coconstructive) in nature and considered crucial to successful child narratives (Ninio & Snow, 1996).

To establish a comparable data base for monologic and dialogic narrative productions, the initial three narrative productions from each activity were analyzed. A note of caution, however, is that while only talk about past experiences was analyzed, talk about past experiences is nonetheless woven in with talk about the present and other non-narrative talk, particularly in mother–child interactions (i.e., dialogic narratives). All narrative (or conversational narrative) segments were transcribed verbatim for analysis into computer files in accordance with the guidelines of Codes for the Human Analysis of Transcripts (CHAT) conventions for analysis by the Child Language Analysis (CLAN) software available through the Child Language Data Exchange System (CHILDES) (MacWhinney & Snow, 1985, 1990). The Key Word and Line (KWAL) program of CLAN was specifically used to extract linguistic items for further analysis.

Linguistic Items/Narrative Devices

In this section, examples told by children are primarily used. Sometimes, however, adult examples are also included, (1) for a comparative purpose or (2) in cases in which no child examples are available. I am particularly interested in what Maynard (1993) calls discourse modality indicators, emotive signs deployed in the Japanese language (e.g., interactional particles, modal adverbs, and verb forms),[4] which, in turn, reflect Japanese culture and society. Furthermore, when applied to language development, the acquisition of such paralinguistic and syntactic indicators inevitably leads to the acquisition of Japaneseness.

Two Types of Particles

Children learn how to convey their ideas to their interlocutors in language. Effective deployment of two different particles, (1) the interactional/rapport particle *ne* (you know) and (2) the assertive and/or emphatic particle *yo* (I tell you, I'm sure), adds sophistication to narratives. The functions of these two particles, however, differ greatly, particularly in terms of psychological orientation. By uttering the sentence-final particle *ne* (or *nee* when elongated), the narrator seeks the listener's agreement (mostly in the form of back-channels), expresses the narrator's psychological and emotional dependence on the listener, and thus tries to establish narrator–listener rapport or intersubjectivity, which, following Ninio and Snow (1996), means "a state in which two or more persons share a feeling of 'togetherness'" (p. 23):

Example 1 (Ryota, boy, age 3;8)[5]

Mari, you know,	*Mari chan wa **ne**,*
to that park, you know,	*asoko no kōen de **ne**,*
(I) went to play a swing, you know,	*buranko ittete **ne**,*

with a bang, you know,	*dobōn tte **ne**,*
(I) fell.	*ochita no.*

In the above example, *ne* is frequently used when the narrator provides background information (note that background information is defined as referring to either orientation [e.g., the setting, people, time, features of environment, conditions, and ongoing behavior in the narrative] or evaluation or both). Although not shown in the example, the listener (the interviewer in this case), by showing brief vocal acknowledgments (i.e., back-channels), signals that he or she is attentive to what the narrator is narrating. Using the particle *ne* facilitates the process of interpretation based on the assumption that the narrator and the listener share common ground; more importantly, it suggests that even a monologic narrative is dialogic to some extent.

In contrast to *ne*, the narrator uses another particle, *yo,* if the narrator assumes that (1) he or she knows something that the listener does not know or that (2) the listener has different views. In other words, the narrator uses *yo* when he or she believes that he or she is the sole possessor of certain knowledge or information.

Example 2a (Yumi, girl, age 4;4)

But (I) wasn't drowned, I tell you.

*demo oborenakatta **yo**.*

Example 2b (Akira, boy, age 4;6)

(That) was this big, I tell you.

*konna ookikatta **yo**.*

In this way, although the particles *ne* and *yo* both illustrate the interactional nature of the Japanese language, *ne* is more interaction-focused, whereas *yo* is more information-focused (Maynard, 1993; Young & Nakajima-Okano, 1984). Thus, these two types of particles function differently and enrich narratives in different ways.

The Quotation-Final Particle tte

The quotation-final particle *tte* is primarily used for either one of the following two purposes: First, the formation of onomatopoeias is completed by simply adding the quotation-final particle *tte* (e.g., *dokaan tte*, which means "with a bang"). Second, reported speech in Japanese is completed by simply adding the quotation-final particle *tte* at the end (but before the verb *itta* [said]). Examples 3a and 3b give the formation of onomatopoeia and reported speech, respectively.

Example 3a (Ryota, boy, age 3;8)

In a sandbox,	*sunaba de,*

| with a bang, | *dokān **tte**,* |
| with a bang, (I) fell. | *patān **tte** ochita.* |

Example 3b (Yumi, girl, age 4;4)

| "(It) hurts, (it) hurts," | *"itai itai" **tte**,* |
| (I) was crying. | *naiteta.* |

The Use of Causal Connectives

The narrative connective *dakara* (so, therefore, that's why) almost always appears when the narrator provides the listener with background information (once again, note that background information includes orientation and evaluation). This connective gives a conclusive tone to what the narrator has stated, as can be seen below.

Example 4a (Sho, boy, age 4;6)

That's why (I) painted (it) black.

***dakara** kuroi no nutta.*

Example 4b (Sae, girl, age 4;8)

That's why (we) went to the wrong river.

***dakara** chigau kawa itchatta no.*

What the narrator has stated should be interpreted by the listener as a sufficient cause/explanation for a result/consequence. In other words, by using *dakara*, the narrator conveys her personal position, attitude, and, moreover, emotion toward the fact in a very brief way. As a manifestation of Japanese consciousness, it seems that, in adult narratives in particular, the listener who is brought up in Japanese culture is naturally expected to understand the narrator's strong emotional feelings and to empathize easily with the narrator.

Example 4c (Mari's mother)

That's why (I) have a faint memory (of grandmother's) face and the contour (of her face), though.

***dakara** sobo no kao mo rinkaku mo ussura nan desu kedo.*

Like *dakara* (so, therefore, that's why), *datte* (but, because), which is another connective, provides the listener with certain information. Unlike *dakara*, *datte* often appears when a child interacts with his or her parents or other adults with whom he or she has established the *amae* psychological and emotional dependence (and he or she expects *omoiyari* [which means "empathy" (Clancy, 1985) or "consideration for others" (Donahue, 1998; Maynard, 1989)] from his or her parents or other intimate adults).[6]

Example 5a (Mari, girl, age 4;0)

Because a middle-aged woman [someone's mom in this case] said so.

datte obachan ga sō itta mon.

Example 5b (Takato, boy, age 5;1)

Because I didn't know that.

datte sonna no wakannai mon.

The Use of Adverbs

Like the examples of uses of *dakara*, the adverb *yappari* (after all) adds the narrator's emotion and attitude toward what he or she has previously narrated. In the following example, *yappari* refers back to a variety of pastime activities in the neighborhood that an adult narrator has described. In other words, the adverb *yappari* serves some kind of referential or anaphoric function in narrative.

Example 6 (Minori's mother)

After all, it was fun (for me) to have an opportunity to play with all [the children] in the neighborhood.

yappari kinjo no minna to asoberu koto ga tanosikute.

Two Types of Verbs in Relation to Narrative

Sophistication in adults' narrative, however, is most manifest in the manipulation of "informal/abrupt" verb forms such as the copula *da* (a linking verb like the English verb "to be") and "formal" *des(u)/mas(u)* verb-ending forms (i.e., suffixes) in Japanese. Note that *des(u)* is the polite form of *da*. Examples of these two verb-ending forms are shown below:

Example 7a (Sho, boy, age 4;6)

That's Uncle Shinobu.

Shinobu ojisan da.

Example 7b (Akira, boy, age 4;6)

This is the one, I tell you.

kore desu yo.

Example 7c (Mari, girl, age 4;0)

(I) am sorry, but I feel sleepy. . .

sumimasen, nemuri . . .

Within the inner circle (e.g., mother–child interactions), "informal/abrupt" styles such as *da* are regularly used, whereas outside the inner circle, in order to maintain personal distance, the "formal" *des(u)/mas(u)* styles are preferred. When an adult speaker addresses an outsider, he or she uses the "formal" *des(u)/mas(u)* styles because the outsider is usually placed in a higher position than the speaker; thus, the distinction between *des(u)/mas(u)* and *da* is based on complex, culturally specific, elaborated rule systems for social exchange, involving asymmetries of power in some cases. However, there are certainly exceptions, as can be seen in Examples 7b and 7c in which both the children address their mothers using the formal verb-ending forms. These instances seem to indicate that preschool children have already acquired culturally specific politeness routines. At the same time, however, the examples seem to suggest that the social/cultural underpinnings of these markings are so complex that children use the formal verb-ending forms only in the performance of limited social-communicative acts (i.e., socially routinized set formulas). In other words, while drawing a clear a boundary between children's developing linguistic skills and their developing sociability is certainly difficult, it seems that preschoolers are either simply developing sociability/politeness or packaging the complete communicative event into words in an unanalyzed or unsegmented manner, such as *ohayoo gozaimasu* (Good morning), *asobimashoo* (Let's play), and *gochisoosama deshita* (Thank you for a nice dish). Thus, regardless of whether they interact with an individual within the inner circle or outside, young children, preschoolers in particular, are likely to use these words in formulaic speech patterns when participating in routinized interactions.

Preschoolers' understanding of the distinction between *des(u)/mas(u)* and *da* or, more specifically, between "inside" and "outside" is, however, less than complete. In the narrative context, the concept of "inside" and "outside" should eventually be understood as a reflection of a narrator's conceptualization about the narrative event (Maynard, 1993). When a narrator who has access to a certain distant topic tells a narrative about that topic, a triangular relationship emerges among the narrator, the narrative topic, and the listener (Toolan, 1988). That is, as the narrator is increasingly engrossed in the topic, he or she takes more distance from the listener; a shift occurs from narrative external (i.e., the closer relation between the narrator and the listener rather than the relation between the narrator and the topic) to narrative internal (i.e., the closer relation between the narrator and the topic than the relation between the narrator and the listener). In the case of Japanese, as the narrator's perspective has shifted toward narrative internal, the narrator tells a narrative without using the formal *des(u)/mas(u)* styles. The narrator, however, at times becomes aware of the existence of the listener and addresses him or her directly. The narrator then takes a narrative-external perspective, using the formal *des(u)/mas(u)* styles. Thus, this language-specific device—the choice of the verb-ending forms—suggests the position the narrator is taking.

Linguistic research concerning point of view has demonstrated that speakers naturally take a particular point of view (e.g., Bamberg, 1997a, 1997b). In the context of discourse, Kuno (1987) proposed the notion of empathy perspective; the speaker represents his or her attitude toward event characters in different ways, as if changing camera angles. In relation to this perspective taking, one of the classic studies that calls our attention to children's language development is Piaget's (1959) pioneering work on young children's developmental constraints. Piaget pointed out that young children are egocentric; they are limited in perspective taking, ignoring the particular angle from which certain things are viewed.

The present data—preschoolers' use of the formal verb-ending forms only in set formulas, not in narrative perspective taking—seem to support this limited perspective taking. Control over the rules for taking different points of view in narratives as well as for expressing intentions politely have not yet fully developed during the preschool years. Certainly, preschoolers can intentionally take on the point of view of people around them, more specifically, a narrative external position. For example, by frequently uttering *ne* (you know), Japanese preschoolers negotiate with the listener about the stance they are taking. As far as the present data are concerned, however, children have failed to use the formal *des(u)/mas(u)* styles for representing a narrative-external perspective. As becomes clear later, in whichever context—monologic or dialogic—preschool children have not yet mastered the effective use of *des(u)/mas(u)* styles in telling personal narratives. The underpinnings of these *des(u)/mas(u)* and *da* markings in terms of perspective taking seem not only socially but also cognitively too complex for preschoolers in order to convey consciousness in linguistically specific ways. In other words, these narrative devices are beyond children's cognitive and linguistic capability at the preschool level.

Adult narratives stand in contrast to children's narratives with respect to narrative perspective taking. Adults are obviously capable of producing narrative with proper perspectives. Linguistically, as they are increasingly involved in narratives, adults are capable of effectively differentiating between the formal and informal verb-ending forms. In the following narrative example, an adult narrator does not use the formal *des(u)/mas(u)* styles initially because she is absorbed in the narrative (i.e., her classmate's death). Toward the end, however, she uses the formal *des(u)/mas(u)* styles because she takes a distance from the topic, becomes fully aware of the listener, and addresses him or her directly.

Example 8 (Akira's mother)

"On the first day of the season when the sea was open to the public, (he) jumped into the water. Because of heart failure, (he) died" said [a friend of mine].

*"umi biraki ga hajimatta hi ni, umi e tobikonde itte, shinzoo mahi de, shinjattan **da**," toka itte.*

At that time first, (I) formed the recognition that [human beings] die, (I) think.

*sono toki ni hajimete kurai shinutte yuu ninshiki ga, dekita gurai datta, to omōn **desu**.*

Cook (1997) aptly called the distinction associated with verb-ending patterns "public/social" versus "private." In narrative contexts, because the narrator is aware of the listener, narrative external is considered "public/social." In contrast, narrative internal is considered "private" because the narrator is inside of his or her world without being fully aware of the listener. It then seems that only those who have mastered how to encode narrative external/internal perspective taking can convey Japanese consciousness to others in linguistically appropriate ways. In like manner, it seems that only those listeners who fully appreciate the narrator's verb-encoded perspective taking can comprehend language-specific manifestations of Japanese consciousness.

RESULTS

Uses of Linguistic Items in Monologic Narratives: Differences Between Children and Adults

The data for seven measures were analyzed:[7]

1. Interactional/rapport particle *ne* (you know)

2. Assertive and/or emphatic particle *yo* (I tell you)

3. Quotation-final particle *tte*

4. Connective *dakara* (that's why)

5. Adverb *yappari* (after all)

6. Formal *des(u)/mas(u)* verb-ending forms

7. Copula *da*

The mean frequencies of the linguistic items are presented in Table 13-1. The informal verb-ending style *da* and the particle *yo* each appear only twice in children's narratives, and *yappari* (after all) and *des(u)/mas(u)* do not appear at all. Another connective *datte* (but, because), which, like *dakara* (so, therefore, that's why), provides the listener with information, appears only once in children's narratives. However, *dakara* does not appear at all in the children's monologic narratives.

In terms of the use of the interactional/rapport particle *ne* (you know), no difference reached statistical significance between preschoolers and adults. Comparisons of mean frequencies by *t* tests, however, revealed that except for *ne*, children's uses of linguistic items are very limited when telling personal narratives.

What is evident here is that uses of linguistic items—both morphological and lexical—differed significantly between children and adults. In children's monologic narratives, except for the interactional/rapport particle *ne* (you know), they have not yet learned to deploy certain grammatical items (e.g., *dakara*, which means "so, therefore, that's why" and *yappari*, which means "after all") that encode evaluation. Conversely, the adult group used the linguistic devices more frequently and effectively than did the preschoolers. In other words, by deploying the linguistic items, the adults succeeded in including more evaluative comments in their narratives.

Children's Uses of Linguistic Items: Differences Between Monologic and Dialogic Narratives

Differences in children's narrative performance in different contexts—monologic and dialogic—were considered next. Table 13-2 presents the mean frequencies of the linguistic items the children used in the monologic and dialogic narratives. For example, the children used the assertive/emphatic particle *yo* (I tell you) and the quotation-final particle *tte* more frequently in mother–child interactions. A connective, *dakara* (so, therefore), which did not appear at all in monologic narratives, was used by four children. Further, another connective, *datte* (but, because), which appeared only once in monologic narratives, was used by nine children. Similarly, the formal *des(u)/mas(u)* styles were used by five children.

Separate two-way analyses of variance (type of narrative interaction x gender) were carried out for each of the following seven dependent measures:

Table 13-1

Uses of Linguistic Items in Monologic Narratives: Differences Between Children and Adults

	Children ($n = 20$)		Mothers ($n = 20$)		
	Mean	(SD)	Mean	(SD)	t^a values
Particles					
ne	7.75	(6.69)	9.90	(6.46)	1.03
yo	0.10	(0.31)	2.90	(2.85)	4.38[***]
tte	0.85	(1.35)	8.00	(5.34)	5.81[***]
Connectives					
dakara	0.00	(0.00)	1.45	(1.73)	3.75[**]
Adverb					
yappari	0.00	(0.00)	1.35	(2.01)	3.01[*]
Verbs					
des(u)/mas(u)	0.00	(0.00)	13.50	(8.24)	7.33[***]
da	0.10	(0.45)	3.00	(2.29)	5.55[***]

[a]Degrees of freedom = 38
*$p < 0.01$
**$p < 0.001$
***$p < 0.0001$

Table 13-2
Children's Uses of Linguistic Items: Differences Between Monologic and
Dialogic Narratives

| | Monologic | | | | Dialogic | | | | F^a values for main effect of CONTEXT |
| | Male | | Female | | Male | | Female | | |
	Mean	(SD)	Mean	(SD)	Mean	(SD)	Mean	(SD)	
Particles									
ne	8.10	(5.71)	7.40	(7.85)	15.90	(21.76)	25.30	(20.55)	6.67*
yo	0.10	(0.32)	0.10	(0.32)	2.10	(3.04)	2.10	(2.47)	10.32**
tte	0.90	(1.45)	0.80	(1.32)	5.10	(5.17)	7.30	(7.54)	13.09***
Connectives									
dakara	0.00	(0.00)	0.00	(0.00)	0.20	(0.63)	1.00	(2.49)	2.17*
datte	0.10	(0.32)	0.00	(0.00)	0.50	(0.71)	0.80	(0.92)	9.97**
Verbs									
des(u)/mas(u)	0.00	(0.00)	0.00	(0.00)	0.20	(0.42)	0.30	(0.48)	6.08
da	0.20	(0.63)	0.00	(0.00)	1.80	(3.05)	2.30	(3.62)	6.67*

a Degrees of freedom = 1, 36
*$p < 0.02$
**$p < 0.01$
***$p < 0.001$

1. Interactional/rapport particle *ne* (you know)

2. Assertive and/or emphatic particle *yo* (I tell you)

3. Quotation-final particle *tte*

4. Connective *dakara* (that's why)

5. Connective *datte* (but, because)

6. Formal *des(u)/mas(u)* verb-ending forms

7. Copula *da*[8]

Interestingly, in spite of the fact that Japanese is often cited as a language that is particularly rich in words, phrases, and formulations of politeness that only women use (e.g., Shibatani, 1990), there were no significant main effects or interactions associated with children's gender. Instead, ANOVAs revealed significant effects involving the type of narrative context (monologic or dialogic), in almost all of the linguistic items examined (see Table 13-2).

DISCUSSION

Language can be thought of as a manifestation of culture, and verbal communication is an important tool in our lives, for instance, for the development, maintenance, and transmission of culture from one generation to the next. Emotions, which are one of the most important aspects when conducting verbal communication, give meaning to events. The goal of the present study has been to demonstrate that how we package emotion is culturally dependent. That is, personal narratives enable people to make sense of their experiences in a culturally satisfying manner. With an aim of exploring transitions from child speaker to native speaker, this study has specifically examined how Japanese children learn linguistic devices and strategies to express Japanese consciousness through conversational interactions with their mothers. In the process of development, all of us are expected to learn how to operate as individual agents of culture in a variety of interactions (Matsumoto, 1996). Narrative discourse is one such interaction. The linguistic items and devices examined in this chapter are also considered necessary for Japanese to acquire for the coherency of narrative discourse. And in this study we have identified that, while they might have sufficient command to produce grammatically correct sentences, as they grow, preschool children need to continue to improve narrative discourse coherency in order to become capable of encoding emotion in a sophisticated manner.

There are certain exceptions, however. As seen in the uses of the linguistic items in monologic narratives, Japanese narrators, regardless of their age, try to communicate by frequently using the interactional/rapport particle *ne* (you know), which, I believe, is an emergent manifestation of Japanese consciousness. This particle probably emerges in early stages of language development and, moreover, comes to be used in the narrative context because of the mother's strong emphasis on a culturally preferred interactional style. That is, Japanese culture is characterized by interdependence, as seen in the reciprocal nature of *amae* (dependence) and *omoiyari* (which means "empathy," following Clancy [1985], and "consideration for others," according to Donahue [1998]). Because people tend to attach a significant meaning to rapport and empathy/consideration for others in Japanese society, and because children learn *amae*-related feelings and behaviors through mother–child interactions (Doi, 1973; Lebra, 1976), it is understandable that young children use the interactional/rapport particle in their early narrative production. To summarize, the interactional/rapport particle *ne* is an effective device to facilitate coconstruction of narrative discourse, particularly in a society in which social relativism (Holloway & Minami, 1996) is emphasized.

The study of preschool children's monologic narrative production, however, has revealed that except for *ne*, they have not yet learned to deploy certain grammatical terms (e.g., *dakara*, which means "so, therefore, that's why" and *yappari*, which means "after all") that encode background information, evaluation in particular (see Table 13-1). The differences between adults and preschool children represent, as Berman and Slobin (1994) put it, how "experiences are filtered—(a) through choice of perspective, and (b) through the set of options provided by the particular language—into verbalized events" (p. 611). Thus, although preschool children seem to be developing a sense of their voice and learning how to take audience into account while narrating, they do not seem to have mastered how to manipulate linguistic devices for the best effect to convey Japanese consciousness; or they simply have not yet acquired Japanese consciousness in some respects.

The linguistic items used by the preschoolers in mother–child interactions exhibit both similarities to and differences from those they used in telling their personal experience on their own. But, in many cases, differences in situation seem to let the same narrator employ different narrative devices. The children frequently used *ne* in both contexts, but more frequently in mother–child interactions. Likewise, the distributions of other linguistic items in the dialogic narrative context are strikingly different from those in the monologic narrative context. To understand these differences, we must consider how the contexts of narrative-telling activities affect the narrator's language use. Developmentally, talking about topics related to the past should be within the preschool children's cognitive and linguistic capabilities. Yet the children's more effective deployment of a variety of lexical items in dialogic narrative situations than in monologic narrative situations seem to suggest that telling personal narratives alone (i.e., monologic narratives) is much more difficult than coconstructing narratives (i.e., dialogic narratives), in terms of encoding emotion. This is probably because, in telling monologic narratives without any help, young children tend to be preoccupied with sequential recapitulation. In mother–child interactions, in contrast, children collaborate with their mothers in the creation of shared meaning; that is, mothers and children focus jointly on a past event so that mothers can help children include evaluative comments in their narratives, in addition to sequential information. More generally, following Vygotsky's (1978) social interaction approach, when their abilities are low or primitive, the adult's support is helpful, or even necessary, for them to reach the full potential of their narrative/storytelling. As children grow, however, they need decreasing support from the environment around them. In this way, mothers help children to provide enough background information and evaluate the events they are narrating. The results thus seem to indicate the importance of parents' sensitivity to children's competence, in this case, in order to raise Japanese consciousness effectively in narrative discourse.

In the past, Bruner (1990) hypothesized that: (1) at an early stage of development the child, interacting with the caregiver, enters into the world of meaning construction; and (2) the meaning-creation process is closely related to specific forms of cultural representation. Mother–child conversations thus seem to form the beginning of children's developing culture-specific meaning-making, which will eventually lead to the development of Japanese consciousness. These interactional practices illustrate what Bruner (1977) termed "scaffolding"—the temporary help that parents give children to perform a task, and, more specifically, the verbal means, either explicit or implicit, by which parents give this help. Claiming that "by using language first for limited ends the child comes finally to recognize its more powerful, productive uses" (p. 7), Bruner (1983) emphasized that, in the process of interacting with others, individuals construct their own logic so that they can successfully communicate their intended meanings to others.

Obviously, the differences in monologic and dialogic narrative contexts seem to highlight the fact that preschoolers, to some extent, perceive the difference between "inside" and "outside." In order to use formal styles effectively in narrative, children may need to get more accustomed to the transition from home to school, a move from the *amae*-based inside world to some kind of outside world, where social relativism—the meaning of life in a group and a social hierarchy— are emphasized (Lewis, 1995). Linguistically, moreover, when children need to produce connected discourse autonomously in school settings—telling stories and reading stories in a textbook on their own—their skills in expressing their own state of mind as well as assessing others' states of mind become increasingly important. Telling stories through interactions (with mothers or other sensitive adults who know something about the narrated event) is no longer enough in school settings.

Cognitively, the question still remains. Is it that "Due to the development of linguistic devices children come to talk about emotion in socioculturally appropriate manners" or that "Because of the need to talk about emotion in socioculturally appropriate manners, certain linguistic devices develop"? This might be one of those timeless questions, like the one about the chicken or the egg. Who can say which is the cause of which? One thing seems clear, however. Cognitive, linguistic, conversational, and social-interactional dimensions are not necessarily separable, but rather they are related to each other; social development affects cognitive and linguistic development and vice versa. These factors interact in a complex fashion in narrative development. At the risk of sounding somewhat contradictory, however, they take different courses in the process of language acquisition, as we have observed in this study. In telling personal narratives—monologic narratives in particular—preschoolers have not yet mastered certain linguistic devices and manipulative strategies that encode the narrator's perspective as well as emotion, which are both manifestations of Japanese consciousness.

Overall, unlike talking about the here-and-now, preschoolers have a long way to go in the development of narrative skills. Narrative-telling activities are places that provide children with opportunities to develop interactionally, socioculturally, and cognitively in increasingly sophisticated ways. But it is much later in the course of development that they can become fully adept at expressing their communicative intents, emotion in particular. As Reilly (1992) suggests, we might, in fact, need to wait for children to become 10 or 11 years old in order for them to be able to integrate emotion in their narratives in an effectively interesting and engaging way. As we observed in this study on cultural consciousness, preschool children's narrative skills are rudimentary and inefficient in terms of encoding emotion; they have not yet mastered the full array of means for expressing their emotions with optimal effectiveness in their narratives in socioculturally appropriate ways. Their narrative skills need to undergo considerable expansion and refinement to reach the level of proficiency exhibited by adults, who can convey their intentions to others with culture-specific consciousness (which are possibly subtle but which cultural insiders explicitly understand). It thus seems that children gradually become capable of using narrative devices that have a full array of means for expressing emotion. Telling a narrative on their own does not seem to be an easy task for young children; a considerable time span is needed to reach the adult level of proficiency, particularly in terms of expressing emotion effectively in culturally appropriate ways.

NOTES

1. The distinction between foreground information and background information was originally suggested by Hopper (1979). Foreground information refers to the parts of the narrative that relate a sequence of events with respect to a timeline. In other words, foreground information consists of plot-advancing events/main line event clauses. In contrast, background information includes plot-motivating comments and contextualizing clauses. Background information thus refers to supportive narrative (e.g., orientation, which presents static descriptions of the scene, and evaluation, which describes the agent's motives) that does not itself narrate the main events.

2. Although differences between the children in the 4-year-old classrooms and the children in the 5-year-old classrooms were initially examined, no age differences were identified. In this chapter, therefore, age differences in the preschoolers are not discussed.

3. Note that scaffolding, which is discussed more extensively later in the discussion section, means the temporary help that adults give children to perform a task (Bruner, 1977).

4. As previously stated, for the writing of this chapter I was greatly inspired by Maynard's (1993) study on emotion. I would like to note, however, that I chose certain linguistic devices and strategies because of my intuitive notion of their importance in narrative and/or because of their prominence in the literature.

5. This is psycholinguistic notation meaning "3 years, 8 months."

6. Following leading Japanese psychiatrist Takeo Doi (1973), there is a reciprocal relationship between *amae* and *omoiyari*; *amae* means the state of dependency on the indulgence or benevolence of another person, whereas *omoiyari* is an aspect describing consideration for others.

7. Note that the connective *datte* (because) is not included for this analysis because it is primarily used when interacting with family members.

8. Since children used *yappari* in neither context—monologic or dialogic—the adverb was not included for the analyses.

REFERENCES

Azuma, H. (1986). Why study child development in Japan? In H. Stevenson, H. Azuma, & K. Hakuta (Eds.), *Child development and education in Japan* (pp. 3–12). New York: Freeman.

Bamberg, M. G. W. (1997a). Positioning between structure and performance. *Journal of Narrative and Life History, 7,* 335–342.

Bamberg, M. (1997b). Language, concepts and emotions: The role of language in the construction of emotions. *Language Sciences, 19,* 309–340.

Berman, R. A., & Slobin, D. I. (1994). *Relating events in narrative: A crosslinguistic developmental study.* Hillsdale, NJ: Lawrence Erlbaum.

Brown, P., & Levinson, S. C. (1987). *Politeness: Some universals in language usage.* Cambridge, UK: Cambridge University Press.

Bruner, J. (1977). Early social interaction and language development. In H. R. Schaffer (Ed.), *Studies in mother–child interaction* (pp. 271–289). London: Academic Press.

Bruner, J. (1983). *Child's talk: Learning to use language.* New York: Norton.

Bruner, J. (1986). *Actual minds, possible worlds.* Cambridge: Harvard University Press.

Bruner, J. (1990). *Acts of meaning.* Cambridge: Harvard University Press.

Clancy, P. M. (1985). The acquisition of Japanese. In D. I. Slobin (Ed.), *The crosslinguistic study of language acquisition, Volume 1: The data* (pp. 373–524). Hillsdale, NJ: Lawrence Erlbaum.

Cook, H. M. (1997). The role of Japanese *masu* form in caregiver–child conversation. *Journal of Pragmatics, 28,* 695–718.

Doi, T. (1973). *The anatomy of dependence* (J. Bester, Trans). Tokyo: Kodansha International. (Original work published 1971)

Donahue, R. T. (1998). *Japanese culture and communication: Critical cultural analysis.* Lanham, MD: University Press of America.

Feldman, C. F., Bruner, J., Renderer, B., & Spitzer, S. (1990). Narrative comprehension. In B. K. Britton & A. D. Pellegrini (Eds.), *Narrative thought and narrative language* (pp. 1–78). Hillsdale, NJ: Lawrence Erlbaum.

Hall, E. T. (1989). Unstated features of the cultural context of learning. *The Educational Forum, 54,* 21–34.

Holloway, S. D., & Minami, M. (1996). Japanese childrearing: Two generations of scholarship. In D. Shwalb & B. Shwalb (Eds.), *Japanese child development: Classics studies, responses, and prospects* (pp. 164–176). New York: Guilford Press.

Hopper, P. (1979). Some observations on the typology of focus and aspect in narrative language. *Studies in Language, 3,* 37–64.

Kuno, S. (1987). *Functional syntax: Anaphora, discourse and empathy.* Chicago: University of Chicago Press.

Labov, W. (1972). *Language in the inner city.* Philadelphia: University of Pennsylvania Press.

Lebra, T. S. (1976). *Japanese patterns of behavior.* Honolulu: University of Hawaii Press.

Lewis, C. (1995). *Educating hearts and minds: Reflections on Japanese preschool and elementary education.* New York: Cambridge University Press.

LoCastro, V. (1987). *Aizuchi*: A Japanese conversational routine. In L. E. Smith (Ed.), *Discourse across cultures* (pp. 101–113). New York: Prentice Hall.

MacWhinney, B., & Snow, C. E. (1985). The Child Language Data Exchange System. *Child Language, 12,* 271–296.

MacWhinney, B., & Snow, C. E. (1990). The Child Language Data Exchange System: An update. *Child Language, 17,* 457–472.

Mandell, C., & McCabe, A. (Eds.). (1997). *The problem of meaning: Cognitive and behavioral approaches.* Amsterdam: North-Holland.

Matsumoto, D. (1996). *Culture and psychology.* Pacific Grove, CA: Brooks/Cole.

Matsumoto, Y. (1993). Linguistic politeness and cultural style: Observations from Japanese. In P. M. Clancy (Ed.), *Japanese/Korean linguistics: Volume 2* (pp.

55–67). Stanford, CA: Stanford University.

Maynard, S. K. (1989). *Japanese conversation: Self-contextualization through structure and interactional management*. Norwood, NJ: Ablex.

Maynard, S. K. (1993). *Discourse modality: Subjectivity, emotion and voice in the Japanese language*. Amsterdam, The Netherlands: John Benjamins.

McCabe, A., & Peterson, C. (1991). Getting the story: Parental styles of narrative elicitation and developing narrative skills. In A. McCabe & C. Peterson (Eds.), *Developing narrative structure* (pp. 217–253). Hillsdale, NJ: Lawrence Erlbaum.

Minami, M. (1990). Children's narrative structure: How do Japanese children talk about their own stories. Unpublished paper, Harvard Graduate School of Education, Cambridge, MA.

Minami, M. (1996). Japanese children's personal narratives. *First Language, 16*, 339–363.

Minami, M. (1997). Cultural constructions of meaning: Cross-cultural comparisons of mother–child conversations about the past. In C. Mandell & A. McCabe (Eds.), *The problem of meaning: Cognitive and behavioral approaches* (pp. 297–345). Amsterdam: North-Holland.

Minami, M. (1998). Politeness markers and psychological complements: Wrapping-up devices in Japanese oral personal narratives. *Narrative Inquiry, 8*(2), 351–371.

Minami, M., & McCabe, A. (1991). Haiku as a discourse regulation device: Stanza analysis of Japanese children's personal narratives. *Language in Society, 20*, 577–599.

Minami, M., & McCabe, A. (1996). Compressed collections of experiences. In A. McCabe (Ed.), *Chameleon readers: Some problems cultural differences in narrative structure pose for multicultural literacy programs* (pp. 72–97). New York: McGraw-Hill.

Ninio, A., & Snow, C. E. (1996). *Pragmatic development*. Boulder, CO: Westview Press.

Peterson, C., & McCabe, A. (1983). *Developmental psycholinguistics: Three ways of looking at a child's narrative*. New York: Plenum.

Piaget, J. (1959). *The language and thought of the child*. London: Routledge & Kegan Paul.

Reilly, J. S. (1992). How to tell a good story: The intersection of language and affect in children's narratives. *Journal of Narrative and Life History, 2*, 355–377.

Sachs, J. (1979). Topic selection in parent–child discourse. *Discourse Processes, 2*, 145–153.

Shibatani, M. (1990). *The languages of Japan*. New York: Cambridge University Press.

Toolan, M. J. (1988). *Narrative: A critical linguistic introduction*. London: Routledge.

Vygotsky, L. S. (1978). *Mind in society: The development of higher psychological processes*. Cambridge: Harvard University Press.

White, S. (1989). Back-channels across cultures: A study of Americans and Japanese. *Language in Society, 18*, 59–76.

Yamada, H. (1992). *American and Japanese business discourse: A comparison of interactional styles*. Norwood, NJ: Ablex.

Young, J., & Nakajima-Okano, K. (1984). *Learn Japanese: New College Text, Vol. 1*. Honolulu: University of Hawaii Press.

Chapter 14

The Impact of English on the Japanese Language

Bates L. Hoffer

The Japanese language is often cited as an example of Japan's cultural unique-ness. The claim is an interesting one in light of the massive borrowing of Chinese language items early in Japanese history and the recent borrowing of tens of thousands of words from American English. As these recent borrowings have increased, some Japanese scholars have been worried about the potential loss of the Japanese language. An analysis of the patterns of uses of the borrowings sug-gests that any anxiety is unwarranted. The basic features of the English borrow-ings are indeed similar to language borrowing in other languages. Yet some grammatical features and some of the functional uses of the borrowings are particular to Japanese. In other words, the English borrowings are being Nipponicized into the Japanese language. The language is thus being enriched with a larger vocabulary, yet is still unique among the world's languages.

In *The Japanese Mind,* Christopher (1983) discusses what he terms the cher-ished Japanese sense of belonging to a unique and impenetrable culture. The Japanese language in particular has been cited as an example of Japan's cultural uniqueness. The claim is an interesting one in light of the massive borrowing of Chinese language items early in Japanese history and in light of the last 50 years of borrowing of tens of thousands of words from American English. While lan-guages such as Spanish and English have absorbed vocabulary from many lan-guages over the centuries, Japanese primarily has absorbed loanwords from China and much more recently from English (Hoffer, 1990, 1996, 1997; Loveday, 1996; Miller, 1967). In the case of Chinese, by the beginning of the 8th century,

Chinese loans had been so completely absorbed into Japanese that to most Japanese they were no different from any other Japanese vocabulary (Miller, 1967). In the case of English, over the past five decades, the number of English loans has grown geometrically from near zero to some 40,000 and counting. Most of the English loans are still written either in *katakana* (the syllabary used primarily for new nonnative words) or in the alphabet. Thus, they are marked and visible as loanwords. English has diffused into almost all aspects of the society, from ordinary conversation to government documents. In neither the Chinese nor the English borrowing situation was there any strong or prolonged intimate contact between the two cultures. Perhaps the voluntary nature of the absorption has muted, to at least some degree, the predictable, if limited, reactions against the pervasive presence of English in the school system and the presence of borrowed words in almost all areas of Japanese life.

The historical Chinese influence and the more recent Western/American influence on Japanese culture and language have some similarities and some even more interesting differences. Those topics are treated below, followed by a discussion of the reactions to the 20th-century influences of American culture and language on Japanese.

CHINESE IN THE JAPANESE LANGUAGE

A millennium and a half ago, Japan encountered China at arm's length, so to speak (Hoffer, 1997). Almost no direct contact was made between Chinese and Japanese in the early centuries of contact. Chinese culture was transmitted into early Japan primarily through the Japanese and Korean scholars of China's heritage. The rather indirect contact of Japan with an advanced world culture led Japan to absorb much of Chinese culture, adapt it over the centuries, and make parts of it components of their own culture. Religions, architecture, science, and so on were studied and the Chinese language was adopted by the court of Japan. The Chinese writing system became the basis for the Japanese writing system, which now uses a subset of Chinese written characters and two syllabaries that were derived from those characters over the centuries. More recently, of course, alphabetic symbols were absorbed into the writing system as well.

Along with the Chinese writing system, the Japanese who were educated in Chinese learned the tens of thousands of vocabulary items. Many of these vocabulary items entered the Japanese lexicon, were absorbed into the native system, and are still in use. Dictionaries of Japanese that are based on the Chinese written symbols are many hundreds of pages long and contain a quite large number of words from Chinese.

Chinese became the language of officialdom when it first arrived. The court and officials were well trained in Chinese, and in fact, the ability to handle Chinese was the mark of an educated, literary person into the beginning of this century. The great Japanese novelist Natsume Soseki of the Meiji period (1868–1912) was perhaps the last great literary figure who wrote Chinese verse as an avocation.

ENGLISH IN JAPANESE EDUCATION

A major development in Japan's knowledge of the world took place during the Meiji period, when Japan reopened to the West after two and a half centuries of no contact between the two. Japanese sent young scholars to Europe to study and bring back the knowledge of the West. For example, Soseki studied in England, returned, and for a time taught English at the Imperial University. Western languages for the first half of the 20th century remained to some extent "scholastic" languages. English vocabulary was used to a small extent in the early decades of the Meiji period. For example, Soseki used several English words in his many famous novels, which were read by people across Japan. However, in the second half of the 20th century, the major influx of English and its use across the social spectrum began.

The rapid growth of the borrowing of English vocabulary began in 1947 when the program of teaching English as an international language in Japan started in junior high schools. Learning English was considered then a necessity for new Japan's young generation if they were to obtain a clear picture of the world and to make Japan a great trading country, which requires international knowledge and communication. The time spent learning English was eventually extended from three to six years, as more and more students chose to go to senior high school. In 1991, over 94% of the nation's 15-year-olds went to senior high school. There is now in Japan a strong majority of people who have had six years of English at school by the time they complete their schooling. Competence in at least written English soon became a critical factor at the entrance examinations for higher education after the universities added an entrance requirement in written English. More recently some have been adding an oral component as well. Dozens of magazines and journals are devoted to the study of English and the related Western culture. To a high degree, these publications are studied as part of the goal of learning English.

With a high test mark as almost exclusively the only purpose, Japanese students spend an astonishing amount of time and energy in the study of English. The critical importance of a college education in Japan spawned the development of a variety of lucrative testing industries including cram schools and proficiency certification organizations that deal with the English language.

For one example, during the period 1979–1994, more than 600,000 persons have taken TOEIC (Test of English for International Communication) tests. TOEIC is administered by a corporation endorsed by the Ministry of International Trade and Industry. The STEP (Standard Test of English

Proficiency), which is supported by the Ministry of Education, is even more popular, attracting more than 1,310,000 examinees in the first of a twice-a-year series of tests in 1994 (Honna, 1995).

This commitment to an educated public, which is able to handle the world's major international language, has had a predictable impact on Japanese over these decades. Loanwords from English have become more and more frequent as the English requirement gave more and more Japanese a level of facility in the language. The current estimate of English loans in the total vocabulary of Japanese is high. As many as 11% of the words spoken in daily conversation in Japan are from English (Honna, 1995). In fact, 60–70% of new words in the annually revised dictionaries of neologisms are from English. Several loanword dictionaries have documented the influx of English into Japanese language use (Gaikoku Kara Kita Shingo Jiten Henshūbu, 1965; Sanseido Henshūbu, 1987).

With this influx of English words and the centuries of use of Chinese loanwords, the Japanese dictionary has a high percentage of borrowed vocabulary. Yet each edition of the major dictionaries moves more words that were originally English into the regular (non-loanword) dictionaries. Japanese scholars long ago suggested that this "Nipponicization" of English loans and other cultural elements would follow the pattern of the Chinese loans. Hasegawa (1938/1983) noted that Japan since the Meiji Restoration (1867–1868) has had the problem of absorption of cultural elements including language from abroad. He noted that, once again, the real question is not whether the new elements would change Japanese culture, but rather the real question is how Western civilization would be Nipponicized. One thing that seems certain is that Japan will never stop at out-and-out imitation of the West.

ENGLISH IN JAPAN

The use of Chinese did not extend beyond the elite classes to ordinary farmers and others of the general population. In this area of language use, the comparison between the absorption of Chinese and the absorption of English is no longer parallel. The use of Latin as a language of education after Latin had been transformed into the Romance languages would be a better parallel between Chinese and Japanese, although that parallel is limited as well. Chinese was used at court, in the government, in certain Buddhist activities, and in the education of persons involved in those and related activities. In contrast, at least some level of proficiency in English has spread through all segments of Japanese society, from ordinary citizens' daily conversations to the official bureaucratic vocabulary of governmental documents.

Over the past few decades, the high percentage of Japanese who have studied at least a few years of English has facilitated the absorption process. The use of English language texts in colleges, the international travel and study that was made possible by Japan's growing economy, and the contact through the international media all have contributed to the easy use of new words from abroad. In the technical fields such as computers, the terms are less English per se than they are international terms. English is the native language of hundreds of millions of people, and English is also the second or third language of an even greater number of people. As an international language, English is the language of much modern technology, such as computers. Thus, the advanced state of Japan's technology has also added to the number of new words. Just three decades ago, many of the new words, even in technology, were being written in Chinese characters. For example, *kikai honyaku* was based on the older Chinese loans, although the English phrase "machine translation" soon became the preferred term.

To some extent, then, the status of English as one of the world's international languages must be kept in mind when evaluating the impact of the use of the English language and of the borrowing in English vocabulary. Japan's commitment to the international marketplace requires high levels of ability in the primary international language of business, English. In the next few sections, some examples are given of borrowed terms and of some interesting adaptations of those terms.

ENGLISH ABSORBED INTO JAPANESE

The English vocabulary items that are used in Japanese are often used as substitutes for the Japanese word. However, the more interesting examples are those that are adapted in various ways. Some of the ways that are discussed are shortening, compounds of shortenings, compounds using both languages, and English roots with Japanese grammatical endings; other types of uses are covered elsewhere (Hoffer, 1990; Hoffer & Honna, 1988).

English speakers shorten all sorts of words in English, as in the use of acronyms such as "scuba" for "self-contained underwater breathing apparatus" and first syllables such as "ad" for "advertisement." The Japanese use both these processes (Miura, 1979) with English words. An example of an English-only acronym, which is pronounced as a word is *mipuro*, which is the Japanese pronunciation of MIPRO. The acronym stands for Manufactured Imports Promotion Organization. An example of an acronym that includes words from both languages is NEC for Nippon Electric Company. A relatively recent loanword dictionary from Sanseido Publishing Company (Sanseido Henshubu, 1987) has about 200 pages of alphabetic acronyms which the daily reader encounters in reading the Japanese newspapers.

Japanese also shortens many English words that are not usually shortened in English. Some examples are:

apāto	apart(ment)
depāto	depart(ment)
famikon	fami(ly) com(puter)

Compounds made of shortened English words are especially difficult for native English or non-Japanese English speakers to interpret. Japanese who are speaking English to native English speakers may expect the listener to understand such compounds, but the compounds are often opaque to the listener because they are not used by native speakers. Two examples are:

puroresu	pro(fessional) wres(tling)
wāpuro	wo(rd) pro(cessor)

Thousands of these shortened compounds are found in Japanese usage.

An example of a shortened mixed language compound is from International Christian University in Tokyo, where a *honjapa* is the term for a native Japanese and a *hanjapa* has one non-Japanese parent. Depending on the writer, these compounds can be written with various combinations of written symbols.

honjapa	*hon* ("true, real")	japa(nese)
hanjapa	*han* ("half")	japa(nese)

Some English items have been in use long enough to have entered the Japanese dictionary decades ago. The more recent ones appear in special loanword dictionaries before—in many but not all cases—achieving the status of a regular Japanese vocabulary item. Such items may be used with the Japanese inflectional endings. An earlier example is:

daburu	from "double" (increase) plus the verbal ending "u"

The present progressive form of this word occurs in print as *dabutte iru* (is increasing). A somewhat more recent example of an English root with Japanese inflection is the adjective "now" as in "the Now generation":

naui	"now" plus "i," the present tense adjectival ending
naukatta	"now" plus "katta," the past tense adjectival ending

The examples of this kind are especially interesting because English adjectives cannot be inflected for past tense as can the Japanese ones.

Another type of double-language example shows how ordinary citizens know English so well that they often have little difficulty in understanding puns, humorous misusage, and various types of word play. One well-cited example is *an-shinji-raburu*, which consists of the Japanese word for "believe" (*shinji*) and the English prefix "un-" and suffix "-able" and the result is a dual-language "unbelievable."

What is conspicuous in these borrowing patterns (Hoffer, 1997), as well as the other patterns not treated here, is the drive for Nipponicization, or Japanization. Although foreign loans are almost always visually recognizable in reading because of their representation in the special *katakana* syllabary, they are structurally and semantically treated as Japanese words. They have been and are being incorporated into the grammatical structure of the Japanese language. They have become an integral part of the Japanese lexicon and grammar and are frequently used in diverse ways and called on to play an important set of roles in contemporary Japanese society.

These examples also serve, among other things, to demonstrate that English is a living language in Japan. While the ability to handle English as an independent language varies with the individual and with the amount of time spent in study, the ability to use English loanwords in new and creative ways is pervasive in Japan.

ENGLISH ACROSS SOCIETY

In addition to encountering the English loans usually written in the *katakana* syllabary in the newspapers, Japanese encounter English in all types of advertisements, as the titles of many dozens of Japanese magazines, as slogans from travel agencies and other businesses, and on countless T-shirts worn by the younger generation. Those non-Japanese who have traveled around Tokyo may have seen those areas where signs in English seem to outnumber those in Japanese. Clearly the businesses would not be using English loans if they thought that use would hurt business. While English is not a prestige language in Japan in the sense of prestige as "reverence," English may be used as a prestige language to sell certain types of items in the same way that French is used in English to sell perfume, fashions, and other merchandise.

Business and commerce in general seem to hold this view. For example, ad campaigns by major travel agencies for travel within Japan may use English-only slogans, such as "Discover Japan." In the many international companies, an ability in English is essentially a requirement. While it is not unusual for an American stationed at a branch in Japan to know no Japanese at all, it is unthinkable that a Japanese in a similar position in America would not know English reasonably well.

The degree of diffusion of English terms can be seen clearly in the growing acceptance of officially approved loans in the government documents. One early example is the approved official use in architecture of an acronym DK based on the English compound "dining/kitchen." The term is used in Western-style houses, where the cooking and eating areas are arranged differently from traditional Japanese ones which retain the original *daidokoro*.

In short, for generations the Japanese have studied Japanese in school and have encountered English or at least English loans in the papers, in magazines, on television shows, in ads, on businesses, in official documents, and on and on. The process of adoption and adaptation of English has advanced to an astonishing degree in only five decades. One of the few areas where English has not made an impact is in religious ceremonies where the sacred languages are preserved.

English has impacted most areas of language usage in Japan and it fills several functions or roles in that usage.

THE FUNCTIONS OF ENGLISH LOANS IN JAPANESE

A few of the functions of borrowed terms are simple to state. One of the most frequently encountered English loans is simple code-switching, a process that may occur in any situation in which speakers and listeners know two languages or "codes." Words or phrases from the second language are substituted for a variety of reasons and rhetorical effects that are outside the scope of this treatment.

The new borrowings are often the terms for new items and concepts, as is usual in borrowing situations. A subset of those terms includes the terms used in internationalized fields, such as computers and math. A country that decided to use native terms within its own scholarship would have to translate them into the international terms for use abroad. This internationalization of terminology helps scholarship in general, as well as science and business.

Historically borrowed words can also be used for prestige terms, in the loose sense described previously. For example, a *meido* ("maid," as in household servant) carries more prestige than a *jochū,* which is the traditional word for the occupation.

In Japanese, English also functions at times for euphemism. In English, a "garbage collector" may become a "sanitation engineer," which sounds much better. Japanese can use its own vocabulary for such euphemisms, but English is employed as well. For one example, the trains have seats designated as "silver seat" (English words written in syllabary), which are for senior citizens and others who may require a seat. An intriguing example at the highest level of government occurs in the Ministry of Construction. The ministry sponsors a council whose task it is to map out what is intradepartmentally referred to as the "charming construction identity" (CCI). It has presided over a change in the terminology of construction work from traditional Japanese terms to English loans. Thus, *kōjigenba* (construction site) is renamed as "station," *sagyōin* (worker) as "outdoorman," *hanba* (eating place) as "outdoor residence," and *genba kantoku* as "supervisor." Obviously, the purpose is for euphemistic effect, since the work and working conditions are exactly the same as before the change. The names have been "charmingly" rephrased from terms that suggest the dirty, dangerous, and painstaking nature of the work (Honna, 1995).

All of these uses and functions of English in Japan have been directly or indirectly the result of the decision several decades ago to require English in the schools. Another type of result was the reaction to the decision and its results.

REACTIONS TO THE STUDY AND SPREAD OF ENGLISH

In terms of a positive impact on Japanese international business, Japanese scholarship, and international communication, the commitment to an international language has been conclusively proved beneficial to Japan. The Japanese economy has gone from essentially zero five decades ago to the top ranks of world economies. Japanese students, business people, and tourists can handle themselves in any country where English is used as one of the languages. However, there are critics of the English language education policy based on another criterion. The huge commitment of the students to the study of English has not had the effect of producing a commensurably large number of bilinguals. In the views of those critics, the actual results have been inadequate. An insufficient percentage of people have developed proficiency in English as a language for international communication. In fact, these critics point out that the TOEFL (Test of English as a Foreign Language) scores of Japanese students have been too low considering the time, energy, and money spent on the efforts to learn. According to one international comparison, Japan ranked among the very lowest group of seven countries that were in the ranking.

As noted previously, in recent years, some of the top universities in Japan have begun to require an English oral component in their entrance examination. This decision may have the effect of producing a somewhat higher proficiency level, but it is too early to make predictions. Although the original goal was not that of producing a nation of bilinguals, the critics have perhaps a valid point in terms of the current results. However, a fact that cannot be overlooked is that the English education policy has received total support from the general public. In any democracy, such support is crucial. Although criticism of the national commitment to English has existed since the government's decision half a century ago, the criticism of the results of the policy has not reached a level significant enough to cause universal reconsideration. The most recent major change is not one away from English but toward it. Students in Japan will soon begin English in late elementary school.

Another type of criticism that has existed for several decades is that of the "corruption" of the Japanese culture by the intrusion of foreign elements. Many Japanese consider English loanwords in Japanese as the most important, serious, and grave problem that faces the Japanese language today. Simply put, these people believe that the influx of a tremendous amount of foreign words into Japanese is an intrusion and will inevitably lead to the corruption and decay of their national language. As Hiroshi Mizutani, Director of the National Language Research Institute, said of the current influx of foreign words into Japanese, the official opinion is that this trend must be contained or at least rationalized (Honna, 1995). Media commentators at times deride those Japanese who make "inconsiderate" use of foreign words in situations where "beautiful, authentic" Japanese could be used instead. Letters to the editors' pages of major national newspapers at times contain similar comments. Some influential government office holders occasionally rail against the assimilation of English into Japanese.

Yet there is an inherent irony here. The written and oral criticism of English education and of English loanwords in Japan uses borrowed words from

Chinese and from English. A few government office holders rail against English, but their rhetoric is usually filled with English loans. As Miller (1967) pointed out during a similar outcry, the articles by Japanese scholars a half century ago protesting the "invasion" of foreign words contained this same linguistic irony. The articles were written in Japanese that consisted primarily of written characters borrowed from China in the middle of the first millennium. By the time of their protests, the "Japanization" of the Chinese written system and vocabulary loans had been complete for centuries. It may have appeared that Chinese would replace Japanese during the time of borrowing, yet far from disappearing under the rapid borrowing of Chinese vocabulary, Japanese thrived and made use of the richness of the Chinese language as the overall culture did of various elements from China.

In addition to worrying about the possible "corruption" of the Japanese language, some scholars sounded a warning about the potential loss of the Japanese language. As Christopher (1983) noted, because the Japanese have borrowed so heavily from other cultures, they have, throughout their modern history, lived in fear of losing their own special identity. An analysis of the patterns of uses of the borrowings suggests that the anxiety is misplaced. The basic features of the English borrowings are indeed similar to language borrowing in other languages. Yet the grammatical features and some of the functional uses of the borrowings are particular to Japanese. In other words, just as happened with the Chinese borrowings earlier, the English borrowings are being "Nipponicized" into the Japanese language.

CONCLUSION

The process of learning and adapting English is so advanced that a complete reversal would be reactionary to a high degree and it is, in fact, probably irreversible. Adaptations of the current educational policy may be made in terms of potential university students, yet the tens of millions of Japanese who have had years of English training and who support the policies cannot be ignored. As a side issue, the positive effects of having a population that is competent to at least some degree in an international language are the objects of envy of many countries.

The real issue is not how Japan should relinquish the influx of international vocabulary, but how to accommodate the new words for the enrichment of the Japanese language. The key point in this discussion is that Japan has already absorbed and Nipponicized tens of thousands of English loanwords into the Japanese grammatical system. The result is a Japanese language and culture that is enriched with a large and flexible vocabulary and a Japanese language that has been, is, and will remain unique in the inventory of the world's languages.

REFERENCES

Christopher, R. (1983). *The Japanese mind.* New York: Fawcett Columbine.

Gaikoku Kara Kita Shingo Jiten Henshubu. (1965). *Gaikoku kara kita shingo jiten* [Dictionary of new words from foreign countries]. Tokyo: Shueisha.

Hasegawa, N. (1983). *The Japanese character: A cultural profile.* Tokyo: Kodansha. (Original work published 1938)

Hoffer, B. (1990). English loanwords in Japanese: Some cultural implications. *Language Sciences, 12*(1), 1–22.

Hoffer, B. (1996). Language borrowing. In H. Goebl, P. Nelde, S. Zdenek, & W. Wölck (Eds.), *Contact linguistics: An international handbook of contemporary research.* New York: Walter de Gruyter.

Hoffer, B. L. (1997). Borrowing at arm's length: Japanese borrowing from English. In W. Mäder, W. Wölck, & P. Weber (Eds.), *Current research in contact linguistics.* Brussels: Research Centre on Multilingualism.

Hoffer, B. L., & Honna, N. (1988). The influx of English into the Japanese language. *Southwest Journal of Linguistics, 8*(2), 15–33.

Honna, N. (1995). English in Japanese society: Language within language. In J. Maher & K. Yashiro (Eds.), Multilingual Japan. A special issue of the *Journal of Multilingual and Multicultural Development, 16*(1 & 2), 45–62.

Loveday, L. J. (1996). *Language contact in Japan.* London: Oxford University Press.

Miller, R. A. (1967). *The Japanese language.* Chicago: University of Chicago Press.

Miura, A. (1979). *English loanwords in Japanese.* Rutland, VT: Tuttle.

Sanseido Henshubu. (1987). *Konsaisu gairaigo jiten* [Concise Loanword Dictionary] (3rd ed.). Tokyo: Sanseido.

part VI

Japanese Rhetoric

Chapter 15

Japan's Attempted Enactments of Western Debate Practice in the 16th and the 19th Centuries

Roichi Okabe

This chapter outlines the rise and fall of the formal *practices of argumentation and debate in Japan's pre-Meiji era of the late 16th century as well as the 19th-century Meiji era. Argumentation is defined as the process of advancing, supporting, and criticizing claims; debate as the argumentative and confrontational process in which matched contestants argue in equal and adequate time on a stated proposition to gain an audience decision. First, the chapter traces the European Christian missionaries' efforts to enact the Western practice of disputation (defined as the educational practice in which one student is given a claim on a religious topic and speaks in its defense and oppositions are then voiced against his/her position) on the Japanese rhetorical stage in the late 16th century. It then delineates the Japanese intellectuals' failed endeavors to transplant the Western rhetorical tradition of argumentation and debate practices in the 19th-century Meiji era, and finally explicates why the Japanese rhetorical theorists and practitioners' enactments failed in their attempt to transplant the Western concept of debate on Japanese soil.*

As far as argumentation and debate practices are concerned, Japan represents one of the most paradoxical countries in the world: on one hand Japan has been characterized by Morrison (1972) as a "rhetorical vacuum" (p. 89) with no tradition or role for debate and argumentation (Becker, 1983),[1] while on the other she has gone to great lengths to introduce the theory and practice of Western oratory and debate to her knowledge-hungry people since the mid-19th century (Okabe, 1973, 1990), obviously with little success. In bridging the gap between Western and Eastern rhetorical practices of argumentation and debate, Japan provides a unique case of her attempted, though failed, cultural enactments of Western rhetorical activities, which deserves a closer examination and analysis.

The main purpose of this chapter, therefore, historically and rhetorically outlines the rise and fall of argumentation and debate practices in the pre-Meiji era of the late 16th century and the 19th-century Meiji era of Japan. It first traces the European Christian missionaries' efforts to enact the Western practice of disputation on the Japanese rhetorical stage in the late 16th century. It then delineates the Japanese intellectuals' endeavors to transplant the Western rhetorical tradition of argumentation and debate practices in the 19th-century Meiji era and finally explicates why the Japanese rhetorical theorists and practitioners failed in their attempt to transplant the Western concept of debate on Japanese soil.

THE RHETORICAL SCENES IN LATE
16TH-CENTURY JAPAN

The first encounter of the Japanese people with Western rhetorical theory and practice of public speaking and/or debate can be traced back to the late 16th century, when European Jesuit missionaries introduced the Christian doctrine as well as the humanistic tradition, including the theory and practice of Western rhetoric. Sato (1987), a renowned rhetoric scholar in contemporary Japan, suggested that while the average Japanese after the Meiji Restoration in 1868 were noted for their lack of rhetorical sense, their predecessors in the Edo era (1590–1868) "were living in an extremely rhetorical culture" (p. 44).[2]

The first reference to the term "rhetoric" in Japan was made in the story on Christian saints titled *Santosu no gosagyo* (Santos's divine work) printed in Romanized characters in 1591 at the province of Kazusa, Saga Prefecture, by a Jesuit missionary named Alejandro Valignano. The section on Saint Catherina recorded the following reference:

One senior scholar came forward from among a group of learned men and spoke reverently to His Majesty. As His Majesty most aptly remarked, this woman, though knowledgeable, was after all nothing but a woman and therefore had no command of oratory or *rhetorica*. In arguing and disputing with us scholars, she looked like a lone mantis fighting against a formidable axe. (Anesaki, 1976, p. 614)

Another publication, *The Latin–Portuguese–Japanese Dictionary* (*Ra-Po-Nichi,* 1973), first printed in Nagasaki in 1595, listed as entries with proper Japanese definitions such rhetorical key terms as *rhetorica, rhetor,* eloquence, oratory, orator, argument, logic, *inventio, dispositio, elocutio, memoria, pronun-*

tiatio, Aristotle's *Topica*, and Cicero's *Orator*. It is clear, therefore, that late 16th-century Japan witnessed the introduction, though limited in scope, of Western rhetorical and logical terms into the Jesuit training of Japanese ministers-to-be.

One may wonder, then, what sort of training, both theological and rhetorical, the Jesuit Society offered the Japanese seminarians of the day. As Cieslik (1963), who extensively studied the Christian mission in Japan, stated: "Like their prototype in Europe, the Latin classes and humanities were part of the curriculum" (p. 44). The Jesuit Society clearly modeled the clergy training in Japan after the European tradition. The Educational Course Plan, originally approved and adopted by the society in 1546 and revised and approved in 1586 and 1599 respectively, consisted primarily of grammar, philosophy, and theology, with the first area including humanities and rhetoric.

According to one contemporary Western history scholar, the Jesuit Society established its Christian seminaries and colleges in western Japan after 1580 and taught, among other things, philosophy, humanities, rhetoric, and scholastic disputation (Sawada, 1983, p. 276). Father Valignano, who was among these early Jesuits in Japan, stressed the importance of offering practical training to Japanese missionary trainees. Cieslik (1963) described disputation as a rhetorical training method as follows:

most of the Bishop's candidates for the seminary had already had a year or more of experience in catechizing and preaching. . . . Besides these, the disputations and repetitions usual in the theological schools of the time were conducted, albeit in a curtailed form. (p. 57)

HOW THE WESTERN MISSIONARIES OBSERVED THE JAPANESE WAY OF THINKING AND ARGUING

Despite the efforts of the 16th-century Western Christian missionaries to enact Western rhetoric and disputation practices, they found the Japanese unable to adapt to this mode of argumentation. They discovered, among other things, that the Japanese way of communication and argumentation was entirely different from their own. Alejandro Valignano (1583/1973), who in his day came to Japan as a "special inspector," reported back to the president of the Jesuit Society that the Japanese people regarded it as a virtue not to engage in a direct refutation against another in person. He went on to observe:

It is a common practice among the Japanese people that to avoid becoming too emotional, they should refrain from speaking directly to another on important matters, negotiate all in writing, or do so through the third party. This procedure is followed not only between parents and children and between masters and subordinates, but also between husbands and wives. This is because whenever indignation, refutation, and disagreement may possibly arise, the Japanese people think it more prudent to discuss matters through the third party. Consensus and harmony will thus be preserved among them. (p. 13)

In addition to an indirect way of Japanese communication either in writing or through an intermediary, the Western missionaries noticed some differences in Japanese ways of thinking and arguing. Father Luis Frois, a Jesuit priest, for example, observed in 1575 that the Japanese in general, and the Buddhist monks in particular, practiced a very different mode of arguing:

It would take too long to recount the disputes, arguments and questions of the heathens here. Anybody fond of arguing has plenty of material here, although the form of their arguments and their way of proceeding in them are very different from what we learn in our studies. As many of them, especially the bonzes [Buddhist monks], are most eloquent in their speech, anybody who did not know about the basic principles on which their religions are founded, might often well think that both we and they are preaching the same thing . . . you would think that they are talking about the one, supreme, true God, Saviour of the world. But in their reasoning and conclusions, all this is a delusion. (Cooper, 1965, pp. 373–374). (Cooper's translation)

Valignano also witnessed the Japanese lacking in logical and enthymemic thinking, in generalizing fundamental principles out of particular phenomena, and in reasoning logically about the unknown from the known. Father Frois supported the validity of Valignano's observation with an episode of his debating with one Buddhist priest named Nichijo concerning the mortality or immortality of the soul after death:

As regards the immortality of the soul and its continuing to exist after the death of the body, I said that he [Nichijo] could understand this by the use of reason, if he so desired. . . .

Now if the soul, being as it were in a prison, still retained all its vigour, it would have even more vigour after being freed from this bondage. And so it was clear the soul continued to exist after death.

At this the bonze [Buddhist priest] rose up gnashing his teeth and the colour of his face changed in his rage and frenzy.

"You say that the soul remains, but you must show it to me now," he shouted. "So I'm going to cut off the head of your disciple (this was Lourenco, who was close by me) so that you can show me the substance that remains."

"I have already said many times that it isn't a thing that can be seen with the eyes of the body," I answered.

At these words he rushed over in an unbelievable rage to one of the king's *naginata* [a long sword], which was lying in the corner of the chamber, and began to unsheathe it. (Cooper, 1965, p. 379). (Cooper's translation)

Frois thus vividly portrayed the impatient rage that a Japanese monk felt because of his inability to engage in abstract thinking unless presented with things concrete.[3]

The Western theory and practice of disputation and argumentation came to Japan with an introduction of Christian culture from Portugal and Spain in the late 16th century, but it met only the limited needs of training the Japanese clergy candidates and failed to produce a substantial influence of Western (in this case European) rhetoric in an alien culture of the East. Japan's Edo rulers took advantage of their natural geographic isolation to fix on the country a firm policy of seclusion from the outside world. For more than two centuries, from 1638 to 1853, the Japanese were almost completely sequestered from foreign contacts and influences. It took another 250 years after this first encounter with Western rhetoric in the late 16th century before the flower of Western (this time British and American) rhetoric actually bloomed in the enlightenment movement of the Meiji era (1868–1912).

THE SECOND ATTEMPTED ENACTMENT OF WESTERN RHETORICAL PRACTICES ON THE JAPANESE STAGE

The main impetus behind the enlightenment movement to modernize a feudalistic Japan in the Meiji period was practicality. Urgent necessity dictated swift enactments of Western techniques and ideas on the part of the Japanese in such a way as to make their country an equal match for the rest (in this case Western) of the nations of the world. Soon after the Meiji Restoration in 1868, a group of scholars began to urge the Japanese people to rethink some of the unquestioned assumptions behind their way of life, their traditional body of knowledge, and their scheme of values.

Doubtless the most popular and comprehensive exponent of the doctrines of the enlightenment and enactment movement in Meiji Japan was Yukichi Fukuzawa (1834–1901), a philosopher, moralist, educator, political scientist, economist, natural scientist, reformer, and rhetorician all rolled into one. Of particular relevance to students of speech communication was his strenuous efforts to enact the practices of Western rhetoric in general and of speech and debate in particular on the rhetorically barren stage of a feudalistic Japan. Because of this pioneering contribution, he is even now called the father of Western speech and debate in Japan.

Japan's second encounter with Western (that is, British and American) theory and practice of rhetoric as spurred by Fukuzawa came to a climax in the latter part of the 19th century with an extensive promulgation of Western rhetorical practices enacted on the Japanese stage by the rhetoric writers and translators. This development constituted part of the modernization and enactment movement for reforming Japanese society—to open it to Western ways of thinking and arguing.

Okabe (1986, 1988) identified a total of 145 Japanese books on rhetorical theory, practice, and criticism published during the Meiji era. Some were originally written in Japanese, while some others were translations primarily from original sources in English. Thirty-eight of these works addressed the theoretical aspects of Western rhetoric. Seven of these 38 dealt with debate either in *toto* or in part. Ten texts out of the total of 145 conformed to the Western tradition of elocution, and 16 were written along the lines of Western *belles lettres*. Okabe also located 60 collections of speeches, including more than 10 that reported the whole or partial transcriptions of debates for young Japanese students of the day to learn from. He likewise tracked down 16 Japanese translations of Western works on rhetorical theory and practice, 2 of which specifically addressed British and American debate respectively, and 5 critical works on oratory, 2 of which analyzed the speeches of orators of classical Greece and Rome and their 18th- and 19th-century British and American descendants. The following section sketches the nature of argumentation and debate instructions provided during the Meiji era in 19th-century Japan by analyzing 13 textbooks (Chuto Kyoiku Gakkai, 1912; Ikushima, 1882; Ito, 1889; Iwai, 1904; Ohata, 1902, 1904a, 1904b; Rinjido-Shujin, 1897; Rowton, 1881; Sugiyama, 1883; Tsuboya, 1897; Ubaoka, 1901; Yamada, 1907) which wholly or partially deal with argumentation and debate.

Why Argumentation and Debate Books Suddenly Proliferated

Several reasons account for this sudden surge of rhetorical enactments taking place after 250 years of total seclusion from Western influence. The writers of debate books in the Meiji era contended, first of all, that debating could function as a means of promulgating the learning and knowledge of the Western world, thus meeting the intellectual needs of the day. Arguing and debating could play an important role in enacting Western learning for the people of the Meiji era. "Speech and debate," Iwai (1904) asserted, "are indispensable for advancing knowledge and learning. Your mastery of the knack of these means will advance you to the status of a Demosthenes or a Pitt" (p. 73). Tsuboya (1897) went a step farther in presenting his view of debate as a means of advancing civilization, when he expounded: "It is needless to say that oratorical speech and debate will contribute greatly to furthering civilization" (pp. 1–2).

Second, the debate textbook writers of the Meiji era argued that the muscle power was to a wild society what the debating power was to an advanced society. Tsuboya (1897) put it this way:

The power of an arm predominates in a barbarian society, while that of oratory dictates in a civilized society. The tendency of the present world is toward speech and debate by which to decide on everything. None disputes the fact that oratory now plays an important part in advancing civilization. (pp. 1–2)

The Meiji writers of rhetoric, therefore, contended that public speaking and debating would meet the social needs of reforming and modernizing the feudalistic country where the freedom of speech and the exchange of ideas were discouraged because of the stern Chinese, or more specifically Confucian, ethics and values. Rinjido-Shujin (1897), for instance, offered the following rationale for promoting debate in a feudalistic society such as Japan:

Confucius tells us that debate is of no necessity because those who have reason always win and those who do not always lose. But in our active society, regardless of whether there is reason or not, success or failure of so much depends on the power of oratory. We should therefore know something about debate. (p. 60)

In this connection, the rhetorical power as represented by debate, the Meiji writers reasoned, could surpass that of a fist or arm. Ohata (1902) sounded pragmatic when he referred to debate as the power of mastery over others:

Any country armed with the power of speech and debate can compete with strong countries, even if its size is small, its army and its arms are fragile, and its food supply is poor. The tongue of eloquence can bring any powerful kingdom under control. (p. 2)

Above all, public debate was widely accepted as a means of training young intellectuals of the day who aspired to go into politics, thus fulfilling the pragmatic or political needs of the Meiji era. The first 10 years of the era witnessed the growing agitation of the people's rights movement. It was in 1874 that Fukuzawa translated *Kaigiben* (How to Hold a Meeting) into the vernacular, thus acquainting the Japanese with Western parliamentary procedures. Increasing demands for the people's rights and suffrage and for more representative government eventually saw the Meiji Constitution adopted in 1889 and put into operation the following year. The constitution's most significant accomplishment was the establishment of the national Diet, or parliament, with its popularly elected Lower House of Representatives.

The opening of the national Diet particularly motivated the writers of debate books to edit or compile sample models for young political aspirants of the day. A case in point of this view was Ikushima's (1882) assertion:

Civilization in Japan has advanced so remarkably these days that it now surpasses that of England, America, Germany, and France. With the proclamation of the opening of the national Diet, it has now become the duty of the learned and the intellectuals to be able to discuss political topics of common interest by means of speech and debate so that they can promote Japanese civilization. (p. 1)

Ubaoka (1901) echoed the same sentiment when he referred to a close relationship that existed between the political system and the value of debate: "Under a constitutional government it is both the right and the duty of every citizen to be able to speak and debate on topics of common interest. Every citizen should therefore strive to learn and master proper methods of speaking and debating" (pp. 1–2). This view was also shared by Yamada (1907), another writer of a popular debate book, who expounded:

Whether at a national parliament or at prefectural, municipal, or town meetings, it is incumbent upon every member of the legislative body and every citizen of the nation to cultivate and improve the ability of debating. It is the only means available of advancing civilization. (p. 1)

The political developments such as these in the 1880s thus provided impetus for Japanese enactments of Western debate practice. As Suzuki (1989) aptly summarized,

In order to run this new political system effectively, there was an urgent need to train politicians who would be good at public speaking in Japan . . . Fukuzawa . . . provided the first training program in Japanese-language debate and public speaking based on Western rhetorical principles and rules of parliamentary procedure. (p. 17)

How the Japanese Writers Viewed Western Debate

How did the Japanese writers of the Meiji era under review here conceptualize debate? Devoting one chapter to the theory of debate, Iwai (1904), for instance, defined it as "a mode of communication through which two or more people either defend or refute one proposition from either pro or con perspective" (p. 69). Ito (1889) further delineated the nature of debate from its purpose, which should be "to discuss one topic among several people from different points of view in order to arrive at and further truth of the matter" (p. 93).

Most of the 13 books on debate that Okabe (1986, 1988) examined shared one characteristic in common concerning their form and/or organization: they all contained, within one book, instructions in and models of both speeches and debates. This meant that the writers unanimously noted the similarity of speech and debate. As Iwai (1904) put it, "As far as it is a mode of expressing one's thoughts by means of language, debate is also one kind of speech" (p. 69). He therefore advised his young readers to learn the methods of speechmaking he had outlined in his book as well. Ito (1889) likewise stated: "While speech and debate are different in form and in appearance, they are similar modes of communication in essence" (pp. 94–95). Ubaoka (1901) followed suit in stating that "Debate and speech are similar in organization, logic, pronunciation, speaking manners, and delivery" (p. 157). The only difference, though, that existed between speech and debate, the writers of debate books in the Meiji era pointed out, lay in the number of participants. Some writers such as Ubaoka (1901) and Iwai (1904) specified the number of debate participants thus: "Whereas speech is engaged only by one person, debate is conducted between two or more people" (Ubaoka, 1901, pp. 157–158).

The debate writers and compilers classified debate into two types: *gijitai* (parliamentary debate type) and *benrontai* (oratorical debate type). Iwai (1904) offered the following definitions which were widely shared by other writers as well. He specified the first type:

The parliamentary debate takes place at the national Diet where many members gather together and discuss topics on the agenda. Each speaker asks for the permission to speak from the chairperson. After the debate is concluded, the topic debated will be put to the vote for a majority decision. (p. 37)

Iwai then elaborated on the second type as follows:

The oratorical debate is conducted between two or more people on one topic. One of them takes the affirmative position and the other takes the negative position. The topic to be debated should always be approached from either the affirmative or the negative. . . . At the conclusion of this debate, the chairperson will ask the audience members to decide the winning side, or the judges, if any, to make a final decision with proper comments and critiques. (pp. 72–73)

One typical example of this oratorical debate could be found in courtroom speaking in which the prosecutor and the attorney present their own arguments from their points of view on a matter at issue (Ubaoka, 1901, pp. 158–159).

The specific purpose behind the Japanese writers' enacting the Western debate practice for aspiring Japanese of the Meiji era was to provide young potential debaters with source materials readily available to them. They offered complete or abridged versions of actual or imaginary debate models and transcriptions for the readers to emulate as well as handy topics for debate and discussion practices. Sugiyama (1883), for instance, stated in his preface that although speech and debate were widely practiced, they failed to achieve their fullest potential, because the speakers and debaters lacked source materials. He therefore set out to meet this need by compiling a source book. He listed historical allusions, aphorisms, proverbs, and maxims that were easily available for speakers and debaters (pp. 1–4). Ikushima (1882) likewise arranged possible topics of political interest for debate and outlined the main arguments, pro and con, of the suggested topics so that young intellectuals of the day could learn the essence of debate (p. 3).

A list of sample debate topics suggested by the Meiji writers can give us a glimpse into how they conceived of the nature of debate. They included "comparative" topics of political, social, economic, and academic interest such as: Which is more important / necessary / essential for life / government / nation, learning or oratory, armament or disarmament, money or intellect, commerce or agriculture, writing or speaking, universal or limited suffrage, or voting with or without names? Another typical group of topics for debate concerned the pros and cons, or the advantages and disadvantages, of something such as: equal rights between husband and wife, ban on drinking, early marriage, nationalization of railway, abortion, suffrage of women, and abolition of death penalty.

Debate Tactics the Meiji Writers Recommended

The Japanese debate writers of the Meiji era all followed the identical pattern of organizing their theoretical discussions along the line of the Western rhetorical tradition. They started with the inventional process, then on to the dispositional aspect, to be followed by the stylistic and pronunciational dimensions of rhetoric. Their explanations generally followed the tenet of Western debate theory, but at times their observations sounded uniquely Japanese. A case in point was what Rinjido-Shujin (1897) suggested concerning a method of countering the opponent in debate. He saw a true secret to success in debate lying in the strategy of not revealing everything from the beginning of the debate. As he reasoned, "It would be extremely dangerous in debate to reveal all of your main arguments from the start. It would be more advantageous, therefore, first to present your minor arguments so that you could sound for the feedbacks of your opponent before presenting your main arguments" (p. 60). In a similar vein, Ohata (1904a) offered young debaters the following pieces of advice: "Don't speak before your opponent does. Let your opponent speak more, so that you can spot his[4] contradictions in his argument. Strive to attack your opponent's weak spots and contradictions with a cool mind. Never be hot-tempered. Remain cool in debate" (p. 1).

In countering the opponent's arguments in debate, the Japanese young debaters were advised, in the words of Tsuboya (1897), "to try to find contradictions, attack the argumentative bases on which the opponent has built his case" (p. 30). He reasoned that this would in essence be "like stabbing the opponent in his back with a sword of his own" (p. 30). Ohata (1904a) also listed several ways of countering the opponent's arguments and attacks flexibly. The following includes some pieces of advice:

Use your opponent's arguments as your own and counterattack them. Disregard your weak spots totally, even if they are pointed out by your opponent. Counter his arguments with proper metaphor, humor, wit, ridicule, and sometimes even silence; face his arguments with boldness sometimes, with sincerity and humility at times, with great care at other times, depending on the situation you happen to be in. (pp. 9–10)

All of the debate books cited thus far were written or compiled along the Western rhetorical tradition. One unique publication in the Meiji era was Nishimura's (1881) translation of a British debate book into Japanese. The original was Frederic Rowton's *The Debater* published in London in 1850. Rowton criticized the practice of elocution-based public speaking in vogue at that time and instead recommended systematic instructions in debate. The plan and organization of Rowton's book clearly reflected his concern. He first wrote 10 "Complete Debates" which would hopefully convey general information, provoke thoughts, and establish debate principles.

Next followed another 10 "Outlines of Debates" with ample references to the most accessible sources of information on each topic. Rowton presented some of the chief arguments that might be used by the affirmative and negative sides. In the last section of the book, the original author listed 109 "Questions for Discussion" which the students might profitably select in practicing debate.

Nishimura (1881), however, did not translate all of the original, but only selected pertinent portions—two complete debate transcriptions, two outlines of debate, and 21 topics for discussion. He also appended a translation of Western parliamentary procedures to his book. The reasons for his uneven selection included the limitation of the pages available and the relevance of the content for potential Japanese readers. The criteria by which Nishimura chose the materials from the original for his translation was not clear enough, but a perusal of his actual selections gives us some clues to understanding the translator's value orientation or preference.

The title of one of the two complete debate transcriptions Nishimura translated for his Japanese readers was "Which Does the Most to Make the Orator—Knowledge, Nature, or Art?" (Nishimura, 1881, pp. 5–48; Rowton, 1850, pp. 210–230). The reason for this particular selection might be that this topic would acquaint the Japanese readers both with the theory of oratory in general and with the art of debate in particular. The other complete debate concerned the question: "Does Morality Increase with Civilisation?" (Nishimura, 1881, pp. 48–72; Rowton, 1850, pp. 73–95). Nishimura included this selection presumably because he wanted to remind the young Japanese readers of a close relationship that existed between the development of civilization and that of morality in the Western world.

One of the two outlines of debates translated for the Japanese version addressed the following moral question: "Which Does the Greater Injury to Society, the Miser or the Spendthrift?" (Nishimura, 1881, pp. 72–75; Rowton, 1850, pp. 231–233). The other one concerned a historical topic: "Was the Execution of Charles the First Justifiable?" (Nishimura, 1881, pp. 75–81; Rowton, 1850, pp. 257–260). The reason for these selections should only be conjectured, since Nishimura did not append a preface. I only surmise that they were intended to provide the Japanese debaters with knowledge and information on things, moral or historical, of the Western world such as Britain and the United States.

Some of the representative questions for discussion Nishimura selectively translated for the Japanese version included the following assortment of political, social, historical, and literary topics: Which was the greater man, Oliver Cromwell or Napoleon Bonaparte? Is cooperation more adapted to promote the virtue and happiness of mankind than competition? Should the press be totally free? (Nishimura, 1881, pp. 81–83; Rowton, 1850, pp. 264–297).

Nishimura's translation of Rowton's *The Debater* was thus a unique publication in that it provided the young Japanese intellectuals of his day with the theory of Western oratory in general and the practice of British and American debate in particular, and newer knowledge and information on things Western.

WHY JAPAN'S ATTEMPTS AT ENACTING WESTERN DEBATE PRACTICE FAILED

Contrary to the popular assertion that "speech survived and debate failed," (Suzuki, 1989, pp. 17–18),[5] it should be contended that Japan's serious attempts to introduce Western principles and practices of *both* speechmaking and debating to young intellectuals of the Meiji Japan eventually resulted in failure. One might wonder, then, why the popularity of Western speech and debate declined all of a sudden at the turn of the century. One obvious reason was political. Japan headed toward militarism early in the 20th century, when the imperialistic government enforced a stiff control over freedom of speech and expression. This political climate curbed the publication of books on oratorical speech and debate and instead provided impetus for more "innocuous" rhetoric books such as collections of stylistic devices based on the tradition of *belles lettres*. Because they disregarded the inventional and dispositional aspects of rhetoric, these books were completely devoid of political substance and influence and therefore incapable of politically and rhetorically indoctrinating the Japanese people.

The second reason was psychological. The publication of many works on rhetorical theory and practice during the Meiji era could be described as part of Japan's mass enactments of Western knowledge and ideas on the stage of a feudalistic Japan. The problem, however, was that these rhetorical ideas had not been properly "precocked" or "predigested," so to speak, so as to facilitate a smoother digestion on the part of the Japanese people. Because they were an emotionally and "heart"-oriented, harmony-loving people, the Japanese were not yet ready to adapt to those logically, cognitively, and "mind"-based concepts of Western speech and debate (Sawada, 1977, pp. 225–226).

The third reason for decline of debate at the end of the Meiji era was ideological. By the time of the promulgation of the Meiji Constitution in 1889 and the opening of the national Diet the following year, Japan had been conspicuous by the total absence of the tradition of deliberative oratory. In order to fill this rhetorical vacuum, the Meiji writers of debate went to great lengths to introduce speaking- and eloquence-based theories of rhetoric in large quantities to their contemporaries who found themselves hard put to practice Western ways of speaking and arguing in a culture of *nemawashi* (root-binding or prior consultation) and *sasshi* (intuitively catching on to the other's feelings). The Japanese people, however, eventually found Western speech and debate quite antithetical to Japanese concepts and practices of *nemawashi* and *sasshi*. They felt some ideological gap between the ideality of Western debate and the reality of a unique Japanese culture.

To these three reasons outlined thus far, Becker (1983) added a rhetorically and linguistically based reason for the debate decline that took place at the end of the Meiji period. He explicated it as follows:

First, the importance of argument had not yet been recognized in either law or government, much less business circles. Similarly, there were not yet enough educated Japanese to overcome popular prejudices against any forms of confrontation, to make the idea of amicable argument comprehensible. Both Confucian *Analects* and Buddhist sutras, the "Bibles" of the Japanese society, looked with suspicion and distrust at silver-tongued rhetoricians. Finally, the Japanese language itself favored vague rather than blunt denials, and tended to become highly fettered with honorifics. (p. 144)

CONCLUSION

Ever since the late 16th century, Japan has come a long way on the road of enacting the Western debate instruction and practice for the Japanese people. She experienced two major waves of encountering with Western oratory and debate, obviously with little success. First came the influence of Western rhetoric through the Christian instruction by Portuguese and Spanish missionaries. After total seclusion from the outside world for more than two centuries, from 1653 to 1853, Japan then encountered a surge of British and American books on speech and debate in the late 19th century.

As a responsible nation of the international community, Japan now faces a challenge of searching for a better way of communicating with the rest of the world. More than one century later after the second encounter, now is the time for the creation of a consensus of opinion that despite the emphasis on group harmony, debate can function in Japanese society as a good debate can function in any society, independent of culture or language. It should be realized that debate, whether in Japanese, English, or in any other language for that matter, can lead to the perspective that one way of coming closer to truth is to juxtapose ideas against each other and defend them until one emerges as superior. If an institution is advancing truth or knowledge, to whatever slight degree, it is fulfilling a useful role in society. Debate can do at least this much in a contemporary Japan as well.

NOTES

1. Ever since Morrison (1972) published his thesis that Japan had been rhetorically barren, Japanese students of rhetoric have responded in several ways to his contention concerning the paucity of a rhetorical tradition in Japan. One group of scholars argue that Western rhetorical theory and practice strongly influenced intellectuals of Meiji Japan, including Yukichi Fukuzawa and Emori Ueki. This response comes from such students of rhetorical communication as Hashimoto (1982), Hirai (1991, 1993), and Okabe (1973). Another group reacts to Morrison's conclusion by contending that Japan has nurtured its own seeds of indigenous rhetorical theory and practice. This line of argument is advanced by Ishii (1992) and most recently by Itaba (1995). Still a third line of response is offered by Japanese students of rhetoric as represented by Kakita (1994) who reinterprets from a rhetorical perspective the thoughts of prominent Japanese philosophers, including Kitaro Nishida and Kiyoshi Miki.

2. English translations of all Japanese quotations are mine, except where otherwise indicated.

3. I must admit that there is some truth in Valignano's and Frois's observations on Japanese logic and thinking, but I do not suggest that the failure of the Japanese people to conform to the expectations of Western (mostly Aristotelian) logic makes them "illogical." Based on the only available sources, I am here reporting their perceptions and observations to recount how the outsiders looked at the Japanese ways of thinking and arguing in the 16th century.

4. In the text that follows, the male singular pronoun is used when referring to a speaker/debater of the Meiji era, not because this "sexist" writing reflects the Japanese language habit, but because speech and debate training was solely limited to the male members of the Meiji society. The language used in the following text recognizes this fact.

5. A similar view was expressed by Nakazawa (1987) who stated that "debate . . . could not gain much popularity. On the other hand, oratory . . . was welcomed and has been practiced in many different occasions" (p. 1).

REFERENCES

Anesaki, M. (1976). *Kirishitan shukyo bungaku* [Christian religious literature]. Tokyo: Kokusho Kankokai.

Becker, C. B. (1983). The Japanese way of debate. *The National Forensic Journal, 1,* 75–91.

Chuto Kyoiku Gakkai (Ed.). (1912). *Yuben enzetsu toronkai* [Oratorical speech and debate]. Tokyo: Shugakudo Shoten.

Cieslik, H. (1963). The training of a Japanese clergy in the seventeenth century. In J. Roggendorf (Ed.), *Studies in Japanese culture: Tradition and experiment* (pp. 41–78). Tokyo: Sophia University.

Cooper, M. (1965). Discussion and debate. In: *They came to Japan: An anthology of European reports on Japan, 1543–1640* (pp. 361–373). Berkeley: University of California Press.

Hashimoto, M. (1982). *Baba Tatsui to yubenho* [Tatsui Baba and his oratory]. *Speech Education, 9,* 45–55.

Hirai, K. (1991). *Fukuzawa Yukichi to enzetsu* [Yukichi Fukuzawa and speech], *Otsuma Joshi Daigaku Kiyo* (Academic Journal of Otsuma Women's University), *23,* 57–72.

Hirai, K. (1993). *Fukuzawa Yukichi no "giron ron"* [Yukichi Fukuzawa's "argument on argument"]. *Otsuma Joshi Daigaku Kiyo, 25,* 47–66.

Ikushima, H. (Ed.). (1882). *Seidan toron hyakudai* [One hundred topics for political debate]. Tokyo: Matsui.

Ishii, S. (1992). Buddhist preaching: The persistent main undercurrent of Japanese traditional rhetorical communication. *Communication Quarterly, 40,* 391–397.

Itaba, Y. (1995). *Reconstructing Japanese rhetorical strategies: A study of foreign-policy discourse during the pre-Perry period, 1783–1853.* Unpublished doctoral dissertation, University of Minnesota.

Ito, Y. (1889). *Yuben hiketsu jitsuyo enzetsuho* [Secret way of oratorical speech]. Nagoya: Miwa Seikando.

Iwai, S. (1904). *Sekijo toron enzetsu mohan* [Models of public debate and speech]. Tokyo: Kyukokaku Shoten.

Kakita, H. (1994, November). *Nishida philosophy and the Japanese wartime ideology: A postmodern rhetoric.* Paper presented at the Speech Communication Association Convention, New Orleans, Louisiana.

Morrison, J. L. (1972). The absence of a rhetorical tradition in Japanese culture. *Western Speech, 36,* 89–102.

Nakazawa, M. (1987, June). *English debate activities in Japan during the 1980s.* Paper presented at the Communication Association of Japan Convention, Tokyo.

Nishimura, G. (Trans.). (1881). *Seiyo toron kihan* [Theory of western debate]. Translation of Rowton's *The debater*. Tokyo: Maruya Zenshichi.

Ohata, Y. (Ed.). (1902). *Gunjin seinen toron enzetsu gosendai* [Five thousand topics for debate by adolescent military personnel]. Tokyo: Kyukokaku Shoten.

Ohata, Y. (1904a). *Toron komon: Toronsha kokoroe* [Advice on debate: Hints for a debater]. Tokyo: Kyukokaku Shoten.

Ohata, Y. (1904b). *Yuben renshu seinen toron taikai* [Oratorical debate for adolescents]. Tokyo: Kyukokaku Shoten.

Okabe, R. (1973). Yukichi Fukuzawa: A promulgator of western rhetoric in Japan. *Quarterly Journal of Speech, 59,* 186–195.

Okabe, R. (1986). *Meiji jidai no supichi kyohon ni arawareta seiyo retorikku riron no eikyō ni kansuru kosatsu* [A study of the influence of western rhetorical theory as exhibited in speech textbooks published in the Meiji era]. A grant-in-aid for scientific research report, Ministry of Education.

Okabe, R. (1988). Meiji jidai ni okeru retorikku rironsho no keifu. [A survey of rhetorical theory books published in the Meiji era]. *Ibunka Komyunikeishon Kenkyu* (Intercultural Communication Studies), *1,* 39–78.

Okabe, R. (1990). The impact of western rhetoric on the east: The case of Japan. *Rhetorica, 8,* 371–388.

Ra-Po-Nichi taiyaku jiten [The Latin–Portuguese–Japanese dictionary]. (1973). Tokyo: Bunka Shobo Hakubunsha. (Original work published 1595)

Rinjido-Shujin. (1897). *Enzetsu toron sanzendai* [Three thousand topics for speech and debate]. Tokyo: Tokyo Tosho Shuppan.

Rowton, F. (1850). *The debater: New theory of the art of speaking, being a series of complete debates, outlines of debates and questions for discussion with references to the best sources of information on each particular topic.* London: Longmans, Green, and Co.

Rowton, F. (1881). *Seiyō toron kihan* [Theory of western debate] (G. Nishimura, Trans.). Tokyo: Maruya Zenshichi.

Sato, N. (1987). *Retorikku no shosoku* [Whereabouts of rhetoric]. Tokyo: Hakusuisha.

Sawada, A. (1977). *Ronbun no kakikata* [How to write a research paper]. Tokyo: Kodansha.

Sawada, A. (1983). *Ronbun no retorikku* [The rhetoric of writing a research paper]. Tokyo: Kodansha.

Sugiyama, T. (1883). *Seiji gakujutsu enzetsu toron tanehon* [Sources for political and academic speech and debate]. Tokyo: Chisando.

Suzuki, T. (1989). *Japanese debating activities: A comparison with American debating activities and a rationale for the improvement.* Unpublished master's thesis, University of Kansas.

Tsuboya, Z. (1897). *Enzetsu toron kihan* [Principles for speech and debate]. Tokyo: Hakubunkan.

Ubaoka, S. (1901). *Dokutoku yuben enzetsu toronho* [Unique ways of oratorical speechmaking and debating]. Osaka: Aoki Kozando.

Valignano, A. (1973). *Nippon junsatsuki* [Inspection reports on Japan]. Tokyo: Heibonsha. (Original work published 1583)

Yamada, T. (1907). *Shisei zukai kokai enzetsu yuben toronho* [Public speech and debate with illustrations of posture and gesture]. Tokyo: Shugakudo Shoten.

Chapter 16

Japanese Identities in Written Communication: Politics and Discourses

Ryuko Kubota

This chapter explores Japanese linguistic self-identities perceived by scholars and educators through review of their discussions on Japanese language and rhetoric published in Japan since the 1960s. Paralleling North American contrastive rhetoric research that underscores cultural differences between Japanese and English rhetoric, many authors discuss the distinctiveness of Japanese language and rhetoric. While one view regards the distinctiveness as defective compared to Western languages, another champions it as reflecting Nihonjinron. *Conversely, composition handbooks and Japanese language education promote logic and clarity, modeling the English mode of communication. These contradicting views are harmoniously blended in the discourse of* kokusaika, *which promotes both nationalism and Westernization. Influenced by* kokusaika, *the educational reforms during the 1980s and 1990s placed a greater educational emphasis on logical thinking, self-expression, and debate. This trend demonstrates the dynamic nature of the Japanese language influenced by economics, politics, and discourses. It also questions the pervasive image of Japanese written communication as indirect and ambiguous.*

Characteristics of written discourse patterns, or rhetoric, in different cultures have been a research theme since "contrastive rhetoric" was introduced by Robert B. Kaplan (1966) as a field within applied linguistics. Kaplan proposed that there are culturally specific thought patterns that affect the organization of written texts in different languages. This research focus derived from a need to teach academic writing in English as a second language (ESL) to international students in the United States, and has prompted many studies on the rhetorical characteristics of various languages, including Japanese (cf. Connor, 1996). A number of studies that compared Japanese and English have concluded that the Japanese written discourse organization is generally different from English. These studies largely describe Japanese written texts as indirect and inductive, while English texts are described as direct and deductive. However, some researchers have criticized this binary characterization and the essentialization of cultural rhetoric. Also, a post-structuralist understanding of knowledge as constructed by discourse rather than as apolitical objective reality challenges the notion of cultural differences as neu-tral scientific truths in the applied linguistics research paradigm.

The essentialization of cultural rhetoric found in contrastive rhetoric research parallels the discussions found in various publications in Japan that promote the uniqueness of the Japanese language and culture. Some authors view the Japanese language and culture as inherently defective, whereas others, as in the discourse of *Nihonjinron* (theories on the uniqueness of the Japanese), view them positively. Despite such descriptions of a distinct Japanese cultural and linguistic identity, many handbooks on academic writing in Japanese promote the conven-tions similar to those of English academic writing. This contradiction between the description and prescription of Japanese rhetoric can be understood within the larger political, economic, and ideological context, particularly in terms of the power relations between Japan and the West. What further makes this contradic-tion comprehensible is the discourse of *kokusaika* (internationalization), which has influenced Japanese educational reform since the mid-1980s. Related educa-tional policies promote characteristically English modes of communication as the model for speaking and writing in Japanese, further problematizing the concep-tion of the Japanese uniqueness.

This chapter focuses on discourses on Japanese language and rhetoric that under-lie the writings of Japanese scholars and educators and explores the ways in which these Japanese linguistic identities are perceived, constructed, and transformed. It is important to stress that this chapter is not concerned with determining empirical "truths" about Japanese linguistics features or justifying any specific claimed char-acteristics of language and culture. Rather, it aims to critically examine discourses that produce particular Japanese cultural and linguistic identities. The main interest here is to explore how various views about Japanese culture and language are exploited to construct certain linguistic identity, how these views are implicated in politics and power, and how contradictions are resolved by a unity of discourse (Foucault, 1972). Thus, various arguments on Japanese culture and language pre-sented in this chapter should not be regarded as objective truth but as discursive constructs implicated in political and ideological underpinnings.

In view of the fact that contrastive rhetoric research began in the 1960s, a review of Japanese publications generally focuses on those published since the 1960s. Also, as contrastive rhetoric focuses on written texts, this chapter mainly explores Japanese identities in written communication. However, it also examines discussions on oral communication, because many authors express their opinions on multiple aspects of the Japanese language from sentence structure to both oral and written communication. Obviously, oral and written modes of language are not completely inseparable and they influence each other. Although there has been criticism of the tendency to conflate oral and written language in the discussion of the characteristics of Japanese rhetoric in writing (Donahue, 1998), examining arguments on both oral and written communication does serve to provide a broader source of information on the construction of Japanese linguistic identities. To reiterate, the focus here is not to pursue the true rhetorical characteristics of written Japanese but to explore how various characteristics are conveniently used and conflict each other in constructing a certain identity. Before examining discussions on the Japanese language among Japanese scholars and educators, the following section provides a summary of studies on Japanese rhetoric within the contrastive rhetoric research framework.

CONTRASTIVE RHETORIC STUDIES ON JAPANESE

The seminal work of contrastive rhetoric by Kaplan (1966) compares the thought patterns in different languages or language groups (i.e., English, Semitic, Oriental, Romance, and Russian) which influence the rhetorical features of written texts. In Kaplan's model, the English thought pattern is linear and represented by a straight line, whereas the "Oriental" thought pattern observed in Chinese and Korean is indirect and represented by a circle turning around toward the center. Although his model did not include Japanese in his "Oriental" language group, this general characterization of Asian languages has been applied to Japanese, as seen next.

Since Kaplan's seminal work, textual features of Japanese and English have been compared by a number of studies, many of which focused on expository writing (e.g., Hinds, 1983a, 1983b, 1987, 1990; Kobayashi, 1984; Kobayashi & Rinnert, 1996; Maynard, 1996; Oi, 1984). These studies have shown a preference among Japanese writers for induction, or placing the main idea toward the end rather than at the beginning of a text. The inductive tendency has been perceived as an "indirect" characteristic of Japanese written texts as well as a manifestation of the *ki-shō-ten-ketsu* organization. Hinds (1990) further argues that induction, as used by Japanese writers, is different from induction as used by English writers. He argues that the Japanese type of induction is better termed "quasi inductive" because the paragraphs preceding a conclusion present observations only loosely connected to the main idea. Hinds's observations underscore differences between Japanese and English text organization. In fact, the studies listed above, as well as contrastive rhetoric studies focusing on other languages, characterize features of English rhetoric—i.e., deductive, logical, direct, and assertive—as opposite to Japanese (cf. Kubota, 1998a).

However, such dichotomized characteristics of Japanese and English have been challenged. For instance, McCagg (1996) argues that what makes a text organized with Japanese rhetoric difficult for native English speakers to understand is not necessarily the text's culturally specific rhetorical style but the reader's lack of cultural and linguistic knowledge. Additionally, Donahue (1998) points out methodological problems in contrastive rhetoric studies such as neglecting the situational context in which a text appears and failing to present characteristics as genre-specific. He also presents counter-examples and states that characterizing Japanese written expository discourse as nonlinear, inductive, and vague seems unwarranted. Kubota (1997) argues that characterizing Japanese rhetoric through *ki-shō-ten-ketsu* (Hinds, 1983a, 1983b, 1987, 1990) is inappropriate because of its multiple interpretations. She also points out an influence of English rhetoric on Japanese by presenting a history of the development of contemporary Japanese language. A study that compared the rhetorical patterns of Japanese and English essays according to the level of quality perceived by evaluators found that Japanese essays shared certain characteristics with English essays (Kubota, 1998a). A longitudinal case study by Spack (1997) revealed a complex and evolving nature of a Japanese female college student's strategies to cope with academic content and discourse in English, questioning the static notion of second language writers as a product of their native culture.

Another critique of the cultural dichotomy comes from a poststructuralist understanding of knowledge as constructed by discursive practices rather than as apolitical objective truths. In this view, cultural representation as knowledge is neither true, scientific, nor neutral, but rather it is produced by discursive practices in which power is circulated, exercised, and attached to such knowledge. In this perspective, an emphasis on cultural differences supported in applied linguistics literature (including contrastive rhetoric) echoes Orientalism (Said, 1978), which demonstrates the Western will to construct the image of the Orient as the static, exotic, and monolithic Other and to legitimate Western superiority over the Orient. Here, cultural images are viewed as discursive constructs rather than objectively determined truths. Also, an emphasis on Japanese cultural uniqueness, which is discussed in more detail in the following sections, manifests *Nihonjinron* or self-Orientalism, which demonstrates Japan's struggle for power in the international community, as well as Japanese political and business leaders' interest in domestic control (cf. Kubota, 1999). This cultural critique provides an important insight into discursive formations of linguistic identity discussed in this chapter.

DISCOURSES ON THE UNIQUENESS OF JAPANESE WRITTEN COMMUNICATION

Paralleling the general conclusion of contrastive rhetoric research that native speakers of Japanese prefer inductive and indirect styles in writing, many

Japanese scholars support the view that English is characterized by a logical, assertive, and objective mode of communication, whereas Japanese speakers prefer a nonlogical, nonverbal, indirect, and emotional mode, reflecting groupism and homogeneity. While contrastive rhetoric studies tend to have a neutral tone, arguments on the uniqueness of Japanese language made by Japanese scholars are often accompanied by value judgments. Some scholars negatively view the distinctiveness of the Japanese language. They perceive nonlogical indirect ways of communication as less developed than Western languages (particularly English). Conversely, other scholars argue against such negative views and attach positive meanings to the distinctiveness of the Japanese language and communication. I elaborate on these different positions next.

"English Is Logical and Japanese Is Indirect"—Negative Views of Japanese

Differences between Japanese and English in terms of linguistic and rhetorical structures have been a topic of interest among Japanese scholars who are involved in English language teaching, linguistic studies, and other fields. These scholars generally support dichotomies between Japanese and English, such as subjective versus objective; emotional, sentimental, and intuitive versus logical and analytic; vague versus clear; and indirect versus direct (e.g., Araki, 1986; Nakajima, 1987; Nishida, 1987; Nozaki, 1988; Okihara et al., 1985; Saisho, 1975; Takefuta, 1982; Tobioka, 1999; Ujiie, 1996). Some of these authors cite Kaplan (1966) and support his argument. For instance, Okihara et al. (1985) cite the dichotomous features of Japanese and English suggested by Takefuta (1982) as well as the model proposed by Kaplan (1966), and state that English speakers construct their arguments in a logical and straightforward manner, whereas the Japanese tend to write lengthy opening remarks before reaching conclusions, which are often vague. Nozaki (1988) also mentions Kaplan's model and states that the English used by native Japanese speakers is often unclear to native speakers of English. According to Nozaki, English texts written by the Japanese are difficult to comprehend because logical development is lacking or the topic sentence in a paragraph is absent or inappropriate.

Underlying these arguments is the conception that English is more advanced than Japanese. Nishida (1987), in his handbook on translating from Japanese into English, argues that stating the conclusion unambiguously is often inappropriate in Japanese, whereas English always requires writers to state the main point clearly in the beginning. Nishida maintains, "English is a language that requires a great amount of logic. As it is a logical language, it deserves its international use" (p. 131). Saisho (1975) argues that since English is more logical and analytical than Japanese, the Japanese language used by native speakers of English who are fluent in Japanese exhibits logical organization, and thus would enrich the Japanese language. However, she recommends that Japanese people not use Japanese logic in English because a greater amount of logic is required in using English. Here the logic of English is viewed as a model for improving the Japanese language. Nakajima (1987) states that, reflecting the syntactic structure of English (i.e., the subject precedes the predicate), English is better equipped for persuading the audience. Nakajima maintains that "English is superior to Japanese as a language for academic writing" (pp. 192–193). In her short essay, Tenma (1990) claims that teaching English to native Japanese speakers would improve their use of the Japanese language. She observed that her students began to develop their ideas in a logical and unambiguous manner in their Japanese essays after they had learned English paragraph organization. Tenma argues that Japanese, for which ambiguity has been a virtue for centuries, needs to improve because we now live in an age that requires a logical way of conveying one's opinions.

These views reflect a discourse that views Japanese as backward, defective, inferior, and therefore in need of change; whereas English is viewed as advanced, positive, and superior. Here, Japanese is devalued while English is glorified.

"Japanese Is Unique"—Positive Views of Japanese

The discourse discussed above is contrasted with another discourse that views Japanese positively. The positive views of Japanese reflect cultural relativism and highlight the positive aspects of the uniqueness of the Japanese language. For instance, Nomoto (1978) criticizes the claim that Japanese is an illogical language by arguing that every language entails its own logic and Japanese cannot be measured by the yardstick for Western languages. Suzuki (1975) maintains that despite the persistent condemnation of Japanese as an inferior language, the Japanese have always appreciated circumlocution and complication. Suzuki (1987, 1995) also suggests that Japanese people should abandon the misconception that Japanese is an inferior language. He constructs an argument that Japanese is in fact a superior language compared to others that use the roman alphabet, because its logographic nature allows easy access to the meanings of technical terms.

Umesao (1988) criticizes the view that Japan lost World War II because the Japanese language lacked logic and prevented Japan from technological development (see the next section). Although he agrees that well-developed logical thinking has been absent in Japanese, he argues that this is because Japanese culture has not acknowledged superiority or absoluteness of logic. According to Umesao, Japanese has developed emotional rather than logical expressions due to the geographical and cultural isolation of the country. He further argues that intricate emotional expressions in Japanese are finer than logical expressions in an "artless language" that only functions as a means to solve conflicts between individuals. Umesao also argues that Japanese can express logic as well, and moreover, what is considered to be a logical feature of many European languages, such as the obligatory sentential subject, is not the manifestation of logic but simply a convention.

Toyama (1973) argues that each language, including Japanese, has its own logic. According to Toyama, Japanese has a dot-like logic, which consists of a series of dots with no apparent links among them, whereas European languages have a linear logic. Characteristic of the dot-like logic, according to the author, is an abundance of abridgment and implicitness, which results in ambiguity. However, for Toyama, ambiguity in itself is a form of logic. He argues that discovering a line of logic by linking isolated dots involves creativity, but tracing a firm linear logic results in boredom.

The argument that English and Japanese have different logic is also made by Nishimura (1997), who argues that *ronriteki* (logical) expressions in Japanese are complete and accurate but not necessarily easy to understand, whereas "logical" expressions in English make messages comprehensible. Nishimura does not believe that Japanese can or should be expressed "logically" because of social cohesiveness and status consciousness. Thus, he recommends that Japanese people debate in English making logical use of language, which ironically echoes the argument for replacing Japanese with English discussed in the next section.

Positive values to Japanese also appear in the discourse of *Nihonjinron* (literally, "studies on Japanese people"), a discourse that champions the uniqueness of the Japanese culture. This discourse has become popular since the 1960s when Japan experienced rapid economic growth. Scholars both in and outside of Japan have attempted to find explanations as to why Japan achieved such economic success. Among many books that promote *Nihonjinron*, the following are considered to be representative: *Amae no kōzō* (*The Anatomy of Dependence*) by Doi (1971, 1973) and *Tate shakai no ningen kankei* (*Japanese Society*) by Nakane (1967, 1973), although these works have been criticized from methodological and ideological points of view. Next, I review both works in terms of the authors' views on the Japanese language.

Doi (1971, 1973), promotes the notion of "dependence" as a key concept for explaining the psychology of the Japanese people and society. According to Doi, the nonlogical and intuitive nature of the Japanese thought pattern is not unrelated to dependence, because dependence, which underlies isolation of self from objective facts and identification of self with the other, has a nonlogical nature. Doi maintains that although the nature of dependence may be viewed critically as "illogical," "closed," and "egoistic," it can also be positively evaluated as "nondiscriminatory" and "tolerant." The positive values of "dependency" are further illustrated by the philosophies of Zen Buddhism and aestheticism in Japan.

Nakane (1967, 1973) maintains that what underlies the Japanese value system is a relative, rather than logical, principle that is based on socially and emotionally "vertical" human relationships. For Nakane, the nonlogical and anti-intellectual everyday language use in Japanese is observed in no other cultures and is a reason that makes Japanese culture unintelligible to foreigners. Nakane claims that while such language use has disadvantages in academic and political debates, it offers people a sort of relaxation in a highly stratified society.

Both of these authors do not overtly praise the nonlogical nature of the Japanese thought pattern, but they regard it as one of the factors that distinguish the Japanese from other people. What is championed here is the distinctiveness of the Japanese and Japanese culture.

CONSTRUCTION OF NEGATIVE/POSITIVE VIEWS OF THE JAPANESE LANGUAGE

Both negative and positive views of the uniqueness of the Japanese language thus reviewed seem implicated by particular political and economic conditions, ideologies, and international relations of power. The negative view of the Japanese language and culture symbolizes a political, cultural, and military defeat by the United States and the West since the Meiji Period (1868–1912), whereas the positive view reflects Japan's military strength under imperialism during World War II and its postwar economic development.

Negative Views

As pointed out by Minami (1994), Mouer and Sugimoto (1986), and Sugimoto and Mouer (1982), who offer overviews of the history of *Nihonjinron*, modern Japan has tended to be dominated by a discourse that views Japan negatively, especially after its experience of political and military conquest by the West. Some Japanese viewed the defeat as caused by a defect of the Japanese people, culture, language, and society.

An extremely negative view of the Japanese language can be found in the proposals for replacing Japanese with other languages. An often cited example is a proposal made in the 1870s by Arinori Mori, the first Minister of Education (Suzuki, 1987, 1995). Mori, realizing the importance of Western knowledge and technology, suggested the adoption of English as the language of Japan. This happened soon after Japan was urged by the United States to open its doors to the rest of the world. Although Mori's proposal needs to be interpreted within a particular historical context in which there was neither an established form nor concept of Japanese as a "national language" and there was a large discrepancy between the spoken and written language (Lee, 1996),[1] Mori's radical proposal carries a legacy of viewing Japanese as incomplete and underdeveloped.

Suzuki (1987) mentions two other proposals for abolishing Japanese. In 1946, immediately after World War II, Naoya Shiga, a writer, expressed his criticism of Japanese in a journal called *Kaizo* (Reformation) (Suzuki, 1987). For Shiga, Japanese was an incomplete and inconvenient language, which prevented a fine development of culture. He maintained that if English had been adopted as the national language as Mori had suggested, World War II would not have broken out. Shiga then advocated the adoption of French as the national language, because France, to him, had advanced culture and a literature close in sentiment to Japanese literature. Also, between 1947 and 1950, Gakudō Ozaki, a politician, advocated the adoption of English as the national language. Ozaki argued that modern democracy was born and developed in Britain and the United States and in order to make it grow in Japan, their language must be adopted (Suzuki, 1987).

These recommendations seem to flow from historical incidents that made Japan surrender to Western power. The negative views of Japanese language reviewed previously can be understood on this historical continuum. Although recommendations for replacing Japanese with a Western language are rarely heard today, the idea that the Japanese mode of communication needs to improve still exists in certain educational reforms discussed later.

Positive Views

Contrary to the view that regards Japanese language and culture as inferior, a discourse that champions the uniqueness and superiority of Japan has tended to emerge out of Japan's economic or military prosperity in the world. Most relevant to the contemporary formation of Japanese linguistic identity found in *Nihonjinron,* is Japan's economic success in the 1960s and 1970s. Certainly, the 1960s was not the first time when the Japanese began to seek their positive identity. Even more affirmative views of the Japanese culture and language, which Minami (1994) calls "fascist *Nihonjinron"* was formed between the 1920s and 1940s under Japanese imperialism. This was also the time when Japanese was taught as the language of the Japanese Empire in occupied territories in Asia and the South Pacific. While the Pacific War (World War II) brought an end to Japan's military and political domination of Asia, its postwar economic expansion has created an economic domination of Asia and other parts of the world. The post–Pacific War *Nihonjinron* needs to be understood in this context.

There have been critiques of *Nihonjinron* since the 1980s (e.g., Befu, 1987; Dale, 1986; Iwabuchi, 1994; Kawamura, 1980; Lummis & Ikeda, 1985; Mouer & Sugimoto, 1986, 1995; Sugimoto & Mouer, 1982, 1989), which offered several explanations of the construction of this discourse. Yoshino (1992, 1997) presents four prevailing theories for the emergence of *Nihonjinron*:

1. To rescue the threatened Japanese identity,
2. To promote the cultural superiority of Japan by explaining its economic success and social stability,
3. To function as an ideology that controls Japanese citizens, and
4. To reflect the national character of being interested in self-identity.

Yoshino critiques each of these perspectives mainly in light of his findings that the consumers of *Nihonjinron*, such as business people and educators, exhibit different levels of understanding and react to it in different ways. He also questions a direct flow of knowledge from the producer of this discourse to the consumer. Nonetheless, these theories, particularly the first three, are worth elaborating here, because they demonstrate how *Nihonjinron* and its explanations are linked to political, economic, and cultural contexts.

First, *Nihonjinron* can be explained as an attempt to rescue Japanese national identity from the threat of Westernization and industrialization. Befu (1987) argues that a large influence of Western lifestyle, which is a result of Japan's attempt to adopt things "Western" in order to overcome the perceived inferiority of things "Japanese," threatened Japanese traditional identity. One means to alleviate the threat was to construct a discourse that viewed Japan not as inferior but as unique among nations. This explanation indicates that the notion of Japanese uniqueness is constructed vis-à-vis the West. Indeed, critics point out that *Nihonjinron* tends to emphasize Japan's uniqueness compared only to the West (e.g., Befu, 1987; Lummis & Ikeda, 1985; Sugimoto & Mouer, 1982). Also, according to Befu (1987), since the emphasis on superiority/uniqueness of Japanese culture emerged from a fear of losing "Japaneseness," the national characteristics described in *Nihonjinron* are often traditional "pure" forms of culture, which are obviously distinctive compared to the West.

The second theory posits that *Nihonjinron* was constructed to explain Japan's economic success, whereby it legitimates the uniqueness of Japanese culture. Sugimoto and Mouer (1982), for instance, argue that both Japanese and non-Japanese scholars, such as Doi (1971, 1973), Nakane (1967, 1973), Ouchi (1981), and Vogel (1979) sought explanations of Japan's economic success by focusing on its unique cultural and sociological characteristics such as harmony and homogeneity. Cultural differences also serve as an excuse for applying Japanese "unique" ways in international politics and business. *Nihonjinron* indeed has created international business manuals—some Japanese businesses have published crosscultural manuals that describe Japanese unique customs in English (Yoshino, 1997).

The third theory argues that *Nihonjinron* is an ideological device used by the dominant political and business leaders. For instance, a belief in harmony, groupism, and homogeneity works to reduce conflicts between the employer and the employee or between the government and the citizen (Befu, 1987; Mouer & Sugimoto, 1986; Sugimoto & Mouer, 1982).

These explanations of the positive views in *Nihonjinron* demonstrate political, economic, and cultural contexts in which this discourse emerged. They highlight Japan's economic boom that has enhanced international business and brought Westernization to various aspects of Japanese life. These contexts imply Japan's increased contact with people from other cultures, which prompted a discourse of *kokusaika* (internationalization), which is discussed later.

HOW TO COMPOSE ACADEMIC TEXTS IN JAPANESE

While the review of literature thus far has demonstrated contrasting views on the distinctness of Japanese and English, the issue of how Japanese academic texts should be written seems to be less controversial. In fact, Japanese composition handbooks rarely recommend using indirect, vague, ambiguous, or nonlogical rhetoric, but instead emphasize logic, unity, clarity, the use of a topic sentence for each paragraph, and in some cases, stating the thesis at the outset (Baba, 1988; Furugori, 1997; Imai, 1980; Kabashima, 1980, 1984; Kinoshita, 1990, 1998; Morioka, 1977; Morioka et al., 1995; Sawada, 1977; Yoshida, 1997). Furthermore, the relevant *Course of Study*, the national curriculum guideline issued by the Ministry of Education (1998a), includes the following achievement objectives for writing skills:

1. Pay attention to the connection between paragraphs while clarifying the main point of the message (Grades 3 and 4);
2. Consider the effect of the overall text organization in order to express one's idea clearly (Grades 5 and 6);
3. Clarify facts, contents, topic, opinions, and feelings that one wants to convey (Grade 7); and
4. Make supporting reasons clear and develop a logical organization in order to effectively convey one's opinion to readers (Grades 8 and 9).[2]

Also, one of the overall goals for Grades 8 and 9 includes having students acquire the ability to clarify their own position and express themselves logically in writing. This emphasis on logical thinking and expression in Japanese language education is discussed further in the section on educational reforms.

The emphasis on logic and clarity seems to indicate a perceived need to overcome linguistic inferiority. Even the authors cited who promote *Nihonjinron* uniqueness beliefs of Japanese culture do not overtly support the use of the nonlogical communication style. Instead, they seem to have ambivalent feelings. For instance, Nakane (1967, 1973), as reviewed above, deplores a lack of logic in academic and political debates, but at the same time celebrates the nonlogicalness as something unique. Doi (1973) regards *amae* or "dependence" as a factor that is related to the nonlogical Japanese thought pattern and celebrates it as a foundation of Japanese traditional philosophies. However, at the same time, he states, "The aim from now on . . . must be to overcome *amae*. . . . [It] will be necessary to transcend *amae* by discovering the subject and object: to discover, in other words, the other person" (p. 84). Toyama (1973) states that Japanese dot-like logic exhibits sophistication superior to the boredom of tracing a line of formal logic. In contrast, when discussing principles of organizing texts in Japanese, Toyama argues:

The reason why the Japanese lack writing skills is because they cannot skillfully organize a paragraph expressing a unified idea. This problem may be identified as "inept in logic" or "excessively emotional or literary." . . . The basic principle of text organization is to formulate ideas. This will be done by clarifying the key issue, developing it logically and turning dots into a line. (1973, p. 43)

Umesao (1988), as reviewed earlier, contends that although the Japanese language can express logic, its users have preferred emotion over logic. Yet he argues that Japanese is incomplete compared to the languages of other civilizations because of its unsystematic orthography, and thus he makes a proposal for a reform.

This kind of ambivalence is realized by Suzuki (1975), who points out the love/hate feelings that many Japanese people have toward their language. While Suzuki states that to avoid clarifying one's argument is a suicidal act in argumentative writing, he recognizes Japanese people's preference for ambiguity, complexity, and indirectness over clarity and directness, which are regarded as stale and immature. Suzuki speculates that such ambivalent feelings are rooted in the cultural inferiority that the Japanese feel vis-à-vis the West. Another author who expresses ambivalence is Morita (1998). Morita describes unique characteristics of the Japanese language observed from teaching Japanese as a second language. He argues that although Japanese has treasured elegance, reservation, and emotional nuance, today's internationalized world requires the Japanese to use logic in both oral and written discourse rather than remaining quiet and reserved. According to Morita, Japanese language and culture operate within a closed circle, which enables people to treasure contexts, subjectivity, and intricate feelings but does not allow them to build up logical arguments to expand creativity. Morita identifies his feelings toward the Japanese language as both regret and intimacy.

The Descriptive versus Prescriptive Contradiction

So far this chapter has reviewed both negative and positive descriptive views of the Japanese language and prescriptive views as to how Japanese academic texts should be written. The review demonstrates a descriptive/prescriptive contradiction in that Japanese communication is often described as intuitive, nonlogical, and ambiguous (either in a positive or a negative sense), whereas practitioners underscore clarity and logic in composing Japanese academic texts. This gap is contrary to Befu's (1993) view that *Nihonjinron* functions as a prescriptive model. According to Befu, the descriptive images of the Japanese people in *Nihonjinron* behoove them to act and think as described. Thus, the idealized descriptive model works as a prescriptive one. However, in the case of the claimed distinctness of the Japanese language, the descriptive model does not seem to be transformed into a prescriptive one. This paradox is unsettling because in *Nihonjinron,* language is made integral to a unique Japanese identity (Befu, 1993; Yoshino, 1992, 1997). How can we reconcile this descriptive/prescriptive paradox? Why isn't the "Japanese" mode of communication enthusiastically promoted? Isn't promotion of the "English" mode of communication contradictory with Japanese uniqueness? To explore answers to these questions, I now turn to *kokusaika* discourse.

DISCOURSE OF *KOKUSAIKA*

Nihonjinron can foster nationalism by creating positive images for cultural identity and giving confidence to Japanese people. Some critics indeed regard *Nihonjinron* as passive nationalism (Befu, 1993) or cultural nationalism (Yoshino, 1992, 1997). To understand this type of nationalism, however, one must consider the international political and military situation in which Japan lies. Unlike previous Japanese nationalism under imperialism sustained by Japan's military power, present *Nihonjinron* exists in Japan's postwar military subordination to the United States. Also, a global capitalist economy and multinational corporations depend on open markets under the protection of multinational military alliances that counter any one nation from colonizing another for its own capitalist expansion (Watanabe, 1998). This condition requires Japan not to exercise power by itself in the international community but to negotiate power with the United States and its Western allies. A discourse of *kokusaika,* or internationalization, enables Japan to achieve such accommodation. In the following section, I discuss *kokusaika* and educational reform in the 1980s and 1990s.

Kokusaika and Educational Reform in the 1980s

As stated above, what needs untangling is how the Japanese simultaneously foster belief in the uniqueness of the Japanese language while promoting that the Japanese language follow an English (or perhaps more broadly, Western) mode of communication. This contradiction seems to be resolved in a discourse of *kokusaika* in the 1980s, which embraces both celebration of Japanese traditions and promotion of Western logic. *Kokusaika* envisions Japan's Westernization, membership into the industrialized countries of the West, and contribution to the international community by instilling the Japanese traditional spirit (Morita, 1987, 1988). *Kokusaika* aims to both accommodate the power of the West, particularly the United States, and strengthen the economic power of Japan (Shindo, 1988).

The construction of this discourse is closely related to political, economic, and military conditions. First, we must understand that the U.S.–Japan military alliance largely determines the political and economic relations between Japan and other countries, including the United States. The military alliance aims at promoting not only military cooperation but also mutual understanding of international economic policies and economic cooperation. Thus, the U.S.–Japan reciprocal support in terms of military, political, and economic issues affects not only bilateral but also international relations (Kudo, 1988). The decline of the American economy in the 1970s and the involvement in the Vietnam War, on the one hand, and the continuing prosperity of the Japanese economy, on the other, created economic and political conflicts between the two nations. The Western praise of Japan's miracle economic growth soon shifted to "Japan Bashing."

This situation led the Japanese government and large corporations to avoid conflict and possible world isolation, while continuing to seek economic growth through international investments. The strategy employed was to neither subjugate themselves to the West nor to seek dominance through military buildup. Rather, Japanese political and corporate leaders sought to accommodate the Western power by joining the West as an equal member and convincing the West and other nations of their position.

For the government and large corporations, this vision was to be accomplished by educating the younger generation. Thus, Rinji Kyōiku Shingikai, the Ad Hoc Committee for Education Reform was established. It consisted of members appointed by the prime minister and compiled four reports on educational reform between 1985 and 1987. An image of the ideal Japanese person envisioned in the committee's reports is sarcastically portrayed by Morita (1988):

An English-speaking Samurai warrior carrying a computer on his back advances to Asia and Pacific under the Stars and Stripes with a flag of the Rising Sun tied around his head singing *Kimigayo* (The Era of Your Highness), the national anthem. (p. 8)

Here, the mentality of the Japanese to be fostered is patriotism, love of traditions, as well as worship of the Emperor. The use of the national flag and the national anthem at school ceremonies was mandated by the Ministry of Education in the *Course of Study* issued in 1989 despite opposition from concerned teachers and citizens who argued that they symbolize Japanese imperialism, which drove Japan into the Pacific War. The ability required of the younger generations, on the other hand, is a command of the language and logic of the West (especially English) as members of the Western industrialized community. What is reflected here is a harmonious blend of nationalism and Westernization. Indeed, one of the committee reports stated that patriotism, which is the love of ethnic tradition and identity, does not conflict with internationalization (Yamaguchi, 1993).

The proposed Westernization is based on the following view of Masakazu Yamazaki, whose input, according to Morita (1988), is reflected in the committee's reports:

The world we face today is the production of cultural and economic enterprises of the West. . . . As a result, the order and knowledge of the world civilization have come to be dominated by the Western criteria of judgment and value. . . . As the lingua francas in the world are a few Western languages including English, there is an implicit expectation that the world politics and economy be discussed through the logic of the West and that the mentality of the leaders of international corporations be Western as well. (*The report from the discussion group on "Japan in the world"* cited by Morita, 1988, p. 141)

What is expected for a Westernized Japanese citizen is to be able to explain Japanese perspectives to the rest of the world through English logic. This perspective is reflected in the committee's proposal that one should develop "language ability that enables communication with people from other cultures, ability to express oneself, as well as international manners, knowledge and education." At the same time, the proposal expects one to develop "a broad and deep understanding of Japan that enables persuasive explanation in the international community on Japanese history, traditions, culture and society" (*The Second Report of the Committee for Education Reform,* 1986, as cited in Gyōsei, 1987).

Of interest here is the emphasis on fostering the ability to express oneself. The first report suggests that the current emphasis on memorization should be replaced by creativity, ability to think with logic, abstraction, imagination, and ability to express oneself. The ability to express oneself in global communities is to be developed particularly through learning English, but it is also to be developed in Japanese. The *Summary of the Discussion Process (No. 3)* of the *Second Report* states, "In order to develop ability to express oneself, teaching the Japanese language is to be promoted as language education (i.e., focusing on developing communication skills)" (Gyōsei, 1987). The view here is that it is important to foster the ability to think and express oneself in both English and Japanese "in order to explain Japanese culture in accordance with the logic and mentality of the people addressed" (*The Third Report*). Indeed, the new definition of "academic ability" announced by the Ministry of Education a few years later included the ability to think, judge, and express oneself (Gyōsei, 1987).

Kokusaika, which combines coherently both Westernization and nationalism, manifests Japan's struggle for power within the dominance of the West. As such, it is closely related to *Nihonjinron.* As mentioned earlier, *Nihonjinron* tends to emphasize Japanese uniqueness as compared to only the West. *Kokusaika* also shares a similar tendency of equating internationalization with Westernization or even Americanization with an emphasis on acquiring the English mode of communication (Kubota, 1998b; Tanaka, 1993). It seems that such inclination toward English inevitably shifts Japanese communication closer to the English-type mode.

Educational Reform, *Kokusaika*, and Nationalism in the 1990s

The revised *Course of Study* based on the reports of the Ad Hoc Education Committee was put into effect in elementary schools in 1992, junior high schools in 1993, and high schools in 1994. The trend of Japanese language education in the 1990s under the new curriculum guidelines includes an emphasis on *hasshin-gata* (expressive mode) rather than *jushin-gata* (receptive mode) and the use of *dēbēto* (debate) in Japanese language classrooms. It has been argued that the expressive mode fosters communicative skills necessary for expressing oneself in the international community, and that debates foster logical thinking and logical ways of communicating one's ideas (cf. Kitaoka, 1990). The 1998 report of *Chūō Kyōiku Shingikai* (Ministry of Education, 1998b), the Central Council for Education, which became the basis of the newly revised *Course of Study*, continues to emphasize teaching Japanese as "language education" to foster abilities to express one's opinion logically, while recommending that educators not place too much emphasis on the detailed analysis of literary texts as traditionally has been done. Also, the *Course of Study* released in 1998 stresses "ability to live," which can be interpreted in the context of Japanese language education as the ability to express oneself logically in the international community for survival. Also stressed is "ability to learn and think by oneself," which requires language skills based in logical thinking (Kitagawa, 1999). Again, there is no emphasis here on indirect and ambiguous ways of communication. What is contrary to the focus on the Western style of communication is a clearly nationalistic trend in education that greatly enforces the use of the national flag and anthem in school ceremonies.

Learning English is another area that is given a greater emphasis in this *Course of Study*. For the first time, public elementary schools have the option to teach a foreign language (English).[3] Although the *Course of Study* treats teaching English as part of "international understanding," the public discussion promoting English language teaching at the elementary school emphasizes the benefit of developing communicative skills in English, regarded as important for survival in the international community (Higuchi, 1997). Similarly, for the first time, foreign language has become a required subject in the junior high school and the senior high school,[4] and English is recommended for the junior high school.

The emphasis on communicative skills in English seems to continue its influence on Japanese language instruction as well. For instance, Watanabe (1995) suggests that, although the Japanese often prefer vagueness in communication and are inept at speaking in a straight line of logic, they need to acquire internationally accepted (i.e., English) rules for paragraph organization in order to communicate with people from different cultures. Referring to some rules of English paragraph writing, he suggests that a paragraph have only one idea and demonstrate unity, coherence, continuity, and adequate development. He then proposes a cross-curriculum for both Japanese and English which includes Japanese and English paragraph writing training for developing logical thinking.

As evident from the above discussion, *kokusaika* discourse in the 1990s and its educational implications basically followed the guideline established in the 1980s. In the 1990s, the world witnessed the end of the Cold War, the outbreak of the Gulf War, and various other ethnic conflicts. *Kokusaika* in Japanese foreign policies emphasized Japan's "international contribution" through participating in the United Nations' peace-keeping missions and cooperating with the United States in regional security. A stronger alliance between Japan and the

United States was established in the 1999 Japan–U.S. Defense Cooperation Guidelines. This implies a continued strong relation between Japan and the United States, which would enhance the teaching of English as well as the adoption of Western (especially English) modes of communication in Japanese language education.

Also worth mentioning is a nationalistic discourse on Japanese history education that emerged in the 1990s. This discourse, promoted by a group called the Japanese Society of History Textbook Reform, led by scholars, business leaders, critics, and so forth, has decried the post-Pacific War history curriculum as being masochistic and self-deprecating of Japanese history (Japanese Society for History Textbook Reform, 1998). For instance, according to their view, the claim that "comfort women" during the Pacific War were transported to battlefields against their will has reflected and produced a masochistic view of Japan's past. Thus, they reject this historical incident as false information and claim, instead, that these women were simply prostitutes. The group maintains that the current biased history education depicts the war-time Japanese as criminals and deprives Japanese citizens of their national pride. Interestingly, a pedagogical approach advocated for history education is formal debate to deal with such controversial topics as whether the Pacific War was an act of aggression or defense by Japan. While critics argue that debating about an already accepted historical fact like this could misinform students (e.g., Sanuki, 1997), an intriguing point here is that debate, a method of argument imported from English, is used as a means to advocate an extremely nationalistic view promoting an idealized Japanese identity. This appropriation of a communication practice in English to teach nationalistic content seems to be an inevitable choice for Japan given the current economic and political situations created by the existing international relations of power.

CONCLUSION

Different discourses of language and culture construct images of Japanese rhetoric in different ways. Contrastive rhetoric research has highlighted the cultural uniqueness of Japanese rhetoric compared to English through positivistic investigation. Different cultural discourses construct images of Japanese rhetoric in different ways. The field of contrastive rhetoric has tended to conclude that Japanese rhetoric is fundamentally different from English rhetoric, discursively constructing Japanese cultural "uniqueness." The conception of cultural uniqueness has also been prevalent in the discourses on language and culture found in Japanese publications in Japan. While one view condemns the culturally distinct discourse style as an inherently defective feature of Japanese compared to Western languages, another champions the uniqueness of Japanese language and rhetoric. Contrary to this emphasis on cultural/linguistic distinctness, composition handbooks and the national curriculum promote clarity and logic, which parallel aims held for English writing. These competing discourses are harmoniously blended in the discourse of *kokusaika* in which both nationalism and Westernization are promoted. Reflecting *kokusaika*, the reforms of Japanese language education envisioned during the 1980s and 1990s have promoted logical thinking, self-expression, and debate. Thus, at least in the mind of most educators, the Japanese language is moving away from an "indirect" and "ambiguous" mode of communication, which, traditionally, has characterized Japanese discourse.

The discussions presented in this chapter offer some predictions. First, as long as the alliance between the United States and Japan, as well as the current political and economic status of Japan, continue to exist, Japanese education will probably continue to incorporate the often claimed characteristics of English mode of communication; that is, logic, clarity, self-expression, and debate. This will probably influence Japanese vocabulary, oral communication, and written discourse organization. This trend might be further strengthened if advocates of Japanese nationalism continue to appropriate the method of debate as a means to promote their points of view.

Second, teaching English as a second/foreign language to Japanese students might create the following two possibilities. With a greater emphasis on teaching English, the negative view of Japanese rhetoric could further transform the Japanese language closer to English. In other words, if the claimed uniqueness of the Japanese language and rhetoric is considered an obstacle for acquiring an English mode of communication, teachers might try to place a greater emphasis on logic and clarity in public speaking and writing in Japanese. The second possibility is confusion created by cultural relativism in English writing classes, particularly those taught by non-Japanese teachers. If the teacher takes a relativistic stance and disseminates the binary opposition of Japanese and English rhetoric (e.g., indirect versus direct), some students might believe that Japanese and English should be written in different ways (cf. Kubota, 1992), which could contradict the possible trend toward Anglicization of Japanese rhetoric.

What has been discussed in this chapter questions the cultural and linguistic dichotomy between Japanese and English and the static notion of rhetorical differences constructed by contrastive rhetoric research. Previous investigations on rhetorical characteristics of Japanese and English have been obsessed with the notion of "difference" and placed rhetoric and language in a void divorced from the larger political and economic contexts. This chapter, however, has indicated that language is far from monolithic, fixed, or neutral but always has been implicated in its political, economic, and ideological conditions, shifting its forms and identities. Also indicated is the possibility that apparently contradictory views about language could be unified by a certain discourse at a deeper political and ideological level. It is necessary for researchers and educators to recognize the perspective that people's identities with regard to language, communication, and rhetoric are discursively produced. This perspective sheds light on political and ideological forces that influence the construction of these identities, which further impact educational policies and evolution of Japanese written communication in dynamic ways.

NOTES

1. Lee (1996) also points out that what was proposed by Mori was "simplified English" because he was aware of the complexity of English including irregular verb conjugations and inconsistent sound and spelling correspondence.

2. The claim that composition is taught only to the sixth grade in Japan (Hinds, 1983b, cited in Leki, 1991) lacks credibility.

3. Although the *Course of Study* mentions teaching a "foreign language," public discussion tends to equate "foreign language" with "English" (e.g., Higuchi, 1997).

4. In the past, foreign language was an elective subject, although almost all schools opted to offer English.

REFERENCES

Araki, H. (1986). *Nihonjin no eigo kankaku* [The uses of English by the Japanese]. Tokyo: PHP Kenkyūjo.

Baba, H. (1988). *Shōronbun no kaki kata* [How to write essays]. Osaka: Sōgensha.

Befu, H. (1987). *Ideorogī to shite no Nihon bunkaron* [The theory of Japanese culture as an ideology]. Tokyo: Shisō no Kagakusha.

Befu, H. (1993). Nationalism and *Nihonjinron.* In H. Befu (Ed.), *Cultural nationalism in East Asia: Representation and identity* (pp. 107–135). Berkeley: The Regents of the University of California.

Connor, U. (1996). *Contrastive rhetoric: Cross-cultural implications of second-language writing.* New York: Cambridge University Press.

Dale, P. (1986). *The myth of Japanese uniqueness.* London: Croom Helm.

Doi, T. (1971). *Amae no kōzō* [Anatomy of dependence]. Tokyo: Kōbundō.

Doi, T. (1973). *The anatomy of dependence* (J. Bester, Trans.). Tokyo: Kōdansha International.

Donahue, R. T. (1998). *Japanese culture and communication: Critical cultural analysis.* Lanham, MD: University Press of America.

Foucault, M. (1972). *The archaeology of knowledge and the discourse of language.* New York: Pantheon Books.

Furugori, T. (1997). *Ronbun repōto no matome kata* [How to organize theses and reports]. Tokyo: Chikuma Shobō.

Gyōsei. (1987). *Rinkyōshin to kyōiku kaikaku. Dai 5 shū: Dai 4 ji tōshin (saishū tōshin) o megutte* [The Ad Hoc Committee on Education and Education Reform Vol. 5: On the 4th (final) report]. Tokyo: Gyōsei.

Higuchi, T. (Ed.) (1997). *Shōgakkō kara no gaikokugo kyōiku* [Foreign language education from the elementary school]. Tokyo: Kenkyūsha.

Hinds, J. (1983a). Contrastive rhetoric: Japanese and English. *Text, 3,* 183–195.

Hinds, J. (1983b). Linguistics and written discourse in English and Japanese: A contrastive study (1978–1982). In R. B. Kaplan, (Ed.), *Annual review of applied linguistics, III* (pp. 78–84). Rowley, MA: Newbury House.

Hinds, J. (1987). Reader versus writer responsibility: A new typology. In U. Connor & R. B. Kaplan (Eds.), *Writing across languages: Analysis of L2 text* (pp. 141–152). Reading, MA: Addison-Wesley.

Hinds, J. (1990). Inductive, deductive, quasi-inductive: Expository writing in Japanese, Korean, Chinese, and Thai. In U. Connor & A. M. Johns (Eds.), *Coherence in writing: Research and pedagogical perspectives* (pp. 87–109). Alexandria, VA: TESOL.

Imai, M. (1980). *Bunshō kian no gijutsu* [Techniques for drafting texts]. Tokyo: Gakuyō Shobō.

Iwabuchi, K. (1994). Complicit exoticism: Japan and its other. *Continuum: The Australian Journal of Media & Culture, 8*(2). Available online: http://wwwmcc.murdoch. edu.au/ReadingRoom/8.2/Iwabuchi.html

Japanese Society for History Textbook Reform (1998). *The restoration of a national history: Why was the Japanese Society for History Textbook Reform established, and what are its goals?* Tokyo: Japanese Society for History Textbook Reform.

Kabashima, T. (1980). *Bunshō kōseihō* [Methods of text organization]. Tokyo: Kōdansha.

Kabashima, T. (1984). Kaku tame no gijutsu [Techniques for writing]. In Bunkachō (Ed.), *"Kotoba" shirīzu 20: Bunshō no kakikata* [Series "Language" 20: Writing] (pp. 49–58). Tokyo.

Kaplan, R. B. (1966). Cultural thought patterns in inter-cultural education. *Language Learning, 16*, 1–20.

Kawamura, N. (1980). The historical background of arguments emphasizing the uniqueness of Japanese society. *Social Analysis, 5/6*, 44–62.

Kinoshita, K. (1990). *Repōto no kumitate kata* [How to structure academic essays]. Tokyo: Chikuma Shobō.

Kinoshita, K. (1998). Ronriteki bunshō to wa [What is a logical text?]. *Nihongogaku* [Japanese Language Studies], *17*, February, 4–13.

Kitagawa, H. (1999). Shin gakushū shidō yōryō de motomerareru kokugo ryoku [Japanese language ability required by the new Course of Study]. *Gekkan Kokugo Kyōiku Kenkyū* (Monthly Studies in Japanese Language Education), *3*(323), 4–9.

Kitaoka, T. (1990). *Dēbēto nōryoku no jidai* [The age of the ability to debate]. Tokyo: Sannō-dai Shuppanbu.

Kobayashi, H. (1984). *Rhetorical patterns in English and Japanese.* Unpublished doctoral dissertation, Teachers College, Columbia University, New York.

Kobayashi, H., & Rinnert, C. (1996). Factors affecting composition evaluation in an EFL context: Cultural rhetorical pattern and readers' background. *Language Learning, 46*, 397–437.

Kubota, R. (1992). *Contrastive rhetoric of Japanese and English: A critical approach.* Unpublished doctoral dissertation, Department of Education, University of Toronto, Canada.

Kubota, R. (1997). Reevaluation of the uniqueness of Japanese Written Discourse: Implications to Contrastive Rhetoric. *Written Communication, 14*, 460–480.

Kubota, R. (1998a). An investigation of Japanese and English L1 essay organization: Differences and similarities. *The Canadian Modern Language Review, 54*, 475–507.

Kubota, R. (1998b). Ideologies of English in Japan. *World Englishes, 17*, 295–306.

Kubota, R. (1999). Japanese culture constructed by discourses: Implications for applied linguistic research and English language teaching. *TESOL Quarterly, 33*, 9–35.

Kudo, A. (1988). *Teikoku shugi no atarashii tendai* [A new development of imperialism]. Tokyo: Shin Nihon Shuppansha.

Lee, Y. (1996). *"Kokugo" to iu shisō* [Philosophies of "national language"]. Tokyo: Iwanami Shoten.

Leki, I. (1991). Twenty-five years of contrastive rhetoric: Text analysis and writing pedagogies. *TESOL Quarterly, 25*, 123–143.

Lummis, D., & Ikeda, M. (1985). *Nihonjinron no shinsō* [The reality of the uniqueness of the Japanese]. Tokyo: Haru Shobō.

Maynard, S. (1996). Presentation of one's view in Japanese newspaper columns: Commentary strategies and sequencing. *Text, 16*, 391–421.

McCagg, P. (1996). If you can lead a horse to water, you don't have to make it drink: Some comments on reader and writer responsibilities. *Multilingua, 15*, 239–256.

Minami, H. (1994). *Nihonjinron: Meiji kara konnichi made* [*Nihonjinron*: From Meiji to today]. Tokyo: Iwanami Shoten.

Ministry of Education. (1998a). *Gakushū shidō yōryō.* [Course of study]. Available online: http://www.mext.go.jp/b_menu/shuppan/sonota/990301.htm#top

Ministry of Education. (1998b). *Atarashii jidai o hiraku kokoro o sodateru tame ni: Jisedai o sodateru kokoro o ushinau kiki* [To cultivate a spirit for the new age: A crisis of losing the spirit to nurture the next generation]. Available online: http://www.mext.go.jp/b_menu/shingi/12/chuuou/toushin/980601.htm

Morioka, K. (1977). *Bunshō kōsei hō: Bunshō no shindan to chiryō* [Methods of text organization: Diagnoses and remedies of texts]. Tokyo: Shibundō.

Morioka, K. (Ed.). (1995). *Shinpan bunshō kōsei hō* [Methods of text organization: A new edition]. Tokyo: Tōkai Daigaku Shoppankai.

Morita, T. (1987). Rinkyōshin to "nihonbunkaron" [The Ad-Hoc Committee for Education Reform and "Japanese cultural studies"]. In Kyoto Education Center (Eds.), *"Nihonbunkaron" hihan to rinkyōshin* [Criticisms of "Japanese cultural studies" and the Ad-Hoc Committee for Education Reform] (pp. 74–93). Tokyo: Azumino Shobō.

Morita, T. (1988). *Rinkyōshin to Nihonjin, Nihonbunkaron* [The Ad-Hoc Committee for Education Reform and the studies on the Japanese people and culture]. Tokyo: Shin Nihon Shuppansha.

Morita, Y. (1998). *Nihonjin no hassō, Nihongo no hyōgen* [Thoughts of the Japanese people and expressions of the Japanese language]. Tokyo: Chūō Kōron Sha.

Mouer, R., & Sugimoto, Y. (1986). *Images of Japanese Society.* London: Kegan Paul International.

Mouer, R., & Sugimoto, Y. (1995). *Nihonjinron* at the end of the twentieth century: A multicultural perspective. In J. P. Arnason & Y. Sugimoto (Eds.), *Japanese encounters with postmodernity* (pp. 237–269). London: Kegan Paul International.

Nakajima, F. (1987). *Nihongo no kōzō: Eigo to no taihi* [The structures of Japanese: A comparison with English]. Tokyo: Iwanami Shoten.

Nakane, C. (1967). *Tate shakai no ningen kankei* [Human relations in vertical society]. Tokyo: Kōdansha.

Nakane, C. (1973). *Japanese society.* Harmondsworth, England: Penguin Books.

Nishida, T. (1987). *Jitsuyō Eigo no ronri* [The logic of practical English]. Fukuoka: Sekifūsha.

Nishimura, H. (1997). "Ronri teki na" hyōgen to "rojikaru na" hyōgen ["Ronri teki" expressions and "logical" expressions]. *Gengo* [Language], *26*, 3, 27–37.

Nomoto, K. (1978). *Nihonjin to Nihongo* [The Japanese people and language]. Tokyo: Chikuma Shobō.

Nozaki, K. (1988). Stilted English: *Nihonjin eigo no sutairu* [Stilted English: The style of English used by the Japanese]. *Gendai Eigo Kyōiku* [Modern English Teaching], *25*(5), 12–13.

Oi, M. K. (1984). *Cross-cultural differences in rhetorical patterning: A study of Japanese and English*. Unpublished doctoral dissertation, State University of New York at Stony Brook.

Okihara, K. (Ed.). (1985). *Eigo kyōikugaku monogurafu shirīzu: Eigo no raitingu* [English teaching monograph series: English Writing]. Tokyo: Taishūkan.

Ouchi, W. G. (1981). *Theory Z: How American business can meet the Japanese challenge*. Reading, MA: Addison-Wesley.

Said, E. W. (1978). *Orientalism*. New York: Pantheon Books.

Saisho, F. (1975). *Nihongo to Eigo: Hassō to hyōgen no hikaku* [Japanese and English: A comparison of thoughts and expressions]. Tokyo: Kenkyūsha.

Sanuki, H. (1997). Kyōiku ni okeru kachi sōtai shugi to "jiyū shugi shikan" [Value relativism in education and "liberalist view of history"]. In E. Matsushima & F. Shiromaru (Eds.), *"Jiyū shugi shikan" no byōri* [The pathology of a "liberalist view of history"] (pp. 250–267). Tokyo: Ōtsuki Shoten.

Sawada, A. (1977). *Ronbun no kakikata* [How to write academic papers]. Tokyo: Kōdansha.

Sawada, A. (1983). *Ronbun no retorikku* [The rhetoric of academic papers]. Tokyo: Kōdansha.

Shindo, M. (1988). "Kokusaika" ron no keifu: "Kokusaika" no kokunai kōzō o kangaeru [A history of "internationalization": Thoughts on domestic structures of "internationalization"]. *Sekai* [World], *513*(April), 58–64.

Spack, R. (1997). The acquisition of academic literacy in a second language: A longitudinal case study. *Written Communication, 14* (1), 3–62.

Sugimoto, Y., & Mouer, R. (1982). *Nihonjin wa "Nihonteki" ka* [Do the Japanese act like Japanese?]. Tokyo: Tōyō Keizai Shinpōsha.

Sugimoto, Y., & Mouer, R. (1989). Cross-currents in the study of Japanese society. In Y. Sugimoto & R. Mouer (Eds.), *Constructs for understanding Japan* (pp. 1–35). London: Kegan Paul International.

Suzuki, T. (1975). *Tozasareta gengo: Nihongo no sekai* [A closed language: The world of Japanese]. Tokyo: Shinchōsha.

Suzuki, T. (1987). *Kotoba no shakaigaku* [Sociology of language]. Tokyo: Shinchōsha.

Suzuki, T. (1995). *Nihongo wa kokusaigo ni nari uru ka* [Can Japanese become an international language?]. Tokyo: Kōdansha.

Takefuta, Y. (1982). *Nihonjin Eigo no kagaku: Sono genjō to asu e no tenbō* [Science of English used by the Japanese: The current use and future prospects]. Tokyo: Kenkyūsha.

Tanaka, K. (1993). *Kotoba no ekoroji: Gengo, minzoku, "kokusaika"* [Ecology of word: Language, ethnicity and "internationalization"]. Tokyo: Ningen Sensho.

Tenma, M. (1990). Eigo ga Nihongo o kaete iku [English is changing Japanese]. *Eigo Kyōiku* (The English Teachers' Magazine), *38*(13), 5.

Tobioka, K. (1999). *Nihonjin no mono no kangae kata: Sono ketten, jakuten, mazushisa*

[Japanese people's ways of thinking: Their flaws, weaknesses, and poverty]. Tokyo: Jitsumu Kyōiku Shuppan.

Toyama, S. (1973). *Nihongo no ronri* [The logic of Japanese]. Tokyo: Chūōkōronsha.

Ujiie, Y. (1996). *Gengo bunka gaku no shiite* [Perspectives of linguistic cultural studies]. Tokyo: Ōfū.

Umesao, T. (1988). *Nihongo to Nihon bunmei* [The Japanese language and civilization]. Tokyo: Kumon Shuppan.

Vogel, E. (1979). *Japan as number one: Lessons for America*. Cambridge, MA: Harvard University Press.

Watanabe, K. (1995). Wagakuni ni okeru gaikokugo (Eigo) ka kyōiku no genjō to kadai [The current status and issues in foreign language (English) education in Japan]. *Nihongogaku* [Japanese Language Studies], June 14, 66–73.

Watanabe, O. (1998). *Nihon to wa dō iu kuni ka, doko e mukatte iku no ka* [What is Japan and where is it going?]. Tokyo: Kyōiku Shiryō Shuppan Kai.

Yamaguchi, K. (1993). *Shin kyōiku katei to dōtoku kyōiku: "Kokusaika jidai" to Nihonjin no aidentiti.* [New curriculum and ethics education: "International age" and Japanese identity]. Tokyo: Eideru Kenkyūjo.

Yoshida, K. (1997). *Daigakuin sei to daigaku sei no tame no repōto, ronbun no kaki kata* [Report and thesis writing for graduate and undergraduate students]. Kyoko: Nakanishiya.

Yoshino, K. (1992). *Cultural nationalism in contemporary Japan*. London: Routledge.

Yoshino, K. (1997). *Bunka nashonarizumu no shakai gaku* [Sociology of cultural nationalism]. Nagoya: Nagoya Daigaku Shuppan Kai.

Chapter 17

Frames in American and Japanese Political Discourse[1]

Hiroko Furo

Based on a comparison of political discourse broadcast in the United States and in Japan, this chapter explores the disparate frames of discourse followed by American and Japanese politicians within their own respective countries. Analysis reveals that (1) the American politicians violate the ritual turn-taking sequence of political discourse more frequently than the Japanese politicians, and when they do so, the American politicians attack their opponents, or show disagreement directly, whereas the Japanese politicians, when they violate the turn-taking system, they assert themselves with linguistic politeness strategies; (2) the politicians also differ in the rhetorical structure—responses by American politicians to the moderator's critical questions often consist of three layers (a partial agreement, supporting evidence, and conclusion), whereas the Japanese politicians' responses consist of four parts (a start, development, change, and conclusion); and (3) an American politician moves to an emotional frame when the opponent does not play fairly while a Japanese politician does so when his "face" is threatened. These results indicate that expectations of political discourse differ between the two countries, in that Americans follow an agonistic schema, whereas the Japanese follow an irenic one.

As the closeness and importance of the bilateral relationship between the United States and Japan grow, interactions between American and Japanese politicians are viewed as crucial in determining the future relationship between the two countries. Communication between the two parties becomes important since it can increase or decrease the psychological distance between them. For example, there is a famous story about crosscultural miscommunication between U.S. President Richard Nixon and Japanese Prime Minister Eisaku Sato during the summit conference in 1969. President Nixon was concerned about the excessive amount of textile imports from Japan and proposed a limit on them to Prime Minister Sato. Prime Minister Sato reportedly answered, *Zensho shimasu* (I will try my best). Not knowing that this answer was an indirect way of saying "no" in Japanese, President Nixon over the next few weeks became furious at what he considered an unfulfilled promise and felt hostility toward Japan. This incident caused friction in the relationship between the two men and consequently between the two countries.[2]

There have been a great number of studies on differences in communication styles between American and Japanese politicians. For instance, Ishihara and Morita (1988) in their book, *Japan That Can Say "No,"* contend that Japanese politicians do not say "no" when they should. They also state that in American political debates, Americans "agree to disagree" and that Japanese politicians can become real political partners with American politicians only when they gain the courage to challenge them. Yamamoto (1993) claims that the negotiation style between Japanese and American politicians is different, and he encourages Japanese politicians not only to confront their American counterparts, but also to present their arguments logically. In this way, American politicians can understand what Japanese politicians are thinking and consequently address each other effectively. These discussions point out that there are differences in format, communication styles, and discourse strategies between American and Japanese politicians. These differences seem to result from the disparate expectations or frames in a speech event of political discourse between the two parties. Ong (1992) argues that the concept of "ritual combat" or "agonism" is prevalent in confrontational settings such as debate, whereas the contrasting term "irenicism" is used to refer to "ritual harmony." American politicians seem to follow an agonistic frame in political discourse while Japanese politicians follow an irenic frame. These opposing frames can cause miscommunication in crosscultural political negotiations.

Thus, this chapter explores disparate frames of American and Japanese politicians, using two political news interviews broadcast in the United States and Japan: an American political news interview from *Meet the Press,* and a Japanese political news interview from *Sunday Project.* Both segments were video recorded and transcribed to show linguistic features that signal distinct frames of the participants. The results of the analysis show the following findings. First, the American politicians violate the ritual turn-taking sequence of political news interviews more frequently than the Japanese politicians, and when they do so, the American politicians attack the opponents or show disagreement in a direct manner. On the other hand, when the Japanese politicians violate the turn-taking system, they assert themselves with linguistic politeness strategies. Second, responses of the American politicians to the moderator's criticizing questions often consist of three-layered structure (a partial agreement, supporting evidence, and conclusion) while those of the Japanese politicians have a rhetorical structure (a start, development, counter-argument, and conclusion). Third, an American politician moves to an emotional frame when the opponent does not play fairly while a Japanese politician does so when his "face" is threatened. These results indicate that the American politicians and Japanese politicians have different expectations in political discourse: the agonistic schema of the American politicians and the irenic schema of the Japanese politicians.

In this chapter, the first section reviews previous literature on frames theory, agonism in political discourse, and irenicism in Japanese communication. Next, American and Japanese political news interviews are analyzed, with focus on the violation of the ritual turn-taking system in institutional settings, the structure of politicians' responses to the moderators' criticizing questions, and the motives of a frame shift. Then, the frame differences in American and Japanese political discourse are discussed.

FRAME THEORY

The concept of "frame" has been discussed by various scholars, including Baston (1972), Goffman (1981), and Tannen (1993). According to Tannen and Wallat (1993), the term "frame" is used for two notions: interactive meta-message, called interactive frame ("frame" in this chapter) and structured expectation, called knowledge schema (hereafter, "schema"). These two concepts of frames, that is, "frame as interactive meta-message" and "frame as structured expectation" are worth reviewing.

The concept of "frame" in the category of "interactive meta-message" can be traced back to Baston (1972), who states that the abstract level of communication consists of meta-linguistic and meta-communicative signals. The meta-communicative signal or meta-message is what is called a "frame" in interaction. He presents an example of this "frame" in interaction among monkeys. When monkeys are playing, they are sending meta-communicative messages, signaling that "this is a play, not a combat," so they can enjoy playing while hitting each other. Goffman (1981) discusses the concept of frame by using the phrase "participants framework" (p. 157), which refers to "alignment" among participants in a speech event, that is, how each participant is aligned to each other and situated in inter-action. This interactive frame can shift depending on a moment-by-moment inter-action in a speech event. Tannen and Wallat (1993) define this frame as "a sense of what activity is being engaged in, how speakers mean what they say" (p. 60). Furthermore, Tannen (1984) regards this frame as "a superordinate message about how the communication is intended" (p. 23). We can observe and analyze frame as interactive meta-message by tracking the verbal and nonverbal signals that the participants send each other in a speech event. These signals show participants' alignment in interaction, and the participants have to interpret their interlocutor's signals correctly in order to avoid miscommunication.

The second category of frame is "frame as structured expectation (knowledge schema)." Tannen and Wallat (1993) define schema as "participants' expectation about people, objects, events and settings in the world, as distinguished from alignments being negotiated in a particular interaction" (p. 60). Tannen (1993) also discusses this kind of frame, comparing the different expectations held by Americans and Greeks for a film viewed in an experiment. She reports that Americans consider themselves "film viewers," whereas Greeks "film interpreters." She further points out that people from different cultures have different expectations in a speech event. Markus and Tanter (1972) argue that the discrepancy between expectation and reality is the biggest cause of interpersonal conflict. Therefore, because people from different cultures structure their expectations differently, and because conflicts can result from the mismatch between expectation and reality, conflicts can occur more frequently in crosscultural communication.

There is an interactive relationship between the two frames, the interactive frame and knowledge schema. Tannen and Wallat (1993) present an instance in which a mismatch in schemas triggers frame shifts. They discuss the dialogs in which a pediatrician is examining a cerebral palsied child. The mismatched schemas between the pediatrician and the child's mother make the pediatrician shift her frames among three interactive frames: a frame to examine the child, a frame to consult with the mother, and a frame to report the examination findings to the video audience. In sum, the concept of frame has two categories: frame as an interactive frame and schema as a structured expectation. Mismatched schemas in participants as well as the incorrect interpreting of an interlocutor's frames can create unintentional miscommunication.

AGONISM IN POLITICAL DISCOURSE

This section explores three agonistic characteristics related to political discourse: combative, ritualistic, and contest-like. Ong (1992) explains the origin of the term "agonism" by saying that it comes from the Greek word, *agōnia:*

agōnia is pretty well the ancient Greek word for what we mean by "contest" in English. It comes from the Greek *agōn,* which means an assembly, an arena, an action at law, a contest, and which in turn comes from *agein,* meaning to lead, bring, drive, weigh, celebrate (a festival or the like). . . . The assembly came together to debate, to match pros and cons, to struggle, not fatally, but seriously and in dead earnest, man against man. . . . Contest can be ceremonial. (pp. 43–44)

Ong uses the term agonism to refer to "ritual combat," which includes three characteristics, that is, combative, ritualistic, and contest-like.

Political discourse can be one of the agonistic situations where verbal combat is carried out ritualistically. It is combative, ritualistic, and contest-like. First, political discourse is combative, having a militant nature, relating to muscular-

ity. This combative characteristic traces back to "the Socratic dialogues reconstructed by Plato" (Ong, 1992, p. 125), in which people fought verbally in order
to win arguments. This traditional way of verbal fighting bloomed in the
medieval era in European history. Nobel (1992) states that after the long period
of wars, young scholars in academic institutions worked off their energy by fighting verbally in the form of debate, that is, verbal fight had replaced physical war.
Arguments are used to attack, ruin, and/or refute the other party's arguments.
Debate is a competition between two opposing parties, which form polarity and
dichotomy. This format is what Ong (1992) calls "adversative paradigms" (p.
116). There are two opposing parties involved as participants in debate, who have
different opinions. What they claim is not necessarily what they actually believe,
in analogy to a soldier fighting for what he may not believe. In addition, the purpose of the debate is to win, so the result is either win or lose with possible humil-
iation. Tannen (1998) discusses the argument culture in the United States as the
result of this tradition and states that the loser of debate "usually attribute[s] that
loss to poor performance or to an adversary's unfair tactics" (p. 274). Therefore,
the claim by the winner does not necessarily have to be right. The eloquence and
prowess, not the truthfulness, is the key to victory.

Second, just as agonism is ritualistic, so is political discourse. Political discourse is usually held in a ritualistic setting, where there are rules for the participants to follow. For example, in political news interviews, a moderator leads the
interviews and controls the turn allocation (Greatbatch, 1992). Another example
of ritualistic characteristics in political discourse is the argument structure. As
Kruger (1960) points out, an argument generally consists of two parts, a proposition and its supporting evidence. This argument structure is ritualistic in a sense
that it is generally carried out. These ritualistic aspects of argument result from
the fact that agonism has a game-like nature, and the participants share the common rules to follow, in a sense, fighting collaboratively. For example, their argument in debate must relate to the previous argument, so that there is interaction
between the two opposing parties. Also, because political discourse is ritualistic,
emotional comments are necessarily discouraged. It is a ritual, intellectual game,
where logic is highly valued and emotion is scorned. Violation of rules by being
emotional is not considered good manners.

Third, agonism is a contest, which Ong (1992) refers to as "a confrontation by
witnesses" (p. 98). A third party, say, the audience in mass media, observes the
contest as a witness or judge. Victory or loss is judged by the third party. Thus,
participants in political discourse have to pay attention to how they are viewed
by the third party. For example, in political news interviews, the participants
often ignore or dodge the moderator's questions, so that they can present their
proposition in a most appealing way to the third party, who enjoys the verbal
fight as a kind of entertainment. In other words, the contest-like characteristic of
argument includes elements of show or entertainment, which may contribute to
the participants' eloquence and prowess, as well as aggressiveness. In addition,

the verbal fight is a face-to-face, impromptu interaction between the participants; thus it rarely occurs in written form, as Ong (1992) argues that "words are essentially an oral event" (p. 26). Since written form of communication does not have the same elements of contest, agonism in the sense of ritual combat can rarely occur in written form.[3]

IRENICISM IN JAPANESE COMMUNICATION

The term "irenicism" is used to refer to "ritual harmony" (Ong, 1992), contrasting it with agonism. One of the societies that puts high value on irenicism is Japan, where harmony is the emphasis in interpersonal relationships (c.f. Yamada, 1992). We can find at least three cultural elements in Japanese society that provide the background for irenicism: the Confucian influence, the hierarchical structure in interpersonal relationships, and *amae* of psychological dependency among Japanese people.

First, irenicism in Japanese society results from the Confucian influence that emphasizes social harmony. Yum (1988) discusses the influence of Confucianism in East Asian countries, including Japan. She states that the four main principles of Confuciansm are "humanism, faithfulness, propriety, and wisdom" (p. 177). These principles influence the interpersonal relationships of East Asian countries, where social relationships are highly valued (vs. individualism in North America). The focus on social relationship is reflected in a harmonious communication pattern, such as preserving one another's face and indirect communication, as found in the East Asian countries, especially Japan (cf. Hirokawa, 1987).

Second, irenicism of Japanese society results from the hierarchical structure of interpersonal relationships in Japanese society. Nakane (1967) claims that Japanese society is structured hierarchically and that Japanese people are very conscious of their relative positions in the society. Because interpersonal relationships in Japanese society are hierarchically structured and because Japanese society exerts a strong pressure to conform to the norm (Nakane, 1967), it is considered rude to disagree directly with superiors, colleagues, or even with subordinates. Japanese people think that they must refrain from disagreeing because it may disrupt the hierarchy. Nakane (1967) presents an example of this disagreement avoidance in academic conferences where superiors and their subordinates participate. In these conferences, they can neither logically argue about their ideas nor even present their own ideas for fear of being seen as a rebel, who disorders the established hierarchy in the group. This phenomenon of disagreement avoidance in Japan sharply contrasts with the tradition of argumentative Socratic dialogue in Western academia.

Third, irenicism of Japanese society results from the psychological dependency on others among Japanese people. This interdependency among the Japanese is called *amae* (Doi, 1972), which is translated in English as "the tendency to presume upon another adult" (p. 18). Presenting an example, Doi quotes Caudill and

Weinstein's (1969) comparative study of the mother and infant relationships among Japanese and Americans. This study concludes that Japanese infants learn a nonverbal and passive communication pattern by the time they reach 3–4 months old. In other words, Japanese people are habituated to expect others to understand them without much explanation or verbal interaction, so that they grow up less unaccustomed to outspokenness and disinclined to confront others verbally. Doi also explains Japanese people's tendency in avoiding "no" as follows.

Unanimous agreement is a very important social function for the Japanese. It is a token that the mutuality of all the members has been preserved. In other words, it is a token satisfaction of *amae*. The Japanese hate to contradict or to be contradicted—that is, to have to say "No" in the conversation. They simply don't want to have divided opinions in the first place, for if such an outcome appears to be inevitable, they will get so heated emotionally that it becomes almost impossible to continue reasoned discussion among themselves. (1972, p. 22)

People of *amae* tend to put high value on agreement with others because they have a tendency to depend on others psychologically. This tendency results in the harmonious communication pattern of the Japanese.

So far three characteristics of Japanese society, the Confucian influence, the hierarchical structure in interpersonal relationships, and *amae* among the Japanese have been discussed. These characteristics are the bases of the harmonious communication pattern among the Japanese people. We see these harmonious characteristics in actual communication in Japanese society. However, their conflict-avoidance strategies could be harmonious only at the surface level. They avoid direct confrontation by not saying a direct "no" and by using linguistic politeness strategies. In shunning direct confrontation, the strategies used in conflicts are subtle. For example, Lebra (1984) discusses the behavioral norm of nonconfrontational strategies in interpersonal conflicts in Japan. She presents seven behavioral strategies that Japanese people employ when they are involved in discord: anticipatory management, negative communication, situation code-switching, triadic management, displacement, self-aggression, and acceptance. The common feature in these strategies is subtle conflict avoidance. Two parties in conflict seem to agree to preserve harmonious relationship on the surface, and thus outsiders cannot see the conflict at first sight. Japanese behavioral strategies of interpersonal conflict management are oriented toward the nonconfrontational and harmonious, at least, on the surface.

Also, Japanese people try to avoid saying "no" even when they have to. There are highly conventionalized ways to avoid saying "no" in Japanese. Ueda (1972) discusses linguistic strategies of conflict management in Japanese in her chapter, "Sixteen Ways to Avoid Saying 'No' in Japan." She claims that the Japanese think about others' feelings and therefore avoid direct expressions to hurt others' feelings. Namely, the Japanese avoid a direct "no" because it sounds too informal and straightforward. She then presents 16 expressions that are used conventionally to mean "no" in Japanese. These expressions are more likely used in formal settings since the avoidance of "no" functions primarily in formal hierarchical relationships where face-saving is of great concern. Therefore, these strategies make the Japanese interpersonal communication harmonious, at least on the surface, especially in formal situations.

In addition, the Japanese use linguistic politeness strategies as conflict-avoidance strategies. Park (1990) discusses these linguistic politeness strategies with examples, such that Japanese people do not use the second-person pronoun "you," which sounds impolite in Japanese. They use a number of hedges as well as honorifics to maintain the hierarchical structure in interpersonal relationships even in conflicting situations. Thus, the politeness of the Japanese is due to their various linguistic politeness strategies that serve as conflict-avoidance strategies.

We can infer from these discussions that the Japanese have highly conventionalized strategies to avoid direct confrontation. These strategies are used almost ritualistically to maintain harmony on the surface in Japanese society. However, this harmony does not correlate straightforwardly with the underlying feeling of the speaker. Matsumoto (1988) discusses the discrepancies between superficial realization of interaction and underlying principle of human behavior, saying, "one must be aware that the same underlying principle may produce superficial differences, but one must equally be aware that superficial similarity can result from different underlying principles" (p. 404).

In sum, the Confucian influence, the hierarchical structure in interpersonal relationships, and *amàe* can result in ritualistic conflict-avoidance strategies and linguistic politeness to maintain harmony in interpersonal relationships, at least superficially, in Japan. This ritual harmony as a conflict-avoidance strategy may be one of the instances of irenicism. The question remains: How can the concept of irenicism be maintained in an agonistic situation such as political discourse? In the following section, American and Japanese political news interviews are analyzed, and interactional frames in each culture as well as agonistic and irenic schemas in the United States and Japan are examined comparatively.

ANALYSIS

This study employs two types of discourse derived from American and Japanese political news interview programs on television. Several hours of political news interview programs were randomly video recorded both in the United States and in Japan, and one TV program from each country was selected for this study. Selection was based on the comparability of the American and Japanese programs in terms of format, participants, and topics. Then, one interview from each program had been selected for this study, in which each interview follows a similar format: the interview situation and discussion of controversial issues.[4] In each of the two interviews, a moderator asked questions to two guest politicians who had opposing ideas about political and economic issues. All the participants in both interviews were male.

The American interview came from *Meet the Press,* aired every Sunday morning on one of the biggest TV networks in the United States. In the selected segment, the Republican national chairman, Haley Barbour, and the Democratic national chairman, Don Fowler, debate about the issues for the upcoming 1996 presidential election. The moderator, who leads the interview, is Stone Phillips, who is joined by two panelists, Robert Novack and Albert Hunt, in interviewing the chairmen.

The Japanese interview was taken from *Sunday Project,* also aired every Sunday morning in Japan on one of the biggest TV networks there.[5] In this segment, two candidates for leadership of the Liberal Democrat Party (LDP) discuss Japanese economic policy. This version of the program was recorded a few weeks before the election for the LDP leadership. The two candidates are Ryutaro Hashimoto and Junichiro Koizumi, interviewed by the moderator, Souichirou Tawara. Hashimoto is older and a more experienced politician, so Koizumi is considered the challenger in this campaign.

Violation of Turn-Taking System

Quantitative Analysis

Greatbatch (1992) states that the turn-taking system in news interviews proceeds according to the framework of institutional roles of interviewers and interviewees. Namely, an interviewer asks questions and interviewees respond to them, but not necessarily answer them since interviewees can avoid answering the questions (cf. Bull & Mayer, 1993; Harris, 1992). When responding to the questions, they often violate the institutional turn-taking system, especially when showing disagreement with their interlocutors. Greatbatch (1992) presents four kinds of turn-taking sequences that a guest interviewee takes in interview programs:

1. An interviewee responds to the interviewer's question, the ritual turn-taking sequence,

2. An interviewee responds in the middle of the interviewer's question,

3. An interviewee responds after a co-interviewee's turn, and

4. An interviewee responds in the middle of a co-interviewee's response.

The interview segments that this study examines also includes these four kinds of interviewees' turn-taking patterns. The following section presents these four turn-taking patterns with examples.

The first type of interviewees' turn-taking pattern is a smooth turn-transition from the moderator to an interviewee without any overlap or interruption. The following excerpt shows the sequence that Phillips, the moderator, asks Barbour,

Republican national chairman, about the result of the straw poll in Iowa in line 1. Responding to Phillips's question, Barbour starts responding in line 2. (See Appendix A for a list of transcription conventions.)

Excerpt 1: moderator to interviewee

    1 Phillips: But both Dole and Gramm took this seriously, didn't they?
—>2 Barbour: They all did, it is a test of organizational strength. . . .

In this sequence, Barbour starts responding in line 2 without any overlap. This is an example of smooth turn-transition from a moderator to an interviewee. Both the American and Japanese political news interviews start with this type of turn-taking sequence, therefore, we can consider this type the ritual turn-taking pattern in political news interviews.

The second type of interviewees' turn-taking pattern involves interruption or overlap with the moderator, as shown in Excerpt 2 below. Fowler, an interviewee, starts his response in line 2 before Phillips, the moderator, is finished in line 1. In the sequence, the participants talk about Bill Bradley leaving the Democratic Party and its impact on the Democratic Party.

Excerpt 2: interviewee interruption of moderator

    1 Phillips: Well he hasn't left the party yet but <he's certainly in the door.
—>2 Fowler: <He wants to continue to be a player
                   and that's one way to make himself a player.

In Excerpt 2, responding to Fowler's comment on Bill Bradley leaving the party, Phillips starts his utterance in line 1. In line 2, Fowler starts his utterance in the middle of Phillips's utterance, resulting in an overlap. This is the second type of interviewee turn-taking pattern, an interviewee starting in the middle of the moderator's turn.

The third type of interviewees' turn-taking pattern in political news interviews is an interviewee responding to the other interviewee. Although this type of turn-taking sequence is smoothly implemented without overlap or interruption, the interviewees respond to each other's comments, ignoring the moderator. The following is an excerpt of an instance of one interviewee starting after the other interviewee's comment; that is, in line 5, Fowler responds to Barbour. In the sequence, the participants discuss the opinion poll for the 1996 presidential election.

Excerpt 3: interviewee to the other interviewee

    1 Phillips: Does this-<does this put some pressure on Bob Dole?
    2 Fowler: <It's a pretty clear indication too I think.
    3   (pause)

4 Barbour: I'm sorry?

->5 Fowler: Does it put pressure on Bob Dole?

In line 1, Phillips, the moderator, poses a question to Barbour. However, Fowler overlaps with him in line 2. Because of the overlap, Barbour is unable to hear the question, indicating this by his words "I'm sorry" in line 4. Fowler, however, goes ahead and repeats the question in place of the moderator in line 5.

The fourth type of interviewees' turn-taking pattern is an interviewee interrupting or overlapping with the other interviewee. In the following excerpt, Fowler overlaps with Barbour in line 3. In the excerpt, the participants discuss Medicare reform.

Excerpt 4: interviewee to the other interviewee with interruption

1 Barbour: . . . that is a step in the right direction, but <it's not enough to meet the standard.

->2 Fowler: <I want to say something, that's the wrong figure.

While Barbour answers the moderator's question in line 1, Fowler overlaps with Barbour in line 2. This is the fourth type of interviewees' turn-taking pattern in political news interviews; an interviewee interrupts or overlaps with the other interviewee.

Based on the categorization of the four types mentioned above, the interviewees' turn-taking patterns in the interview segments of this study are quantitatively examined. The quantitative analysis focuses on the most argumentative segment in each political news interview (PNI), each of which lasts approximately 15 minutes. Table 17-1 shows the number of each type of interviewees' turn-taking patterns. The number in parentheses indicates the percentage of the four types of turn-taking patterns in each interview segment.

Table 17-1
Frequency of Turn-Taking Patterns

Turn-Taking Sequences	U.S. PNI	Japanese PNI
Moderator to interviewee	16 (25.0%)	44 (80.0%)
Interviewee interrupts moderator	35 (55.7%)	1 (1.8%)
Interviewee to interviewee	1 (1.6%)	5 (9.1%)
Interviewee interrupts interviewee	12 (18.8%)	5 (9.1%)
Total	64 (100%)	55 (100%)

Table 17-1 shows that the Japanese political interviewees follow the ritual ideal of turn-taking in political news interviews at the high rate of 80%; whereas the same pattern occurred for only 25% of American turn-taking, indicating the Americans had much more violations of the ideal model for political news interviews. Furthermore, the American political guests frequently interrupt both the moderator and the other interviewee (73.5%), something the Japanese politicians rarely do (10.9%). We can infer from these results that the U.S. political news interviews are more agonistic, showing the politicians' aggressiveness while the Japanese political news interviews are more irenic, with the political guests maintaining an orderly turn-taking at a high rate.

Qualitative Analysis

A quantitative analysis on turn-taking in political news interviews has shown a major difference between the Japanese and U.S. interviewees: whereas U.S. interviewees violate the turn-taking system on 75% of their turns, the Japanese interviewees do so on only 20% of their turns. In addition to the frequency of turn-taking violations, the ways in which they do so differ in the American and Japanese political news interviews. This section examines how the American and Japanese politicians violate the turn-taking system.

When the American politicians violate the canonical turn-taking patterns, they present their argument in a direct manner or attack the co-interviewee with few softening devices. The following sequence is a typical example of the U.S. politicians violating the turn-taking system. The excerpt takes place after a panelist, Novack, asks a question of the Republican national chairman, Barbour, about a Medicare plan. Barbour and Fowler overlap with each other after line 15.

Excerpt 5: violation of turn-taking pattern

1 Novack: Chairman Barbour er- Chairman Barbour er- the criticism I hear of the Republicans is that you don't even have a plan yet. Why- why are the Republicans so late in putting out a plan?

4 Barbour: Bob, what we're talking about here is saving Medicare from bankruptcy, it's very important. It's the Clinton administration, that announced in April, Medicare will be bankrupt in seven years, and Republicans are not going to let Medicare go bankrupt.

8   (*pause*)

9   We held 39 public hearings on Medicare, and our members of Congress and senators are spending the August recess going to their constituents and saying, "Here are the things that have been recommended to save Medicare from bankruptcy." The good news is Medicare is-

13 Fowler: Boy <I'll tell you what giving Medicare to the Republicans- yeah.

->14 Barbour: <I'll tell you what Don I'll let you talk when it's your turn to talk, and if you want to interrupt, that's your manners or your business. But when I get through you can talk.

17 Hunt: Chairman Bar <bour let me ask you-

—>18 Fowler: <Well I want to have something to <say about that.

—>19 Barbour: <The fact of the matter
            is Medicare spending is <going to go up to $4,800 to $6,734.

—>21 Fowler: <I want to have something to say about that.

Fowler's interrupting comment in line 13, "Boy I'll tell you what giving Medicare to the Republicans- yeah," functions to sarcastically attack the Republicans, making fun of their ability to make a plan on Medicare in a timely manner. Then, Barbour overlaps with Fowler in line 14, scolding Fowler for his interruption. In lines 18 and 21, Fowler tries to take a turn, resulting in Barbour and Fowler overlapping with each other.

In the Japanese political news interviews, on the other hand, violation of the regular turn-taking pattern is carried out more irenically with various softening devices. The following excerpt is one of the most aggressive instances of over-lapping in the Japanese interview. Hashimoto overlaps with Koizumi in line 6. Preceding Hashimoto's utterance, the moderator, Tawara, asks a question of Koizumi about an abuse in the postal system. (See Appendix B for a list of abbre-viations used in Japanese transcription.)

Excerpt 6: interruption

  1 Tawara: *chotto honto desu ka*

            little   true   be   Q

  2 Koizumi: *honto desu.*

            true   be

  3 Tawara: *sono ranmyaku tte   iuno   wa?*

            that abuse   QT   about TP

  4 Koizumi: *sorya ranmyakumo hidoi   desu.*

            oh   abuse   terrible be

—>5   *dakara <mesu   wo   irenakyaikan.*

            so   operate OM must

—>6 Hashimoto: *<chotto sore wa watashi wa iisugi   da to   omoimasu.*

                  little   that TP I   TP exaggeration   be QM think

[Translation]

  1 Tawara: Is it true?

  2 Koizumi: It's true.

  3 Tawara: They are abusing the system?

  4 Koizumi: It is a terrible abuse of the system.

—>5   That is <why we have to change the system.

—>6 Hashimoto: <I think that's a little bit of an exaggeration.

Regarding the violation of the turn-taking system in the Japanese interview, there are two points that show Japanese irenicism in Hashimoto's overlapping comment in line 6, "I think it's a little bit of an exaggeration." First, Hashimoto shows disagreement with the way in which Koizumi responds to the moderator's question by saying that it was an exaggeration, but Hashimoto does not completely deny Koizumi's point. In other words, Hashimoto does not attack Koizumi nor his point, but attacks how Koizumi spoke about the postal system. Second, Hashimoto's overlapping comment, "*Chotto sorewa iisugi dato omoimasu*" (I think it's a little bit of an exaggeration), has four mitigating or linguistic politeness devices:

1. *Chotto* (little) is a mitigating strategy to downgrade the aggressiveness of the comment.
2. *Watashi* (I) is used by Hashimoto to refer to himself. According to Ide (1982), *watashi* in Japanese men's language is considered a formal form.[6] Hashimoto uses *watashi*, which is a formal usage of the first-person pronoun in Japanese, in the overlapping and disagreeing comment in line 6.
3. *Omoimasu* (I think) is another mitigating device, a hedge to make the comment less aggressive.
4. The *masu* verb-ending is a form of politeness in Japanese. The participants in the interview segment do not always use polite verb endings, as we can see in line 5 of Koizumi's comment that ends with *ikan*, which is a casual form of negative imperative *ikenai*.

Hashimoto does not abandon the use of the polite verb-ending *masu* even when he expresses his disagreement in line 6. Thus, these four linguistic politeness strategies in Hashimoto's disagreeing comment can be viewed as an indicator of irenicism in an agonistic setting of Japanese political news interviews. Even when the Japanese politicians disagree with the other interviewee and violate the turn-taking system of political news interviews, they employ various politeness strategies to mitigate the force of conflicts.

In sum, the quantitative analysis of the violation of the turn-taking system shows that the American politicians violate the ritual turn-taking system more frequently than the Japanese politicians. The qualitative analysis shows that when violating the ritual turn-taking system, the American politicians attack the opponent or disagree with him in a direct way while the Japanese politicians show disagreement with various mitigating and linguistic politeness strategies. These differences between the American and Japanese politicians indicate that the American politicians are combative while the Japanese politicians are harmonious in taking turns in the political news interviews.

Structure of Responses

In this section, the structure of politicians' responses in the American and Japanese political news interviews is analyzed and compared. The analysis shows that the American politicians' responses often consist of a partial agreement, evidence, and conclusion whereas the Japanese politicians often use responses that consist of a start, development, counter-argument, and conclusion, which is a rhetorical structure in Japanese. While the moderator's questions can be categorized into information-eliciting questions and criticizing questions, the analysis in this section focuses on the politicians' responses to moderators' criticizing questions. The reason is that sharp criticizing questions are a way for the moderators to attack the interviewees in order to elicit more information or to stir up the debate, and thus is more agonistic.

The American politicians' responses to the moderator's criticizing questions often consist of partial agreement with the moderator's previous comment and an independent argument with evidence and conclusion. The following excerpt includes a question from the moderator, Phillips, asking Fowler, the national Democratic chairman, about the damage created by Bill Bradley leaving the Democrat Party, and Fowler's response to the question.

Excerpt 7: responses to criticizing questions

1 Phillips:	Mr. Fowler, let's turn to your party for moment, and the story about Bill Bradley, always a bit of a loner, but a team player loyal to his teams both in politics and in basketball. But this past week he delivered a rather serious blow to your party.
5	<Assess the damage.
6 Fowler:	<Bill Bradley is one of the finest members of the United States Senate. He's made a great contribution, not only to the Democratic Party but to the United States Senate, and we'll miss his service there. But let me point out, that Bill Bradley has been concerned about the same kind of central issues that have concerned President Clinton: education, health care, tax reform, making government work better. Bill Clinton and- and Bill Bradley are together.

Phillips's question consists of three parts:

1. A comment about Bill Bradley that he is somewhat a "loner" but still loyal to his party;
2. The "fact" that he will leave the Democrat Party; and
3. A directive asking Fowler to "assess the damage."

Phillips's directive, "Assess the damage," is agonistic for two reasons. First, his directive is used without any linguistic politeness strategy to mitigate its face-threatening force. Second, the directive presupposes that the Democratic Party has been damaged by Bradley's leaving. If Fowler were to assess the damage within this formulation, Fowler would end up admitting that the Democrat Party was indeed damaged by Bradley's action. If Fowler did not assess the damage, however, he would not be cooperating with the moderator, Phillips, and would therefore be viewed as an uncooperative participant.

Fowler instead counters with a contrary proposition that Bradley and Clinton are together. He does so by using a three-layered structure in his response that includes

1. Praise for Bradley,

2. Evidence of Clinton and Bradley being concerned about the same issues, and

3. The statement that they are together.

At the same time, Fowler acts as a cooperative participant by keeping to the topic initiated by Phillips and expanding a good point made by Phillips about Bradley. This compliment appeals to not only Bradley, but also to his supporters, who might be watching this program. This compliment also functions as praise of the Democratic Party for which Bradley has been working. Any praise for Bradley is also praise for his party, making the party look good. Fowler goes on to dodge Phillips's presumption by his counter-argument of "evidence," and his conclusion that "Clinton and Bradley are together." This conclusion emphasizes a positive aspect of the Democratic Party, that is, collaboration. In the end, Fowler ignores Phillips's directive to "assess the damage" and instead changes the focus about Bradley from negative to positive. This kind of response structure is often used by American politicians to present their own argument and thereby put themselves in a good light.

In contrast, the Japanese politicians often use a four-layered structure of responses. This structure functions as equivocation as a conflict-avoidance strategy. The following excerpt is a sequence of the moderator, Tawara, who challenges an interviewee, Hashimoto, about an economic plan by the government. In the sequence, Hashimoto's response consists of four parts:

1. A direct response to the question, "There is no single best plan" in line 8,

2. An example about a well-worked economic plan in lines 8–14,

3. Another example about a Japanese economic plan in lines 14–24, and

4. The conclusion in line 25.

Excerpt 8: responses to criticizing questions

1 Tawara:	Well if you say so, I would like to ask you a specific question. Well so far,
2	the Murayama Administration, the Murayama Cabinet, has been propos-
3	ing various economic plans. But the situations have not improved at all.
4	The government has already stopped using the word "recovery." The situ-
5	ations have not improved at all. In order to improve the situations, in other
6	words, Mr. Hashimoto, there are various economic plans but we don't
7	understand them. What's the most important plan?
8 Hashimoto:	There is no single plan that cures everything. However, for example,
9	on August 2nd, the Ministry of Finance proposed the promotion plan
10	for the foreign investment loan. In fact this is, from the end of last year

11	till this April- (*pause*) February, what we had been asking the Ministry
12	of Finance to do. The announcement was well timed, and they inter-
13	vened the foreign exchange skillfully by cooperating with the United
14	States, the money exchange rate has been improving by now. On the
15	other hand, when we investigated the small business industry in Japan,
16	last July, we found out that, the profit point in exporting was 113 yen.
17	When the exchange rate was rising this March, we found out that the
18	profit point moved back to 110 yen then. But that was when the small
19	business industry was in discouraged mood. When we investigated it
20	once again on August 29th, the profit point moved further back to 108
21	yen. I admire the power of the small business industry, but, that's not
22	it. The number of bankruptcies still outnumbers that of starting busi-
23	ness. We have to propose plans for those who are starting new busi-
24	ness, we have to prepare the funds for them, too. There are many
25	things that should be done. There is no single plan that cures everything.

Hashimoto's response to Tawara's question forms the four-layered structure, which is parallel to the structure of a Japanese rhetoric. According to Takemata (1976), a rhetorical structure that consists of four parts of *ki* (start), *shō* (development), *ten* (change/counter-argument), and *ketsu* (conclusion) is prevalent in Japanese writing.[7] In the excerpt above, Hashimoto starts with a direct response to the moderator's question, by saying, "There is no single plan that cures everything." This proposition functions as a start that bridges Tawara's question and Hashimoto's response. Next, Hashimoto introduces a story about a well-working economic plan, starting with *tatoeba* (for example), which indicates an upcoming topic shift. This story serves as "development" of the direct answer to the moderator's question. Then, he introduces another example of a struggling economic plan with a discourse marker, *ippoude* (on the other hand), which indicates that the topic is about to change. This example, contradicting the previous example, functions as counter-argument. Finally, he repeats the proposition, "There is no single plan that cures everything." This repeated proposition functions as the conclusion of his response, as well as the link to the start, providing his response with consistency.

In contrast with the three-layered structure in the American politicians' responses, this four-layered structure is equivocal and potentially ambiguous. This structure can function as a conflict-avoidance strategy that hinders an intense argument for two reasons. First, because it has the four parts that are tangentially connected, not by a topic but by the rhetorical structure, we find it difficult to identify the point in the response, which the opponent can attack. Second, the four-layered structure includes counter-argument, which makes the responses inclusive and thus functions as a conflict avoidance strategy. Watanabe (1993) claims that in an argument, the Japanese include a contradictory account not in order to weaken the argument, but to reinforce it by demonstrating the speaker's wholistic perspective. She states as follows:

In order to make a conclusion as inclusive as possible, hence, perfect, from the Japanese standpoint, they include a contradictory account in advance. To exclude a contradictory account suggests that one is being neglectful of a weak point and one may be attacked on it. Thus, to be inclusive is, in a sense, a defensive way to present one's argument. (pp. 201–202)

Therefore, the four-layered structure of the Japanese politicians' responses functions as a conflict-avoidance strategy because it equivocates by including the contradicting point that makes the response wholistic. In sum, the American politicians often use the three-layered structure in their responses while the Japanese politicians use the four-layered structure of rhetoric. The three-layered structure in the American politicians' responses shifts the topic and presents their own arguments logically while the four-layered structure in the Japanese politicians' responses makes the responses equivocal and then works as a conflict-avoidance strategy.

Fairness versus Face

As the discussion becomes heated in the political news interviews, the ritualistic norm of logical argument is abandoned, and the participants move to an emotional frame (frame shift from ritual to emotional). In other words, the participants in the political news interviews shift their interactive frames from "ritual combat" to "real combat" and begin to express their negative emotions openly. We can see this kind of frame shift by paralinguistic features such as raised tone of voice as well as nonlinguistic features such as facial expression and gesture. Although this type of frame shift occurs in both American and Japanese interviews, the motivation that triggers the frame shift seems to differ. Namely, the frame shifting is motivated by the concept of "fairness" in the American political news interviews while the concept of "face" plays the important role in the frame shift of the Japanese politicians. In other words, an American politician shows emotion when the opponent plays unfairly while a Japanese politician does so when his face is threatened.

For an example of a frame shift in the U.S. political news interviews, we saw in Excerpt 5 how Fowler abruptly interrupted Barbour in line 13, violating the turn-taking system of interview or discussion settings. While the panelists, Robert Novack and Albert Hunt, ask Barbour about a Medicare plan, Barbour emotionally shouts to Fowler in lines 14–16 after being abruptly interrupted by Fowler. In other words, Fowler played unfairly by doing so. Then, Barbour replied in a raised tone of voice showing that he had moved to an emotional frame. In these lines, he promised that he would not interrupt and admonished Fowler for doing so. He further ordered Fowler to cease. In other words, Barbour promised to play fairly if Fowler did, too. Therefore, Barbour's frame shifting seemed to be motivated by the concept of fairness, a matter Americans are well conscious of in interpersonal relationships (Yamamoto, 1993). This instance shows that unfair treatment can disrupt "ritual combat" or logical argument and eventuate emotional display in the American political discourse.

In the Japanese case, a Japanese politician moves to an emotional frame motivated by the concept of face. Let's take a look at an excerpt with this kind of instance. In the excerpt, Hashimoto shows strong emotion after Koizumi teased him and the audience laughed at him.

Excerpt 9: frame shift

1 Hashimoto:	But Koizumi said that the privatization of the three postal businesses
2	was good. I don't agree with that kind of strategy.
3 Koizumi:	That [Hashimoto's voicing his opinion on the reform] is great
4	progress, compared with the former politicians in the LD Party.
5 Hashimoto:	No, no.
6	(*Audience laughter*)
7 Hashimoto:	That's what I have been saying for a long time.
8 Koizumi:	It was an unthinkable thing [for an LD Party politician to voice his
9	opinion]. The politicians in the LD Party were not able to say the
10	things like that.
11 Tawara:	We will pause for a commercial break.
12 Hashimoto:	It's strange.
13	I have been saying that for a long time.

Koizumi mentioned previously in the interview that it has been considered a taboo for the LDP politicians to talk about postal reform. So after Hashimoto expresses his opinions on the postal reform, Koizumi makes a sarcastic comment that compliments Hashimoto's courage in voicing his own opinion about the postal reform although it is against Koizumi's idea. Responding to Koizumi's sarcastic comment, the audience bursts into laughter in line 6. Then, Hashimoto becomes emotional, "No, no. That's what I have been saying for a long time." In other words, Hashimoto moves to an emotional frame, with his tone of voice raised. At this moment, his normally smiling face changes to a grimace. Even after the moderator cues for a commercial break, Hashimoto continues talking in lines 12–13, protesting against Koizumi's sarcastic comment. We can infer that Hashimoto moves to an emotional stance because Koizumi teases him and because his face is threatened by the audience laughing at him. Hirokawa (1987) claims that the Japanese are very sensitive about the concept of face and avoid by any means "loss of face" of not only the speaker but also that of an interlocutor. Shillony (1973) also claims that Japanese people are conscious about face in interpersonal relationships even in a conflict situation. Hashimoto may be offended by being teased and laughed at in the contest situation with a big live audience as well as TV viewers, so he breaks the ritualistic nonemotional frame of political news interviews and moves to an emotional frame. Clearly Hashimoto's frame shift seems to be motivated by the concept of face.

In sum, both American and Japanese politicians may at times move to an emotional frame in political discourse. However, the motives of the frame shifting by the American politician and the Japanese politician differ: the American politician moves to an emotional frame when the opponent plays unfairly, while the Japanese politician does so when his face is threatened. These different motives of frame shift imply disparate schemas between American and Japanese politicians in political discourse, that is, American politicians value fairness while Japanese politicians put high value on face.

CONCLUSION

This study compares U.S. and Japanese political news interviews to investigate interactive frames and schemas of U.S. and Japanese politicians in political discourse. As the analysis shows, the American politicians violate the ritual turn-taking system more frequently and aggressively than the Japanese politicians. Also, when violating the turn-taking system, the American politicians show disagreement in a direct manner while the Japanese politicians do so politely. Examining the structure of responses to the moderators' criticizing questions reveals that responses of the American politicians often consist of a partial agreement, proposition, and its supporting evidence while those of the Japanese politicians consist of a rhetorical structure, that is, a start, development, counter-argument, and conclusion. Examining motivations of frame shifts reveals that an American politician moves to an emotional frame triggered by the concept of fairness while a Japanese politician expresses his emotion when his face is threatened. These results suggest that the American politicians and Japanese politicians have different interactive frames resulting from their different expectations in political discourse: the agonistic schema and irenic schema, respectively. These different schemas can trigger miscommunication in crosscultural communication between American and Japanese politicians.

In the 1969 summit, Prime Minister Sato said, "I will do my best" as an indirect "No," to President Nixon's proposal. This indirect response may have resulted from Sato's interactive frame of "saving Nixon's face" by not turning down his offer publicly. In other words, Sato's consideration for Nixon's face relates to irenic schema to be harmonious, at least on the surface, even in a conflicting situation such as a bilateral political negotiation. Nixon, on the other hand, had an agonistic schema that expected Sato to play fairly and to interact with him openly in a direct manner. This expectation may be the reason why Nixon got furious when he thought that Sato had not kept his promise and had acted deceptively. This is an example where a miscommunication in a crosscultural political discourse as a result of the different frames of the parties had a great impact in international diplomacy.

APPENDIX A: TRANSCRIPTION CONVENTIONS

The transcription conventions used in this study are an adaptation of those found in Tannen (1984).

.   sentence-final falling intonation

?   yes/no question rising intonation

-    glottal stop or abrupt cutting off of sound

<   overlapping speech

->   point of the analysis

APPENDIX B: ABBREVIATIONS USED IN JAPANESE TRANSCRIPTION

These abbreviations are adapted from Watanabe (1993).

TP for *wa*	topic particle marking the preceding noun phrase as theme or a topic
SP for *ga*	subject particle marking the preceding noun phrase as a subject
Q for *ka*	question particle that marks the sentence as a question
QT for *to*	quotation particles, which are equivalent to "that" for English verbs "think," "feel," "seem," "say," etc.
FP for *ne*	sentence-final particle, which assigns extra meaning of the preceding sentence
ONO	onomatopoetic expressions
PO	polite form
past	past form

NOTES

1. I would like to thank Deborah Tannen and Julie Parandie for their insightful comments. This chapter is the revised version of the paper, "Different frames in Japanese and American Discourse," presented at Georgetown Linguistic Society Conference in 1996 as well as a part of my doctoral dissertation in 1998. This research was supported by an Illinois Wesleyan University ASD grant.

2. Barnlund (1988) reports this incident in detail.

3. Agonism can be seen as attack in academic writings that criticize the works of certain experts or authorities.

4. Although there are panelists who ask questions to the political guests in both programs, the segment chosen from the U.S. political news interview includes the panelists' questions while that from the Japanese interview does not. However, the panelists in the Japanese interview do so in the later segment of the program.

5. I would like to show my sincere appreciation to Atsuko Honda, who let me use her recorded news interview for this research.

6. Men's language and women's language can differ greatly in Japanese.

7. Takemata (1976) regards *ten* as "change"; however, in this context, *ten* is most properly explained as "counter-argument," and therefore, *ten* is translated as "counter-argument" in this study.

REFERENCES

Barnlund, D. C. (1988). Communication in a global village. In L. A. Samovar & R. E. Porter (Eds.), *Intercultural communication: A reader* (5th ed., pp. 5–14). Belmont, CA: Wadsworth.

Baston, G. (1972). *Steps to an ecology of mind.* New York: Ballantine.

Bull, P., & Mayer, K. (1993). How not to answer questions in political interviews. *Political Psychology, 13,* 651–666.

Caudill, W., & Weinstein, H. (1969). Maternal care and infant behavior in Japan and America. *Psychiatry, 22,* 367–389.

Doi, T. (1972). Some psychological themes in Japanese human relationships. In J. C. Condon & M. Sato (Eds.), *Intercultural encounters with Japan* (pp. 17–26). Tokyo: Simul.

Greatbatch, D. (1992). On the management of disagreement between news interviewees. In P. Drew & J. Heritage (Eds.), *Talk at work* (pp. 268–301). Cambridge: Cambridge University Press.

Goffman, E. (1981). *Forms of talk.* Oxford: Blackwell.

Harris, S. (1992). Evasive action: How politicians respond to questions in political interviews. In P. Scannel (Ed.), *Broadcast talk* (pp. 76–99). London: Sage.

Hirokawa, R. Y. (1987). Communicating with the Japanese business organization. In D. L. Kincaid (Ed.), *Communication theory: Eastern and western perspectives* (pp. 137–149). San Diego, CA: Academic Press.

Ide, S. (1982). Japanese sociolinguistics: Politeness and women's language. *Lingua, 57,* 357–385.

Ishihara, S., & Morita, A. (1988). *Japan that can say "no."* Tokyo: Shin-Nihon.

Kruger, A. N. (1960). *Modern debate: Its logic and strategy.* New York: McGraw-Hill.

Lebra, T. S. (1984). Nonconfrontational strategies for management of interpersonal conflicts. In E. S. Krauss, T. P. Rohlen, & P. G. Steingoff (Eds.), *Conflict in Japan* (pp. 41–60). Honolulu: University of Hawaii Press.

Markus, G. B., & Tanter, R. (1972). A conflict model for strategist and managers. *American Behavioral Scientist, 15*(6), 809–836.

Matsumoto, Y. (1988). Reexamination of the universality of face. *Journal of Pragmatics, 12,* 403–426.

Nakane, C. (1967). *Tate-shakai-no ningen-kankei* [Human relationship in a hierarchical society]. Tokyo: Kodansha.

Nobel, D. F. (1992). *A world without women.* Oxford: Oxford University Press.

Ong, W. J. (1992). *Fighting for life.* Cornell, NY: Cornell University Press.

Park, M. (1990). Conflict avoidance in social interaction: A sociolinguistic comparison of the Korean and Japanese honorific systems. In H. Hoji (Ed.), *Japanese/Korean linguistics* (pp. 111–127). Stanford, CA. The Stanford Linguistics Association.

Shillony, B. (1973). Victories without vanquished. In B. Shillony (Ed.), *Revolt in Japan* (pp. 127–137). Princeton, NJ: Princeton University Press.

Takemata, K. (1976). *Genkō shippitsu nyūmon* [An introduction to writing manuscripts]. Tokyo: Natsumesha.

Tannen, D. (1984). *Conversational style: Analyzing talk among friends*. Norwood, NJ: Ablex.

Tannen, D. (1993). *Framing in discourse*. Oxford: Oxford University Press.

Tannen, D. (1998). *The argument culture: Stopping America's war of words*. New York: Ballantine.

Tannen, D., & Wallat, C. (1993). Interactive frames and knowledge schemas in interaction: Examples from a medical examination/interview. In D. Tannen (Ed.), *Framing in discourse* (pp. 57–76). Oxford: Oxford University Press.

Ueda, K. (1972). Sixteen ways to avoid saying "No" in Japan. In J. C. Condon & M. Saito (Eds.), *Intercultural encounters with Japan* (pp. 185–192). Tokyo: Simul.

Watanabe, S. (1993). Cultural differences in framing: American and Japanese group discussions. In D. Tannen (Ed.), *Framing in discourse* (pp. 57–76). Oxford: Oxford University Press.

Yamamoto, S. (1993). *Nihonjin to Amerikajin* [The Japanese and Americans]. Tokyo: PHP.

Yamada, H. (1992). *American and Japanese business discourse: A comparison of interactional styles*. Norwood, NJ: Ablex.

Yum, J. O. (1988). The impact of Confucianism of interpersonal relationships and communication patterns in East Asia. *Communication Monographs, 55*, 174–388.

part VII

Japanese Pragmatics

Chapter 18

Speech Act Realization Patterns of Japanese Social Refusal: The Question Strategy

Nagiko Iwata Lee

This chapter reveals certain characteristics of Japanese native speakers as realized in their speech act of refusal. These revelations about Japanese character arise from a series of studies involving native speakers of Japanese—children and adults—and native speakers of English in Australia and in Canada. Major findings from the studies show that: (1) Japanese adult speakers tend to use questions when refusing a request from someone of equal or higher status; (2) the type of questions used differ according to relative social status; and (3) overall, Japanese use a question strategy in refusal much more than native speakers of English in comparable situations. These findings help to explain and characterize how Japanese social speech can manifest "indirectness," a feature long held about Japaneseness but much less substantiated.

Japanese are often characterized as being indirect and ambiguous in their speech (see Rose, 1996, for a good summary). Ueda (1974), for instance, presents 16 ways to avoid saying "no" in Japanese, such as lying, delaying an answer, and being silent. Some argue, however, that the view of Japanese indirectness is oversimplified (Beebe & Takahashi, 1989; Rose, 1996). To what degree, if at all, the Japanese are indirect and vague in their speech becomes an empirical question. Such issues are addressed in the area of linguistic studies called contrastive pragmatics and interlanguage pragmatics. In these studies, data from more than two languages are examined quantitatively and qualitatively to discover speech act realization patterns, which may be specific to some cultural groups or universal as a form of human communication.

This chapter presents findings from such studies. It identifies a Japanese strategy of indirectness realized through their speech act of refusal. An initial observation made in Lee (1998) is that Japanese speakers often use questions as a strategy for refusal while English speakers do not. The basis of this finding is presented herein and then expanded by previously unreported data derived from experiments that extend from the original adult population to Japanese children. The scope is extended in other directions by changing test sites from Canada to Australia for English speakers, and by using a variety of observational measures overall. The chapter concludes by discussing the nature of questions in communication.

CULTURE-SPECIFIC FEATURES REALIZED IN SPEECH ACTS

Speech act theory claims that speakers perform certain kind of acts, such as complaining, apologizing, and thanking through direct or indirect usage of language (Austin, 1962; Searle, 1969, 1975). This notion of speech act is compelling and has stimulated extensive research in various disciplines, such as literature, anthropology, communication, and linguistics. One good example is the Cross-Cultural Speech Act Realization Project (CCSARP) (Blum-Kulka & Olshtain, 1984; Blum-Kulka, House, & Kasper, 1989), which empirically has examined the ways language is used to perform speech acts of request and apology in as many as 10–14 varieties of language. This project stimulated the area of studies in contrastive pragmatics and interlanguage pragmatics. Contrastive pragmatics studies the use of language in separate speech communities to determine how they differ. For instance, Coulmas (1981) contrasts the functioning of highly routinized speech acts, such as thanks and apologies, in Japanese and a number of European languages. Barnlund and Araki (1985) and Daikuhara (1986) examine the management of compliments in Japanese and English. These studies reveal culture-specific features of speech within those communities.

Interlanguage pragmatics, on the other hand, studies speech act performance by nonnative speakers. Such studies reveal aspects of second language development, including the phenomenon of pragmatic transfer—a transfer of pragmatic knowledge from a speaker's first language (L1) to his or her second language (L2). Beebe, Takahashi, and Uliss-Weltz (1990) examined the Japanese use of their L2, English, in performing speech acts for invitation, offer, suggestion, and refusal. They present evidence that pragmatic transfer exists in the order, frequency, and content of semantic formulas used by Japanese making refusals in English. For instance, Japanese displayed no positive opinion, while American English speakers did, in a situation where the refuser was of lower status than the requester. Such items identified as pragmatic transfer are assumed to reveal culture-specific features of the L1 speech community in contrast to that of the L2 community.

SPEECH ACT REALIZATION PATTERNS OF JAPANESE

Use of Question in Refusal to a Request

Lee (1998) studies the interlanguage pragmatics between Japanese and English using a modification of the Discourse Completion Test (DCT) (Beebe, Takahashi, & Uliss-Weltz, 1990). The key modification was to allow speakers to make free responses as opposed to limiting them to a predetermined set of choices. In Beebe et al. (1990), the DCT was conducted in such a way that the researchers presented utterances of an interlocutor (e.g., those of the requester in refusal situation) and allowing participants only one turn to respond in discourse. Lee (1998), however, simply gave the description of situations involving a speech act of refusal and left participants free to create discourse on their own, at least up until six turns of interactions—three turns each for the requester and the refuser. The participants tested were native speakers of Japanese and native speakers of English who were studying at a university in Canada in January 1997. Participants numbered as follows:

Japanese native speakers who responded in Japanese (JJ) 23

Japanese native speakers who responded in English (JE) 47

English native speakers who responded in English (EE) 35

Three situations given in Lee (1998) were:

Situation 1. A boss of a travel agent asks you to work overtime, but you refuse

Situation 2. Your classmate asks you to lend him/her lecture notes, but you refuse

Situation 3. You, a teacher of a language class, are asked to change the content of the class by your students, but you refuse

As is evident from these descriptions, the variable tested here is the relative social status between the interlocutors. In situation 1, the refuser is lower than the requester in relative status, while in situation 2 the refuser and the requester are equal, and in situation 3 the refuser is higher than the requester.

Following Beebe, Takahashi, and Uliss-Weltz (1990), Lee (1998) assumes that frequency counts of DCT responses provide evidence of pragmatic transfer. For instance, if the number of a particular type of response by JJ is greater than that of EE, and JE is placed in between as in the pattern (a) below, we assume that the type of response is a characteristic of Japanese speakers. JE, here, exhibits a pragmatic transfer, carrying the L1 habit into the performance of L2. The variety of such patterns follow:

(a) JJ > JE > EE

(b) JJ < JE < EE

(c) JJ = JE < EE or JJ ≅ JE < EE (where ≅ reads "almost =")

(d) JJ = JE > EE or JJ ≅ JE > EE

The result of the DCT reported by Lee (1998) has uncovered an interesting pattern. Japanese native speakers present a clear tendency to use questions when refusing a request from someone considered of higher or equal status than their own. Tables 18-1 through 18-3 present the number of occurrences of such patterns among JJ, JE, and EE. Examples for each situation follow tables.

Table 18-1
Number of Questions Observed in Situation 1
(Refusal to Someone of Higher Status)

	Participants n	Questions Observed n (%)
JJ	23	12 (52%)
JE	47	11 (23%)
EE	35	2 (6%)

Table 18-2
Number of Questions Observed in Situation 2
(Refusal to Someone of Equal Status)

	Participants n	Questions observed n (%)
JJ	23	10 (43%)
JE	47	16 (34%)
EE	35	4 (11%)

Table 18-3
Number of Questions Observed in Situation 3
(Refusal to Someone of Lower Status)

	Participants n	Questions observed n(%)
JJ	23	7 (30%)
JE	47	7 (15%)
EE	35	0 (0%)

Examples of situation 1:

JJ

(1) Boss: *Warui kedo, konban zangyō shite kure nai?*
               I'm sorry, but can you work overtime tonight?
Employee: *E, komban desu ka?* [Use of question]
               Oh, tonight?

JE

(2) Boss: Could you work late tonight?
Employee: Oh, do we have much work left? [Use of question]

EE

(3) Boss: Sally, could you work late tonight?
Employee: Well, normally I would be happy to, but my husband and I are going out to dinner.

Examples of situation 2:

JJ

(4) Student A: *Kōgi no nōto kashite.*
               Please lend me your lecture notes.
Student B: *Dōshite?*
               Why? [Use of question]

JE

(5) Student A: Can I borrow your notes?
Student B: My notes? Did you absent the lectures? [Use of question]

EE

(6) Student A: Could I borrow your notes from last class?
Student B: No, I don't think so.

In both situations 1 and 2, the percentage figures by JJ and JE are considerably higher than for EE. Manifesting a pattern of JJ > JE > EE, the result meets the criteria of pragmatic transfer from Japanese to English presented earlier. Thus, Lee (1998) concludes that native speakers of Japanese have a tendency to use a question when refusing a request from someone higher or equal in status.

In situation 3, where the refuser is considered higher in status than the requester, the use of questions was found in a lesser degree than in situations 1 and 2. Many responses were instead explanations, such as "*Bumpō no kiso ga taisetsu desu*" (Foundation of grammar is important). Nonetheless, the pattern of JJ > JE > EE was still observed in the use of questions as shown in Table 18-3. It is interesting to note that no use of questions was found among EE.

Examples of situation 3:

JJ

(7) Student:	*Sensei, motto kaiwa no renshū o shite morae masen ka.*
	Sir, could you please give us more practice in conversation?
Instructor:	*Dōshite da ne?*
	Why? [Use of question]

JE

(8) Student:	I want you to practice conversation, not grammar.
Instructor:	How come? [Use of question]

Further Data

A similar DCT was conducted in September 1998 involving Japanese native speakers of the age group 10–11, and the same DCT was conducted in August 1999 involving native speakers of English in Australia to supplement the partic-ipants available from the EE group in Lee (1998). Data from oral role-play and naturally occurring examples were also collected in response to criticisms of the DCT method of data collection. First we consider the Japanese speakers.

Data for Japanese Speakers Aged 10–11

The Japanese participants consisted of 29 fifth-grade primary school students in Japan. The situations given in the DCT were modified in such a way that chil-dren of this age group could identify with them as follows:

Situation 4: A student refuses a request made by a teacher to stay after school to finish an essay. (The refuser has lower status.)

Situation 5: A student refuses a request to let a classmate to borrow homework. (The refuser has equal status.)

Situation 6: A student refuses a request made by a student junior to him or her to use a part of the school ground. (The refuser has higher status.)

The initial responses by the refuser in the three situations are presented in Tables 18-4, 18-5, and 18-6, respectively. Examples for each situation follow the tables.

Table 18-4
Initial Responses and Number of Respondents in Situation 4

Initial Response Made	Respondents, *n*
Interjection "*Eee*" (Aw!)	19
Excuse	4
Counter request	2
Direct refusal	2
Protest	1
Question "*Nandō*?" (Why?)	1

Table 18-5
Initial Responses and Number of Respondents in Situation 5

Initial Response Made	Respondents, *n*
Direct refusal	20
Order/suggestion	3
Hesitation "*Ee demo* . . ." (Well, but . . .)	2
Question "*Nandō*?" (Why?)	2
Interjection, "*Eee*" (Aw!)	1
Excuse alone	1

Table 18-6
Initial Responses and Number of Respondents in Situation 6

Initial Response Made	Respondents, *n*
Direct refusal	20
Question "*Nandō*?" (Why?)	5
Excuse	4

Example of situation 4 (containing the most predominant strategy, uttering an interjection "Eee"):

(9) Teacher: *Kyō chanto yatte kaetta hō ga raku da yo.*

It's better for you to finish it before you go home.

Student: *Eee*

Aw! [Interjection]

Teacher:	*"Eee" ja nai.*
	Don't say "Eee."
Student:	*Kyē wa asobu yakusoku ga aru no ni.*
	I promised to play with my friend today.
Teacher:	*Kaette kara asondara..*
	Why don't you play after you get home?
Student:	*Eee.*
	Aw! [Interjection]

Example of situation 5 (containing the most predominant strategy, direct refusal):

(10) Student A:	*Kyō no shukudai misete kureru?.*
	Can you show me your homework answer for today?
Student B:	*Iya da.*
	No.
Student A:	*Onegai.*
	Please.
Student B:	*Demo jibun ga shinakatta kara deshō?*
	It's your fault that you didn't do it.
Student A:	*Hontō ni onegai.*
	I beg you, please.
Student B:	*Jibun de yareba?*
	Why don't you do it by yourself?

Example of situation 6 (containing the most predominant strategy, direct refusal):

(11) Junior student:	*Undōjō tsukawashite.*
	Please let me use the school ground.
Senior student:	*Iya ya.*
	No.
Junior student:	*Nandē.*
	Why?
Senior student:	*Saki kita hō ga kachi.*
	First come, first served.
Junior student:	*Demo ii yan ka.*
	That doesn't matter, does it?
Senior student:	*Hoka n toko itte.*
	Go and use somewhere else.

Observing the above results, we can see that children of the age group 10–11 years old are as sensitive to the variable of social status as adult speakers in performing a speech act of refusal. They make different responses according to the relative social status of the interlocutor. This social acuity by the young Japanese is not surprising and is similar to Ervin-Tripp's (1982) finding that young American children also vary their speech depending on to whom they speak: they use more imperatives with their mothers than with their fathers, and give orders to siblings, but make requests politely to strangers.

As compared with adults, Japanese children's responses, however, turned out to be different in content. Unlike adult speakers, children aged 10–11 did not show a tendency to use questions in refusing a request made by someone higher or equal in status. They instead employed the utterance "*Eee*" (Aw!) as a sign of reluctance to someone higher, and refused directly to someone equal in status.

Data for English Speakers

As noted, data was also collected from eight native speakers of English in Australia in August 1999. They were all university students, including two maturer in age. My modified DCT, which was used in Canada in January 1997, was used without any further modifications, as the subjects tested at both sites were university students. A wide variety of responses by the refuser was observed in situation 1 where the refusal was made to a boss who asked an employee to work overtime the same night. Examples of the semantic formula for such utterances is indicated by brackets:

(12) Any other time I would, but tonight I'd already made plans for the evening meal.

    [positive comment]   [excuse]

(13) Sorry, I've made plans already.

    [regret]   [excuse]

(14) I know we've got to get a lot of work done, but I've got other commitments.

    [sympathy]   [excuse]

(15) Tonight? That's a bit difficult. I've got some things planned.

    [echo question] [indirect refusal]   [excuse]

What is notable here and in the data in Lee (1998) is that English native speakers do not simply respond with "no." They usually express regrets, saying "sorry," which is usually followed or preceded by excuses. As had been expected, use of a question was not a predominant strategy among them. It is rather surprising to find the example (15), "Tonight?" among the eight subjects. The subject who used the question strategy was a mature female student.

Like situation 1, many instances of excuses appeared in situation 2 where the refusal was made to a classmate asking for lecture notes. Unlike situation 1, however, there were two subjects who responded with the direct refusal "no" at the initial turn of the interaction. It is also interesting that one subject refused with an accusing question, "Why weren't you at the lecture?"

Unlike situations 1 and 2, no expressions of regret were found in situation 3 where a teacher refused a student for more conversation practice than grammar. The majority of the responses consisted of explanations such as "I really think we should go over some grammar." Examining the results of the data obtained here, it is reasonable to conclude that English native speakers do not typically use questions when refusing a request.

Data from Other Methods of Data Collection

The DCT has often been criticized for its nonauthenticity. The DCT was used by the CCSARP because they were interested in getting a large sample, in seven countries, of two specific speech acts used in the same context. They argue that the virtue of authenticity in naturally occurring speech must be weighed against its reflection of speaker's sociolinguistic adaptations to very specific situations.

Using written elicitation techniques enables us to obtain more stereotyped responses. It is precisely this more stereotyped aspect of speech behavior that we need for cross-cultural comparability. (Blum-Kulka, House, & Kasper, 1989, p. 13)

I happen to agree, but I also believe that our findings made from the DCT eventually must be verified by naturalistic, or at least experimental, data. I have worked toward collecting such data for my hypothesis about the Japanese use of a question in refusal.

Oral role-play was conducted in October 1997. Five pairs of Japanese university students were asked to conduct a role-play for the same situations as those tested in the DCT conducted in January 1997. Two out of the five pairs made use of questions in situation 1 (refusal to someone of higher status).

A note-taking method also recorded the refusers who repeated part of the requesters' utterances in the form of a question. I classify this kind of question as an "echo question." A young man who was requested by his girlfriend to go and make a complaint to a shop owner produced the echo question. He responded by saying, "*Ore gaa?*" (Me?), which was repeated twice. Another incidence was observed when a student asked his professor to write a reference for him in his application for a scholarship. The student requested it to be done by the end of the week. The professor's initial response was "*Konshū jū ni desu ka?*" (By the end of the week?) He then went on to ask the student, "*Senmon no sensei ni kiki-mashita ka?*" (Have you asked a professor of your major subject?)

In brief, further data presented here confirm that Japanese adult speakers, in contrast to English speakers, tend to use questions in refusal to a request. Still, some evidence of this question strategy, though small, was found among English speakers. Thus, this use of questions may form a continuum as that of directness, which is better perceived as one of degree (Rose, 1996). Japanese speakers would be placed on the frequent end of question-refusals while English speakers would be placed on the opposite end of the continuum. Similarly, older speakers could be placed on the frequent end while the younger speakers would go on the other end of the continuum when age is a variable. Gender was excluded from the study here, but this could be a variable as well.

Data collected from young Japanese speakers aged 10–11 disconfirmed the hypothesis that Japanese have a tendency to use a question in refusal to a request. Instead, predominant strategies used were the interjection "*Eee*" (Aw!) when responding to someone higher, and a direct refusal to someone equal or lower in status. Directness by children may come as little surprise. This phenomenon is, however, interesting when combined with another observation from the DCT conducted in Australia. In addition to the eight English speakers reported above, there was one nonnative speaker of English (a native speaker of Chinese) who participated in the data collection session. Her response to a request in situation 1 (refusal to someone of higher status) was a direct refusal, "No, I'm sorry, I can't." This presents a contrast to responses by native speakers of English, such as example (12) introduced earlier. Direct and possibly impolite usage of English by nonnative speakers has been reported (Fukushima, 1990; Tanaka, 1988). Issues involving directness and politeness form a separate research topic.

A question may be raised as to the differences among varieties of English. The 1997 data were collected in Canada, while the 1998 data are from Australia. As far as the refusal strategies are concerned, no remarkable differences were found between them. Similar results are likely in the United Kingdom and United States as well.

ON THE USE OF QUESTIONS

In examining the content of questions and its frequency count, Lee (1998) found a correlation between situations and the types of question used by Japanese speakers. In situation 1 where the refusal was made to a boss asking the employee to work overtime that night, the refuser used either an echo question or asked for further information regarding the request. For example, "*Komban desu ka?*" (Tonight?) is an echo question, and "*Isogi no shigoto desu ka?*" (Is it an urgent job?) is seeking further information.

On the other hand, in situation 2 where the refusal was made to a classmate asking for lecture notes, questions demanding a reason for the request or those regarding the requester, such as "*Dōshite?*" (Why?) and "*Jibun no nōto wa dō shita no?*" (What happened to your own notes?) were frequently observed. Similarly, some of the Japanese primary school students used a question demanding a reason for the request, "*Nande ya?*" (Why?) in situation 6, where the refusal was made to a student lower in grade asking for the use of the school ground. This question "*Dōshite/Nande ya?*" (Why?) is to be classified here as an "accusing question" because its illocutionary force is really accusing in nature.

Some of the questions observed here may be considered rhetorical questions. A rhetorical question is one to which the speaker does not expect an answer. It not only mitigates potential loss of face (Brown & Levinson, 1978) but also has persuasive effects. It is thus often observed in conflict situations, such as in a sociable conversational argument or in a therapeutic counseling setting (Shiomi, 1998). As a matter of fact, use of (rhetorical) questions by Japanese speakers has been observed in other face-threatening speech acts, such as complaining and correcting an interlocutor's errors. Beebe and Takahashi (1989) report a case in which a Japanese speaker used a rhetorical question to correct an interlocutor's error. Hajikano, Kumatoridani, and Fujimori (1996) studied complaint strategies used by native and nonnative speakers of Japanese. They report a case in which questions, whether rhetorical or not, were used more frequently by native speakers than nonnative speakers whose first languages were English, Chinese, Indonesian, and Thai, among others.

Whether the question strategy in refusal discussed in this chapter is a rhetorical question used to mitigate potential loss of face or for persuasive effects is still debatable. I recall my own experience of using an echo question, "*Watashi ga?*" (Me?) to a request asking me to write a letter of reference. At that time, I knew the request was coming. Therefore, it was not a genuine sign of surprise. I was willing to comply with the request, hence it was not a strategy to win an argument either. Rather, it seemed to be a sign of modesty, implying that I might not be a person worthy of writing a letter of reference for the requester. Forms and functions of rhetorical questions are complex. Frank (1990) concludes that speech act theory and discourse analysis, even if used in combination and augmented by the insights of cognitive psychology, are insufficient to identify and explain the multiple communicative functions of rhetorical questions in spontaneous conversation.

CONCLUSION

This chapter has reviewed a finding made in Lee (1998) that Japanese speakers have a tendency to use questions in refusal to a request. The nature of individual questions used for refusal have been more carefully examined here, and at least three kinds of questions are identified: echo questions, questions to request further information, and accusing questions.

Further data collected from English speakers did not show the same strategy and thus confirmed the tendency of using a question to be a characteristic of Japanese. However, data collected from young Japanese speakers aged 10–11 showed that the question strategy might be limited to adults. Instead of using a question, young Japanese used an interjection "*Eee*" (Aw!) to someone higher in status and directly refused someone equal or lower in status.

Other variables such as gender, the degree of imposition involved with a request, the sense of obligation to the requester (Beebe, Takahashi, & Uliss-Weltz, 1990), and the psychological distance between the interlocutors might further modify the finding. If a speaker is using his or her second or a foreign language, the picture becomes more complex because speech acts could be a function of pragmatic transfer from the L1 or a phenomenon related to L2 development. Many questions remain to be examined.

A conclusion can be made at this stage that Japanese adult speakers have a tendency to use echo questions and questions to request further information in a refusal to someone of higher status, whereas they tend to use accusing questions to someone of equal status. To someone of lower status, the question strategy was used less frequently than to someone of higher or equal status. The question strategy is, however, still a characteristic of Japanese speakers when compared with English speakers, who displayed no or little use of questions in the same situations.

REFERENCES

Austin, J. L. (1962). *How to do things with words*. Oxford: Clarendon Press.

Barnlund, D., & Araki, S. (1985). Intercultural encounters: The management of compliments by Japanese and Americans. *Journal of Cross-Cultural Psychology, 18,* 9–26.

Beebe, L. M., & Takahashi, T. (1989). Do you have a bag? In S. Gass, C. Madden, D. Oreston, & L. Selinker (Eds.), *Variation in second language acquisition, vol. 1.* Clevedon, Avon (U.K.): Multilingual Matters.

Beebe, L. M., Takahashi , T., & Uliss-Weltz, R. (1990). Pragmatic transfer in ESL refusals. In R. C. Scarcella, E. S. Andersen, & S. D. Krashen (Eds.), *Developing communicative competence in a second language* (pp. 55–73). New York: Newbury House.

Blum-Kulka, S., & Olshtain, E. (1984). Requests and apologies: A cross-cultural study of speech act realization patterns (CCSARP). *Applied Linguistics, 5,* 196–213.

Blum-Kulka, S., House, J., & Kasper, G. (Eds.). (1989). *Cross-cultural pragmatics: Requests and apologies.* Norwood, NJ: Ablex.

Brown, P., & Levinson, S. (1978). Universals of language usage: Politeness phenomena. In E. Goody (Ed.), *Questions and politeness* (pp. 256–289). Cambridge: Cambridge University Press.

Coulmas, F. (1981). Poison to your soul: Thanks and apologies contrastively viewed. In F. Coulmas (Ed.), *Conversational routine* (pp. 69–91). The Hague: Mouton.

Daikuhara, M. (1986). A study of compliments from a cross–cultural perspective: Japanese vs. American English. *Working Papers in Educational Linguistics, 2,* 103–135.

Ervin-Tripp, S. (1982). Ask and it shall be given to you: Children's requests. In H. Byrnes (Ed.), *Georgetown University Roundtable in Language and Linguistics* (pp. 235–245). Washington, DC: Georgetown University Press.

Frank, J. (1990). You call that a rhetorical question? *Journal of Pragmatics, 14,* 723–738.

Fukushima, S. (1990). Offers and requests: Performance by Japanese learners of English. *World Englishes, 9,* 317–325.

Hajikano, A., Kumatoridani, T., & Fujimori, H. (1996). Fuman hyomei sutoratejii no shiyoo keikoo [Patterns of complaint strategies]. *Nihongo Kyoiku* [Journal of Japanese Language Teaching], *88,* 128–139.

Lee, N. (1998). Hatsuwakōi ni arawareru gengobunka: Nihongo Bogowasha no Tokuchō [A linguistic and cultural characteristic of Japanese speakers realized in their speech acts]. *Ritsumeikan Journal of Economics, 46*(6), 150–164.

Rose, K. R. (1996). American English, Japanese, and directness: More than stereotypes. *JALT Journal, 18,* 67–80.

Searle, J. (1969). *Speech acts.* Cambridge: Cambridge University Press.

Searle, J. (1975). Indirect speech acts. In P. Cole & J. Morgan (Eds.), *Syntax and semantics, Vol. 9: Speech acts* (pp. 59–82). New York: Academic Press.

Shiomi, K. (1998). Multi-functions of conversational devices: Speech acts, pragmatics, and discourse studies. *Ritsumeikan Studies in Language and Culture, 10*(3), 23–34.

Tanaka, N. (1988). Politeness: Some problems for Japanese speakers of English. *JALT Journal, 9,* 81–102.

Ueda, K. (1974). Sixteen ways to avoid saying "no" in Japan. In J. Condon & M. Saito (Eds.), *Intercultural encounters with Japan—contact and conflict* (pp. 185–195). Tokyo: Simul Press.

Chapter 19

Japaneseness Manifested in Apology Styles

Naomi Sugimoto

Aspects of Japaneseness are identifiable through a close study of Japanese apology styles. In order to do so, the chapter first examines cultural connotations of apology in Japan, such as a weak relationship between apology and responsibility, as well as the interchangeability between apology and thanks. Then the chapter turns to unique features of Japanese apology: (a) exaggeration of remorse felt and offense committed, (b) vague offers of repair and prevention, (c) dislike of accounts, and (d) reciprocated or denied apology. The chapter ends by pointing out the possible correspondence between these unique features of Japanese apology and "Japaneseness": (a) truthfulness is understood in relation to the perception of the message recipient, (b) autonomy is not automatically presupposed, and (c) deference is important in Japanese culture and communication.

Japan is often characterized as a "culture of apology" (Kato & Rozman, 1988; Kitagawa, 1990; Naotsuka, 1990), where people are more "apologetic," than in other cultures such as the United Kingdom (Miyake, 1994), Canada (Takagi, 1997), South Korea (Ogoshi, 1993), Thailand (Horie, 1993), and the United States (Sugimoto, 1997). Indeed, apology carries a significant weight in Japanese social life (Barnlund & Yoshioka, 1990; Sugimoto, 1998). To a Japanese, an adequate apology, not just atonement of the original harm, is a requirement for the "offended" to change the negative evaluation of the offender (Ohbuchi, Kameda, & Agarie, 1989). Given this cultural emphasis, this chapter explores aspects of "Japaneseness"[1] manifested in the Japanese patterns of apology.[2] Toward that end, the chapter first reviews the cultural connotations of apology in Japan; second, it discusses important features of Japanese apology; and third, it considers the implications of, and changes in, these features.

CULTURAL CONNOTATIONS OF APOLOGY IN JAPAN

While the *concept* of apology is universal,[3] its *referents* are not: what is considered as "apology," as well as its implications and consequences, depends on where it is practiced or studied. Special meanings and functions assigned to apology in Japan create situations where Japanese apologize differently than do members of other cultures. Thus, knowledge of cultural connotations of apology in Japan is crucial to our understanding of Japanese apology patterns. This section discusses two of such cultural connotations, a weak relationship between apology and responsibility as well as an intertwined relationship between apology and thanks.

Apology and Responsibility: A Weak Relationship

Japanese are often said to apologize for situations for which they are not directly responsible (Sugimoto, 1997). Some may argue that a collectivistic notion in the culture forces Japanese to feel responsible for many offenses other than their own. Others may conclude that Japanese are insincere because they apologize on the *tatemae* (surface) level, even when at the *hon'ne* (internal) level, they do not see the need to do so.

While these explanations may well be true, it should be kept in mind that apology and responsibility do not have a strong relationship with each other in Japan. Responsibility is implied in the English verb, "apologize," but not in "*ayamaru*," a Japanese word most commonly translated as "apologize" (Wagatsuma & Rosett, 1986). This does not mean, of course, that apology and responsibility are completely detached; in most cases, Japanese do feel responsible when apologizing. Yet it is not a requirement for an apology: Japanese do not *have to,* but *are free to,* apologize even when they are not directly responsible for the offensive act. In other words, the extent to which the prospective "apologizer" is responsible for the offense, is not a criterion for offering apology. Thus, it is somewhat pointless to analyze Japanese apology patterns from the perspective of responsibility.

Apology and Thanks: An Intertwined Relationship

"In Japanese, a remedial move [apology] is appropriate, whereas in English, thanks would be appropriate" (Owen, 1983, p. 176). This seemingly perplexing tendency can be better understood with the knowledge that apology and thanks are strongly related with one another in Japanese connotations.

The character used in *ayamaru, sha* is also used in a noun, *kansha*, the word for thanks in Japanese. Etymologically, this character, *(sha)* refers to the sense of indebtedness felt in various situations. In the case of apology, it is a sense of debt incurred by the offense or inconvenience (often involuntarily) experienced or endured by the other. In the case of thanks, the sense of indebtedness results from the other's voluntary act of kindness. While this close relationship between apology and thanks itself is not uncommon in other cultures, it is played out in a unique manner in Japan. Japanese tend to (or at least pretend to) interpret most of the situations as calling for apology.

In Japan, expressing one's sense of indebtedness to the other with thanks would imply that the speaker is deserving of such kindness by the other. In the society where the "polite fiction" of "I'm your inferior" (Sakamoto & Naotsuka, 1982) must be maintained, giving thanks would appear presumptuous, pretentious, or even arrogant. For that reason, it is safer for Japanese to apologize, implying that it was the speaker's fault that the other was forced to endure such a situation.

FEATURES OF JAPANESE APOLOGY

As seen above, apology has certain connotations for Japanese people. This section examines specific features of Japanese apology in which these assumptions are played out.

Remorse Statements and Evaluation of Damage: Exaggerated

Japanese tend to express their remorse repeatedly and strongly emphasize the negative consequences of their act, contributing to their image as apologetic. The following sections explain why this kind of exaggeration is safe, if not preferred, in Japan.

"Sorry, Sorry, I'm Sorry": Repetitious Expressions of Remorse

Japanese tend to repeat the same formulaic apology phrases (e.g., *gomen*) within the same utterance rather than add modifiers or intensifiers. In fact, some Japanese respondents in a study (Sugimoto, 1997) simply wrote "*Warui*"[3] or "*Gomen* x 10," indicating the number of times they would repeat the given phrase in proportion to the magnitude of offense they felt. Such repetition in Japanese apology takes place for two reasons.

The first reason is that the Japanese language is quite receptive to repetitions. In fact, "onomatopoeic expressions in Japanese mostly consist of the same syllable[s] repeated twice or more; adjectives and adverbs in the Japanese language can be intensified by simple repetition instead of using special modifiers" (Sugimoto, 1999, p. 75). This practice of repetition is further reinforced by the fact that "it is 'safe' to rely on time-proven formulaic expressions in a culture like Japan where strict norms exist for appropriate word usage" (Sugimoto, 1999, p. 75).

The second possible reason for repetition is interference in L2 conversation (Sugimoto, 1999). Japanese are often seen as apologetic when they are interacting in English with members of other cultures. Apology situations, stressful as they are, can be quite nerve-wracking to deal with in English to ill-prepared non-native speakers. Since not much instruction is provided as to how to properly apologize in English (Coulmas, 1981; Fraser, 1981; Tanaka, 1985; Yamada & Tanaka, 1986), Japanese apologizers may simply resort to repeating whatever English apology expressions they know (most typically "sorry") just as the Japanese norm of repetition in apology dictates. This repeated "sorry" stands out even more strikingly in English conversation, in which such repetition is generally discouraged, hence forming an impression of Japanese as apologetic.

"What a Dorky Thing I Have Done!": Exaggerated Evaluation of Damage

Japanese also seem to dwell on the offense they committed, an insistence generally discouraged in cultures like the United States (Sugimoto, 1998). In fact, Japanese strive to come up with an exhaustive list of possible negative consequences of the offending act, no matter how remote the possibility is. Four such strategies of "exaggeration" are explained in the sections that follow.

First, the negative impact of the offense can be emphasized rhetorically. Examples of this tactic abound in sample apology provided in Japanese books on etiquette (Sugimoto, 1998). When apologizing for missing a visitor who came to their home unexpectedly (in many other cultures, this may not even constitute an offense that requires apology), the "offenders" acknowledged the fact that the visitor came "all the way" or "in the rain/wind/cold/heat." A questionnaire study (Sugimoto, 1997) reports a similar trend: When late for a trip with friends, a significantly large number of Japanese answered that they would say things like "Oh, I don't even know how to apologize for what I've done"; American respondents tried to lighten the damage by saying "Look, we still have all of spring break to enjoy. Let's party!"

The second method of exaggeration is to focus on the irreversibility of the damage. In the "unexpected visitor" situation above, the writers speculate on how critical the visit might have been by saying "it could have been an emergency" or "it was the first time we could have seen each other in five years" (Sugimoto, 1998). This type of "empathic exaggeration" was found also in the survey data. When causing a friend to miss a movie they had planned to see together, almost 12% of the Japanese respondents employed this strategy by saying "I know *how much you wanted to see this*" or "I realize that *we just missed the last showing* of the movie" (Sugimoto, 1997).

The third way to focus on the imposition caused by the offense is to refer to "secondary damage" or inconveniences which could possibly extend from the original offense and may affect other parties or situations beyond the immediate offending situation. For instance, when late for an appointment, some Japanese may go so far as to say things like "This may mess up your schedule for the rest of the day" or "I feel bad about your next appointment, which may be shortened because of my tardiness" (Sugimoto, 1997).

Finally, "hindsight" is the fourth exaggeration tactic. It is not just an objective declaration of afterthoughts, but implies self-blame. In one situation (Sugimoto, 1997), where the offender, president of a club, canceled a meeting and failed to notify a member, 16.8% of Japanese respondents said something to the effect of "I should have told you about the cancellation in the class we both attend," in addition to apologizing for the initial offense of cancellation. In another situation (Sugimoto, 1997), where the offender failed to show up for a meeting because of a friend's car accident, 7.7% of Japanese shared a hindsight with a self-blaming tone, such as "though it was unavoidable that I had to stay with my friend and miss the meeting, at least I could have called to let you know." By doing so, the respondents appear to focus on the secondary offense of not calling the other rather than the initial offense of not attending the meeting. As illustrated by this example, hindsight in Japanese apology is not necessarily used to refer to random afterthoughts, but used to rhetorically expand the magnitude with a tone of self-blame.

Reasons for Exaggeration in Japanese Apology

Traditionally, Japanese have been seen as "minimalists" in communication, reticent and passive partners in conversation. In sharp contrast to this image, Japanese seem quite verbose when emphasizing the negative impact of their offense. Why is this "apologetic tone" safe, or rather, acceptable, or even expected in Japan? While these acts of exaggeration may further aggravate people from other cultures, the same message features seem greatly satisfying to Japanese.

A "*sunao-na*" apology, one that embraces the other's feelings about, or perceptions of, the situation, is the ideal apology in Japan. With that cultural undertone, underestimating the victims' perceived magnitude of offense runs a much higher risk of offending them than does overestimating it. Thus, a Japanese apologizer needs to emphasize the negative aspects of the situation, in an effort to stay ahead of the victim in the game of damage estimation.

Another reason for effectiveness of exaggeration in Japanese apology is that the ability to do so helps prove the offender's capability to take the other's perspective without being told. This perspective-taking skill, highly prized in Japanese communication, helps alleviate the negative image of the offender; assures that the offense would not be repeated; and therefore shows that the offender deserves a second chance.

Offers of Remediation and Promises of Forbearance: Quick and Vague

Another reason for the apologetic image of Japanese is their tendency to quickly and readily offer restitution and promise not to repeat the same offense. These promises of remediation and forbearance, however, are not always concrete: vague promises seem equally effective in Japanese apology as long as they send a clear message that the speaker genuinely cares about the recipient. In fact, vague offers, such as "I don't know how but somehow (I'll make it up to you / I'll never let this happen again)" with "somehow" stressed may sound more assuring than concrete offers like "I'll buy you a new one" or "I'll set the alarm next time." In the latter, remediation and promise are "reduced" to the physical and immediate level, while the former indicates the apologizer's commitment to the recipient above and beyond the immediate and physical reparation or future prevention.

This is because the basic assumption in Japan is that people should be able to satisfy others' needs and wants without being explicitly told. As such, Japanese are often evaluated by the extent to which they can intuitively attend to needs of others. They are expected to recognize, beyond what is obvious from the immediate context, highly contextualized, personal needs. Thus, Japanese find it safer to assume the need for repair or forbearance for every damage, in order to avoid the risk of being labeled "someone who needs to be told," making them a less than competent member of the culture.

Thus, asking what the victim prefers by way of remediation or prevention can be considered an imposition in Japan. As argued above, Japanese are supposed to know or at least best guess the other's wishes. They find beauty in this type of internal search on the actor's part, this making use of all the information about the other individual and coming up with the best plan of action.

To carry this line of reasoning a step further, asking for the other's preference could imply that one does not care enough to undertake this intricate process of guessing, and would rather take the easy way out by blatantly asking. Below, Doi (1973) recalls his frustration with his hosts at dinner parties, who constantly asked for his preferences, from beverage to dessert, during his first stay in the United States:

I soon realized that this was only the American's way of showing politeness to his guest, but in my own mind I had a strong feeling that I couldn't care less. What a lot of trivial choices they were obliging one to make—I sometimes felt—almost as though they were doing it to reassure themselves of their own freedom. (p. 13)

The Japanese host, too, occasionally asks for a guest's preference, but Doi (1973) argues that the two must be very close before the host feels comfortable asking. More typically, people offer "something with a deprecatory 'it may not suit your taste but . . .'" (Doi, 1973, p. 13).

Similarly, Japanese tourists are often perplexed when ordering at a restaurant abroad. They feel that instead of customers deciding whether they should get soup or salad, or instructing on how their eggs and potatoes should be cooked, the management should offer the best combination. The Japanese customers may not appreciate being "imposed on" when they pay extra to go out to eat. As these examples illustrate, being asked for preference can be a bother or a burden to a Japanese, and thus not too frequently practiced in Japanese apology.

Dislike of Accounts

One of the standard apology expressions in Japanese, *mōshiwakenai* (and its politer derivatives, *mōshiwake arimasen* and *mōshiwake gozaimasen*) literally means "there is no excuse for what I have done." Though Japanese speakers may not be aware of this etymological meaning every time they use the phrase, it symbolizes their dislike of excuses in apology. At the root of their dislike is the fear that they may seem rather self-serving in the eye of the apology recipient. Accounts (e.g., excuses or justifications) are perceived as inconsideration for the victims' perception of the offense, or cruel rationalization with no respect for their feelings. In fact, Japanese children have been taught traditionally that an apology followed by accounts is not really an apology.

It may seem rather counterintuitive that, in Japan, where the view that people can have little control over their own fate dominates, accounts do not serve a powerful role in apology. Actually, accounts are more frequently employed and better received in other cultures where autonomy is more readily presupposed. In those cultures, the excuse of having no control has greater mitigating power, because it enables the apologizer to explain the infraction as a rare case, one that will not be repeated. In contrast, when lack of control is generally presupposed, such an appeal will only be met with reactions like "Nobody does!": thus, it has very limited mitigating power in Japanese apology.

However, when apologizers must clarify factors that contributed to the offense, they can avoid projecting the self-serving or self-preserving image by: (a) hedging (e.g., "this is just an excuse . . ." or "this is no excuse but . . ."), or (b) including "anti-self-serving" statements that immediately precede or follow accounts (e.g., "my flight was canceled *but it is still my fault that I did not make it to the meeting*"). These tactics help assure the recipient that the apologizer is not giving excuses for the self-serving purposes.

Apology Not Accepted, But Denied or Reciprocated

Another standard apology expression in Japanese is *gomen,* and this phrase— along with its more formal variation, *gomennasai*—has a literal meaning of "please forgive me." However, forgiveness may not be the most preferred reaction to a given apology. Rather, apology is often denied or reciprocated: "the Japanese offer an apology so easily and casually because they can count on the other party to say 'Don't mention it. I am the one who should apologize'" (Kato & Rozman, 1988, p. 123). The above example illustrates reciprocated apology; an example of denied apology would be statements such as "Oh, that wasn't your fault at all" or "You don't need to apologize for that."

In an interview study on conflicts due to culturally different norms about apology (Kotani, 1999), a Japanese informant, Rie, shares an incident in which her American roommate violated this expectation.

One day, I scorched her oven mitt by mistake. . . . I thought, "Oh, no! I did it!" I said to her, "I'm sorry. This gets like this, blah blah blah. Sorry." And she just said, "Oh, that's OK." That was it. Then I said, "But I'll replace it. I'll buy a new one." Then she said, "OK." Well, of course that's OK, but . . . the mitt could still be used. I'm not making an excuse, but it wasn't totally damaged, like burned to rags. So when I said I'd buy a new one, she could have said, "No, no, that's not necessary." Then this could have been over. But she didn't say it. (p. 145)

Rie offered remediation even though she didn't find it necessary. Why? If asked, Rie would probably answer, "Oh, just to be polite." In reality, this offer might have been Rie's way of "fishing for" denial of her apology. Rie must have felt intuitively that her roommate did not do so because the level of her initial apology did not quite match the roommate's expectation. Thus, Rie might have tried to "upgrade" it by adding an offer of reparation, also providing another opportunity for her roommate to dismiss any importance in the offense. Nonetheless, the roommate did not pick up on Rie's cue but simply "accepted" the apology[4] and "forgave" her. That appeared rude and arrogant to Rie, who was expecting more assurance that she really did not have to apologize any further.

With this sort of expectation of automatic redemption, apology becomes less face-threatening to Japanese. However, Japanese usually do not publicly acknowledge this assumption lest they appear presumptuous or pretentious. Thus, a Japanese apologizer may say "*gomennasai*" ("please forgive me") while asserting that the matter will never be settled or he or she will never be forgiven. This enables Japanese to enact the cultural fiction of "Oh, what I've done is so awful that I never expect you to forgive me."

CONCLUSION

The first part of this chapter examined cultural connotations of apology in Japan. Then, the chapter turned to unique features of apology: (a) exaggeration of remorse felt and offense committed, (b) vague offers of repair and prevention, (c) dislike of accounts, and (d) reciprocated or denied apology. These specific features of Japanese apology may seem unrelated to one another, but they actually revolve around three facets of "Japaneseness."

The first facet, "truthfulness," is understood in Japan in relation to the recipient's perception, not in relation to physical reality (if such a thing exists) as in some other cultures. Thus, exaggeration and apology for something one is not directly responsible for are not necessarily considered as insincere in Japan.

Second, in Japanese communication, autonomy, or having control over one's circumstances, has been neither automatically presupposed nor considered perfectly positive. Thus, the claim of temporary loss of control does not work as well in Japan as in other cultures. Also, asking for the other's preferences is not considered as thoughtful or caring as is anticipating every wish of the other. Blatant questions may only make the other feel reduced to an object of a materialistic exchange.

"I'm your inferior" (Sakamoto & Naotsuka, 1982), the third facet of Japaneseness, is the image to project in Japan in order to enhance one's public esteem. Giving thanks can be taken as arrogant because the act implies putting oneself on the same or even higher ground than the person to whom the debt is felt. With words of apology, Japanese can remain within the realm of "I'm your inferior." Similarly, accepting the other's apology, especially when he or she was not directly responsible for the offense, might project a pretentious image of the apology recipient. This act automatically puts the recipient in the position of a "merciful forgiver," and in turn labels the volunteer apologizer as a "real culprit." Rather, a Japanese apology recipient often denies the need for apology or reciprocates it with his or her own, which will keep the recipient in line with the "I'm your inferior" cultural fiction.

This chapter presented mainly traditional mainstream views and patterns of Japanese apology. Yet the culture is rapidly changing, and so are norms dictating apology. For instance, as early as the 1960s (Saiga, 1966), Japanese, influenced by beliefs and values of other cultures, started criticizing themselves for "apologizing when they *should* give thanks." As a result, more and more thanks are heard now in situations where apologies dominated in the past. Autonomy, likewise, has been assigned more positive meaning in recent years. Consequently, students give more excuses when apologizing, and menus in restaurants give increased freedom of choice to individual customers.

Despite these changing norms, apology will retain its place of power in Japanese communication. Just as corporate apology, once feared to be on the road to extinction, survived the Product Liability Law introduced to Japan in 1995, interpersonal apology will survive, reflecting many facets of "Japaneseness" in communication.

NOTES

1. "Japaneseness" is defined as what "bearers" of the Japanese culture consider to be the essence of being Japanese, or what is tacitly or intuitively understood by the "bearers." Yet, this chapter does not hold, as many Japanese do, that Japanese culture is so superbly unique that no outsiders can possibly begin to capture its essence. Further, while this chapter focuses on uniqueness of Japanese thoughts and behavior, the arguments should be understood more in terms of degree, not in kind. Likewise, the argument that follows may sound as if treating "bearers" of Japanese culture (for brevity and style, hereafter referred to as "Japanese" or "members of Japanese culture") as one homogeneous group, but this does not mean that individual differences within the culture should be disregarded.

2. Apology is defined herein as "restoring social balance once overturned by the offense in question."

3. In the sense that the concept exists in almost every culture.

4. "That's OK" could serve multiple functions in English. The roommate, in her first response, seems to me to be declining Rie's apology, an interpretation Rie does not share. Apparently, she took the phrase quite literally just as do those who have not quite mastered conversational English.

REFERENCES

Barnlund, D. C., & Yoshioka, M. (1990). Apologies: Japanese and American styles. *International Journal of Intercultural Relations, 14,* 193–206.

Coulmas, F. (1981). "Poison to your soul": Thanks and apologies contrastively viewed. In F. Coulmas (Ed.), *Conversational routines* (pp. 69–91). The Hague: Mouton.

Doi, T. (1973). *The Anatomy of Dependence* (J. Bester, Trans.). Tokyo: Kodansha International.

Fraser, B. (1981). On apologizing. In F. Coulmas (Ed.), *Conversational routines* (pp. 259–271). The Hague: Mouton.

Horie, I. P. (1993). Shazai no taishou kenkyū: Nittai taishou kenkyu [A Japa–Thai comparison of apology]. *Nihongo Gaku, 12,* 22–28.

Kato, K., & Rozman, M. (1988). *Kotobade saguru America* [The American mentality]. Tokyo: Japan Times.

Kitagawa, K. (1990). *How to 101: Otonano aisatsu* [How to 101: Greetings for adults]. Tokyo: Nippon Jitsugyo Shuppan.

Kotani, M. (1999). The feel-good apology as a cultural category. In N. Sugimoto (Ed.), *Japanese apology across disciplines* (pp. 125–154). Commack, NY: Nova Science.

Miyake, K. (1994). Kansha no taisho kenkyū: Nichiei taisho kenkyu—bunka / shakai o hanei suru gengo kodo [Thanks in Japanese and English]. *Nihongo Gaku, 13,* 10–18.

Naotsuka, R. (1990). *Obeijin ga chinmoku surutoki: Ibunka no communication.* [When Westerners become silent: Intercultural communication]. Tokyo: Taishukan.

Ogoshi, M. (1993). Shazai no taishou kenkyuu: Niccho taishou kenkyuu [A Japanese–Korean comparison of apology]. *Nihongo Gaku, 12,* 29–38.

Ohbuchi, K., Kameda, M., & Agarie, N. (1989). Apology as aggression control: Its role in mediating appraisal of and response to harm. *Journal of Personality and Social Psychology, 56*(2), 219–227.

Owen, M. (1983). *Apologies and remedial interchanges: A study of language use in social interaction.* Berlin, Germany: Mouton.

Saiga, H. (1966). Sunao ni arigatō to iou [Say *arigato* more often]. *IDE, 54,* 44–45.

Sakamoto, N., & Naotsuka, R. (1982). *Polite fictions: Why Japanese and Americans seem rude to each other.* Tokyo: Kinseido.

Sugimoto, N. (1997). A Japan–U.S. comparison of apology styles. *Communication Research, 24*(4), 349–269.

Sugimoto, N. (1998). Norms of apology depicted in U.S. American and Japanese literature on manners and etiquette. *International Journal of Intercultural Relations, 22*(3), 251–276.

Sugimoto, N. (1999). "Sorry we apologize so much": Linguistic factors affecting Japanese and U.S. American styles of apology. *Intercultural Communication Studies, 8*(1), 71–78.

Takagi, N. (1997). "Saying I'm sorry": Cross-cultural comparison of apology expressions. *Tokyo Kasei Daigaku Kenyuu Kiyou, 37*(1), 239–254.

Tanaka, Y. (1985). Kinouteki shiten karano kyouzai bunseki: Excuse me / I'm sorry no baai [An analysis of teaching materials from the functionalist perspective: The case of excuse me and I'm sorry]. *Chuugoku Chiku Eigo Kyoiku Gakkai Kenkyū Kiyō, 15,* 7–11.

Wagatsuma, H., & Rosett, A. (1986). The implications of apology: Law and culture in Japan and the United States. *Law and Society Review 20*(4), 461–498.

Yamada, M., & Tanaka, Y. (1986). Amerika eigo ni okeru shazaino hyogen [Apology in American English]. *Shimanedaigaku Kyōikugakubu Kiyō (jinbun / shakaikagaku), 20,* 47–54.

Chapter 20

Vagueness Is Not Always Polite: Defensive Concession in Japanese Everyday Discourse

Reiko Hayashi

Analysis of two separate discourses of Japanese indicates that a speaker's vagueness may be variously interpreted by the listener depending on how he or she frames the speaker's intention. Politeness is not always positively received. Focusing on a particular linguistic expression common to both discourses—de ii (that's okay)—analysis reveals disagreement by the subjects studied about the conventional use of Japanese. By focusing on such disagreement, this study hopes to trace processes involved in the interpretation of metamessages in Japanese while revealing a common aspect of social speech in Japanese—the duality of meanings of politeness in Japanese.

In social interaction, people commonly seek information about each other. They want to know if they can expect ongoing interaction, how to act with the person, and how to maintain the relationship. Ideally, they confirm this information through further observation and analysis of behavior. Inferences are then made based on the person's conduct and appearance. Goffman (1959) explains that people consciously or unconsciously express themselves at two different levels of sign activity, enabling others to narrow their perceptions of the behavior and interpret the information conveyed. These two sign levels are essentially content and process, respectively. The content level consists of verbal symbols and other equivalents by which the individual conveys a message. The process level includes the behavior that tells how a content message is to be interpreted. The notion of the process level is close to what Bateson (1972) calls metamessage, a message a speaker conveys about the meaning relationships for the message and for the other interactants. For example, Tannen (1990, p. 32) explains that the content message of helping, such as "This is good for you," may send the metamessage "I am more competent than you," or it may send the metamessage "I am more concerned about you," at the process level. The reason why the act of giving helps to send such metamessages is that it also implicitly conveys the social relations such as status or connection.

As Tannen (1990) points out, how the metamessage is interpreted depends on how the things are said or done at the process level. The verbal and nonverbal cues that signal in prominence how the metamessage is interpreted are called "contextualization cues" (Gumperz, 1982, 1992, 1996). While contextualization cues help people apprehend the particular nuances related to the interpersonal relations, they also help "frame" (Goffman, 1974) an "interactional floor" (Hayashi, 1996) with regard to how to interpret the activity of the content message and how the speaker aligns the social relations of the interactants in the floor. For example, if a speaker says to the recipient, "This is good for you," in a pressing tone with a stern face, these contextualization cues may frame the floor of this utterance assuming that the recipient takes it as an order. By doing so, the speaker may align their relation, assigning the recipient as an inferior. Furthermore, the speaker's alignment with regard to the recipient also frames the speaker him- or herself. Therefore, in this floor, the recipient may perceive the speaker's way of talking as pompous or less confident.

These theories of communication suggest that the content message cannot be interpreted successfully without the process message being properly understood. They also advise that the utterances are inferential and convey multiple perspectives to the receivers, and therefore the receivers interpret messages according to their own frames of reference. Elsewhere (Hayashi, 1997), I argue that hierarchy and interdependence are conditions that frame Japanese social interaction. Indeed, hierarchical interdependence is an ethical value in Asia, which has been influenced by Confucianism. As any communicative action constructs dual meanings, so does Japanese hierarchy, which maintains vertical social relations, and Japanese interdependence, the horizontal. Both hierarchy and interdependence are always two-sided and on a continuum (Hayashi & Hayashi, in press), as well as mutually reinforcing: When one is expressed explicitly as a strong process message, the other functions implicitly as a weak process message in support. Another, but yet inherent, Japanese social ethic is defensive concession, which is also two-sided and functions either as a content message or a process message. These social conventions are intricately intertwined, and complementary to each other. For example, interdependence might convey a strong process message while hierarchy frames it as a weak process message. Concession expressed as a strong process message might be framed by the defense as a weak process message, and hierarchy is disguised by the weak process message of defense, and so on. Sometimes they can become a power to unite and cope with odds, and at other times, the power to control.

To validate such theory, I started to observe whether Japanese people share my assumptions and how they observe these social conventions in their everyday social practice, if they do. I happened to come across two written discourses in which the Japanese writers express their concerns and thoughts about these social ethics. Both were concerned about social conflict involved with the Japanese expression "*de ii desu*" ([something] will do or suffice) and the related contextualization cues they had observed. Their accounts not only put a spotlight on an essential aspect of Japaneseness, but also reveal the writers' own critical sensitivity for these conventions that reflect Japanese language and society.

My task in this chapter, once their observations are presented, is to trace the impact of contextualization cues for the participants in question, showing how the social conversations became constructed and how they can be explained. At center is debate about Japaneseness, to which I hope to contribute further by systematizing how language and society interact in use of the *de ii desu* structure. Through this system, we can gain insight into Japanese social interactions and how they are judged by Japanese themselves.

EVERYDAY DISCOURSE

This section presents data from two different genres of discourse, one from an ordinary housewife published in a readers column for a newspaper, and the other, a novelist published in a literary magazine. Both independently present similar accounts of the *de ii desu* expression, while they conveniently represent two widely different socioeconomic backgrounds. Prior to data analysis, I provide the linguistic basis for this expression. The linguistic knowledge involves the issues of form, use, and relevant meanings, and the data reveal that the meaning of form and that of the situated use are not necessarily consistent in actual communication. This discrepancy in communication becomes the common and practical resource for people to make their communication meaningful in everyday situations.

Linguistic Background of the Particle *de* and the Form *de ii desu*

The particle *de* is equivalent to English prepositions such as *by, on, in,* and *with,* and it is attached to nouns to indicate a method, a tool, a location, or a material of substance. For example, *de* is used in phrases such as "*basu de kaeru*" (go back by bus), and "*teeburu o hana de kazaru*" (decorate the table with flowers). The particle *de* also constructs the form of "*de ii,*" which is a contracted style of "*de mo ii.*" According to *Kojien* (1971) dictionary, the propositional particle *de mo* in "*de mo ii*" is used to attach a broad or vague idea to the referent to avoid a precise definition or decision. For example, the expression "*Ocha de mo nomou ka*" (I am thinking to drink something like tea./Let's drink something like tea, shall we?) implies that tea is not the speaker's exact referent but just one of a number of drinks the speaker is considering. Makino and Tsutsui (1986, pp. 471–472) explain that "*te mo/de mo*" used in the form of "*te mo/de mo ii*" also means "even if." As an adjective, "*ii*" is the colloquial form of "*yoi*" and means "good," "suitable," and "right." The phrase "*te mo/de mo ii*" expresses permission or concession. For example, Makino and Tsutsui present examples such as "*Takaku te mo ii desu*" (It is all right if it's expensive) and "*Gakusei de mo ii desu*" (It is all right even if you are a student). At a discourse level, they give the example such as:

A: *Nanika tsumetai mono o nomitai n desu ga.*

(I want to drink something cold.)

B: *Biiru de mo ii desu ka?*

(Will beer do?)

As the particle *mo* in the usage of "*de/te mo ii*" indicates emphasis (Makino & Tsutsui, 1986, p. 251) and expresses an affirmative attitude while implicating a concession (*Kojien* dictionary, 1971), the contracted form of "*de ii*" becomes more indirect and implicit, diversifying its interpretation.

The meaning of the phrase "*de ii*" can be also be explained by comparing the "*ga ii*" phrase, which normally forms the construction of "A *wa* B *ga* C," as shown in the following example:

Watashi wa biiru ga ii desu.

(Talking about me/To me, beer is good.)

The particle *wa* in this construction marks a topic or a contrastive element; therefore, *watashi* (I)—which corresponds to element A—refers to what the rest of the sentence is about with regard to her. *Watashi* can also be contrasted with other people as *ga* indexes the particularity of A and means that "I don't know about other people but at least I think beer is good."[1] According to Makino and Tsutsui (1986, p. 526), "B *ga* C" in the "A *wa* B *ga* C" construction expresses A's physical and/or mental state, such as ability or desire. Therefore, the sentence "*Watashi wa Biiru ga ii desu*" means, "I, but no one else, desires beer." As is also the case, the topic and topic marker "*watashi wa*" is often omitted in an informal situation, but "*Biiru ga ii desu*" still encodes the speaker's explicit preference for beer.

People's Accounts for the Use of the *de ii desu* Expression

The two sets of discourse I consider here are written by Japanese who express their own views about the use of the particle *de*. Text 1 is from a housewife who wrote it as a letter to the editor of a newspaper, and Text 2, from a novelist who happens to be living in Germany, and who wrote it as part of a short essay for the literary magazine, *Chuuoukouron*. Their discourse shows how they observe the grammar of *de,* and how they account for the related grammatical norm in a situated conversational exchange.

Text 1 *Yasaisarada de ii wa* (Vegetable salad will do)

Suupaa ni kaimono ni ikou to shite, otto ni "ohiru, nani ga ee?" to kiku to, "zarusoba de ee—wa" to, dare (katakana) ta henji ga kaette kuru. Shuutome nimo "ohiru nani ga yoroshii?" to kiku to, "souyane, kudamono ga notta yasai sarada de ii wa" to iu dewa naika. Soroi mo sorotte "zarusoba de ii" "sarada de ii" to wa douiu koccha. "Zarusoba ga yoi" "sarada ga tabe tai" to nazeien.

Kakka shinagara kankan deri no naka, jitensha o kogu. Futari ga ie no naka de, kuuraa o kake te nekoron de terebi o miteru to omou to, masu masu hara ga ta tte kuru.

Reji de tenin ga hyouhakuzai ippon demo fukuro ni ire you to suru node, "teepu (o haru dake) de ii desu" to ii kake te, "teepu ni shite kudasai" to ii naoshi te shinamono o uketotta.

"XX de ii desu" to iu ii kata. Watashi wa dai kirai desu. (Reader's Column, 1999)

(Translation)

When I was ready to go shopping at the supermarket, I asked my husband, "What do you want to eat for lunch?" [lit. What is good for your lunch (nani ga ee)?] Then, a response with a slackening voice came, "Zarusoba [cold noodles] is gooood (zarusoba de ee—wa)." I asked my mother-in-law, "What would you like to eat for lunch?" [lit. What is good for your lunch (polite form) (nani ga yoroshii)?] "Well, vegetable salad with fruit topping will do" (yasai sarada de ii wa), she says to my surprise. Both together said, "zarusoba is good" (zarusoba de ii) "salad will do" (sarada de ii) but how come they say "will do" (de ii)? Why can't they say (more directly), "zarusoba is good" (zarusoba ga yoi), "I want to eat salad" (sarada ga tabe tai)?

Burning with anger under the blazing sun, I pedal the bicycle. Thinking of them lying down and watching TV with the air-conditioner on at home, my anger swells.

At the cashier counter, the salesperson will even put a bottle of bleach in a bag. I was about to say "Just a sticker will do" (teepu de ii desu) (a proof-of-purchase sticker, that is). But I stopped and corrected myself, and said "Please attach a sticker" (teepu ni shite kudasai) [lit. I decide on/make it a sticker instead of a bag and please attach it], and received the bottle.

The way of saying such as "XX de ii desu." I hate it. [my translation]

Descriptive Explication

The use of the particle *de* in the "*de ii*" expression is deeply conventionalized in Japanese language use and, of course, is unconsciously used. In this particular situation, however, the woman came to disagree with its use and makes her own personal account for its referential perspective. First, she views it as inappropriate when receiving a favor from someone. She criticizes her husband and mother-in-law for the contextualization cues they sent for interpreting their "*de ii*" expressions as framing their relationships in an assymetrical manner. She reconstructs her husband's response with epithets, such as "*dare* (in *katakana* script) *ta*" (slackening*)* and "*ee—wa*" (gooood), and indirectly charges that his way of responding sounds like he evades responsibility or lacks sincerity. These descriptions reveal her negative evaluation about her husband's mode of responding arrogantly. Furthermore, the husband and the mother-in-law implicitly frame the social arrangement as if they take things for granted. The expression "*de ii*" placed the housewife in a subordinated role of service provider for the husband and the mother-in-law. She directly expresses her negative attitude against this framing. In her discourse, she reconstructs it with such emotional wordings as "*kakka shinagara*" (burning with anger), "*futari ga ie no naka de, kuuraa o kake te nekoron de terebi o miteru to omu to, masu masu hara ga ta tte kuru*" (Thinking of them lying down and watching TV with the air-conditioner on at home, my anger swells). She reacted to her mother-in-law's response with negative surprise, as the adverbial reflection "*dewa naika*" in her indirect narrative "*to iu dewa naika*" (says to my surprise) reveals. She also showed her embarrassment of nearly using *de* herself at the market. She framed herself in the same metamessage—a process message—that she thought she had received from her family in nearly saying to the shop attendant "*tepu de ii desu*" (just a sticker will do).

Second, she claims that the phrase, "*de ii*" obscures the speaker's individuality. Her following discourse reveals this criticism: "How come they say 'will do'? (*de ii*) Why can't they say, '*Zarusoba* is good' (*Zarusoba ga yoi*), 'I want to eat salad'? (*Sarada ga tabetai*)." She contends that there is no individuality in their way of requesting what they want to eat. She also regards "*de ii*" not only defensive but wrong in its use because it evades responsibility. She reconstructs this criticism in her verbal behavior: "I stopped and corrected it," saying "Please attach a sticker" [lit. I decide on/make it a sticker instead of the bag, and please put it on the bottle] (*teepu ni shite kudasai*) to a shop attendant. As the English translation shows, the verbal phrase *ni suru* expresses the speaker's speech act, as implying that she made the decision. The verb *suru* (decide) requires that the subject and its actor become explicit; therefore, the speaker expresses her individuality through this verb. The verb requires the speaker's sincerity and responsibility (Searle, 1969) as it clarifies who is an actor. *De ii,* in contrast to *ni suru,* does not require a grammatical subject; therefore, by saying *de ii* the speaker can speak implicitly, something for which the housewife criticizes herself, for having evaded her own responsibility.

Text 2 *Koohii de ii desu* (Coffee will do)

Doitu de kurashi hajime te 16 nen ijou ni naru ga, kono aida, ninen buri de Toukyou ni kaette mite, oyatto omou koto ga iroiro atta. Kissaten de hito o matte iru to, tonari no hito ga, ueitoresu ni "koohii de ii desu" to itte, koohii o chuumon site iru. "De" no tukai kata ni iwakan o oboeta. "Amarimono de mani awasemasu," "semai heya de gaman shimasu," "kono hen de dakyou shimasu," "aachisuto e no orei wa, nashi de ii desu," nado, "de" niwa, akirame to jouho no nioi ga tukimatou. . . .

Sakki no "koohii de ii desu" to iu iikata ni hanashi o modosu to, kore wa, moji douri ni tore ba, hontou wa betu no mono ga nomitai keredomo, souiu kimochi o osae te koohii ni shimasu, to iu imi ni naru. Demo, dou iu riyuu de, jibun ga ichiban nomitai to omou mono o chuumon shinai de, jouho site koohii ni sita no ka, sono riyuu ga mattaku wakara nai to iu tokoro ga mondai nano da. Nihongo no tukai kata o machigaete iru no dewa naku, mushiro, akirame, jouhoshi, enryoshi, ki o tukai, jibun o gisei ni suru youna monogoshi dake ga, bachigai na tokoro de nan no imi mo naku hitori aruki shi teiru youna bukimi na inshou o ataeru. . . .

Doitu de wa, arayuru chansu o riyou site jibun no kosei o kakuritu suru koto ga ningen no gimu da to iu, koremata myou na kangae kata ga aru node, "naninani de ii" de wa naku, "naninani ga ii" to iu. Sore dokoro ka, "koohii ga ii" hito wa, futuu wa koucha wa nomanaishi, koucha no suki na hito ni wa koohii o zettai kuchi ni shinai hito mo sukunaku nai. Jouho wa hajirubeki haiboku de ari, nomimono o dasu gawa mo, jibun ga kyaku ni jouho o shiita to nare ba haji to naru. Dakara, kyaku ni wa kanarazu nani ga nomitai no ka tazune nakere ba naranaishi, sonotoki, nihon de yoku mimi ni suru "koohii de ii desu ka" nado to iu tazune kata wa hidoku shiturei ni ataru. Kore wa, koohii o nomu no ga ippan teki da kara anata mo soushi nasai, to iu imi na no ka, mou koohii o wakashi te shimatta kara kore o non de kureru to tasukaru to iu imi na no ka, tonikaku shiturei na iikata de aru koto ni kawari wa nai. (Tawada, 1999, pp. 14–16)

(Translation)

Since I began living in Germany, more than 16 years have passed. Recently, after a two-year absence from Tokyo, I went back and found that there were many things about which I thought, "Why?" When I was waiting for someone in a coffee shop, a patron beside me ordered a coffee, saying to the waitress, "Coffee will do." I had a feeling that the use of *de* does not fit in such a case. As in the following expressions, there is always an indication of resignation and concession: "I will make the leftover do," "I will compromise with the small room," "I will come to the settlement at this stage." "With regard to the gratitude to the artist, no payment will do," etc. . . .

Returning to the story, I mentioned the way of saying, "Coffee will do." If we interpret it literally, its meaning is that, "though I want to drink something else, I suppress such emotion and will have coffee." However, the problem with this is that—for whatever reason—the person makes a concession and decides on coffee without ordering what he/she wants most to drink. The speaker does not make a grammatical mistake with regard to the syntax, but rather, such speech gives a certain impression of giving up, making a concession, hesitating, caring, and sacrificing oneself. . . .

In Germany, because there is also a belief that it is a person's duty to make use of every possible chance to establish one's individuality, they may say "I like such and such," but not "such and such will do." It is more than that. A person "who prefers coffee" usually does not drink tea, and conversely quite a few people like tea but not coffee. Concession is a defeat that one should be ashamed of. For a host to serve a drink, it would be shameful if he/she forced the guest to make a concession. So, the host always has to ask the guest what he/she wants to drink, and if "Don't you mind drinking coffee?"

(*Koohii de ii desu ka*) were asked as it is often heard in Japan, it would be very impolite. Its implication will be that "as it is common to drink coffee, you also have to drink it, and that it will be helpful if you drink coffee because I have already made it." However, whether you believe it or not, it is an impolite expression.

Descriptive Explication

Tawada (1999) critically analyzes the Japanese use of *de* in certain situations by comparison with speakers of German. According to her, the use of *de* in the sentence "*Koohii de ii desu*" (Coffee will do) at a café is unusual and pragmatically wrong. She explains that such an expression implies that the speaker does not want to take personal responsibility for a decision. If such verbal behavior is made excessively, she contends that it will implicate defensiveness and be interpreted as laziness on the part of the speaker by seeming to avoid serious thought about his or her own preference. She adds that it conveys the message of peddling a favor because he/she has kindly chosen the second preference and dodges responsibilty if the kindness is unwelcomed. She defines its use as the manner of "giving up, making a concession, hesitating, caring, and sacrificing oneself" and it is "nonsense for a customer to worry about causing trouble by requesting a drink at a café because the customer pays for it and no one gets in trouble simply for taking an order" (p. 15).

Tawada's analogy is based on her linguistic knowledge of two different languages. She observes that German speakers place the discretion and responsibility on one's self; therefore, they speak with individuality when they make a request (e.g., "I want to drink coffee" and "I care for coffee"). Based on this observation, she extends her analogy. She makes a linguistic and cultural comparison and claims that Japanese speakers, when they use such expressions, assume a defensive stance about their behavior. She hypothesizes that Japanese defensiveness is embedded in the usage of "*de ii*" and reflects the speaker's attitude, such that he or she yields to the interlocutor the decision making. She also hypothesizes that a sense of concession is embedded in the defensive attitude, and "behind the concession a hungry-look is visible from time to time" (p. 14).

While the Japanese think that a concession is a practical strategy of defensiveness, she claims that Germans think that it "is a defeat that one should be ashamed of," because in Germany, "it is a person's duty to make use of every possible chance to establish one's individuality" (p. 15). Here, she brings the issue of "self" to explain the difference of the ethno-conception about individualism. She claims that in Germany it is acceptable for

a host to ask the guest about his/her preference first, even if he/she does not have anything else but coffee. If the guest says "green tea," then the host will reply "I do not have any." If the guest replies "tea," then the host replies, "I don't have tea either." They (German speakers) reply this way because a person's desire should not be altered or corrected according to a temporary change of physical conditions such that there is nothing other than coffee. (p. 15)

Then, Tawada displays her own identity with regard to this conception. She claims that "there is no reason to erase one's desire from the beginning. Even at dessert, if one wants to eat fish, he or she ought to say that he or she wants to eat fish" (p. 15).

Tawada extends her analogy to other examples that include the sentences such as "Coffee will do" (*Koohii de ii desu*), "No vacation will do" (*Kyuuka nashi de ii desu*), "This person will do" (*Kono hito de ma ni awase masu*), "Being a house-wife will do" (*Shufu de ii desu*), and "Regular will do" (*Futuu de ii desu*). She concludes that if a speaker chooses such expressions, the speaker indicates that what is spoken (i.e., coffee, vacation, this person) is not his or her first choice.

SOCIAL MARKERS AND MULTIPLE PERSPECTIVES

Researchers may come to consider Japanese speakers' use of the particle *de* as polite because being implicit is often considered polite in Japanese society. However, as Texts 1 and 2 show, this linguistic feature evidently indexes differ-ent social meanings; there is a gap between what is expressed by the particle and what is interpretable. Although the rhetoric of the texts differ, their writers share a common insight into the phenomenon of *de*. They refer to the indexical aspect of the language: how a speaker frames his or her message and the metamessage that is perceived. In Text 1, the speakers (the husband and the mother-in-law) may implicitly convey a concession by using the particle *de*, but the writer iden-tifies its metamessage as conveying asymmetrical social relations and obscuring individuality. In Text 2, the speaker presumably conveys politeness or concern, but the writer identifies the speaker's attitude and linguistic sensitivity with terms such as "concession," "defensive," "hungry-looking," and "giving-up." These cases of everyday discourse provide support for Goffman's (1959) claim that the content message by a speaker and the process message given off are fundamen-tally asymmetrical in communication. That is, even if speakers are likely to pre-sent themselves in a favorable light (and others, as well), listeners who are aware of the process message given off may be little concerned about it or will receive the message in other frames. To account for these social significances they per-ceived, I reexamine the *de ii* expression in interactional exchange, and will dis-cuss what social marking this particle inherently postulates in interaction. I first discuss the ways in which the expression is most plausibly accounted for in sociopragmatic theory.

Politeness, Deference, and Implicitness

The speakers' social attitudes about using this particle, as well as other parti-cles such as *ne* and *yo,* are often discussed in the disciplines of pragmatics and sociolinguistics, because many Japanese particles inherently index social mark-ers that are assumed related to the social norm of politeness. For example, according to the theory of politeness (Brown & Levinson, 1987) the *de ii* expression would be characterized as a strategy for performing off-record politeness, because making a request threatens the face of the recipient (and the speaker's as well), something the speaker tries to minimize. If valid, the speakers in Texts 1 and 2 may use this politeness strategy to make their request vague and save the recipient's face. The *de* particle also may be used to observe the Tact Maxim, one of the maxims that comprise the Politeness Principle (PP), proposed by Leech (1983). According to this view, the maxim states that speakers minimize the expression of beliefs that imply an imposition on another. If the speakers of our texts believe that making a request imposes on the recipients, then they would try to reduce the implied cost to the recipients by being vague.

Other researchers of Japanese language and culture may argue that the use of the particle *de* reveals how the speakers orient themselves in relation to others (Lebra, 1976). In a society like Japan, harmony and dependency become important values reflective of Japanese collectivism rather than individualism, and so people behave accordingly by honoring the group ahead of themselves. Thus, use of the particle *de* in the above cases would be considered as displaying an attitude favorable to group harmony.

Frame of the Particle in Interactional Structure

When we examine the use of the particle *de* in interactional structure, it also encodes a reading that differs from those mentioned above. To show this, I incorporate the notion of frame and analyze the semantic relations (Fillmore, 1982) that the particle develops by contrast with the particle *ga* in the *ga ii* construction.[2] Consider this contrast between B-1 and B-2 responses by B to a question by A:

A: *Nomimono wa nani ga ii desu ka*? (With regard to the drinks, what is good to you?)

B-1: *Koohii ga ii desu* (Coffee is good)

B-2: *Koohii de ii desu* (Coffee will do)

As I explained earlier, the particle *ga* in the *koohii ga ii* construction in B-1 indicates speaker B's explicit preference for coffee over other drinks. The particle frames the utterance and constructs a semantic relation between speakers A and B, and their common referent, the coffee. By indicating the referent as a first choice, normally what the speaker gives off is that the selected object is the best among other selections. Thus in B-1, the particle *ga* frames the coffee such that the coffee is credited more highly than other drinks. What I wish to point out is that this high regard for coffee becomes extended to A and B also. Involvement with such a well-regarded entity ought to rub off on its users as well. Conversely, if the entity were discredited as in B-2, by indicating that coffee is dispreferred, then this framing could cast A and B in a light less favorable than that found in B-1. Although this perspective may not readily become an issue today with Japanese interpersonal relations, it will do so, however, the more that Japanese embrace individualism in the future, a matter that is not entirely unlikely.

Social and Cultural Indexing in Interactional Floor

Through frame theory, as has been developed in linguistics,[3] and related notions from Goffman (1974) and Tannen (1990), the mapping of social images that emerge in interactional structure helps us to understand what kind of expectation the particle *de* engenders for the interactants involved. A way to map these social images is by observing how an interactional floor is developed in social interaction. Floor is a cognitive space shared by the interactants, where they construct their participation structure, develop interpersonal relations between them, and behave with regard to what is going on within the structure (Hayashi, 1991, 1996). Related social expectations grow out of the immediate context of the interpersonal encounter and are rooted in one's background of sociocultural experience.

For example, the context of the writers' floor in the texts quoted earlier includes service encounters at a store where events of service-giving and -receiving take place. This immediate context involves a variety of contextual features that the interactants must utilize to stay aligned together within the floor, and thus carry out their respective roles. Japanese, as well as speakers of other languages, are sensitive to the concept of *ba* (event), for it influences how a floor becomes socially constructed. The conventional expectation about the event of service-giving and -receiving in Japan generally aligns the service-giver in a lower status and the receiver of the service in a higher status. This alignment of role status is sometimes reversed, even going out of the established social hierarchy. One example is the mother–child relation, by which the mother holds the power and is in a higher position. However, this conventional mother–child relation in status reverses when the mother takes the role of service-giver. Social convention expects the event to frame the participation structure of the floor for conversation and aligns the mother (respondent) in a lower position and the child (speaker) in a higher position. Therefore, the mother often asks questions about the child's preference using the particle *de,* whereas *ga* may be more structurally appropriate. In reply to a child's request, such as "*Nanika nai*" (Is there anything [to drink]?), mothers are often heard to reply by saying, "*Omizu de ii*" (Will water do?). Conventionally, the event frames the mother's participation in this conversation as a service provider, which elicits her *de* face-saving function. Yet, structurally, the semantic connection frames the relation between the mother and the child in the ways that she subtly discredits herself and even the water despite that she says water (*mizu*) with the *o-* honorific affixed. Although her service role shifts power to the child, the discrediting by the *de* particle of the water extends even to the child. The very fact that this "discrediting" of the parties concerned goes generally unnoticed in Japan is telling of Japaneseness. Politeness is so highly valued that it comes with certain "costs" to the Japanese themselves. Moreover, as Texts 1 and 2 suggest, an awakening of individualism in Japan may cause Japanese to question related social conventions, giving rise to social change.

The general rationale within Japanese collectivism is that vagueness by a speaker accommodates the receiver. That is, one avoids possible imposition on the other, as seen with the Tact Maxim previously. Thus, the *de* particle comes to be used. At a deeper level of analysis, however, *de* comes at the cost of individuality by suppressing one's real preferences. It even is discrediting for the parties involved. As long as social harmony is the target goal, benefits will accrue. But not always, as Texts 1 and 2 illustrate. These texts show that a tension between collectivism and individualism may be budding in Japan, which parallels the bicivilization cited in chapter 1. The potential duality or multiplicity of perspectives is a common attribute of Japanese social relations and to this extent demonstrates an important feature of Japaneseness. Research of this phenomenon not only will enlarge our knowledge of Japanese culture but also pragmatics as a field in general.

CONCLUSION

Despite the burgeoning interest in the study of the relationships between language structure, beliefs, attitude, and states of mind, there are few analyses on Japanese discourse that investigate the affects with regard to how a speaker provokes a listener to feel cast within a certain interactional frame. In this chapter, I showed how people display and interpret social attitude through language in everyday discourse, and demonstrated through natural data that the social markers Japanese language is often thought to bear, do not necessarily index positive attitudes, such as politeness to the addressee. Negative, as well as positive, attitudes accompany social interactions, and their interpretation depends on how the addressee frames them when language is used. Events carry significant social information in Japanese communication, and the uses of language must accord with it. Yet, in a language like Japanese, the social significance is marked in any utterance, and such significance does not often accord with what events mark and what expectations the addressee(s) have, leading interactants to implicate dual messages in interaction. Such duality may be particularly relevant to Japanessness as an acute condition of Japanese social interactions and so merits all the more attention.

ACKNOWLEDGMENT

The author wishes to thank Yoko Tawada and *Chuuou Kouron* for permission to use Tawada's essay.

NOTES

1. In linguistic convention, the particle *ga* marks the new information as a topic, that is, the coffee has never been discussed before. When a transitive adjective follows as a predicate as shown in the utterance B-1, it marks the topic element (coffee) presented as a subject, though it corresponds to a direct object in English (Makino and Tsutsui, 1986, p. 120). The sentence, "*Watashi wa koohii ga ii desu*" (To me, coffee is desirable) presents *Watashi* (I) as a topic and *koohii* (coffee) as a subject (though it is considered to be a direct object).

2. The discussion on the relational coherence of the logical relationship between statements within the theory of frame semantics is given in Hayashi and Hayashi (1995) and the similar argument is made here to explain how the particles construct the specific relational coherence with the referents.

3. The linguistic theory of frame semantics has been developed by Fillmore (1975), who has incorporated the ideas of the frame theories in different fields or disciplines, including the one discussed in this paper. See Tannen (1990) for the detailed explanation.

REFERENCES

Bateson, G. (1972). *Steps to an ecology of mind.* New York: Ballantine Books.

Brown, P., & Levinson, S. C. (1987). *Politeness: Some universals in language usage.* Cambridge: Cambridge University Press.

Fillmore, C. J. (1975). An alternative to checklist theories of meaning. In *Proceedings of the first annual meeting of the Berkeley Linguistics Society* (pp. 123–131). Berkeley: University of California Press.

Fillmore, C. J. (1982). Frame semantics. In The Linguistic Society of Korea (Eds.), *Linguistics in the Morning Calm* (pp. 111–137). Seoul: Hanshin Publishing.

Goffman, E. (1959). *The presentation on self in everyday life.* New York: Doubleday.

Goffman, E. (1974). *Frame analysis.* New York: Harper & Row.

Gumperz, J. J. (1982). *Discourse strategies.* Cambridge: Cambridge University Press.

Gumperz, J. J. (1992). Contextualization and understanding. In A. Duranti & C. Goodwin (Eds.), *Rethinking context* (pp. 229–252). Cambridge: Cambridge University Press.

Gumperz, J. J. (1996). The linguistic and cultural relativity of conversational inference. In J. J. Gumperz & S. C. Levinson (Eds.), *Rethinking linguistic relativity* (pp. 374–406). Cambridge: Cambridge University Press.

Hayashi, R. (1991). Floor structure of English and Japanese conversation. *Journal of Pragmatics, 16,* 1–30.

Hayashi, R. (1996). *Cognition, empathy and interaction: A floor management of English and Japanese conversation.* Norwood, NJ: Ablex.

Hayashi, R. (1997). Hierarchical interdependence expressed through conversational styles in Japanese women's magazines. *Discourse and Society, 8*(3), 359–389.

Hayashi, R., & Hayashi, T. (in press). Duality and continuum in indirect talk: Linguistic style and gender in clinical supervision. In D. C. S. Li (Ed.), *Discourses in search of members in honor of Ron Scollon.* Washington, DC: University Press of America.

Hayashi, T., & Hayashi, R. (1995) A cognitive study of English loanwords in Japanese discourse. *World Englishes, 4*(1), 55–66.

Kojien [Japanese dictionary]. (1971). Tokyo: Iwanami.

Lebra, T. S. (1976) *Japanese patterns of behavior.* Honolulu: University of Hawai'i Press.

Leech, J. N. (1983). *Principles of pragmatics.* London: Longman.

Makino, S., & Tsutsui, M. (1986). *A dictionary of basic Japanese grammar.* Tokyo: Japan Times.

Reader's column. (1999, September 7). *Mainichi Shimbun.*

Searle, J. R. (1969). *Speech acts.* Cambridge: Cambridge University Press.

Tannen, D. (1990). *You just don't understand.* New York: Ballantine.

Tawada, Y. (1999). Essay: *yuzuru monogoshi monohoshige* [Manner of making a concession with a hungry look]. In *Chuuou Kouron, 3,* 14–16.

part VIII

Japanese Mass Media
and Internet Communications

Chapter 21

Japanese Advertising Discourse: Reconstructing Images

Brian Moeran

This chapter discusses distinctive features of Japanese advertising as finished products and as social processes. In the first part, the common assertion that Japanese advertising constitutes a unique and indirect style is examined and called into question. Does it really reflect Confucian or collectivist values, adopt a soft-sell approach designed to appeal harmoniously to the consumer, or prefer an emotional to an informational format? For the most part, no. At the same time, there are certain ways in which language, design, and aesthetics are presented in Japanese ads which do make them different from advertisements found elsewhere. In the second part of the chapter, the social processes surrounding the production of advertising are examined and a number of differences between Japanese and American and European advertising agencies are highlighted. In particular, the adoption of the split-account system encourages a somewhat unusual relationship between agency and client on the one hand, and between agencies and other media organizations on the other.

Japan has the largest economy in the world after that of the United States, and its advertising market, too, is second only to America's.[1] Unlike other countries whose advertising industries have been, for the most part, dominated by American agencies, Japan has managed to create and sustain the growth of its own powerful and independent advertising agencies. As a result, it has been able to carve out for itself a certain socioeconomic space whose products (the advertisements themselves) have been seen by many analysts—in particular by those employed in other advertising industries, as well as in academic environments—to be peculiarly "Japanese."

In this chapter, I examine this discourse of Japaneseness in two rather different, but interrelated, spheres. Most studies of advertising focus on the *products* of advertising, that is, on the finished *advertisements* put out by the industry as a whole. Just how these advertisements reach their final, public, analyzed form, however, remains woefully obscure. I have also argued, therefore, that we need to examine the social *processes* behind the creation and media placement of ads, that is, *advertising*. For example, it is the negotiations between agency and client, on the one hand, and those among different divisions—specifically account services, marketing, and creative—within an advertising agency, on the other hand, which crucially affect a particular campaign's "tone" and "voice" (that is, its linguistic and communicative forms; its choice of Chinese, Japanese, and/or Roman scripts; color, design, aesthetics, and use of model or celebrity; and overall subject matter and cultural style). Although I have gone into such micro-level social processes in my monograph on a Japanese advertising agency (Moeran, 1996), I wish here to look rather more generally at the production of advertisements in Japan and to suggest certain ways in which they might be affected by the structure and organization of the Japanese advertising industry as a whole.

JAPANESE ADVERTISEMENTS

Let me start by addressing the advertisements themselves. There are certain themes that crop up time and time again in non-Japanese people's interpretations of what makes Japanese ads "Japanese." For example, in a recent book, *Global Marketing and Advertising*, Marieke de Mooij writes:

Japanese advertising reflects Confucian and collectivist values. Concepts of face and harmony lead to an indirect communication style. . . . The goal of Japanese advertising is to make friends with consumers and get them to trust and rely on the seller, to win their respect . . . by telling a story or by entertaining the audience. Identification of the brand, company name, or product in a commercial is less important than pleasing the consumer. . . . The soft-sell approach is meant to induce the consumer to be kind enough to take a close look at the product in the store. . . . The result is overall mood, advertising that is entertaining, has fantasy appeals, and is low on facts. Thus advertising does not explicitly provide the product benefits, and "advertising liking" plays an important role. (Mooij, 1998, p. 281)

I have quoted this passage at length because it neatly delineates certain traits that are often seen to constitute a "Japanese advertising style": for instance, indirectness, soft-sell, and mood, rather than product information. In the eyes of many observers, these traits—together with an emphasis on "the Asian value of harmony," man's "oneness with nature," and use of celebrity endorsement further noted by Mooij—characterize advertising in Japan as, if not unique, at least very different from that found in other societies (see, for example, Burton, 1983; Day, 1984; Fox, 1990, p. 48; Knibbs, 1992; Mosdell, 1986). Advertisements are seen somehow to be more "intuitive" or "atmospheric" in Japan (Schein, 1991, p. 2) than they are elsewhere in the world.

Clearly, such an approach needs a critical eye rather than simple (celebrity) academic endorsement. After all, every advertisement "tells a story" of some sort; every advertisement is also designed to attract attention and thus to "entertain." In principle, much advertising also tends to make use of situations in which concepts like trust, reliance, and friendship are deployed to persuade consumers to buy the products and services advertised. It may be that in Japan such concepts are sometimes given more emphasis than they currently are in Europe or the United States, but this does not mean that they are, or have been, absent in the work of advertising industries outside Japan (cf. Marchand, 1985). There are other countries, particularly in Asia, where the focus on alliances, networks, and exchange as a preferred mode of social organization makes trust, reliance, and mutual reciprocity crucial social norms (see, for example, Yang, 1994). We would thus expect the advertising in such countries to exhibit similar tendencies to those remarked here for products of the Japanese industry. In other words, Japan's geographical and cultural proximity to other east and southeast Asian societies—its very "Asianess"—should make us beware of comparing Japanese (or other Asian) with specifically American and other Western advertising, since the latter invites us to pose an "orientalist" discourse of difference that is not so readily apparent *within* the Asian region.

It is with this in mind that we should address the remaining "unique" features of Japanese advertising picked out by Mooij. So-called Confucian values, for example, are found not only among Japanese businessmen and educators, but are consciously used by fellow Asians from Korea and Taiwan in the east to Malaysia and Singapore in the west (see, for example, Cauquelin, Lim, & Mayer-König, 1998), which means that we can expect to—and do—find some Confucian values contributing to those societies' advertising styles. Similarly, many other "collectivist" peoples in Asia value harmony over confrontation, mood to information advertising, and prefer soft- to hard-sell, so that once again these qualities in themselves do not tell us anything about what makes Japan's advertising style particularly "Japanese."

At the same time, however, anyone with a reasonably broad understanding of the different kinds of advertising found in various media in Japan can also point out that ads do not necessarily aim at creating "harmony" between consumer and producer or between one product and another. Examples of comparative advertising do occur in Japan from time to time, although not so often as they do in the United States.[2] Moreover, as to whether a soft- or hard-sell approach that relies on "mood" rather than "information" is adopted depends very much on the type of product advertised and type of media used. Foods, for example, tend to be more information driven than alcohol ads. Bargain sales are always going to be more "in the consumer's face" than advertisements for art exhibitions. Print ads in general, especially perhaps those found in magazines, are always going to provide far more information than 15-second television commercials which may be—as Nakanishi points out in chapter 22—more effective in Japan than, for example, in the United States.

There are two interrelated simple and pragmatic points to be made here. Depiction of an advertising "style" cannot be based simply on a limited knowledge of advertisements in a *single* medium because almost all advertisements are part of *multi*media campaigns. Thus, print advertising generally is used to pinpoint particular consumers (defined by gender, age group, interests, and so on) and to add depth to the broad scope, or reach, of television commercials, while point-of-purchase advertising is designed explicitly to facilitate the ultimate aim of all advertising: the purchase of the product or service advertised. So, as Varda Langholz-Leymore (1987, p. 324) points out, "individual advertisements are nothing but isolated pieces in a jigsaw puzzle." This means that judgments of advertising style—in the manner generally carried out by semioticians—have to take account of three things. First, a single advertisement or commercial only makes sense vis-à-vis all other advertising in the *campaign* of which it is a part *synchronically*. Second, that campaign itself must be located in the *diachronic* context of previous campaigns for the same product. And third, it also must be fitted into the synchronic and diachronic structures of the advertising of all other similar products or product ranges (contact lenses, for example, or shampoos, family sedans, low-alcohol lagers, and so on), since each campaign has a knock-on effect on the campaigns of all competing products which themselves then affect the way in which the next campaign for the product in question is carried out. Advertising thus ends up as a kaleidoscope of meanings and product styles (Langholz-Leymore, 1987, p. 325).

Let me take as a concrete example an advertising campaign for contact lenses produced by the agency in which I conducted my research (Moeran, 1996). In trying to distinguish a new product—the *Ikon Breath O$_2$*—from competing lenses, the agency's account team came up with two concepts, "soft–hard" (describing a characteristic of the lens itself) and "serious" (an appeal both to the self-image of the manufacturer—a formerly prestigious corporation that had been at the forefront of Japan's postwar economic revival—and to consumers who took their eyesight seriously enough to want to buy this particular lens). Once the campaign was launched, other manufacturers of similar brands of contact lenses (including Menicon, Bausch & Lomb, Seed, and Johnson-Johnson) found themselves having to review and once or twice slightly change the meanings and values already attributed to their products in separate advertising campaigns. Thus, one manufacturer began to emphasize "softness" as a new quality of its product; another followed *Ikon Breath O$_2$* in making the visual of a lens cut green rather than blue as previously. This, in turn, led the agency to change subtly one part of the "softness" attributed to its client's lens by making use of a soft-focus portrait of a trendily dressed, "hard" Miho Sekine (the celebrity used) in its second campaign. This development obliged the other manufacturers to turn to their agencies for new ideas, and so on, as each tried to give its product one or more distinctive properties that would keep it apart from, preferably ahead of, its competitors. But this game of distinction was not confined to the contact lens market for, within a year, the image changes taking place within this particular product line (contact lenses) also began to affect neighboring product ranges for eyeglasses, accessories, and fashion, where the "soft–hard" look was also consciously adopted by one or two manufacturers. Such changes themselves set off a chain reaction among existing values and meanings within these partially separate sets of objects so that once again a number of moves were made in this different, but parallel, game of advertising chess.

Given this structural logic by which advertising presents products as both material objects and "cultural exercises" (Baudrillard, 1981, p. 57), as well as the aims and purposes of advertising in different media forms, we can begin to appreciate the difficulties involved in lumping together all Japanese advertising and calling it "atmospheric," "indirect," or whatever. At the same time, however, I think it is fair to say that there are certain areas where it does display particular cultural dispositions.

One of these is connected with "nature." Here I do *not* wish to suggest that Japanese advertisements achieve a certain "oneness with nature" as described by Mooij above. Rather, as Lise Skov and I have argued elsewhere (Moeran & Skov, 1993, 1997), they are part of a particular marketing pattern which makes use of special events (Christmas, Valentine's Day, *o-chūgen* midsummer gift giving, and so on) and seasonal references in general to promote consumer goods.[3] Some of the visual references used for such events are "natural": Mount Fuji, for example, symbolizes the New Year, cherry blossoms the spring, bamboo midsummer, maple leaves late autumn, and so on. Such images are made to symbolize as wide a variety of events and emotions as possible in their attempt to persuade people to buy the products or services advertised and, clearly, changes in the seasons are related to cycles of both production and consumption. Print advertisements for skin creams and face tonics, for example, often are situated in a language and visuals that emphasize winter and dryness, while summer is heralded by ads for deodorants that—along with other headlines and visuals for swimwear, for example—emphasize "nudity" (*hadaka* and *nūdo*).[4] Such "summer" ads are also clearly marked by extensive use of blue skies and blue water. Some campaigns, like that for Royal Doulton in the early 1990s, consist of one advertisement for each of the four seasons in the dominant colors of green, blue, red, and grey (spring, summer, autumn, and winter, respectively). Others, however, like that for Tokyo Beauty Salon in the winter of 1991–1992, juxtapose opposing seasons by using such headlines as *Midwinter Midsummer* (*Mafuyu no Manatsu*) to show how young women should start thinking of, and working on, their bodies in midwinter if they want to look attractive in their summer bikinis on the beach.

We need to be careful about assuming from these examples that Japanese ads are culturally peculiar in their usage of nature. After all, blue (sky or water) is likely to be the dominant "summer" color of all advertising throughout the world, while dark tones are often used in the winter months.[5] In addition, we need to remember that—as suggested above—some products and industries (of which fashion is the most notable example) are seasonally oriented. What makes the use of nature slightly special in the case of Japanese ads, perhaps, is the frequency with which it is actively exploited in marketing and used to appeal to individual consumers' tastes—tastes that already have been socialized through both family and education systems to "appreciate" nature. Japanese nature thus can be seen as part of what Bourdieu (1984) has referred to as distinction (here at both social and national ideological levels), and it is in this sense that advertisements making use of natural imagery can be said to exhibit a certain "Japaneseness."

Another area in which Japanese advertisements have been thought to convey a sense of "Japaneseness" is in their use of *aesthetics* and design (see Mosdell, 1986, pp. 18, 75–76). Again, this claim may be said to be partially true, in the sense that there are some advertisements that clearly are constructed with a view to emphasizing one visible aspect of their design through proximate or surrounding blank space, in a manner that might not be readily appreciated by a non-Japanese. At the same time, however, we should realize that there is no one "Japanese aesthetic." Not surprisingly, therefore, we can find plenty of advertisements in Japan that are definitely not "zen-like" in their approach and that will do their utmost to clutter all kinds of linguistic and visual information into the available space within a particular ad's frame. Moreover, we should recognize that global communication and information make the idea of a "pure" Japanese aesthetic untenable, and that nowadays designers and art directors in agencies throughout the world have beside their desks dozens of books of visual images (art, photography, design, and so on) from which they plunder at will as they seek to find the perfect solution to the advertising problem at hand. In this respect, European and American art directors are as likely to borrow "Japanese" images as Japanese are from elsewhere. When it comes to design, therefore, we are faced with what some might see as a postmodern pastiche or aesthetic bricolage—witness, for example, how Japanese ads make indiscriminate simultaneous use of multiple languages and scripts—in which it is virtually impossible to define precisely what constitutes "Japaneseness," "Frenchness," or whatever.

Use of the aesthetic (or poetic) function in language, however, may well be a different matter.[6] In earlier work, I have argued that Japanese—unlike, say, English or American—advertising has tended to make use of a limited number of keywords, which exist in numerous cultural domains and whose meanings are condensed to reflect certain cultural tensions (Moeran, 1984). I also have noted that, whereas English advertising language tends to favor proverb-like, quadripartite structures (such as "Long on resources. Short on red tape"), Japanese advertising does not, with the singular exception of lexical parallelism found in the juxtaposition of Chinese characters (*kanji*) in some ads.[7] Following Jakobson's important work on the link between linguistics and poetics (Jakobson, 1960), and taking account of ways in which Japanese ads sometimes make allusions to Japanese literature and folklore (Moeran, 1989, pp. 123–131), I hypothesized further that, whereas English advertising tends to emphasize alliteration, assonance, and structural completeness in its use of headlines and slogans, Japanese would seem at times to prefer association, suggestion, and structural incompleteness of the kind generally seen to be central to Japanese aesthetics (Keene, 1972; Moeran, 1985). While such a hypothesis is clearly linked to the perceived emphasis on mood advertising discussed earlier, we should note again that it is only true of some, not all, kinds of advertising. It is in this area of language use and "cultural play" that I see Japanese advertisements as being distinctive, particularly, perhaps, in those areas like onomatopoeic duplications (*sara sara*, *pichi pichi*, *fuwa fuwa*, and so on) which are particularly resistant to translation.

Yet another area in which we find obvious representational differences is in the ways in which bodies and gestures are used in Japanese advertising. Like all advertising throughout the world, Japanese advertisements tend to fragment the body, by presenting partial images: for example, legs only are portrayed in ads for stockings, hands for jewelry, hair (with or without partial face) for shampoos, rinses, and hair products, and so on.[8] Precisely because many advertising campaigns for major cosmetics and fashion houses make use of global images that originate in the West, Japanese advertisements, too, have their abundance of models running one hand through their hair, looking back or sideways across a bare shoulder, folding their arms, putting hands on hips, revealing belly buttons, caressing thighs, and so forth. At the same time, however, there are certain body gestures that are much more specifically Japanese. One obvious example is that of a woman's hand across her laughing mouth; another, somewhat stranger posture adopted by female models consists of bending the torso forward and sticking out the rear, while keeping both legs together and straight. There are other uses of the face and body—in particular, of the hands and legs—exemplifying the "cute" (*kawaii*) style discussed by, among others, Sharon Kinsella (1995), while there are also certain visual preferences (like that for the back of a woman's neck) that are not so commonly found in Western advertising.

All in all, we may well agree with John Clammer (1995, p. 210) that "the favored female body is young, firm, fair, middleclass, average and cute" and that the presentation of the body in Japanese ads (and other media) tends to be regulated by a strong sense of what is "appropriate," so that the body ends up being somewhat "disciplined" in appearance (Clammer, 1995, p. 215). Given advertising's general lack of restraint in the portrayal of consumption practices and dreams, this may help explain another feature of Japanese advertising noted by foreign observers: the prevalent use of Caucasian models,[9] although why Japanese ads should so often use a non-Japanese to promote products remains somewhat of a mystery. William O'Barr (1994, p. 176), for example, suggests that Western models are associated in Japanese consumers' minds with action, freedom, and flexibility and so "signify an alternative to the expectations and conventions of Japanese society." Clammer (1995, p. 213) suggests that Western models "either promote the consumption of that which is hidden (underwear), or that which is distinctly exotic (such as French perfumes) and, as such, that which is by definition not Japanese, but enjoyable by the Japanese woman as an indicator of her internationalization and sophistication."[10] These seem to be reasonable assumptions. We might add further, though, that Japanese models are almost invariably used in advertisements related to tourism. They are also frequently found endorsing health and internal body products, as well as for those that are taken into the body (in particular, Japanese, and not necessarily Western, foods and drinks). The more products are disconnected from the body, it seems, the more likely Western models are to be used.

JAPANESE ADVERTISING PROCESSES

Now that we have looked at Japanese advertisements themselves, I want to turn to the social processes surrounding their production and look at the way in which the Japanese advertising industry is structured. My aim here is to see what, if any, of these processes are particularly "Japanese" and how, if at all, such processes may be related to the style of the advertisements described above.

Let us start with advertising agencies. American agencies have come to dominate the global advertising scene for a simple reason connected with the activities of their clients, on the one hand, and with the very nature of the agency–client relationship, on the other. As a company grows big, it tends to look outside its own country for new business opportunities. Because it already makes use of an agency to handle its advertising at home, and because it is usually unaware of how advertising functions in those countries in which it is developing new business opportunities, that company generally asks that same agency to handle its business abroad. Thus, the internationalization of American advertising agencies has gone hand in hand with the internationalization of the American economy. Once an agency finds that not just one of, but several, perhaps a large number of, its clients is establishing offices overseas, it, too, tends to do the same. In other words, the strength of American agencies overseas—in particular, in various parts of Latin America, Europe, Africa, and, more recently, Asia—has been closely related to the presence of American corporations overseas and thus to the overall strength of the American economy. It is possible, just possible, that this economic strength has been reflected in a communicative style of advertising first developed in the United States (hard-, rather than soft-sell, for example, with its perceived concomitant emphasis on directness, comparison, and language over image).

This simple economic fact enables us to understand why American agencies have not been as successful in the world's second largest advertising market as they have been elsewhere. Precisely because of Japan's own phenomenal postwar economic growth, Japanese agencies have been able to resist the influx of American agencies and to maintain control over the domestic market. It is the growth of Japanese corporations and affiliated groups—like Shiseido, Toyota, Suntory, Matsushita, and so on—that were advertising actively in Japan throughout the second half of the 20th century that has enabled Japanese agencies to grow and resist the arrival of American and other foreign agencies. And these advertising clients have, as we are all aware, developed into powerful transnational conglomerates that have competed successfully with their American and European rivals in the world's markets. Without the resilience and strength of these clients, therefore, we might surmise that Japanese agencies would almost certainly have succumbed to the influence of their American counterparts and thus have been unable to assert the cultural peculiarities of the market in which they operate.

This in itself, however, is not sufficient explanation for the independence of the Japanese advertising industry and, concomitantly, of its advertising style. Here we need to outline two further economic factors underpinning its communicative forms. The first of these concerns agencies' embeddedness in other media organizations. Although Japanese advertising agencies are no different from advertising agencies elsewhere in the world in the manner in which they started out as brokers of space (and later, time) selling media to their clients, some of them have, over the years, invested heavily in media organizations which have themselves, in turn, invested in advertising agencies. As a result, there is a complex set of interlocking relations among agencies, newspaper and magazine publishers, and radio and television stations, which includes the sharing of media content on the one hand, and mutual shareholding on the other (Westney, 1996) and which enables some agencies to establish and maintain special lines of "communication" with particular media organizations. These lines of communication—for example, the ability of Dentsu to purchase prime-time commercial spots on NTV (Nihon Television) as a result of its investment in the station when it was established in 1953 (Moeran, 1996, pp. 259–260)—enable agencies to offer their clients preferential treatment of one sort or another, a treatment that is clearly not available to the clients of American agencies operating in Japan.

This brings us to the second, and in my opinion crucial, economic factor: the account system. Unlike anywhere else in the world, Japanese advertisers have not handed over the whole of their advertising appropriations to a single agency, but have preferred to divide them into a number of different accounts, according to product line, media, and/or a combination of the two.[11] As I argued in my monograph on the Japanese advertising industry (Moeran, 1996), what is known as the split-account system is a clever divide-and-rule mechanism that enables advertisers to exert considerable control over the activities of their agencies. At the same time, by maintaining control over the amount of marketing and other information given out to each of its agencies, an advertiser virtually obliges those agencies to interact with one another and with the media organizations in which they are placing their client's advertising, so that the split-account system also makes for a much tighter-knit organization of the institutions that make up the advertising industry in Japan. This means that networking and personal contacts take on a slightly greater significance than they would seem to do in advertising industries elsewhere, and that personal likes and dislikes, rather than detached professionalism, tend to guide both business and creative decisions in agency–client relations.

This is an important point because it is sometimes hinted by those in the industry that Japanese advertising is not as "creative" as that found in, say, Britain or the United States. Of course, definitions of what constitutes "creativity" are problematic and tend to be culture bound (especially when defined for Asians by Westerners), but there is a further point connected with the organization of the Japanese advertising industry that may be relevant here. Precisely because the competing account rule is not followed in Japan—that is to say, because, unlike in Europe or the United States, a single agency may handle the advertising accounts of any number of competing automobile, beer, or cosmetics manufacturers—large Japanese advertising agencies find themselves taking on several hundred different accounts. (By way of comparison, we should point out that American agencies with equivalent billings to such Japanese agencies probably handle fewer than three or four dozen accounts at any one time.)

As a result, those working in Japanese agencies are not assigned to a single account over a long period of time, but find themselves attending to a variety of different accounts and working with numerous account teams (made up of account executives, planners, marketers, media, and creative personnel) over much shorter, and more intense, overlapping periods of time. This means that "creativity" as such is not allowed to take on the kind of importance attributed to it in some European and American agencies, since people just cannot spare the time to indulge in such a luxury (a word used by my Japanese informants to describe their situation). Those working in Japanese agencies tend instead to adopt a fairly down-to-earth, pragmatic approach to the production of advertisements. Precisely because the split-account system encourages close cooperation and negotiation between client and agency, there is a tendency for the latter to be guided rather more by marketing aims and situations than by the kind of creative impulses outlined by advertising gurus like David Ogilvy and others.

CONCLUSION

I have outlined some of the distinctive features of the products and processes of the Japanese advertising industry. In the first part of this chapter, I discussed ways in which Japanese advertisements have been seen and commented on by scholars and those working in advertising industries around the world. I then tried to show how some of the generalizations made—especially those classifying Japanese advertising as soft-sell, mood-oriented, and lacking information—need to be reconsidered in the light of the particular marketing aims and media adopted in different advertising campaigns. While, like all "myths," such ideas contain

their kernels of truth, they provide in the end no more than broad sweeping categories that may tell us rather more about American and European stereotypes of
"Japan" and the "Japanese" than about Japanese advertising itself. I argued, further, that all studies of advertising have to move beyond individual advertisements to take account of current and previous campaigns, both of the products
advertised and of all competing products and product lines.

I proceeded to discuss certain aspects of the contents of Japanese advertising
which I saw as being culturally specific: in particular, its use of nature for marketing purposes, its adoption of a particular style of language based on keywords,
and an overall aesthetic that focuses on association, suggestion, and structural
incompleteness. I then remarked on how Japanese advertising also makes use of
distinctive cultural representations of the (female) body, which I then related to
the pervasive use of Western (primarily Caucasian) models in ads and television
commercials.

From this I moved to the second part of the chapter in which I outlined certain
distinctive features of the organization of the Japanese advertising industry.
These included the virtual absence of major American advertising agencies on
the Japanese scene, a fact which I suggested might possibly have had some
impact on Japanese advertising content. I then pursued this possible connection
between advertising processes and products by examining how advertisers split
their accounts in an effort to control the agencies working for them. I argued that,
in fact, the split-account system obliges agencies and media to interact more
closely than they do elsewhere in the world, and encourages a reliance on personal networking and contacts rather than objective professionalism in decisions
about what is or is not included in any one advertising campaign. Finally, I suggested that the sheer number of accounts generated by the split-account system
might have a negative effect on "creativity" in the Japanese advertising industry.

Clearly, such hypotheses are extremely tentative, especially in view of my
attempt to place Japanese advertising within the development and overall context
of the American and other advertising industries. In a world that now begins to
believe in the efficacy of global communication, local differences should be seen
as more of a marketing ploy by local agencies wishing to attract foreign business
than of actual cultural uniqueness.

Moreover, given my emphasis on seeing advertisements as part of both synchronic and diachronic structures, we should also note that many of the conclusions reached can only be partial since they are based on a limited sustained study
of Japanese advertising over a period of 10 years. It is more than likely, therefore,
that certain features noted—for example, the use of visual parallelism, changes
over time in the popularity of certain keywords, a preference for allusion and
puns, gestures, body positions, even prevalence of foreign models—will change
in emphasis over time. Some of these may remain more or less constant, others
may fade away, yet others, not noted here, may become dominant features at
some time in the future. After all, advertising industries are chameleons that

somehow have to keep one step ahead of the social groups that they address. If nothing else, the discourse of advertising is always on the run, trying to free itself of constraints, and to be imprisoned by none.

NOTES

1. For the time being. It is estimated that the Chinese advertising market will be the largest in the world by the year 2015 (Hong Kong Trade Development Council, 1998, p. 2).

2. Comparative advertising is forbidden by law in Belgium, France, Germany, Italy, and some other European countries (Usunier, 1993, p. 344).

3. Thus, we find in Japan that numerous advertisements are linked to particular cyclical events. The most obvious and most frequently remarked on of these is that of Valentine's Day, which is the focal point of all chocolate advertising. Similarly, Christmas is used to advertise jewelry, food, drink, restaurants, hotels, travel, and so on. March and April provide the occasion for all kinds of advertisers to promote pens, bank accounts, cars, mobile phones, even wedding services to new university graduates, company employees, and would-be brides, since this is the time when major social changes in family, education, and company organization take place every year.

4. Mosdell (1986, p. 21) suggests that nudity in Japanese ads is not erotic, since "sex in Japan is essentially a part of nature. . . . It is natural." This is why, in his opinion, Japanese advertising is "sensuous" rather than erotic. For his part, Usunier (1993, p. 350) notes that French advertising has more nudity than nearly any other country and that this is accepted because "the meaning conveyed by nudity there is very much related to beauty, excellence and nature."

5. At the same time, we need to recognize that colors in general tend to be perceived and expressed in culturally different ways. In Japan, blue, for example, symbolizes immaturity rather than sadness; red, happiness and good luck, rather than pleasure, or nobility (Mosdell, 1986, pp. 66–70); and pink, a kind of sexy cuteness.

6. Myers (1994, p. 92) suggests that in English ads the use of foreign languages is "generally restricted to a few products, a few effects, and a very few languages." Although the number of languages used in Japanese advertising is indeed small, their use is widespread and for a wide variety of effects, from puns (*Happy Bathday,* Kōse) to visual shock (through combining scripts).

7. It should also be added that there was a period from the late 1980s into the very early 1990s when a number of Japanese ads made use of visual parallelism and opposition, through reversed writing, mirror images, and so on. My impression, however, is that this was a passing phase that coincided more or less with the culmination of Japan's bubble economy and that this trend—for such it was—has passed for now.

8. Surrealist images abound in such fragmented body images, particular those that play on Man Ray's photographs of a woman with long flowing hair.

9. We should also note the widespread use of Westerners in celebrity endorsement.

10. We should recall here that perfume ads are generally global campaigns that make use of standard images throughout the world.

11. Procter & Gamble announced in 1999 that it would similarly divide its advertising appropriation into nine product lines or brands, and at the time of writing it would seem

that some of the largest American advertisers might move toward the Japanese split-account system.

REFERENCES

Baudrillard, J. (1981). *For a critique of the political economy of the sign.* St. Louis, MO: Telos Press.

Bourdieu, P. (1984). *Distinction: A social critique of the judgement of taste.* London: Routledge & Kegan Paul.

Burton, J. (1983, October 24). Lintas executive learns lesson in compromise. *Advertising Age.*

Cauquelin, J., Lim, P., & Mayer-König, B. (Eds.). (1998). *Asian values: Encounter with diversity.* London: Curzon.

Clammer, J. (1995). Consuming bodies: Constructing and representing the female body in contemporary Japanese print media. In L. Skov & B. Moeran (Eds.), *Women, media and consumption in Japan* (pp. 197–219). London: Curzon.

Day, B. (1984). The advertising of ambiguity. *Ads Magazine, 3,* 8–18.

Fox, S. (1990). *The mirror makers: A history of American advertising.* London: Heinemann.

Hong Kong Trade Development Council. (1998). *Advertising & market research in Chinese mainland: Opportunities for Hong Kong.* Hong Kong: Author.

Jakobson, R. (1960). Closing statement: Linguistics and poetics. In T. Sebeok (Ed.), *Style in language.* Cambridge, MA: MIT Press.

Keene, D. (1972). *Landscapes and portraits: Appreciations of Japanese culture.* London: Secker & Warburg.

Kinsella, S. (1995). Cuties in Japan. In L. Skov & B. Moeran (Eds.), *Women, media and consumption in Japan* (pp. 220–254). London: Curzon.

Knibbs, D. (1992). The *kansei* factor: Image making in Japanese advertising. *The Japan International Journal, 2,* 18–23.

Langholz-Leymore, V. (1987). The structure is the message—The case of advertising. In J. Umiker-Sebeok (Ed.), *Marketing and semiotics: New directions in the study of signs for sale* (pp. 319–331). Berlin: Mouton de Gruyter.

Marchand, R. (1985). *Advertising the American dream: Making way for modernity, 1920–1940.* Berkeley: University of California Press.

Moeran, B. (1984). Individual, group and *seishin:* Japan's internal cultural debate. *Man, 19,* 256–266.

Moeran, B. (1985). When the poetics of advertising is the advertising of poetics. *Language & Communication, 5.*

Moeran, B. (1989). *Language and popular culture in Japan.* Manchester: Manchester University Press.

Moeran, B. (1996). *A Japanese advertising agency: An anthropology of media and markets.* London: Curzon.

Moeran, B., & Skov, L. (1993). Cinderella Christmas: Kitsch, consumerism and youth culture in Japan. In D. Miller (Ed.), *Unwrapping Christmas* (pp. 105–133). Oxford: Oxford University Press.

Moeran, B., & Skov, L. (1997). Mount Fuji and the cherry blossoms: A view from afar. In P. Asquith & A. Kalland (Eds.) *Japanese images of nature: Cultural perspectives* (pp. 181–205). London: Curzon.

Mooij, M., de. (1998). *Global marketing and advertising: Understanding cultural paradoxes.* London: Sage.

Mosdell, C. (1986). *The mirror makers: Cultural differences between America and Japan seen through the eye of advertising.* Tokyo: Macmillan Language House.

Myers, G. (1994). *Words in ads.* London: Edward Arnold.

O'Barr, W. (1994). *Culture and the ad.* Boulder, CO: Westview.

Schein, J.-E. (1991). Hello Kitty as stylemaker: Advertising and popular culture in Japan. *Japan Society Newsletter, XXXIV,* 2–5.

Usunier, J.-C. (1993). *International marketing: A cultural approach.* London: Prentice-Hall.

Westney, E. (1996). Mass media as business organizations: A U.S–Japan comparison. In S. Pharr & E. Krauss (Eds.), *Media and politics in Japan* (pp. 47–88). Honolulu: University of Hawai'i Press.

Yang, M. (1994). *Gifts, favors and banquets: The art of social relationships in China.* Ithaca, NY: Cornell University Press.

Chapter 22

TV Commercials as Cultural Performance: The Case of Japan

Masayuki Nakanishi

*From the perspective of cultural performance, this chapter presents a compara-
tive study between Japanese and American TV commercials to highlight certain
features of Japaneseness. (Cultural performance refers to the processes by which
to demonstrate the structural features of a culture that might influence communication patterns within that culture.) These findings will aid practitioners or
leaders of intercultural training: The understanding of and respect for the host
culture is a key to successful advertising in a foreign market, and Japan is no
exception. These findings also promise to be useful for researchers in the fields of
communication, media, advertising, and marketing.*

The remarkable growth of international business during the past few decades
has underscored the importance of crosscultural orientations in doing business
overseas. Successful foreign companies and businesspeople operating in or planning to enter the Japanese market must realize the fact that the kinds of business
practices that are considered effective in their own cultures may not necessarily
produce the same results when dealing with Japanese consumers. The same
applies to commercial advertising and marketing. Each culture has its own value
system and assumptions. Increasing effectiveness in advertising and marketing
requires a keen awareness of intercultural communication, which necessarily
"occurs whenever a message that must be understood is produced by a member
of one culture for consumption of by a member of another culture" (Porter &
Samovar, 1997, p. 21).

What is effective or acceptable as a marketing strategy or advertising campaign tactics varies across cultures, and sensitivity to cultural diversity had to be learned the hard way. Many of us probably can recall an ad that was highly successful in one country or culture only to fail in another. Advertisers today generally recognize that they must speak to the local consumer: "Every global brand finally reaches the consumer at a particular time and place and a particular intersection of meanings, so there remains a need for all sorts of local knowledge in the agency and local modifications in the campaign" (Myers, 1999, p. 56).

Sony Corporation is one of the first multinational corporations that have adopted the idea of "global localization." In fact, Sony has long made it a policy to promote local production in the markets where its products are sold. In addition, Sony has been striving to "Think Globally and Act Locally" in the entire spectrum of its corporate functions, including research and development (R&D), design, and production as well as sales and marketing (Sony International, 1997). As a global company, Sony is keenly aware that the understanding of and respect for basic cultural orientations and assumptions is the key to successful crosscultural marketing.

Based on the premise that culture is one of the most significant parameters for effective marketing strategies, this chapter discusses the Japanese cultural expectations of consumers and advertisers which might affect the advertising messages being produced and disseminated. Whereas Moeran in chapter 21 takes a multinational and broad view of advertising, I narrow the focus by keeping to a binational study of TV commercials between Japan and the United States. Both broad and narrow approaches are necessary. The latter approach can lock on to cultural difference, while the broad view can help keep perspective. Thus, Moeran rightly cautions against overgeneralized views of Japanese advertising, a point well taken especially in contemplation of what I have to show. Two nation's TV commercials could not seem more different than those between Japan and the United States. This difference is attributable at least partly to culture, which should become evident as we proceed.

ADVERTISEMENTS AS CULTURAL PERFORMANCE

Advertisements are everywhere, and the primary objective of advertising is to sell things. Life would be much simpler and easier for advertising agencies and copywriters if the size of the advertising budget or the amount of exposure in the mass media were directly correlated with the sales of a given product. That is not necessarily the case. Reviewing a series of case studies involving such well-known brands as Coca-Cola, Pepsi, Volkswagen, Levi's, among others, Schudson (1984) concluded that increased advertising support could not guarantee higher sales or larger market share gains. His findings suggest that aggressive, multi-million-dollar advertisement campaigns surely help, but other factors such as cultural differences, as well as market shifts and consumer trends, must be examined carefully to ensure successful ad campaigns.

Culture generally refers to those common or similar characteristics shared by the members of a certain group. Indeed, these different groups can be "identified with shared characteristics and attributes to distinguish from other groups which do not share similar characteristics" (Sarbaugh, 1987, p. 26). A universal definition of culture is offered by Kroeber and Kluckhohn (1952), which reads as follows:

Culture consists of patterns, explicit or implicit, of and for behavior acquired and transmitted by symbols, constituting the distinctive achievements of human groups, including their embodiments in artifacts; the essential core of culture consists of traditional (i.e., historically derived and selected) ideas and especially their attached values; cultural systems may, on the one hand, be considered as products of action, on the other as conditioning elements of further action. (p. 181)

An important implication of this definition of culture is that it presupposes the interdependent nature of the relationship between culture and communication. Just as culture is not static, but dynamic, so is communication. A generally held principle is that people behave as they do according to the way in which they perceive the world, and culture functions as a perceptual filter. In an attempt to conceptualize communication unfolding within formal organizations as cultural performance, Pacanowsky and O'Donnell-Trujillo (1983) argue that instead of focusing on static, structural features of culture that might influence communication, the cultural processes by which these structures are created should be examined. Furthermore, Turner (1986) generally defines "cultural performances" as being "not simple reflectors or expressions of culture or even of changing culture but may themselves be active agencies of change, representing the eye by which culture sees itself and the drawing board on which creative actors sketch out what they believe to be more apt or interesting 'designs for living'" (p. 24). These cultural processes or cultural performances create a variety of discourses, and advertising is, of course, "one of the institutions within which discourses are constituted" (Myers, 1999, p. 211).

According to Wernick (1991), advertising constitutes "promotional culture," for the rhetoric or language of advertising has permeated throughout our culture. Different nations, ethnic groups, age groups, genders, organizations, and so on represent their own unique promotional cultures and compete against one another for our attention. When these groups send messages to "sell" their products, views, opinions, whatever, to people outside of their own groups, they are "performing" intercultural communication, as if in a face-to-face situation.

Impact of Culture on Advertising Messages

Nakanishi (1996) conducted a preliminary study comparing and contrasting American and Japanese TV commercials, and its findings are partially presented in this article. This crosscultural study was conducted to examine some of the distinctive features of Japanese TV commercials, which might reflect important cultural assumptions and attitudes (see Table 22-1).

Table 22-1
American Perception of Japanese TV Commercials

Nonstudent Males		Nonstudent Females	
1. Few public announcements	57%	1. Few public announcements	50%
2. Boring	28%	2. Exaggerated	45%
3. High-quality	25%	3. Fun	36%
4. Don't understand the message	20%	4. Boring	33%
5. Exaggerated	16%	5. Useful	32%
Male Students		**Female Students**	
1. Fun	68%	1. Fun	60%
2. Don't understand the message	50%	2. Don't understand the message	45%
3. Exaggerated	25%	3. Exaggerated	35%
4. Not worth watching	19%	4. High-quality	25%
5. Few public announcements	17%	5. Not consumer-oriented	20%

Note: $n = 100$ each. The top five responses are listed here. *Source:* Nakanishi, 1996.

In order to obtain a reasonably representative sample of Japanese TV commercials, Nakanishi (1996) randomly recorded a total of 136 different TV commercials aired during prime time (7:00 p.m. to 10:00 p.m.) over a 1-week period. These TV commercials were then content-analyzed to identify the key elements of these advertising messages. In addition, a short questionnaire was given to American college students and working people (males and females) in Tokyo to get their general impressions about Japanese TV commercials (see Table 22-2).

This study examined how these components are combined differently in Japanese TV commercials and attempted to answer the following questions:

1. What may be the key features of Japanese advertising, especially TV commercials?
2. How do various aspects of Japanese culture influence the manner in which advertisements and TV commercials are made and presented to the target audience?
3. What may be the key parameters for effective advertising and marketing in Japan?

The results revealed six areas in which there appeared to be crosscultural differences:

1. Use of imperatives,
2. Comparative advertising/attack commercials,
3. Use of proofs,
4. Featuring celebrities,
5. Lack of concern for cultural diversity, and
6. Few public advertisement or public service announcements (PSAs).

Use of Imperatives

Imperatives are often used in American TV commercials such as "Buy one and get one free," "Drink Coke!" and so on. This reflects American culture's preference for directness in communication. Directness and straightforwardness are some of the key characteristics of communication in low-context cultures where "the mass of information is vested in explicit codes" (Hall, 1976, p. 76). In contrast, Japanese TV commercials seldom use imperatives. American TV commercials urge consumers to take action immediately, whereas Japanese consumers seem to find this approach pushy and emotionally disturbing. The reason may be because Japanese are used to high-context communication, "in which most of the information is either in the physical context or internalized in the person, while very little is in the coded, explicit transmitted parts of the message" (Hall, 1976, p. 91). Moreover, high-context communication emphasizes the importance of the perceiver. Mushakoji (1976) describes the high receiver-orientation characteristic of the Japanese message sender in terms of *awase* ("adjustive") logic, which depends not on standardized word meanings, but on expressions that "have multifarious nuances and are considered to be only signals that hint at reality rather than describing it precisely" (p. 43). In other words, the Japanese receiver is expected to adjust to the sender's real intent before it is logically and clearly enunciated.

Table 22-2
Comparison of Basic Cultural Orientations

United States	Japan
Culture of "doing" (action/change)	Culture of "being" (reaction/status)
Emphasis on achievements	Emphasis on family/social background
Individualism ("We are all unique.")	*Kanjinshugi* (Interdependence, mutual trust, inherent value of interpersonal relationships)
Self-concept	Group identification
Equality/fairness	Role differentiation/complementality
Competition	Cooperation (by compromise/accommodation)
"Conflict is not necessarily bad."	"Conflict should be avoided."
Direct communication style	Indirect/use of circular logic
Pursue maximum clarity	Ambiguity acceptable
Low-context culture	High-context communication
Rely on verbal communication	Rely on shared experiences
Emphasis on logical appeal	Emphasis on affective appeal
Use of numbers/facts as evidence	Personal anecdotes/feelings/images (confusing facts and subjective views)
Result-oriented (targets)	Process-oriented (no specific targets)
Convince/conquer by argument (winner and loser)	Apparent consensus (no winner/loser)
Source credibility (knowledge/authority, goodwill dynamism, trustworthiness)	Source credibility (brand image, familiarity, social status, popularity or celebrity appeal)

Comparative Advertising/Attack Commercials

In many American TV commercials, direct comparisons with competing products are used at great frequency as an attempt to clarify the relative advantages of the product being advertised, while pointing out weaknesses of the competitors' products (e.g., Coke vs. Pepsi, Ford vs. Chrysler, Apple vs. Microsoft, etc.). This is similar to negative campaigning in political communication (Cutbirth, Monroe, Kirch, Case, & Mikesell, 1989; Pfau & Kenski,1990). For example, in the 1980s, Pepsi launched a direct, confrontational advertising campaign against Coca-Cola to increase its market share in Japan using street-corner taste tests. In Japan, too, comparative advertising is allowed, having received its legal basis in 1987 when Japan's Fair Trade Commission established regulating guidelines. Japanese consumers, however, reacted negatively to such aggressive approaches. The campaign flopped and Pepsi later switched to a more positive advertising campaign featuring Michael Jackson dancing and singing merrily with a can of Pepsi. More recently, Japan Railway, the biggest passenger railway service in Japan, ran a TV commercial showing airline pilots in their uniforms riding on a train while telling each other that "it is safer than flying and it is as fast." This commercial might seem like comparative advertising, but it did not identify a competitor by its brand or company name. Moreover, while trains and airplanes compete directly for passengers, such competition, if depicted, was done so only generically. Mention of this commercial is made because this is about the closest a Japanese ad comes to comparative advertising. Knowing full well about the potential objection among Japanese consumers toward comparative advertising and attack commercials, it must have been as far as the advertising agency or the ad creator could go.

There are several culture-specific reasons for the large crosscultural variability in the use of comparative advertising or attack commercials. Confrontation carries a positive connotation in American culture, and open conflict is a function of the direct communication style, which predominates in individualistic cultures (Levine, 1985). The Japanese, on the other hand, value harmony and view its maintenance as one of the key functions of communication. As Okabe (1983) observed, Japanese "seek to achieve harmony by a subtle process of mutual understanding, almost by intuition, avoiding any sharp analysis of conflicting views" (p. 38). Furthermore, Hamaguchi (1977) argues that the opposing concept of Western individualism is not collectivism as Westerners define it, but *kanjinshugi,* in which the development and maintenance of interpersonal ties or network is always given priority over the fulfillment of the needs of individuals. More specifically, *kanjinshugi* is premised on three principles of interdependence, mutual trust, and inherent value of interpersonal relationships. The corollary to all this is that Japanese advertising generally relies on a tacit awareness by consumers; in that sense, it is intuitive, affective, and adaptive, rather than logical, confrontational, and argumentative.

Use of Proofs

As Shepherd (1992) notes, in humanistic, social scientific, and critical perspectives on communication, "interaction processes have typically been characterized essentially and primarily in terms of persuasion, influence, and power" (p. 204). Advertising is no exception. If companies and advertisers want to sell certain products, they must be able to persuade consumers effectively that these products are beneficial. Since the days of Aristotle, most Western rhetoric and persuasion theories have been concerned with three types of proofs or appeals: *logos* (or logical appeal), *pathos* (or emotional appeal), and *ethos* (ethical appeal). The concept of logos and how logical appeals are used in persuasive advertising messages represent interesting crosscultural differences.

Westerners value specificity, objectivity, and precision, and tend to rely on factual evidence, statistics, or numbers, and expert testimonials. Accordingly, Nakanishi (1996) found that price tags constitute a highly visible part of American TV commercials. The price of a given product is a major concern for American consumers but not necessarily for Japanese. In Japanese TV commercials product prices are seldom shown, and if they are, they appear inconspicuously in small print in the corner of the TV screen. This suggests that Japanese people are less enamored with numbers and statistics as compared to Americans, viewing them as just part of the picture of product description. In philosophical terms, the Japanese perception of the world is "profoundly holistic, dynamic, and spiritual" (Kim, 1991, p. 415) being the product of Japan's "unique fusion of Confucian, Shinto, and Buddhist beliefs" (Cushman & King, 1985, p. 120). This holism, dynamism, and spirituality carry over to the commercial realm in that Japanese tend to seek a holistic orientation utilizing affective and intuitive messages in their ads while downplaying the "materialistic" aspect—price—in Japanese commercials.

The commercial message as a whole creates an image, such as "product image" and "brand image." These images are not precisely defined, but are often very powerful. Katahira (1999) argues that the so-called "brand power" cannot be measured by price tags alone. He noted that "no one will disagree that a Toyota Corolla [an economical model] is an excellent car in terms of 'value for money,' but owning an old Corolla will never give its owner a sense of pride or affection" (p. 3). In a nationwide survey conducted by the Japan Adverting Agencies Association (JAAA) (1994), a stronger preference was found among Japanese consumers for "fun" and "interesting" commercials, rather than "simple informative" commercials. Moreover, Nakanishi (1996) reported that many Japanese TV commercials opted for positive affective proof, which acts on basic human emotions such as love, happiness, and excitement by combining attractive visuals and sound effects, and that there are many TV commercials that are produced as 30-second sitcoms or romantic films. A story develops in everyday settings, such as the home, office, or place of amusement, where viewers can easily identify. The product is often just one of the stage properties along with performers, music, and so on, while the setting becomes conspicuously highlighted. The purpose of such commercials is to link positive affect or emotion with the product by emphasizing the sensory and aesthetic aspects of the setting or atmosphere. Table 22-3 presents some of the descriptors (image components) derived from affective or "image-oriented" Japanese TV commercials used in Nakanishi's study (1996). Although not every Japanese commercial is affective in nature, the results suggest a Japanese general preference for positive affect and images as depicted in those commercials over rational approaches through logical appeals.

Ethos, or ethical proof, is believed to be closely related to source credibility, giving weight to assertions of a message, while increasing trustworthiness, sincerity, goodwill, moral character, and reputation (Anderson & Clevenger, 1963). In Western culture, dynamic communicators who are experienced, knowledgeable, and authoritative in their fields of specialty are considered to be credible sources (McCroskey, 1986). Nakanishi (1996) observed that brand, popularity, and familiarity are among the factors that determine the credibility of advertising message sources. This also explains the frequent uses of celebrities in Japanese TV commercials, which is discussed in more detail in the next section.

Table 22-3
Image Components Derived from Popular TV Commercials

Positive Image Components	Negative Image Components
Good music/sound effect = "Big-name" pop musicians compose and play commercial music/songs. Many top-selling CD singles are originally made for TV commercials. Also, hit pops and oldies are used as ambience music to create positive brand image and familiarity.	Not realistic Too much exaggeration, hard to believe Noisy, condescending, pushy Repetitive, lack of good taste/sensibility
Beautiful pictures/scenes	
Heart-warming, relaxing, pleasant	
Sensible, comfortable, overall positive feelings	
Stimulate empathy (*kyōkan,* such as sharing perceptions at the emotional level)	
Upbeat/fun	
Familiar, the scene/story easy to identify with	
Not pretentious	
Cute (use of animals, comical characters, children, etc.)	
Comical, for good laughs	

Source: Nakanishi, 1996.

Featuring Celebrities

In Japan, big-name "stars" (movie actors/actresses, pop singers. entertainers, athletes, and other celebrities) are featured in most TV commercials. They do not directly endorse the product; rather, they help enhance the product's brand image by being seen using the product. These so-called "talent commercials" have proliferated in Japan. Alperstein (1991) found that the use of celebrities captures the attention of viewers who often become precariously involved with them in a kind of imaginary social interaction by shared use of a product. Thus, Japanese advertisers believe that the popularity or positive public image of a celebrity can be effectively merged with the product or brand image (Kobayashi & Shimamura, 1997). A survey by J. W. Thompson, a U.S. consulting firm, showed that celebrities are featured in nearly 80% of Japanese TV commercials, as opposed to less than 20% in the United States (Nikkei Advertising Research Institute, 1984, p. 90). While in 1997 the Japanese percentage dropped to 63% (Blair, 1999), it is still quite high.

Nakanishi (1996) also observed that the same individual endorsed a variety of products for different companies (more than 10 in some cases). These popular TV commercial stars, who are often female actresses or singers ("The Queens of TV Commercials"), are highly sought after by advertising agencies, which reap these stars bigger roles in movies and TV shows.

The Japanese interest in things Western is well known. Aoki (1990) argues that Japan's desire for Western culture may be attributable to the fact that "the modernization and industrialization of the Japanese society has been accomplished through Americanization or adoption of Western ideas" (p. 17). Advertising in Japan is no exception, making great use of Western loan words, especially English, Western personalities, and Western popular music. TV commercials in Japan can enhance a film star's career in contrast to the opposite view held by many top stars in Hollywood. Japanese TV commercials capitalize on the popularity young movie stars or singers have for youths and their power to set trends in the youth market for products. Hollywood stars have found Japanese commercials to be advantageous for them as well as a way to avoid notice in the United States while reaping benefits. This influx of American celebrities has been on the increase since the 1970s (Shiga, 1990). The latest examples include Leonardo DiCaprio (Suzuki Motor Corp./mini-van and Orient Corporation/credit card) and Meg Ryan (Daihatsu Motor Co./compact car, Suntory Limited/canned soft drink). Shiga (1990) attributes the popularity of these foreign celebrities in Japanese TV commercials to several factors, including (1) large advertising effects; (2) the international fame of such celebrities; and (3) exotic tastes not found domestically. As for these Hollywood stars, big guarantees, the quality of Japanese TV commercials, Japan being a big market for Hollywood films, and most importantly, no negative impact on their reputation or popularity as celebrity figures at home, have all motivated them to come to Japan to shoot TV commercials.

Lack of Concern for Cultural Diversity

The United States is a society characterized by cultural diversity. Cultural diversity does not just mean ethnic or racial diversity alone but also refers to the great diversity of "co-cultures" or "influential cultures that simultaneously exist" (Orbe, 1998, p. 1). Concern for such co-cultures seems to be a major factor in American advertising. Since the American culture values equality and egalitarianism, and also from the viewpoint of "political correctness," American advertisers are concerned about how co-cultures such as different races, ethnic groups, and women, among others, are represented in their advertisements (O'Barr, 1994). However, as a monolingual, monocultural society, such concern for co-cultures is inherently absent in Japan. As mentioned earlier, Japanese people show favorable attitudes toward foreigners. However, most of the foreigners appearing in Japanese TV commercials are American or European white males or females, whereas very few Asians are used as product endorsers. Moreover, members of each co-culture are assigned fixed roles. Potter (1998) states that there has been public criticism of advertising for various reasons, and one of which is the tendency of advertising to perpetuate stereotypes. In fact, the few people of color seen in Japanese TV commercials are usually world-class athletes (Sammy Sosa, Carl Lewis, Michael Jordan, among others) or popular musicians (e.g., Michael Jackson, Stevie Wonder). Elderly people are portrayed as grandfathers or grandmothers, while women are depicted as housewives or young attractive women. These age- and gender-related stereotypes were identified by Professor Masatake Yamanaka of Seijo University in his study of 612 TV commercials aired the same day in 1998. He found that over 50% of them showed traditional gender-role stereotypes of men as professional workers and women as housewives, and that 142 of them featured older people in their 50s or above but were simply described as typical senior citizens (cited in "Komasharu," 1999).

Although these results suggest that Japanese TV commercials lack awareness of diversity, Japanese collectivism likely preconditions it. "Unlike other cultures or societies where each individual's autonomy is highly valued, Japanese people express their individuality in a 'strategically' limited way to maintain homeostasis within the relational context of the supra-systems (i.e., family, community, or organization) to which they belong" (Hamaguchi, 1977, p. 275). In other words, Japanese people may be culturally conditioned to perceive others primarily in terms of their group memberships or the interpersonal relationships they have, and not necessarily as individuals. It might make good sense, then, for these TV commercials to depict members of various co-cultures in terms of the primary groups to which they belong.

Few Public Advertising/PSAs

The primary purpose of advertising is to create a positive image about a product or brand and the desire to actually use it. Advertising is also used to raise consciousness about social problems such as drug abuse, domestic violence, or environmental pollution, and to shape or change our beliefs and attitudes regarding nutrition, smoking, and aging, to name but a few. This type of advertising is generally called public advertising or public service announcements (PSAs). They are sponsored by government agencies and various public organizations, as well as private companies. When asked why there are so few public advertising campaigns or PSAs on TV in Japan, Aoba (1999) explained that "Japanese people were not used to explicitly giving their own opinions or views and debating over issues in public" (p. 31). For most Japanese people, proving who is right or who is wrong, particularly in public, is displaying a lack of concern for others. Barnlund (1989) found that "the motive promoting such behavior derives from the value attached to congeniality and consensus, the importance of preserving and promoting a harmony of a feeling" (p. 156). Public advertising or PSAs can become provocative and confrontational in nature, and their realism is so overwhelming with blood and other shocking scenes that Japanese people would find them difficult to view. Therefore, even in serious PSAs, Japanese celebrities will appear on the screen and say, for example, "Please do not do drugs" with a grin. Ozaki (1978) warns that such overemphasis on harmony "can become a form of tyranny, limiting the free flow of ideas on even the most vital personal and public issues" (p. 232). Moreover, Ward (1999) went so far as to criticize these Japanese "talent public commercials" as being "hard to understand" and "questionable in terms of effectiveness" (p. 38).

Aoki (1990) also points out the fact that the lack of presence of public advertising campaigns or PSAs in Japanese media may be attributable to the rather weak public awareness of the Japanese people. It has been observed that Japanese have "a very strong sense of who is on the inside [*uchi*] and who is on the outside [*soto*]" (Taylor, 1983, p. 67; see also chapter 2 in this book). More precisely, the public sphere for the Japanese consists of those who belong to *soto* and *yoso* groups, and they tend to detach themselves from society at large or local communities as *soto* or *yoso* worlds. Japanese people exhibit high levels of loyalty and identification for their own groups and fellow group members (*miuchi* or people from their *uchi* group), whereas they are basically indifferent to *tanin* (strangers) or other people from their *soto* group, or even hostile to *yoso-mono* or people from groups in conflict with their own. Due to this "group-think," public advertising or PSAs have a hard sell to make if promoting increased public good will or consciousness.

CONCLUSION

Conceptualizing advertising as cultural performance and marketing as intercultural communication, this chapter highlights how basic Japanese cultural assumptions can influence the types of TV commercials produced and broadcast in Japan. Culture provides a context by which messages are interpreted, and if it is "high-context" as in Japan, meanings and social realities can be shared that much more easily. This high-context aspect encourages advertisers to rely heavily on sensory images, rather than detailed explanations of product features. Blair (1999) found that the majority of Japanese TV commercials targeted consumers by:

1. Stimulating consumer interest with effective attention-getters (e.g., "talent commercials"),
2. Entertaining consumers and providing topics of conversation, and
3. Bridging brands and prospective consumers through interactive communication.

A reasonable caveat for considering Japanese TV commercials is that they may not provide the kind of information needed for consumer decision making because they emphasize the "brand image" and rely merely on celebrity appeal. These brand-image–based, affective approaches work in Japan because they are based on Japanese cultural assumptions, values, beliefs, and attitudes shared by most Japanese people. As a result, the general consensus among Japanese advertisers and consumers is that TV commercials are a form of entertainment (i.e., TV "drama" played in 15 or 30 seconds), and that they need not be informative about the product being advertised.

This study has discussed Japanese TV commercials as cultural performances based on the premise that the understanding of, and respect for, basic cultural orientations/assumptions in the Japanese culture is the key to successful intercultural marketing/advertising in Japan. The study identified some distinctive cultural features of Japanese TV commercials by comparing and contrasting them with American counterparts, which might be of interest to both practitioners and scholars in the fields of intercultural communication, media, advertising, and marketing. Although as Moeran shows in chapter 21 that some interpretations of Japan can overwork the influence of traditional Japanese cultural values, a useful point to be made, it is also true that some foreign business people fail to note such values when they should. Overall, our perspectives—Moeran's and mine— are complementary in casting a wider scope on the subject.

If there is a difference between our views of TV commercials, it would be largely attributable, I believe, to Europeans having more similar views with Japanese about commercials than what Japanese share with Americans. For example, as Moeran points out, some European countries disapprove of comparative advertising, as does Japan. Moeran rightly identifies such points of similarity, which may help clarify actual cultural differences. A greater cultural gulf, however, seems to exist between Japan and the United States, at least in regard to TV commercials, so the relative differences I present ought not to be too surprising. Such issues present future avenues for research.

REFERENCES

Alperstein, N. M. (1991). Imaginary social relationships with celebrities appearing in television commercials. *Journal of Broadcasting & Electronic Media, 35*, 45–58.

Anderson, K. E., & Clevenger, T., Jr. (1963). A summary of experimental research in ethos. *Speech Monographs, 30,* 59–78.

Aoba, M. (1999, April). Paburikku to iu ishiki ga kawaranakereba kōkoku wa kawaranai [Without public awareness, advertising will not change]. *Brain, 39*(4), 30–32.

Aoki, T. (1990). *Nihon bunkaron no henyo: Sengo Nihon no bunka to aidentiti* [Changing perspectives on Japanese culture: The culture and identity of Japan during the post-war period]. Tokyo: Chuo Koronsha.

Barnlund, D. C. (1989). *Communication styles of Japanese and Americans: Images and realities.* Belmont, CA: Wadsworth.

Blair, M. (1999). Burando kōchiku to kōkoku biggu ban [Brand building and advertising big bang]. In M. Shimaguchi, H. Takeuchi, H. Katahira, & J. Ishi (Eds.), *Burando kōchiku: māketeingu kakushin no jidai* [Brand building for the age of marketing innovation] (pp. 326–339). Tokyo: Yuhikaku.

Cushman, D. P., & King., S. S. (1985). National organizational cultures in conflict reso-lution: Japan, the United States, and Yugoslavia. In W. B. Gudykunst, L. P. Stewart, & S. Ting-Toomey (Eds.), *Communication, culture, and organizational processes* (pp. 114–133). Newbury Park, CA: Sage Publications.

Cutbirth, C. W., Monroe, P. S., Kirch, M., Case, J., & Mikesell, B. (1989, April). Negative campaigning. Paper presented at the annual meeting of the Central States Communication Association, Kansas City, MO.

Hall, E. T. (1976). *Beyond culture.* New York: Doubleday.

Hamaguchi, E. (1977). *Nihonjin-rashisa no saihakken* [The rediscovery of what it means to be Japanese]. Tokyo: Nikkei Shimbun

Japan Advertising Agencies Association (JAAA). (1994, July). Seijukushitekita shōhisha no kōkokukan—Kōkoku no kino to yakuwari ni kansuru ankēto [The maturation of consumers' views on advertising: A survey on the functions and roles of adver-tising]. *JAAA Reports,* pp. 8–11.

Katahira, H. (1999). Burando o tsukuru to iu koto [On building a brand]. In M. Shimaguchi, H. Takeuchi, H. Katahira, & J. Ishi (Eds.), *Burando kōchiku: māketeingu kakushin no jidai* [Brand building for the age of marketing innovation] (pp. 1–15). Tokyo: Yuhikaku.

Kim, Y. Y. (1991). Intercultural personhood: An integration of Eastern and Western per-spectives. In L. A. Samovar & R. E. Porter (Eds.), *Intercultural communication: A reader* (6th ed.) (pp. 401–410). Belmont, CA: Wadsworth.

Kobayashi, T., & Shimamura, K. (1997). *Atarashii kōkoku* [New advertising]. Tokyo: Dentsu.

Komasharu ni otoshiyori inaino? [Aren't there any elderly people in commercials?] (1999, August 6). *The Asahi Shimbun,* p. 15.

Kroeber, A. L., & Kluckhohn, C. (1952). *Culture: A critical review of concepts and defi-nitions.* Cambridge, MA: Harvard University Press.

Levine, D. (1985). *The flight from ambiguity.* Chicago: The University of Chicago Press.

McCroskey, J. (1986). *An introduction to rhetorical communication.* Englewood Cliffs, NJ: Prentice Hall.

Mushakoji, K. (1976). The cultural premises of Japanese diplomacy. In Japan Center for International Exchange (Ed.), *The silent power: Japan's identity and world role* (pp. 35–49). Tokyo: Simul Press.

Myers, G. (1999). *Ad worlds: Brands, media, audiences.* London: Arnold.

Nakanishi, M. (1996). The role of intercultural communication in the international market place: A Japanese perspective. Unpublished research report.

Nikkei Advertising Research Institute. (1984). *Amerika no kōkoku hyōgen* [American advertising expressions]. Tokyo: Author.

O'Barr, W. (1994). *Culture and the ad: Exploring otherness in the world of advertising.* Boulder, CO: Westview Press.

Okabe, R. (1983). Cultural assumptions of East and West: Japan and the United States. In W. B. Gudykunst (Ed.), *Intercultural communication theory: Current perspectives* (pp. 21–44). Beverly Hills, CA: Sage Publications.

Orbe, M. P. (1998). *Constructing co-cultural theory: An explication of culture, power, and communication.* Thousand Oaks, CA: Sage Publications.

Ozaki, R. (1978). *The Japanese: A cultural portrait.* Tokyo: Tuttle.

Pacanowsky, M. E., & O'Donnell-Trujillo, N. (1983). Organizational communication as cultural performance. *Communication Monographs, 50,* 126–147.

Pfau, M., & Kenski, H. C. (1990). *Attack politics: Strategy and defense.* New York: Praeger.

Porter, R. E., & Samovar, L. A. (1997). An introduction to intercultural communication. In L. A. Samovar & R. E. Porter (Eds.), *Intercultural communication: A reader* (8th ed.) (pp. 4–26). Belmont, CA: Wadsworth.

Potter, W. J. (1998). *Media literacy.* Thousand Oaks, CA: Sage Publications.

Sarbaugh, L. E. (1987). *Intercultural communication* (rev. ed.). New Brunswick, NJ: Transaction Books.

Schudson, M. (1984). *Advertising: The uneasy persuasion—Its dubious impact on American society.* New York: Basic Books.

Shepherd, G. J. (1992). Communication as influence: Definitional exclusion. *Communication Studies, 43,* 203–219.

Shiga, N. (1990). *Showa terebi hōsōshi (ge)* [The history of Japanese TV broadcasting in the Showa era (Vol. II)]. Tokyo: Hayakawa Shobo.

Sony International (Singapore) Ltd. (1997, April). *Sony global materials business forum.* Retrieved August 29, 1999, from the World Wide Web: http://www.sony-asia.sg/procurement/whatsnew/announce.html

Taylor, J. (1983). Shadows of the rising sun. New York: Harcourt Brace Jovanovich.

Turner, V. (1986). *The anthropology of performance.* New York: PAJ Publications.

Ward, B. (1999). Nihon no kokyo kōkoku heno teigen [Suggestions for Japanese public advertising]. *Brain, 39*(4), 38.

Wernick, A. (1991). *Promotional culture: Advertising, ideology, and symbolic expression.* London: Sage.

Chapter 23

Projecting Peer Approval in Advertising: Japan versus U.S. *Seventeen* Magazine

Michael L. Maynard

Examining advertisements can illuminate how assumptions about and under-standings of self are culturally shaped. This chapter addresses the crosscultur-al variability of how peer groups are presented in advertising to adolescent females by analyzing advertisements appearing in eight issues of Seventeen *magazine, four Japanese and four American. The study approaches peer approval from a perspective that investigates the cultural codes of independ-ence/dependence and focuses on the broadly acknowledged descriptions of Japan as a collectivistic culture versus the United States as an individualistic one. Culture-based differences in advertising are discussed with a specific focus on how advertising constructs the image of adolescent females, and how, in turn, adolescent females are encouraged to identify with their mediated images of selves—their peer groups.*

In the Japanese *Seventeen* magazine, no less than seven young Japanese females are featured in an advertisement for Kyowa Contact lenses in the June 1996 issue. In contrast, only one young American female is featured in an adver-tisement for Bausch & Lomb's Envision contact lenses in the June 1996, American *Seventeen* magazine. The manner in which these models are portrayed offers even more contrast.

The Japanese girls are grouped in a tight-knit ensemble of chummy intimacy with playful embraces and arms casually slung around each other's shoulders. All are smiling. Again, in contrast, only the decontextualized face of the American female is presented, and in her mannequin-like role, she is unsmiling.

Certainly the ads are designed to strategically communicate different benefits. Kyowa's headline, "*Kontakuto wa doko de katte mo onaji ja arimasen*," ("Contacts are not the same wherever you buy them" [my translation]) is making the claim that Kyowa dealers offer important benefits other contact lens dealers do not. This message is further explicated with each of the Japanese females specifying, in speech balloons, Kyowa's exclusive guarantee, assurance of safety, offer of selection, and so forth.

Bausch & Lomb's headline, "Stop wishing you could wear contacts. Try ENVISION" is appealing to people who have had problems wearing contact lenses either because they find them uncomfortable or because the lenses have not improved their vision. The solid block of ad copy offers compelling reasons to try Envision. The product offers more oxygen, and more oxygen means healthier eyes. Envision has a unique, patented design precisely matching the shape of one's cornea and the like.

Although different communication strategies typically may follow different executions, Kyowa's *quality* story also may have been told in the direct manner of the Bausch & Lomb ad. Equally so, Envision's *comfort* story also may have been told through the personae and voices of several female teenagers. Advertising messages, that is, can be presented in a variety of manners.

In fairness, a casual glance through the two June 1996 magazines reveals that some U.S. ads have more than a few models in them, and, indeed, some Japanese ads have but one model in them. Yet the reverse appears to be the norm. Japanese messages directed to young women tend to be presented with multiple images of young women, whereas U.S. messages to young women tend to be presented with singular images of young women. The purpose of this chapter is to test this assumption.

PEER GROUP APPROVAL

An often repeated axiom in advertising claims that a recommendation from a friend, through word of mouth, offers a powerful sales tool. Leveraging this, advertising discourse in the mass media generally attempts to simulate "a friend's recommendation" through a written style approximating friendly, casual conversation. The advertiser, of course, assumes the role of the friend who knows the product well, and cannot help but wish to share the good news with the reader. By proxy, a peer member of the reader's social group addresses the reader on behalf of the advertiser. Sometimes the proxy is a celebrity—someone who the reader wishes to emulate. Most often, however, the peer is not a celebrity but someone who closely mirrors the demographic characteristics of the reader.

So, when targeting young females, the models in the advertising are posed and costumed to look very much like the females in the target audience. This creates a selling environment in which the reader feels comfortably at ease among friends, and with her defenses down, more susceptible to the advertisement's message. Ample research on teens and persuasion strongly affirms the centrality of peer pressure in influencing attitude, behavior, and buying patterns (see, for example, Cotterell, 1996; Seltzer, 1989; White, 1993).

The appeal of the peer approval may be actualized through copy alone. The headline may be phrased along the lines of "Your friends won't recognize you when you. . . ." Or, "Be the first in your group to use. . . ." The intensity of the peer pressure may be greater when the appeal is stated in the negative, such as, "Everybody *else* is wearing the new fashion. . . ." More subtly, however, the *Seventeen* reader sees others in the ad with whom she readily identities with, and thus she is more receptive to the sales message. Peer approval thus operates wordlessly and does its work through like-association.

But how many peers in the advertisement are necessary to reflect the reader's "peer group"? One? Or as many as half a dozen? This study assumes that manifestations of "peer approval" are culturally determined. Accordingly, this study approaches the peer group phenomenon from a crosscultural perspective. Employing the cultural codes of independence/dependence, this study focuses on the broadly acknowledged descriptions of Japan as a collectivistic culture versus the United States as an individualistic culture.

The importance of this study is that it adds perspective on the variable of peer pressure in how it is idealized as a social value, and how it may differ across cultures. Given that advertising is a cultural force that helps shape our self-image, contributing to how our identity is defined in society, this empirical study sheds light on how adolescent females are encouraged to present themselves in their respective societies. Examining the staged worlds of advertisements can illuminate how assumptions about, and understandings of, self are culturally constrained—how, for example, adolescent female images are marketed in Japanese and American mass media.

ADVERTISING AND CULTURE

This study interrogates a particular image of U.S. society versus a particular (yet matching) image of Japanese society as reflected in the ads in teen magazines directed to young women. Specific focus is on the comparative cultural traits of U.S. "individualism" versus Japanese "group-orientation." Are these broad generalizations gross overstatements, merely simpleminded clichés? Or can these cultural assertions be supported through empirical evidence?

If even moderately true, controlling for product category and ad size, one anticipates a higher frequency of multiple-person ads in the Japanese sample because this supports Japan's assumed high-context communication style many previous studies have regarded as characteristic of collectivistic cultures. Alternatively, one hypothesizes a greater number of ads in the American sample that portray one female model because this supports the assumed valorization of the individual.

Following the logic of Leiss, Kline, and Jhally (1990, p. 5) that "advertising is a discourse through and about objects which bonds together images of persons, products and well-being," advertising may be seen as a cultural force that continually shapes and reinforces the values around us. Given that a large number of people take in advertising messages, "advertisements enter significantly into the fabric of meaning that constitutes culture" (Ohmann, 1996, p. 212). Despite the strategic character of advertising discourse to persuade, a miniature reproduction of the culture into which the ad is placed is inevitable.

Ads may be individually unique, but their creation is inevitably shaped and constrained by the cultural environment of their makers. The images portrayed in magazine advertisements are determined by advertising professionals such as copywriters and art directors. They, of course, mediate words and images for the target audience. Their task is harnessing the appropriate cultural cues—including the most current edgy phrases and visual styles—toward the communication objectives of attitude change, information giving, or awareness building.

Marchand's (1985, p. 185) "social tableaux" describes ads as the space wherein persons are depicted in such a way as to suggest their relationships to each other or to a larger social structure. The social tableaux is an *index*, linking the people in the ad not merely to the headline's message and product, but also linking their image to the culture's structure. A degree of abstraction in place or setting highlights the people portrayed in the advertisements as social types with which the viewer is encouraged, through a fantasy of choice, to make a connection. The more expensive the ad, which means four-color, high production values, and a special photo shoot—typical characteristics of the magazine ad—the more likely it is to emphasize values other than product features.

One of those values, social belonging, appears to be fostered by elevation of the peer group. With Coke and Pepsi, for example, the youth-centric theme of solidarity with a whole generation is evoked (Wernick, 1991). The peers depicted in contemporary advertising that is aimed at the young are what Wernick (1991) calls unigenerational—people of the same age who have no fixed roles.

Background: Self and Society in Japan and the United States

The general sense of self that a Japanese develops is thought to differ from that developed in the West. Many observers characterize Japan as a culture that emphasizes social hierarchy, group belonging, harmony, modesty, and obligations. A prominent characteristic of Japanese society has been defined as "group-oriented" (versus American "individual-oriented"). While the group-orientation of the Japanese people has been suggested and advocated by more than a few scholars (for example, Reischauer, 1970), Chie Nakane's work, *Japanese Society* (1970), has made a decisive impact. According to Nakane, Japanese society is characterized by hierarchical organizations whose group membership is determined in terms of frame, rather than attribute. For example, a Japanese person identifies himself or herself as a member of a particular organization or an insti-tution ("I work for Sony"), while a typical American identifies himself or herself by a universal attribute such as a type of profession ("I am an engineer").

The group orientation of Japan has been criticized for its inability to account for some of the defining aspects of Japanese society (Befu, 1980; Mouer & Sugimoto, 1986). While recognizing shortcomings of the group theory, however, it is reasonable to believe that the average Japanese person is, or at least desires to be, more concerned about his or her primary group than the average American.

According to Smith (1983, p. 74), the Japanese self in such a society is an "interactionist self." Plath (1980, pp. 3–5) contends that the Japanese interac-tionist self emerges in social relations, and that awareness of self is continuously recreated as one responds to others.

According to Rosenberger (1992, p. 67), Japanese self is not "transcendental with an ultimate meaning within itself." The meaning of self, or more appropri-ately "selves," derives from its interrelationship to others. Self is not a rigid, sta-ble, constant matter that stands alone. Lebra (1992) discusses three dimensions of the Japanese self, "the interactional self," "the inner self," and "the boundless self." The multiple dimensions of the Japanese self advocated by Lebra also con-tribute to the concept of self as a shifting and changing experience. Self in Japan, then, is a changing, forming, fluid awareness based on social relationships and bears meaning in relation to one's thought, as well as to others and context.

Concepts of self and society in the United States offer a contrast. The term usu-ally associated with self in the United States is "individual." In *Habits of the Heart*, Bellah and colleagues (1985) state that Americans are described as believ-ing in the dignity, indeed the sacredness of the individual. According to them, Americans hold dear to their hearts the dignity and autonomy of the individual; Americans do this to prescribe to "an individualism in which the self has become the main form of reality" (1985, p. 143).

Yet Americans remain ambivalent in their pursuit of the autonomous individ-ual self. According to Bellah and colleagues (1985), when it comes to the con-cepts of self and society, Americans experience a classic case of ambivalence. Americans "strongly assert the value of our self-reliance and autonomy" and yet "deeply feel the emptiness of a life without sustaining social commitments" (Bellah et al., 1985, p. 150). And still, they maintain, Americans are hesitant to articulate that they need one another as much as they need to stand alone, for fear that if they did they would lose their independence altogether.

Although the issues surrounding self and society in Japan and the United States are complex, for the purpose of this study, it seems reasonable to assume the following. A Japanese person finds balance between self and society by being *inter*dependent, while an American finds balance between self and society by being *in*dependent. Cultural forces in Japan and the United States sustain oppos-ing directions pulling Japanese and Americans toward different ends of the group/individual continuum. Indeed, Hofstede's (1984) seminal study on work-related values offers a stark contrast between cultures that are low versus high on the Individualism scale. In summary, Hofstede (1984) dichotomizes Low Individualism Japan versus High Individualism United States as a "we" consciousness versus an "I" consciousness, respectively.

The Japanese tendency toward a stronger sense of psychological accommodation marks another aspect differentiating the self-identification process in Japan and in the United States. For Japanese people, "secondary control," where one enhances rewards "by accommodating to existing realities and maximizing satisfaction or goodness of fit with things as they are" (Weisz, Rothbaum, & Blackburn, 1984, p. 955), is primary. Emphasis on "primary control," where one enhances rewards by influencing existing realities (Weisz et al., 1984, p. 955), more closely approximates the American value system. In contrast, Japanese materialism tends to be influenced by a psychological preference for group-based self-identification. Accordingly, one of the basic rationales for both the construction and consumption of the advertising text in Japan is a strengthening of the sense of group belonging.

Hypotheses

All of the above leads to two hypotheses:

H1. The Japanese sample will present more advertisements with two or more peers in them than will the U.S. sample.

H2. The U.S. sample will present more advertisements with one peer in them than will the Japanese sample.

METHOD

This chapter content-analyzes the number of female peer-group images appearing in each advertisement and compares the Japanese sample with the American sample. Given the crosscultural analysis the study intends, controlling for title, target, and time offers the opportunity for lexical, audience, and temporal equivalence. Data for this study come from eight issues of young women's magazines, four *Seventeen* in Japan and four *Seventeen* in the United States. They share three important characteristics: same title, same target, and same year and months of publication.

Despite the identical title, the two *Seventeen* magazines are completely independent of each other in content: neither one is an adaptation nor a "version" of the other. The American *Seventeen*, a monthly, has a circulation of about 1.4 million with a target age range of 12–20. The Japanese *Seventeen*, aimed at a comparable age group, is a semi-monthly, with an unaudited circulation of about 550,000 (*Zasshi Shimbun Sōkatarogu*, 1994). The shared time of publication are the four matching issues of June 1995, June 1996, January 1997, and July 1997.

This controls for history (change) as a threat to validity. A count of all ads in the eight magazine issue samples was conducted. Advertisements appearing in the four American *Seventeen* issues totaled 206, and advertisements appearing in the four Japanese *Seventeen* issues, 148.

Two bilingual coders, proficient in both English and Japanese, independently content-analyzed the ads after having determined through trial analyses and mutual discussion what constituted an advertisement (as opposed to other magazine content) and what counted as a peer to the magazine's target audience of young women readers. Although most ads present themselves as such, and the cues that inform the reader that "this is an ad" are quickly perceived, some advertisements are designed deliberately to create an ambiguous identity, requiring the reader to puzzle its meaning and thereby engendering reader involvement. After resolving such issues, coders began the task of independently assessing the sampled ads for the presence or absence of the targeted peers with "peer" defined as a person who looked similar to the *Seventeen* reader in age, appearance, or manner, as found in graphic elements of the ads. Graphic elements included not just photographs, but also drawings and cartoon material. Intercoder reliability was high, measuring above the .85 standard for percentage of agreement recommended (Kassarjian, 1977): photographic images, 94.3; illustrations and cartoons, 90.4.

Findings

Table 23-1 shows that the highest percentage of advertisements in the Japanese sample featured two or more people ($N = 63$; 42.6%). In contrast, the highest percentage of advertisements in the American sample featured one person ($N = 108$; 52.6%). A relatively smaller number of ads in the Japanese sample featured just one peer ($N = 47$; 31.7%). A relatively smaller number of U.S. ads featured two or more peers ($N = 51$; 24.65%). Both samples indicate near equivalency in number of ads without people (Japan, $N = 38$; 25.7%) (U.S., $N = 47$; 22.8%).

Table 23-1
Frequency of Person Ads in Japanese and U.S. *Seventeen*

	Japanese ($N = 148$)		United States ($N = 206$)	
	n	%	*n*	%
No person	38	25.7%	47	22.8%
One person	47	31.7%	108	52.6%
Two or more	63	42.6%	51	24.6%
Total	148	100.0%	206	100.0%

$x^2 = 17.02, p < .001.$

DISCUSSION

Hypotheses 1 and 2 are supported by chi square measurement. There is a significant difference between the two samples in the frequency of ads featuring two or more peers, and the frequency of ads featuring just one peer (Table 23-1). As predicted, the Japanese sample showed more peers in more advertisements than did the American sample.

Emblematic of the redundancy in peer representation evident in the Japanese sample, a two-page ad for Fuji Film featured 43 peers. The ad, presenting snapshots of girls on their school excursion, is literally wall-to-wall with group shots, quotations, drawings, handwritten notes, and other scribbles that give it the look of an annotated school yearbook. The message suggests that the reward of using a camera derives not merely from capturing precious moments with friends, but capturing *many* precious moments with *many* friends. Another campaign in the Japanese sample featuring more than a modest number of peers is the Morinaga chocolate campaign. The June 1995, two-page Morinaga ad, for example, features over 50 images of Japanese female teens.

The opposing tendencies of the two cultures are evident in beverage ads, as well. A Kirin beverage ad in the June 1996 issue for Kiriris, an orange soft drink, for example, features nine peers. The idea centers around a female recreational baseball team. With Kiriris inscribed on an orange-colored baseball in the center of the ad, circular head shots of the nine players are arranged in a triangle around it. In yet another execution of this same baseball motif, an ad for Kiriris in the July 1997 issue shows the nine Kiriris players plus the other team as well as several spectators, so that a total of 24 people, mostly peers, are in the ad.

In contrast, an ad for Coca-Cola in the June 1996 U.S. issue, which appears to be a slumber party, features only three girls. The girls are relaxing (hanging out) in one girl's bedroom, with a bowl of popcorn and a couple of prominently displayed Coca-Cola bottles.

Based on the findings in this study, we might speculate that even had the themes of baseball and slumber party been reversed such that the Kirin ad showed a slumber party and the Coca-Cola ad showed baseball, the cultural tendencies for Japanese advertising to display more peers and for American advertising to display fewer peers would hold. One can imagine for the U.S. ad a solitary young female in baseball attire sitting on the end of a dugout bench, sipping Coca-Cola. One can also imagine for the Japanese ad 10–12 girls at a slumber party, each brandishing a can of Kiriris.

In addition to the Coca-Cola ad, advertisements for Advil, Soft & Dri, Airwalk, Always, Urban Decay, and so forth, for example, in the January 1997 issue of U.S. *Seventeen,* bear testimony to the claim that U.S. ads tend to feature just one model in them.

Comparing the aggregate number of peers in all the ads of all the issues offers yet another way of comparing the two samples. In raw numbers, there were more

Japanese girls than American girls in the respective samples—even though there were more American ads! A total of 349 female teens were presented in the Japanese sample. A total of 305 female teens were presented in the U.S. sample.

The difference in aggregate representation may be expressed by dividing the number of ads into the total number of people in the ads. The ratios of 349/148 (Japan) versus 305/206 (U.S.) yield the following: On average, there were 2.35 peers per Japanese ad. In contrast, there were 1.33 peers per U.S. ad.

CONCLUSION

Advertisements in both *Seventeen* magazines targeting adolescent females promote a sense of membership in a group to which one already thinks one belongs, or to which one wishes to join. Since "identifying with" is key to the process, physical appearance and facial expression of the spokesperson become determinant factors. Through transposition of the mirror-like image of one's idealized self, the text producer hopes that the reader identifies with the image being advertised. Identity and rapport, two defining attributes of one's peer group, are achieved by closely matching the physical appearance, dress, style, and expression of the spokesperson with the intended reader, or with the reader's idealized self.

One can understand this process of the mediated construction of self from the perspective of mediated interpersonal communication. Cathcart and Gumpert (1983) suggest that the media play a significant role in the development of one's self-image or self-identification. They even suggest that an individual's self-concept is dependent on the media. Since a person's self-image is, in large part, media-dependent, the media-projected images that a person looks at contribute to how that person perceives what is acceptable, normative, or even "perfect." According to Cathcart and Gumpert (1983), the more advertisers project the images the reader has been taught to value, the more the reader will see himself/herself in them, and this, in turn, creates a striving to produce a self-concept, or identity, which confirms that same image.

It seems apparent, then, that in general, what Japanese teens are being taught to value is identity with their peer group, whereas what American teens are being taught to value is identity with one's self, or in its idealized societal expression, independence from others. The scarcely populated ads in the American sample may be the result of the ad makers cognizance of the belief that, "Peer pressure in America is popularly seen as a negative force" (White, 1993, p. 37).

In contrast, according to White (1993, p. 37), "Peer pressure . . . in Japan [is seen as] . . . a source of support and socialization for adult roles." It might even be said that the image of a solitary Japanese teen raises more fear in adults (and thus in teens themselves) than the image of a gang of teens. Not belonging, then, carries a stigma in Japanese society.

Further explanation for the overabundance of girls in the Japanese *Seventeen* ads derives from Japanese consumer psychology. According to Dynax, a

Japanese marketing research group specializing in teenager behavior, "Children in their early teens are more open to each other than at any other age, and thus more influenced by each other in purchasing as well" (White, 1993, p. 109).

It seems fair to conclude that one way of understanding why more Japanese ads portray groups (often large groups) of girls whereas more American ads portray just one girl is that these outcomes correspond to how each culture understands self.

Here I return again to the idea of self and society in Japan and the United States. Miller (1993), in her discussion of Japanese selfhood and subjectivity, introduces the concept of "gender-independent co-subjectivity." By this Miller means that Japanese men and women are, regardless of gender, constructed as subjects in a relationship between two subjects (co-subjectivity) rather than between subject and object. According to Miller (1993, p. 482), in Japan subjectivity seems to coexist routinely with a genuine sense of shared identity, which yields co-subjectivity, that is, "the formation of the subject through identification with a group or community."

Although this understanding of the difference in subjectivity, that is, self, between Japan and the West is critical for appreciating the mediated self-image marketed in the mass media, I must hasten to add that the image of the Japanese self being portrayed here is not "unique" to the Japanese people. In fact, scholars such as Markus and Kitayama (1991) have suggested that the interdependent view of self finds expression in many other Asian cultures, African cultures, Latin American cultures, and many southern European cultures.

We have observed in this study that the Japanese and American mass media tend to portray the peer-group dimension of adolescent females in different ways, and those differences correspond to each country's controlling concepts of self and society. Based on the data, although limited to four magazines from each culture, it appears that the message delivered to young American females is one of individual identity apart from the controlling influence of a peer group.

The U.S. *Seventeen* reader sees, in the mirror of advertising, one other female, alone, and generally unattached to any social grouping. Some ads clearly model a group peer image, but most do not. The image of individualism is portrayed, in part, by the absence of peer groups. The Japanese ads, however, appear to hold up a fairly consistent model of the peer group. This peer-group model reinforces the value of belonging to a social set that extends beyond one's self.

REFERENCES

Befu, H. (1980). The group model of Japanese society and an alternative. *Rice University Studies, 66*, 169–187.

Bellah, R. N., Madsen, R., Sullivan, W. M., Swindler, A., & Tipton, S. M. (1985). *Habits of the heart: Individualism and commitment in American life*. New York: Harper & Row.

Cathcart, R., & Gumpert, G. (1983). Mediated interpersonal communication: Toward a new typology. *Quarterly Journal of Speech, 69,* 267–277.

Cotterell, J. (1996). *Social networks and social influences in adolescence.* London: Routledge.

Hofstede, G. (1984). *Culture's consequences.* Beverly Hills, CA: Sage.

Kassarjian, H. H. (1977). Content analysis and consumer research. *Journal of Consumer Research, 4,* 8–18.

Lebra, T. S. (1992). Self in Japanese culture. In N. Rosenberger (Ed.), *Japanese sense of self* (pp. 105–120). Cambridge: Cambridge University Press.

Leiss, W., Kline, S., & Jhally, S. (1990). *Social communication in advertising: Persons, products and images of well-being* (2nd ed.). London: Routledge.

Marchand, R. (1985). *Advertising the American dream: Making way for modernity, 1920–1940.* Berkeley: University of California Press.

Markus, H. R., & Kitayama, S. (1991). Culture and the self: Implications for cognition, emotion and motivation. *Psychological Review, 98,* 224–253.

Miller, M. (1993). Canons and the challenge of gender. *The Monist, 76,* 477–493.

Mouer, R., & Sugimoto, Y. (1986). *Images of Japanese society.* London: KPI.

Nakane, C. (1970). *Japanese society.* Berkeley: University of California Press.

Ohmann, R. (1996). *Selling culture: Magazines, markets and class at the turn of the century.* London: Verso.

Plath, D. W. (1980). *Long engagements: Maturity in modern Japan.* Stanford, CA: Stanford University Press.

Reischauer, E. (1970). *The Japan: The story of a nation.* New York: Knopf.

Rosenberger, N. (1992). Tree in summer, tree in winter: Movement of self in Japan. In N. R. Rosenberger (Ed.), *Japanese sense of self* (pp. 67–92). Cambridge: Cambridge University Press.

Seltzer, V. C. (1989). *The psychological worlds of the adolescent: Public and private.* New York: Wiley.

Smith, R. J. (1983). *Japanese society: Tradition, self and the social order.* Cambridge: Cambridge University Press.

Weisz, J. R., Rothbaum, F. M., & Blackburn, T. C. (1984). Standing out and standing in: The psychology of control in America and Japan. *American Psychologist, 39,* 955–969.

Wernick, A. (1991). *Promotional culture: Advertising, ideology and symbolic expression.* London: Sage.

White, M. (1993). *The material child: Coming of age in Japan and America.* New York: The Free Press.

Zasshi shimbun sōkatarogu. (1994). Tokyo: Media Research Center.

Chapter 24

Global and Local in Computer-Mediated Communication: A Japanese Newsgroup

Jane W. Yamazaki

Globalization, or the spread of certain practices around the world, is a well-noted feature of contemporary life. This chapter focuses on the global/local interaction of technological communication on a Usenet discussion group populated by Japanese users. To what extent does the communication in a Japanese newsgroup reflect particular (local) communication mechanisms and styles of the Japanese speech community? On the other hand, how and to what extent do the global—universal or common—characteristics of technology and the Usenet environment influence the communication of the (mostly) Japanese participants? Observation suggests that the influence goes both ways; that (1) Japanese users have particular ways of dealing with the limitations and constraints of newsgroup communication; and (2) the technological and English environment in which the communication occurs is reflected in the language used, Japanese.

The Internet provides fertile ground for students of communication to investigate how people of different cultures adopt and adapt practices from the global environment. The interaction between global and local culture is especially visible in computer-mediated communication (CMC) when participants are not from an English-speaking background. The culture of technology and the Internet is global; participants' language and national/geographical background are local.

This study focuses on a Usenet newsgroup populated by Japanese[1] users. Usenet is an Internet facility for online public discussion that allows users with access to a newshost and a newsreader to discuss certain topics with others in a newsgroup.[2] Newsgroups are open to the general public; by attaching one's newsreader to a particular named newsgroup, anyone can participate.

To what extent does communication in a Japanese newsgroup reflect the particular (local) communication mechanisms and styles of the Japanese speech community? On the other hand, how and to what extent do the universal or common (global) characteristics, limitations, and conventions of the Usenet environment influence the communication of the Japanese participants?

Baym (1996) has described Usenet interaction as "a hybrid between oral, written, interpersonal, and mass communication" (p. 320). This study extends this idea by presenting computer-mediated communication, especially for participants from non–English-speaking, non-Western cultural backgrounds, as a hybrid of cultures as well as, in this case, between the technological—largely Western and English—environment of Usenet and Japanese communication practices. Although preliminary in nature, the evidence presented here suggests that Japanese users react to the Internet environment in some very culturally specific ways; furthermore, the international and technological environment can be seen to affect certain communication practices among the Japanese participants. The influence is bidirectional. The resulting discourse is a hybrid.

In this chapter, I first introduce the Usenet group with a brief description of the general nature of the group and the participants before dealing with global and local issues. Then, focusing on verb forms and politeness, I demonstrate how this newsgroup discourse particularizes commonly recognized characteristics of CMC, in particular, its interpersonal, interactive, and expressive nature. Finally, to illustrate how the global environment may be affecting Japanese communication practices, I look at personal names and self-introductions in the Japanese discourse.

THE USENET GROUP "FJ.SOC.MEN-WOMEN"

Of the thousands of Usenet discussion groups, there are over 100 whose titles begin with the prefix "fj" ("from/for Japanese").[3] Unlike other newsgroups, most discussions in "fj" newsgroups are conducted in the Japanese language. Although participants are not necessarily Japanese, they must be fairly proficient in Japanese in order to participate, although other languages, most often English, sometimes appear.[4]

I observed five Usenet groups over a 2-month period before deciding to focus on the newsgroup "fj.soc.men-women."[5] This group discusses issues of gender, women, and sex. From February 13 to April 14, 1999, I collected 146 messages from 61 contributors.

Based on information in the message headers, most participants seem to be male Japanese citizens posting from Japan, although there are some exceptions.[6] Most identify themselves with plausible, "real-life" names, although 11 of the 61 participants use names that are obviously fictional, such as, for example, "synsyr" and "myaw." Four participants have feminine sounding names. Sixteen work in technological or university environments. Many participate in multiple Usenet groups, usually in the "fj" category.

All Usenet forums are not alike, even when participants share the same language and cultural background.[7] Depending to a large extent on the subject matter, different discussion groups attract people with different backgrounds, interests, and motivations. The only thing participants in "fj.soc.men-women" share in common, other than their Japanese backgrounds, is their access to computers and their interest in discussing the specific issues addressed by this newsgroup.

To give some idea of the nature of the issues discussed, the most popular subject during the period I collected messages was the declining Japanese birth rate, attracting 30 participants and 64 messages within a 10-day period. The topic led to discussions of marriage age, the responsibility of fathers for bringing up children, worldwide population pressures, immigration, and even the proper Japanese script for "father."

Participants in this newsgroup use standard Japanese with frequent use of *kanji* (Japanese characters), fairly long sentences and messages, as well as sophisticated vocabulary and detailed argument. These characteristics deserve more detailed treatment than I am able to provide in this chapter, but even on a superficial level and allowing for individual variation, the text seems fairly serious and adult in nature especially in comparison with "fj.yoso" and "fj.chat," two other newsgroups I had followed.

GLOBAL CHARACTERISTICS

What I mean by global characteristics of the Usenet environment in this discussion are the universal and functional characteristics that hold true for all users, no matter what nationality or language. Although much of the technical environment can be considered global, I focus on several aspects of technology, newsgroup structure, and process that have particular relevance for multilingual and international participation.

Technology

Technological characteristics of the Usenet communication environment include first the standard system of addressing required for transmission of messages across computers and physical boundaries. At the individual level, electronic mail (e-mail) addresses are used to identify individual users and provide a common scheme for routing messages. For example, an address such as "s.smith@state.edu" identifies a user "S. Smith" at State University, allowing messages to be sent from anywhere on the network. All e-mail addresses follow a standard scheme, using alphanumeric characters, the "@" sign, and "." to delineate fields.

Technological characteristics also include the individual terminal/keyboard interface, the lack of physical presence of those with whom one is communicating, and a temporal delay between messages. Like e-mail, messages are composed in private and at one's leisure, thus allowing a degree of reflection and deliberation. However, unlike e-mail or private correspondence, messages are available for public perusal.

Although the audience is invisible and to a large extent unknown to the writer, discourse is clearly visible in the explicit trail of language. In newsgroup communication, messages are textual rather than visual or graphic as one would find, for example, on Web pages. The textual basis puts a premium on literacy and articulate expression, requiring participants to be competent in the language of the newsgroup audience in addition to computer manipulation of text.

The predominant technology of text representation for both e-mail addressing and general text is the standard ASCII character set based on the roman alphabet. The ASCII character set contains 256 characters, including upper- and lowercase alphabets, numbers, and specialized characters such as %^&*(.

Organization/Message Structure

Another global feature of newsgroup communication concerns method of access. Using any of several network programs such as Netscape, participants indicate the name of the newsgroup they wish to access. Newsgroups are organized and named hierarchically according to topic, mostly in English, although often abbreviated. For example, "rec.sports.golf" might identify a newsgroup focused on golf, a subset of sports, a subset of recreation. Although Japanese newsgroups could be named using romanized Japanese words, most seem to prefer a title in English like "fj.soc.men-women," the newsgroup in the present study.[8]

Individual messages also follow a prescribed pattern, following e-mail conventions. At the beginning of every message is a header containing information about the sender, when and where the message was created, the subject of the message and certain network and technical information. The sender is identified by e-mail address. Most newsreaders allow users to specify a personal name for use in the header in addition to the required e-mail address. Similarly, a "signature file" can be created and appended to messages. These features allow participants to develop online identities and personal expression.

Process

The communication process is the same for all newsgroup users. Participants may simply read messages, or they may write or post messages, frequently in response to earlier messages, and thus join in the conversation. Newsreaders provide the ability to quote, edit, rearrange, and attribute text from previous messages, thus providing context for ongoing dialogue.[9] The quotation system adds coherence and cohesion to the discourse over time and compensates to some extent for the lack of face-to-face cues and temporal delays (Baym, 1998, p. 45).

Communication Implications

Among the characteristic features of newsgroup communication noted by communication scholars are hybridity (Baym, 1996), interactivity (Rafaeli & Sudweeks, 1997; Sproull & Faraj, 1997), and expressivity (Baym, 1998; Danet, 1993; Witmer & Katzman, 1997). The phenomena of anonymity and politeness have also received considerable attention.[10] These features frame our inquiry.

LOCAL CHARACTERISTICS

Written Japanese Language

Local aspects of Japanese newsgroups refer first and foremost, of course, to the use of Japanese language and especially to the written language. Written Japanese uses four scripts: *kanji* (Japanese characters), of which there are perhaps 4,000–8,000 different characters in regular use; *hiragana* and *katakana*, two phonetic syllabaries, each with 50 characters or syllables; and *roomaji*, the Western alphabet which can be used to write Japanese words as well as, of course, Western words. Thus, the name Yamazaki (*roomaji*) can also be represented as やまざき (*hiragana*), ヤマザキ (*katakana*), and 山崎 (*kanji*). All four scripts are frequently mixed in text, often within the same sentence.

The use of Japanese language in a computer context presented a considerable technical challenge. First, a coding system had to be designed to accommodate literally thousands of characters instead of the comparatively brief repertoire of the standard Western alphabet. Then, a method of keyboard entry that would allow users to type in syllables and convert to *kanji* using a computerized dictionary lookup was needed. Finally, in order to read a Japanese message—or, more correctly, to view Japanese characters on the screen and to print the Japanese text—software must exist to recognize and print/display the Japanese character set.[11]

In Japanese newsgroup messages, Japanese is confined largely to the text portion of the message. The header contains mostly technical terminology in a standard format, frequently expressed in English or alphanumeric text. The body of the message is, on the other hand, mostly Japanese, decoded and displayed by special software on the reader's local system.

Politeness

Another local feature closely intertwined with language is politeness. Japanese is often characterized as rich in the forms of politeness (Niyekawa, 1991). In spoken language, appropriate language depends largely on the particular, situated relationships of the two (or more) participants as well as the occasion. One is usually either speaking "up," so to speak, or "down," depending on the age, sex, role, and status of the person to whom one is speaking. These distinctions are frequently dropped among close friends and in informal discussion, indicating an intimacy and equality that would be inappropriate outside one's closest friends (Shibamoto, 1985).

A major indicator of these differences in style is the sentence-final verb form (Maynard, 1993, pp. 150–182). Informal speech uses the "plain," sometimes called the "*da*" or "abrupt" form. The standard "polite" form or the "*masu-desu*" form is a mid-level politeness form, polite, but neutral in its evaluation of status levels.[12] It also implies a certain distancing between speakers. Politer forms, of which there are many, require a knowledge of status and a desire to form a relationship based on reciprocal and hierarchical ties (Niyekawa, 1991).

Written discourse also varies considerably in politeness and formality according to genre and target audience (Maynard, 1993, 1998; Smith & Schmidt, 1996). For example, personal letters are generally more formal than spoken conversation. However, publications intended for a general audience such as newspaper articles, essays, and government publications generally use the plain form. Commercial advertisements, on the other hand, often use humble and polite forms to show deference to the intended customer.

A JAPANESE USENET COMMUNICATION ENVIRONMENT

So how does Japanese newsgroup communication fit into this complex pattern of style and formality? In fj.soc.men-women, the sentence-ending forms of verbs are overwhelmingly of the standard polite form; of the 61 participants, only 7 use the plain form regularly; another 6 showed mixed usage.[13] Polite usage recognizes the interpersonal nature of the communication. Nevertheless, the politeness level does not suggest intimacy or close relationships, but rather a distanced and respectful stance. This politeness level is consistent with the anonymity of one's communication partner(s), suggesting at the same time an egalitarian environment by treating everyone with the same polite language.

As another indication of the interpersonal dimension and politeness level, participants frequently address each other directly by name, always appending the honorific *san* to those names. This is usually the family name although respondents will generally use whatever name is indicated, even when the names are obviously pseudonyms, as in, for example, "synsyr-*san*."

Exceptions exist to the general rule of neutral politeness as shown by the ultra-polite language by Akiko[14] (female) and Uchida (male) in this exchange:[15]

>*Machuka sama no **o-shimeshi kudasatta** URL (www) o mite **itadake** wa inai no kashira?*
>I wonder if you have not seen the URL (www) that Mr./Ms. Machuka has indicated?
Haiken shimashita.

I have seen it.

In this post, Akiko has accorded Machuka the higher honorific of *sama* instead of the more typical *san*. The verb forms in bold are highly inflected for courtesy and respect. Although Uchida usually uses the standard polite forms, in this case he echoes Akiko's ultra polite language. There are several other instances of ultrapolite expressions in the discourse, namely, *orimasu* (polite form of "to be") and *ossharu* (polite form of "to say"), but they are rare.

Participants who regularly use the plain form demonstrate a more informal, sometimes playful style that sounds more conversational at the same time it is less polite. One participant uses language that can only be described as very colloquial, if not vulgar.[16] These informal uses may simply reflect personal taste or background, but they may also be related to age. When one participant complains to Uchida, "Can't you take a joke?"[17] in very informal language, Uchida suggests that jokes should be sent to fj.jokes, and sarcastically comments:

Gakubusei-san desu ka? Mō sukoshi yo no naka o shirō ne.
Are you a (college) student? You should learn a little more of the world, don't you think?

Thus, Uchida evaluates the language and attitude as that of an uneducated undergraduate. In other words, "Is your youth an excuse for such poor manners? Grow up!"

Other instances of less polite language occur when participants become angry. One irritated and exasperated participant mixes plain and polite forms with the abrupt ending *gozonji nai*? (Aren't you aware that . . .?). In one long message exchange between Nakayama and Uchida, both writers use the plain form from time to time. This may suggest a lapse in manners or a dropping of formality as they become involved in the argument; or it may reflect the development of camaraderie and intimacy between people who have, so to speak, gotten to know each other well after extended conversations. Even so, for both these writers, as for the newsgroup in general, this represents a departure from their usual polite verb endings. Perhaps the best example of the general tendency toward polite language is this statement:

Watashi wa anata no go-iken ni hedo ga demasu.
Your opinion(s) make me throw up.

Using the polite "*-masu*" verb form along with *go-iken* (your honorable opinion) may be considered ironic in this case; nevertheless, the writer maintains the formal politeness level even when expressing strong disagreement.

Interactivity

Despite the generally polite and distanced language, communication is clearly interactive. One indication of interactivity is the degree to which messages are direct replies to previous messages. All but 9 of the 146 messages (93%) begin by quoting from a previous message.[18] A common pattern is to interweave previous text with current comments in such a way as to mimic conversation, most frequently as a dialog between two people. In an extended message (221 lines) in which Nakagawa responds to Uchida after several previous exchanges, the number of new lines written by Nakagawa is only 105. First, Nakagawa quotes several lines from Uchida's previous post, then he comments, followed by more lines of Uchida's text, and so on. The resulting text is very conversational, both visually and linguistically.

Both Nakagawa and Uchida frequently use direct address, further enhancing the sense of ongoing dyadic exchange as evidenced in this comment by Nakagawa: "As I have repeatedly tried to explain, Mr. Uchida, I cannot agree with you."

Another indication of interactivity and the conversational nature of the discourse is the frequency of so-called "interactional particles" (Maynard, 1993, pp. 183–220). These are linguistic markers at the ends of sentences such as *ka* (question), *ne* ("isn't it?" expecting or showing agreement), *yo* (masculine emphasis), *wa* (emphasis, usually feminine), and *na* ("you know"; "say, listen"; "look here"). These interactional particles explicitly recognize and invoke audience response, suggesting camaraderie and joint construction of dialogue.

In this discourse, statements ending in interactional particles account for approximately one out of four statements.[19] The interactional particle *wa* does not occur at all, perhaps because of the small number of female participants; but the masculine *yo*, meaning "I insist" or "for sure" also occurs infrequently, suggesting perhaps a general dispreference for strong assertive and unequivocal statements.

Personal Attitude/Opinion

In addition to interactional particles that call for a response from the reader/listener, a large number of sentences end with the verbs *deshō* (potential/probable), *darō* (I wonder), *omou* (to think), *kamo shirenai* (perhaps), and similar indications of qualification. Consequently, statements not only sound like conversations, but conversations in which opinion, often qualified and tentative, is both offered and solicited.

As Maynard (1998) has noted, such expressions are frequent in Japanese speech, allowing and encouraging the explicit expression of personal attitude toward factual content (p. 116). Clear distinctions are made between factual statements and opinions. Degree of certainty is explicitly noted. Thus, these expressions are not simply matters of politeness or unassertiveness, but habitual methods of evaluating and commenting, of indicating one's personal involvement and commitment.

In the discourse of fj.soc.men-women, the combination of sentence-ending strategies using interactional particles and tentative constructions account for approximately half of the statements. The frequency of "I think that" and "don't you think that" and "isn't it probably so that" suggests that this newsgroup is primarily a forum for expressing opinion, not for exchange of information or affiliation.[20] This is not to say that information exchange and affiliation do not occur, but that the primary motivation here is the satisfaction of having one's opinions aired in the public arena—to see one's ideas in print, to challenge others' opinions, and to defend one's opinions without the deterrent of real-life social repercussions. The opinion-centered motivation is also supported by the strategies used to invite the opinions of others, as if to say, "This is my opinion, what's yours?" Politeness and active probing of opinion encourages participation.

This may invite comparison with the acronym IMHO (In My Humble Opinion) used commonly in English-speaking newsgroups. Ignoring the humorous and ironic connotations of IMHO, we would not expect, of course, the use of alphabetic acronyms of English phrases in non-English discourse. In this case, however, Japanese have no need to develop special acronyms or techniques for indicating "in my humble opinion"; the standard language and habitual usage contains ample capabilities for this already. Similarly, there is no system of capitalization in the Japanese script to indicate shouting or emphasis, another convention in CMC circles. For strong emphasis in Japanese, the particle *yo* (masculine emphasis) and the *katakana* script might be used but even these strongly assertive mechanisms are used sparingly by the participants in this study.

Another mechanism used by many of the Japanese participants is the "aside," indicated by the use of "#" to preface statements.[21] This illustrates another way of distinguishing between off-the-record internal thinking and externally defensible and assertive statements. Ostensibly addressed to oneself, these statements are frequently in plain form and contain incomplete thoughts and sentences. For example, in a message responding to Nakayama, Uchida wonders about his reaction:

Nakayama-san no iken wa nan darō ka?
I wonder what Mr. Nakayama's (your) opinion about that is?

Expressivity

Another often-noted feature associated with personal expression in CMC is the use of emoticons, graphic symbols and character combinations that supplement the text with nonverbal communicative content (Baym, 1998; Witmer and Katzman, 1997). Most well-known is the so-called smiley face ":-)" to indicate that the writer is "just kidding." This icon occurs twice in our data along with several other emoticons: ";_;" (crying?) and "^^" (raised eyebrows?).

Perhaps more interesting is the use of *kanji* like an emoticon, as in the Japanese version of the smiley face using 笑 (*wara[u]*, to smile or laugh). This occurs five times in the text as in this aside, as Uchida comments on his study of *karate*:

#*Mi ni tsuku ka dō ka wa gimon desu ga* (笑) . . .
#Whether I've learned it or not is debatable (Smile) . . .

There are several other unusual ways in which attitude and emotion are expressed in these messages. One is the use of *kigo*, literally, "picture symbols" such as, for example, a musical note ♪ that occurs twice in the discourse:

"Macska no kiji o yonda kara anshin ♪" nante hito ga iru to wa omoemasen.
I can't think there's anyone who says "I've read Macska's article and so I'm safe, Tra la!"

There are a number of other expressive devices that appear from time to time in the discourse. Exclamation points (!!!!), question marks (???), and ellipsis (. . .) occur as well as other, more Japanese-like expressions such as *guaa* (Oops), *aatsu* (Oh!), *un, un,* (yes, yes), and *uumu* (hmm).[22]

In summary, communication in fj.soc.men-women demonstrates many of the same characteristics noted in other newsgroups, namely, a strong interpersonal nature, interactivity, and expressivity. These global features are, however, demonstrated in linguistically specific ways, through politeness levels and mechanisms of personal expression that differ from those of English. Thus, common attributes of CMC become transformed under the influence of the Japanese environment—still present, but visible in a different way.

INFLUENCE OF CMC ON JAPANESE LANGUAGE AND CULTURAL PRACTICES

In this section, I consider how Japanese language and practices themselves seem to be influenced, perhaps transformed, by participation in the global environment of CMC. I shall consider two areas where the influence of the global environment is quite visible: self-introduction and personal names. One area that deserves attention but is not considered here is vocabulary and the choice of script, especially the use of the roman alphabet for English words instead of the traditional *katakana*. The evidence of script and vocabulary influence from the technological Internet environment is considerable and deserves further research.

Introductions

How messages begin and end—greetings and goodbyes, for example—probably deserve more attention from CMC scholars as these conventions imply certain assumptions about the nature of the communication and its relationship with other types of communication. Should one say in English, "Hello everyone!" thus recognizing the "one-to-many" nature of CMC? Or should one say, "Dear Joe," or simply, "Joe," emphasizing the parallels to letter writing and the response to a single person? Is this like a letter or even a face-to-face meeting where there is some form of initial address or introduction? Or would we say, "This is Jill Smith," as in a telephone conversation?

In fj.soc.men-women, 16 of the 61 contributors and 40% of messages begin with simple, one-sentence introductions. Most participants who introduce themselves have a particular style that they use all the time. In an English e-mail environment, self-introduction is rare except for first-time posters, perhaps because one would be repeating information already found in the header.[23] In the Japanese case, of course, self-introduction in Japanese may not seem redundant. This is especially true if the writer uses *kanji*, thus providing the Japanese "spelling" of the name.

Three of the participants follow the example of Uchida who begins every message with:

内田と申します。(*Uchida to mōshimasu.*)
My name is Uchida.

Using the humble verb *mōsu* (to be named) and his family name written in *kanji*, this is a rather formal and ultrapolite method of self-introduction. Thirteen participants use a less-formal self-introduction, as illustrated here:

宮野です。(*Miyano desu.*)
This is/I am Miyano.

As in the previous example, Miyano follows the standard Japanese practice of identifying himself with family name in *kanji*. This greeting/introduction sounds like a typical phone identification in Japanese and Miyano introduces himself this way in every message.

Three people modify Miyano's format using the *hiragana* phonetic syllabary to write their names rather than *kanji*. The use of *hiragana* is perhaps akin to "baby talk," that is, a "cute" way to present oneself. It is not typical in an adult context, although it is not uncommon to supply *hiragana* for pronunciation purposes. It might indicate that the writer is a woman, because women tend to use more *hiragana* in general (Smith & Schmidt, 1996).

The examples given so far follow characteristic Japanese patterns of self-introduction albeit with some variation. The following examples alter the form itself:

とも@和大です。(*Tomo @ Wa-dai desu.*)
This is Tomo at Wakayama University.
小野寺@トロントです。(*Onodera @ Toronto desu.*)
This is Onodera in Toronto.
こんにちは takao @ sophia です。(*Konnichi wa takao @sophia desu.*)
Hello. This is Takao at Sophia.
高森@ラベル撲滅委員でした。(*Takamori @ raberu bokumetsu i-in deshita.*)
This was Takamori from the Anti-Discrimination League.

These four examples use the "This is . . ." format, as does Miyano earlier. Two use *kanji* (Takamori and Onodera); the other two *hiragana*. However, the use of the @ sign, clearly modeled on Internet e-mail address conventions, departs from traditional introductions. This new format is not simply technological shorthand. Rather than referring to a technical e-mail address, the @ refers to geographical location or, in the case of Tomo, Takamori, and Takao, organizational affiliation. In Japanese, this kind of information can be indicated in a number of elementary constructions, all of which put location or affiliation *before* the name as in, for example, *Fōrdo no Takeda desu* identifying Mr. Takeda as working for Ford Motor Company. Onodera provides an example of the more typical construction in an earlier introduction:

Toronto zaijū no Onodera desu.
This is Onodera, living in Toronto.

Thus, the sentences using the @ designation to establish location or affiliation are not influenced simply by the symbol @ to mean "in" or "at" but also by Western patterns of presentation order inherent in e-mail address formulation. The information order has been altered to present the name followed by the location or affiliation. In the case of Takao, Western influence includes the use of romanization of his name, use of his school's international name (Sophia University instead of the Japanese name Jochi), and use of his given name rather than his family name (Yamanaka).

Although these three examples identify company affiliation, most introductions and other personal references in fj.soc.men-women do not specify company or organizational affiliation, unlike typical face-to-face introductions. This may indicate the degree to which participation in newsgroups is being undertaken on an individual and informal basis as well as the fact that one's work affiliation is simply not relevant in this communication situation.

In summary, these Japanese self-introductions suggest that it is polite to identify oneself, usually at the beginning of the message, much as one would when joining a group that had people unknown to you. Even if redundant due to the address in the message header, self-introduction establishes one's "Japanese" identity. The introductions also demonstrate the influence of the technological environment of CMC on the form and content of the Japanese introduction. The varied combinations using Western and Japanese scripts, personal nicknames, and the @ sign make these introductions rather specialized and, indeed, even peculiar Japanese introductions.[24] Moreover, the variety in practice demonstrates personal expression and idiosyncratic practice.

Personal Names

Personal names offer further evidence of Western influence on Japanese practices. The order of personal names in Japan is family name followed by the given name. Furthermore, given names are rarely used as forms of address. Thus, Tanaka Hiroko whose family name is Tanaka would typically be called Tanaka *san* (Ms. Tanaka) or some other designation of title or role. This presents an area of difficulty for Japanese participants in a global setting. Should they conform to Western custom in order to be perceived correctly? Or should they maintain the Japanese method of self-presentation?

In the message headers in this sample, Japanese and Western naming order occur almost equally. Of the 30 users who provide personal names in the header, 14 put the family name first (standard Japanese) and 16 reverse the order to follow Western conventions. Some examples of different solutions to self-identification in the header are as follows:

UCHIDA Ryoichi (Japanese order, capitalized family name),

YOKO UEJIMA (Western order),

HiRoShi TaKaDa (Western order, with syllables indicated),

synsyr (fabricated name),

Toshiko KOUNO (Western order, capitalized family name), and

Ken Terada (Western order and capitalization).

Conforming to Western order in the header makes sense if one sees the header as Western or international, suggesting appropriate compliance with international standards. In other words, "When in Rome . . ."—that is, in the message header—"do (communicate) as the Romans (Westerners) do." Still, about half continue to follow the Japanese naming order as does Uchida, but even they recognize the ambivalence and difficulty by making special efforts to indicate their last name by capitalization.

Most of those who choose to represent their names in the Western order in the header switch back to the Japanese order in the text, that is, in the Japanese portion of the message. Thus, Hiroshi TaKaDa (Western order) becomes 高田 (Takada), as he introduces himself in *kanji* at the beginning of the message text and 高田浩 (Takada Hiroshi) in his signature file (family name first).

Others are less traditional. As indicated above, three people introduce themselves in the Japanese text using the *hiragana* syllabary rather than *kanji*. Tomoyuki Satō (Western order) as identified in the header introduces himself in the Japanese text as "Tomo" using *hiragana* for an abbreviation of his given name. The atypical use of his abbreviated given name brings to mind the case of the Japanese student abroad who truncates his name to make pronunciation easier for fellow students. In another variation, Mr. Akizawa abbreviates his family name and writes it in roman letters:

Aki です。(*Aki desu.*)
This is Aki.

Again, the abbreviation, as well as use of alphabetic characters, is reminiscent of some Japanese who simplify their names for the benefit of non-Japanese friends and for whom these names may come to represent a new identity. Nevertheless, incorporating these clearly internationally stylized names into the Japanese text in discussion with fellow Japanese represents a clear departure from cultural traditions.

A final example of variation is synsyr, an obviously fictitious name. Synsyr maintains the formal Japanese form by beginning every message as follows:

synsyr と申します。 (*Synsyr to mōshimasu.*)
My name is synsyr.

This represents, it seems to me, a new approach to identity, the creation of an identity that is neither Japanese nor Western/English except for the alphabetic representation of "synsyr."

Other members of the newsgroup accept or at least make no comments regarding these unusual naming practices. In responses, names are used as indicated in self-introduction, or if that is not given, then the name as indicated in the header, always with the polite appellation "*san.*" One exception is Uchida's reference to Macska. Macska is identified in the header as Macska but he introduces himself as *Machuka* (using *katakana*) in the Japanese text. This is a typical rendering of Western alphabetic words into the Japanese phonetic system. What makes this interesting is that Uchida does not use Macska's version of his name in Japanese. Instead, Uchida refers to Macska as "Macska さん" (Macska *san*). In other words, Uchida uses the Western spelling despite Macska's self-identification in Japanese as "Machuka."

These examples illustrate various attempts to negotiate the boundaries of Japanese/Western interaction in the dialog. They illustrate first that Western practices are creeping over the boundaries of the header and outside the Internet environment into the Japanese territory of the message text and perhaps into the wider domains of Japanese society. These are not traditional naming and introduction patterns. Nevertheless, the degree of variation in how these standard conventions are being modified at the very least suggests that these practices are in a state of flux. Communication in the technological environment of the Internet is an evolving environment and new standards and practices for social behavior have not yet crystallized.

CONCLUSION

Baym (1998) recognizes the importance of cultural factors in her discussion of external influences on CMC:

The preexisting speech communities in which interactants operate provide social understandings and practices through and against which interaction in the computer-mediated context develops. The CMC use always is nested in the national and international cultures of which its participants are members. From this they draw a common language (usually but not always English), common ways of speaking, and a good deal of shared understandings. (p. 40)

My focus in this chapter can thus be seen simply as a particular instance of "external" influence on CMC. Rather than seeing culture as an external factor influencing the communication, however, I see the two aspects, external and internal, global and local, as two overlapping and, to some extent, clashing cultures with influence going in both directions. More than an influence, Japanese language and culture are central to the discourse. The resulting CMC is an expression of Japanese culture in a new setting. At the same time, Japanese language and cultural practices are changing under the influence of global interaction.

This study would seem to support both sides of the global/local debate over the consequences of globalization. On the one hand, Japanese accommodation to the Western environment seems evident, especially in areas in which cultural practices differ, such as the order of personal names. On the other hand, technology has made it possible, somewhat ironically, to incorporate the Japanese language into the global environment. Rather than losing one's identity to global homogeneity, sophisticated technology supports the use of the Japanese language and thus supports the continuation of cultural differences. Indeed, with the table lookup functions for *kanji* at one's fingertips, it can be argued that Japanese language is more accessible than ever before, even for the Japanese.[25]

Perhaps we make too much of the global/local distinction. As Featherstone (1990) suggests,

Globalization [should be seen] . . . less in terms of alleged homogenizing processes (e.g., theories . . . of cultural imperialism, Americanization and mass consumer culture . . . riding on the back of Western economic and political domination) and more in terms of the diversity, variety and richness of popular and local discourses, codes and practices which resist and play back systemicity and order. (p. 2)

This study has only scratched the surface of "the diversity, variety, and richness of popular and local discourses" that can be studied in the global environment of CMC. Both intercultural and crosscultural research can benefit from a close look at the changing world of Usenet communication.

NOTES

1. The word "Japanese" has many different uses in English, including ethnicity, national origin, and political citizenship. As I use the term, to be Japanese includes citizenship plus ethnic ancestry plus language capability of a native speaker, that is, someone brought up in Japan. Thus, despite my last name and the fact that I speak (some) Japanese, even if I were to obtain Japanese citizenship, I doubt that I would be considered Japanese by most Japanese because I am Caucasian.

2. Usenet and its characteristics have been described by, among others, Baym (1996, 1997) and Sproull and Faraj (1997, pp. 41–47).

3. A list of current Usenet groups can be found on the website www.dejanews.com, which provides access and information about the Usenet network.

4. English words appear from time to time throughout the Japanese text. Occasionally, extended excerpts from other languages appear as when Italian and English news articles concerning an Italian court decision on rape were posted to the group. A man named Vladimir wrote in Japanese in his initial postings, but later messages were in somewhat broken English and two people responded at some length in English. Another participant responded to the English discussion by asking what certain of the English words meant, saying his English was poor.

5. The other newsgroups I monitored were fj.soc.law, fj.soc.history, fj.chat, and fj.yoso. Fj.chat and fj.yoso proved difficult for me to understand, perhaps because they focused on popular culture. My guess is that the participants were younger than the participants in the other groups. Fj.soc.history seemed somewhat esoteric and there were few messages. Both fj.soc.law and fj.soc.men-women had considerable participation but I found fj.soc.men-women to have the most interesting examples of language and communication hybridity.

6. One participant, self-identified as Japanese, posted from California; another person with a Japanese surname posted to the group twice from Toronto. Vladimir introduced himself as a visitor to Japan who had learned Japanese in Vladivostok. The name "Macska" does not sound Japanese and his organization, "American Organization of Anarchists," seems to be a joke (he says so in one post), but his e-mail address is Tokyo. He writes long messages in Japanese, but in one exchange, he wrote in colloquial American English. My guess is that he is an American living in Japan who knows Japanese well.

7. For comparison, see Denzin (1999), who describes an alcoholics anonymous Usenet discussion group and Baym (1996, 1997, 1998), who studies a close-knit, supportive group, consisting mostly of women, which derives much of its energy and reason for existence from a common interest in soap operas.

8. If one wanted to use Japanese words, the group might have been named "nihon.sha.otoko-onna" (*Nihon* = Japan; *shakai* = society; *otoko* = man; *onna* = woman). Fj.yoso is an example of newsgroup that uses Japanese words in the title.

9. Newsreaders vary in their formatting and presentation capabilities so that how the header information is displayed and the way that quotations are noted may differ, although the information is the same.

10. The phenomena of anonymity (identity) and politeness (behavior norms) arise in almost every study of CMC; for example, see Kendall (1999), Baym (1997), and McLaughlin, Osborne, and Smith (1995).

11. There are several different coding schemes in use although "iso-2022-jp" seemed standard here. Print and display capability is provided with specialized fonts.

12. Niyekawa (1991) calls this form the "P0" form, or minimum politeness form. She uses "P1" and "P2" to indicate higher levels of politeness.

13. Mixed usage, indicating subordinate information (Maynard, 1998, pp. 101–103) and copies of government reports that are generally in plain form, are not counted here.

14. I have changed the names of participants to maintain their privacy.

15. I have transcribed this and later excerpts into Western alphabetic representation except in cases where the original script is critical to the argument. The original is, of

course, written with *kanji, hiragana,* and *katakana* as well as some *roomaji*; for example, "URL (www)" is represented in the text just as you see it here, with alphabetic capital letters.

16. For example, sentences ending in *ssuyonee* (isn't it?) or *ii ssu* (it's okay).

17. *Karakatten no ga wakannai?*

18. This is a much higher percentage than what is reported for other Usenet groups by Sproull and Faraj (1997) and Rafaeli and Sudweeks (1997). Their definitions of interactivity are somewhat different from my focus on simple response to previous messages.

19. Counting "statements" is problematic with this data. There is much overlap in the use of interactional particles and other sentence-ending strategies.

20. Sproull and Faraj (1997) list motivations/rewards for participation in Usenet discussion groups as information, entertainment, and affiliation (pp. 43–46). Baym's (1997) emphasis on the performance aspects of newsgroup discourse comes close to my sense of the rewards of giving one's opinion and waiting for response.

21. It is not clear whether this convention is particular to Japanese discourse. I have not seen it used in English text, although the use of parentheses provides similar functionality.

22. I suspect there is a connection between these expressions and the *manga* (comic book) genre. These kinds of words appeared much more frequently in fj.yoso and fj.jokes.

23. Although most English-speaking Usenet and e-mail users do not formally identify themselves, other forms of greeting are common. For me, it always seems somewhat abrupt to start an e-mail without some kind of greeting. Internet real-time groups (MUDs /MOOs) are more dynamic and people frequently introduce themselves, as if to say they've just arrived.

24. Of course the seepage of Internet culture and in particular the use of @ in real world life is not confined to Japanese users. I recently bought a tourist T-shirt in Leland, Michigan, with the expression "@leland.com" printed on the front.

25. Smith and Schmidt (1996) note that *kanji* usage may be increasing among the Japanese because of computer capabilities (p. 51ff).

REFERENCES

Baym, N. K. (1996). Agreements and disagreements in a computer-mediated discussion. *Research on Language and Social Interaction, 29,* 315–345.

Baym, N. K. (1997). Interpreting soap operas and creating community: Inside an electronic fan culture. In S. Kiesler (Ed.), *Culture of the internet* (pp. 103–120). Mahwah, NJ: Lawrence Erlbaum.

Baym, N. K. (1998). The emergence of on-line community. In S. Jones (Ed.), *Cybersociety 2: Revisiting computer-mediated communication and community* (pp. 35–68). Thousand Oaks, CA: Sage.

Danet, B. (1993). Books, letters, documents: The changing materiality of texts in late print culture [on-line]. Available e-mail: msdanet@pluto.mscc.huji.ac.il.

Denzin, N. (1999). Cybertalk and the method of instances. In S. Jones (Ed.), *Doing internet research: Critical issues and methods for examining the net* (pp. 107–126). Thousand Oaks, CA: Sage.

Featherstone, M. (1990). Global culture: An introduction. In M. Featherstone (Ed.), *Theory, culture and society, Vol. 7* (pp. 1–14). London: Sage.

Kendall, L. (1999). Recontextualizing "cyberspace": Methodological considerations for on-line research. In S. Jones (Ed.), *Doing internet research: Critical issues and methods for examining the net* (pp. 57–74). Thousand Oaks, CA: Sage.

Maynard, S. K. (1993). *Discourse modality: Subjectivity, emotion and voice in the Japanese language*. Amsterdam: John Benjamins.

Maynard, S. K. (1998). *Principles of Japanese discourse: A handbook*. Cambridge: Cambridge University Press.

McLaughlin, M. L., Osborne, K. K., & Smith, C. B. (1995). Standards of conduct on Usenet. In S. G. Jones (Ed.), *Cybersociety: Computer-mediated communication and community* (pp. 90–111). Thousand Oaks, CA: Sage.

Niyekawa, A. (1991). *Minimum essential politeness: A guide to the Japanese honorific language*. Tokyo: Kodansha International.

Rafaeli, S., & Sudweeks, F. (1997). Networked interactivity. *Journal of Computer-Mediated Communication, 2*(4). Available online: http://www.ascusc.org/jcmc/vol2/issue4/rafaeli.sudweeks.html.

Shibamoto, J. S. (1985). *Japanese women's language*. Orlando, FL: Academic Press.

Smith, J. S., & Schmidt, D. L. (1996). Variability in written Japanese: Towards a sociolinguistics of script choice. *Visible Language, 30*, 46–71.

Sproull, L., & Faraj, S. (1997). Atheism, sex, and databases: The net as a social technology. In S. Kiesler (Ed.), *Culture of the internet* (pp. 35–51). Mahwah, NJ: Lawrence Erlbaum.

Witmer, D., & Katzman, S. (1997). On-line smiles: Does gender make a difference in the use of graphic accents? *Journal of Computer-Mediated Communication, 2*(4). Available online: http://www.ascusc.org/jcmc/vol2/issue4/ witmer1.html.

Index

About the Contributors

Christopher Barnard is associate professor at Teikyo University, Tokyo. His research is in critical linguistics, most notably on the issue of Japanese state ideology and its reflection in school history textbooks, in the journals *Functions of Language* and *Revista Canaria de Estudios Ingleses*, and in his book, *Nankin-Gyakusatsu wa 'Okotta' no Ka—Kōkōrekishi e no Gengogaku-teki Hihan* (translated by E. Kaji).

Ray T. Donahue is Professor of Intercultural Communication (jointly appointed) in Foreign Studies and in the Institute for Japanese Studies at Nagoya Gakuin University. His publications include the books *Japanese Non-Linear Discourse Style, Diplomatic Discourse: International Conflict at the United Nations* (coauthored with Michael H. Prosser), and the award-winning *Japanese Culture and Communication: Critical Cultural Analysis*.

Hiroko Furo is Assistant Professor of Japanese at Illinois Wesleyan University. She received her PhD in linguistics with a concentration in sociolinguistics from Georgetown University. She specializes in crosscultural communication between the United States and Japan, discourse analysis, language and gender, and pragmatics.

Sylvie Guichard-Anguis, geography research fellow at the French National Center for Scientific Research (CNRS), belongs to the Space and Culture laboratory at Paris IV Sorbonne. She also heads the Center of Research on the Far-East of Paris Sorbonne (CREOPS). She has published widely on the cultural heritage in Japan, the evolution and perception of Japanese urban landscapes, and other topics.

Masako Hamada is assistant professor and Director of Japanese Studies at Villanova University where she teaches both language and area studies. She has published articles on language education, crosscultural communication and conflict resolution, and Japanese aesthetics and art. She is completing her doctorate in International Education and Transcultural Studies at Columbia University.

Reiko Hayashi is Professor of English and Linguistics at Konan Women's University. Her research interests include discourse and identity, particularly in relation to the issues of society and the individual; English language in Japan; and conversational managements, and has published widely on these topics.

Bates L. Hoffer teaches linguistics and Japanese culture at Trinity University in San Antonio, Texas. He has authored or edited over 200 books, articles, and reviews. He currently edits *Intercultural Communication Studies* and *Language and Literature.* He is Director of the International Association for Intercultural Communication Studies.

Rotem Kowner is senior lecturer in the Japanese Studies Cluster at the University of Haifa, Israel. He has written on Japanese national behavior and Japanese racial images in the West and is currently engaged in research on the Japanese reaction to the West during the Meiji era.

Ryuko Kubota teaches Japanese as a foreign language and second language teacher education at the University of North Carolina at Chapel Hill. She has published on second language writing, issues of culture in teaching second languages, and critical approaches to applied linguistics.

Nagiko Iwata Lee is Professor of Japanese at Ritsumeikan University. Her publications include *Nihongo no Hobunkōzō*, chapters in *Kotoba to Ningen to Shakai to*, journal articles on Japanese language and education, and translations of haiku collections.

Soo-im Lee is currently associate professor in the Department of Business Administration, Ryukoku University, and her main research interests are teaching English as a foreign language, crosscultural communication, and computer-assisted language learning.

Seiichi Makino is Professor of Japanese and Linguistics at Princeton University. His major books include *Some Aspects of Japanese Nominalization, Kotoba to Kūkan, Kurikaeshi no Bunpō, Uchi to Soto no Gengo-bunka-gaku,* several standard dictionaries, and his recent *Nakama: Communication, Context, Culture, Vols. 1 & 2* (with Y. Hatasa & K. Hatasa). His current research interest is the cognitive linguistic analysis of universal metaphors.

Michael L. Maynard is Associate Professor of Advertising at Temple University. He has extensive advertising experience with major agencies in Japan, New York, and Chicago. His areas of research include mass media analysis, the relationship between mass communication and culture, as well as textual and semiotic analysis of television and print advertising in Japan.

Senko K. Maynard is Professor of Japanese and Linguistics at Rutgers University. Her recent publications include *Discourse Modality, Kaiwa Bunseki, Japanese Communication: Language and Thought in Context, Danwa Bunseki* *no Kanōsei, Principles of Japanese Discourse: A Handbook, Jōi no Gengogaku* (Kuroshio), and *Linguistic Emotivity* (in press).

Eamon McCafferty graduated from a master's program in area studies (Japan) from the School of Oriental and African Studies, University of London. He currently teaches at Tokai University in Japan and recently has begun study for a doctorate in education with a focus on language in social context.

Brian J. McVeigh is Chair of the Cultural and Women's Studies Department of Tokyo Jogakkan University. His major publications include *Life in a Japanese Women's Junior College: Learning to Be Ladylike, The Nature of the Japanese State: Rationality and Rituality,* and *Wearing Ideology: State, Schooling and Self-Presentation in Japan.*

Masahiko Minami is Assistant Professor of Japanese at San Francisco State University. His research interests include crosscultural comparisons of narrative/discourse structure. He has published a number of articles and presented papers on this subject, and has coauthored *Language Issues in Literacy and Bilingual/Multicultural Education.*

Brian Moeran is professor in the Department of Media, Communication, and Japanese Culture at the Copenhagen Business School and has written widely on Japanese society and culture. His recent books include *A Japanese Advertising Agency, Folk Art Potters of Japan,* and *A Far Valley.*

Masayuki Nakanishi is currently Professor of Communication at Tsuda College in Tokyo. His areas of interest include interpersonal, small group, and intercultural communication. His work has appeared in the forums *Human Communication Research* and *Women & Language,* among others.

Roichi Okabe is Professor of Speech Communication at Nanzan University in Nagoya, Japan. He has published several books in international communication, including rhetorical studies of American political discourse: *Ibunka o yomu: Nichibeikan no, Seiji komyunikeishon: Amerika no settoku kozo o saguru,* and *30-byo no settoku senryaku: Amerika daitōryosen no terebi komasharu.*

Tomoko Sekiguchi is currently a visiting researcher and an adjunct assistant professor at the School of Humanities for Environmental Policy and Technology at Himeji Institute of Technology. Her research interests include intercultural communication, educational anthropology, and ethnic minority studies.

Noriko Akimoto Sugimori, a doctoral candidate in applied linguistics at Boston University, holds several master's degrees: in TESOL (Columbia University); in English (Michigan State University); and in CAS in Human Development and Psychology (Harvard Graduate School of Education). She has taught advanced communication and reading in Japanese at Massachusetts Institute of Technology.

Naomi Sugimoto is associate professor in the Faculty of Nursing and Medical Care at Keio University. Her research interests include intercultural (especially Japan–U.S.) communication, interpersonal communication, and communication training for medical professionals.

Jane W. Yamazaki is a PhD candidate in communication at Wayne State University and holds an M.A. in East Asian history from the University of Virginia, as well as an M.A.T. in mathematics from Northwestern University. Her research interests include rhetoric, language, and reality/identity/morality.

Tsutomu Yokota recently joined the faculty at Ohkagakuen College in Toyota City, where he now teaches TEFL and culture learning, after having spent a career as a Professor of Foreign Language Education at Yamagata University. His works include *Foreign Language Learning in Multicultural Society*.